Package on the Market!

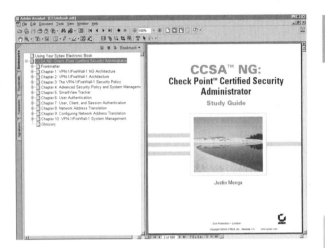

Search through the complete book in PDF!

- Access the entire *CCSA Study Guide*, complete with figures and tables, in electronic format.

- Search the *CCSA Study Guide* chapters to find information on any topic in seconds.

- Use Adobe Acrobat Reader (included on the CD-ROM) to view the electronic book.

Use the Electronic Flashcards for PCs or Palm devices to jog your memory and prep last minute for the exam!

- Reinforce your understanding of key concepts with these hardcore flashcard-style questions.

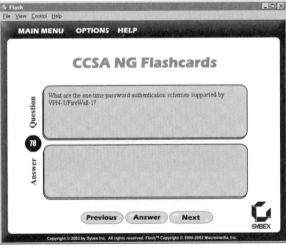

Prepare for the CCSA exam on the go with your handheld device!

- Download the Flashcards to your Palm device and go on the road. Now you can study for the CCSA exam anytime, anywhere.

CCSA NG:
Check Point Certified Security Administrator
Study Guide

CCSA™ NG:
Check Point™ Certified Security Administrator
Administrator
Study Guide

Justin Menga

San Francisco • London

SYBEX

Associate Publisher: Neil Edde
Acquisitions Editor: Maureen Adams
Developmental Editor: Heather O'Connor
Editor: Cheryl Hauser
Production Editor: Dennis Fitzgerald
Technical Editors: Ted Snider, Gareth Bromley
Graphic Illustrator: Tony Jonick
Electronic Publishing Specialist: Interactive Composition Corporation
CD Coordinator: Dan Mummert
CD Technician: Kevin Ly
Proofreaders: Emily Husan, Dave Nash, Laurie O'Connell, Nancy Riddiough
Indexer: Ted Laux
Book Designer: Bill Gibson
Cover Design: Archer Design
Cover Photograph: Bruce Heinemann, PhotoDisc

Library of Congress Card Number: 2002113565

ISBN: 0-7821-4115-3

SYBEX and the SYBEX logo are either registered trademarks or trademarks of SYBEX Inc. in the United States and/or other countries.

Screen reproductions produced with FullShot 99. FullShot 99 © 1991–1999 Inbit Incorporated. All rights reserved. FullShot is a trademark of Inbit Incorporated.

The CD interface was created using Macromedia Director, COPYRIGHT 1994, 1997–1999 Macromedia Inc. For more information on Macromedia and Macromedia Director, visit http://www.macromedia.com.

TRADEMARKS: SYBEX has attempted throughout this book to distinguish proprietary trademarks from descriptive terms by following the capitalization style used by the manufacturer.

ClusterXL, ConnectControl, FireWall-1, FireWall-1 GX, FireWall-1 SecureServer, FireWall-1 SmallOffice, FireWall-1 VSX, FireWall-1 XL, FloodGate-1, INSPECT, INSPECT XL, IQ Engine, Open Security Extension, OPSEC, Provider-1, SecureKnowledge, SecurePlatform, SecureXL, SiteManager-1, SmartCenter, SmartCenter Pro, SmartDashboard, Smart-Defense, SmartLSM, SmartMap, SmartUpdate, SmartView, SmartView Monitor, SmartView Reporter, SmartView Status, SmartView Tracker, SVN, UAM, User-to-Address Mapping, UserAuthority, VPN-1, VPN-1 Accelerator Card, VPN-1 Net, VPN-1 Pro, VPN-1 SecureClient, VPN-1 SecuRemote, VPN-1 SecureServer, VPN-1 SmallOffice and VPN-1 VSX are trademarks or registered trademarks of Check Point Software Technologies Ltd. or its affiliates.

The author and publisher have made their best efforts to prepare this book, and the content is based upon final release software whenever possible. Portions of the manuscript may be based upon pre-release versions supplied by software manufacturer(s). The author and the publisher make no representation or warranties of any kind with regard to the completeness or accuracy of the contents herein and accept no liability of any kind including but not limited to performance, merchantability, fitness for any particular purpose, or any losses or damages of any kind caused or alleged to be caused directly or indirectly from this book.

Manufactured in the United States of America

10 9 8 7 6 5 4 3 2 1

SYBEX

To Our Valued Readers:

The Check Point certification program well deserves its position as the leading vendor-specific security certification in the IT arena. And with the recent release of the Check Point NG exams, current and aspiring security professionals are seeking accurate, thorough, and accessible study material to help them prepare for the new CCSA and CCSE exams.

Sybex is excited about the opportunity to provide individuals with the knowledge and skills they'll need to succeed in the highly competitive IT security field. It has always been Sybex's mission to teach exam candidates how new technologies work in the real world, not to simply feed them answers to test questions. Sybex was founded on the premise of providing technical skills to IT professionals, and we have continued to build on that foundation. Over the years, we have made significant improvements to our study guides based on feedback from readers, suggestions from instructors, and comments from industry leaders.

Check Point's certification exams are indeed challenging. The Sybex team of authors, editors, and technical reviewers have worked hard to ensure that this Study Guide is comprehensive, in-depth, and pedagogically sound. We're confident that this book, along with the collection of cutting-edge software study tools included on the CD, will meet and exceed the demanding standards of the certification marketplace and help you, the Check Point certification exam candidate, succeed in your endeavors.

Good luck in pursuit of your Check Point certification!

Neil Edde
Associate Publisher—Certification
Sybex, Inc.

This book is dedicated to my first child, Chloe.

Contents at a Glance

Contents

Table of Exercises

Introduction

Welcome to the exciting world of Check Point certification! You have picked up this book because you want something better; namely, a better job with more satisfaction. Rest assured that you have made a good decision. Check Point certification can help you get your first networking or security job, or more money or a promotion if you are already in the field.

Check Point certification can also improve your understanding of how network security works for more than just Check Point products. For instance, currently over 300 products integrate VPN-1/FireWall-1 through protocols such as voice over IP (VoIP) and Lightweight Directory Access Protocol (LDAP), as well as technologies such as network address translation (NAT) and content filtering. Check Point's Open Platform for Security (OPSEC), located at www.opsec.com, is the foundation responsible for creating the standards used to incorporate products from third-party vendors with Check Point products.

It certainly can't hurt to have Check Point certifications, considering Check Point is the worldwide market leader in firewalls and VPNs and has been since 1995. According to their website, Check Point's solutions are "sold, integrated and serviced by a network of 2,500 certified partners in 149 countries." Obtaining a Check Point certification makes you a CCP (Check Point Certified Professional), which in turn makes you eligible to use the Certified Professional password-protected website. Here you'll find tools, features, transcripts, and other information not available to the general public. Other benefits of being a CCP include access to the Secure-Knowledge database, notification of product updates, use of logos and credentials, and invitations to seminars and other Check Point events. For more information about the CCP program, visit www.checkpoint.com/services/education/certification/index.html.

While pursuing Check Point certifications, you will develop a complete understanding of networking security. This knowledge is beneficial to every network security job and is the reason that, in recent times, Check Point certification has become so popular. Check Point is one of the leading and most respected firewall and VPN vendors in the world. To ensure that organizations can measure the skill level of Check Point administrators and engineers, Check Point provides various levels of certification that quantify network security knowledge and an administrator's ability to implement network security using Check Point products.

How to Use This Book

If you want a solid foundation for the Check Point Certified Security Administrator (CCSA) exam, then look no further. We have spent hundreds of hours putting together this book with the sole intention of helping you to pass the VPN-1/FireWall-1 Management I NG (156-210) exam.

This book is loaded with valuable information, and you will get the most out of your studying time if you understand how we put this book together.

To best benefit from this book, we recommend the following study method:

1. Take the assessment test immediately following this introduction. (The answers are at the end of the test.) It's okay if you don't know any of the answers; that is why you bought this book! Carefully read over the explanations for any question you get wrong, and note which chapters the material comes from. This information should help you plan your study strategy.

2. Study each chapter thoroughly, making sure that you fully understand the information and the test objectives listed at the beginning of each chapter. Pay extra-close attention to any chapter where you missed questions in the assessment test.

3. Complete the exercises included in each chapter on your own equipment if possible. If you do not have Check Point VPN-1/FireWall-1 equipment and software available, be sure to study the examples provided in the book carefully.

4. Answer all of the review questions related to each chapter. (The answers appear at the end of each chapter.) Note questions that confuse you and study those sections of the book again. Do not just skim these questions! Make sure you understand completely the reason for each answer.

5. Try your hand at the practice exams that are included on the companion CD. The questions in these exams appear only on the CD. These exams will give you a complete overview of what you can expect to see on the real VPN-1/FireWall-1 Management I NG exam.

6. Test yourself using all the flashcards on the CD. There are brand new and updated flashcard programs on the CD to help you prepare completely for the VPN-1/FireWall-1 Management I NG exam. These are great study tools!

 The electronic flashcards can be used on your Windows computer, Pocket PC, or Palm device.

7. Make sure you read the Key Terms and Exam Essentials lists at the end of the chapters. These study aids will help you finish each chapter with the main points fresh in your mind; they're also helpful as a quick refresher before heading into the testing center.

To learn every bit of the material covered in this book, you'll have to apply yourself regularly, and with discipline. Try to set aside the same time every day to study, and select a comfortable and quiet place to do so. If you work hard, you will be surprised at how quickly you learn this material.

If you follow the steps listed above, and really study and practice the review questions, CD exams, and electronic flashcards, it would be hard to fail the VPN-1/FireWall-1 Management I NG exam.

What Does This Book Cover?

This book covers everything you need to pass the VPN-1/FireWall-1 Management I NG exam.

- Chapter 1 introduces you to Check Point's Secure Virtual Network, which is a framework that provides a total end-to-end network security solution. This chapter is a high-level overview of Check Point VPN-1/Firewall-1.

- Chapter 2 discusses the different types of firewall architectures and takes a closer look at the architecture of VPN-1/FireWall-1.

- Chapter 3 covers the basics of VPN-1/FireWall-1 security policy, introducing you to each of the components that make up the security policy database. Security objects, policy properties, and security rules are all introduced in this chapter. By the end of the chapter, you will be able to configure a complex security policy using security rules and install the policy to VPN-1/FireWall-1 enforcement modules.

- Chapter 4 discusses advanced security policy topics, such as optimizing the performance of your security policy and learning how to manage security rule bases more efficiently. You will also learn about many of the useful CLI utilities that can be used to manage and monitor VPN-1/FireWall-1.

- Chapter 5 shows you how to use the SmartView Tracker application, to ensure that you can harness the native security logging features of VPN-1/FireWall-1, detect security threats, and block connectivity to suspected security threats.

- Chapter 6 discusses authentication in VPN-1/FireWall-1 and how VPN-1/FireWall-1 supports many popular authentication schemes. You'll also learn how to configure the users database, which holds all user and group objects—important features when defining authentication rules.

- Chapter 7 provides in-depth analysis of each of the authentication types supported on VPN-1/FireWall-1, how to implement each type, and when to implement them.

- Chapter 8 introduces you to the concept of network address translation (NAT), why it is such an integral component of Internet connectivity today, and discusses the various types and advantages and disadvantages of NAT.

- Chapter 9 shows you how to configure network address translation on VPN-1/FireWall-1. You will learn how to configure automatic and manual NAT. The differences between and caveats of each type of NAT will also be explored in depth, so that you know when you should implement the appropriate type of NAT.

- Chapter 10 provides the information you need to back up and restore VPN-1/FireWall-1 so you can ensure the ongoing availability and reliability of your VPN-1/FireWall-1 installation. You will also learn how to uninstall VPN-1/FireWall-1, as this may be required during the restoration procedure. Finally, you will learn about the SmartView Status SMART client, which is used to provide real-time system monitoring of VPN-1/FireWall-1 systems and products, ensuring that you are notified in real-time of any immediate or potential issues.

- The glossary is a handy resource for Check Point and other security terms. This is a great tool for understanding some of the terms used in this book.

Each chapter begins with a list of objectives covered by the VPN-1/ FireWall-1 Management I NG test. Make sure to read them over before working through the chapter. In addition, each chapter ends with review questions specifically designed to help you retain the information presented. To really nail down your skills, read each question carefully, and if possible, work through the chapters' hands-on exercises.

Within Check Point NG, there are periodic updates to the software. In the past, Check Point released service packs to improve the current product with patches and code enhancements. With NG, Check Point releases feature packs (FPs) that not only include patches, but also offer significant feature and code improvements. The most current version of FireWall-1 at the time of this writing is Check Point NG Feature Pack 3. Due to its broad enhancement of features, this version should be your minimum choice for deployment and is the deployment on which this book is based.

What's on the CD?

We worked hard to provide some really great tools to help you with your certification process. All of the following tools should be loaded on your workstation and used when studying for the test.

The All-New Sybex Test Preparation Software

The test preparation software, made by experts at Sybex, prepares you to pass the VPN-1/FireWall-1 Management I NG exam. In this test engine, you will find all the review and assessment questions from the book, plus two additional bonus exams that appear exclusively on the CD. You can take the assessment test, test yourself by chapter or by topic, take the practice exams, or take a randomly generated exam comprising all the questions.

Electronic Flashcards for PC, Pocket PC, and Palm Devices

To prepare for the exam, you can read this book, try the hands-on exercises, study the review questions at the end of each chapter, and work through the practice exams included in the book and on the companion CD. But wait, there's more! You can also test yourself with the flashcards included on the CD. If you can get through these difficult questions and understand the answers, you'll know you're ready for the VPN-1/FireWall-1 Management I NG exam.

The flashcards include 150 questions specifically written to hit you hard and make sure you are ready for the exam. Between the review questions, practice exams, and flashcards, you'll be more than prepared for the exam.

CCSA Study Guide in PDF

Sybex offers the *CCSA Study Guide* in PDF format on the CD so you can read the book on your PC or laptop. This will be helpful to readers who travel and don't want to carry a book, as well as to readers who prefer to read from their computer. (Acrobat Reader 5 is also included on the CD.)

Check Point—A Brief History

Founded in 1993 by Gil Shwed, Marius Nacht, and Shlomo Kramer, Check Point Software Technologies quickly rose to the top as an industry and worldwide leader in Internet and network security and in the VPN and firewall markets. What started out as a small software company has grown into an international leader in the security marketplace with over 1,000 employees and revenue of over $500 million dollars in 2001. Their international headquarters is in Ramat-Gan, Israel, and their U.S. base of operations is in Redwood City, California.

With products such as Check Point VPN-1/FireWall-1, Provider-1, and FloodGate-1, which are based on the Secure Virtual Network (SVN) architecture, Check Point is constantly updating its security offerings and providing valuable solutions to Internet and network security. OPSEC partner alliances expand Check Point's capabilities with integration and interoperability with over 325 leading companies.

Check Point has been honored with awards every year since 1997, and in October 2000, they were named in the top 10 of the "Most Important Products of the Decade" by *Network Computing*.

Check Point VPN-1/FireWall-1 has received countless certifications, both in the United States and internationally, by meeting the requirements of strict security standards set by government and commercial bodies worldwide. Check Point NG has achieved the following certifications:

- The Common Criteria for Information Technology Security Evaluation (CCITSE). This is a set of evaluation criteria agreed to by the U.S. National Security Agency/National Institute of Standards and Technologies and equivalent bodies in 13 other countries. The Common Criteria for Information Technology Security Evaluation (CCITSE or "Common Criteria") is a multinational effort to write a successor to the previous Trusted Computer System Evaluation Criteria (TCSEC), or "Orange Book" criteria. The CCITSE is available on the Internet at `www.radium.ncsc.mil/tpep/library/ccitse/`.

- The Federal Information Processing Standard (FIPS) 140-1 level 2 certification, administered by the U.S. National Institute of Standards and Technology's (NIST) and the Communications Security Establishment (CSE) of the Government of Canada, specifies security requirements designed to protect against potential threats such as hacking and other cybercrimes. FIPS information can be found at `www.itl.nist.gov/fipspubs/index.htm`.

- IT Security Evaluation Criteria (ITSEC E3), awarded by the Communications Electronics Security Group (CESG) of the United Kingdom, is equivalent to the Common Criteria EAL 4 standard. For more information visit: `www.cesg.gov.uk/assurance/iacs/itsec/index.htm`.

Check Point VPN-1/FireWall-1 Security Certifications

Check Point sponsors a number of different certifications for their products. The first certifications to tackle include the Check Point Certified Network Associate (CCSA), Check Point Certified Network Expert (CCSE), and CCSE Plus, based on the VPN-1/FireWall-1 product. From there, candidates can advance to Check Point Certified Quality of Service Expert (CCQE) for the Floodgate-1 product and Check Point Certified Addressing Expert (CCAE) for the Meta IP product. Finally, for those implementing VPN-1/FireWall-1 and Provider-1 Internet security solutions, Check Point offers the advanced Check Point Certified Managed Security Expert (CCMSE), which requires passing the CCSA, CCSE, and Managing Multiple Sites with Provider-1 exams.

Check Point Certified Security Administrator (CCSA)

Check Point Certified Security Administrator (CCSA) is the base certification that validates a candidate's ability to configure and manage fundamental implementations of FireWall-1. Before pursuing this certification, you should possess the skills to define and configure security policies that enable secure access in and out of your networks. You should also be able to monitor network security activity and implement measures to block intruder access to networks.

The first step in obtaining a CCSA is to obtain the recommended six months of experience with VPN-1/FireWall-1. After that, candidates may take Exam 156-210: VPN-1/FireWall-1 Management I NG. CCSA candidates will be tested on the following:

- The ability to administer and troubleshoot a security policy

- Testing and improving VPN-1/FireWall-1 performance

- Creating network objects and groups

- The ability to log management operations

- Configuring anti-spoofing on the firewall to prevent intruders from accessing the network

- Creating users and groups to be implemented for user, client, and session authentication

- Configuring network address translation (static NAT and hide NAT)

- Backing up VPN-1/FireWall-1

- Uninstalling VPN-1/FireWall-1

Candidates who successfully pass the VPN-1/FireWall-1 Management I NG are awarded their CCSA and can go on to gain other worthwhile Check Point certifications.

Check Point Certified Security Expert (CCSE)

Before taking the Check Point Certified Security Expert (CCSE), exam (Exam 156-310) you should possess the knowledge and expertise to configure VPN-1/FireWall-1 as an Internet security solution as well as the ability to configure virtual private networks (VPNs). CCSE certification builds on the CCSA certification, and therefore you must pass the CCSA exam before taking the CCSE exam. You will be tested on your ability to configure content security, setup user defined tracking, and protect against SYN floods, among other things.

Check Point demands a certain level of proficiency for its CCSE certification. In addition to mastering the skills required for the CCSA, you should be able to do the following:

- Use scanning and network assessment tools to look for weaknesses and then modify your security policy to close any holes.

- Be able to define a secure network architecture with components such as VPNs and DMZs, as well as using Content Security to filter HTTP, SMTP, FTP, and TCP traffic.

- Install VPN-1/FireWall-1 along with the pre- and post-installation tasks that go along with it, such as loading and hardening the operating system.

- Be able to edit system files such as `smtp.conf` and `objects_5_0.C` as well as importing and exporting users from your database.

- Configure Secure Internal Communications (SIC) in a distributed environment as well as between VPN-1/FireWall-1 and OPSEC products.

- Perform basic troubleshooting using the logs and basic network tools such as TCPDUMP.

- Be familiar with OPSEC partners and their ability to integrate with VPN-1/FireWall-1.

 Sybex offers the *CCSE™ NG: Check Point™ Certified Security Expert Study Guide* (ISBN 0-7821-4116-1) as a preparation solution to the CCSE exam (Exam 156-310). Check out www.sybex.com for more information.

Other Check Point Certifications

Once you have obtained your CCSE, you may feel compelled to advance to the Check Point Certified Security Expert Plus: Enterprise Integration and Troubleshooting (CCSE Plus). This is the highest level of certification for VPN-1/FireWall-1 and builds on CCSA and CCSE certifications. The CCSE Plus certification validates your in-depth technical expertise with Check Point's VPN-1/FireWall-1. This certification requires extensive knowledge of troubleshooting, network planning, and implementing complex VPN-1/FireWall-1configurations. To obtain the CCSE Plus, a candidate must pass the VPN-1/FireWall-1 Management I NG (Exam 156-210), VPN-1/FireWall-1 Management II NG (Exam 156-310), and a third exam: VPN-1/FireWall-1 Management III NG (Exam 156-510). Check Point offers two other certification tracks beyond the VPN/Security Track: Performance/Availability and Management.

Check Point's Performance/Availability certification is the Check Point Certified Quality of Service Expert (CCQE) certification, which focuses on network bandwidth management. CCQEs are expected to configure, implement, and manage bandwidth policies using Check Point's FloodGate-1 software as well as the VPN-1/FireWall-1 software. To become a CCQE, candidates must pass Exam 156-605: Quality of Service Using FloodGate-1.

In the Management track, Check Point offers two certifications: Check Point Certified Addressing Expert (CCAE) and Check Point Certified Managed Security Expert (CCMSE). The CCAE certification requires the ability to implement and configure Check Point's Meta IP software in a corporate network and the ability to streamline IP address management. CCAEs must also be able to configure and manage DNS and Dynamic DNS. CCAE status is earned by passing Exam 156-705: Introduction to Meta IP/ Deploying and Troubleshooting Meta IP.

CCMSE candidates acquire certification by becoming CCSAs as well as CCSEs. After earning a CCSE, candidates must be able to implement VPN-1/FireWall-1 as an enterprise security solution and deploy Provider-1 software in a Network Operating Center environment as a centralized policy management solution. CCMSEs are held in the highest regard. They are the premier experts for managed security services based on Check Point solutions.

To earn the CCMSE certification, candidates must pass: VPN-1/FireWall-1 Management I NG (Exam 156-210), VPN-1/FireWall-1 Management II NG (Exam 156-310), and Managing Multiple Sites with Provider-1 NG (Exam 156-810).

For more information about Check Point's certification offerings, updates and certification news, visit: www.checkpoint.com/services/education/certification/index.html.

Remember that test topics and tests can change at any time without notice. Always visit the Check Point website for the most up-to-date information (www.checkpoint.com/services/education/certification/index.html).

Where Do You Take the Exams?

You may take the exams at any of the more than 3,300 authorized VUE testing centers in over 120 countries (www.vue.com). Calling is not the way to register for an exam because they'll tell you to register on the Web. So go to www.vue.com, click IT Certification, select Check Point from the list of certifications, and click Go. From this page (www.vue.com/checkpoint/), you can register with VUE and setup your exam for a testing center near you.

To register for the Check Point Certified Security Administrator exam:

1. Create your VUE username and password and then sign in. Determine the number of the exam you want to take.

2. Register with the nearest VUE testing center. At this point, you will be asked to pay in advance for the exam. At the time of this writing, the exams are $150. You can schedule the exam in advance but if you want to schedule the exam for the same day, you must call the VUE testing center directly. If you fail the exam, you must wait until the next day before you will be allowed to retake the exam. If something comes up and you need to cancel or reschedule your exam appointment, contact VUE one business day prior to your exam appointment. Canceling or rescheduling an exam less than 24 hours in advance is subject to a same-day forfeit exam fee. Exam fees are due for no-shows.

3. When you schedule the exam, you'll get instructions regarding all appointment and cancellation procedures, the ID requirements, and information about the testing-center location.

Tips for Taking Your CCSA Security Exam

The CCSA exam contains approximately 75 questions to be completed in 90 minutes if the exam candidate is from Australia, Bermuda, Canada, Japan, New Zealand, Ireland, South Africa, the United Kingdom, or the United States. All other candidates are allotted 120 minutes. You must get a score of 69% to pass this exam. As was stated before, check the Check Point website for more information on the specifics before you take your exam.

There are no upgrade exams if you are certified on a previous version of VPN-1/FireWall-1. The exam is not adaptive and consists of multiple-choice and true/false questions. Remember to read each question carefully. Also, never forget that the right answer is the Check Point answer. In many cases, more than one appropriate answer is presented, but the *correct* answer is the one that Check Point recommends. Don't let common sense and experience cloud your answers.

Check Point does not subtract points for incorrect answers, so even if you don't know the answer, give it your best shot. Each subject area, which corresponds to the chapters in this book, pulls questions from a pool of questions. Not every objective is represented on the exam and therefore each exam is unique. The exam also contains a series of questions pulled from common events and questions encountered in Check Point's Technical Assistance Centers.

Certifications are valid for a minimum of 18 months and are considered current if they are for the current major product release or the product release immediately prior to the current release.

Here are some general tips for exam success:

- Arrive early at the exam center, so you can relax and review your study materials.

- Read the questions *carefully*. Don't jump to conclusions. Make sure you're clear about *exactly* what each question asks.

- When answering multiple-choice questions that you're not sure about, use the process of elimination to get rid of the obviously incorrect answers first. Doing this greatly improves your odds if you need to make an educated guess.

- You can move forward or backwards during the exam. You can also mark questions for review if you're not immediately sure of your answer. We find this most helpful because something later in the exam may trigger a memory that will enable you to answer the question you marked for review.

After you complete an exam, you'll get immediate, online notification of your pass or fail status, a printed Examination Score Report that indicates your pass or fail status, and your exam results by section. (The test administrator will give you the printed score report.) If you pass the exam, you'll receive confirmation from Check Point within four to six weeks, in the form of a letter that outlines the benefits of your certification as well as your username for the SecureKnowledge website and your Professional ID. Your password will be distributed via e-mail.

About the Author

Justin Menga is a Check Point Certified Security Expert (CCSE) and Cisco Certified Internetworking Expert (CCIE) employed as a network design consultant for Logical Networks Ltd in New Zealand, a global network integration company. Previously, Justin was employed by Compaq Computer as a network solution architect.

Justin provides network and security design/consulting services to a wide variety of clients with large, enterprise networks. To contact Justin, you can e-mail him at jmenga@hotmail.com.

Assessment Test

1. What are the minimum rights required to block intruders?

   A. Read-only access to the Log Consolidator component

   B. Read-write access to the Log Consolidator component

   C. Read-only access to the Monitoring component

   D. Read-write access to the Monitoring component

2. Which of the following describes the information on which control decisions can be made using stateful inspection? (Choose all that apply.)

   A. Application-derived state.

   B. Evaluation of flexible expressions based on application-derived state, communication-derived state, and communication information.

   C. Application-layer proxying.

   D. Inspection of Layer 2 parameters.

   E. Connection table.

3. Which of the following protocols is compatible with hide NAT? (Choose all that apply.)

   A. ICMP

   B. IPSec

   C. TCP

   D. UDP

4. Which of the following applications can be used to configure security objects? (Choose all that apply.)

   A. SmartDashboard

   B. SecureUpdate

   C. System Status

   D. Visual SmartDashboard

5. What is the quickest way to only view accounting log entries in Check Point NG?

  A. Use the Account log mode

  B. Use the Audit log mode

  C. Use the Account predefined log query in log mode

  D. Apply a log query to the Type field including only accounting log entries

6. You are using SmartView Status to monitor an enforcement module, and you notice a status of Untrusted on the FireWall-1 module. What is the most likely cause?

  A. SIC has not been established with the enforcement module.

  B. The FireWall-1 services on the enforcement module have failed.

  C. No security policy is installed on the enforcement module.

  D. The network connection to the enforcement module has gone down.

7. Which of the following *best* describes the function of a firewall?

  A. Provides address translation to connect the internal network to the Internet.

  B. Provides stateful inspection to ensure secure remote access communications.

  C. Protects the internal network from the Internet.

  D. Protects the internal network from external customers networks.

8. You hide a rule in your security rule base and install the rule base onto an enforcement module. Which of the following statements is *not* true?

  A. The hidden rule is displayed as a gray line in SmartDashboard.

  B. The hidden rule is not enforced by the enforcement module.

  C. The hidden rule can be displayed by selecting Rule ➢ Hide ➢ Unhide all.

  D. The hidden rule is logged in the security log if the tracking option is set to log.

9. What are the advantages of stateful inspection over other firewall types? (Choose all that apply.)

   A. Provides filtering of Layer 3 and Layer 4 parameters.

   B. Combines the performance of a packet filtering firewall with the security and application awareness of an application-layer gateway.

   C. Protects clients by proxying connections on behalf of clients.

   D. Cheaper than other firewall types.

10. Which of the following is true regarding implicit client authentication? (Choose all that apply.)

    A. It is the same as partially automatic client authentication.

    B. Users must manually authenticate to the TELNET or HTTP security server.

    C. Users can authenticate via user authentication to authorize the client authentication rule.

    D. Is the same as fully automatic client authentication

11. What is the recommended memory requirement for a VPN-1/FireWall-1 NG enforcement module?

    A. 16MB

    B. 64MB

    C. 128MB

    D. 256MB

12. Which of the following authentication types are transparent from a users perspective? (Choose all that apply.)

    A. User authentication

    B. Client authentication

    C. Implicit client authentication

    D. Session authentication

13. Which of the following describes the term client side? (Choose all that apply.)

  A. When a packet is transmitted out of an interface

  B. When a packet is received on an interface

  C. Where source NAT is performed

  D. Where destination NAT is performed

14. Where does the ICA reside?

  A. Enforcement module

  B. Management client

  C. Management server

  D. External CA

15. What are the two types of Check Point NG licenses?

  A. Central

  B. Local

  C. Remote

  D. Distributed

16. What are the functions of an enforcement module? (Choose all that apply.)

  A. Store the user database.

  B. Authenticate users.

  C. Maintain security logs of traffic.

  D. Inspect traffic against a security rule base.

  E. Provide network address translation.

17. You attempt to install a policy onto a remote enforcement module from a management server. You get a connection timeout error. You can still access the Internet from a PC via the enforcement module. What is the *most likely* cause of the problem?

    A. SIC is not established with the enforcement module.

    B. The implied VPN-1 control connections rule has been disabled.

    C. The Check Point enforcement module service has crashed.

    D. The stealth rule is applied too high in the security rule base.

18. A customer phones you, complaining that he has configured automatic NAT for a security object, added the appropriate security rules, and installed the policy; however, external devices using the rule can't connect to internal devices configured for automatic NAT. The customer has checked the ARP cache of his border routers and verified that the correct MAC address is associated with the valid IP address configured for automatic NAT. Which of the following could be the cause of the issue? (Choose all that apply.)

    A. The customer has configured hide NAT for the object.

    B. The customer has disabled automatic ARP.

    C. The customer has configured static NAT for the object.

    D. The customer has disabled client-side destination translations.

19. What are the default objects present in the users database? (Choose all that apply.)

    A. Default

    B. Default User

    C. Default Users

    D. All Users

20. An administrator wishes to block access using a security rule, with a notification sent to the system attempting access. What action should be specified for the rule?

A. Accept

B. Deny

C. Encrypt

D. Reject

21. Which of the following types of NAT is required for enabling external devices to connect to internal devices with private IP addresses? (Choose all that apply.)

A. Destination NAT

B. Hide NAT

C. Source NAT

D. Static NAT

22. Which of the following requires backup on a SmartCenter server? (Choose all that apply.)

A. $FWDIR/bin

B. $FWDIR/conf

C. $FWDIR/lib

D. $FWDIR/state

23. You wish to configure anti-spoofing for the internal interface of your VPN-1/FireWall-1 NG module. Three separate networks reside behind the inside interface. Which of the following must you do to define anti-spoofing? (Choose all that apply.)

A. Define the addresses behind the interface as External.

B. Define the addresses behind the interface as Internal.

C. Configure a group object that includes each of the internal networks.

D. Configure the addresses behind the interface as Specific.

E. Configure the addresses behind the interface as Defined by the interface.

24. Users on your network are complaining of slow Internet access to web sites. You narrow the problem down to your enforcement module. You notice that the web access rule has a rule number of 100, and that numerous anti-spoofing log messages are being generated. What should you do to rectify the problem?

    A. Place the web access rule near the top of the rule base.

    B. Configure a hosts file on the SmartCenter server.

    C. Disable NAT rules.

    D. Disable anti-spoofing.

25. What is the mechanism used by Check Point NG to ensure log unification?

    A. Log ID

    B. LUUID

    C. GUID

    D. SID

26. You create a user object called `jimmy` from a user template called `engineering`. After creating the user, you modify the engineering template so that access is only permitted between 8:00 A.M. and 5:00 P.M. (it previously did not restrict login times). An authentication scheme of RADIUS is configured for `engineering`. When can Jimmy log in?

    A. Between 8:00 A.M. and 5:00 P.M.

    B. Between 5:00 P.M. and 8:00 A.M.

    C. Any time

    D. Never

27. An intrusion has been detected by your organization and law enforcement authorities require logging events related to the incident that they can import into their Oracle database. You create a log query in SmartView Tracker and display the required log entries. What should you do next?

    A. Choose File ➢ Export.

    B. Choose File ➢ Log Switch.

    C. Choose File ➢ Print.

    D. Choose File ➢ Save As.

28. Which of the following ports can you use to perform manual client authentication via TELNET?

    A. 23

    B. 80

    C. 259

    D. 900

29. You wish to restart VPN-1/FireWall-1 services but not the SVN foundation. Which command or commands should you use (choose all that apply)?

    A. cprestart

    B. cpstart

    C. cpstop

    D. fwrestart

    E. fwstart

    F. fwstop

30. Which of the following are features of session authentication? (Choose all that apply.)

    A. Authentication is required per connection.

    B. Authentication is required once per IP address.

    C. Works with a small set of services.

    D. Works with any service.

31. When would you configure manual NAT instead of an automatic NAT?

    A. You don't want to configure local.arp.

    B. You don't want NAT to apply for all services.

    C. You don't want to configure host routes.

    D. You don't want to configure address translation rules.

32. Which SmartView Tracker feature would you use to display all the information contained within a field in SmartView Tracker?

A. Find

B. Width

C. Log query

D. Record Details window

33. In address translation rules for automatic static NAT, which of the following represents the private IP address of an object? (Choose all that apply.)

A. Original Packet ➤ Source

B. Original Packet ➤ Destination

C. Translated Packet ➤ Source

D. Translated Packet ➤ Destination

34. Where are user objects stored?

A. Security objects database

B. Security policy database

C. Security servers

D. Users database

35. You restore the `$FWDIR/conf` directory on a Windows-based enforcement module and install the security policy OK. Users now complain that they can not establish connections that have manual NAT configured and were previously working. What is the most likely cause of the problem? (Choose all that apply.)

A. Proxy ARP configuration has not been restored.

B. OS routing configuration has not been restored.

C. `$FWDIR/lib` folder has not been restored.

D. Security rules are not configured for the NAT rule.

36. Which of the following are components of an enforcement module?

　A. Inspection module

　B. Log database

　C. Object database

　D. Security Servers

37. Which of the following authentication schemes are supported by hybrid mode authentication? (Choose all that apply.)

　A. RADIUS

　B. TACACS

　C. OS Password

　D. S/Key

Answers to Assessment Test

1. D.   You must have read-write access to the Monitoring component if you want to block intruders. See Chapter 5 for more information.

2. A, B, E.   Control decisions can be made based on communication information, communication-derived state, application-derived state, and the information manipulation of the each of these. Communication-derived state is based on information contained within a connection table, hence E is correct as well. See Chapter 1 for more information.

3. A, C, D.   ICMP, TCP, and UDP are compatible with hide NAT, as they include Layer 4 identifiers that can be used to uniquely identify connections. See Chapter 8 for more information.

4. A, D.   Both SmartDashboard and Visual SmartDashboard can be used to configure security objects. See Chapter 3 for more information.

5. C.   In Check Point NG the previous account mode view has been removed, with all accounting records placed in the Log mode view. An accounting predefined log query allows you to view only accounting records with the single click of a button. D will work, but takes longer that C. See Chapter 5 for more information.

6. A.   The Untrusted status indicates SIC has failed between the Smart-Center server and the enforcement module. See Chapter 10 for more information.

7. C.   The primary purpose of a firewall is to protect the internal network or information assets of an organization from external threats. The most notable of these threats is the Internet. See Chapter 1 for more information.

8. B.   Hidden rules are still enforced by enforcement modules. They are merely used to tidy up the SmartDashboard display. See Chapter 4 for more information.

9. B.   Although stateful inspection provides A, it is not an advantage over other firewall types. Option C describes an application-layer gateway, and Option D is incorrect, as stateful inspection firewalls tend to be more expensive than packet filter firewalls. See Chapter 1 for more information.

10. A, C.   Implicit client authentication is also known as partially automatic client authentication. It enables users to authenticate transparently using the user authentication security servers in order to authorize a client authentication rule. See Chapter 7 for more information.

11. C.   The minimum memory requirement for an enforcement module is 128MB. See Chapter 2 for more information.

12. A, C, D.   User authentication is considered transparent, because the user connects to the desired target behind an enforcement module and is then authenticated, instead of having to authenticate separately with the enforcement module prior to connecting to the desired target (this describes client authentication in its default state, which is non-transparent). Implicit client authentication enables client authentication to be transparent if the service desired by the user is a user authentication service. Session authentication is transparent also, as the user connects to the desired target and is then prompted for authentication. See Chapter 7 for more information.

13. B, D.   Client side and server side refers to the point at which the INSPECT engine inspects a packet as it passes through an enforcement module. Client side is when a packet has been received on an interface (ingress) and is passed to the INSPECT module. In VPN-1/FireWall-1 NG, destination NAT is performed at the client side. See Chapter 8 for more information.

14. C.   The internal certificate authority (ICA) resides on the management server, and is designed to provide certificates for Check Point SVN components. See Chapter 2 for more information.

15. A, B.   Central licenses are the new licensing model for NG and are bound to the SmartCenter server. Local licenses are the legacy licensing model and are bound to the enforcement module. See Chapter 4 for more information.

16. B, D, E.   The enforcement module is responsible for enforcing policy defined on a management server. This enforcement includes the inspection of traffic against a security rule base and the authentication of users. An enforcement module also provides network address translation. See Chapter 2 for more information.

17. B.   The implied VPN-1 control connections rule enables all required communications between the management server and enforcement module. If SIC was not established, you could not even begin the process of installing a policy. If the enforcement module had crashed, Internet access would not work as all IP traffic is blocked if the module is down. The stealth rule can be applied as the first rule in the rule base, as the implied VPN-1 control connections rule is always applied before explicit rules. See Chapter 3 for more information.

18. A, D.   The issue here is with destination NAT. Remember that hide NAT cannot be used for external devices (with valid IP addresses) to establish connections with internal devices (with private IP addresses), only static NAT supports this. The question indicates that ARP is working, so this is not an issue. The customer may have disabled the client-side destination NAT parameter, which means the customer would need to add a host route for the valid IP address of the internal device to the enforcement module operating system. See Chapter 9 for more information.

19. A, D.   By default, a user template called Default and a group called All Users exists. The All Users group is hidden and cannot be deleted. The Default template can be modified and deleted. See Chapter 6 for more information.

20. D.   The deny action drops traffic silently, while the reject action drops traffic and sends a notification to the sending system. See Chapter 3 for more information.

21. A, D.   For enabling external connectivity to internal devices, static NAT (one-to-one mapping) must be used. Destination NAT is also required, as the destination IP address of the connections must be translated from a valid IP address representing the internal device to the private IP address of the internal device. See Chapter 8 for more information.

22. B, C.   The $FWDIR/conf directory requires backup on an enforcement module, while the $FWDIR/lib directory requires backup if any files in this folder have been modified. See Chapter 10 for more information.

23. B, C, D.   Because the interface faces the internal network, you must define the addresses behind the interface as internal (B). You can't use E, as this is only applicable when a single network resides behind the interface. Because multiple networks are behind the interface, you must create a group that includes each network first, and then choose the Specific option and specify the group. See Chapter 3 for more information.

24. A.   Always place your most commonly used rules near the top of the rule base. The first rule in the rule base is numbered 1. Clearly 100 is a long way down the list. Disabling NAT will prevent privately addressed hosts from accessing the Internet. Disabling anti-spoofing can leave you vulnerable to DoS attacks. See Chapter 4 for more information.

25. B.   The Log Unique Unification ID (LUUID) is used to identify log records associated with a specific connection. See Chapter 5 for more information.

26. C.   If you modify a user template object, any user objects previously created from the template are not modified. If you modify an LDAP user template object, any user objects previously created from the template are modified. Because the authentication scheme for engineering is RADIUS, jimmy is not modified. See Chapter 6 for more information.

27. A.   Using the log switch feature will close the current log file and create a new file. Using the save as feature will save the current log entries into a new file; however, the file will be in a Check Point proprietary format. Using the print feature will require manual import of the log entries. Using the export feature will save the log entries in a generic ASCII format. See Chapter 5 for more information.

28. C.   Client authentication via the TELENT security server uses port 259. See Chapter 7 for more information.

29. E, F.   The cprestart and fwrestart options do not exist. Using cpstop and then cpstart will restart *all* Check Point components, including the SVN foundation. Using fwstop and then fwstart will only restart VPN-1/FireWall-1. See Chapter 4 for more information.

30. A, D.   Session authentication works with any service and requires authentication per session or connection. See Chapter 7 for more information.

31. B. Manual NAT requires you to configure the `local.arp` file and configure host routes on the enforcement module operating system. You must also configure address translation rules yourself. Manual NAT does allow you to configure NAT to apply for specific services. See Chapter 9 for more information.

32. D. The Record Details window displays all information for all fields of a single log entry. See Chapter 5 for more information.

33. A, D. With automatic static NAT, two rules are created for each object that you configure it for. The first rule defines the translations performed on connections initiated from the private IP address of the object to the public IP address of the destination. Hence, the original packet source element represents the private IP address of the object. The second rule defines translations performed on connections initiated from external devices to the valid IP address of the object. For these connections, the valid IP address of the object is the destination IP address of the original packets and must be translated to the private IP address of the object; hence, the Translated Packet ➤ Destination element also represents the private IP address of the object. See Chapter 9 for more information.

34. D. All user objects are stored in the users database on the management server. See Chapter 6 for more information.

35. B. The enforcement module requires OS routing configuration to be restored to ensure manual destination NAT will work. Because the enforcement module is Windows-based, proxy ARP configuration is stored in the `$FWDIR/conf` directory, which has been restored. The `$FWDIR/lib` folder does not require backup on an enforcement module. The question indicates that connections were working beforehand, so it is not related to security rules. See Chapter 10 for more information.

36. A, D. The VPN-1/FireWall-1 NG enforcement module consists of an inspection module, Security Servers, and synchronization module (for high availability). See Chapter 2 for more information.

37. A, B, C, D. Hybrid mode authentication enables IPSec-based SecuRemote and SecureClient VPN connections to use any authentication scheme. See Chapter 6 for more information.

Chapter

1

VPN-1/FireWall-1 NG Architecture

THE CCSA EXAM OBJECTIVES COVERED IN THIS CHAPTER INCLUDE:

- ✓ Explain the purpose of a firewall.
- ✓ Compare firewall architectures.
- ✓ Identify the different components of Check Point VPN-1/FireWall-1.

Check Point VPN-1/FireWall-1 represents one of the leading *firewall* and *virtual private network (VPN)* products in the market today. Since its inception in 1993, Check Point has led the Internet security market, incorporating many enhanced features that enable organizations to apply network security policy in a robust and manageable fashion. Check Point VPN-1/FireWall-1 *Next Generation (NG)* is the most recent release of the VPN-1/FireWall-1 product set. VPN-1/FireWall-1 NG is a revolutionary release in many facets. For example, performance capabilities now exceed 1Gbps for both firewalls *and* VPNs, reliability and availability has been increased with enhanced load-sharing tools, and the centrally managed network security policy can now be extended to reach even mobile users situated in the most remote of locations. Check Point VPN-1/FireWall-1 NG forms a key component of the Check Point Secure Virtual Network (SVN), which is a framework that unifies network security policy across the entire organization, enabling organizations to use e-business applications securely and transparently.

In this chapter, we'll discuss the Secure Virtual Network, how to secure a network, and also introduce virtual private networks (VPNs). You'll learn about the SVN architecture, why it is important for organizations, and the components that comprise the SVN architecture. We'll examine Check Point's stateful inspection technology, showing you how it exceeds the performance, manageability, and security of other firewall technologies. Finally, there are several different types of VPNs that can be deployed to service different types of communications, and we'll discuss these VPN architectures and explain how each is important in various situations.

Securing E-Business Applications

Before examining Check Point VPN-1/FireWall-1 NG as a product, it is important to understand *why* we need the product in the first place. The reason why, in two words, is the Internet. Without doubt, the Internet has become an essential component of global commerce. The Internet provides global connectivity to millions of businesses and their customers, and for extremely low cost compared to traditional communication networks. The power of the Internet provides enormous opportunity for businesses to increase customer base, improve efficiency, and enable closely knit operations and relationships with other partners and vendors. The Internet has redefined how many organizations conduct business. The business models used by these organizations have been totally reengineered to harness the power of the Internet. Conducting business over the Internet is called *e-business*. E-business applications enable organizations to communicate with customers, partners, vendors, and remote employees, phenomenally increasing accessibility to an organization's products and services.

The openness of the Internet introduces dangers for organizations that are connected to the Internet. The Internet is a public network; however, the information that forms the intellectual property of an organization is considered private and confidential. Organizations must ensure the privacy and confidentiality of their information systems is maintained, at the same time ensuring they can maximize the benefits of the Internet. E-business applications that are provided for remote employees, customers, partners, and vendors must also be protected to ensure they are not affected by infamous *denial of service (DoS)* attacks. An e-business application being brought offline can immediately cost a large organization millions, and also causes perhaps a greater cost due to customers and partners losing confidence in the organization's network security. To protect private information assets and ensure the ongoing availability of e-business applications, an organization must deploy a robust security infrastructure. The security infrastructure must protect the organization, while at the same time be as transparent as possible, so as to not hinder the usability of services provided to (and from) the Internet. The best security infrastructures don't just implement a single security device (also referred to as a point solution) and not worry about the security of other network devices, hosts, and applications—they approach security in layers. Applying security to multiple layers of the network (for example, to networks, systems, applications, and users) makes it much more difficult for an attacker to breach the security of your network. Although an attacker may breach the first line of defense, other security measures are in place introducing another obstacle for the attacker.

The Check Point *Secure Virtual Network (SVN)*, which you will learn about in the next section, takes a holistic approach to security, allowing you to define a global *security policy* that can be distributed to the networks, systems, applications, and users that comprise a network. This represents much more than just providing a point solution for network security, or implementing multiple discrete security devices that each require their own security policy configured independently.

Before implementing security configuration on devices in the network, an organization should define and document a security policy that recognizes key systems and services and identifies threats to these entities. The cost of data theft or loss of service from threats versus the cost of securing the network to protect against threats must be considered, which determines the risk to business and how viable it is to mitigate that risk. A good security policy should also provide acceptable usage guidelines for users, implement best practices where possible, and define how an organization should respond to security breaches. The security policy must by signed off by your top-level management to ensure the rest of the organization accepts the security policy.

The Secure Virtual Network Architecture (SVN)

The Check Point Secure Virtual Network is a security architecture that provides a unified framework for implementing and maintaining network security, right across the network and its systems, applications, and users. This unified framework allows you to configure and manage the various components of your organization's network security, all from within a common management umbrella. The SVN serves as a central *policy definition point* and *policy distribution point* that defines security policies centrally and then distributes them to *policy enforcement points,* which are devices that enforce the security policy received from the policy distribution point, located throughout the network. The SVN allows you to centrally configure and manage firewall security, virtual private networks (VPNs), allocation of bandwidth resource, IP addressing, and much more. Because of its integrated nature, the Check Point SVN provides a total network security solution that represents best-of-breed security, reliability, scalability, and manageability.

Security policies are the rules that drive the security requirements of an organization—the SVN provides management interfaces that allow you to easily apply security policy *independent* of the physical security devices, applications, and users in your network. The abstraction of security policy from the security devices that enforce policy ensures the security policy of the organization is maintained throughout the network, independent of the number and location of the devices that enforce security. Taking this approach is crucial for scalability. Networks are not static entities. Rather they are dynamic and changing constantly, which increases the importance of the ability to extend security policy to new networks or to quickly adjust policy for network topology changes.

For many organizations, a firewall is the single (and only) security device considered sufficient to protect the security of the network from external networks such as the Internet. Figure 1.1 shows the concept of using a firewall to protect the internal (protected) network and the information assets located on the network from an external network.

FIGURE 1.1   Using a firewall to secure information assets

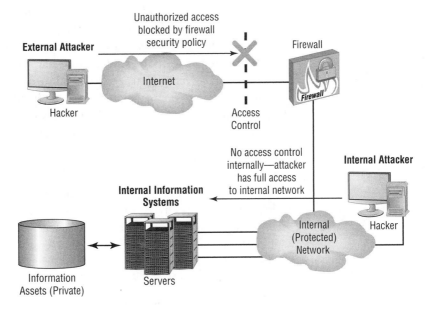

In Figure 1.1, all traffic that must pass from the external network to the internal network (and vice versa) must pass through the firewall. The mandatory flow of traffic through the firewall enables security policy to be defined on the firewall, which determines the internal systems and applications that can be accessed from external parties. Although the topology of Figure 1.1 may protect against unauthorized external access, it cannot protect against an *internal* threat. In Figure 1.1, an internal threat (which might be a contractor or disgruntled employee) is located on the inside of the network and has full local area network (LAN) connectivity to the internal systems and applications that house the information assets of the organization. The firewall has no way of controlling network access for internal communications— the network in Figure 1.1 is vulnerable to any internal threats that may exist. In order to ensure complete security policy enforcement across the entire network, the Check Point SVN architecture extends security to four key elements that comprise any organization:

Networks   Networks combine to form the infrastructure that systems, applications, and users use to communicate with each other. The SVN architecture provides security solutions that protect networks and control access between the various networks in an organization.

Systems   Systems are typically divided into servers and clients. A server hosts applications, which provide an interface for users to access the information assets of an organization. Servers also host the databases and files that comprise the information assets of an organization. A client system provides a vehicle for users to access the information stored electronically on server systems located on the network. Many types of devices comprise the client and server systems of an organization— for example, servers, desktops, laptops, personal digital assistants (PDAs), and cell phones. The SVN architecture allows each individual device to be protected, and also allows devices to securely communicate over insecure (public) networks such as the Internet.

Applications   Applications are the programs running on systems that provide a mechanism for accessing, communicating, and storing information. Applications deliver services; an e-commerce application provides a service that allows an organization's customers and vendors to engage in commercial transactions. The SVN architecture understands network traffic at an application level, allowing security devices to enforce security policies intelligently.

Users   Users provide the human aspect of networks. Security policy and access control are ultimately based on users or groups of users. When defining access to systems and applications, security policy documents will often refer to a group of users that represent a function of the organization. Many security devices represent a user as a system by controlling access based on the network address of a system—this approach is inaccurate as often multiple users may share systems. The SVN architecture allows you to define security policy rules that define users rather than just systems, ensuring you can control access on a per-user level.

By extending the security policies of your organization to these essential elements, you ensure that the security of your organization's information assets is maintained, regardless of the location of security threats. Figure 1.2 shows how the SVN architecture allows for the distribution of security policy throughout an organization's network:

FIGURE 1.2   The Secure Virtual Network

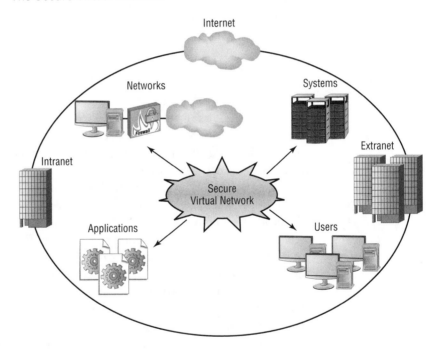

The security of the SVN architecture is not restricted by the physical topology of the network or other constraints. By abstracting the security policy from these constraints, the SVN architecture allows organizations to maintain security policy, regardless of location or topology. This is a very important feature for modern networks—the security boundaries of organizations are being blurred by the increasing need for features such as mobility. Figure 1.3 demonstrates an example of the blurring of the security boundaries of an organization.

FIGURE 1.3 Blurring the security boundaries

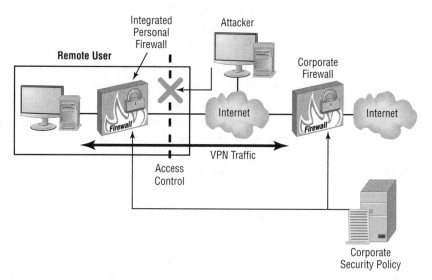

In Figure 1.3, a traveling employee accesses internal information systems back at head office by using a VPN connection on a laptop connected to the Internet. By using VPN technology, the head office network can be extended securely to the user—however, the user's laptop is also connected directly to the Internet. The user's laptop could be compromised, with the authorized VPN connection to the head office being used to gain unauthorized access to the head office network. The SVN architecture is capable of extending the security policy of the organization to a personal firewall running on the user's laptop. This option provides the benefits of being able to extend the network to remote users while ensuring the security of the network is not compromised. The key to the SVN architecture is that the policy applied to the laptop is created and distributed from the central management SVN framework, allowing for easy deployment and ongoing management.

To maintain the privacy of information of communications between geographically separated locations within an organization, traditionally expensive private wide area network (WAN) links have been provisioned to securely and reliably transport these communications. The SVN allows an organization to leverage the Internet to interconnect all components of an organization's networks in a secure and reliable fashion, allowing an organization to emulate a private, dedicated network for a fraction of the cost.

SVN Components

The SVN architecture consists of a base management framework from which different SVN components are managed. The SVN components can be categorized into four different functional product types: VPN/Security, management, performance/availability, and *OPSEC* applications.

 OPSEC stands for Open Platform for Security, which is designed to extend the SVN framework to include third-party products and services. OPSEC provides an application programming interface (API) to which third-party vendors can write applications that enhance or complement the functionality of the base Check Point SVN components. The OPSEC API exposes SVN component objects, services and data—for example, third-party applications that allow web traffic (HTTP, FTP and SMTP) to be forwarded from Check Point FireWall-1 to the application for virus checking and content filtering.

Table 1.1 describes the various products that comprise the SVN architecture.

TABLE 1.1 Check Point SVN Products

Functionality	Product	Description
VPN/Security	VPN-1	Provides authentication, encryption, and integrity to secure communications across an unsecured network.
	FireWall-1	Fully featured stateful inspection firewall.
	VPN-1/FW-1 SmallOffice	Provides the same VPN-1/ FireWall-1 features for networks with a small amount of users.
	Safe@Home	Provides a home user firewall/ VPN solution.
Management	Visual Policy Editor	Provides a visual topology representation of security policy and objects.

TABLE 1.1 Check Point SVN Products *(continued)*

Functionality	Product	Description
	Reporting Module	Analyzes VPN-1/FireWall-1 logs and provides consolidated reporting in a graphical format.
	Meta IP	Provides a total IP address management solution.
	UserAuthority	Enables a secure method of authenticating users against applications.
	Provider-1	Service provider product that allows hosting of multiple management servers on a single server.
Performance	FloodGate-1	Provides Quality of Service for different types of Availability traffic, including different streams within a VPN tunnel.
	High Availability Module	A redundant fail-over solution that ensures firewall/VPN uptime.
	VPN-1 Accelerator	Card that increases VPN throughput and simultaneous tunnel support.
	ConnectControl	Allows for intelligent load distribution of traffic to multiple application servers.
OPSEC Applications	Various	Hundreds of OPSEC applications are available that extend the functionality of the base SVN components. Categories include content security, reporting, and high availability.

Check Point has recently redefined the SVN architecture, creating new categories of products, renaming a few products, and providing some new products:

Connect Consists of the VPN-1 product family, used to securely communicate using VPNs. The VPN-1 product range has been renamed—VPN-1 Net is a dedicated VPN gateway (no firewall features), while VPN-1 Pro is the equivalent of the previous VPN-1/FireWall-1 product.

Protect Consists of FireWall-1, VPN-1 Pro, and other firewall products.

Accelerate Consists of FloodGate-1, ClusterXL (integrated high availability and load sharing solution), PerformancePack (uses SecureXL feature to accelerate performance), and others.

Manage Includes Meta IP, Reporting Module, SmartMap, and more.

Securing the Network

It is important for an organization to connect internal networks, systems, applications, and users to the Internet and to also secure that connection, ensuring the internal network is not compromised from unauthorized parties. The most basic security device used to provide Internet security is the firewall. A *firewall* is a security device that provides a gateway between an external, untrusted network (most commonly the Internet) and internal, protected networks that contain the systems and applications that house an organization's private information. In Figure 1.1 you saw how a firewall acts as a gateway between the internal (protected) networks of an organization and external (untrusted) networks such as the Internet. Because all traffic to and from the external network(s) must travel through the firewall, access control mechanisms configured on the firewall restrict the systems and applications that can access the internal network. There are two traditional approaches to firewalling: packet filters and application-layer gateways. Each has its advantages and disadvantages. Once we've discussed packet filters and application-layer gateways, we'll compare these firewalls with the firewall technology used for Check Point FireWall-1, stateful inspection technology.

Packet Filters

A *packet filtering* firewall represents the first generation of firewalls. The most basic packet filter firewall inspects traffic based on Layer 3 parameters (such as source or destination IP address). Packet filtering rules determine the *types* of traffic that are permitted access or denied access based on these parameters. Traffic types can be defined by the following:

- Layer 3 parameters such as source/destination IP address and IP protocol type (e.g., TCP, UDP, or ICMP)

- Layer 4 (e.g., TCP, UDP, or ICMP) parameters such as TCP/UDP source or destination port. TCP/UDP ports identify the upper-layer application protocol data contained within the packet (e.g., HTTP, DNS, or FTP).

Throughout this book, I may reference *layers*, for example, Layer 3 or Layer 7. Each layer refers to layers defined in the Open System Interconnection (OSI) model. TCP/IP consists of four layers: the application, transport (e.g. TCP or UDP), IP, and physical (e.g. Ethernet) layers, which can be loosely mapped to the seven layers of the OSI model.

Figure 1.4 shows the OSI model and demonstrates how packet filtering firewalls work.

FIGURE 1.4 Packet filtering firewall

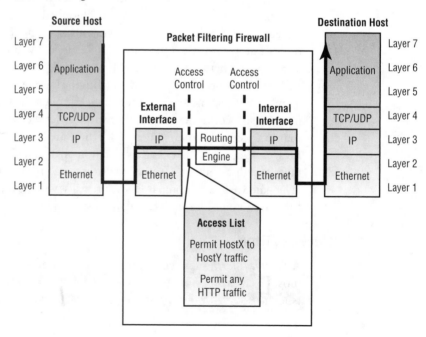

All traffic arriving into the external interface of the firewall is analyzed against an access list (a list of rules) that define which traffic flows should be permitted or denied. The firewall processes each rule until a match is made against the packet being inspected, and the appropriate action (permit or deny) is then applied. If the action is permit, the packet is forwarded to the routing engine of the firewall, which determines the egress interface and next hop where the packet should be sent to reach its final destination. If the action is *deny*, the packet is simply dropped, preventing unauthorized access from the external network.

A packet filtering firewall is essentially a *router* with access control rules configured. Routers are normally configured via a command line interface that is complex to configure, with the configuration being stored as a list of configuration commands, which makes it difficult to visualize and manage your security policies. Routers also typically do not support logging locally as they do not possess sufficient file storage space, so logging is required to an external system, which makes it more complex to maintain logs for auditing and reporting purposes.

A packet filtering firewall only operates up to Layer 3 (some can inspect Layer 4 parameters as well) of the OSI model. It does not understand the higher layer levels such as the application layer (Layer 7). By only having to inspect Layer 3 and possibly Layer 4 information contained within each packet, a packet filtering firewall can process traffic much more quickly than if it was inspecting Layer 7 information as well. This means that packet filtering firewalls can operate much faster than another type of firewall called the *application-layer gateway*, which operates up to Layer 7 in the OSI model.

Although a packet filtering firewall can restrict traffic *flows* (or communication sessions) between systems sent or received on a particular interface, it does not understand that traffic flows are *bidirectional* and maintain *session state*, which tracks events such as connection setup and data transfer associated with each traffic flow. By not understanding session state, it is easy for attackers to send attack traffic that may conform to the access rules defined on the firewall, but does not conform to the connection setup or data transfer rules of the service being accessed on the target system. An attacker can easily implement denial-of-service attacks by sending repeated connection setup requests that consume resources on target systems, or send illegal data that causes target systems to crash. Because a packet filtering firewall does not understand bidirectional communications, this makes it hard to ensure that a connection initiated by an internal system to an external system (e.g., a web server on the Internet) can succeed by permitting the return traffic of the connection from the external system to the internal system. Figure 1.5 illustrates why it is difficult to configure a packet filtering firewall to support bidirectional communications.

FIGURE 1.5 Bidirectional communications

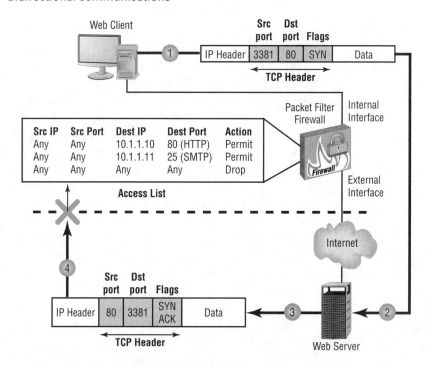

In Figure 1.5, a user on an internal PC (the web client) initiates an HTTP connection to a web server on the Internet. The following steps indicate how the connection is set up:

1. The initial connection request packet (also known as a TCP SYN or synchronize packet) is sent to the IP address of the web server with a TCP destination port of 80, which is the TCP port the web server listens on for new connections. The TCP source port of the packet is a free port (normally greater than 1024) chosen randomly on the web client. In Figure 1.5, the source port is 3381.

2. When the connection request packet arrives at the firewall, because no packet filters are configured on the internal interface or outbound on the external interface, the packet is routed towards the web server.

3. The web server receives the connection request packet, allocates memory for the new connection, and sends a connection acknowledgment packet (also known as a TCP SYN ACK, or synchronize and acknowledge packet) back to the web client, which informs the client that the connection request has been accepted. To ensure the client can track the connection that the acknowledgment is associated with, the source TCP port of the packet is 80 (because this is the TCP port the connection request was sent to) and the destination TCP port of the packet is 3381 (because this is the TCP port the connection request originated from).

4. The firewall receives the connection acknowledgment packet on the external interface. Because packet filtering is enabled for inbound traffic on the firewall, the packet is inspected against the access rules configured for the interface. The packet is dropped, because it does not match any of the permit rules. The permit rules only allow inbound traffic to a web *server* (not client) and a mail server. Because the web client chose a random source port in Step 1, there is no rule that can be defined on the firewall that specifies a static destination port.

Here is where the problem resides: an access rule could simply specify a rule that permits the IP address of the web server as the source and the IP address of the web client as the destination. However, that would allow any IP traffic from the web server to the web client, which would expose the web client. Alternatively, the firewall could use Layer 4 parameters to make the rule less open. A rule could permit TCP traffic with a source IP address of the web server and a source TCP port of 80, with a destination IP address of the web client and any destination TCP port (because the web client chooses a random TCP port for its side of the connection, the firewall must allow any destination TCP port for return traffic). Although this second rule is more restrictive than the first rule, the web client is still vulnerable because an attacker on the web server can send TCP connection requests to any port listening on the web client, as long as the attacker uses a source TCP port of 80.

Some packet filtering firewalls possess the ability to examine the TCP flags of packets to determine if traffic is part of an established session. Any traffic that has the *ACK* flag set is considered part of an established session under normal circumstances (I stress the word *normal*). In Figure 1.5, if the access rule permits TCP traffic from the web server with a source port of 80, any destination port, and a TCP flag of ACK set, it prevents the web server from sending a connection request to the web client, because a TCP connection request only has the SYN flag set. This strategy does not prevent an attacker from sending malformed data that might crash the web client (after all, the attacker only needs to ensure the ACK flag is set), and also does not work for traffic because UDP traffic is connectionless.

Although TCP allows for some restriction by allowing only established connections as described above, enabling bidirectional communications for UDP traffic represents an extremely serious security issue for packet filtering firewalls.

One solution for security risks of allowing UDP traffic is to not allow any UDP-based communications through the firewall whatsoever. However, DNS name resolution (which is a fundamental component of web browsing) uses UDP, so prohibiting UDP traffic represents a major restriction for the organization. Applications that communicate using UDP are responsible for establishing connections at the application layer, and a packet filtering firewall has no visibility of the application layer.

Because packet filter firewalls are simple, they are normally faster and cheaper than application-layer gateways—an advantage in certain environments. This is because packets that are processed by a packet filter firewall only need to be processed up to Layer 3 or Layer 4 of the OSI model, before being either forwarded or dropped. With an application-layer gateway, all packets must be processed right up to Layer 7 of the OSI model, which reduces the throughput capabilities of an application-layer gateway. When compared to application-layer gateways, packet filtering firewalls are also transparent to the traffic being inspected, which means end-devices are not aware of the packet filtering firewall. This transparency ensures that any type of traffic can be processed by the packet filtering firewall. The following summarizes the advantages of a packet filtering firewall:

- Transparent to the systems and applications sending traffic through the firewall.

- Higher performance (packet throughput) than application-layer gateways.

- Inexpensive.

Although packet filter firewalls are cheaper and faster than application-layer gateways, they do not possess adequate security or flexibility to meet the security requirements of modern networks. They typically do not possess sophisticated management tools, which makes them harder to manage on an ongoing basis. Modern hackers possess the tools and knowledge to bypass simple packet filtering firewalls, making their effectiveness limited. Because application-layer gateways process traffic up to the application layer, it is much harder for attackers to break through the security of an application-layer gateway. The following summarizes the disadvantages of a packet filtering firewall:

- No visibility of the application content of traffic.

- Lack of understanding of session state and bidirectional communications.

- Limited logging and alert information.

- Access to only basic header fields restricts packet modifications to only these fields.

- Difficult to configure and manage.

- Typically packet filtering is a feature bolted on to a multi-purpose device not designed with security in mind.

Application-Layer Gateways

An *application-layer gateway* firewall is commonly referred to as a proxy-based firewall, because it *proxies* application-layer connections on behalf of other clients. The application-layer gateway is vastly different from a packet filtering firewall in approach—all access is controlled at the application layer (Layer 7 of the OSI model), and no client system ever communicates directly with a server system.

Most applications and services that run on the Internet are referred to as client/server applications. A server hosts applications/services that provide access to data (e.g., a web server provides access to web content) while a client requests data residing on a server (e.g., a web client requests a web page from a web server).

An application-layer gateway provides *daemons* or services (server-side components) that emulate the services on the destination server that a client wishes to connect to. This allows clients to connect to the application-layer gateway rather than the destination server (the application-layer gateway accepts the connections on behalf of the destination server). The application-layer gateway also provides client-side components that allow the gateway to connect to destination servers on behalf of clients. To understand how an application-layer gateway works, consider Figure 1.6.

FIGURE 1.6 How an application-layer gateway works

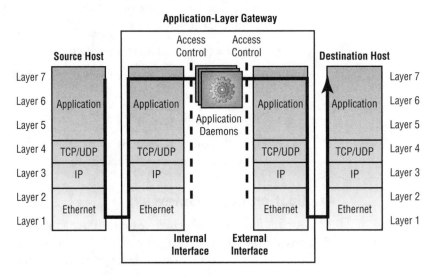

In Figure 1.6, notice the existence of application daemons. For each application that needs to be supported through the gateway, an appropriate application daemon must be available for and installed on the gateway. Most application-layer gateways also provide access control, regulating which hosts can use which services.

To compare how a real-life connection is made through an application-layer gateway, consider Figure 1.7, which shows the topology of Figure 1.5 using an application-layer gateway.

FIGURE 1.7   Example of an application-layer gateway

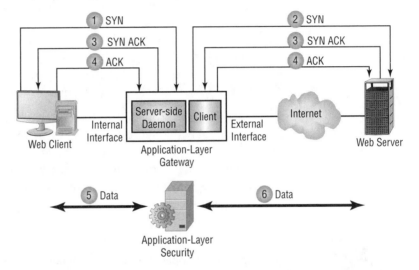

In Figure 1.7, the same connection demonstrated in Figure 1.5 is shown, this time using an application-layer gateway:

1. The initial connection request packet from the web client is sent to the application-layer gateway—in essence the client is establishing a connection with the application-layer gateway.

2. The application-layer gateway accepts or rejects the connection request based on the security policy configured. If the connection request is permitted, the application-layer gateway then establishes a new connection to the web server on behalf of the client.

3. The web server receives the connection request and sends back a connection acknowledgment to the application-layer gateway. The application-layer gateway sends an acknowledgment on behalf of the web server to the web client.

4. The web client sends an acknowledgment packet (known as a TCP ACK) to the application-layer gateway, which indicates the connection setup is complete. The application-layer gateway sends an acknowledgment packet to the web server on behalf of the web client.

5. The client starts sending data to the application-layer gateway (e.g., an HTTP GET request). The data is forwarded to a proxy web daemon (or service), which is essentially a web server running on the application-layer gateway. Because the application-layer gateway is running a web server, it understands the HTTP requests from the client and can ensure the traffic sent from the client is proper web traffic that conforms to the HTTP protocol standard. Assuming the traffic from the web client is legitimate, the application-layer gateway then sends the data to the web server on behalf of the client.

6. The web server processes the data received and responds to the data appropriately (in Figure 1.7, the client sends an HTTP GET request, and the server returns the web content associated with the URL). Return data is sent to the application-layer gateway, which ensures the traffic is legitimate. This data is then sent to the web client on behalf of the web server.

A non-transparent application-layer gateway requires configuration on the client in order to forward connection requests to the application-layer gateway. A common example of a non-transparent application-layer gateway is a SOCKS proxy server or a web proxy server. Some application-layer gateways can operate transparently, where they "pretend" to act as the server for clients, sending requests on behalf of the client and server to the appropriate destination without requiring configuration on the client.

The application-layer gateway introduces a greater level of security than a packet filtering firewall, because all connections to the outside world are made by the application-layer gateway and the application-layer gateway ensures all received traffic from either client or server at the application layer is legitimate. With a packet filtering firewall, although the firewall may understand that traffic is from a particular application, it does not understand the application protocol and what is considered legitimate traffic.

Although application-layer gateways are very secure in principle, they do raise issues with scalability and flexibility. For each connection a client makes to a server, the application-layer gateway must maintain a server connection (for the real client) and a client connection (to the real server). This consumes memory and processing time. An application-layer gateway scales to a much lower level than a packet filtering firewall due to the large amount of system resources required to maintain many connections through the gateway. In terms of flexibility, the application-layer gateway is somewhat limited, as the gateway must support every application protocol used by clients on the network. If an organization is using a few common services such as SMTP and HTTP, this does not represent a problem for the application-layer gateway. However with the increasing number of applications on the network and the convergence of voice and video onto data networks, many modern networks require application support for much more than just basic protocols. Each time an organization needs to use a new application through the gateway, support for the application protocol on the gateway must be present otherwise the application cannot be used.

An application-layer gateway also becomes a target for attackers because the gateway is directly accepting connections from the outside world. The operating system on the application-layer gateway must be very secure; however, it is still vulnerable to buffer overflow attacks and other unknown software bugs that might give attackers access to the gateway. If an attacker manages to compromise an application-layer gateway, the security of the entire network has been breached as the attacker now has direct access to the internal network.

Often application-layer gateways are used for common services, to separate the main firewall of the network, which can be a packet filtering firewall for performance reasons. An example is a web proxy server, which acts as an application-layer gateway for HTTP, HTTPS, and FTP traffic. The web proxy sits behind the firewall and makes web connections on behalf of internal web clients to web servers on the Internet. The main firewall has access rules that allow web connections from the web proxy—using this approach provides the speed and flexibility of a packet filtering firewall combined with the application-layer security of an application-layer gateway.

Because application-layer gateways operate all the way up to the application layer of traffic, it is very difficult for an attacker to bypass the security of the gateway. An application-layer gateway also proxies connections on behalf of clients, ensuring internal devices are not exposed directly to the Internet. The following summarizes the advantages of an application-layer gateway:

- Higher security than a packet filtering firewall.

- Understand application-layer protocols.

Although the application-layer gateway is very secure in principle, in the real world it does possess some severe limitations. The most notable limitation is performance—an application-layer gateway must allocate memory and resources for every connection passed through, as well as providing both client-side and server-side functions for each connection. This means that the total system throughput is limited, and expensive hardware is required to provide reasonable levels of performance. Another major limitation is the support for complex and obscure protocols. Because the security model of an application-layer gateway requires the gateway to proxy all connections, the gateway must understand each protocol from both a server-side and client-side perspective. Other limitations include non-transparency for end-devices and the increased complexity of the software required. The following summarizes the disadvantages of a packet filtering firewall:

- Performance is limited.

- Limited support for complex or less common protocols.

- Most application-layer gateways are non-transparent, meaning client systems must be reconfigured to use the gateway.

- Inefficient—doubles the number of connections required to achieve a single client/server session.

- High complexity increases the chances of bugs in the application-layer daemons on the gateway.

- Depending on the gateway vendor's interpretation of an application protocol, the gateway and clients/servers may have interoperability issues.

- Because application-layer gateways work at the application layer, the underlying operating system must provide security at lower layers (such as the network layer). Many operating systems are designed for flexibility, which can add many security vulnerabilities to the operating system. This means that the application-layer gateway itself may be susceptible to compromise.

Stateful Inspection Technology

So what's the alternative to packet filtering firewalls and application-level gateways? *Stateful inspection* operates in a manner similar to a packet filtering firewall, except that it possesses much more sophisticated access control algorithms. Both stateful inspection firewalls and packet filtering firewalls essentially provide security by making *control decisions*. An example of a control decision is whether to accept or reject a connection. Another example might be to encrypt a packet. Check Point FireWall-1 uses a patented and innovative *stateful inspection technology*, which is designed to provide the speed and efficiency of a packet filtering firewall and the application state awareness and high security provided by an application-layer gateway.

On a packet filtering firewall, control decisions are made purely on the Layer 3 and/or Layer 4 parameters of each packet received. Each packet is either permitted or denied, and is processed independently of any other packet, with no logical relationship being established between packets that belong to the same connection. If the parameters match an allowed traffic type, a control decision is made to permit the traffic. A stateful inspection firewall on the other hand can make control decisions based on much more that just the information contained within each packet received. The following lists the types of information on which a stateful inspection firewall can make control decisions:

Communication information   Information from the Layer 3 and Layer 4 parameters of a packet (this is the only type of information a packet filtering firewall makes decisions on).

Communication-derived state   Information derived from that passed within a connection. This can include Layer 3/4 information (such as TCP ports, sequence numbers, and so on) through to Layer 7 information (such as dynamic port allocations for new connections).

Application-derived state   Information derived from other applications. For example, Check Point FireWall-1 possesses a user authentication service that allows users to be identified. Once a user has been successfully authenticated, this information can be passed to the stateful inspection engine, which allows access to authorized services for the users. This feature allows for access rules to be defined based on users or groups, rather than IP hosts or networks.

Information manipulation   Decisions can be made based on all of the above—communication information, communication-derived state, and application-derived state. This allows for an enhanced level of flexibility and very granular security policy.

The most important difference between the packet filtering firewall and the stateful inspection firewall is the ability to make control decisions based on communication-derived state. By understanding the communication-derived state, the firewall not only permits or denies traffic with certain Layer 3/4 parameters, it also understands the current state of the connection (e.g., connection is in setup phase or data transfer phase). All traffic processed by the firewall is passed to a stateful inspection engine, which possesses the appropriate access rules. By maintaining a connection table that identifies each active connection through the firewall and the associated Layer 3/4 parameters, the stateful inspection engine can allow the return traffic of a connection, avoiding the issues with packet filtering firewalls demonstrated in Figure 1.6. Once a connection is established, the firewall verifies that traffic matching the basic Layer 3/4 parameters (such as source/destination IP address and TCP ports) of a connection are legitimate and not spoofed, by checking more advanced connection attributes such as TCP sequence numbers. A communication-derived state also encompasses application-layer intelligence, which allows the firewall to ensure complex protocols such as FTP or H.323 are passed through the firewall correctly. For example, FTP uses a control connection to send commands, while a data connection is used to return data. The data connection is established by using the PORT command to dynamically specify a port on the FTP client to which data should be sent. The stateful inspection engine examines FTP control traffic for the PORT command so that it can permit the data connection back to the FTP client.

Figure 1.8 demonstrates how a stateful inspection firewall works.

When comparing a stateful inspection firewall to an application-layer gateway, because the stateful inspection engine is application-layer aware, a stateful inspection firewall possesses a security level that is similar to an application-layer gateway. The stateful inspection firewall is much more flexible and can scale much higher than an application-layer gateway, as it can ensure communications integrity at an application level, without having to proxy all connections on behalf of the client/server endpoints of a connection.

FIGURE 1.8   How a stateful inspection firewall works

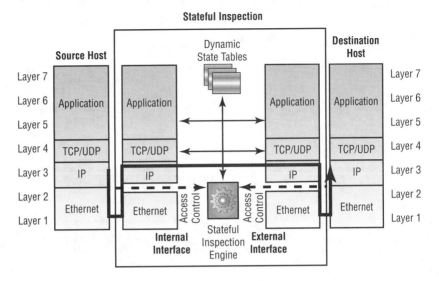

Fragmented Packets

The IP protocol allows packets to be fragmented when the maximum transmission unit (MTU) of a Layer 2 media over which the packet is being transported is smaller than the size of the packet. For example, Ethernet has an MTU of 1500 bytes, which means any Layer 3 protocol packet (such as an IP packet) transported in an Ethernet frame cannot exceed 1500 bytes. Assuming a 1500-byte IP packet was sent from a host on an Ethernet network, if the network path to the destination IP host included a Layer 2 link (e.g., a serial WAN link) that had an MTU of say 500 bytes, this IP packet (greater than 500 bytes in size) poses a problem for the devices communicating over the serial WAN link. In order to meet the MTU of the link, the devices attached to the serial WAN link can fragment (chop) the packets into smaller units to ensure the IP packets sent across the link are less than or equal to the MTU (500 bytes). In the example of a 1500-byte packet, it could be fragmented into three 500-byte packets and then transported across the link.

Once a packet has been fragmented, it stays fragmented until it reaches the destination host. The following graphic demonstrates how a packet is fragmented.

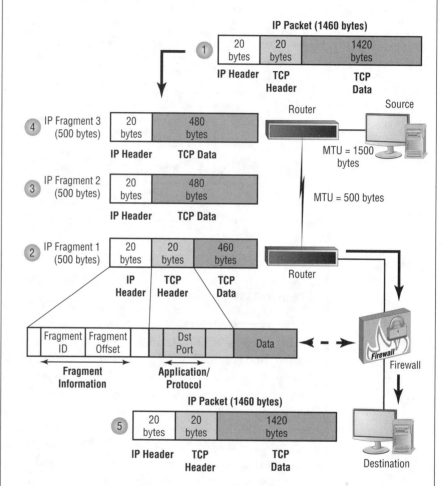

As illustrated above, a host sends a packet to the destination host indicated. The packet arrives at a router that must fragment the packet in order to meet the MTU of the WAN link to the next hop towards the destination host. Once the packet has been fragmented, it remains fragmented until it reaches the destination. Notice in the graphic fields exist within the IP header of a packet that identify whether a packet is a fragment, to which set of fragments the packet belongs and which part of the fragment a packet includes. To understand the problems fragments cause for firewalls, you must understand how a firewall examines packets to either permit or deny traffic. In the illustration above, the fields in the first fragment (labeled ②) that are examined by a firewall are indicated. Notice that these fields are all located within the IP header or TCP header of the packet.

The issue with fragments is that the Layer 4 headers (e.g., TCP or UDP headers) containing information about the applications/protocols the packet represents (e.g., HTTP or FTP) are only contained in the *first* fragment (labeled ②). Subsequent fragments only contain the data portion of the IP packet and have no Layer 4 fields that identify the application/protocol the packet represents. By examining subsequent fragments, the firewall has no way of knowing what application/protocol the fragment represents. The firewall can only read the *fragmentation* fields in the IP header to link the fragment to the first fragment within a fragmented IP packet. Attackers can exploit this by masking attacks using fragments. The attacker can send an initial fragment that has a TCP/UDP header that defines an allowed application, but then send attack traffic in subsequent packets. Because the firewall allowed the first fragment, subsequent fragments are permitted, even though these fragments may contain unauthorized or attack traffic. Many denial-of-service attacks also use fragmented traffic that is illegal (e.g., overlapping fragments, oversized packets) as denial-of-service weapons—the illegal traffic is designed to confuse and crash the TCP/IP stack or operating system of the target system.

To work around the issue of fragmentation, a stateful inspection firewall such as Check Point FireWall-1 maintains the state of a fragmented IP packet by caching each fragment until all fragments are received and then reassembling the fragment. By reassembling the fragment, Check Point FireWall-1 can perform application-layer analysis, and also ensure that the fragments are not illegal. This prevents attackers from bypassing the firewall or using fragments as a denial-of-service technique.

A stateful inspection firewall provides the speed and flexibility of a packet filter firewall, as well as the high security of an application-layer gateway. This means that you gain the best of both worlds in a single, high-performance platform. The following summarizes the advantages of a stateful inspection firewall:

- High performance.
- Understands both transport-layer (e.g., TCP/UDP) and application-layer (e.g., FTP) connections rather than just packets.

- Understands application-layer protocols.

- Maintains a dynamic connection table that is continuously updated with the state of each connection. This ensures the firewall enables the return traffic of allowed connections only as long as the connection is active, and also ensures that only legitimate traffic consistent with the expected state of the connection is permitted.

- Fragment reassembly allows the firewall to reassemble fragmented packets and inspect them, defeating a common method used by attackers to bypass firewall security.

- The underlying operating system of the firewall is protected, because the stateful inspection engine processes packets before they reach the TCP/IP stack of the operating system.

Of course the advanced technology provided by a stateful inspection firewall does not come cheaply. This means that the stateful inspection is typically more expensive than other firewalls, although for most organizations this expense is justified by the extra benefits gained. Another disadvantage relates to the fact that an application-layer gateway is not affected by issues with network address translation, which is increasingly becoming popular due to limitations with the current Internet IP addressing schemes. A stateful firewall often provides network address translation (NAT) to ensure internal private hosts are represented with a valid Internet IP address. Some protocols are broken by NAT. Because an application-layer gateway makes a new connection using a valid Internet IP address on behalf of a client, NAT is not required and is not an issue. The following lists the disadvantages of a stateful inspection firewall:

- Cost.

- Lacks some benefits related to an application-layer gateway, such as NAT.

NOTE   Although Check Point FireWall-1 is classified as a stateful inspection firewall, it does possess limited application-layer gateway functionality for a few common protocols. FireWall-1 possesses separate HTTP, FTP, SMTP, TELNET, and RLOGIN daemons that can be used to proxy connections for these protocols. FireWall-1 overcomes issues of NAT for many protocols by possessing an application-layer understanding of how to apply NAT for these protocols.

Virtual Private Networks

The most fundamental component of the Check Point SVN is FireWall-1, which provides a stateful inspection firewall that allows enforcement of network security policy at Internet and other external network access points. The next most fundamental component of the Check Point SVN is Check Point VPN-1, which provides virtual private networking (VPN) features. This section introduces you to virtual private networks, what they provide, and common types of VPNs.

A *virtual private network* (VPN) in the most generic sense refers to a private network connection that is overlaid onto a public network. For example, consider Figure 1.9—a service provider may offer a frame relay network that is considered public because multiple customers share the network. Frame relay permanent virtual circuits (PVCs) represent a VPN connection, as each PVC is logically separated from other PVCs and has no visibility of other (customers) PVCs. Although a physical link that forms part of the frame relay network may be shared by multiple customers, a PVC allows each customer to view the connection as private. Frame relay is an example of a Layer 2 VPN technology, as it operates at the data-link layer (Layer 2) of the OSI model.

FIGURE 1.9   A frame relay VPN

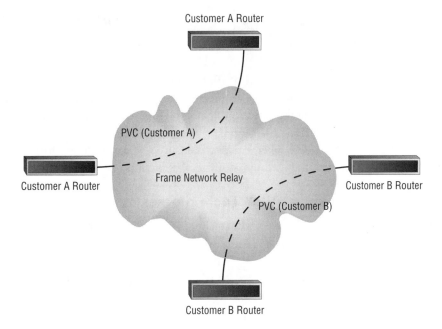

Customer A Router

PVC (Customer A)

Frame Network Relay

Customer A Router

Customer B Router

PVC (Customer B)

Customer B Router

When referring to the Internet, the term VPN usually refers to overlaying a private network connection onto the Internet. Because the Internet is the most public data network available, it is important to secure communications between remote offices and users when using the Internet as the transport medium. By using VPN technology, you not only secure information, but you also emulate a private network link for each VPN connection. Because VPNs on the Internet operate over an IP network (Layer 3), these VPNs are referred to as Layer 3 VPNs. Figure 1.10 demonstrates the concept of Layer 3 VPNs.

FIGURE 1.10 Layer 3 VPNs

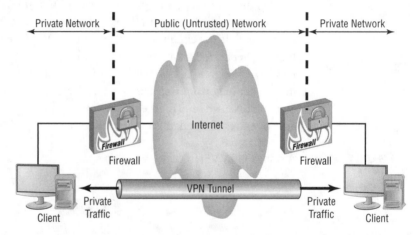

In Figure 1.10, the tunnel between each office represents a VPN connection—these connections appear essentially as private network links to each of the offices. VPN technologies used on the Internet provide logical separation of VPN traffic from other traffic by encapsulating IP packets in another IP packet. Privacy is ensured by encrypting information and authenticating the endpoints of each VPN connection.

Internet VPN Technologies

The main VPN technology used on the Internet today is the *Internet Protocol Security (IPSec)* standard. IPSec is defined in various IETF (Internet Engineering Task Force) Request for Comment (RFC) documents (see RFC 2411 for a guide as to which RFC documents relate to IPSec) and is designed to allow network devices and hosts to secure IP transmissions with a remote network device or host. IPSec addresses the following key requirements of securely transmitting information in a private fashion across a public IP-based network such as the Internet:

Authentication   To begin securely exchanging information between two parties, both parties need to be able to identify themselves, so that each party can verify the opposite party is an authorized party to exchange information with. IPSec provides authentication using either a shared secret (both parties must know a common password shared between the parties) or by using certificates, which are part of the *public key infrastructure (PKI)*.

Confidentiality   A VPN must provide privacy and confidentiality for information being transmitted via the VPN connection. IPSec provides a protocol called the *Encapsulating Security Protocol (ESP)*, which can provide encryption using various encryption standards. The most common encryption protocol used is called *DES (Data Encryption Standard)*, which uses a 56-bit key to encrypt information. Triple-DES (or 3DES) is a more secure encryption protocol that uses three 56-bit keys to encrypt information. More recently, the *Advanced Encryption Standard (AES)* has been developed which supports 128-bit or 256-bit keys.

Integrity   Even though you might encrypt information that if intercepted is very hard to decrypt, that information can still be used to compromise systems. For example, a banking transaction might be sent between two systems across a VPN. The transaction is encrypted, and a hacker on the Internet intercepting the transaction will find it very difficult (it will take a long time) to decrypt the transaction. However, the hacker could send multiple copies of the encrypted transaction. If the transaction was transferring $1,000 into the bank account of the hacker, by replaying the transaction multiple times, the hacker could deposit much more than $1,000 illegally. To prevent this sort of activity from occurring, IPSec includes *integrity* security features that allow a receiving party to verify IPSec communications were not tampered with in transit. IPSec uses sequence numbers to protect against replay attacks, and uses *message digests* (similar to a signature) to ensure an entire IPSec packet or the data contained within has not been altered in transit.

Non-repudiation   *Repudiation* is the ability to deny responsibility. For example, somebody may accuse you of doing something. If there is no evidence to support that accusation, you can successful repudiate the accusation. *Non-repudiation* is the opposite—with VPN communications, it refers to the ability to categorically confirm communications have been sent (and only sent) by a specific remote party. Certificates, which form a part of public key infrastructure (PKI) technologies, provide non-repudiation. A certificate contains the public key of a system or user, which is the only key that can be used to decrypt any information encrypted by the private key of the system/user. The private key is only ever known to the system/user that the key belongs to, which means that no other party could ever encrypt information in the exact identical fashion. It also means it is impossible for the party encrypting information with its private key to ever deny in the future that it sent the encrypted information. (Of course, this assumption breaks down if the private key is compromised and known to another party.)

In addition to the above, IPSec also has the ability to tunnel traffic, meaning it can encapsulate traffic in a totally new IP packet, and then secure the packet by encrypting it. This tunneling feature essentially allows IPSec to create VPN links—traffic between two organizations tunneled securely across the Internet. The VPN link appears to each organization as a single private link connecting the other organization. Each organization can communicate with each other's internal hosts, regardless of whether private addressing (illegal on the Internet) is used.

VPN Deployments

An IP-based VPN can provide secure and private communications for a variety of network topologies. There are three basic deployment types for VPNS:

- Intranet

- Remote access

- Extranet

Intranet VPN

The *intranet VPN* is designed to secure communications between different functional groups within an organization. For example, an organization may have a corporate headquarters located in one city, with several branch offices located in other cities. To enable data communications between the headquarters and the branch offices, the organization could use dedicated, private WAN links from a service provider. This approach is normally very expensive. An alternative approach is to implement VPN connections across a public network such as the Internet. Using a VPN emulates a private link, and uses encryption to ensure the privacy of intranet communications. Because the cost of a local Internet connection at each office is much lower than private WAN links spanning large geographic distances, an organization can gain considerable ongoing savings by using intranet VPNs.

Private international dedicated WAN circuits are phenomenally expensive, to the extent that many organizations have adopted the use of intranet VPNs to provide international connectivity at a fraction of the cost.

When designing an intranet VPN, you must take into consideration the following requirements:

Strong data encryption   Because an organization is sending encrypted data between *internal* groups across the Internet, the information being transmitted is of a highly sensitive nature. You should always ensure the strongest possible encryption algorithms are used to make it almost impossible to decrypt any encrypted communications that might be intercepted.

Scalability   As organizations grow and expand, the need to add more VPN connections to the intranet VPN increases. The head office VPN gateway that concentrates the VPN connections must be scalable to incorporate future growth and bandwidth upgrades.

Reliability   Because of the business critical nature of many intranet VPNs, the VPN devices used must be reliable and the network may also require a level of redundancy to ensure continued operation in the event of a single network device failure.

Figure 1.11 illustrates an intranet VPN. In Figure 1.11, two international offices of an organization are linked to the head office via VPN tunnels. If traffic needs to be routed between Tokyo and London, either the traffic can be routed via New York, or a dedicated VPN connection could be configured between Tokyo and London.

FIGURE 1.11 Intranet VPN

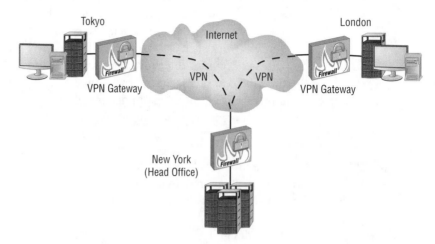

Remote Access VPN

A *remote access* VPN is used to provide remote access to an organization for employees that are located outside the organization. Most remote access VPNs are implemented over the Internet. For example, an employee may be out of the country, located in an area where there is no local office. The employee can use an Internet connection (e.g., one provided by a hotel) to establish a VPN connection to the organization VPN gateway, authenticate using his or her credentials, and then be granted access to the internal network. The VPN essentially extends the internal network out to the user in a secure fashion—all information transmitted is encrypted. When designing a remote access VPN, you must take into consideration the following requirements:

Strong authentication   Remote access VPNs are used to allow remote users to gain access to the internal network of an organization. A remote access VPN must be able to support at least the same levels of authentication required to access the network when connected locally. Ideally, because a remote user is not within the physical boundaries of the organization, the authentication technologies used should be stronger than that required for local users connecting to the network.

Scalability   An organization can potentially have hundreds or thousands of users that may be located remotely and each require a separate remote access VPN connection. The VPN gateway device(s) that terminate these connections must be capable of scaling to hundreds or thousands of simultaneous connections.

Management   Because of the large numbers of remote access users, management of these users must be centralized and should integrate as tightly as possible with existing databases that contain user accounts and passwords. For example, if your internal organization had 10,000 user accounts for users located internally, it would be administratively prohibitive to create another database on your VPN gateway and assign new passwords. At this scale, the VPN gateway needs to be able to utilize the internal authentication databases to ensure users don't need to remember too many passwords, and to reduce administrative overhead of maintaining users for remote VPN access.

Figure 1.12 illustrates a remote access VPN. In Figure 1.12, several remotely located users are connected via VPN tunnels across the Internet to head office—to each user it is as if they are back at head office connected directly to the internal network. VPN client software is loaded on each user's machines. This software is responsible for providing the VPN tunnel on the client side. When a user establishes a VPN connection to the VPN gateway, the user must send authentication credentials, which are passed to an authentication server (either locally or remotely) for authentication. Assuming the user's credentials are correct, the user is then permitted access.

FIGURE 1.12   Remote access VPN

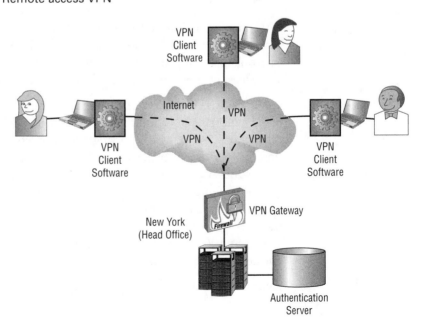

Extranet VPN

An *extranet VPN* is used to provide private communication links between an organization and another external organization, such as a vendor, partner, or customer. Traditionally, when an organization needs to establish communications with a third party, a dedicated private link is required. Although this link is private, it is also costly because it is not shared by anybody else. Another approach is to use an extranet VPN to emulate private links by using VPN connections between an organization and third parties. The VPN connection provides privacy and confidentiality by encrypting data between a VPN gateway located at the organization and a VPN gateway located at the third party. When designing an extranet VPN, you must take into consideration the following requirements:

Use of standards-based encryption When setting up VPNs between an organization and third parties, it is important that the organization VPN gateway supports standards-based VPN technologies, rather than proprietary vendor-specific VPN technologies. This ensures that the organization can form VPNs with any other third party that supports the standards-based VPN technology, regardless of the actual vendor of the VPN gateway device at each end of the VPN connection. The standards-based VPN technology primarily used on the Internet is the Internet Protocol Security standard (IPSec).

Performance Often extranets support business critical communications between various organizations that are critical to ongoing functions of the each organization. Extranet VPNs must be able to support the throughput of business critical traffic as well as deliver that traffic in a timely manner.

Quality of service (QoS) Because of the business critical nature of many extranet VPNs and the fact that this VPN traffic is shared with other traffic normally over a single Internet connection, an organizations network/security devices must be able to ensure that less important traffic does not starve the business critical VPN traffic of network resources. For example, if an organization has a T1 (1.5Mbps) Internet connection and a user downloads a large file from a web server and all traffic is treated as equal across the connection, the web traffic may starve the VPN traffic of its bandwidth needs, ultimately disrupting business for the organization.

Figure 1.13 demonstrates an extranet VPN.

FIGURE 1.13 Extranet VPN

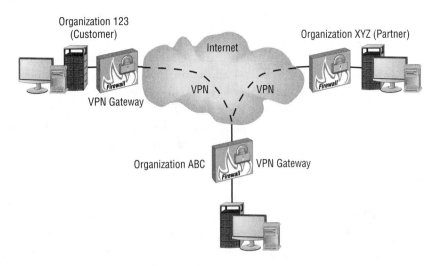

The Check Point VPN Implementation

Check Point VPN-1/FireWall-1 provides all VPN types (intranet, remote access, and extranet), allowing an organization that uses Check Point VPN-1/FireWall-1 to secure internal network communications, provide access to the network for roaming mobile users and establish links with external customers, partners, and vendors. Check Point VPN-1/FireWall-1 integrates the high security associated with the FireWall-1 product with the VPN functionality provided by VPN-1. By integrating both products, the following benefits are gained:

Security   Integrating FireWall-1 enhances the security of VPN deployments by introducing access control and user authentication in addition to the authentication, encryption, and integrity features offered by VPN-1.

Quality of service (QoS)   Because VPN traffic may be used for business critical applications, it is important to be able to provide *quality of service (QoS)* to these applications, ensuring other less important traffic does not starve critical applications of network resources such as bandwidth. FloodGate-1, an optional integrated component of VPN-1/FireWall-1 provides these QoS features. Having FloodGate-1 integrated with VPN-1 also allows for very granular QoS policy. For example, you might want to differentiate between different types of traffic *within* a

VPN tunnel—because FloodGate-1 can process the traffic before it is placed into the VPN tunnel, it can provide differentiated QoS to each type of traffic.

Performance and management   The integrated nature of VPN-1/ FireWall-1 allows firewall and VPN policy to be combined into a single security policy. Having a single policy for both network security and VPNs allows the network to scale easily. The integrated nature of the security policy also means that access control and encryption mechanisms can be merged into a single process, rather than being split into separate processes, improving performance.

Check Point has recently re-branded their VPN products. VPN-1 Net is a new product that only includes VPN-1 functionality and does not include FireWall-1 functionality. VPN-1 Net is designed to be a low-cost, purpose-built VPN deployment platform. Check Point has also renamed the VPN-1/FireWall-1 product as VPN-1 Pro, which is essentially VPN-1/FireWall-1 with a few enhancements that make VPNs easier to set up and manage.

Summary

The Internet has revolutionized the way in which organizations across the world conduct business. The openness and global connectivity allow organizations to reach new markets, form closer relationships with partners and vendors, and provide access to information for remote offices and workers. E-business applications are the mechanisms used to take advantage of the Internet. The openness of the Internet comes at a price—security. Because of the public nature of the Internet, it is important that organizations ensure security measures are in place to prevent unauthorized access to private information assets. By securing the network, you secure the e-business applications that leverage the Internet.

Check Point provides the Secure Virtual Network (SVN) architecture, which consists of various security products all unified by a common management framework. The SVN allows an organization to define a global security policy and apply it end-to-end across the network, systems, applications, and users that comprise an organization, regardless of the location of each. This architecture ensures security is easy to manage and is scalable enough for change and growth. The most common SVN component is Check Point VPN-1/FireWall-1, which provides a firewall device with integrated virtual private networking functions.

A firewall is a device that is used at the gateway of an organization's internal network and an external untrusted network such as the Internet. The firewall employs some form of access control to ensure that unauthorized hosts or applications can access the internal protected network. There are three types of firewalls: packet filtering, application-layer gateway, and stateful inspection. Check Point FireWall-1 uses a patented stateful inspection engine that provides the high performance of a packet filtering firewall with the application-layer capabilities of an application-layer gateway.

A VPN is a virtual private network, which emulates a private, dedicated service provider link used across a public network such as the Internet. The most common IP-based VPNs today are IPSec VPNs, and various types of VPNs exist to meet different communication requirements. The intranet VPN allows offices within an organization to communicate using a VPN connection, replacing the need for expensive dedicated private WAN links. The remote access VPN allows remote workers/teleworkers to connect to the enterprise in a secure fashion from any location in the world that has Internet access. The extranet VPN allows organizations to connect in a secure fashion to third parties such as customers, vendors, and partners. Check Point provides integrated VPN connectivity through the VPN-1 component of VPN-1/FireWall-1. Integrated VPN capabilities with firewall capabilities allow VPN traffic to be secured to a much greater extent; access control and quality of service can be applied to native traffic before it is placed into a VPN connection. The VPN-1/FireWall-1 integration also allows for firewall and VPN policy to be configured from the same security policy.

Exam Essentials

Understand the need for a firewall.   Firewalls provide a gateway typically between the Internet (an untrusted network) and the internal network of an organization that contains information assets private to the organization. To prevent unauthorized access to information assets from intruders on the Internet, a firewall implements access control, which typically comprises a set of rules defining which hosts and applications/services are permitted in or out of the internal network.

Know each of the three types of firewalls and the pros and cons of each. There are three basic firewall technologies: packet filtering, application-layer gateways, and stateful inspection firewalls. Packet filtering firewalls are simple, and therefore inexpensive and fast; however, they only examine packets on a one-by-one basis and have no understanding of the logical relationships (i.e., sessions or connections) between packets. Application-layer gateways provide full application-layer security by proxying connections on behalf of clients; however, this approach requires the gateway to run server-side components for each application, reducing flexibility, scalability, and performance. Stateful inspection provides the best of both firewall types. It combines the performance of packet filtering firewalls with the application layer visibility of application-layer gateways.

Know the types of information on which stateful inspection can make control decisions. The types of information on which control decisions are made are communication information (information from top five layers), communication-derived state (state information derived from the previous communications), application-derived state (information derived from other applications), and information manipulation (flexible expressions based on communication information, communication-derived state, and application-derived state).

Know what type of firewall Check Point VPN-1/FireWall-1 NG is. VPN-1/FireWall-1 NG uses a patented stateful inspection engine to provide stateful, application-layer aware inspection of traffic.

Understand what a virtual private network (VPN) is. A VPN provides a private and isolated connection over a shared network infrastructure such as the Internet. VPNs provide isolation (by tunneling traffic) and security (by encrypting VPN traffic). Most Internet VPNs are based on the Internet Protocol Security (IPSec) standard.

Know the different types of VPNs. The three types of VPNS are intranet VPNs, which link networks within an organization; remote access VPNs, which provide connectivity for remote users and teleworkers; and extranet VPNs, which provide connectivity to third party customers, partners, and vendors.

Key Terms

Before you take the exam, be certain you are familiar with the following terms:

Advanced Encryption Standard (AES)

message digests

application-layer gateway

Next Generation (NG)

bidirectional

Non-repudiation

Control decisions

Open Platform for Security (OPSEC)

Daemons

packet filtering firewall

denial of service (DoS)

policy definition point

Data Encryption Standard (DES)

policy distribution point

e-business

policy enforcement point

Encapsulating Security Protocol (ESP)

public key infrastructure (PKI)

extranet VPN

quality of service (QoS)

Firewall

remote access VPN

Flows

Secure Virtual Network (SVN)

Fragmentation

security policy

Integrity

session state

Internet Protocol Security (IPSec)

stateful inspection technology

intranet VPN

virtual private network (VPN)

maximum transmission unit (MTU)

Review Questions

1. The Secure Virtual Network describes which of the following?

   A. A virtual private network that uses encryption.

   B. An architecture for providing secure remote access to data center networks.

   C. A security product such as VPN-1/FireWall-1 that integrates both VPN and firewalling features onto a single platform.

   D. A common management framework that allows organizations to extend a central security policy end-to-end across the enterprise.

2. Which of the following describe the entities to which the security policy provided by SVN can reach? (Choose all that apply.)

   A. Networks

   B. Firewalls

   C. Systems

   D. Users

   E. VPN gateways

   F. Applications

3. Which of the following firewall types only operates up to Layer 3/4 of the OSI model? (Choose all that apply.)

   A. Application-layer gateways

   B. Packet filtering

   C. Stateful inspection

   D. SOCKS proxy

4. Which of the following firewall types would need to run daemons? (Choose all that apply.)

    A. Application-layer gateways

    B. Packet filtering

    C. Stateful inspection

    D. SOCKS Proxy

5. Which of the following firewall types breaks the client/server model?

    A. Application-layer gateways

    B. Packet filtering

    C. Stateful inspection

    D. Content security server

6. VPN-1/FireWall-1 makes control decisions based on which of the following? (Choose all that apply.)

    A. Layer 2 attributes of a packet

    B. Layer 3 attributes of a packet

    C. The state of a TCP connection

    D. The use of the FTP PORT command

7. Which of the following is an example of a VPN protocol?

    A. SSL

    B. IPSec

    C. Internet Protocol

    D. PPP

8. Which of the following are types of VPNs? (Choose all that apply.)

    A. Extranet

    B. Internet

    C. Intranet

    D. Remote access

9. An organization uses a VPN to provide connectivity to a customer network. What type of VPN is described above?

   A. Extranet

   B. Internet

   C. Intranet

   D. Remote access

10. A VPN requires user-level authentication to permit access via the VPN. What type of VPN is described above?

    A. Extranet

    B. Internet

    C. Intranet

    D. Remote access

11. Which of the following are examples of SVN products? (Choose all that apply.)

    A. VPN-1/FireWall-1

    B. Apache web server

    C. OPSEC applications

    D. Sun Solaris

12. Check Point VPN-1/FireWall-1 is an example of which of the following types of firewall?

    A. Application-layer gateway

    B. Packet filtering

    C. Stateful inspection

    D. Content security server

13. A firewall normally provides security between which two types of networks? (Choose all that apply.)

   A. Extranet

   B. Internet

   C. Internal

   D. Remote access

14. An organization uses a VPN to provide access to the network for a user located in a hotel. What type of VPN is described above?

   A. Extranet

   B. Internet

   C. Intranet

   D. Remote access

15. Which of the following describes a firewall?

   A. Policy definition point

   B. Policy enforcement point

   C. Policy distribution point

   D. Policy configuration point

16. What does OPSEC stand for?

   A. Open Security

   B. Outstanding Security

   C. Open Platform for Security

   D. Open Platform for Securing External Connectivity

17. If a TCP connection is established, which flag is always set in the TCP header?

   A. SYN

   B. ACK

   C. URG

   D. RST

18. Which of the following firewalls can detect attacks masked by IP fragments? (Choose all that apply.)

    A. Stateful inspection

    B. Packet filter

    C. Perimeter router

    D. Application-layer gateway

19. A company requires that all internal client connections to the Internet must not be direct connections. Which type of firewall would you implement?

    A. Stateful inspection

    B. Packet filter

    C. Perimeter router

    D. Application-layer gateway

20. Which of the following describes Check Point VPN-1/FireWall-1? (Choose all that apply.)

    A. Stateful inspection

    B. Filtering based on MAC address

    C. Application-layer gateway support for common protocols

    D. NAT Support for complex protocols

Answers to Review Questions

1. D.   As the answer states, the secure virtual network (SVN) provides a framework for Check Point and third-party OPSEC applications to be managed from a single enterprise-wide security policy.

2. A, C, D, F.   The SVN extends security to the networks, systems, users, and applications that comprise an organization.

3. B.   A packet filtering firewall only operates up to Layer 3/4 (network layer).

4. A, D.   Application-layer gateways proxy application-layer connections for clients, meaning they must run server-side daemons for each application/service that a client wishes to use. The SOCKS proxy is an example of an application-layer gateway.

5. A.   An application-layer gateway breaks the traditional client/server model by accepting connections from the actual client by acting as a server, and then establishing the connection (on behalf of the client) to the actual server by acting as a client.

6. B, C, D.   Check Point VPN-1/FireWall-1 makes security decisions based on many aspects of IP communications, such as communication information (e.g., Layer 3 attributes of a packet) and communication-derived state (e.g., TCP connection state and dynamic connection information communicated at the application layer such as the use of the FTP PORT command).

7. B.   IPSec is the IETF standard for providing secure VPN features using IP.

8. A, C, D.   Intranet, extranet, and remote access are all types of VPNs.

9. A.   An extranet VPN provides connectivity to third parties such as customers, partners, and vendors.

10. D.   Because a remote access VPN provides access for users, user-level authentication is used to ensure authorized users only are permitted access via the VPN.

11. A, C.   VPN-1/FireWall-1 and all OPSEC applications are examples of SVN products.

12. C.   Check Point VPN-1/FireWall-1 uses a patented stateful inspection engine.

13. B, C.   The most basic firewall provides a security gateway between the Internet and an organization's internal network.

14. D.   A remote access VPN provides access for remote users and teleworkers.

15. B.   A firewall *enforces* security policy by inspecting traffic and accepting or rejecting the traffic based on the security policy applied to the firewall.

16. C.   OPSEC is the open platform for security that is used to extend the functionality of VPN-1/FireWall-1 and allow interoperation with other third-party security applications.

17. B.   The ACK flag is always set for TCP packets that are part of an established connection.

18. A, D.   Both stateful inspection firewalls and application-layer gateways possess the ability to reconstruct fragmented data streams, which allows them to detect masked attacks.

19. D.   The application-layer gateway is non-transparent and protects internal clients by proxying connections on behalf of each client.

20. A, C, D.   VPN-1/FireWall-1 supports stateful inspection; application-layer gateway functionality for HTTP, FTP, SMTP, TELNET, and RLOGIN; and NAT support for complex protocols. MAC addresses are Layer 2 addresses, which are not inspected by VPN-1/FireWall-1.

Chapter

2

VPN-1/FireWall-1 Architecture

THE CCSA EXAM OBJECTIVES COVERED IN THIS CHAPTER INCLUDE:

- ✓ Compare firewall architectures.
- ✓ Identify the different components of Check Point VPN-1/FireWall-1 NG.

The previous chapter gave a high-level overview of why you need to secure networks and how you can go about doing so by using firewalls and VPNs. You were also introduced to the Check Point SVN architecture, including VPN-1/FireWall-1 NG, which is the focus of this book and the CCSA exam. Before learning about the specifics of configuring and managing VPN-1/FireWall-1 NG on a day-to-day basis, it is important to understand the internal architecture of VPN-1/FireWall-1 NG, and how the communications between various components of VPN-1/FireWall-1 NG can be distributed across the network in a secure fashion. In this chapter you will learn about the VPN-1/FireWall-1 NG product itself, examining the distributed set of components that comprise VPN-1/FireWall-1 NG and then learning how each of these components communicates in a secure manner across the network. The distributed architecture of VPN-1/FireWall-1 ensures that network security can scale as required, yet still remain manageable from a central administration point. To ensure that you understand at a low level how VPN-1/FireWall-1 NG provides network security and access control, we'll cover the internal operations of the firewall component of the VPN-1/FireWall-1 NG. This will aid in your understanding of how packets are processed by VPN-1/FireWall-1 NG in a manner that is fast and efficient but does not compromise security for the sake of performance.

VPN-1/FireWall-1 NG Components

Check Point VPN-1/FireWall-1 NG consists of a modular architecture that separates the administration, management, and enforcement functions of the product into separate components. Taking this approach enhances the scalability and performance of the product, allowing for a central security policy to be applied to distributed enforcement points throughout the network. For example, security policy configuration and auditing information collection can be managed on a device separate from a firewall device that enforces security policy. This allows the firewall device to concentrate on its job (security enforcement), removing the overhead of policy management functions.

In essence, VPN-1/FireWall-1 NG provides a three-tier model that consists of the following components:

- SMART Clients

- SmartCenter server

- Enforcement modules

In addition, an *SVN foundation* component resides on the SmartCenter server and enforcement module components (and also optionally on the management client), and provides common Check Point functionality to each component. Figure 2.1 demonstrates each of the components and how they interface with each other.

FIGURE 2.1   VPN-1/FireWall-1 NG components

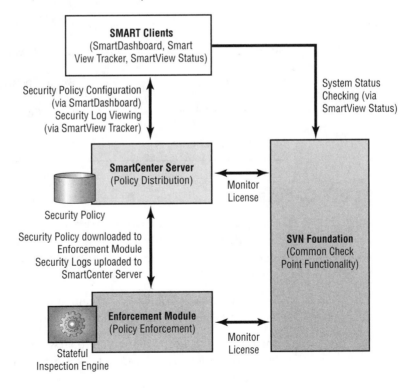

It is important to note that this book is based upon the VPN-1/FireWall-1 NG Feature Pack 3 release. A Feature Pack is similar to a service pack, however also provides new features in addition to software bug fixes. In the VPN-1/FireWall-1 NG Feature Pack 3 release, many of the components that comprise VPN-1/FireWall-1 have been rebranded, which may cause you some confusion if you are familiar with the old naming of components. Table 2.1 lists all of the new component names, along with the naming previously used.

 For the CCSA exam, make sure you understand both naming conventions.

TABLE 2.1 NG Feature Pack 3 Product Name Changes

Previous Name	Feature Pack 3 Name
Policy Editor	SmartDashboard
Visual Policy Editor	SmartMap
Log Viewer	SmartView Tracker
System Status	SmartView Status
SecureUpdate	SmartUpdate
Management Server	SmartCenter Server
Management Clients	SMART Clients

SMART Clients

The Check Point *SMART Clients* are a set of GUI applications that allow security administrators to configure and manage the global security policy for the entire organization. The fundamental SMART Clients include the following:

SmartDashboard   Allows you to configure security policy. In versions prior to NG Feature Pack 3, SmartDashboard is referred to as *Policy Editor*.

SmartView Tracker   Allows you to view security audit and event logs. In versions prior to NG Feature Pack 3, SmartView Tracker is referred to as *Log Viewer*.

SmartView Status Allows you to monitor status of enforcement modules. In versions prior to NG Feature Pack 3, SmartView Tracker is referred to as *System Status*.

The main SMART Client application used is called *SmartDashboard*, which is used to configure the security policy of the network. SmartDashboard runs on all Windows platforms (as well as on Sun SPARC Solaris-based platforms) and allows you to visually define security policy rules and the objects that comprise those rules. SmartDashboard interfaces with the *SmartCenter server* (look back at Figure 2.1), which houses the actual security policy database of rules and objects. Figure 2.2 shows an example screen shot of the Smart-Dashboard on Windows 2000.

FIGURE 2.2 SmartDashboard

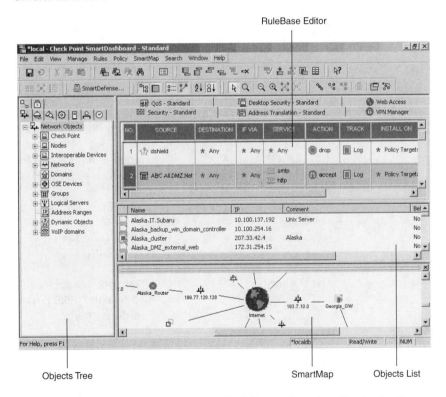

In Figure 2.2, various panes provide different functionality in the Smart-Dashboard window. The layout is quite different from previous versions, which only contained the Rule Base Editor pane. SmartDashboard NG introduces an Objects Tree and Objects Lists pane, which allows you to quickly search for objects in the security policy database, as well as the SmartMap pane, which displays security policy and objects from a network topology point of view. SmartMap aids administrators in visualizing the traffic flows that security rules will permit through the firewall and also represents an alternative method of finding objects within the security policy database.

SMART Client System Requirements

VPN-1/FireWall-1 allows you to distribute where to place SMART Clients in the network. If you are installing the SMART Clients on a separate machine from the SmartCenter server, you must ensure that the host machine meets certain hardware and software requirements. Table 2.2 lists the system requirements for installing Check Point SMART Clients on a separate machine (refer to Table 2.3 later in this chapter if you are installing SMART Clients on a SmartCenter server).

TABLE 2.2 Check Point SMART Client System Requirements

Component	Requirement
Operating Systems	Microsoft Windows 98, ME, NT, 2000, or XP; or Sun Solaris SPARC
CPU	Intel Pentium II 300MHz or higher (Windows) UltraSPARC II (Sun Solaris)
Memory	128MB
Disk Space	55MB (Windows) 100MB (Solaris)
Other	Network interface configured for TCP/IP 16-bit color (65,536 colors) with large monitor for SmartMap

SmartCenter server

The SmartCenter server contains the global security policy for an organization. This policy is defined using the SmartDashboard—however, the policy is actually saved on the SmartCenter server. The SmartCenter server contains the following databases, which together form the ingredients of the overall global security policy:

Object database   The object database represents the various network devices, systems, and services (applications) present in the network. For example, a workstation object can be used to define a server or PC, while a service object can be used to define an application-layer protocol such as HTTP.

User database   The user database holds user and group accounts that are used for user-based security rules.

Security rules   Security rules define the global rule sets that are applied to the various enforcement modules in the network. Each rule comprises objects or users that are defined in the object/user databases. You can store multiple rule sets; however, only one rule set can be applied for the entire network at any one time.

Log database   The SmartCenter server collects logging information from each enforcement module, information that can be used for auditing purposes. Logging information is stored in various log database files and can be viewed visually using the SmartView Tracker application on a system that has the Check Point SMART Clients installed.

The SmartCenter server interacts with enforcement modules by uploading security rule sets specific to the enforcement module and by receiving logging information from enforcement modules. The SmartCenter server also monitors the status of each enforcement module, which can be graphically viewed using the Check Point SmartView Status SMART Client.

The Check Point SMART Client applications can be installed on the same machine as the SmartCenter server, or on a separate machine.

SmartCenter Server System Requirements

The SmartCenter server is obviously a central component to your network security policy. When you are selecting a server on which to install the SmartCenter server, it is recommended that the server only acts as a VPN-1/FireWall-1 SmartCenter server, and does not perform other functions. This is especially important if you have configured a lot of logging in your security rule base. Table 2.3 lists the system requirements for installing the Check Point SmartCenter server:

TABLE 2.3 Check Point SmartCenter server System Requirements

Component	Requirement
Operating Systems	Microsoft Windows NT Server 4.0 (SP6a)
	Microsoft Windows 2000 Server/Advanced Server (SP1 or SP2)
	Sun Solaris 2.8 with patches 108434 (32-bit), 108424 (64-bit) and 108528-06, 109147-18, 109326-07 (32-bit and 64-bit mode)
	Sun Solaris 2.9 (64-bit mode only)
	Red Hat Linux (7.0, 7.2 or 7.3)
CPU	Pentium II 300MHz or higher (Windows or Red Hat Linux)
	UltraSparc II (Sun Solaris)
Memory	128MB
Disk Space	40MB
Other	Network interface configured for TCP/IP

Solaris 2.7 is no longer supported as an operating system for NG Feature Pack 3.

Enforcement Module

A Check Point VPN-1/FireWall-1 enforcement module is installed on network access points where network security rules must be applied. The most common example of such a network access point is the Internet access point, where the enforcement module protects the internal (protected) networks from the Internet (untrusted). Each enforcement module in the network has a rule set downloaded from the SmartCenter server that is specific to the enforcement module. Rules that are only applicable to other enforcement modules are not required and hence are not included in the rule set received. The rule set is represented as an *inspection script*, which is a file written in a proprietary language called *INSPECT*. This file is generated on the Smart-Center server for each specific enforcement module from the global security policy, and then distributed to the appropriate enforcement modules.

The enforcement module comprises two main components:

Inspection module   Determines access for all traffic based on the inspection script generated from the global security policy. The inspection module also performs network address translation functions to ensure devices with private IP addresses can connect to the Internet.

Security servers   Used to provide user authentication services as well as application-layer gateways for common services such as HTTP and SMTP.

The enforcement module is a software application that can be installed on a wide variety of operating systems, which include the following:

- Microsoft Windows NT 4.0/2000

- Sun Solaris (SPARC)

- Linux (Intel-based)

- Nokia IPSO

Check Point has recently released SecurePlatform, which is a bootable CD-ROM that installs a custom, security hardened Red Hat Linux build, which also includes VPN-1/FireWall-1 NG Feature Pack 2 or Feature Pack 3 software. The installation process takes approximately 10 minutes, which means that you can easily build a secured VPN-1/FireWall-1 gateway much more quickly than if you were installing a standard operating system.

Most enforcement modules are installed on what might be considered *general-purpose* operating systems, which by default include many features that are not required for enforcement module operation. All unnecessary features should be disabled, and best-practice security configuration for the applicable operating system should be applied to ensure the underlying operating system is as secure and as least vulnerable as practically possible. Many vendors offer Check Point firewall appliances, which are purpose-built firewalls that are essentially based on one of the above operating systems, with the operating system having already been secured and modified for firewall only use.

The system requirements for installing an enforcement module are identical to the system requirements of the SmartCenter server, listed in Table 2.3.

SVN Foundation

All Check Point products (excluding the SMART Clients) are installed with a base SVN foundation component, which is often referred to as *CPShared*. CPShared offers the following components:

cpstart/cpstop utilities   Allow you to stop and start Check Point component services.

Check Point registry   Common cross-platform registry for Check Point and OPSEC products.

Check Point daemon (cpd)   Cross-platform manager for all Check Point internal communications.

Watchdog for critical services   Monitors SVN component services such as cpd, fwd (FireWall-1 service), and vpnd (VPN-1 service). The watchdog ensures all monitored services are running and attempts to restart any failed services.

cpconfig   Provides a command-line utility that allows you to configure the base configuration properties for SVN components installed on a device.

License utilities   Manages the licensing of SVN components installed on the local system.

SNMP daemon   Provides an SNMP agent that can forward SNMP traps to an SNMP manager based on network security events

The SVN foundation essentially represents the background system management tasks and communication components that are common to each of the different SVN components. The SVN is a new component that was not present in versions of VPN-1/FireWall-1 prior to NG. By wrapping the core services and functions common to the various Check Point products into a separate module, they are easier to maintain and provide a common interface that can be used to enable better interoperability and management of all Check Point products. An example of a SVN component that utilizes the SVN foundation is *SmartUpdate*, which is a centralized software and license management tool for Check Point SVN applications. SmartUpdate communicates with CPShared components, allowing for licenses to be uploaded or new software updates to be distributed to the SVN applications running on a device. For example, SmartUpdate allows you to manage all licenses for all enforcement modules, and also allows you to apply software updates as required from a central distribution point. All current licensing and software information is stored centrally, eliminating the need to separately manage licenses and software upgrades for each device.

Three-Tiered Management Architecture

Check Point VPN-1/FireWall-1 provides a three-tiered architecture that enhances the manageability of security policy and also ensures a global security policy can be applied end-to-end. In this section you have learned about the three main components (excluding CPShared) that comprise Check Point VPN-1/FireWall-1:

- SMART Clients
- SmartCenter server
- Enforcement module

Each of these components can be installed on the same device, or they can be distributed across multiple devices, depending on the scalability and performance requirements of the organization. Figure 2.3 demonstrates how each of the components above can be distributed across the network.

FIGURE 2.3 Distributed VPN-1/FireWall-1 deployment

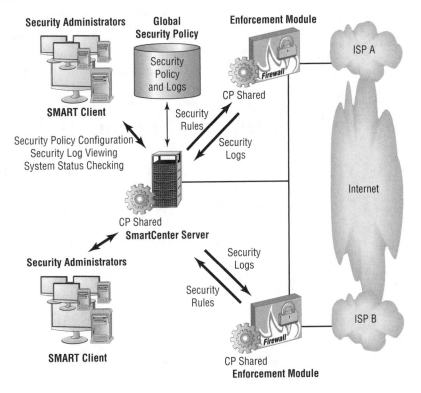

In Figure 2.3, SMART Clients can reside on security administrators' machines, separate from any other Check Point components. The Smart-Center server is installed on a dedicated server and houses the security policy database and logging database. SMART Clients communicate with the SmartCenter server in order to configure and manage the organization's security policy. The network consists of multiple Internet access points, which are each protected by separate, dedicated enforcement modules. The SmartCenter server distributes rule sets to each enforcement module, ensuring the security policy of the organization is adhered to. In Figure 2.3, the distributed nature of the Internet access points is covered by distributing multiple enforcement points, while the need for a central security policy is met by using a single SmartCenter server that can distribute the security policy to each enforcement point. If the SmartCenter server and enforcement module functions were combined with each other and installed on each firewall, multiple security policy configurations would exist and administrators would need to ensure each security policy was identical with all the others, making it much harder to manage the network security for the organization.

Check Point VPN-1/FireWall-1 SmartCenter servers can also manage router access control lists. This feature requires an *Open Security Extension (OSE)* license, which is purchased separately from the core VPN-1/FireWall-1 product.

Secure Internal Communications

In the previous section, you learned about the components that make up Check Point VPN-1/FireWall-1 NG. Each of these components is a separate entity that can be distributed across the network to ensure a global security policy is applied end-to-end. Because of the distributed capabilities of Check Point VPN-1/FireWall-1 NG, in order to communicate with each other, each VPN-1/FireWall-1 component must use the network to transport these communications. The network communications between the VPN-1/FireWall-1 components must be secure. For example, if administrative account information that has rights to configure the security policy of an organization is sent in cleartext across the network between a host running SmartDashboard and a SmartCenter server, this information can easily be captured and used to provide unauthorized modification of the organization's network security policy.

Check Point VPN-1/FireWall-1 NG employs a feature called *secure internal communications (SIC)* to ensure administrative communications between SVN components (such as a SmartCenter server and enforcement module) are secure. SVN components that use SIC include the following:

- Check Point SMART Clients (e.g., SmartDashboard)

- SmartCenter servers

- Enforcement modules

- OPSEC applications

- VPN-1 clients

SIC essentially uses a PKI (public key infrastructure) model to initially authenticate communicating components and then encrypt communications between components using *secure sockets layer (SSL)* encryption, protecting the privacy and confidentiality of the communications. SIC also ensures the integrity of communications by ensuring that communications are not altered in transit by another party and arrive in their original state. PKI is designed for scalability and ease of management; hence, SIC substantially reduces the administration of large, distributed installations by reducing the amount of configuration required to initialize SIC between each component.

Previous versions of Check Point VPN-1/FireWall-1 used a proprietary mechanism to ensure secure communications. To initialize each component, the use of the (sometimes troublesome) fw putkey command-line utility was required locally on each device. The new SIC model is much easier to initialize and configure, can be managed centrally and is also much less error-prone.

Securing Communications

As stated previously, SIC is based on the use of a PKI model to ensure the security of communications. The major feature of SIC is the use of *certificates*, which essentially certify (or authenticate) the identity of an entity. The use of certificates to authenticate identity is based on an important premise—all parties trust a *certificate authority*, which is a third party that signs certificates indicating each entity does indeed represent that particular entity. In SIC, the Check Point SmartCenter server includes an internal certificate authority (ICA), which is responsible for issuing certificates to all other SVN components within the organization. Certificates are not only used for authentication—they are also used to verify data integrity and to ensure the confidentiality of communications.

All security features provided by certificates revolve around a central concept—the use of *public/private key* encryption, also known as *asymmetric encryption* (because different keys are used to encrypt and decrypt data). Each entity possesses a public/private key pair, which is a set of keys that are mathematically related, yet cannot be derived from each other. The public and private keys share a unique relationship. Information encrypted using one key can only be decrypted by the opposite key, and vice versa. For example, if a message is encrypted using the private key, only the public key can be used to decrypt the message. No other key, including the private key, can be used to decrypt the message. The public key is freely distributed to other entities via certificates—however, the private key is known only to the entity the private key belongs to. Based on the simple relationship of public/private keys and the free distribution of public keys, entities can both verify the identity of each other (authentication), and ensure that communications have not been altered in transit (integrity). Certificates are used to authenticate each party of a communications session and establish a secure communications channel. Once this secure channel has been established, *symmetric encryption* (which uses a shared secret key securely negotiated by both parties for encryption and decryption) is used to provide data confidentiality.

This section provides an overview of the processes of authentication, data integrity, and confidentiality and describes how the use of certificates provides these features. Each of the examples looks at the features from the perspective of unidirectional communications—the concepts can be extended to provide authentication, data integrity, and confidentially for communications in both directions.

Understanding how certificates provide security is important, not just for Check Point's secure internal communications. The operations fundamentally form the basis of many forms of other secure communications mechanisms such as IPSec and HTTPS.

Authentication and Data Integrity

The first step in any secure communications transaction is for at least one party to identify or *authenticate* the remote party. This is similar to when you go to a bank to perform a financial transaction. Before the transaction is processed, you must identify yourself using some form of identification. With remote networking communications, mechanisms must also be in place to ensure that all communications between the parties are not tampered with in transit. This is referred to as maintaining the integrity of the data transmitted. Once both parties have been authenticated, a secure channel can be established that allows each party to ensure the confidentiality of data transmitted by using encryption.

To provide authentication and data integrity features using certificates, public/private key (asymmetric) encryption is used. An example of the use of public/private keys for providing both authentication and data integrity is shown in Figure 2.4.

FIGURE 2.4 Authentication and data integrity using public/private keys

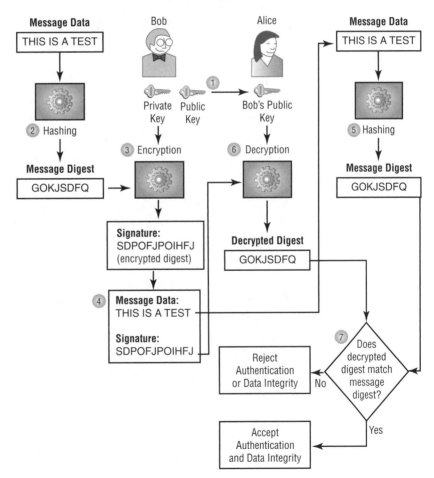

Let's assume that Bob wants to send a message (THIS IS A TEST) to Alice. Alice wants to verify that Bob is the sender of the message, and that the message is not altered in transit. The following events take place:

1. Bob sends Alice his public key via some mechanism. Normally this is contained within a certificate, which verifies that the public key does indeed belong to Bob.

2. Bob applies a *one-way hashing* function to the message data (THIS IS A TEST), producing a unique, fixed-length output called a *hash* or *message digest* (GOKJSDFQ). The hashing function is irreversible—it is virtually impossible to derive the original message from the message digest. The message digest produced is also guaranteed to produce a unique output for each message. This ensures the same digest is not produced from different messages.

3. Bob encrypts the digest (GOKJSDFQ) using his private key. This produces an encrypted output of SDPOFJPOIHFJ. This output is also known as a *signature*, as it is unique data derived from the message data (via the *message digest*) and Bob's private key. Because Bob's private key is only known to Bob, the signature uniquely identifies Bob—only Bob could have produced the signature data.

4. Bob sends a message to Alice, which includes the message data (THIS IS A TEST) and the signature (SDPOFJPOIHFJ).

5. Alice receives the message, and passes the message data through the same hashing algorithm used in Step 2. If the message data is the same as what Bob originally sent, this should output the same digest produced in Step 2.

6. Alice decrypts the signature (SDPOFJPOIHFJ) using Bob's public key that was sent in Step 1. Remember only a public key can decrypt the encrypted output derived from the associated private key and vice versa. In this example, the decryption process produces a value of GOKJSDFQ.

7. Alice compares the decrypted output of Step 6 with the hashed output of Step 5. If these values match, then Alice knows that Bob is who he claims to be. Bob's message has been authenticated because only Bob's private key could produce an encrypted output that is successfully decrypted by Bob's public key to the correct message digest. Matching outputs also confirm data integrity. If the message contents were

changed in transit, then the hashed output generated by Alice in Step 5 would be different, and would not match the decrypted hash output of Step 6. If the phrases do not match, then somebody is impersonating Bob or has altered the message in transit.

The processes outlined in Figure 2.4 depend on a couple of important trust relationships:

- The public key received by Alice must be trusted by Alice. Using certificates allows for this as a trusted third party (that has verified Bob is who he claims to be) is responsible for issuing certificates. The third party (also known as a certificate authority) signs the certificate, validating that the public key belongs to the user Bob. Because Alice trusts the certificate authority, it trusts the certificate and the public key attached to it.

- Bob's private key must only be known to Bob—if somebody else knew Bob's private key, then they could impersonate Bob using the processes described for Bob in Figure 2.4.

Notice that using authentication and data integrity alone does not protect the privacy of the data. The message data in Figure 2.4 is sent in cleartext across the network. Anybody who captures the traffic can see the data contained within.

Securely Negotiating Session Keys

Once each party that participates in a secure communications transaction has been authenticated, the next phase is to negotiate a shared session key that will be used to provide symmetric encryption and decryption of data. Symmetric encryption is much faster than asymmetric encryption, and hence is used for encrypting the data stream of a communications session. Encrypting data provides confidentiality for the data, ensuring that anybody who eavesdrops on the communications will find it virtually impossible to decipher the encrypted data. Before symmetric encryption can commence, each party must agree on an identical shared session key, which must be only known to each party and no one else, for the duration of the communications session. An algorithm called the *Diffie-Hellman* key exchange is normally used to negotiate a shared session key in a secure fashion. This mechanism is very secure, as the shared session key is actually never transmitted across the wire. Instead, public keys and other random values are exchanged, and a complex mathematical formula is used to derive the same session key on each party. Once the session key has been generated, it can be used for providing data confidentiality using symmetric encryption. Symmetric encryption algorithms include the Data Encryption Standard (DES), Triple-DES, and the Advanced Encryption Standard (AES).

Data Confidentiality

To obtain totally secure communications, the authentication and integrity features of public/private key encryption are combined with the confidentiality features of symmetric encryption, to ensure communications are authorized, authentic, and confidential. To provide confidentiality via symmetric encryption, the Diffie-Hellman key exchange process described previously is used to securely negotiate the session key for both parties. This session key is then used for the ongoing encryption and decryption of session data. Using the same session key for encryption and decryption is described as *symmetric* encryption. Figure 2.5 illustrates symmetric encryption.

FIGURE 2.5 Symmetric encryption

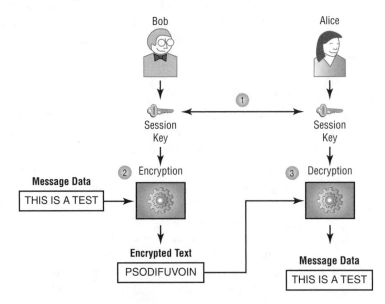

In Figure 2.5 Bob and Alice wish to communicate via a secure channel. Figure 2.5 shows the process of Bob sending a message (THIS IS A TEST) to

Alice and the processes that occur to ensure the privacy of the data while in transit. The following events take place:

1. Bob and Alice securely negotiate a session key via some mechanism. Typically this is performed using the Diffie-Hellman key exchange algorithm.

2. Bob encrypts the message data (THIS IS A TEST) by combining it with the session key and passing it through a symmetric key encryption algorithm, which produces an encrypted output of PSODIFUVOIN. This data is then sent across the wire to Alice. Any party intercepting this transmission will find it extremely difficult to derive the original message from the encrypted output.

3. Alice receives the encrypted message and decrypts the message using the session key negotiated with Bob in Step 1. This produces the original message data (THIS IS A TEST).

The process described in Figure 2.5 is used for the encryption of all data associated with a communications session. Notice in Figure 2.5 that authentication and data integrity are *not* provided. Somebody can send false data to Alice, and Alice will decrypt the data and think that it is from Bob (the data will most likely be garbled, and that could be used to crash the system that Alice is operating). To combine data confidentiality (as shown in Figure 2.5) with authentication and data integrity, the encrypted data generated in Step 2 of Figure 2.5 is used as the message data in Figure 2.4. This verifies the authenticity and integrity of the encrypted data that Bob sends.

Symmetric Encryption versus Asymmetric Encryption

You might be wondering why symmetric encryption is used for encrypting data, as opposed to asymmetric encryption. Symmetric encryption uses much smaller keys (e.g., DES uses 56-bit, Triple-DES uses 168-bit) and has much less computational complexity than asymmetric, meaning it can be performed faster. Asymmetric encryption uses keys in the order of 512 bits and 1024 bits, and is therefore much slower (but much more secure). By using the very secure asymmetric encryption processes to securely negotiate a session key, and then using the session key for symmetric encryption of data, devices can communicate in a secure and scalable fashion.

Certificates

You learned earlier that a public key must be the trusted in order for the whole authentication and data integrity processes to work. Certificates provide a means of establishing identity and trust. A certificate is essentially an electronic document that contains information about the identity of an entity (for example the name of a person or system, IP address, and so on), the public key of the entity, and a signature from a trusted certificate authority, which verifies the certificate is authentic. The signature of the CA is created in the same manner as the signature created in Figure 2.3—an entity viewing the certificate knows that the certificate is authentic and has not been tampered with by hashing the certificate contents and comparing the computed digest with the digest computed by decrypting the signature using the CA's public key. PKI uses *transitive* trust to achieve security. By trusting the key component of a PKI infrastructure (the certificate authority), you trust any certificate that has been signed by the certificate authority.

Public/private encryption and certificates are used for secure sockets layer (SSL) encryption, which provides security for many types of applications and protocols. The most common use of SSL is in conjunction with HTTP (also known as Secure HTTP or HTTPS). Most consumers using Internet banking or placing credit card transactions over the Internet demand security, and HTTPS is used to provide that security. Check Point SIC similarly uses SSL encryption to secure the Check Point management protocol used for administrative communications. After the identity of each communicating party has been authenticated, the parties then begin to negotiate a shared session key, which is used for a symmetric encryption algorithm such as DES, Triple-DES, or AES. Public/private key encryption is still used during data transfer to authenticate and verify the integrity of the data being transmitted.

SIC Operation

Check Point VPN-1/FireWall-1 NG provides an *internal certificate authority (ICA)*, which resides on a SmartCenter server. This is useful as you do not need an external certificate authority, which can be costly and is not required for the needs of SIC. Figure 2.6 demonstrates how SIC is initialized in the network.

FIGURE 2.6 SIC initialization

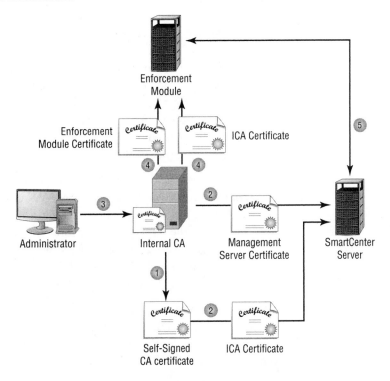

In Figure 2.6, the following events take place:

1. During installation of the SmartCenter server, an ICA is automatically created, and a *self-signed* certificate is issued that represents the ICA. This certificate is required by all entities to verify the authenticity of any certificates issued by the CA.

2. The ICA issues a certificate that identifies the SmartCenter server. This certificate is distributed to the SmartCenter server, so that it can send the certificate to other SVN components in order to identify itself. The ICA also sends the ICA's own self-signed certificate to the SmartCenter server, which allows the SmartCenter server to authenticate other SVN components.

3. After installation of the SmartCenter server, an administrator installs the enforcement module. During installation of the enforcement module, a one-time password (activation key) is configured, which is used to authenticate initial communications with the SmartCenter server.

4. An administrator creates a certificate on the SmartCenter server for the enforcement module. The administrator must specify the one-time password configured in Step 3 to authenticate the SmartCenter server to the enforcement module. As soon as a certificate is created for the enforcement module, the SmartCenter server and enforcement module authenticate each other using the one-time password. The ICA then signs the certificate and delivers it to the enforcement module (this allows the enforcement module to identify itself to other SVN components). The ICA also sends the ICA's own certificate to allow the enforcement module to authenticate other components.

5. Once all SVN components possess certificates signed by the ICA, each component can authenticate other SVN components by checking the ICA signature on each certificate. Because every SVN component trusts the ICA, if the signature is authentic, the component trusts the remote party. Each SVN component uses the authentication/data integrity mechanism described in Figure 2.4 to verify the certificate is authentic and unaltered while in transit from the ICA to the SVN component.

It is important to note that the ICA is a part of the SmartCenter server and cannot be separated out into a separate component. The SmartCenter server in Figure 2.6 refers to the component of the entire SmartCenter server that communicates with other SVN components.

You cannot use the ICA to form the basis of a PKI solution where you issue certificates to many types of devices. The ICA can only be used to manage certificates for Check Point and OPSEC products.

The certificate that is created is written in X.509 format, which is a standards-based format for producing certificates. Each certificate includes information such as the entity name (also known as the *distinguished name* or *DN*), IP address, and other information.

Once you have created a certificate for an object using SmartDashboard, you cannot rename the object. Make sure you carefully define your naming conventions before issuing certificates.

Although Check Point VPN-1/FireWall-1 NG supports SIC, previous versions of Check Point do not. All SVN NG components are backward compatible with the previous `fw putkey` shared secret method used. Each Check Point VPN-1/FireWall-1 component possesses a special configuration file that lists the methods of authentication supported. SIC will only be used between two Check Point components if they both support it. This means they must be of the appropriate version, agree on using certificates for authentication, and also agree on the encryption algorithm (e.g., DES, Triple-DES, or AES) used to encrypt the communications session.

SIC Communications with SmartDashboard

SIC communications between a SmartCenter server and an enforcement module are authenticated using certificates signed by the ICA and installed on both the SmartCenter server and the enforcement module. When using the SMART Clients to communicate with the SmartCenter server, you can authenticate the connection using certificates (which operate identically to how the SmartCenter server and enforcement module communicate) or by just using a username/password, eliminating the requirement for certificates. The username/password authentication process used between the SmartDashboard SMART Client and the SmartCenter server is illustrated in Figure 2.7.

FIGURE 2.7   SIC communications with SmartDashboard

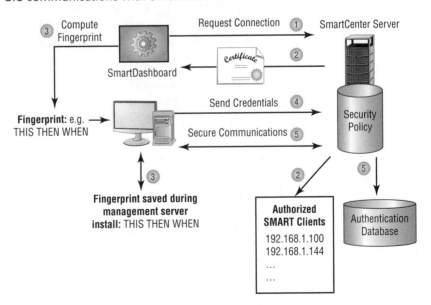

Notice in Figure 2.7 that the SmartDashboard SMART Client does *not* require a certificate, unlike an enforcement module or other SVN components. In Figure 2.7, the following events take place:

1. The SmartDashboard application is started and an administrator types in the appropriate IP address of the SmartCenter server, an account name with rights to configure the SmartCenter server as well as the appropriate password for the account. The SmartDashboard initiates an SSL connection with the SmartCenter server.

2. The SmartCenter server verifies that the IP address of the SMART Client is authorized to configure the SmartCenter server. If the SMART Client is authorized, the SmartCenter server sends its certificate to the SMART Client.

3. The SmartDashboard GUI calculates a fingerprint from the received certificate and displays the fingerprint to the user. During installation of the SmartCenter server, the same mechanism is used to generate a fingerprint for the SmartCenter server certificate. This fingerprint is also displayed to the installer for future reference (see Figure 2.8). By comparing the fingerprint calculated by SmartDashboard with the fingerprint calculated during installation, an administrator can verify they are communicating with the correct SmartCenter server. If the calculated fingerprint matches the fingerprint generated during installation of the SmartCenter server, then the administrator knows it is communicating with the correct SmartCenter server.

4. The SmartDashboard SMART Client and SmartCenter server negotiate a session key that is used to encrypt data for the management session. The username and password specified in Step 1 is encrypted with this key, ensuring authentication information is securely passed to the SmartCenter server.

5. The encrypted credentials received from the SMART Client are decrypted and checked against the local authentication database. Assuming the credentials are correct and the user is authorized to access the security policy database, the management connection is accepted and the SmartDashboard SMART Client can now configure the SmartCenter server security policy. All subsequent communications are secured using the session key generated in Step 4.

FIGURE 2.8 The Certificate Authority screen

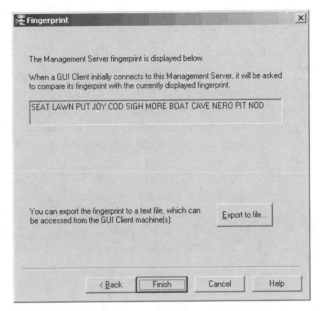

VPN-1/FireWall-1 Enforcement Module Operation

As described in the Chapter 1, Check Point VPN-1/FireWall-1 uses a patented stateful inspection technology to provide access control and network security. The enforcement module is responsible for providing this functionality, and the enforcement module essentially consists of three components, which are listed and described below:

INSPECT module   Provides access control, stateful inspection, network address translation, generation of log records and alerts, as well as encryption features.

Security servers   Provide user authentication and content security for HTTP, FTP, and SMTP traffic.

Synchronization module   Allows the stateful connection table to be shared with other enforcement modules for high availability deployments.

This section describes how the *INSPECT module* operates, which will help you understand how each packet received by a VPN-1/FireWall-1 enforcement module is processed.

Check Point VPN-1/FireWall-1 NG is an application-based or software-based firewall product, meaning it does not include an operating system or hardware to provide a platform for the firewall to run on. Check Point VPN-1/FireWall-1 NG must be installed on one of a variety of common operating systems, including Microsoft Windows NT 4.0/2000, Sun Solaris, Red Hat Linux, or Nokia IPSO. In this section, any references to operating systems refer to any of the above operating systems listed. Interoperability of VPN-1/FireWall-1 components, such as the enforcement module and SmartCenter, server are not dependent on the operating system installed on each, meaning for example you could have a Windows-based SmartCenter server managing a Linux-based enforcement module.

INSPECT Module Operation

The INSPECT module is integrated with the operating system kernel, and receives all packets from the lower-level (Layer 2) network interface card (NIC) drivers, *before* the packets reach the TCP/IP stack of the operating system. This approach ensures packets are inspected and access control is applied, before the operating system can process the packets, protecting the operating system of the enforcement module (firewall) from attack. If a packet is permitted, it is passed by the INSPECT module to the TCP/IP stack of the firewall. The operating system of the firewall performs the routing of the packet to the correct egress interface. The firewall determines the appropriate next hop destination and appropriate egress interface to the next hop for the packet, based on the local routing table.

Because packets are intercepted by the INSPECT module before the operating system, certain issues must be considered. Specifically, communications that the host operating system must participate in. The security policy must make allowances for these packets so that they are allowed in if necessary. A common example would be traffic for routing protocols that the enforcement module may be participating in.

The packet is then passed back to the INSPECT module, where it again can be inspected. Assuming the packet is once again permitted, the packet is then forwarded to the lower-level device drivers of the egress NIC, and the packet is placed on to the wire to its next hop destination. Figure 2.9 demonstrates the process described above.

FIGURE 2.9 Routing a packet through the enforcement module

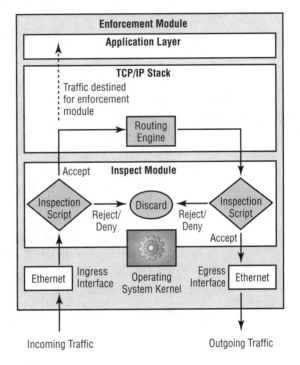

 The packet flow assumes the enforcement module is inspecting traffic being received and sent by the firewall. Check Point FireWall-1 possesses the ability to inspect traffic in the *inbound*, *outbound*, or *eitherbound* (both inbound and outbound) directions. By default, Check Point VPN-1/FireWall-1 NG is configured to perform eitherbound inspection.

As you have learned in previous sections, the SmartCenter server stores the security policy database locally, which includes the security rule bases used for each enforcement module. The INSPECT module contains a rule

base that contains access control policy relevant to the local device location. This rule base is written in a language called INSPECT, which enables the fast processing of packets through the INSPECT module. Each rule has a set of parameters that must all be matched for a packet to be matched against a rule. These parameters include source IP address(es), a destination IP address(es), and services (application-layer protocols). For example, a rule might specify a source IP address of 10.1.1.1, a destination address of 192.168.1.1, and a service of HTTP. This rule matches any packet that has a source IP address of 10.1.1.1, destination IP address of 192.168.1.1, and a destination TCP port of 80 (HTTP), which allows the 10.1.1.1 host to access web services running on the 192.168.1.1 host.

It is important to understand that the rules in the rule base apply to connections as opposed to actual packets. A connection can be defined as the bidirectional packet flow between two end-devices. A connection is always established from one party to the other. The initiating party is called the source of the connection, while the receiving party is called the destination of the connection. The packet flows over a connection include traffic from the source to the destination, as well as return traffic from the destination to the source. For example, with the rule described in the previous paragraph, return packets have a source IP address of 192.168.1.1, a destination IP address of 10.1.1.1, and a source TCP port of 80. The INSPECT module could implement another rule that matched return traffic with the parameters described above. This would permit return traffic for the connection, but it would also permit any traffic that matched the return rule parameters, not just traffic specific to the connection. For example, the 192.168.1.1 host could send any packets to 10.1.1.1, as long as the traffic had a source TCP port of 80.

The key to allowing return traffic without compromising security policy is to permit return traffic only for connections that are currently established. The INSPECT module does this by implementing a connection table (sometimes referred to as a state table), which contains a list of current connections and the current state of those connections. When a packet is received by the INSPECT module, it is first checked against the connection table to see if it is part of an established connection. If it is, the INSPECT module forwards the traffic, and also updates the connection state if required. If the packet is not part of an existing connection, the packet is then processed against the security rule base, which will permit or deny the packet as appropriate.

Figure 2.10 illustrates how each packet received from a Layer 2 NIC is examined to determine whether the packet is to be permitted or dropped.

FIGURE 2.10 INSPECT module packet flow

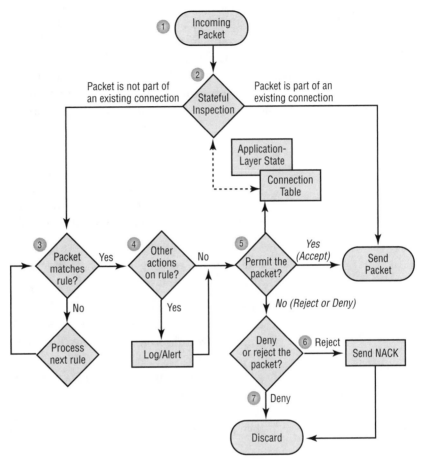

The following events are depicted in Figure 2.10:

1. A packet is received by the NIC of the firewall. The packet is passed to the INSPECT module loaded within the operating system kernel.

2. The packet is evaluated against the stateful inspection connection table, to check if the packet is part of an existing connection permitted through the firewall. If the packet is part of an existing connection, information such as TCP sequence number is checked to ensure the traffic is legitimate, and the packet is then forwarded. If the packet is not part of an existing connection, it is passed to the rule base for inspection.

It is important to note that application-layer state information is also maintained by the INSPECT module, which may have been generated by previous traffic. For example, the connection process for many complex protocols (such as FTP) consists of the establishment of a control connection and the subsequent negotiation of dynamic ports to provide a data connection. The INSPECT module possesses the intelligence to understand these negotiations and can therefore allow the packets of the new dynamic connection to be forwarded.

3. If the packet is not part of an existing connection, it is examined against an inspection script generated from the security policy rule base residing on the SmartCenter server. The packet is evaluated against each security rule until a match is made against the rule. If the packet does not match any rules, it is dropped and no further action is taken.

4. If the matched rule has an optional action of log or alert, logging and/or alerts actions are invoked.

5. The forwarding action for the matched rule is examined. The forwarding actions for a rule include *Accept*, *Reject*, and *Deny*. If the forwarding action of the rule is Accept, a new entry is placed in the connection table (the packet must be part of a new connection, as it did not previously match an existing connection), which includes the various parameters that represent the connection (such as source/destination IP address and source/destination TCP or UDP port). The packet is then passed to the operating system TCP/IP stack for routing and delivery.

VPN-1/FireWall-1 checks that any TCP packet matched against the rule base contains TCP flags that indicate it is a new connection request. This ensures data that matches a rule is not sent without the proper TCP connection sequence being followed.

6. If the forwarding action of the rule is Reject, or the packet is rejected by stateful inspection checks, a NACK (or rejection acknowledgment) is sent to the source host of the traffic, indicating the packet was rejected. The packet is then discarded.

7. If the forwarding action of the rule is Drop, the packet is discarded, and no further action is taken.

Do not use the Reject action for any traffic that originates from an untrusted connection. The Reject action indicates to hackers scanning your systems that a rule actively exists. Depending on the way the Reject action is implemented, hackers can also determine the operating system of the device that rejected the connection, using readily available reconnaissance tools such as nmap. You might use the Reject action internally so that users who attempt an unauthorized connection do not experience lengthy timeouts (the Rejection notification immediately tells the operating system that the connection was rejected, and this is indicated to the user immediately).

Stateful Inspection and Connectionless Protocols

The majority of traffic on the Internet today is TCP-based (TCP is a transport or Layer 4 protocol). TCP is a *connection-oriented* protocol, meaning it provides guaranteed delivery and performs other functions such as sorting out-of-sequence packets. Because of these capabilities, the TCP header contains fields that ensure it can provide connection-oriented functionality. For example, the TCP header contains a set of fields called TCP flags, which indicate whether a packet is a control packet (such as one that might be used to establish or tear down a connection) or a packet that contains application-layer data. The TCP header also contains a field that provides a sequence number, which enables a receiving system to pass TCP packets in the correct order to the application layer. The INSPECT module reads TCP fields to define a connection, track connection state, and ensure the validity of packets claiming to be part of the connection. The following lists the parameters used in the connection table to define a TCP connection:

- Source and destination IP address

- Source and destination TCP port

- TCP sequence number

- TCP flags

Unfortunately, not all traffic on the Internet is TCP-based (connection-oriented). The other major transport-layer protocol is UDP, which is a *connectionless* protocol used for popular protocols such as DNS, SNMP, and VoIP voice traffic. UDP is designed to be fast and efficient, at the expense of not providing connection-based delivery like TCP does. This means that UDP has less overhead, but the application-layer protocols transported by UDP must provide connection-oriented functions such as guaranteed delivery or handle out-of-sequence packets. From a VPN-1/FireWall-1 perspective, UDP only provides identification of a connection—it does not provide any indication of the connection state of the application-layer protocols. The following lists the parameters used in the connection table to define a UDP connection:

- Source and destination IP address
- Source and destination UDP port

Other transport-layer protocol connections, such as IPSec connections, are tracked based on only source and destination IP address, as they do not possess the concept of ports, unlike TCP and UDP.

You could track connection state by implementing application-layer intelligence on the INSPECT module. This would require new code for each application-layer protocol, affecting the complexity and performance of the firewall. Instead, a low connection idle timer (defined as the amount of time that can pass, during which no packets associated with a connection are received, before a connection is considered invalid) is used, which means that if a UDP connection goes idle for a certain amount of time, the connection is considered to have been torn down, and the connection entry is removed from the connection table. By default, on VPN-1/FireWall-1 NG, UDP connections are considered invalid after being idle for 40 seconds, while TCP connections are considered invalid after being idle for 3,600 seconds. In VPN-1/FireWall-1 NG, you can customize these timeouts on a per-service object basis, unlike in previous versions where these timeouts applied globally for all services.

It is preferable for a stateful inspection firewall to only permit TCP-based traffic where possible, as all TCP connections must follow certain rules and the firewall can track the state of each connection.

Summary

In this chapter you learned about the architecture of VPN-1/FireWall-1 NG, which is important in aiding your understanding of how to configure VPN-1/FireWall-1. From a high-level perspective, VPN-1/FireWall-1 NG consists of three separate components, which can be distributed across one or more systems. The SMART Clients provide a GUI front end for administrators to configure, manage, and monitor the security policy of the network. The SmartCenter server hosts the security policy database and security logging database, and communicates with the SMART Clients for configuration/ management, and also communicates with enforcement modules for download-ing security rule sets. The enforcement module is the component that actually enforces security policy. A rule set specific to each enforcement module is downloaded from the SmartCenter server, and includes the necessary rules required to enforce the network security policy. The distributed nature of the VPN-1/FireWall-1 components allows you to build an extremely scalable system that provides easy management of security policy applied end-to-end.

The internal communications between VPN-1/FireWall-1 NG components have been improved to use standards-based secure sockets layer (SSL) encryp-tion. Certificates are used to provide an extremely secure and scalable method of securing communications between VPN-1/FireWall-1 NG components. The new communications model is called secure internal communications (SIC); however NG components are still capable of using older secure communication protocols to support earlier VPN-1/FireWall-1 versions.

Finally, you learned about the internal architecture of the VPN-1/FireWall-1 enforcement module. This module is also commonly referred to as the INSPECT module, as it enforces a rule base called an INSPECT script. The inspection module is part of the operating system kernel, ensuring high speed and inspection of traffic before it reaches the TCP/IP stack of the operating system. This ensures the firewall operating system itself is protected, with unauthorized traffic discarded before the operating system TCP/IP stack receives it. The TCP/IP stack is only used to route traffic to an egress inter-face. The INSPECT module can process traffic both on the inbound and outbound directions. Security rules are defined on the INSPECT module, which determine the permitted connections (rather than packets) allowed through the firewall. During inspection, the INSPECT module first deter-mines whether a packet is part of an existing connection by referencing a connection table, with all packets that are part of an existing connection packet being accepted after validity checks. If the packet is not part of an existing connection, the INSPECT module matches the packet to the appropriate rule in the security policy rule set. If the action of the rule is to deny or reject, the appropriate actions are taken and the packet is discarded. If the action of the rule is to accept, the INSPECT module creates a new entry in the connection table (to ensure return traffic of the new connection is permitted) and then forwards the packet to the TCP/IP stack.

Exam Essentials

Know the basic components of VPN-1/FireWall-1 NG.   SMART Clients (e.g., SmartDashboard) provide GUI front end for administrators. The SmartCenter server stores security databases and distributes security policy to enforcement modules. Enforcement modules enforce network security using a security rule set downloaded from the SmartCenter server.

Know that NG Feature Pack 3 has many product name changes.   Refer to Table 2.1 for a list of products that have been renamed.

Know the system requirements of VPN-1/FireWall-1 NG.   The system requirements for Check Point SMART Clients are covered in Table 2.2 and in Table 2.3 for Check Point SmartCenter servers/enforcement modules.

Understand the basic operation of SIC.   Secure internal communications (SIC) provides secure communications between SVN components. SIC uses certificates to ensure authenticity, integrity, and confidentiality of communications. The Check Point VPN-1/FireWall-1 NG SmartCenter server includes an internal certificate authority (ICA) that assigns certificates to each SVN component.

Understand the basic internal architecture of the VPN-1/FireWall-1 NG enforcement module.   The enforcement module primarily consists of an INSPECT module, which is loaded in the kernel of the operating system on which VPN-1/FireWall-1 is installed. The INSPECT module receives traffic *before* it reaches the operating system TCP/IP stack for routing, to ensure the security of the firewall operating system itself. Stateful inspection is utilized to ensure Layer 3 to Layer 7 security.

Understand how security rules work with connection-based and connectionless transport-layer protocols.   For all IP protocols (e.g., TCP, UDP, and ICMP), you only need to define rules that match the traffic associated with the direction in which a connection is established. Each connection is maintained in a connection table, which includes the appropriate parameters that allow return traffic to be identified and forwarded. Depending on the transport-layer protocol, the parameters that define a connection vary. For example, UDP connections are based on source/destination IP address and source/destination UDP port, while ESP (used for IPSec) connections are only based on source and destination IP address.

Know the transport-layer protocol parameters used by stateful inspection to identify connections for TCP, UDP, and other protocols.   For TCP, connections are defined by source/destination IP address, source/destination TCP port, TCP sequence number, and TCP flags. For UDP, connections are defined by source/destination IP address and source/destination UDP port. For other protocols that do not use the concept of ports, connections are based on source/destination IP address only. For all non-TCP protocols (connectionless protocols), the fact that a connection has been torn down can only be identified when the connection goes idle for a certain amount of time.

Key Terms

Before you take the exam, be certain you are familiar with the following terms:

Accept	external interface
Asymmetric	general-purpose
Authenticate	Hash
binding order	Inbound
certificate authority (CA)	INSPECT
Certificates	INSPECT module
CPShared	inspection script
Deny	internal certificate authority (ICA)
Diffie-Hellman	message digest
distinguished name	one-way hashing
Eitherbound	Open Security Extension (OSE)

outbound

public/private key

Reject

secure internal communications
(SIC)

secure sockets layer (SSL)

seed

self-signed

signature

SMART Clients

SmartCenter server

SmartDashboard

SmartUpdate

SVN Foundation

symmetric

Transitive

Review Questions

1. What are the main components of Check Point VPN-1/FireWall-1 NG? (Choose all that apply.)

   A. Enforcement module

   B. Internal certificate authority

   C. SMART Clients

   D. SmartCenter server

   E. SVN foundation

2. Assuming all VPN-1/FireWall-1 components are version NG, what mechanism is used for internal communications?

   A. FW PUTKEY

   B. PKI

   C. SIC

   D. SSL

3. A VPN-1/FireWall-1 NG SmartCenter server manages a previous version VPN-1/FireWall-1 enforcement module. What mechanism is used for internal communications?

   A. FW PUTKEY

   B. PKI

   C. SIC

   D. SSL

4. What component is used to distribute certificates used for SIC?

   A. Certificate authority

   B. Internal certificate authority

   C. SmartCenter server

   D. SmartDashboard

5. What component of the enforcement module provides application-layer gateway type functionality?

   A. INSPECT module

   B. Security Servers

   C. Synchronization module

   D. CPShared

6. The INSPECT module resides between which layers of the operating system network stack?

   A. Layer 1 and Layer 2

   B. Layer 2 and Layer 3

   C. Layer 3 and Layer 4

   D. Layer 4 and Layer 7

7. What mechanisms can be used to authenticate administrators using Check Point NG SMART Clients? (Choose all that apply.)

   A. FW PUTKEY

   B. User name and password

   C. Certificates

   D. SSL encryption

8. The Security Server is a component of which VPN-1/FireWall-1 component?

   A. CPShared

   B. Enforcement module

   C. SMART Client

   D. SmartCenter server

9. Between which layers does the inspection module reside on the hosting firewall operating system TCP/IP stack?

A. Application layer

B. Network layer

C. Datalink layer

D. Physical layer

10. What is the language used by the enforcement module to permit or reject traffic?

A. C

B. C++

C. INSPECT

D. PERL

11. Which of the following is common to all Check Point VPN-1/FireWall-1 hosts?

A. SmartCenter server

B. Enforcement module

C. SVN foundation

D. SMART Clients

12. You wish to allow web access to a server on the Internet from internal clients. Which of the following should you do? (Choose all that apply.)

A. Create a rule that permits HTTP traffic from the internal clients to the external server.

B. Create a rule that permits return HTTP traffic from the external server to the internal clients.

C. Create a rule that permits SMTP traffic from the internal clients to the external server.

D. Create a rule that permits return SMTP traffic from the external server to the internal clients.

13. UDP is considered a _____ protocol.

    A. secure

    B. non-secure

    C. connection-based

    D. connectionless

14. The inspection module can identify a UDP connection based on the following parameters? (Choose all that apply.)

    A. Source IP address

    B. Destination IP address

    C. Checksum

    D. Source port

    E. Sequence number

    F. Flags

    G. Destination port

15. The Inspection Module can identify a TCP connection based on the following parameters? (Choose all that apply.)

    A. Source IP address

    B. Destination IP address

    C. Checksum

    D. Source port

    E. Sequence numbers

    F. Flags

    G. Destination port

16. You wish to allow internal clients to ping a server on the Internet. Which of the following should you do? (Choose all that apply.)

   A. Create a rule that permits ICMP traffic from the internal clients to the external server.

   B. Create a rule that permits return ICMP traffic from the external server to the internal clients.

   C. Create a rule that permits GRE traffic from the internal clients to the external server.

   D. Create a rule that permits return GRE traffic from the external server to the internal clients.

17. SmartDashboard is available on which of the following operating systems? (Choose all that apply.)

   A. OS 2

   B. Solaris

   C. Windows ME

   D. Windows XP

18. Which of the following ensures VPN-1/FireWall-1 services are always running?

   A. cpconfig

   B. cpd

   C. SNMP daemon

   D. watchdog

19. The VPN/FireWall-1 architecture consists of how many tiers?

   A. 1

   B. 2

   C. 3

   D. 4

20. SIC uses which of the following to authenticate and ensure the integrity and privacy of communications?

A. DES

B. Triple-DES

C. SSL

D. CA certificates

Answers to Review Questions

1. A, C, D, E.   VPN-1/FireWall-1 consists of SMART Clients, a Smart-Center server, and enforcement modules. The SVN foundation is used on SmartCenter servers and enforcement modules to facilitate common system functions, such as SIC.

2. C.   All NG components use secure internal communications (SIC) to communicate internally. SIC uses PKI and SSL features.

3. A.   FW PUTKEY is the legacy method required for securing internal communications for prior versions of Check Point.

4. B.   The internal certificate authority (ICA) is responsible for creating and distributing certificates to VPN-1/FireWall-1 NG components.

5. B.   Check Point VPN-1/FireWall-1 enforcement modules include security servers, which provide application-layer gateway services for common applications such as HTTP, FTP, SMTP, and TELNET.

6. B.   The INSPECT module resides between the NIC and the TCP/IP stack of the operating system. The NIC operates up to Layer 2, while the TCP/IP stack operates between Layers 3 and 7.

7. B, C.   The SMART Clients for NG support the use of certificates or a username/password for authentication.

8. B.   Security servers are application-layer daemons that provide application-layer inspection of common Internet protocols on enforcement modules.

9. B, C.   The inspection module intercepts and examines traffic after it has been received by the Layer 2 interface and before it is passed to the IP stack of the operating system.

10. C.   The INSPECT scripting language is used by enforcement modules to apply rules.

11. C.   The SVN foundation is installed on both SmartCenter servers and enforcement modules, provided common system functions.

12. A.   For TCP-based traffic, you only have to create a rule that defines the traffic flow from the client (source) to the server (destination). Stateful inspection allows the return traffic associated with the connection.

13. D. UDP does not provide any connection-oriented services, such as those provided by TCP. The retransmission of lost packets must be handled by the application layers that are using UDP for transport.

14. A, B, D, G. The UDP header only contains source port and destination port information; therefore the inspection module can only identify a connection based on the unique combination of source/destination IP address and source/destination UDP port.

15. A, B, D, E, F, G. Because TCP is connection-oriented, the TCP header includes information that indicates connection state and allows delivery of application data to be guaranteed by TCP. This information includes source/IP address, source/destination TCP port, sequence numbers, and TCP flags. The checksum of each TCP packet is a representation of the payload of a TCP packet, and hence does not uniquely identify a connection (another connection could send an identical payload).

16. A. For all IP traffic, VPN-1/FireWall-1 NG requires you to only configure a rule for the direction in which a connection is initiated. When a connection is initiated, a new entry is written in the connection table, which ensures return traffic associated with the connection is permitted.

17. B, C, D. SmartDashboard is available for Windows-based machines as well as Solaris on the SPARC platform.

18. D. The watchdog monitors each VPN-1/FireWall-1 service and ensures that each is running.

19. C. Tiers include SMART Clients, SmartCenter server, and enforcement modules.

20. C. SIC uses SSL (secure sockets layer) to provide authentication, data integrity, and confidentially for communications between SIC components.

Chapter

3

The VPN-1/FireWall-1 Security Policy

THE CCSA EXAM OBJECTIVES COVERED IN THIS CHAPTER INCLUDE:

- ✓ Explain the function of a security policy.
- ✓ Describe creating network objects and groups using the Administration GUI.
- ✓ Describe how to configure anti-spoofing on the firewall.
- ✓ Outline process to set up and operate an active security policy.
- ✓ Describe how to install and uninstall a security policy.

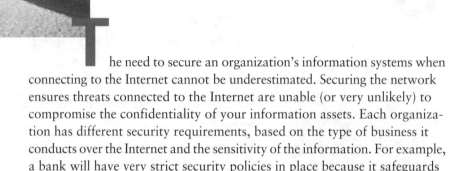

he need to secure an organization's information systems when connecting to the Internet cannot be underestimated. Securing the network ensures threats connected to the Internet are unable (or very unlikely) to compromise the confidentiality of your information assets. Each organization has different security requirements, based on the type of business it conducts over the Internet and the sensitivity of the information. For example, a bank will have very strict security policies in place because it safeguards customers' financial information.

The network requirements of an organization should be well-planned and documented in a *security policy* document. Each access requirement can be summarized as a *security rule* that requires enforcement at each gateway between the organization's internal networks and external networks (such as the Internet). Check Point VPN-1/FireWall-1 NG provides the tool that allows you to enforce security rules that are required for your security policy to be enacted, enabling organizations to conduct business over the Internet in a secure fashion that meets the organization's requirements.

In this chapter you will learn about security policy and how VPN-1/FireWall-1 NG enforces security policy by using security rules. In order for security rules to be created, you must configure VPN-1/FireWall-1 with your network topology, which defines the various networks, systems, users, and applications relevant to the security policy. These topology elements are configured in VPN-1/FireWall-1 as security objects, which you will learn how to configure. Once you create security objects, you can use them to represent the source, destination, service, and other parameters associated with each security rule required to implement the security policy of the organization.

Introduction to VPN-1/FireWall-1 Security Policy

The heart of Check Point VPN-1/FireWall-1 is the VPN-1/FireWall-1 *security policy*, which is a set of security rules, address translation rules, and security policy parameters that enable you to ensure the security of an organization's information systems. Before learning about how to configure VPN-1/FireWall-1 security policy, you must understand what a security policy actually is, from both business and technical perspectives. This section defines security policy, and then introduces you to SmartDashboard, which is the main configuration tool you will use to define VPN-1/FireWall-1 security policy.

What Is a Security Policy?

At the heart of any network security system is the underlying security policy that determines the security rules and checks that they are applied to network traffic. Security policy is driven by the assessment of risk and how to mitigate that risk within a defined cost limit. Risk is related to threat. For example, establishing an unsecured connection to the Internet might be perceived as a high risk, due to the high number of potential threats on the Internet. Any organization with a network (especially a network connected to the Internet or to a third-party network) should have a network security policy document that describes the risks the organization faces and how those risks are mitigated. The network security policy document will describe the rules and procedures for obtaining secure access to the organization's electronic information systems, as well as defining the authorized users, systems, and applications that are permitted access in and out of the organization's security boundaries. As an example of how security policy might be applied to an organization, Figure 3.1 illustrates how an organization might securely deliver Internet access to internal users, systems, and applications.

The organization in Figure 3.1 has a documented security policy that states all access to the Internet must be authorized on an individual basis and access must be used for business purposes only. All content downloaded from the Internet must also be checked to ensure the content is legitimate and will not pose a security threat to the organization. To actually apply the security policy in practice, the organization places a web proxy server on an isolated network segment (also known as a demilitarized zone, or DMZ), which will serve as an application-layer gateway for internal users, systems, and applications (clients) requiring access to the Internet. The firewall will only permit internal clients' access to the web proxy server, and will not permit direct access to the Internet. This ensures that all Internet access is directed through the web proxy server. The firewall will permit the web proxy server access to the Internet, which ensures the web proxy server can service internal client requests. Because the web proxy server has direct access to the Internet, it could potentially be compromised by a threat on the Internet. If it was to be compromised, it has limited visibility of the internal network, making it harder for an attacker to compromise internal information systems. For internal users, systems, and applications to access web resources on the Internet, they must do so via the web proxy. The web proxy authenticates client requests, ensuring only authorized users, systems, or applications are permitted access to the Internet. All content passed through the web proxy is checked for malicious content (e.g., viruses) as well as content appropriateness (e.g., is the content business-related), and then permitted or rejected appropriately. You can see that a couple of sentences of a security policy document require a lot of work over multiple systems to enforce.

FIGURE 3.1 Security policy that secures Internet access

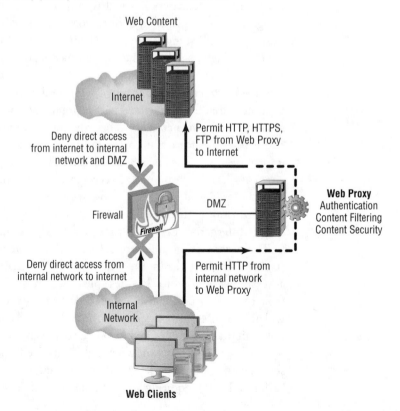

To ensure the security policy is adhered to, a security system is required for security policy enforcement. The most common example of such a security system is a firewall, which is used to enforce the security policy with relation to an Internet or extranet connection. For a firewall to enforce security policy, the security policy of the organization must be defined in a format that the firewall can understand. In the case of Check Point VPN-1/FireWall-1 NG, network security policy is defined and stored in a security policy database, which resides on the SmartCenter server (previously called management server) component of VPN-1/FireWall-1 NG. The security policy database is a collection of security rules, which define the users, systems, and applications that are permitted, denied, or rejected access through the firewall. To enable security administrators to configure and maintain this security policy database, the SmartDashboard SMART client is used. The Smart-Dashboard provides a graphical view of the security policy, visually aiding security administrators in providing a comprehensive and easy-to-use interface. Security administrators only need to define security policy that is enforced over distributed firewalls in one place—the SmartCenter server. The SmartCenter server is responsible for distributing security policy to each enforcement module. The security policy is a set of rules specific to each enforcement module that is used to process all traffic received by the module. This architecture ensures a global security policy can be applied end-to-end throughout the network.

Throughout this book references will be made to enforcement modules and gateways—in the context of this book, these are identical.

SmartDashboard

The *SmartDashboard* application is part of the Check Point VPN-1/FireWall-1 NG SMART clients and enables security administrators to create and manage security policy rules for the entire enterprise. The Smart-Dashboard application provides a user interface into the central security policy database stored on the SmartCenter server. Access to the SmartCenter server via SmartDashboard (and all other Check Point SMART clients) is determined by administrative user accounts, which can possess a set of permissions that allow access to the security policy to be defined at a very granular level. In this section, you will learn how to start SmartDashboard and also learn about administrative permissions.

Starting SmartDashboard

To start SmartDashboard, select Start ➢ Programs ➢ Check Point SMART Clients ➢ SmartDashboard NG. This should present you with an authentication dialog box, which prompts you to specify a username (or certificate), password, and IP address or name of the SmartCenter server that you wish to connect to. Figure 3.2 shows the authentication dialog box that is presented after starting the SmartDashboard application.

FIGURE 3.2 The SmartDashboard authentication dialog box

Check Point NG introduces the option to use a certificate to authenticate an administrator. This method uses SIC in the same manner other Check Point VPN-1/FireWall-1 components communicate.

In Figure 3.2, notice the Read Only and Demo Mode options. The following describes each of these options:

Read Only   Connects to the SmartCenter server with read-only permissions. This option is normally used if another administrator is connected with read-write permissions, as only a single administrator can be connected with read-write permissions to ensure the security policy is not corrupted.

Demo Mode   Runs the SmartDashboard SMART client in Demo Mode, where the application doesn't actually connect to any SmartCenter server, just reads a sample security policy that ships with the

SmartDashboard application. This is useful if you wish to determine how to configure security policy, without having to connect to a valid SmartCenter server.

Once you have specified the appropriate credentials and SmartCenter server IP address/name, click OK to establish a connection. If the SmartDashboard can communicate with the SmartCenter server and this is the first time you have logged onto the SmartCenter server, a *fingerprint* is next displayed, which allows you to verify you are communicating with an authentic Smart-Center server. Figure 3.3 shows an example of the fingerprint of a SmartCenter server being displayed.

FIGURE 3.3   The SmartDashboard fingerprint dialog box

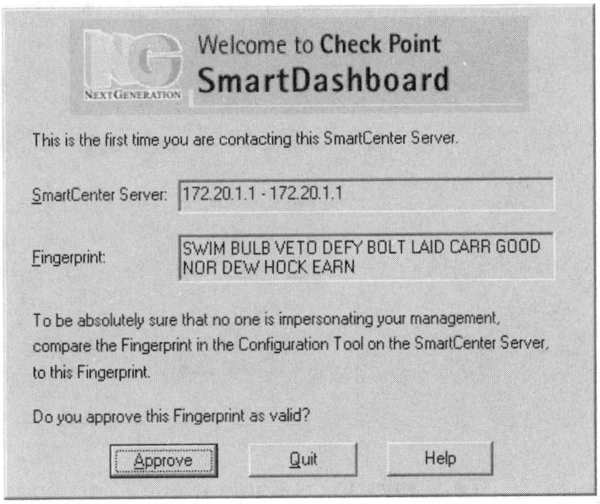

Notice in Figure 3.3 that the fingerprint presented is simply a string of characters. You can view the fingerprint of the actual SmartCenter server by running the *Check Point Configuration Tool* on the SmartCenter server. This tool can be run on Windows-based Check Point SmartCenter servers by selecting Start ➢ Programs ➢ Check Point SMART Clients ➢ Check Point Configuration NG or by running the cpconfig command-line tool (this is the only method on Sun Solaris or Linux-based SmartCenter servers). Figure 3.4 demonstrates the Fingerprint tab on the Check Point Configuration Tool window on a Windows-based SmartCenter server.

If you compare the fingerprint in Figure 3.3 with Figure 3.4, you can see that they are identical. This means that the SmartCenter server being con-nected to in Figure 3.3 is the SmartCenter server being checked in Figure 3.4.

Notice in Figure 3.4 that you can also click the Export to File button to save the fingerprint to a text file, which can then be distributed to a network share point so that administrators can check the fingerprint remotely.

FIGURE 3.4 The SmartCenter server fingerprint

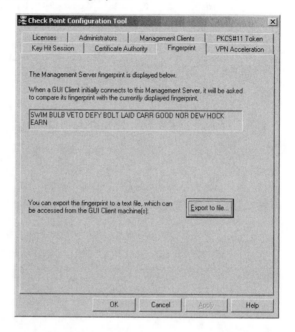

 The Check Point Configuration Tool contains some Check Point parameters on a SmartCenter server or enforcement module that cannot be configured remotely. For example, you can only define GUI clients (systems that can connect to the SmartCenter server via SmartDashboard) on the SmartCenter server console. Other parameters such as licenses and administrators are now configurable via SmartUpdate and SmartDashboard.

If the fingerprint presented during SmartDashboard logon matches the fingerprint stored locally on the SmartCenter server, then you know that you are configuring the correct and authentic SmartCenter server. If the fingerprint presented by the SmartCenter server during logon is correct, click on the Approve button (see Figure 3.3). If you connect from the same SmartDashboard client to the same SmartCenter server again, you will not be presented with the fingerprint, as you have already accepted it and the SmartCenter server is considered trusted. Sometimes you might want to remove the fingerprint trust relationship between a SMART client and SmartCenter server. For example, you might reinstall a SmartCenter server, rebuilding it with the same IP address and hostname. If you attempt to connect to it from the SMART client, the SMART client will reject the connection, as a new fingerprint is generated during the new installation. To remove a trusted fingerprint, you must remove the appropriate entry for the SmartCenter server in the Windows registry of the SMART client. This entry resides in the `HKEY_LOCAL_MACHINE\Software\CheckPoint\Management Clients\5.3\Connection\Known Servers` registry key.

WARNING   If you choose to approve a fingerprint that does not match the fingerprint of the SmartCenter server you are attempting to connect to, your user credentials may be sent to an imposter SmartCenter server.

Once you have established that the SmartCenter server to which you are connecting is authentic, SmartDashboard will send the administrator credentials to the SmartCenter server, which are then checked by the SmartCenter server against an authentication database. The authentication database contains a list of permitted administrators with associated passwords, as well as a list of permissions that determine what the administrator can actually do with the security policy. Assuming your logon authenticates correctly and you have rights to configure the security policy rule base, the SmartCenter server accepts the connection and the security policy is displayed in the SmartDashboard application.

 Real World Scenario

VPN-1/FireWall-1 and Multiple Administrator Connections

If you only have read-only rights to view the Check Point security policy, you must select the Read Only check box in SmartDashboard authentication dialog box before connecting to the SmartCenter server. You will also have to connect with read-only access when another administrator has an open read-write connection to the SmartCenter server. This is because the SmartCenter server only permits a single read-write connection to ensure the security policy database is not corrupted. If another administrator is connected with read-write access, you will be notified and presented with the SmartDashboard Authentication dialog box once again, where you must select the Read Only check box.

Figure 3.5 shows an example of the SmartDashboard application after an administrator has successfully authenticated.

FIGURE 3.5 SmartDashboard after successful authentication

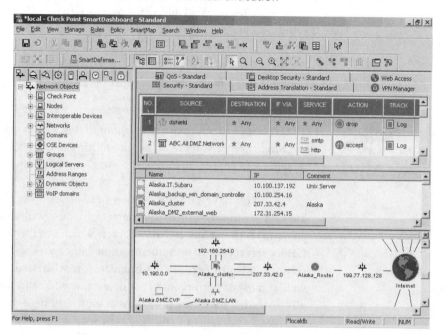

SmartMap

In Figure 3.5, the bottom right pane shows the *SmartMap pane*, which was previously known as *Visual Policy Editor* in NG versions prior to Feature Pack 3. SmartMap provides a visual representation of the network topology. It intelligently maps out the network topology based on *security objects* that represent different elements of the network.

You can print out topology maps from SmartMap.

You can see in Figure 3.5 the existence of an Internet object (which represents the Internet), a 199.77.128.128 object (represents the IP network between the Internet and perimeter router), a perimeter router called Alaska_Router, a 207.33.42.0 object (represents the IP network between the perimeter router and firewall cluster), and an object called Alaska_cluster, which represents a Check Point VPN-1/FireWall-1 enforcement module cluster. All of these objects are linked visually, showing the actual IP topology of the network. You can configure any object via SmartMap by simply double-clicking it, and you can also view security rules via SmartMap that show the source, destination, and direction of traffic flows defined by each rule.

If you wish to disable SmartMap, you can do so by selecting Policy ➢ Global Properties from the SmartDashboard menu, and then selecting the SmartMap screen in the Global Properties dialog box. From here you can enable or disable SmartMap as needed.

You will learn more about SmartMap later in this chapter. It is important to note that SmartMap is an optional component of VPN-1/FireWall-1 NG that you must purchase separately.

Administrator Permissions

Check Point VPN-1/FireWall-1 NG provides a wide range of security permissions that determine the components of the security policy you can access, and the level of access granted for each component. For example, you may be permitted read-only access to security rule base, but could be permitted full (read-write) access to the user database. You can assign each administrator a custom set of granular access rights, allowing an organization to ensure security administrators can only perform actions on the network security policy as required by policy. Permissions affect not only the Smart-Dashboard SMART client; they also affect all other Check Point SMART clients, such as SmartView Tracker, SmartView Status, and SmartUpdate. Three levels of permissions can be granted:

- No access

- Read-only access

- Read-write access

Administrator accounts used for the Check Point SMART clients can be created and managed using the Administrators tab of the Check Point Configuration Tool located on the SmartCenter server, as shown in Figure 3.6.

Check Point provides no authentication for access to the Check Point Configuration Tool, instead relying on the operating system to provide the security for using this tool. For this reason, you must ensure the physical and operating system security of the SmartCenter server.

FIGURE 3.6 Administrators tab of the Check Point Configuration Tool

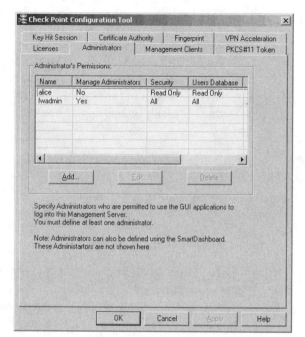

In Figure 3.6, you can see that a table lists each administrator and the access rights each has to various components of Check Point products. To add a new administrator, click on the Add button, which displays the Add Administrator dialog box, as shown in Figure 3.7.

Notice in Figure 3.7 that you can grant permissions to a wide range of components. You can easily grant either full read-write access or read-only access to all components by selecting the appropriate Read/Write All or Read Only all radio buttons. Notice the Manage Administrators check box under the Read/Write All option, which additionally enables the administrator to manage administrator accounts using SmartDashboard (you will learn more about this in Chapter 6). If you choose the Customized option, you can selectively grant read-only access, read-write access, or no access for each component. The components of the Check Point security policy for which you can grant permissions are determined by the Check Point SVN components that you install. For example, if you choose to install the FloodGate-1 SVN component, you are able to define permissions for accessing the Quality of Service (QoS) policy.

Table 3.1 lists the common VPN-1/FireWall-1 SMART clients and describes each of the permissions that are relevant to each client.

FIGURE 3.7   The Add Administrator dialog box

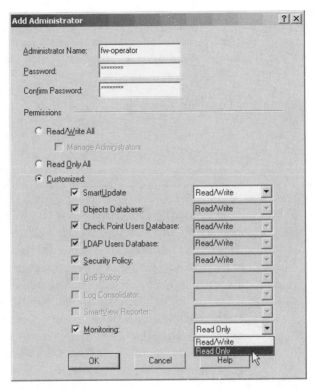

TABLE 3.1   Check Point VPN-1/FireWall-1 Security Object Categories

SMART Client	Permission	Description
SmartDashboard	Objects Database	Permits access to the security objects database
	Check Point Users Database	Permits access to the users database (discussed in Chapter 6)
	LDAP Users Database	Permits access to an external LDAP directory (discussed in Chapter 6)
	Security Policy	Permits access to security policy rules and properties

TABLE 3.1 Check Point VPN-1/FireWall-1 Security Object Categories *(continued)*

SMART Client	Permission	Description
SmartView Tracker	Monitoring	Permits access to security logs. Read/Write All access also enables blocking of connections (discussed in Chapter 5)
SmartView Status	Monitoring	Permits access to status and alerting information about Check Point hosts and gateways

The SmartUpdate permissions control the available rights that can be assigned to other components. If read-write access is granted to Smart-Update, read-write access is granted to the Objects Database, Users Database, LDAP Users Database, and Security Policy, and this cannot be changed. If no access or read-only access is granted to SmartUpdate, read-only access is granted to the Objects Database (and cannot be changed); however, you can choose the access rights for all other components. Notice in Figure 3.7 that the SmartUpdate permission is set to *Read/Write*—the four permissions below are also set to *Read/Write* and cannot be modified, as indicated by the gray shading.

It is important to note that a limitation of the Check Point Configuration Tool (cpconfig) is that it can only be accessed locally on the SmartCenter server console (you can run cpconfig via a remote telnet or SSH session on a Unix-based system). Check Point VPN-1/FireWall-1 NG also allows you to define administrators from within SmartDashboard, which integrates administrator management into the security policy. You will learn more about creating administrators using SmartDashboard in Chapter 6.

GUI Clients

GUI clients represent the IP addresses or hostnames of devices that can connect to the SmartCenter server and can configure, manage, and monitor security policy using Check Point SMART clients. For remote devices to manage a Check Point VPN-1/FireWall-1 SmartCenter server, you must explicitly define each IP address or hostname that wishes to manage the SmartCenter server. To configure GUI clients, you must use the Check Point Configuration Tool. GUI client configuration is configured via the SMART Clients tab of this Check Point Configuration Tool.

Now that you have a solid understanding of how to connect to the Smart-Center server using SmartDashboard, you will now learn how to configure administrators using the Check Point Configuration Tool. Figure 3.8 shows the underlying network topology used for this exercise and all exercises in this book.

FIGURE 3.8   Chapter exercises network topology

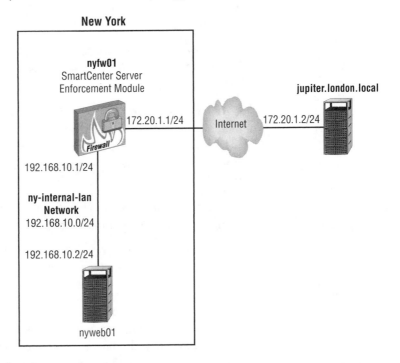

EXERCISE 3.1

Configuring Administrators and GUI Clients

In Figure 3.8, an organization has a network (in New York) connected to the Internet. A firewall called nyfw01 protects the internal network, which hosts a single web server called nyweb01. A web server connected to the Internet called jupiter.london.local is used to simulate Internet connectivity in later exercises. The nyfw01 firewall includes an integrated SmartCenter server, enforcement module, and GUI client. If you are performing the exercises on your own lab at home, you will need to perform the following before beginning the exercises:

- Install VPN-1/FireWall-1 NG Feature Pack 3 on nyfw01. You will need to install the SmartCenter server, enforcement module, and SMART clients. VPN-1/FireWall-1 NG FP3 ships with a 15-day trial license.

- Install Microsoft Windows 2000 with IIS on nyweb01 and jupiter .london.local. IIS will provide web services so that you can test web connectivity.

This exercise shows you how to use the cpconfig utility to configure both administrators and GUI clients (hosts that are authorized to use SMART clients to configure and manage a SmartCenter server). To complete this exercise, you will require access to a VPN-1/FireWall-1 SmartCenter server.

1. Click Start ➢ Run, which will invoke the Run dialog box. Type in the command cpconfig and then press OK.

2. The Check Point Configuration Tool should now appear. Click on the Administrators tab, which will display the list of current administrators configured.

3. Click the Add button to create a new administrator. The Add Administrator dialog box will be displayed, which allows you to configure a new administrator and the permissions assigned to the administrator. Configure the following parameters for the new administrator and click OK to return to the Check Point Configuration Tool.

   - Administrator Name = **jbloggs**
   - Password = **jbloggs**
   - Permissions = Read Only All

4. Click on the Management Clients tab, which displays all hosts that are permitted to configure and manage the SmartCenter server using SMART clients. In the Remote hostname field, type in the IP address 192.168.10.2, and then click the Add button to configure this host as an authorized GUI client. Once you have completed your configuration, click OK to close the Check Point Configuration Tool and apply the changes you have made.

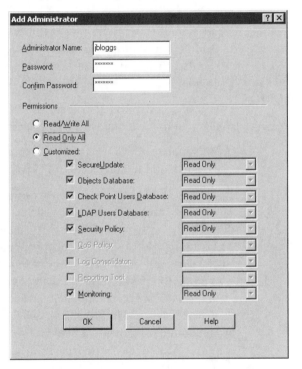

The VPN-1/FireWall-1 Security Policy

So far you have learned about what a security policy is and that you can use SmartDashboard to configure security policy. You have learned how to use SmartDashboard to establish a connection to a SmartCenter server, bearing in mind how administrative permissions affect what you can configure once connected. In this section, you will learn about the VPN-1/FireWall-1 security policy, which resides on the VPN-1/FireWall-1 SmartCenter server. At the most basic level, the VPN-1/FireWall-1 security policy consists of the following components:

Security objects   Provides logical representations of networks, systems, users, and applications that must be defined in the VPN-1/FireWall-1 security policy.

Security rule base   Consists of security rules that define the authorized (and unauthorized) access between security objects. This rule base is the heart of the VPN-1/FireWall-1 security policy.

Address translation rule base   Consists of rules that define how IP traffic should be translated to ensure systems with private IP addressing can communicate on the Internet.

Global security policy properties   Defines many security policy parameters that apply globally to all Check Point components.

VPN manager   Consists of VPN communities that describe intranet, extranet, and remote access VPN connections between devices.

This chapter focuses purely on security objects and the security rule base. The address translation rule base will be examined in detail in Chapter 7, while the global security policy properties will be examined throughout this book (in fact, some global security policy properties are examined in this chapter). VPN Manager is outside the scope of this book and is covered in *CCSE NG: Check Point Certified Security Expert Study Guide* (Sybex, 2003).

In this section you will learn about security objects and how to configure them using SmartDashboard. You will learn about how security objects can be configured to implement *anti-spoofing*, which is used to protect against common DoS attacks. After that, you will learn about security rules—how they are constructed and how to create, manage, and install rule bases. Finally, you will learn how to improve rule base management and the rule processing performance on enforcement modules.

Security Objects

In order to create security rules in the VPN-1/FireWall-1 security policy, you must first create security objects. This section defines security objects, teaches you how to create and configure security objects, and then examines the anti-spoofing security feature that is configured using security objects.

Understanding Security Objects

Security objects are the logical representation of the networks, systems, users, and applications that comprise an organization's information systems and are used to enable configuration of your network security policy on Check Point VPN-1/FireWall-1. Before you can configure a security rule on VPN-1/FireWall-1, you must create security objects that represent the networks, systems, users, and applications that you wish to include in the rule. An example of a security object might be a mail server or an internal network subnet. Another example might be an enforcement module or an employee of your organization. Each security object possesses different properties, depending on the type of security object. Security objects can be categorized into several major categories, which are listed in Table 3.2.

TABLE 3.2 Check Point VPN-1/FireWall-1 Security Object Categories

Object Category	Description
Network Objects	These objects represent SmartCenter servers, enforcement modules, gateways, hosts, networks, and other network or system-related objects.
Services	These objects represent transport-layer protocols (such as ICMP, IPSec, TCP, and UCP) and application-layer protocols (such as HTTP, SMTP, and DNS).
Resources	These objects represent common application-layer protocol traffic (HTTP, FTP, and SMTP) with specific application-layer specific attributes. For example, a resource could define HTTP GET requests for a specific URL.
OPSEC Applications	These objects represent OPSEC applications that VPN-1/FireWall-1 can interact with to extend the functionality of VPN-1/FireWall-1.
Servers	These objects represent authentication servers and databases that provide user authentication services for VPN-1/FireWall-1. These objects include RADIUS, TACACS, Certificate Authority, and LDAP servers.

TABLE 3.2 Check Point VPN-1/FireWall-1 Security Object Categories *(continued)*

Object Category	Description
Users	These objects represent users and groups that are part of your organization or are external to your organization.
Time	These objects represent specific times of the day, week, or month. You can also create scheduled event objects.
VPN Communities	These objects represent an intranet, extranet, or remote access VPN that may consist of multiple enforcement module or gateway objects that participate in the VPN.

All of the object categories listed in Table 3.2 can be managed from the Object Tree, Object List, and SmartMap panes within SmartDashboard, as shown in Figure 3.9.

FIGURE 3.9 The Object Tree and Object List panes in SmartDashboard

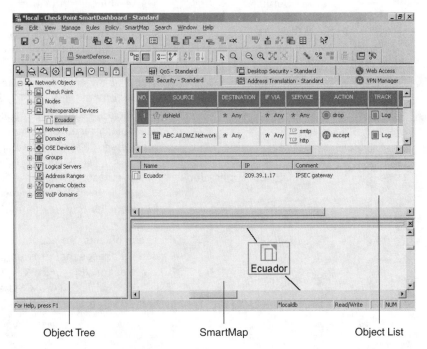

Object Tree   SmartMap   Object List

The Object Tree provides access to the various types of security objects, as described in Table 3.2. The Object List lists all objects associated with the currently selected category in the Object Tree. For example, in Figure 3.9, the Domain category is selected in the Object Tree pane, which means all domain objects are listed in the Object List pane. The SmartMap pane allows you to visually indicate where a particular object exists within the network topology.

At this stage, we will only examine network and service objects, as they constitute the majority of objects that are used in the Check Point VPN-1/ FireWall-1 security policy. We will also look at resource objects as they are mentioned in the exam objectives.

Network Objects

As listed in Table 3.2, network objects generally represent network or system-related entities. Within the network objects category, different types of objects exist. In Figure 3.9 you can see that the *Network Objects* tree is expanded, with each type of network object listed. Table 3.3 describes the common types of network objects.

TABLE 3.3 Common Check Point VPN-1/FireWall-1 Network Object Types

Object Type	Description
Check Point	Describes various types of Check Point systems. The most common Check Point objects include a Check Point *Gateway* object, which defines either standalone enforcement modules or VPN-1/ FireWall-1 Internet gateways (integrated enforcement module and SmartCenter server), a Check Point *Host* object, which normally defines standalone SmartCenter servers (i.e., SmartCenter servers that are installed on a separate system from enforcement modules) and an *Externally Managed Gateway* or *Externally Managed Host* object, which represents a remote enforcement module or remote SmartCenter server that is not managed by the local SmartCenter server.

TABLE 3.3 Common Check Point VPN-1/FireWall-1 Network Object Types *(continued)*

Object Type	Description
Node	Describes two types of hosts. The first is a *Gateway* object, which represents a host that has more than one network interface and can route between those interfaces. An example of a gateway might be a router or a third-party firewall. The second type is a *Host* object, which represents a host with a single network interface. Host objects normally represent servers, workstations, and printers.
Interoperable Device	An interoperable device represents a third-party VPN gateway device that is interoperable with the VPN component of VPN-1/FireWall-1. Used to configure an interoperable device to represent a remote third-party VPN device that enforcement module(s) need to establish a VPN connection to.
Network	The network object is used to represent networks internal or external to your organization. A network object is essentially an IP subnet or supernet, and hence consists of an IP address and subnet mask, which define the subnet represented by the object.
Domain	The domain object is used to represent the networks and systems associated with a domain name system (DNS) domain. For example, the networks and systems associated with the Check Point network might all reside within the checkpoint.com domain. When used in the source or destination element of a rule, an enforcement module performs a reverse DNS lookup on the source or destination IP address of traffic to see whether the IP address of the traffic resolves to a fully qualified domain name (FQDN), for example www.checkpoint.com, that resides within the domain specified in the domain object. The enforcement module must have a local DNS client enabled to provide DNS name resolution.
OSE Device	An OSE device represents a third-party router whose access control lists you wish to manage to implement security on the router. Router vendors that are supported include Cisco, Bay (Nortel), and 3Com.

TABLE 3.3 Common Check Point VPN-1/FireWall-1 Network Object Types *(continued)*

Object Type	Description
Group	A group object is simply used to group other types of network objects into a single, combined object. This allows rule appearance to be improved, and also means that you only have to add objects to a group object to enable access for new objects, rather than modifying rules directly.
Logical Server	A logical server object is used to implement load balancing across multiple physical servers. The logical server has a single virtual IP address that remote clients use to access content associated with the IP address. The logical server definition includes a group of physical servers that actually serve the content to the client. The enforcement module distributes (load balances) incoming connection requests to the virtual IP address out to the physical servers using a variety of load balancing mechanisms such as round robin, random, and server load.
Address Range	An object that defines a list of contiguous IP addresses. Address range objects are commonly used in address translation rules and are discussed in more detail in Chapter 9.
Dynamic Object	A dynamic object is used to describe a logical object that is common in function to different enforcement modules, but resolves to a different physical IP address on each enforcement module. For example, several offices may each have an enforcement module with a local mail server attached. A dynamic object can be created that represents the local mail server at each office, which enables an administrator to create a common rule for all mail servers.
VoIP Domain	An object that represents a voice over IP network or device, such as an H.323 Gateway, H.323 Gatekeeper, or SIP gateway.

Prior to Check Point NG Feature Pack 2, there is no concept of Check Point objects or Node objects. In Check Point NG Feature Pack 1 and prior, only a single Workstation object is defined in the place of Check Point and Node objects, which is used to represent Check Point enforcement modules and SmartCenter servers, interoperable VPN gateways, gateways, and hosts. Interoperable devices and VoIP domain objects were also introduced in Feature Pack 2.

Service Objects

As listed in Table 3.2, *service objects* represent application-layer and transport-layer protocols on the network. Service objects are only used in the Service element of a rule, and normally specify the application or service associated with traffic. There are different types of service objects, most related to the transport-layer protocol associated with each application-layer protocol. Figure 3.10 shows the Services Tree expanded in Smart-Dashboard.

FIGURE 3.10   The Services tree in SmartDashboard

In Figure 3.10, notice that a specific tab in the Object Tree pane represents service objects. You can modify service objects directly from this view, or you can select Manage ≻ Services from the SmartDashboard menu. Table 3.4 describes the common types of service objects.

TABLE 3.4 Common Check Point VPN-1/FireWall-1 Service Object Types

Object Type	Description
TCP	Contains a large amount of common TCP-based application-layer protocols, such as FTP, HTTP, and SMTP. You can create or customize existing TCP service objects. Each TCP service object allows you to specify the destination (server) ports and source (client) ports associated with the application-layer protocol being defined. Check Point NG introduces configuration session timeouts on a per-service object basis, rather than on a global policy-wide basis in previous versions.
UDP	Similar to TCP service objects, except these define UDP-based application-layer protocols.
ICMP	Defines common ICMP message types used for diagnostic (and reconnaissance!) purposes. Examples include objects for ICMP echo requests and ICMP echo replies, which are required for ping testing to work. In Figure 3.10, you can see the expanded ICMP category, which shows the various service objects that represent different ICMP message types.
Group	A group object is simply used to group other types of service objects into a single, combined object. This allows rule appearance to be improved, and also means that you only have to add objects to a group object to enable access for new objects, rather than modifying rules directly.

Resource Objects

As listed in Table 3.2, *resource objects* represent application-layer attributes of common services. Resource objects are associated with HTTP, FTP, and

SMTP traffic. Resource objects using these services are possible because the enforcement module includes an HTTP, FTP, and SMTP security server (application-layer gateway). You use resource objects to provide content security for HTTP, FTP, and SMTP traffic. For example, you can create a resource object that represents the HTTP content associated with a particular URL (uniform resource locator). When traffic is processed against the rule, it is passed to the HTTP security server that is part of the enforcement module. The security server inspects the content, verifying it is associated with the URL permitted—optionally the HTTP content can be passed to an external system for content filtering and malicious content checking (virus checking).

Content Vector Protocol (CVP) is a protocol used for passing content to an external content security system for anti-virus and content checking. CVP is most commonly used for passing SMTP, HTTP, and FTP content to an external OPSEC-compliant anti-virus server. URL Filtering Protocol (UFP) is a protocol used for passing URLs (in HTTP and FTP traffic) to an external OPSEC-compliant UFP server to determine whether access to the URL should be granted. Check Point uses CVP and UFP to interact with external content security servers. These external servers must be OPSEC-compliant.

In another example you create an SMTP resource object that specifies all files with a .VBS (Visual Basic scripts) extension should be stripped from SMTP mail messages, and no message should exceed 10MB in size. When traffic is processed by the rule, it is handed to the internal SMTP security server, which performs the necessary checks and stripping actions, and then forwards it on to the destination SMTP server.

VPN-1/FireWall-1 NG Feature Pack 3 introduces a new resource object type called CIFS (Common Internet File System), which is also commonly referred to as the SMB (Server Message Block) protocol. The SMB protocol is used by Windows 2000 and Windows XP computers to access file shares on Windows 2000 Servers. By defining CIFS resource objects, you can restrict access based on application-layer information contained within the SMB data stream. For example, you can block access to specific file shares on a file server, yet enable access to another file share on the same file server.

 **Real World Scenario**

Using VPN-1/FireWall-1 as a Non-Transparent Proxy

Check Point enforcement modules enforce resource objects in an identical manner to a transparent application-layer gateway (see Chapter 1 for more on application-layer gateways). The communicating devices of the connection are not aware that the connection is being proxied by the Check Point security services. You can configure security servers to be non-transparent. For example, you might specify the enforcement module as a web proxy for internal web browsers (when using this method, no content inspection is available), or you could specify the enforcement module as the SMTP mail exchanger (MX) for your organization's domain.

Configuring Security Objects

After you have installed a Check Point VPN-1/FireWall-1 SmartCenter server and connected to it for the first time using SmartDashboard, you will find that a single security object has been initially created for you. The object that is present is a Check Point gateway or host object, which represents the SmartCenter server itself. In order to actually configure and define a security policy and store it in the security policy database, the SmartCenter server must be represented as a security object. If you installed an integrated SmartCenter server and enforcement module, the initial object created for you represents both of these Check Point components. If you install separate enforcement modules, you must create security objects that represent these before you can install a security rule base from the SmartCenter server onto the enforcement module. Once you have successfully connected for the first time to the SmartCenter server via SmartDashboard, you are ready to start configuring your security policy.

The security policy is made up of various rule bases. The main rule base is the security rule base, which includes rules that define the networks, systems, users, and applications that are permitted through enforcement modules. Before you can create rules, you must create security objects that you can place into the various rule elements. For example, if you wish to specify a particular host IP address as the source element of a rule, you must create the appropriate security object that represents the host. You must also create security objects for other rule elements, such as Destination, Service, Install On, and Time. Once the appropriate security objects have been created, you can then create rules.

Planning a Security Policy

Before you start creating security objects and configuring rules that reference security objects, it is highly recommended that you plan your Check Point security policy configuration fully. Planning your Check Point security policy consists of mapping out your networks, systems, users, and applications and then defining the permitted communication requirements between each of these entities. Once you have clearly mapped out your network topology and access requirements, you can determine the security objects that you must create to place in the rule bases that comprise your security policy. Figure 3.11 illustrates an example of a very simple network and the communications between components of the network that are required.

FIGURE 3.11 Example of planning your security policy

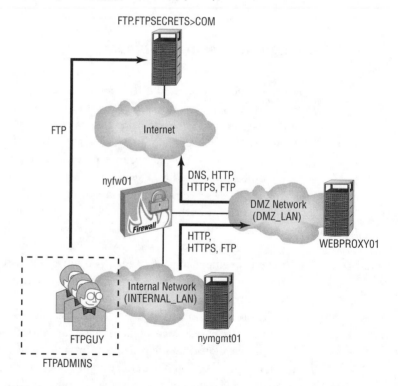

In Figure 3.11, any system on the internal network is permitted web access (HTTP, HTTPS, and FTP) to a web proxy server (WEBPROXY01) on the DMZ network. The proxy server requires DNS and web access to anywhere on the Internet, in order to service web content requests from internal systems. A specific group of users called ftpadmins located internally also requires direct

FTP access to an FTP server called `ftp.ftpsecrets.com`. The `ftpadmins` group consists of a single user called `ftpguy`. Referring to the topology illustrated in Figure 3.11, Table 3.5 lists the security objects that are required to allow configuration of rules that enforce the access requirements.

TABLE 3.5 Check Point Security Objects Required for Figure 3.11

Object Name	Object Type	Description
NYMGMT01	Check Point Host	Represents the NYMGMT01 VPN-1/Firewall-1 SmartCenter server on which the security policy database resides. This is a Check Point Host object, because it has only a single network interface.
NYFW01	Check Point Gateway	Represents the NYFW01 VPN-1/FireWall-1 enforcement module that is responsible for enforcing the network security policy. This is a Check Point Gateway object, because it has more than one network interface.
INTERNAL_LAN	Network	Represents the internal network subnet. This object is required as the source element of a rule that permits any internal system access to the web proxy. It is also required for anti-spoofing purposes to define valid source IP addresses on the internal interface of the enforcement module.
DMZ_LAN	Network	Represents the DMZ network subnet. This is required for anti-spoofing purposes to define valid source IP addresses on the DMZ interface of the enforcement module.
WEBPROXY01	Host	Represents the WEBPROXY01 server that is used for servicing web requests from internal systems.

TABLE 3.5 Check Point Security Objects Required for Figure 3.11 *(continued)*

Object Name	Object Type	Description
FTPADMINS	User (Group)	Represents the ftpadmins user group that requires direct access to the ftp.ftpsecrets.com FTP server.
FTPGUY	User	Represents the ftpguy user that belongs to the ftpadming group.
ftp.ftpsecrets.com	Host	Represents the external FTP server called ftp.ftpsecrets.com.

Once you have created the required security objects, you can define your security policy rules, which define the access permitted through the enforcement module.

Creating a Security Object

To create a security object, you must connect to SmartDashboard using an account that has at least *read-write* access to the Objects Database component (see Figure 3.7 and Table 1.1). Once you have connected, you can create a new object by selecting the Manage item from the main menu and then selecting the appropriate object type, such as Network Objects (i.e., Manage ➤ Network Objects). The Network Objects dialog box is displayed when you select Manage ➤ Network Objects from the main menu.

You can also create a new security object by right-clicking the appropriate object type in the Object Tree and clicking New *<Object Type>* (e.g., New Network).

In the Network Objects Dialog box a list of the current network objects located in the security policy database is displayed. You can click the More >> hyperlink to create filters that only display certain types of network objects (for example, only Check Point gateway objects). You can add, modify, or delete objects as required—to add an object, click the New button. This displays a dropdown menu that allows you to select the type of object you wish to create in the object category you are currently configuring. Figure 3.12 shows an example of clicking the New button in the Network Objects dialog box shown in Figure 3.12.

FIGURE 3.12   Selecting the type of a new security object

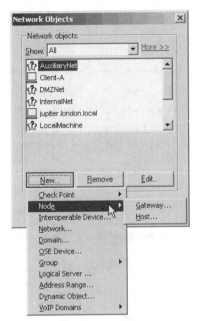

You can choose any one from all of the types of objects associated with the current category of object you are configuring. In Figure 3.12, the types of objects associated with the network objects category are displayed—refer to Table 3.3 for descriptions of some of these object types.

CONFIGURING SECURITY OBJECTS FOR YOUR SMARTCENTER SERVER AND ENFORCEMENT MODULES

When you begin to configure VPN-1/FireWall-1, you must first ensure that an object exists for your SmartCenter server and that objects exist for your enforcement modules. Once you have your SmartCenter server and enforcement module objects correctly configured, the framework to distribute the remaining security objects and security policy to each enforcement module is in place. As discussed previously, when you first install VPN-1/FireWall-1 NG, an object is automatically created that represents the SmartCenter server object. If you have a distributed VPN-1/FireWall-1 topology, you will then need to create objects that represent your enforcement modules. Figure 3.13 shows an example of creating a Check Point gateway object, which is the object used to represent enforcement modules, by selecting

New ➤ Check Point ➤ Gateway from the menu shown in Figure 3.12. The Check Point Gateway dialog box is presented, which allows you to configure parameters such as external IP address, Check Point version, Check Point products installed, and so on.

In Feature Pack 3, if you create a Check Point Gateway object, you are asked if you want to use a new wizard to create the object, which prompts you with the appropriate step-by-step questions to ensure the object is created properly, or whether you want to manually configure the object. You can turn off this prompt from being displayed each time.

FIGURE 3.13 The Check Point Gateway dialog box

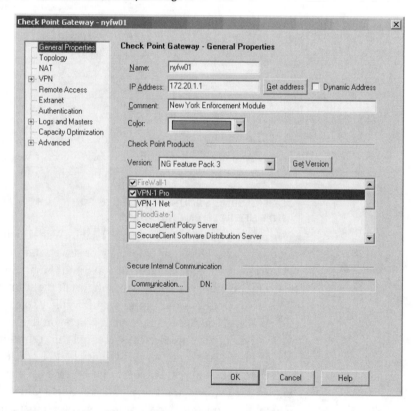

In Figure 3.13, a Check Point gateway object called nyfw01 is being created with an IP address of 172.20.1.1. Notice that the Check Point product version is set to NG Feature Pack 3. Also notice that the VPN-1 Pro and FireWall-1 Check Point products are installed.

It is important that you understand what type of object to create when you want to represent the various types of networks and systems present on your network. Table 3.6 lists common types of systems and the appropriate security objects that you create to represent each.

TABLE 3.6 Configuring the Appropriate Security Objects

System Type	Security Object to Create	Specific Parameters
Check Point Enforcement Module	Check Point Gateway	Select VPN-1 Pro as installed product for VPN-1/FireWall-1
		Select VPN-1 Net as installed product for VPN-1 only
		Select FireWall-1 only as installed product for FireWall-1 (no VPN-1)
		Ensure topology information is configured for SmartMap
Check Point Smart-Center server	Check Point Host	Select Primary Management Station or Secondary Management Station as installed product
		Ensure topology information is configured for SmartMap
Integrated Check Point Enforcement Module and Smart-Center server	Check Point Gateway	Ensure parameters configured for both a standalone enforcement module and SmartCenter server are configured.
External Check Point Enforcement Module	Check Point Externally Managed Gateway	Configure correct Check Point version and indicate installed products
		Ensure topology information is configured for SmartMap
External Check Point SmartCenter server	Check Point Externally Managed Host	Configure correct Check Point version and indicate installed products
Third-party firewall	Gateway Node	Ensure topology information is configured for SmartMap

TABLE 3.6 Configuring the Appropriate Security Objects *(continued)*

System Type	Security Object to Create	Specific Parameters
Third-party VPN gateway	Interoperable Device	Ensure topology information is configured for SmartMap
Server, workstation, or printer	Host Node	Ensure topology information is configured for SmartMap
Subnet or network	Network	Ensure topology information is configured for SmartMap
Domain name	Domain	Ensure topology information is configured for SmartMap

For example, to create objects that represent a VPN-1/FireWall-1 enforcement module, you must create a Check Point object that has a type of gateway, and you must configure the parameters as shown in the Check Point Products section of Figure 3.13.

Prior to Feature Pack 2, you must create a workstation object that represents an enforcement module. In the workstation object type, you have the option of specifying whether or not the module is managed by the local management server. If the enforcement module is managed by the local management server, you must ensure the Managed by this Management Server (Internal) option is selected. When the Managed by another Management Server (External) option is selected, the enforcement module object does not appear on the available list of enforcement modules when you install a policy.

CONFIGURING A HOST NODE OBJECT

After creating the appropriate objects to represent your VPN-1/FireWall-1 SmartCenter server and enforcement modules, you are ready to start creating the security objects that describe the rest of your topology. When creating security objects, you will predominantly work with host node objects (which represent servers, PCs, printers, or any device with a single network interface) and network objects (which represent subnets or summarize a range of subnets). You also may work with service objects, if your network uses custom applications.

Figure 3.14 shows an example of creating a new host node object by selecting New ≻ Node ≻ Host from the Object Properties dialog box.

FIGURE 3.14   The Host Node dialog box

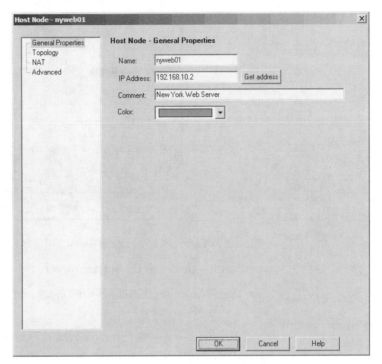

In Figure 3.14, you can see that a host node object has a General Properties screen (defines the name and IP address of the host), a Topology screen (used to determine which network object the host should be connected to in SmartMap), a NAT screen (used to configure automatic network address translation, which is discussed in Chapter 9), and an Advanced screen (used to configure SNMP parameters for the host).

CONFIGURING A SERVICE OBJECT

Figure 3.15 shows an example of creating a new service object, which is used to represent an application-layer protocol. To create a new service object, select Manage ≻ Services from the SmartDashboard menu, which opens the Services dialog box. Click the New button, which allows you to choose the type of service object (e.g., TCP and UDP). In Figure 3.15, a TCP service object is being created.

FIGURE 3.15 The TCP Service Properties dialog box

Notice in Figure 3.15 that the service object has the following parameters:

- Name—describes the service object

- Port—describes the server-side or destination port (applicable for TCP and UDP services)

- Advanced—allows you to restrict the client-side or source ports and specify connection timeouts specific to the service object

Once you have created the appropriate security objects, if you wish to save your configuration before applying a security policy to an enforcement module (when you apply a security policy, any changes are automatically saved), select File ➢ Save from the main menu. This will save the current security policy rule base, as well as save all of your security objects.

You can create multiple security rule bases that each contain different rules. Although multiple security rule bases can be created, a single security object database (represented by files called objects.c and objects_5_0.c) exists for all rule bases. This means that by saving a particular rule base before modification, you can only roll back any rule changes—you cannot roll back any security object changes made. If you wish to enable rollback for your security object database, backup the objects.c and objects_5_0.c file residing in the conf subdirectory of the VPN-1/FireWall-1 SmartCenter server installation directory.

Creating a Security Object Using SmartMap

SmartMap (the bottom pane in SmartDashboard) also allows you to create security objects. If you are using SmartMap, it is recommended that you use it to create security objects where possible, to ensure that the topology generated is accurate. The most important example of when you should use SmartMap to create security objects is for network objects that represent the networks connected to the interfaces of your enforcement modules. If you install VPN-1/FireWall-1 on a combined SmartCenter server/enforcement module, during installation, an object that represents both the SmartCenter server and enforcement module will be created. The interfaces on the server will be auto-detected and added to the Topology screen of the workstation object representing the SmartCenter server/enforcement module. SmartMap builds the network topology by reading the topology information configured for enforcement modules. Figure 3.16 shows the Topology screen for a Check Point gateway object representing a combined SmartCenter server/enforcement module called 1afw01.

FIGURE 3.16 The Topology screen

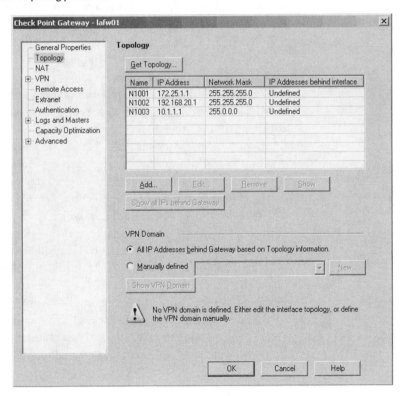

In Figure 3.16, three interfaces have been automatically configured during installation. Each interface is defined by the operating system device name, IP address, and subnet mask. Figure 3.17 shows the SmartMap representation of the lafw01 object.

FIGURE 3.17 The Topology pane

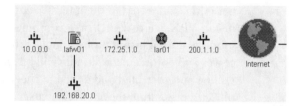

In Figure 3.17, you can see that a Check Point gateway object represents lafw01, and three network objects are attached to each of the interfaces on lafw01. These network objects are calculated by SmartMap based on each interface in the Topology screen. For example, in Figure 3.16, interface N1001 is configured with an IP address of 172.25.1.1 and a subnet mask of 255.255.255.0. Based on this information, SmartMap knows that this interface is connected to the 172.25.1.0 network (with a subnet mask of 255.255.255.0) and hence represents this network in the topology map. A perimeter router has also been defined, with interfaces that attach to the 172.25.1.0 and 200.1.1.0 networks.

The network objects that are automatically generated are referred to as *implied network objects*, as the existence of each is implied from the topology configuration for the enforcement module object. You can't actually configure implied network objects—Figure 3.18 shows what happens when you double-click the 172.25.1.0 implied network object in Figure 3.17.

Notice that all of the object fields are grayed out, indicating that you cannot configure the object. To be able to configure an implied object, you must *actualize* the implied network object, which essentially copies the parameters of the implied network object (these parameters are shown in Figure 3.17) into a new network object, and removes the implied network object. Once you have actualized an implied network object, it is identical to any normal network object that you would create using New ➢ Network Object in the Network Objects dialog box. To actualize an implied network object, right-click on the implied object in SmartMap and select the Actualize Network option from the menu. This will create a new network object and display the Network Properties dialog box for the newly created object, as shown in Figure 3.19.

FIGURE 3.18   An implied network object

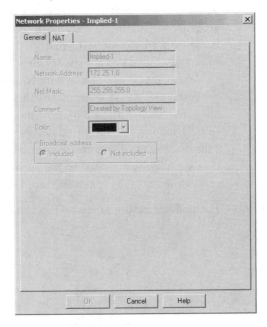

FIGURE 3.19   Actualizing an implied network object

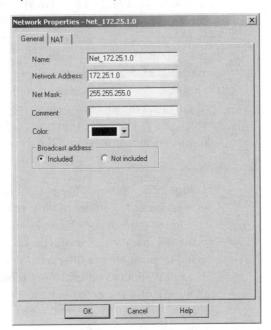

As you can see in Figure 3.19, the actualized object is identical to a normal network object, and you can modify the object as required. Once you have actualized an implied object, the object will still appear in SmartMap as shown in Figure 3.16, except with whatever name you configure (by default, a prefix of Net_ is added to the network IP address, as indicated in Figure 3.19).

You might be wondering why you would actualize a network object and not just create it via the normal method (using Manage ➢ Network Objects in SmartDashboard). The reason is that there is no way currently in SmartMap to tie a manually configured network object to an enforcement module. This means that if you create your network objects manually, the networks that are directly attached to the enforcement module will not be correctly represented visually in SmartMap. Figure 3.20 shows an example of this.

FIGURE 3.20   Manually configured networks in SmartMap

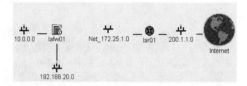

In Figure 3.20, the N1001 interface definition for lafw01 has been removed, and the 172.25.1.0 network object has been manually created. Notice that the 172.25.1.0 network object is not connected to the lafw01 object as it should be, even though the IP address of the lafw01 object is configured as 172.25.1.1. To correctly display the topology, you must create network objects that are attached to any gateway device (a device with two or more interfaces, such as an enforcement module or router) by actualizing the implied network objects generated from topology (interface) information configured for the gateway object. This means that when you create gateway objects, you must ensure that you configure each interface accurately (IP address and subnet mask) on the Topology screen of the object.

Topology information is only generated automatically for a combined Smart-Center server/enforcement module object during installation. For any other enforcement modules or gateways you must configure topology (interface) information manually. A useful tool is the Get Interfaces button, which can be used to populate the interface information for a remote Check Point VPN-1/FireWall-1 NG enforcement module. Clicking this button instructs the SmartCenter server to fetch the interface information using SIC from the enforcement module, which means you don't have to manually find out the information yourself.

Finally, you can also use SmartMap to create new objects manually, in an identical fashion to choosing Manage ➤ Network Objects from the main menu. To create a new object, right-click in any white space in the Topology pane, and select the New Network Object submenu from the menu that appears. From this submenu you can create a new workstation or network object, as well as other more advanced object types.

In this Exercise 3.2, you will create objects in the VPN-1/FireWall-1 security database that represent each of the networks and systems in Figure 3.8.

EXERCISE 3.2

Configuring Security Objects

1. Log on to the nyweb01 SmartCenter server using SmartDashboard. If this is the first time you have logged on, you will be presented with the fingerprint of the SmartCenter server. Ensure the fingerprint is correct and click Approve to continue.

2. By default, VPN-1/FireWall-1 creates a single object that represents the SmartCenter server. When configuring VPN-1/FireWall-1 for the first time, you should always configure this object first. Select Manage ➤ Network Objects from the SmartDashboard main menu. This will display the Network Objects dialog box.

3. Configure the SmartCenter server object called nyfw01 by selecting the nyfw01 object in the Network Objects dialog box and then clicking the Edit button. This displays the Check Point Gateway dialog box. Ensure the object is configured as follows:

   - IP address = 172.20.1.1
   - Comment = New York Firewall
   - Color = Red
   - Check Point Version = NG Feature Pack 3
   - FireWall-1, VPN-1 Pro, Primary Management Station, SVN Foundation, and Log Server are listed as installed Check Point products

4. Click on the Topology screen of the nyfw01 object properties and verify that interface information has been automatically generated during installation.

You can see that the correct interface information has been generated during installation. This will ensure that the topology generated by SmartMap is accurate.

Note: On Windows 2000 installations, you may sometimes encounter an interface called NDISWAN, with an IP address of 0.0.0.0 and subnet mask of 0.0.0.0. This is generated if a modem is present on the Windows 2000 host, as the NDISWAN interface represents a virtual interface that is used to represent a dial-up connection. You should delete this interface (unless of course you are actually using the dial-up connection).

5. Click OK to complete your configuration. The SmartCenter server will generate a certificate for the enforcement module, which will enable you to install a security policy to the internal enforcement module. You will then be returned to the Network Objects dialog box.

6. Create a new workstation object for nyweb01, by selecting New ➤ Node ➤ Host in the Network Objects dialog box. Configure the following parameters for the object and click OK once complete:

   - Name = nyweb01
   - IP address = 192.168.10.2
   - Comment = New York Web Server
   - Color = Green

7. Click Close in the Network Objects dialog box to return to the main screen in SmartDashboard. Create a new host object for jupiter .london.local, by right-clicking in any white space within the SmartMap pane, and selecting New Network Objects ➤ Nodes ➤ Host from the menu that appears. The Host Node dialog box will be displayed. Configure the following parameters for the object and click OK once complete:

   - Name = jupiter.london.local
   - IP address = 172.20.1.2
   - Comment = External Web Server
   - Color = Red

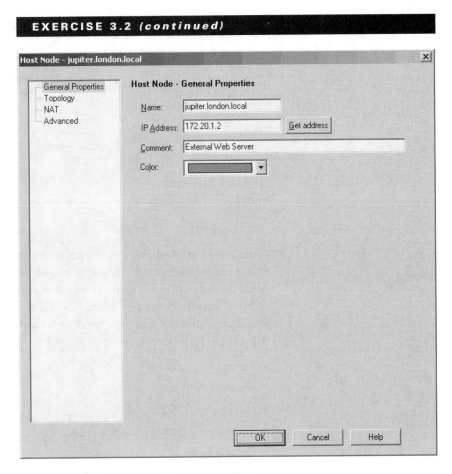

8. You will now create a network object for the internal New York network. You could do this by selecting New ➤ Network in the Network Objects dialog box (similar to creating the nyweb01 workstation object in Step 5), however you can also do this using SmartMap. In the SmartMap pane of SmartDashboard, you should see an object called nyfw01 locale. This object represents a set of collapsed objects situated around the nyfw01 enforcement module. The collapsed view is used to make the topology map easier to read. Right-click the nyfw01 locale object and select Expand from the menu. All of the objects within the locale will be displayed. Practice moving objects around by dragging them with the mouse.

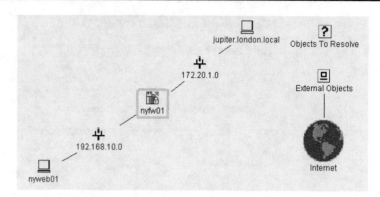

9. Actualize the implied 192.168.10.0 object (which is the New York internal network) by right-clicking on the object and choosing the Actualize Network menu item. A new network object will be created, and the Network Properties dialog box is displayed, which allows you to configure the new network object. Configure the network object with the following parameters and click OK once complete.

   - Name = ny-internal-lan
   - Network Address = 192.168.10.0
   - Net Mask = 255.255.255.0
   - Comment = New York Internal LAN
   - Color = Green
   - Broadcast address = Not included

10. Actualize the implied 172.20.1.0 object (which is the New York Internet DMZ network) by right-clicking on the object and choosing the Actualize Network menu item. A new network object will be created, and the Network Properties dialog box is displayed, which allows you to configure the new network object. Configure the network object with the following parameters and click OK once complete.

    - Name = ny-internet-dmz
    - Network Address = 172.20.1.0
    - Net Mask = 255.255.255.0
    - Comment = New York Internet DMZ

EXERCISE 3.2 *(continued)*

- Color = Red
- Broadcast address = Not included

11. Right-click on the `ny-internet-dmz` network object in the topology
    pane and select Connect to ➢ Internet from the menu that appears.
    This will attach the Internet DMZ network to the Internet, which
    ensures the connection to the Internet is accurately described. The
    following shows how the Topology pane should appear after actu-
    alizing the network objects and connecting the Internet object.

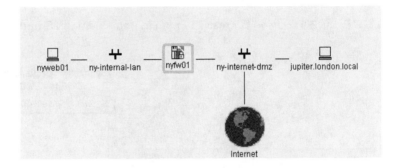

12. Create a group object called `ny-internal-networks`, which is to
    represent any internal networks in the New York office (at present,
    the 192.168.10.0 network is the only internal network). Select
    Manage ➢ Network Objects from the main menu, which will display
    the Network Objects dialog box. Select New ➢ Group ➢ Simple
    Group, which will display the Group Properties dialog box for a
    new group. Configure the group with the following parameters and
    click OK once complete:

- Name = `ny-internal-networks`
- Comment = New York Internal Networks
- Color = Green
- Members (In Group) = `ny-internal-lan`

The group created includes any internal networks at New York, so
therefore must include the `ny-internal-lan` object as a member.

Anti-Spoofing

Anti-spoofing is a security feature that enables a firewall to determine whether traffic is legitimate or if it is being used for malicious purposes. Anti-spoofing specifically detects IP address spoofing—spoofing is when the sender of traffic impersonates someone else. Spoofing techniques are used in many well-known denial of service (DoS) attacks and can also be used to hijack TCP sessions between systems. The most common form of spoofing is the spoofing of the source IP address of a packet—the sender of the packet alters the source IP address of the packet to the IP address of another system. Figure 3.21 shows how a common denial of service attack known as Smurf is implemented using spoofing.

FIGURE 3.21 Using address spoofing to implement the Smurf attack

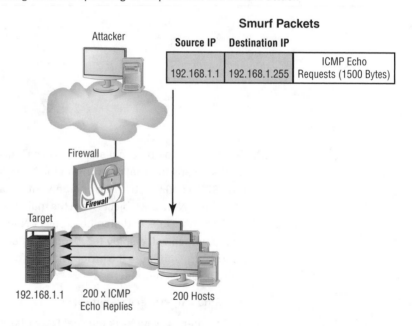

In Figure 3.21, an attacker on the Internet sends numerous large 1500-byte ICMP echo request packets with a source IP address of the target system (192.168.1.1) and a destination IP address of 192.168.1.255. The 192.168.1.255 is a directed broadcast address, which means that the echo request is sent to *all* hosts on the 192.168.1.0 subnet. In Figure 3.21, this represents 200 hosts. Because the source IP address of the echo request is 192.168.1.1, each host sends a reply back to that address. This means that suddenly the target system receives 200 ICMP echo replies at once. This attack is often referred to as an *amplification attack*, because the attacker only has to send one packet to achieve an end result of actually sending 200 packets to the target system. So if the attacker generates 1.5Mbps (T1 speed) worth of ICMP echo packets, the target system must deal with 300Mbps of attack traffic, which will most likely bring the target system to its knees, as well as flood the entire network.

There are many other common DoS attacks and other attacks that use address spoofing. You should always ensure anti-spoofing is enabled correctly on all enforcement modules in your network.

To counter address spoofing, the VPN-1/FireWall-1 enforcement module includes an anti-spoofing mechanism that ensures addresses are not spoofed and traffic is legitimate. In Figure 3.21, because the IP address of the attack packet is 192.168.1.1 and the attack packet is received first on the Internet interface of the firewall, the firewall actually can detect the spoofed address. If the firewall is configured that the 192.168.1.1 address is an internal network address, the firewall can drop the traffic, because there is no legitimate reason why any traffic received on the Internet interface should contain a source IP address of an internal system. Any traffic containing a source IP address of an internal system should only ever be received on the internal interface.

Prior to VPN-1/FireWall-1 NG, anti-spoofing checks both the source IP address of packets received on an interface *and* the destination IP address of packets transmitted out an interface, to ensure these packets are addressed to a valid destination. In VPN-1/FireWall-1 NG, only the source IP address of packets received on an interface is subject to an anti-spoofing check.

The anti-spoofing mechanism is configured via anti-spoofing policy on the SmartCenter server. Each enforcement module workstation object includes a Topology category, which includes information about each of the interfaces installed on the enforcement module. Figure 3.22 shows the Topology configuration screen of a workstation object representing an enforcement module.

In Figure 3.22, you can see information about each interface that is installed on the enforcement module. The name of the interface (operating system device name), IP address, network mask, and IP addresses behind the interface are all listed. The IP Addresses behind interface column determines whether the anti-spoofing mechanism is enforced. This column lists all IP addresses that legitimately exist behind the interface. To visualize this concept, take a look at Figure 3.23.

FIGURE 3.22   The Topology configuration screen

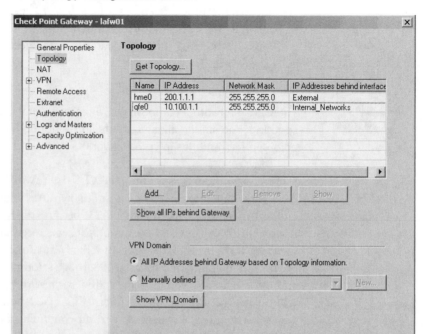

Throughout this book subnets are commonly referred to using subnet mask bit-length notation. For example, in 192.168.1.0/24, the /24 portion refers to a 24-bit subnet mask (255.255.255.0). Another example might be 10.1.0.0/16—the /16 portion refers to a 16-bit subnet mask (255.255.0.0).

In Figure 3.23, three interfaces are present on the enforcement module. The 192.168.1.0/24 subnet is connected to the DMZ interface (qfe1), while the 10.100.1.0/24 and 10.200.1.0/24 subnets are connected to the Internal interface (qfe0). All other IP addresses are considered to be connected to the Internet interface (hme0). Looking at the internal interface, only the subnets that are connected to this interface are considered valid. IP traffic that is received by the internal interface should have a source IP address that falls within the 10.100.1.0/24 or 10.200.1.0/24 subnet. If the source IP address is outside these subnets, the traffic is not considered legitimate and could indicate somebody is spoofing traffic. Similarly on the DMZ interface, all traffic received on this interface should have a source IP address that falls within the 192.168.1.0/24 subnet. On the Internet interface, all traffic received on the interface can have any source IP address, *except* for the subnets connected to the DMZ interface and the Internal interface. If any traffic received on the Internet interface has a source IP address that falls within the 10.100.1.0/24, 10.200.1.0/24, or 192.168.1.0/24 subnets, the firewall considers this traffic to not be legitimate, as the traffic should have arrived on either the DMZ or internal interface, not the Internet interface. If the firewall detects any traffic that is not considered legitimate due to possible spoofing, the traffic is dropped and optionally logged in the security log file or an alert is generated.

FIGURE 3.23 IP addresses behind interfaces

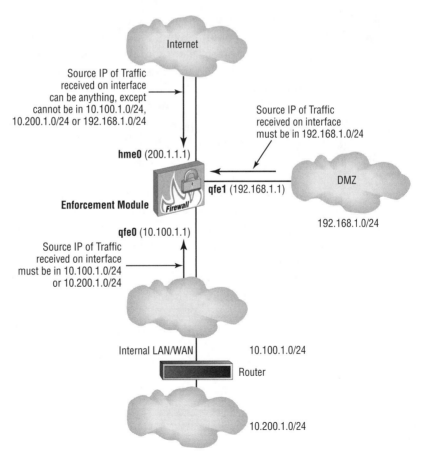

Referring back to Figure 3.22, notice that an entry exists for the hme0 and qfe0 interfaces on the workstation object 1afw01. The IP addresses behind interface column for the hme0 interface specifies External, which means that this interface is facing the Internet and any source IP address (except for addresses defined as legitimate on other interfaces) of traffic received on the interface is considered valid. For the qfe0 interface, notice that the IP addresses behind interface column specifies Internal_Networks, which is the name of a group object that includes network objects repre-senting the 10.100.1.0/24 and 10.200.1.0/24 networks attached to the qfe0 interface. Only source IP addresses within the group object defined are considered valid for traffic received on the qfe0 interface—any traffic carrying a source IP addresses outside of the Internal_Networks group is considered illegal and is dropped.

Before configuring anti-spoofing, make sure that you have a clear under-standing of your network topology. You must ensure that all valid devices behind an interface are represented in your anti-spoofing configuration, otherwise devices that are omitted will not be able to communicate through the firewall, as the enforcement module will think the traffic is spoofed. Many administrators run in to problems when they enable anti-spoofing, as they have not configured it correctly. Because of this, many administrators disable anti-spoofing, thinking it is more trouble than it is worth.

Notice in Figure 3.22 that an entry for the qfe1 interface (DMZ interface) does not exist. To add an interface to the Topology configuration screen, click the Add button shown in Figure 3.22. The Interface Properties dialog box will be displayed, which includes a General tab and a Topology tab, as shown in Figure 3.24. The General tab (see Figure 3.24) allows you to define the interface name, IP address, and subnet mask. In Figure 3.24, an interface called qfe1 has been defined, with an IP address of 192.168.1.1 and subnet mask of 255.255.255.0.

To configure anti-spoofing, click on the Topology tab. Figure 3.25 shows the Interface Properties dialog box with the Topology tab selected.

FIGURE 3.24 The Interface Properties dialog box

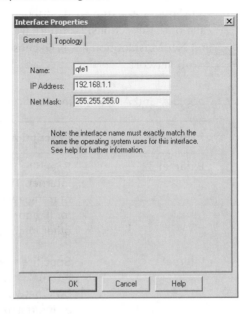

FIGURE 3.25 The Interface Properties dialog box with Topology tab selected

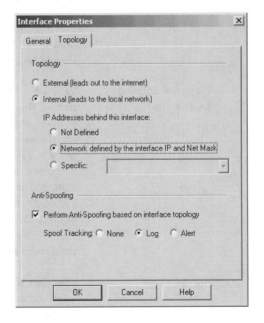

In Figure 3.25, there are two sections you can configure: Topology and Anti-Spoofing. Table 3.7 describes the various configuration parameters for each of these sections. Notice that the Network defined by the interface IP and Net Mask option has been chosen, as the qfe1 interface is connected to a stub network.

TABLE 3.7 Topology and Anti-Spoofing Configuration Parameters

Parameter	Description
External	Specifies that the interface is attached to the Internet. This means that any source IP address of traffic received on the interface is valid, except for IP addresses that are defined as internal on other interfaces.
Internal	Specifies that the interface is attached to an internal network. This network could include DMZ networks and extranet networks, as well as internal networks. There are three options for defining the IP addresses behind the interface (see next three items in this table).
Not Defined	The IP addresses attached to the interface are undefined. This option disables anti-spoofing and should only be used for troubleshooting purposes.
Network defined by the interface	VPN-1/FireWall-1 calculates the valid addresses behind the interface based on the interface's IP address and subnet mask. This option is useful for interfaces attached to *stub* networks—a stub network is a network that only has a single subnet and does not attach to any further networks. For example, if a DMZ interface has an IP address of 192.168.1.1 and a subnet mask of 255.255.255.0, VPN-1/FireWall-1 calculates any address in the 192.168.1.0/24 (192.168.1.1–192.168.1.255) as valid, with all other IP addresses being invalid.
Specific	Specifies that the valid addresses behind the interface are defined by a Check Point security object. Most commonly this is a *group* object, which contains several network objects that represent subnets located behind the interface.

TABLE 3.7 Topology and Anti-Spoofing Configuration Parameters *(continued)*

Parameter	Description
Perform Anti-spoofing	This option enables anti-spoofing based on the topology defined for the interface. You should always enable anti-spoofing.
Spoof Tracking	Specifies the *tracking* action to take if a packet is dropped that has an IP address that is considered spoofed. You can specify that no tracking action be taken (by choosing *None*), an entry should be placed in the security log file (by choosing *Log*), or an alert should be generated (by choosing *Alert*). It is recommended that you either log or alert for anti-spoofing events, to ensure you have a clear picture of possible denial of service or hijacking attempts against your organization.

Anti-spoofing checking is not implemented until the security policy has been installed to an enforcement module.

Configuring Anti-Spoofing for Open Security Extension Devices

You can configure anti-spoofing for Open Security Extension (OSE) devices (routers) that are manufactured by Cisco (IOS version 10.0 and above), 3Com, or Bay (Nortel). A security object representing any of these OSE devices also has a topology configuration screen, which allows you to define the valid IP addresses behind each router interface. There are some restrictions on where anti-spoofing can be enforced:

- Cisco routers can detect anti-spoofing only on the external interface, in both directions (inbound or outbound).

- Bay routers can detect anti-spoofing on all interfaces for inbound traffic only.

- 3Com routers can detect anti-spoofing on all interfaces for traffic in both directions (inbound or outbound).

In the following exercise, Exercise 3.3, you will configure the `nyfw01` enforcement module to implement anti-spoofing. In the network topology (see Figure 3.8), any traffic received on the internal interface should have an internal source IP address, while traffic received on the external interface should not have a source IP address of any internal networks.

EXERCISE 3.3

Configuring Anti-Spoofing

1. Log on to the `nyfw01` SmartCenter server using SmartDashboard. Select Manage ➢ Network Objects from the main menu, which opens the Network Objects dialog box. Select the `nyfw01` object and click the Edit button, which will display the Workstation Properties dialog box for `nyfw01`. Open the Topology screen by clicking the Topology option in the left-hand menu.

2. Notice that the IP Addresses behind interface column lists Undefined for each interface, meaning anti-spoofing is not configured for either interface. Select the internal interface by clicking on it and then click the Edit button, which will display the Interface Properties screen. Click the Topology tab and configure the interface as follows. Once you have completed your configuration, click OK to return to the Topology screen.

    - Topology = Internal
    - IP Addresses behind this interface = Specific (`ny-internal-networks`)
    - Anti-spoofing = Enabled
    - Spoof tracking = Log

3. Select the external interface by clicking on it and then click Edit button, which will display the Interface Properties screen. Click the Topology tab and configure the interface as follows. Once you have completed your configuration, click OK to return to the Topology screen.

    - Topology = External
    - Anti-spoofing = Enabled
    - Spoof tracking = Log

4. At this stage, the IP Addresses behind interface column for each interface in the Topology screen should now indicate that anti-spoofing is enabled.

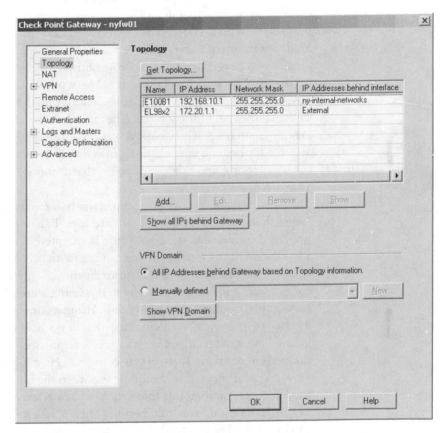

5. Click OK to complete the anti-spoofing configuration of nyfw01, which will return you to the Network Objects dialog box. Click Close to return to the main SmartDashboard view.

Security Policy Rules

Security rules form the major component of the VPN-1/FireWall-1 security policy, and are the feature that you will most commonly work with as a Check Point security administrator. In this section you will learn about how each security rule is constructed, how to configure multiple rules to form a *security rule base* and how to manage and install security rule bases.

Understanding the Security Rule Base

The heart of the security policy database is the security *rule base*, which is an ordered set of rules that define what types of network traffic are permitted between networks, systems, users, and applications. The rule base is configured on the SmartCenter server but actually enforced on the enforcement module, which is receiving traffic from untrusted networks and is responsible for ensuring the security of the internal network. Every rule has criteria that are used to classify traffic and define actions that determine what happens to the traffic. Each rule also specifies if the traffic should be tracked via logging or alerting, which enforcement module(s) the rule applies to, and also the time of the day when the rule should be enforced. The various criteria, actions, and other parameters that comprise a rule are referred to as *rule elements*.

It is important to note that security rules are based on connections rather than packets received on an interface. Each rule defines an accepted or denied connection. If a connection is accepted, the enforcement module will automatically ensure that return traffic that is part of the connection is permitted back through the enforcement module to the sender. The enforcement module does this by maintaining stateful information about each connection through the firewall. Using a connection-based approach means you only need to define rules based on where the connection originates. For example, if you have an access requirement that requires Host X (located on the internal network) to connect to Host Y (located on the external network), the enforcement module (between the internal and external networks) only requires a rule that specifies Host X as the source and Host Y as the destination. This rule permits Host X to establish a connection to Host Y—all return traffic from Host Y back to Host X associated with the connection is permitted back through the enforcement module automatically. With just the single rule in place, Host Y cannot establish connections to Host X. If you mistakenly also created a rule that specified Host Y as the source and Host X as the destination, thinking that this rule was required to enable return traffic, you would actually be allowing Host Y (external) to establish a connection back to Host X (internal).

Figure 3.26 shows an example of the security rule base viewed from SmartDashboard.

You can use the View menu in SmartDashboard to selectively display or hide the various panes. This allows easier configuration of the rule base.

FIGURE 3.26 The security rule base

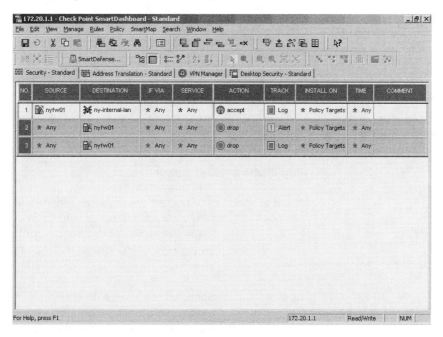

The Desktop Security rule base defines security policy for the firewalling component of SecureClient (a Check Point VPN client).

In Figure 3.26, notice that four rule bases are installed—Security, Address Translation, VPN Manager, and Desktop Security as indicated by the tabs at the top of the rule base. If you have additional SVN components installed, other rule bases may be available via another tab. For example, if FloodGate-1 is installed, a rule base called *QoS* is configurable via a new tab labeled QoS. At this stage, we'll just examine the Security rule base, which determines what traffic is permitted through the enforcement module(s) protecting an organization's network.

Check Point VPN-1/FireWall-1 Feature Pack 2 introduces the VPN Manager rule base, which is a separate rule base used for managing VPNs. Prior to this release, all VPN configurations are controlled by the Security rule base (In Feature Pack 2 and above you can opt to use the security rule base for VPN configuration if you wish).

Notice in Figure 3.26 that each rule has fields (elements) that describe the criteria for the rule, actions to perform, and so on. Each element contains security objects, which represent networks, systems, users and applications. Table 3.8 describes each of the elements that are configured for a rule in the Security rule base.

TABLE 3.8 Rule Elements

Rule Element	Description
Number	Determines the order in which rules are processed. When a packet is processed by the rule base, each rule in the rule base is processed from top (Rule 1) to bottom until a rule is found that matches the packet being examined.
Source	Specifies the source host, source network, or user that traffic is originating from. For example, if a packet has a source IP address of 192.168.1.10 and a rule has a source network of 192.168.1.0 with a subnet mask of 255.255.255.0 (i.e., the source can be 192.168.1.x), the source field of the rule is matched because the source IP address of 192.168.1.10 is part of the 192.168.1.0/24 subnet.
Destination	Specifies the destination host or destination network to which traffic is being sent.
If Via	Used only for VPN rules and indicates the VPN community traffic defined by the rule can pass through and initiate subsequent VPN connections. If you are not configuring a rule that uses a VPN, always leave this field as Any. The If Via element was introduced in Feature Pack 2 and is not present in versions prior to this.

TABLE 3.8 Rule Elements *(continued)*

Rule Element	Description
Service	Specifies the application-layer or transport-layer protocol of traffic being sent. For example, a service called HTTP might match any traffic with a destination TCP port of 80 (HTTP), while a service called ICMP might match any traffic with an IP protocol number of 1 (which indicates ICMP traffic).
Action	Specifies the action the enforcement module should take on traffic matching the source, destination, and services criteria listed above. Actions include accept (permit the traffic), drop or reject (deny the traffic), and other actions related to authentication and encryption.
Track	Specifies a tracking option that is fired if the rule is matched. Tracking options include logging (writing an entry to the security logging database), alerting (e.g., sending an e-mail), or executing a custom script for more complex requirements.
Install On	Specifies which enforcement module(s) the rule is installed on. If you are managing multiple enforcement modules, it is very unlikely that the rule base required for each enforcement module will be the same. You can specify to enforce common rules on all enforcement modules, and then create rules specific to each enforcement module and specify to enforce these rules on specific enforcement modules. This approach allows you to maintain a single security rule base on the SmartCenter server and allows for portability by aggregating a common rule applied to all enforcement modules into a single rule.
Time	Specifies the time during which the rule is effective. If no time is specified, the rule is always in effect.
Comment	Allows for a user-defined description of the rule that aids security administrators in understanding each rule.

The Source, Destination, and Services elements all must be matched to match a rule and invoke the rule action. If one or more of the Source, Destination, or Services elements is not matched, the rule is not matched and processing moves to the next rule.

To understand how security rules are processed by enforcement modules, examine the flowchart shown in Figure 3.27.

FIGURE 3.27 Security rule processing on enforcement modules

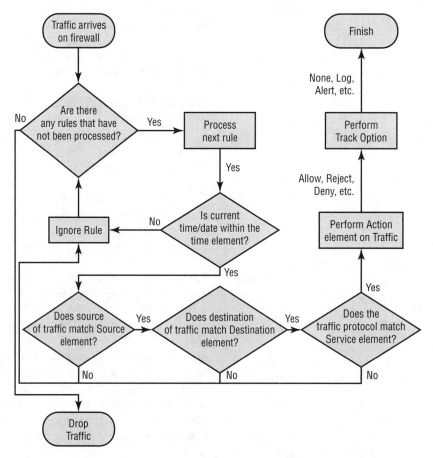

Traffic that the firewall is to inspect is processed against the rule base. A check is made as to whether there are any remaining rules to process. If the traffic has just been received, no rules have been processed, so the first rule is examined. The Time element of the rule is checked for a time object that specifies the date and time the rule should be enforced. If a time object is present and the current system date and time falls within the date/time range of the time object, the next element of the rule is processed. The Source, Destination, and Service (protocols carried by the traffic) of the traffic are all examined against each respective element of the rule. The traffic must match all three of these elements to continue. If the traffic does not match any of the elements, the rule is ignored, and the enforcement module checks if there are any remaining rules to process. Assuming the traffic matches the Source, Destination, and Service elements of the rule, the Action element of the rule is read and the appropriate action (e.g., accept, deny, and so on) is performed. The Track element of the rule is also read and any appropriate tracking actions are performed (e.g. log, alert, and so on). If traffic matches a rule, an action is applied to the rule and no further rule processing is required for the traffic.

Working within Security Rules in SmartDashboard

The security rule base is normally the most heavily configured and managed portion of the Check Point security policy. It is vital that you understand how to use the SmartDashboard application to modify the various elements that make up each rule. In this section you will learn how to configure and modify each element within in a rule. Don't worry about creating, modifying, and removing whole rules just yet, these actions will be examined later in this chapter.

MODIFYING THE SOURCE ELEMENT OF A RULE

To modify any element of a rule, simply position the mouse arrow over the element and right-click. A menu will appear next to the mouse arrow, displaying a menu specific to the element that you are modifying. Figure 3.28 shows the menu displayed when right-clicking within the Source element of a rule.

FIGURE 3.28   Modifying the Source Element of a Rule

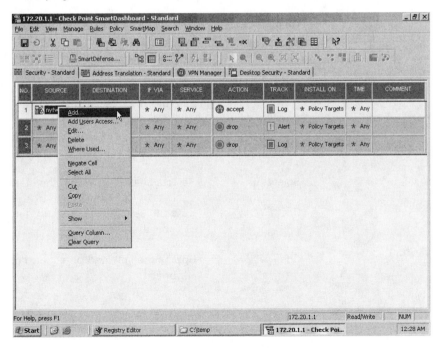

As you can see from Figure 3.28, the menu displays the following menu options described in Table 3.9.

TABLE 3.9 Menu Options for Modifying the Source Element of a Rule

Menu Option	Description
Add	Allows you to add a new network object to the source of a rule. A network object represents hosts, networks, groups, and other types of systems.
Add Users Access	Allows you to add a new user group object to the source of a rule.
Edit	Allows you to modify an existing network or user group object specified in the source of a rule.
Delete	Deletes the selected object from the source element of the rule.
Where Used	Queries the security rule base and indicates where else in the rule base the object you have selected appears.
Negate Cell	Negates the selected network or user group object. This means that the source of the rule matches all network/user group objects, excluding the selected network or user group object. For example, if a user group object called Admins is negated in the source element of a rule, the rule will match all users except for Admins as the source element. If the negate option is selected on an object, a red cross is placed on top of it (see the internal object on the first rule in Figure 3.26).
Select All	Selects all objects within the element.
Cut	Cuts the selected object and places it onto the clipboard.
Copy	Copies the selected object and places it onto the clipboard.

TABLE 3.9 Menu Options for Modifying the Source Element of a Rule *(continued)*

Menu Option	Description
Paste	Pastes the current network or user group object in the clipboard into the source element of the rule.
Show	Highlights the selected object in the SmartMap window.

The last two items in the Source Element menu (Query Column and Clear Query) are outside the scope of the CCSA exam and not discussed here.

MODIFYING THE DESTINATION ELEMENT OF A RULE

To modify the destination element of a rule, simply position the mouse arrow over the destination element and right-click. Table 3.10 describes the menu options available for configuring the destination element.

TABLE 3.10 Menu Options for Modifying the Destination Element of a Rule

Menu Option	Description
Add	Allows you to add a new network object to the destination of a rule. A network object represents hosts, networks, groups, and other types of systems.
Edit	Allows you to modify an existing network object specified in the destination of a rule.
Delete	Deletes the selected object from the destination element of the rule.
Where Used	Queries the security rule base and indicates where else in the rule base the object you have selected appears.
Negate cell	Negates the selected network or user group object for the destination element of a rule.

TABLE 3.10 Menu Options for Modifying the Destination Element of a Rule *(continued)*

Menu Option	Description
Select All	Selects all objects within the element.
Cut	Cuts the selected object and places it onto the clipboard.
Copy	Copies the selected object and places it onto the clipboard.
Paste	Pastes the current network or user group object in the clipboard into the destination element of the rule.
Show	Highlights the selected object in the SmartMap window.

MODIFYING THE IF VIA ELEMENT OF A RULE

The If Via element listed in Table 3.8 is used to support the new VPN communities configuration feature of VPN-1/FireWall-1, which is outside the scope of this book and the CCSA examination.

In versions prior to VPN-1/FireWall-1 NG Feature Pack 2, VPN configuration was implemented by using security rules and specifying actions of Encrypt or Decrypt (referred to as the *traditional mode* VPN configuration method), whereas from VPN-1/FireWall-1 NG Feature 2 onwards, the concept of VPN communities in conjunction with standard security rules using the If Via element is used to implement VPN configurations (referred to as the *simplified mode* VPN configuration method). When configuring security rules (as opposed to VPN rules) in simplified mode, always configure the If Via element as Any to ensure the rule is a security rule and not a VPN security rule.

You can configure your security policy so that the traditional mode VPN configuration method (i.e., using actions of Encrypt and Decrypt) is implemented. This will remove the VPN Manager tab shown in Figure 3.26, and will also remove the If Via element from the security rule base. To configure your security policy to use traditional mode, simplified mode, or either mode, select Policy ≻ Properties from the SmartDashboard menu, which will display the Global Properties dialog box. Within this dialog box, click on the VPN-1 Pro screen, which will allow you to enable simplified mode for all policies, traditional mode for all policies, or simplified or traditional mode per new security policy. Note that this setting only affects new security policies, which means the current security policy will remain in its current mode (simplified mode is the default mode). If you wish to use the new configuration method, you must create a new security policy rule base.

Because VPN configuration is outside the scope of the CCSA exam, all subsequent reference to security rules and related screen shots in this book are based on security policies that are configured using the traditional mode VPN configuration method. If you wish to apply the referenced security rules and screen shots to a simplified VPN configuration method, assume that the If Via element is always configured as "Any."

MODIFYING THE SERVICES ELEMENT OF A RULE

To modify the service element of a rule, simply position the mouse arrow over the service element and right-click. Table 3.11 describes the menu options available for configuring the service element of a rule.

TABLE 3.11   Menu Options for Modifying the Service Element of a Rule

Menu Option	Description
Add	Allows you to add a new service to a rule. A service represents an application-layer or transport-layer IP protocol, such as HTTP or TCP.
Add with Resource	Allows you to add a new resource to a rule. A resource represents HTTP, FTP, or SMTP traffic with some unique application-level parameters. For example a resource might match all HTTP traffic that includes *.com* as part of HTTP URL.
Edit	Allows you to modify an existing service specified in the service element of a rule.
Delete	Deletes the selected object from the service element of the rule.
Where Used	Queries the security rule base and indicates where else in the rule base the object you have selected appears.

TABLE 3.11 Menu Options for Modifying the Service Element of a Rule *(continued)*

Menu Option	Description
Negate Cell	Negates the selected service for the service element of a rule. For example, if you negated a service that represented HTTP traffic, all traffic *except* for HTTP traffic would match the rule.
Cut	Cuts the selected object and places it onto the clipboard.
Copy	Copies the selected object and places it onto the clipboard.
Paste	Pastes the current service in the clipboard into the service element of the rule.

MODIFYING THE ACTION ELEMENT OF A RULE

To modify the action element of a rule, simply position the mouse arrow over the action element and right-click. Figure 3.29 shows this process—notice that each action has an associated icon.

FIGURE 3.29 Modifying the Action element of a rule

Table 3.12 describes the menu options available for configuring the action element of a rule.

TABLE 3.12   Menu Options for Modifying the Action Element of a Rule

Menu Option	Description
Edit Properties	Allows you to edit any properties associated with the action of the rule. This option is not available for the accept, drop, or reject actions.
Add Encryption (Traditional Mode only)	Allows you to add encryption to the action of the rule. This option is only available if the traditional mode VPN configuration method is enabled for the security policy.
Edit Encryption (Traditional Mode only)	Allows you to modify the encryption action specified for a rule. This option is only available if the traditional mode VPN configuration method is enabled for the security policy.
Accept	Permits traffic that matches the source, destination and service elements of the rule.
Drop	Drops traffic silently that matches the source, destination, and service elements of the rule.
Reject	Rejects traffic that matches the source, destination, and service elements of the rule. Rejecting traffic consists of dropping traffic and notifying the source of the traffic that the traffic was rejected.
User Authentication	Specifies that the source user group object defined in the source element of the rule must authenticate for traffic to be passed. This option only applies to HTTP, FTP, TELNET, and RLOGIN traffic.
Client Authentication	Specifies that the source user group object defined in the source element of the rule must authenticate via an out-of-band authentication daemon (service) running on the firewall, before traffic will be passed. This option can be applied to all types of traffic.

TABLE 3.12 Menu Options for Modifying the Action Element of a Rule *(continued)*

Menu Option	Description
Session Authentication	Specifies that the source user group object defined in the source element of the rule must authenticate via an authentication mechanism that runs on both the user's PC (the session agent) and the firewall. This option can be applied to all types of traffic.

MODIFYING THE TRACK ELEMENT OF A RULE

To modify the track element of a rule, simply position the mouse arrow over the track element and right-click. Figure 3.30 shows this process—notice that each tracking option has an associated icon.

FIGURE 3.30 Modifying the Tracking element of a rule

Table 3.13 describes the menu options available for configuring the track element of a rule.

TABLE 3.13 Menu Options for Modifying the Track Element of a Rule

Menu Option	Description
None	Specifies that no logging or alerting should be invoked for traffic matching the rule.

TABLE 3.13 Menu Options for Modifying the Track Element of a Rule *(continued)*

Menu Option	Description
Log	Specifies that an entry should be written to the security log database for traffic that matches the rule. Note that only one entry is written per *connection* rather than an entry being written per packet (this applies to all tracking options).
Accounting	Specifies that an entry should be written to the accounting log database for traffic that matches the rule. Accounting entries include information about the amount of traffic (number of bytes) associated with each connection, allowing administrators to track bandwidth usage.
Alert	Specifies that an alert be generated for traffic that matches the rule. By default, this is a pop-up window for administrators running the SmartView Status SMART client; however, the alert action can be modified to run a custom script that resides on the SmartCenter server.
SNMP Trap	Specifies that an SNMP trap be generated for traffic that matches the rule.
Mail	Specifies that an e-mail alert be generated for traffic that matches the rule. This e-mail alert is generated using a utility called sendmail on Windows-based SmartCenter servers, which has command-line parameters that customize the e-mail and where it is delivered to.
User Defined	Specifies that a user defined alert be generated for traffic that matches the rule. This is a custom script that is specified in the global properties of the security policy. Several user-defined alerts can be configured.

MODIFYING THE INSTALL ON ELEMENT OF A RULE

To modify the Install On element of a rule, simply position the mouse arrow over the Install On element, right-click and expand the Add submenu, which displays the various options that you can specify to control where a rule is enforced. Figure 3.31 shows this process—notice that each install on option has an associated icon.

FIGURE 3.31 Modifying the Install On Element of a Rule

Table 3.14 describes the menu options available for configuring the Install On element of a rule.

TABLE 3.14 Menu Options for Modifying the Install On Element of a Rule

Menu Option	Description
Gateways	Specifies that the rule should be installed on all enforcement modules. The direction in which the rule is enforced can be inbound, outbound, or either-bound. This direction is a global setting configured in the global properties of the security policy.
Dst	This is a special option used to enforce the rule on the inbound direction for enforcement module(s) specified in the Destination element of the rule. Select this option only when you are permitting or denying traffic sent directly to an enforcement module.
Src	This is a special option used to enforce the rule on the outbound direction for enforcement module(s) specified in the Source element of the rule. Select this option only when you are permitting or denying traffic sent directly from an enforcement module.
OSE Devices	Specifies that the rule should be installed on all open security extension (OSE) devices. An OSE device is simply a router which has access control lists managed by the Check Point SmartCenter server, allowing security policy to be extended to perimeter routers.
Embedded Devices	Specifies that the rule should be installed on all embedded devices. An embedded device is a firewall appliance that has a security-hardened operating system and a Check Point enforcement module pre-loaded.

TABLE 3.14   Menu Options for Modifying the Install On Element of a Rule *(continued)*

Menu Option	Description
Targets	Specifies that the rule should be installed on the specified enforcement modules. When you choose this option, you are presented with a dialog box that allows you to choose one or more enforcement modules that you wish the rule to be installed on. This option allows you to selectively apply rules to specific enforcement modules.

By default, the Install On element for each rule specifies Policy Targets. This is a built-in object that represents all possible targets on which a policy can be downloaded, including enforcement modules, OSE devices, and embedded devices. This object is the default Install On element object for all new rules that are created.

MODIFYING THE TIME AND COMMENT ELEMENTS OF A RULE

To modify the Time element of a rule, simply position the mouse arrow over the Time element and right-click, which displays the various options that you can specify to control the time during which a rule is enforced. You can add, edit, or delete time objects, which are special objects that specify the day(s) of the week or month as well as the time during the day when a rule is to be enforced. If no time object is specified, then the rule is always enforced.

To modify the Comment element of a rule, simply double-click within the Comment element, which will pop up a Comment text box that allows you to type in a comment (in free text) that describes the rule.

Creating a Rule Base

Now that you understand how a security rule is composed and understand how to create and configure the security objects that are referenced in security rules, you are ready to create security rules, which implement the security policy of your organization. If you refer back to the topology shown in Figure 3.11, the diagram displays two basic Check Point components—*security objects*, which define the networks, systems, users and applications of the organization, and *security rules*, which define which entities in the organization can communicate through the enforcement module. The security rules define the permitted network access through the enforcement module. These security rules are configured in the Check Point VPN-1/FireWall-1 SmartCenter server security rule base.

When you first install a SmartCenter server, the security rule base is empty. No explicit security rules exist (implicit security rules do exist by default that are not visible in SmartDashboard—these are discussed later in the chapter). To manage rules, you use the Rules menu item on the main SmartDashboard. Figure 3.32 shows the Rules menu.

FIGURE 3.32   The Rules menu

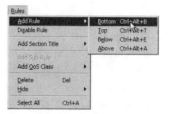

Table 3.15 describes the rules menu options shown in Figure 3.32.

TABLE 3.15   Menu Options for the Rules Menu

Menu Option	Description
Add Rule (submenu)	Allows you to add a rule to the rule base. This submenu specifies four locations where you can insert a new rule—at the Bottom (add a new rule to the bottom of the existing rule base), at the Top (add to the top of the existing rule base), After (add a new rule below the currently selected rule), or Before (add a new rule before the currently selected rule).
Disable Rule	Disables the currently selected rule in the rule base, meaning the rule will not be processed by enforcement modules until the Disable rule is removed. If you select a previously disabled rule, this menu item changes to Enable Rule, which allows you to re-enable the disabled rule.

TABLE 3.15   Menu Options for the Rules Menu *(continued)*

Menu Option	Description
Add Section Title (submenu)	Allows you to partition your security rule base up by including section titles that describe a set of contiguous rules.
Add Sub-Rule	Applies only to QoS rules, which are outside the scope of the CCSA exam.
Add QoS Class (submenu)	Applies only to QoS rules, which are outside the scope of the CCSA exam.
Delete Rule	Deletes the currently selected rule in the rule base.
Hide (submenu)	Allows you to hide and unhide rules in the rule base. Hidden rules are still applied by enforcement modules—hiding rules allows you to improve readability of the rule base when managing a complex rule base.

Creating Rules

To create your first rule, you must select the Rules ➢ Add Rule submenu from the main menu, and then choose either the Bottom (add a new rule to the bottom of the existing rule base) or Top (add to the top) menu item. In this case it doesn't matter, as no other rules exist. Figure 3.33 shows a new security rule base after a new rule has been added.

FIGURE 3.33   Adding a new rule

Notice in Figure 3.33 that the new rule reads as follows:

- Source = Any

- Destination = Any

- Service = Any

- Action = drop

The rule above is known as the *default rule* and tells all enforcement modules to drop all IP traffic. Obviously this is a very secure policy but not very effective in enabling access through the firewall. Once you have added a new rule, you can right-click in any element (e.g., Source or Action) and add the appropriate objects or options applicable for the element (see Table 3.8 through Table 3.14).

To add new rules to a rule base that contains other existing rules, you do not have to necessarily use the Rules menu to add new rules. You can right-click the mouse over the Number element of an existing rule, which presents a submenu as shown in Figure 3.34.

FIGURE 3.34   Right-clicking the mouse over the Number Element of a rule

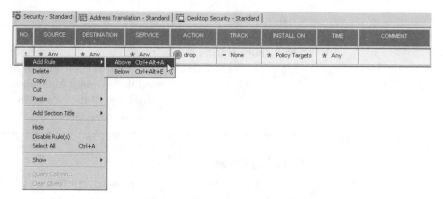

In Figure 3.34, notice that you can add a new rule above or below the selected rule. You can also delete a rule, and copy or cut a rule to the clipboard. The Paste Rule submenu allows you to paste a rule in the clipboard either above or below the selected rule, and you can also hide or disable a rule. Using this method of managing rules is much more intuitive than using the Rules menu.

The Basic Rules

It is important to understand two very basic rules that are normally used in most VPN-1/FireWall-1 implementations. These rules are known as the following:

Cleanup Rule   The *cleanup rule* specifies any IP traffic to drop, and is the rule created by default when you add a new rule. The cleanup rule is always applied at the end of a rule base—meaning any traffic that could not be matched by rules above the cleanup rule is dropped and logged. This ensures any unauthorized traffic that is not defined within your security rule base is always dropped.

Stealth Rule   The *stealth rule* is designed to protect your enforcement module from any attempted direct access by dropping all traffic destined to the enforcement module. This rule is normally placed at the top of a security policy; however, you must place any rules that define authorized access direct to the enforcement module above the stealth rule. For example, you might terminate VPN connections on your enforcement module, meaning that you must add rules that permit this traffic above the stealth rule. You should specify a tracking option of a least Log; however, a real-time notification option such as Alert or SNMPTrap is often defined to ensure you can quickly respond to attacks against your enforcement module.

Figure 3.35 demonstrates a security rule base with just the cleanup rule (Rule 2) and the stealth rule (Rule 1) configured.

FIGURE 3.35   The basic rules

NO.	SOURCE	DESTINATION	IF VIA	SERVICE	ACTION	TRACK	INSTALL ON	TIME	COMMENT
1	✳ Any	🖼 nyfw01	✳ Any	✳ Any	◉ drop	▤ Log	✳ Policy Targets	✳ Any	Stealth Rule
2	✳ Any	✳ Any	✳ Any	✳ Any	◉ drop	▤ Log	✳ Policy Targets	✳ Any	Cleanup Rule

🌐 Real World Scenario

Eliminating Unimportant Events from VPN-1/FireWall-1 Security Logs

Many networks include a lot of harmless, "noisy" traffic, such as broadcast traffic, which can fill up your logs quickly if they match the cleanup rule. This traffic is a part of normal network operation. For example, DHCP broadcast traffic from workstations or periodic NetBIOS broadcasts are a common and normal occurrence on Windows-based machines. If VPN-1/FireWall receives this traffic on an interface, it will process the traffic against the rule base and normally match the traffic against the cleanup rule (unless the traffic has been explicitly permitted for some reason). Although the traffic is dropped, an entry is also generated in the security logs for the event. With hundreds of devices connected to a network, these log entries can quickly clutter the security logs with information about traffic that is a normal and valid part of everyday network operation. It is recommended that you place a "noisy rule" in your rule base, which drops this noisy traffic and does not perform any tracking, ensuring your logs are not filled up with useless information.

EXERCISE 3.4

Creating Basic Rules

When you are first configuring your rule base, you should always create your cleanup and stealth rules first. In this exercise, you will configure the cleanup and stealth rules.

1. Log on to the nyfw01 SmartCenter server using SmartDashboard. At present, you should not have any security policy rules configured. To make configuring the rule base easier, click on the View menu in SmartDashboard and ensure that the only item checked is the Rule Base item. This will only display the rule base, making it easier to configure security rules.

2. Select Rules ➢ Add Rule ➢ Bottom from the SmartDashboard menu. This will create a new rule with the following elements:

   - Number (NO.) = 1
   - Source = Any
   - Destination = Any
   - Service = Any
   - Action = drop
   - Track = None
   - Install on = Policy Targets
   - Time = Any

3. Configure the new rule to be a cleanup rule. Right-click on the Track element and select the Log option. Double-click on the Comment element and configure a comment of "Cleanup Rule."

4. Create a stealth rule by right-clicking in the Number element of the cleanup rule (Rule 1) and selecting the Add Rule Above option from the menu displayed. This will create a new rule with identical parameters to the first rule created in Step 2. Modify the rule as follows to create the stealth rule. Once complete, the security policy should be identical to Figure 3.35.

   - Destination = nyfw01
   - Track = Log
   - Comment = Stealth Rule

Explicit and Implicit Rules

The security rule base that you normally see displayed in SmartDashboard consists of *explicit rules*—these rules have been manually (explicitly) defined by administrators to meet the security requirements of the organization. Check Point also includes *implicit rules* (also referred to as implied rules), which are rules designed to enable common applications and services through enforcement modules, without requiring the creation of explicit rules that define the required access. Implicit rules are controlled by the global properties of the security policy. To access these properties, select the Policy ➢ Global Properties menu item from the main menu. The Global Properties dialog box will be presented, which consists of several configuration screens that allow you to define parameters that are applied globally across the entire enterprise. Figure 3.36 shows the Global Properties dialog box with the FireWall-1 configuration screen selected, which allows you to enable and disable each implied rule.

FIGURE 3.36   The FireWall-1 Configuration screen in the Global Properties dialog box

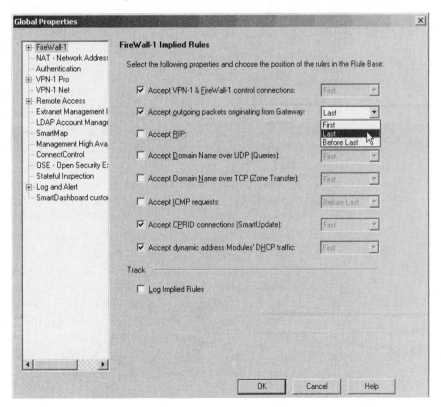

In Figure 3.36, you can see the various implied rules that can be selectively enabled or disabled as required. Each implied rule allows you to specify where in the security rule base the implied rule should be applied as follows:

- First—place the implied rule at the beginning of the rule base
- Last—place the implied rule at the end of the rule base
- Before Last—place the implied rule before the last rule in the rule base

If you define an explicit cleanup rule, any implied rules that have the Last option selected will never be matched, as the cleanup rule will match all traffic and drop it before it reaches the implied rule. If you wish to place an implied rule at the end of a rule base, yet still permit the traffic and still maintain a cleanup rule, choose the Before Last option.

Figure 3.36 shows that the Accept VPN-1/FireWall-1 control connections, Accept outgoing packets originating from the gateway, Accept CPRID connections (SmartUpdate), and Accept dynamic address Modules' DHCP traffic implied rules are enabled by default. The following describes each of the configuration parameters in Figure 3.36.

Accept VPN-1/FireWall-1 control connections.   This implied rule is enabled by default, and permits VPN-1/FireWall-1 control connections. The rules associated with this implied rule are always applied at the beginning of the security rule base if enabled. You cannot alter the position of this implied rule. This implied rule constitutes communications between Check Point SVN components. For example, the communications between a SmartCenter server and enforcement module when downloading a rule base to the enforcement module, or the communications between the SmartDashboard SMART client and the SmartCenter server. This implied rule also permits VPN-1 control connections, which includes IKE (Internet Key Exchange) traffic (used to negotiate, authenticate, and establish IPSec VPNs) as well as RDP (Reliable Datagram Protocol) traffic, which is used to negotiate, authenticate, and establish Check Point FWZ (Check Point's legacy proprietary VPN protocol) VPNs. Finally, any communications with security objects that reside in the Servers category (see Table 3.3—for example, RADIUS or LDAP servers) are also permitted by this implied rule.

You can disable this option; however, you must create explicit rules that permit any required VPN-1/FireWall-1 internal communications, VPN control connections, and security server (e.g., RADIUS) communications. Failure to configure these explicit rules will result in lost connectivity between SmartCenter servers and enforcement modules.

Accept outgoing packets originating from gateway (enforcement module).   This implied rule is enabled by default. You can apply this rule either first, last, or before the last rule in the rule base, by selecting the appropriate option from the dropdown box to the right of the rule. This rule permits any outgoing traffic that originates from enforcement modules only. Normally rules that are enforced on enforcement modules are only applied for inbound traffic only, which poses a problem for traffic originating from the enforcement module (this traffic is never processed inbound by the module). For example, you might log on to the console of an enforcement module, and attempt to connect to some remote system to test connectivity if there are problems. With this implied rule enabled, the test traffic described above is permitted. By default the implied rule is applied *Before Last*, meaning that you can define explicit rules that restrict traffic that might be considered dangerous from being sent by the gateway itself.

By default VPN-1/FireWall-1 enforcement modules enforce security rules eitherbound, meaning both inbound and outbound packets. You can configure the enforcement module to only apply security rules inbound, which means packets originating from the gateway will not be processed by the security rule base. This is not recommended, as it reduces the security of how security rules are processed and your enforcement module.

Accept RIP.   This option is disabled by default. You can apply this rule either first, last, or before the last rule in the rule base, by selecting the appropriate option from the dropdown box to the right of the rule. Enabling this implied rule allows routing information protocol (RIP) traffic between any source and destination to be permitted through the enforcement module.

Accept Domain Name over UDP (Queries). This option is disabled by default. You can apply this rule either first, last, or before the last rule in the rule base, by selecting the appropriate option from the dropdown box to the right of the rule. DNS traffic running over UDP is used for DNS queries, which are used by DNS clients to resolve DNS names via DNS servers. Enabling this option permits any UDP-based DNS traffic through the enforcement module.

Accept Domain Name over TCP (Queries). This option is disabled by default. You can apply this rule either first, last, or before the last rule in the rule base, by selecting the appropriate option from the dropdown box to the right of the rule. DNS traffic running over TCP is used for DNS zone transfers between DNS servers, which are used to synchronize DNS database information. Enabling this option permits any TCP-based DNS traffic through the enforcement module.

Accept ICMP requests. This option is disabled by default. You can apply this rule either first, last, or before the last rule in the rule base, by selecting the appropriate option from the dropdown box to the right of the rule. ICMP is used for diagnostic and monitoring purposes. Enabling this option permits any ICMP traffic through the enforcement module.

Accept CPRID connections (SmartUpdate). This option is enabled by default. You can apply this rule either first, last, or before the last rule in the rule base, by selecting the appropriate option from the dropdown box to the right of the rule. CPRID connections are used by the Smart-Update SMART client for communicating with the SVN foundation components running on SmartCenter servers and enforcement modules, for the purposes of transferring files for remote installation and/or product upgrades. SmartUpdate is used to manage product installations, upgrades, and licensing.

Accept dynamic address Modules' DHCP traffic. This option is enabled by default. You can apply this rule either first, last, or before the last rule in the rule base, by selecting the appropriate option from the dropdown box to the right of the rule. Check Point VPN-1/FireWall-1 NG allows enforcement modules to now be assigned an address dynamically via DHCP (called dynamically assigned IP address or DAIP modules)—this implied rule permits the DHCP traffic required to obtain an IP address lease.

Log implied rules. This option is disabled by default. Enabling this option means that any traffic that matches an implied rule will be logged to the security logs.

WARNING

You are strongly advised not to enable any of the RIP, DNS, or ICMP implied rules, as they permit any source and any destination. ICMP is particularly dangerous, as a large number of denial of service and reconnaissance utilities use ICMP. Unrestricted DNS ports are also commonly used to pass unauthorized non-DNS traffic through the port. If you need to enable access for any of these protocols, it is best to create an explicit rule specific to your requirements. If you do not have any DAIP modules, you should also turn off the DHCP implied rule.

You can view the implied rules enabled for a rule base and also view the location of implied rules by selecting the View ➢ Implied Rules item from the main menu. Figure 3.37 shows the security policy set with the viewing of implied rules enabled.

FIGURE   3.37   Viewing implied rules

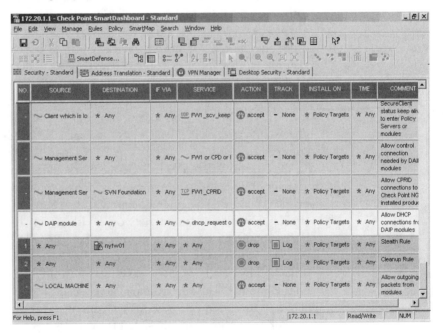

Although you can't see it due to the black and white print, implied rules are indicated by a light green color, while explicit rules are indicated by a gray color. Implied rules also do not have a rule number, as indicated by the dash (-) character in the Number column. In Figure 3.37, you can see the "Accept packets originating from Gateway" implied rule, as indicated by the implied rule above Rule 2 (see the comments element for this rule).

Notice the large amount of implied rules associated with the VPN-1/ FireWall-1 control connections option, which are applied first in the rule base.

The Implicit Drop Rule

The security rule base has an implicit *drop* rule at the end of the rule base, which means that any traffic not matched by a rule in the rule base is dropped. This rule is similar in function to the cleanup rule. One important distinction is that any traffic dropped by the implicit drop rule will *not* be logged. For this reason, it is preferable to always specify a cleanup rule that logs any dropped traffic that matches the rule.

Understanding Rule Base Order

You have learned that rules configured in the security rule base are processed in order from top to bottom (from 1 to *n*), with rule base processing ceasing once traffic being inspected matches a rule and the appropriate action is performed on the traffic. You must also consider implicit rules and where they are processed relative to other rules. It is important to consider rule base order and the effect it has on whether traffic is permitted or rejected. For example, you might have a policy that you wish to deny all traffic from a particular host. You create a rule that explicitly denies all traffic from the host. However, you might have an implied rule above the rule that permits ICMP traffic from *all* hosts. This means that your security policy is not being completely enforced, as the denied host can still send ICMP traffic through the enforcement module.

VPN-1/FireWall-1 also includes network address translation (NAT) and anti-spoofing features which must be considered when evaluating how traffic is processed by enforcement modules. NAT (discussed in Chapter 8) enables systems on internal networks with private (RFC 1918) IP addressing to communicate on the Internet (where RFC 1918 addressing is not permitted), by translating the source and/or destination IP address of traffic generated by or sent to internal systems to/from an IP address that is valid on the Internet. The SmartCenter server security policy includes a separate address translation rule base, which contains a set of rules that define how IP addressing should be translated for various types of traffic. This address translation rule base is configurable via the Address Translation tab in Smart-Dashboard. Anti-spoofing describes the process of determining whether the source and destination IP addressing of traffic is legitimate for the interface on which the traffic was received.

When traffic is processed by an enforcement module, it is important to understand that the traffic is processed by the security rule base first, passed through anti-spoofing checks, and then passed through the address translation rule base. The following lists the order in which traffic is processed by an enforcement module:

- Implied rules configured First in the security rule base

- Stealth rule (normally the first explicit rule)

- All explicit rules except the last rule

- Implied rules configured Before Last in the security rule base

- Cleanup rule (normally the last explicit rule)

- Implied rules configured Last in the security rule base

- Implicit drop rule

- Anti-spoofing check

- Address translation rule base

 By default the rule processing described above is applied at both the ingress interface (where a packet is received, also known as the client side) and at the egress interface (where a packet is transmitted from, also known as the server side). This is discussed further in Chapter 8 "Network Address Translation."

EXERCISE 3.5

Configuring Implied Rules

It is important to understand that VPN-1/FireWall-1 does have implied rules that you may not be aware are enabled in the security policy as they are not displayed by default. In this exercise you will configure implied rules and then verify the implied rule configuration by displaying the implied rules in the rule base.

1. Log on to the nyfw01 SmartCenter server using SmartDashboard. To configure implied rules, select Policy ➢ Global Properties from the SmartDashboard menu. This will display the Global Properties dialog box, and the FireWall-1 Implied Rules should be displayed by default.

EXERCISE 3.5 *(continued)*

2. Configure the implied rules as follows:

   - Disable Accept VPN-1 & FireWall-1 control connections.
   - Disable Access dynamic address Modules' DHCP traffic.
   - Disable Accept CPRID connections (SmartUpdate).
   - Enable Accept ICMP Requests. Ensure this implied rule is applied first by changing the default order for the rule from Before Last to First.

   Once you have completed your configuration, click OK.

3. To view implied rules in the SmartDashboard rule base, select View ➢ Implied Rules from the SmartDashboard menu. You should see the ICMP implied rule at the top of the rule base, and the Accept outgoing packets originating from the gateway implied rule before the last explicit rule (the cleanup rule).

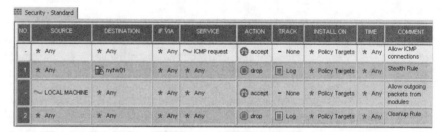

4. Let's assume that the nyweb01 machine is an authorized GUI client that will be used to configure VPN-1/FireWall-1 using SMART clients such as SmartDashboard. Because you have disabled the Accept VPN-1 & FireWall-1 control connections implied rule, you must configure an explicit rule for this management traffic above the stealth rule. Create a new rule above the stealth rule with the following parameters:

   - Source = nyweb01
   - Destination = nyfw01
   - Service = CPMI
   - Action = Accept
   - Track = Log
   - Comment = GUI Client Management Connections

EXERCISE 3.5 *(continued)*

Note: Hide the implied rules in the rule base by unchecking the View ➤ Implied Rules option in the SmartDashboard menu.

NO	SOURCE	DESTINATION	SERVICE	ACTION	TRACK	INSTALL ON	TIME	COMMENT
1	nyweb01	nyfw01	TCP CPMI	accept	Log	Policy Targets	Any	GUI Client Management Connections
2	Any	nyfw01	Any	drop	Log	Policy Targets	Any	Stealth Rule
3	Any	Any	Any	drop	Log	Policy Targets	Any	Cleanup Rule

Installing and Uninstalling a Rule Base

Once you have created your security rule base, you must explicitly install it onto enforcement modules. Once a security rule base is installed, the enforcement module will process traffic based on the rules that form the installed rule base. When you modify your security rule base, you must install the rule base to enforcement modules for the rule change to take effect. If you install a rule base that causes access problems for authorized traffic, you can quickly uninstall a policy if required. In this section you will learn about how to install and uninstall a security rule base.

Installing a Rule Base

After you have completed the configuration or modification of your rule base, you will need to download (or install) the rule base to the enforcement module(s) that protects your organization, after which the security rules will take effect. Before installing a rule base, you can verify that the rule base passes a check that ensures the rule base makes sense and does not include any illegal operations. For example, placing a rule after the cleanup rule does not make any sense, as any traffic not matched by the rules above the cleanup rule will always be matched by the cleanup rule. If you verify your rule base, the rule base is not downloaded to your enforcement modules.

To verify your security rule base, select the Policy ➤ Verify item from the SmartDashboard main menu, or click the Verify Policies button located on the policy toolbar underneath the main menu. Figure 3.38 shows the Policy toolbar and the Policy menu, from which you can verify, install, and uninstall security rule bases. Figure 3.38 also describes the Rules toolbar in SmartDashboard.

FIGURE 3.38   SmartDashboard toolbars

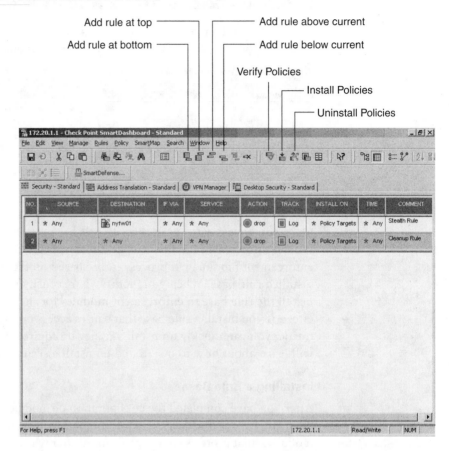

To install your security rule base on enforcement modules, select the Policy ➢ Install item from the SmartDashboard main menu, or click the Install Policies button on the Policy toolbar (see Figure 3.37). At this stage, SmartDashboard Warning dialog boxes may be displayed that provide some form of warning. To stop these warnings from appearing every time you install policy, check the "Don't show this message again" option.

If you disable the VPN-1/FireWall-1 control connections implied rule, you must ensure that the FW1 service (TCP port 256) is permitted on any remote enforcement modules to ensure the policy can be installed from the management.

After you have acknowledged any warnings, the Install Policy dialog box will be displayed, which displays a list of objects representing enforcement modules that the SmartCenter server can distribute the rule base to. All objects representing enforcement modules are Check Point Gateway objects, with at least the FireWall-1 product selected as an installed product (see Figure 3.14). Figure 3.39 shows the Install Policy dialog box.

FIGURE 3.39 The Install Policy dialog box

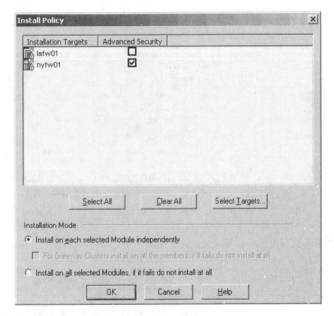

To install the security policy on the desired enforcement modules, enable the check box in the Security column (see Figure 3.39) for each enforcement module. Notice in Figure 3.39, that nyfw01 is selected as an installation target, but not lafw01. Once you have selected the desired enforcement modules, click OK. The Install Policy dialog box will next be displayed, which indicates the progress and success (or failure) of the policy installation, as shown in Figure 3.40.

When you install policy, both the security rule base and address translation rule base are applied to the enforcement module.

FIGURE 3.40 The Install Policy dialog box

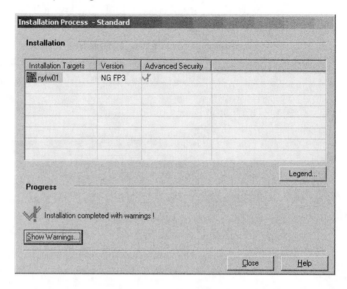

In Figure 3.40 you can see that installation completed, but with warnings. To view the warnings, click the Show Warnings button, which displays the Verification and Installation Errors dialog box, as shown in Figure 3.41.

FIGURE 3.41 The Verification and Installation Errors dialog box

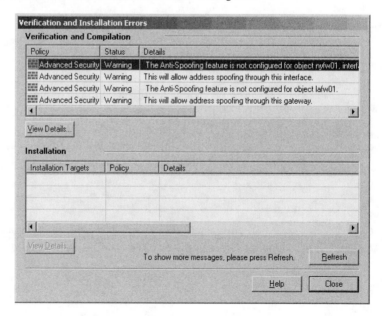

Notice In Figure 3.41 that there are several verification warnings. These warnings are related to anti-spoofing not being configured correctly on the enforcement modules.

In Feature Pack 3, if VPN-1 Pro is installed, you must configure the topology information for at least one interface of an enforcement module, so that the enforcement module can determine what are the internal addresses it protects for VPN connections. If you do not configure any topology information, the policy installation will fail.

EXERCISE 3.6

Verifying and Installing a VPN-1/FireWall-1 Security Policy

In Exercises 3.1 through 3.3 you configured the objects and rules required to implement a basic VPN-1/FireWall-1 security policy. The final step in completing your configuration is to verify and install the security policy to the enforcement module component of nyfw01.

1. Log on to the nyfw01 SmartCenter server using SmartDashboard. There should be three security rules configured (management communications, stealth, and cleanup). Select Policy ➢ Verify from the SmartDashboard menu, which will display the Verify dialog box. Ensure the Security and Address Translation option is checked and then click OK.

2. Verification of the policy will now take place. Once verification is complete, the Policy Verification dialog box will be displayed, which indicates whether or not the policy was verified OK. Click OK to close the Policy Verification dialog box after verification is successful.

3. Select Policy ➢ Install from the SmartDashboard menu. If this is the first time you are installing a policy, the SmartDashboard Warning dialog box will appear, advising you about the default implied rules that you cannot normally see in the security rule base. Check the "Don't show this message again" option and then click OK to continue.

EXERCISE 3.6 *(continued)*

4. The Install Policy dialog box will be displayed, which allows you to choose the enforcement modules that you want to install policy on. Because there is only a single enforcement module in this exercise, only the nyfw01 object is displayed. Ensure nyfw01 is configured as an installation target (as indicated by the check box in the Security column) and then click OK to proceed.

5. Policy installation should now begin. The status of the installation will be displayed, with any problems being reported as they occur. Once installation is complete, a message should be displayed indicating the policy installation is complete. Click OK to close the Install Policy dialog box and return to SmartDashboard.

Uninstalling a Rule Base

If you wish to uninstall a rule base, simply select the Policy ➤ Uninstall item from the SmartDashboard main menu, or click the Uninstall Policies button on the Policy toolbar (see Figure 3.38). The Uninstall Policy dialog box will be displayed, which is identical to the Install Policy dialog box shown in Figure 3.39. Select the enforcement modules for which you wish to uninstall policy, and click OK.

Uninstalling a security policy means that the enforcement module will accept any traffic, with no access control applied. When a security policy is installed, IP routing is disabled by the enforcement module, which means that only your enforcement module is exposed, and not the rest of your network behind the firewall. Only use this feature for emergency situations, such as when you accidentally block all communications to the enforcement module, including VPN-1/FireWall-1 control connections.

Connection Persistence

Connection persistence is a new feature in VPN-1/FireWall-1 NG Feature Pack 3, and describes how an enforcement module handles existing connections after a new policy has been installed to the enforcement module. You can define three options for connection persistence on a per-enforcement module basis, using the Advanced ➤ Connection Persistence screen of a Check Point Gateway object. Figure 3.42 shows this screen.

FIGURE 3.42   Connection Persistence screen

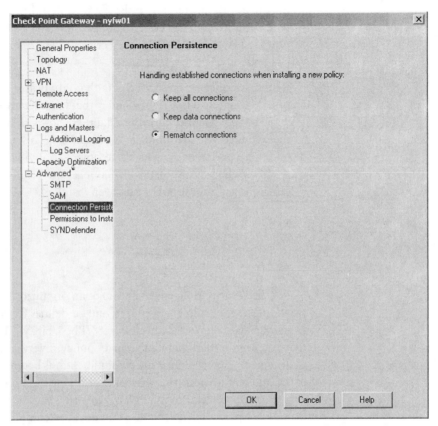

The following describes each of the connection persistence options shown in Figure 3.42:

Keep all connections.   Selecting this option means that all existing connections are kept open until the connections have ended, even if existing connections are no longer permitted by the new policy. The new policy is only enforced for any new connections.

Keep data connections.   All existing data connections are kept open until the data connections have ended, even if existing data connections are no longer permitted by the new policy. Existing control connections, however, are immediately torn down if they are not permitted by the new policy. For example, if a user has an FTP connection open through an enforcement module, with an FTP control connection allowing the user to issue commands and an FTP data connection allowing the user to transfer data, if a new policy is installed that no longer permits the FTP connections, the control connection will be immediately torn down. However, the data connection is kept open until the connection has ended.

Rematch policy. This is the default configuration. All existing connections are matched to the new policy that has been installed. If any existing connections (whether control or data) are not permitted by the new policy, these connections are immediately discarded. This policy can be overridden on a per-service basis, as service objects now include an option that specifies whether or not existing connections related to the service should remain open after a policy has been installed.

Summary

The security policy is the heart of an organization's network security, providing a set of rules, procedures, and guidelines for securing access to and from external networks. Check Point VPN-1/FireWall-1 provides the tools that enable you to implement security policy. Every organization has access requirements, which define the communications between networks, systems, users, and applications that are conducting business with or on behalf of the organization. Check Point VPN-1/FireWall-1 allows these access requirements to be provided in a manner that does not compromise the organization by permitting other unauthorized forms of access. The SmartCenter server component of VPN-1/FireWall-1 holds the security policy database, which is a collection of security rules, security configuration parameters, and other rules. A single SmartCenter server is normally used for an entire organization, allowing a central security policy to be created and then distributed to each firewall or gateway in the organization. SmartDashboard is a Check Point SMART client that provides a GUI application front-end into the security policy database for security administrators. The level of access for administrators using SmartDashboard can be customized, ensuring administrators can only access portions of the security policy for which they are authorized.

The main component of the VPN-1/FireWall-1 security policy is the security rule base, which defines the communications permitted (and denied) between elements internal and/or external to the organization. Each form of communication is defined as a security rule. A security rule is based on parameters of IP traffic such as source/destination IP address and the application protocol carried in the data portion of IP traffic. Traffic is processed by enforcement modules against each rule until the traffic is matched against a rule. At this point, the rule also defines the action that should be taken on the traffic—for example, allow (permit) or deny the traffic. You can optionally configure a rule to be tracked. This means any traffic matching the rule will be either logged or will generate some form of alert, enabling administrators to traffic specific types of traffic.

When configuring a security rule, you must first create security objects that can be placed into the security rule. A security object is simply a representation of a network, system, user, or application internal or external to the organization. Security objects that describe enforcement modules allow you to define anti-spoofing, which is a defensive mechanism designed to detect spoofed traffic that is used in many DoS attacks. After you have created security objects, you can configure security rules. Check Point VPN-1/FireWall-1 has two types of rules—implicit and explicit. Implicit rules are hidden rules that enable common types of communications. By default, VPN-1/FireWall-1 control connections and outgoing traffic from enforcement modules are permitted by implicit rules. Explicit rules are rules that are manually defined and visible in SmartDashboard by administrators. When configuring security rules, it is good practice to define a cleanup rule, which drops and logs all traffic not matched by the rule base, as well as a stealth rule, which drops all traffic directed to your enforcement modules. Once you have configured your security rules, you must explicitly install the policy on enforcement modules.

Exam Essentials

Understand how you configure VPN-1/FireWall-1 security policy. Security policy is configured via SmartDashboard. When starting Smart-Dashboard, you must attach to the SmartCenter server with the appropriate credentials and access rights. Both SmartDashboard and Policy Editor (previous name for SmartDashboard) may be referred to in the exam— they are the same.

Understand administrator permissions and how they control access to VPN-1/FireWall-1 security policy.   Various components of the security policy can be assigned permissions. Permissions include no access, read-only access, and read-write access. Some components are dependent on specific Check Point products being installed. The SmartUpdate component permissions affect many other component permissions.

Know what comprises a basic VPN-1/FireWall-1 NG security policy. The security object database, security rule base, global policy properties, and address translation rule base comprise a basic VPN-1/FireWall-1 policy.

Understand security objects and how to configure them.   Security objects represent networks, systems, users, and applications. You configure them using SmartDashboard via the Manage menu or by using the Objects Tree and Objects List pane.

Understand the common types of security objects.   The most common type of security object is the host node object, which represents servers, PCs, and printers. Check Point objects represent Check Point systems such as the SmartCenter server (host) and enforcement modules (gateways). Other common security objects include the network object, which defines an IP subnet or supernet; the domain object, which defines all hosts associated with a specific domain; and the group object, which allows you to group different objects into a functional group. Another important category of security objects are service objects, which represent transport-layer and application-layer protocols.

Know what anti-spoofing is and how you configure it.   Anti-spoofing detects IP traffic received on an interface that has spoofed IP addressing. This is source or destination IP addressing in traffic that comes from a network that is not present behind the interface. Anti-spoofing is used in many DoS attacks. To configure anti-spoofing, you must configure the topology of enforcement module. The topology lists all interfaces on the enforcement module and defines what networks (IP addresses) are valid behind the interface.

Understand what rule elements are and how a rule is constructed.   A security rule includes various elements that define traffic that is matched by the rule (Source, Destination, and Service elements), the action to take on traffic (action element), whether the rule match should be logged or sent as an alert (track element), what enforcement modules or OSE devices the rule should be installed on (install on element), and the time of day during which the rule should be enforced (time element). Each rule also contains a Number element that defines the order in which the rule is processed and a Comment element that allows you to add comments to a rule. To modify any element of a rule in SmartDashboard, simply right-click over the rule and choose the appropriate option.

Know the recommended rules for all rule bases. The cleanup rule is the recommended last rule in the rule base that drops all traffic and logs the denied traffic. The stealth rule is recommended near or at the top of the rule base and denies and logs/alerts any traffic destined for enforcement modules directly.

Understand implicit and explicit rules. Implicit (or implied) rules are defined in the global properties of the policy and enable common types of traffic through all gateways (enforcement modules). Implicit rules are hidden by default in SmartDashboard. Explicit rules are rules manually created by administrators. Implied rules include VPN-1/FireWall-1 control connections, packets originating from gateways, RIP, ICMP, DNS (UDP), DNS (TCP), and ICMP. You can place an implied rule at the beginning of the rule base (First), before the last explicit rule (Before Last) or at the end of the rule base (Last).

Understand how to view implied rules. Choose the View ➤ Implied Rules option.

Know how to verify, install, and uninstall policies. Choose the Policy menu and choose Verify, Install, or Uninstall from the menu.

Know what SmartMap is. SmartMap provides a graphical topology representation of the network, providing a visual representation of the security objects defined in SmartDashboard and the relationship between them. This aids in configuration of rules and creation of objects. Both SmartMap and Visual Policy Editor (previous name for SmartMap) may be referred to in the exam—they are the same.

Key Terms

Before you take the exam, be certain you are familiar with the following terms:

access rules	Implied network
actualize	Interoperable Devices
aklfw01	Network Objects
amplification attack	Noisy rule
anti-spoofing	read-write
Before Last	rule elements
Check Point Configuration Tool	security objects
cleanup rule	security policy
Connection Persistence	security rule
Content Vector Protocol	security rule base
default rule	service objects
Drop	SmartCenter Server
explicit rules	SmartDashboard
Fingerprint	SmartMap
GUI Clients	Stealth rule
implicit rules	subnet broadcast address

Review Questions

1. Which of the following applications can be used to configure implied rules? (Choose all that apply.)

   A. SmartDashboard

   B. SmartUpdate

   C. SmartView Status

   D. SmartMap

2. Which of the following would be part of an organization's security policy? (Choose all that apply.)

   A. Internet usage guidelines

   B. Remote access for users

   C. Cost of securing the network

   D. Gaining physical access to the office

3. Which of the following components comprise a VPN-1/FireWall-1 NG security policy? (Choose all that apply.)

   A. Object Database

   B. User Database

   C. Security Rule Base

   D. QoS Rule Base

   E. Log Database

4. Which of the following rules is used to protect enforcement modules?

   A. Cleanup

   B. Explicit

   C. Implicit

   D. Stealth

5. Which of the following panes in SmartDashboard represents the network topology visually?

    A. Objects List

    B. Objects Tree

    C. Rule base

    D. SmartMap

6. Which of the following permissions can you grant for Check Point administrators? (Choose all that apply.)

    A. No access

    B. Read-only access

    C. Read-write access

    D. Full access

7. What is the name of the process of creating network objects from implied network objects in SmartMap?

    A. Creating

    B. Visualizing

    C. Actualizing

    D. Cloning

8. A network object of type *network* has which of the following attributes? (Choose all that apply.)

    A. IP address

    B. Check Point installed

    C. Type (host or gateway)

    D. Net mask

9. You need to create an object that represents a TCP protocol that runs over port 2984. What type of object should you create?

    A. Workstation

    B. Resource

    C. Server

    D. Service

10. What configuration screen of a workstation screen is used to configure anti-spoofing?

    A. Anti-spoofing

    B. NAT

    C. Interfaces

    D. Topology

11. Which of the following is used to create a rule?

    A. Rules ➤ Add Rule

    B. Rules ➤ Manage

    C. Manage ➤ Add Rule

    D. Manage ➤ Add Security Rule

12. You create a rule that drops traffic that is considered dangerous. You wish for an e-mail notification to be sent using SMTP to an administrator if the rule is invoked. Which of the following track options should you configure?

    A. Alert

    B. Log

    C. Mail

    D. SMTP Alert

13. You place a rule that denies all ICMP traffic at the top (the first rule) of your rule base; however, users can still pass ICMP traffic through the firewall. What could be the cause of the problem?

    A. The ICMP implied rule is enabled and configured with the option Before Last.

    B. The ICMP implied rule is enabled and configured with the option First.

    C. The Accept outgoing packets implied rule is enabled and configured with the option Before Last.

    D. The Accept outgoing packets implied rule is enabled and configured with the option First.

14. Which of the following is used to install a security policy on an enforcement module?

    A. Policy ➤ Install

    B. Policy ➤ Install Rule Base

    C. Security ➤ Install

    D. Security ➤ Install Rule Base

15. You wish to define a rule that specifies a particular remote enforcement module, but find that you cannot choose the enforcement module from the options available in the Install On element of the rule. What could be the cause of the problem? (Choose all that apply.)

    A. In the gateway object for the enforcement module, the VPN-1 option is not checked.

    B. Secure Internal Communications have not been established with the enforcement module.

    C. The object representing the enforcement module is a Gateway Node object.

    D. Secure internal communications have not been configured on the SmartCenter server.

16. You wish to enable alerting for any packets that are anti-spoofed. Where do you enable alerting for anti-spoofing?

   A. On the Topology tab of the Interface Properties page for each interface on the firewall.

   B. In the Tracking Options section of the Log and Alert screen of Global Properties.

   C. In the Alert Commands section of the Log and Alert screen of Global Properties.

   D. By enabling the logging of implied rules.

17. True or False: By default, ICMP traffic is permitted via implicit rules on VPN-1/FireWall-1 NG.

   A. True

   B. False

18. You disable the VPN-1/FireWall-1 Control connection implicit rule and need to support an environment which has a separate Smart-Center server and enforcement module. Which TCP port should you explicitly permit to ensure the SmartCenter server can install a policy on a remote enforcement module?

   A. 80

   B. 256

   C. 259

   D. 443

19. You wish to ensure SMTP content from the Internet is virus-free. Which of the following do you need to provide this?

   A. CVP

   B. UFP

   C. Anti-virus server

   D. OPSEC-compliant anti-virus server

20. Anti-spoofing performs checks on which of the following? (Choose all that apply.)

A. Source IP Address

B. Source TCP Port

C. Destination IP Address

D. Destination TCP Port

Answers to Review Questions

1. **A.** SmartDashboard can only be used to configure implied rules via Policy ➢ Global Properties.

2. **A, B, C, D.** All of the above can form part of the security policy of an organization.

3. **A, B, C, E.** The QoS Rule Base is part of the FloodGate-1 product.

4. **D.** The stealth rule is used to deny all traffic with a destination of an enforcement module.

5. **D.** The SmartMap pane visually represents the network topology.

6. **A, B, C.** You can configure no access, read-only, and read-write access permissions.

7. **C.** When you actualize an implied network object, you copy the attributes of the implied network object to a new network object that you can configure and manage just like any other network object.

8. **A, D.** Options B and C only apply for workstation objects.

9. **D.** Service objects are used to represent application protocols.

10. **D.** The Topology configuration screen is used to configure anti-spoofing.

11. **A.** The Rules ➢ Add Rule submenu is used to create rules.

12. **C.** The mail tracking option allows VPN-1/FireWall-1 to generate an e-mail message that is sent to a configure recipient, notifying the recipient of the security event. The SMTP Alert option does not exist.

13. **B.** Implied rules that are configured with the option First are applied before any explicit rules. The Accept outgoing packets implied rule only applies to traffic generated by enforcement modules.

14. **A.** The Policy ➢ Install menu item is used to install security policies.

15. **C.** In order for an enforcement module object to become a valid target on which a rule can be installed, a Check Point gateway object must be created, with at least FireWall-1 indicated as an installed product. If SIC has not been established, you can still choose to install the rule on the enforcement module; however, when you attempt to install the rule, you will get an error.

16. A. You configure anti-spoofing tracking on the Topology tab of each interface on an enforcement module.

17. B. In VPN-1/FireWall-1 NG, ICMP is not permitted by default by implicit rules. ICMP was permitted by default in all previous versions of VPN-1/FireWall-1.

18. B. The FW1 service, which operates on a TCP port of 256, is required to allow a SmartCenter server to install a policy on a remote enforcement module.

19. A, D. CVP is used for the passing of HTTP, SMTP, and FTP for content checking. An OPSEC-compliant antivirus server is required to support CVP. UFP is used for content filtering of HTTP and FTP traffic based on URL.

20. A. In VPN-1/FireWall-1 NG, anti-spoofing only checks the source IP address of packets received on an interface. In versions prior to VPN-1/FireWall-1 NG, both the source IP address of packets received on an interface and the destination IP address of packets transmitted out an interface are checked.

Chapter

4

Advanced Security Policy and System Management

THE CCSA EXAM OBJECTIVES COVERED IN THIS CHAPTER INCLUDE:

- ✓ Describe how to manipulate rules in the Rule Base by masking and disabling them
- ✓ List the guidelines for improving VPN-1/FireWall-1 performance using a security policy
- ✓ Outline process to set up and operate an active security policy
- ✓ Identify the different components of Check Point VPN-1/FireWall-1 NG

In the previous chapter, you learned about the VPN-1/FireWall-1 NG security policy and the various components that comprise the policy. Once you have created the security objects that represent the various networks, systems, users, and applications that require representation in the security policy, you create your security rule base, which defines the access permitted and denied through enforcement modules. It is important to understand that the way in which you configure your security rule base can affect the performance of your enforcement modules. In this chapter, you will learn how you can optimize your rule base to ensure that network traffic is processed quickly and efficiently, even against a complex rule base, without taxing your enforcement module. We'll also examine how you can manage and troubleshoot complex rule bases, using techniques such as rule masking and disabling rules.

VPN-1/FireWall-1 NG introduced a new SMART client called *SmartUpdate* (previously known as *SecureUpdate* in Feature Pack 1 and Feature Pack 2), which allows you to manage VPN-1/FireWall-1 products and licenses. Check Point NG uses a totally revamped licensing model that permits central license administration, reducing the headaches associated with license management in previous versions. Also new to NG is the central management of Check Point product versions, software updates, and remote installations. You will learn how you can use SmartUpdate to take advantage of the new centralized management features of VPN-1/FireWall-1.

Finally, you will learn how to use the more common command-line utilities to manage and monitor both the VPN-1/FireWall-1 enforcement module and SmartCenter server. A series of Exercises spread throughout the chapter will demonstrate practically how to implement all of the topics covered by this chapter.

Improving Rule Management and Performance

Managing a large security rule base may leave you feeling overwhelmed by the large amount of information displayed in the security rule base. Displaying a large amount of information makes it difficult to work with specific rules or find specific information in your rule base. VPN-1/FireWall-1 provides security rule management features that can help you filter your rule base, refining the rule base display, easing rule management, and making it easier to find information.

The way in which you configure your rules does have bearing on the ongoing ease of management of rules, as well as the performance of the enforcement module processing the rules. You can decrease the amount of time it takes to configure rules on a SmartCenter server by using simple time-saving techniques. This section looks at how you can improve the management of a complex rule base, how you improve performance on enforcement modules, and how to reduce administrative overhead on your SmartCenter server.

Managing a Complex Rule Base

If you are working with the security rule base for a large and complex security policy, it can often become difficult to manage rules due to the large number of rules. SmartDashboard allows you to both hide and disable rules to increase the manageability of complex rule bases. It is often useful to hide rules during the configuration and troubleshooting of complex rule bases, removing rules from the view of the administrator that are distracting and don't need to be displayed on screen. You can also disable specific rules, which is very useful for troubleshooting access through a firewall that is being incorrectly permitted or denied. VPN-1/FireWall-1 NG Feature Pack 3 also introduces the ability to add *section titles* to your security rule base, which allows you to group rules together that have a common function or purpose, making rule management much easier, especially for complex rule bases.

Working with Rules

SmartDashboard allows you to work much more intuitively with the rules you learned to create in Chapter 3 than just using the menu—you can drag and drop rules and security objects, which allows you to modify the order of the rule base (by moving rules), copy rules, and copy security objects from one rule to another.

Moving Rules

To move a rule, simply click and hold the number element (shown as No. on screen) of the rule you wish to move, and then drag the rule to the position in the rule base that you wish to move the rule to. Once you have positioned the rule as desired, release the mouse button, and the rule will be moved. Figure 4.1 demonstrates moving a rule in the security rule base.

FIGURE 4.1 Moving a rule

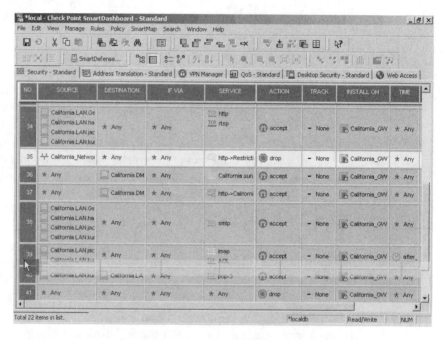

In Figure 4.1, Rule 35 is being dragged to a position in the rule base between Rule 39 and Rule 40. The fact that rule 35 is being dragged is indicated by the white highlighting of Rule 35, and the position in the rule base where it is being moved is indicated by the position of the mouse pointer, and the silhouette of Rule 35 in Figure 4.1.

Copying Rules

To copy a rule, you perform exactly the same procedure used to move a rule, except that you press Ctrl while dragging the rule and until you release it. When you press Ctrl, a small icon with a plus symbol (+) will appear underneath the mouse pointer, indicating you are copying the rule rather than moving it.

You can select multiple rules by Ctrl-clicking on each rule you wish to add to your selection or by Shift-clicking on the uppermost bound rule of a selection range. Once you have selected multiple rules, you can move and copy them as described in this section and the previous.

Copying Security Objects

If you create a new rule that uses security objects currently used in other rules, you can quickly copy those objects into the appropriate element of the rule by simply dragging and dropping the object in an existing rule element into the new rule element. This process does not move the object—it only copies the object.

Hiding Rules

When you are working with a complex and large security rule base, you will often find it easier to hide rules that are not applicable to the task you are trying to achieve. Hiding rules makes the rule base easier to work with, and also makes it easier for you to find the information that you wish to configure or verify. To *hide a rule* (also referred to as masking a rule), you can either use the Rules ➤ Hide submenu in SmartDashboard, or you can right-click in the number element of a rule that you wish to hide. Figure 4.2 shows the Rules ➤ Hide submenu.

FIGURE 4.2 The Rules ➤ Hide submenu

As you can see in Figure 4.2, you can choose from one of the following menu items:

Hide Hides the selected rule in the security rule base. The rule will still be present in the rule base and maintain its number and position, but will not be visible in the security rule base via SmartDashboard.

Unhide All Clears the hidden rule mask, displaying all rules that were previously hidden in SmartDashboard.

View Hidden   Displays all rules that are currently hidden. Each hidden rule is displayed along with unhidden rules, with each hidden rule being indicated by dark gray shading.

Manage Hidden   Allows you to save the current mask (set of hidden rules). Saving the mask allows you to store which rules are currently hidden, allowing you to quickly apply the saved mask at a later date, without having to remember which rules you hid on the previous occasion.

To hide a rule using the Rules menu, ensure the rule that you wish to hide is selected and select the Rules ➢ Hide ➢ Hide menu item. You can also hide a rule by selecting one (or more) rules that you wish to hide and then right-clicking in the number element of the selected rule(s). This will display a menu, which includes an item called Hide, which if selected hides the rule. Figure 4.3 shows this process.

FIGURE 4.3   Right-clicking the number element

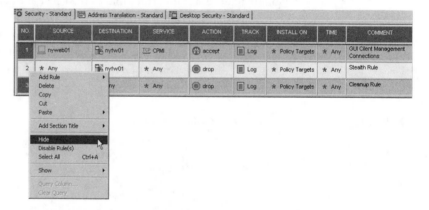

Once you have hidden rules, you cannot see them in SmartDashboard. The hidden rules are still present in the actual security rule base that is enforced—they just cannot be seen in SmartDashboard. It is important that you understand that hiding rules does not mean that they will not be enforced any longer; it just means you can't see them in SmartDashboard, reducing unnecessary rule clutter and making your rule base easier to manage. SmartDashboard does give some indication, however, that there are hidden rules. Figure 4.4 shows a security rule base in SmartDashboard that contains hidden rules.

Notice in Figure 4.4 the line that points to the thick dark gray line. This gray line indicates that one or more hidden rules exist at that point in the rule base. You can right-click on the line and deselect the Hide option to make the hidden rule visible again.

FIGURE 4.4 Detecting hidden rules in SmartDashboard

Hidden Rule(s)

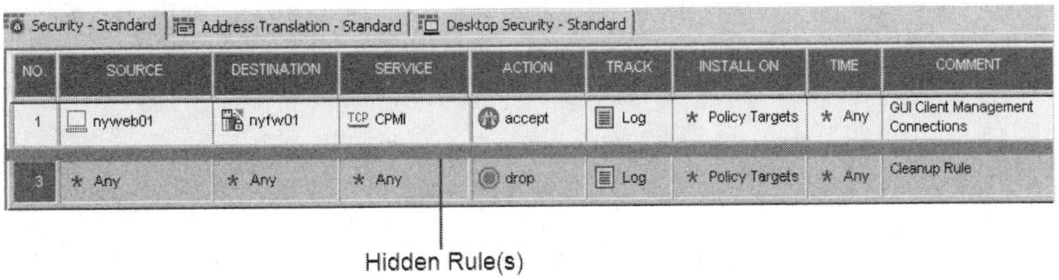

Disabling Rules

Referring back to Figure 4.3, you may have noticed the option *Disable Rule(s)* in the menu. Choosing this option allows you to disable a rule. Disabling a rule means that although it is still present in the security rule base, it is disabled and will not be enforced on any enforcement modules. Disabling is different from hiding a rule, as a hidden rule is still enforced by enforcement modules. Using this feature is very useful for troubleshooting when you have traffic that is being incorrectly permitted or denied. You can also disable a rule by selecting the desired rule and choosing the Rules ≻ Disable Rule menu item. Once you have disabled a rule, a red X is placed over the number element of the rule, indicating the rule is disabled. Figure 4.5 shows a disabled rule in SmartDashboard.

FIGURE 4.5 Disabled rules in SmartDashboard

In Figure 4.5, because rule 1 has been disabled, it will not be enforced on enforcement modules. To re-enable a disabled rule, simply right-click on the disabled rule in the number element. This displays a menu similar to Figure 4.3. However, because the rule is disabled, the Disable Rule(s) option will have a check mark next to it. Choosing the checked Disable Rule(s) option will re-enable the rule (and remove the check mark from the Disable Rule(s) option), meaning it will be enforced on enforcement modules. You can also re-enable a disabled rule by selecting the Rules menu and choosing the checked Disable Rule menu item.

After disabling or re-enabling a rule, you must install the new rule base on the desired enforcement module(s) for the disabled rule (or re-enabled rule) to take effect.

Adding Section Titles

A new feature of the SmartDashboard SMART client introduced in Feature Pack 3 is the use of *section titles*, which provide a method of organizing rules that have a similar function or purpose into a section. Each section includes a title, which describes the rules represented by the section. The most useful feature of section titles is the ability to collapse and expand each section title, making it very easy to quickly view all the rules in your security policy, or a specific subset of rules. Figure 4.6 shows a security policy with section titles.

FIGURE 4.6   Section titles in SmartDashboard

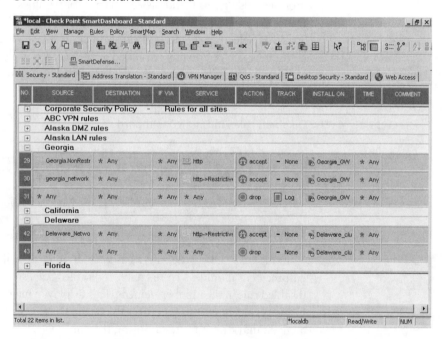

In Figure 4.6, there are several section titles, which include "ABC VPN rules," "Alaska DMZ rules," and so on. The section title text is totally customizable, allowing administrators to describe a set of rules. Notice how section titles can be collapsed (e.g., Alaska DMZ rules) or expanded (e.g., Georgia and Delaware). The rule base in Figure 4.6 actually consists of

47 rules, but by using section titles to partition the rule base, the readability and usability of the rule base is much enhanced.

To add a section title, simply right-click in the Number element of a rule directly above or below where you wish to create a section title, and select Add Section Title ➤ Above or Add Section Title ➤ Below from the menu that appears. You will then be prompted to enter the section title, after which the section title is created. All rules below the newly added section title automatically belong to the section title, until another section title is inserted into the rule base.

A limitation of section titles is that all rules within a section title are contiguous, meaning you can't have a section title that contains Rule 1, 5, 9, and 47, rather only Rule 1, 2, 3, 4, and so on. Section titles have no bearing on how an enforcement module enforces rules, with rules still enforced in order from top (Rule 1) to bottom.

In the last chapter, you created security objects and configured some very simple rules that comprised your first security policy. In this exercise you will actually learn how to configure a complete security rule base, based on a given security policy.

The following lists the security policy that you must configure in this exercise:

- Allow any ICMP traffic unless explicitly denied.

- Do not permit any other firewall management or control communications from any remote devices, except for SMART client communications from ak1web01.

- Allow web access (HTTP, HTTPS, FTP, and DNS queries) from the ny-internal-lan network to the Internet. This access is only permitted during business hours (Monday–Friday, 08:00 until 18:00). The bandwidth utilized per connection must be recorded.

- Permit hosts from the london.local domain web access (HTTP only) to nyweb01.

- Allow access from all internal New York networks to a custom TCP service called Remote Desktop Protocol on jupiter.london.local. This service runs on TCP port 3389.

- Remote access VPN users on the Internet must be able to establish VPN connections to nyfw01.

You have actually already configured the first two requirements in the Chapter 3 exercises. Figure 4.7 illustrates the required security policy for the remaining requirements.

FIGURE 4.7 Security policy for Exercise 4.1

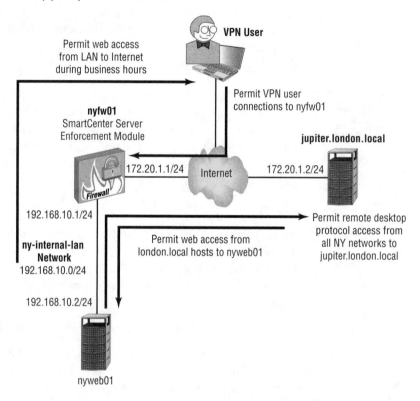

Before you can configure security rules that represent the security policy requirements, you need to ensure that all security objects are created for placement in each rule. The following lists the new objects that are required before you begin creating security rules.

- Domain object representing the london.local domain

- Service object representing the custom TCP service (port 3389) on JUPITER

- Group object represent web access protocols (HTTP, HTTPS, FTP, and DNS queries)

- Time object representing business hours

EXERCISE 4.1

Configuring a Complete Network Security Policy

1. Establish a connection to the SmartCenter server via the Smart-Dashboard application on nyfw01. At present, you should have a security rule base with three rules:

   - Rule permitting SMART client connectivity from nyweb01.
   - Stealth rule
   - Cleanup rule

2. Create a new domain object called london.local by selecting Manage ➤ Network Objects from the SmartDashboard menu and then selecting New ➤ Domain Object in the Network Objects Dialog box. The Domain Properties dialog box will be displayed. Configure the following parameters for the new domain object and then click the OK button.

   - Name = .london.local
   - Comment = The london.local domain
   - Color = Red

3. Click the Close button in the Network Objects dialog box to return to SmartDashboard. To ensure that your SmartCenter server can resolve hosts in the london.local domain, configure the HOSTS file (located in c:\winnt\system32\drivers\etc) with an IP address entry for jupiter.london.local.

4. To create a service object representing the remote desktop protocol that operates on TCP port 3389, select Manage ➤ Services from the SmartDashboard menu, which will open the Services dialog box. Click the New button and select the TCP option from the menu that appears. The TCP Service Properties dialog box will be displayed, which enables you to create a new TCP-based service object. Configure the new service with the following parameters and then click OK.

   - Name = ms-rdp
   - Comment = Microsoft Remote Desktop Protocol
   - Color = Blue
   - Port = 3389

5. Create a new services group object by selecting New ≻ Group from the Services dialog box. The Group Properties dialog box will now be displayed, which allows you to create a group that contains multiple services. The service group you need to configure is for web services, which includes FTP, HTTP, HTTPS, and DNS queries. Domain queries are represented by a service object called domain-udp. Configure the new group with the following parameters and then click OK.

   - Name = web-services
   - Comment = New York Web Services
   - Color = Green
   - Members (In Group) = domain-udp, ftp, http, https

6. You should now be able to see your new web-services group object in the Services dialog box. Click Close to return to SmartDashboard.

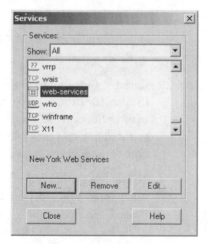

7. To configure a time object that will be used to restrict web access from ny-internal-lan to business hours only, select Manage ≻ Time from the SmartDashboard menu, which will display the Time Objects dialog box. Next, select New ≻ Time. The Time Object Properties dialog box will be displayed, which allows you to create a new time object. On the General screen, configure the following parameters:

   - Name = work-hours
   - Comment = New York Business Hours

- Color = Green
- Time of day = From 08:00 to 18:00

Note that the maximum length of the name of a time object is 11 characters.

8. Click the Days screen of the time object and configure the object such that the only permitted days during the week are Mondays through Fridays. Once you have finished your configuration, click OK to return to the Time Objects dialog box and then click Close to return to SmartDashboard.

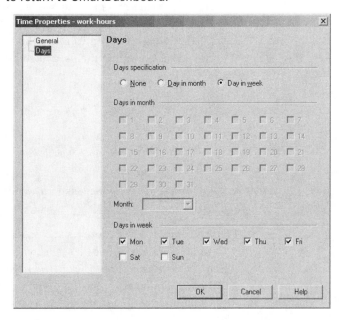

9. You are now ready to create the security rules required to enforce the security policy. First create the rule that permits web access from the ny-internal-lan during business hours. Right-click in the number field of the cleanup rule (Rule 3) and choose the Add rule above option from the menu. Configure the new rule with the following parameters:

- Source = ny-internal-lan
- Destination = Any
- Service = web-services (custom group object you created in Step 5)

- Action = Accept
- Track = Account
- Time = work-hours (time object you created in Step 7 and 8)
- Comment = Web access to Internet during working hours

Note: Because the bandwidth used for each connection must be recorded, you must configure the Track element with a tracking option of Account, which records the number of bytes sent/ received per connection.

10. Create the rule that permits web access from hosts in the london .local domain to nyweb01. Right-click in the number field of the stealth rule (Rule 2) and choose the Add Rule below option from the menu. Configure the new rule with the following parameters:

- Source = .london.local
- Destination = nyweb01
- Service = http
- Action = Accept
- Track = Log
- Comment = Web access to nyweb01 from london.local domain

11. Create the rule that permits access to the remote desktop protocol service running on jupiter.london.local from internal New York networks hosts. Right-click in the number field of the stealth rule (Rule 2) and choose the Add Rule below option from the menu. Configure the new rule with the following parameters:

- Source = ny-internal-networks
- Destination = jupiter.london.local
- Service = ms-rdp (the custom service object you created in Step 4)
- Action = Accept
- Track = Log
- Comment = MS RDP access to jupiter.london.local from ALL internal NY networks

12. Finally, create the rule that permits remote access VPN users on the Internet VPN connectivity to nyfw01 to the remote desktop protocol service running on jupiter.london.local from internal New York networks hosts. Right-click in the number field of the MS RDP access rule (Rule 3) and choose the Copy Rule(s) option from the menu. Next, right-click in the number field of the stealth rule (Rule 2) and choose the Paste Rule(s) ➤ Below option. This should create a copy of the MS RDP access rule below the stealth rule. Modify the new rule as follows:

   - Right-click the ny-internal-networks object in the Source element and choose Negate Cell from the menu. This means that the Source element of the rule matches any traffic *except* for traffic originating from the internal networks (i.e., the New York networks). Because users connected to the New York networks don't require VPN access (they already have internal access), you should take this approach (rather than just leaving the *Source* element as *Any*) to reduce the vulnerability of the nyfw01 enforcement module.

   - Drag the nyfw01 object in the Destination element of the stealth rule (Rule 2) into the Destination element of the new rule. This will copy the nyfw01 object into the Destination element of the new rule. Right-click the jupiter.london.local object in the Destination element and choose Delete from the menu to remove the object.

   - Right-click the ms-rdp object in the Service element and choose Delete from the menu. Add the IPSEC service group object and the FW1_topo service object, which enables SecuRemote VPN users to establish an IPSec-based VPN connection to nyfw01.

   - Comment = SecuRemote VPN Access

13. There is an issue with the rule you created in Step 12. The problem is that the rule is below the stealth rule, meaning that remote access VPN traffic will be matched against the stealth rule first (and immediately dropped) before hitting the remote access VPN rule. Rectify this issue by clicking the number column of the rule and then dragging the rule above the stealth rule.

EXERCISE 4.1 *(continued)*

| Security - Standard | Address Translation - Standard | Desktop Security - Standard |

NO	SOURCE	DESTINATION	SERVICE	ACTION	TRACK	INSTALL ON	TIME	COMMENT
1	nyweb01	nyfw01	TCP CPMI	accept	Log	★ Policy Targets	★ Any	GUI Client Management Connections
2	ny-internal-networks	nyfw01	TCP FW1_topo / IPSEC	accept	Log	★ Policy Targets	★ Any	SecuRemote Access
3	★ Any	nyfw01	★ Any	drop	Log	★ Policy Targets	★ Any	Stealth Rule
4	ny-internal-networks	jupiter.london.local	TCP ms-rdp	accept	Log	★ Policy Targets	★ Any	MS RDP Access to jupiter.london.local from all internal networks
5	london.local	nyweb01	TCP http	accept	Log	★ Policy Targets	★ Any	Web access to nyweb01 from london.local domain
6	ny-internal-lan	★ Any	web-services	accept	Account	★ Policy Targets	work-hours	Web access to Internet during working hours
7	★ Any	★ Any	★ Any	drop	Log	★ Policy Targets	★ Any	Cleanup Rule

14. All that is left for you to do is to install your policy to the enforcement module running on nyfw01. Select Policy ≻ Install from the SmartDashboard menu, ensure that nyfw01 is selected as an installation target and then click OK to install the policy.

Congratulations! You have successfully created and installed a complete security policy from scratch. After you have installed the policy, if you have set up web services on both nyweb01 and jupiter.london.local, you should be able to access the web pages on each from the opposite host. As a final step, you should verify that the security policy is actually providing the access required. From nyweb01, attempt to access the web service running on jupiter.local.london. You can do this by typing in the URL http://172.20.1.2 in a web browser running on nyweb01. Also attempt to access nyweb01 from jupiter.local.london by opening http://192.168.10.2 from a browser on jupiter.local.london. In both scenarios (assuming you have configure web services on each host), connectivity should be established. You should also be able to ping any device in the network by virtue of the ICMP implied rule (configured in Chapter 3 exercises), which is applied before any explicit rules.

Increasing Enforcement Module Performance

It is important to understand that Check Point VPN-1/FireWall-1 processes security rules one by one, from top to bottom. You learned in Chapter 3 that along with security rules, NAT rules and anti-spoofing checks are also applied. When dealing with large security rule bases, these factors may affect the performance of your enforcement module(s), thus it is important that you bear them in mind. It is recommended that you always implement anti-spoofing, as this protects against many common DoS and impersonation attacks. You can increase the performance of your enforcement modules by minimizing the amount of time required to process the NAT rule base. Because NAT is outside the scope of this chapter, we won't discuss optimization of NAT rules here (see Chapter 7 for more information). However, you can apply similar concepts of optimizing your security rule base to your NAT rule base.

Optimizing your security rule base is important, especially in a complex environment that defines many rules or in an environment where the enforcement module must process large amounts of traffic. When creating your security rule base, keep the following points in mind, which should optimize the performance of your enforcement module:

Keep the rule base as simple as possible.   Avoid having a lot of rules and the excessive use of complex services in rules, as this will degrade enforcement module performance by increasing the amount of time required to process traffic against the rule base. Complex services such as H.323 should only be used where required, as traffic being processed by the rule will require much more examination than simple services.

Place the most commonly used rules near the top of the rule base. Because the enforcement module processes rules one by one from top to bottom until a match is found, if the bulk of traffic can be matched in the first few rules, the amount of time required to process traffic is reduced, increasing firewall performance.

Minimize the use of the accounting option in the Track element. Accounting can degrade system performance significantly if used in a large number of rules, because the enforcement module must measure the number of bytes associated with each connection.

Decreasing SmartCenter server Administration Overhead

When you are faced with the task of managing a complex VPN-1/FireWall-1 security policy, you may find that your administration tasks become exceeding complex and prone to error. There are two common methods used to decrease SmartCenter server administrative overhead: configuring a HOSTS file and partitioning a security rule base.

Configuring a HOSTS File

When you are tasked with creating numerous security objects that will be placed in your security rule base, it is useful to maintain a HOSTS file on the SmartCenter server operating system. The HOSTS file allows for the local resolution of hostnames into IP addresses. For example, you might have a host called SMTPGW01 that has an IP address of 192.168.10.100. If you wish to refer to the host by name only, you must have some mechanism of resolving the IP address of the host from the hostname, because all IP communications take place using IP addresses, not hostnames. The HOSTS file contains an entry for each hostname and associated IP address, allowing the system to resolve names to IP addresses. Using a HOSTS file on a SmartCenter server decreases the administrative overhead of creating security objects. You can specify the name of a host for which you are creating a security object, and then ask the SmartCenter server to resolve the name to an IP address, saving you from having to know the IP address of the host. Before you create your security objects for your network topology, it is a good idea to create a HOSTS file with all the appropriate IP addressing for each host. This will speed up security object creation and reduce configuration errors.

The location of the HOSTS file depends on the operating system on which the SmartCenter server is located. On Unix-based platforms (Solaris and Linux), the full path to the HOSTS file is /etc/hosts, while on Windows-based platforms, the full path to the HOSTS file is c:\winnt\ system32\drivers\etc\hosts (assuming the Windows OS is installed in c:\winnt). The syntax for configuring the hosts file is the same on all operating systems. Figure 4.8 shows an example HOSTS file.

FIGURE 4.8 Example of a HOSTS file

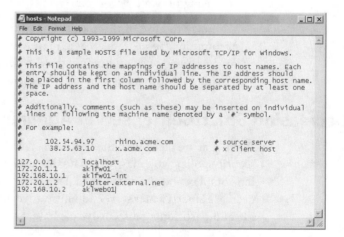

You can also use domain name resolution (DNS) to resolve hostnames to IP addresses. Using this method requires a DNS client to be functional on the SmartCenter server operating system, with correct DNS servers configured.

When creating an enforcement module object, always ensure that the object name is identical to the operating system name of the enforcement module. Also ensure that the enforcement module hostname resolves to external IP address of the module, with other interface IP addresses resolving to a different hostname. For example, if you have an enforcement module called NYFW01 that has an external IP address of 172.20.1.1, this should be the IP address used for the hostname NYFW01. If NYFW01 has an internal interface with an IP address of 192.168.10.1, you could resolve this IP address to the hostname NYFW01-INT as an example.

Partitioning a Security Policy

In a distributed environment, where many enforcement modules are managed by a single SmartCenter server, you may find that your rule bases and objects database becomes very large and unwieldy to manage. In this scenario, you may wish to maintain separate security policies, which makes the overall policy easier to manage by partitioning the security policy into smaller pieces. VPN-1/FireWall-1 saves all security policy information in *policy packages*, which includes the following information:

- Security rule base, address translation rule base, and VPN manager configuration
- QoS rule base
- Desktop security rule base

The security objects database, users database, and all global security properties are components that are common to each policy package, which means you can't use multiple policy packages to store different versions of these components.

All of the components listed above are stored in separate physical files. For example, security rule bases are stored in the $FWDIR/conf directory with a .W extension. VPN-1/FireWall-1 Feature Pack 2 introduced policy packages, which enable you to store multiple versions of the components listed above in a single policy package, which makes version control management much simpler. Prior to policy packages, there was no mechanism that linked the various versions of the security rule base together, making overall management, backup, and version control difficult.

By default, a single security policy package called Standard is created. You can save a security policy package as a separate policy package, which enables you to partition your security policy into separate, more management chunks.

A security rule base file includes security and address translation rules. A separate file is used for Desktop Security rules, as is the case for QoS rules if FloodGate-1 is installed.

For example, if you had ten enforcement modules to manage, you might create a separate security policy package for each enforcement module, allowing you to quickly configure and manage the rules, objects and properties specific to the environment each enforcement module protects. The only disadvantage to using this method is that you must separately load and install each policy package.

When managing multiple policy packages on multiple gateways, it is possible to accidentally push the wrong policy. To prevent a rule base from accidentally being pushed to the wrong enforcement point, use the Install on element within each security rule in a given policy. When attempting to install an incorrect policy you will receive an error message stating that none of the rules apply to the enforcement module in question.

To save a policy package, simply choose File ➢ Save As from the Smart-Dashboard menu, which displays the Save Advanced Security Policy As dialog box that allows you to create a new policy package. Figure 4.9 shows this dialog box.

The policy package name cannot contain spaces.

FIGURE 4.9 Saving a policy package

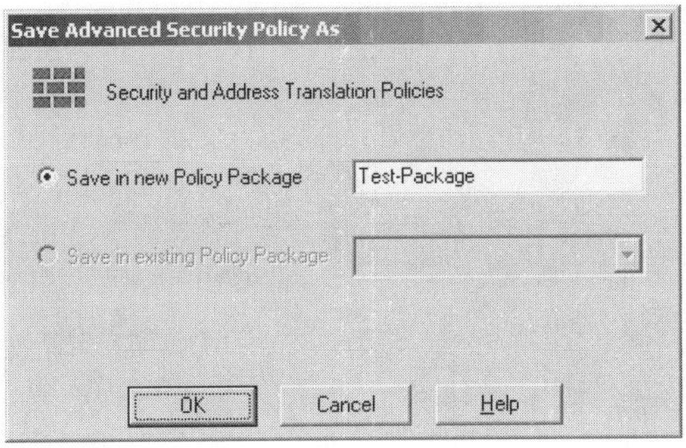

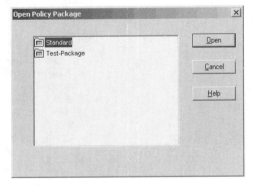

To open a previously saved security rule base, simply choose File ➤ Open from the SmartDashboard menu. This step displays the Open Policy Package dialog box, which allows you to select the appropriate policy package that you wish to open, as shown in Figure 4.10.

FIGURE 4.10 Opening a saved policy package

Database Revision Control

The ability to rollback security policy changes is very important for any organization, as sometimes a change may have undesired or unintended effects. You can configure VPN-1/FireWall-1 NG to automatically create new versions of your security policy after each policy installation, with the ability to rollback to previous versions of the security policy if required. This feature is known as *database revision control*.

To configure database revision control, select Policy ➤ Global Properties from the SmartDashboard menu, and then click on the SmartDashboard customization screen. In this screen, you will see a Database Revision Control section, with a single option to enable the creation of a new version of the security policy after each install policy operation. Figure 4.11 shows the SmartDashboard customization screen in the Global Properties dialog box.

FIGURE 4.11 Configuring database revision control

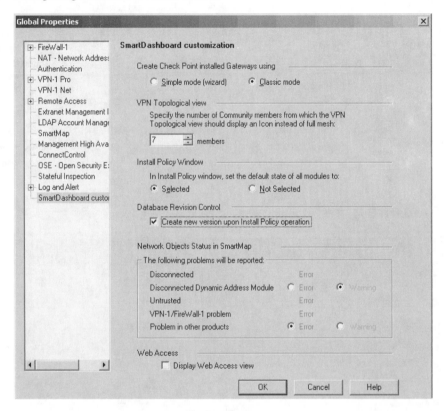

In Figure 4.11, notice that the Create new version upon Install Policy operation option has been checked. By default, this option is disabled. Once you have enabled database revision control, every time you install a security policy, you will be prompted to enter a name and comment for the new security policy. Figure 4.12 demonstrates this after Policy ≻ Install has been selected from the SmartDashboard menu.

If you need to rollback to a previous version of the security rule base, select File ≻ Database Revision Control from the SmartDashboard menu. This opens the Database Revision Control dialog box, which indicates all versions of the security rule base saved within the current policy package. Figure 4.13 shows the Database Revision Control dialog box.

FIGURE 4.12 Creating a new version of security policy

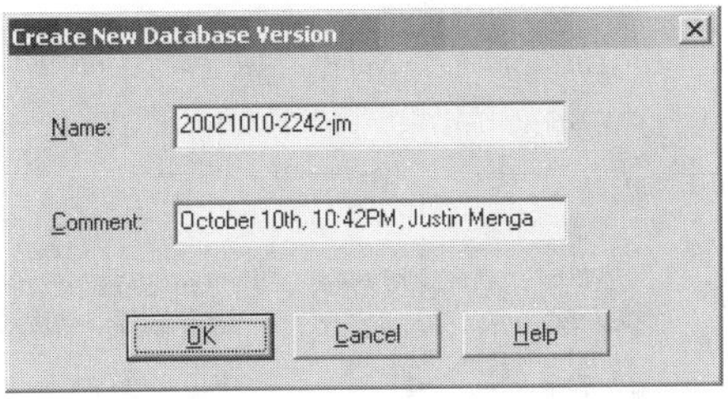

FIGURE 4.13 The Database Revision Control dialog box

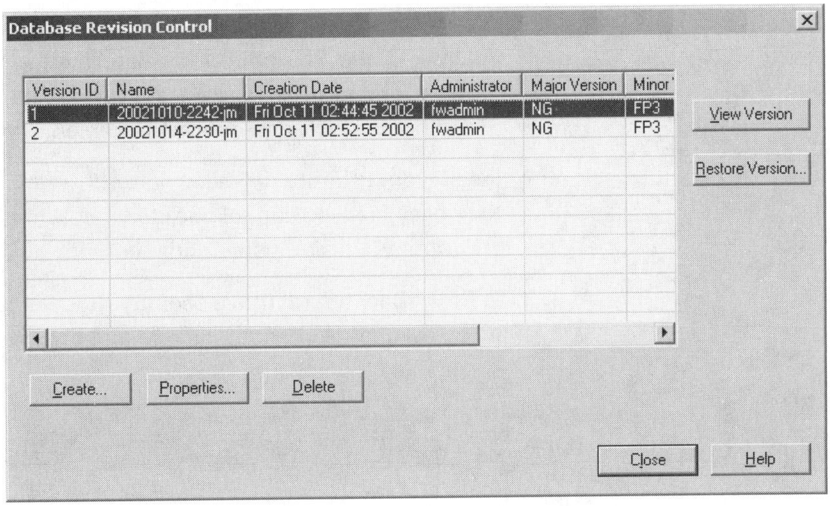

You can select any version stored within the policy package and click on the View Version button, which opens another SmartDashboard session with the selected version of the rule base opened in read-only mode. If you wish to rollback to a previous version, click the Restore Version button.

Optimizing SmartCenter Server Administration and Enforcement Module Overhead

Now that you have some background in SmartCenter server, it's time for to try your hand at optimizing the server by doing Exercise 4.2. Let's assume that the security policy configured in Exercise 4.2 has been in use for some time, and analysis of the log files indicates that the rule permitting web access from the ny-internal-lan object to the Internet is the most frequently matched rule. Currently, this rule is second to last in the rule base (Rule 6), and should be moved as close to the top of the rule base as possible. The closest position to the top possible is as Rule 4, which is directly below the stealth rule. If the web access rule was placed above the stealth rule, internal users would be permitted access to nyfw01 (for web services), which could compromise the security of nyfw01, hence the rule must be placed below the stealth rule.

EXERCISE 4.2

Optimizing the SmartCenter server

1. Before making the modification, you may wish to enable the database revision control feature to ensure you can rollback the change quickly. From the Global Properties dialog box (select Policy ➢ Global Properties to open this), open the SmartDashboard customization screen, and ensure the Create new version upon Install Policy operation option is enabled.

2. Install your security policy, which will create an initial version of the policy that you can rollback to later. When prompted, enter the appropriate version name and comments.

3. In SmartDashboard, move security Rule 6 to be Rule 4 by clicking in the number element of the rule and dragging the rule below the stealth rule (Rule 3).

4. Install your security policy to ensure that the new rule order changes take effect. When prompted, enter a new version name, which will create version 2 of the security policy. If problems were to occur after installing the modified security policy, you can now easily rollback to the prior security policy.

VPN-1/FireWall-1 System Management

This section describes the VPN-1/FireWall-1 system management tasks that allow you to manage Check Point licensing and product installation. Check Point licensing and product installation and management features have been greatly enhanced in VPN-1/FireWall-1 NG, which has a dedicated SMART client called SmartUpdate for performing these tasks. In this section you will learn about VPN-1/FireWall-1 NG licensing and how to use Smart-Update to manage licenses. Next, you will learn how SmartUpdate can be used to track the software versions of all of your Check Point products, and how you can perform remote installations and software upgrades from Smart-Update. Finally, you will learn about the common command-line tools that you can use to manage Check Point VPN-1/FireWall-1 NG.

VPN-1/FireWall-1 NG Licensing

All Check Point products (excluding the Check Point SMART clients) require the purchase of a software license. Check Point products will not run without a valid license, so before installing any Check Point product, ensure that you have purchased the correct license and that you have the license on hand. Check Point VPN-1/FireWall-1 offers several different licensing options, depending on the size and requirements of your organization.

For smaller organizations, Check Point offers an integrated VPN-1/FireWall-1 *Internet Gateway*, which provides you with a license that allows you to install both the SmartCenter server and enforcement module on the same host (you cannot separate these components for this licensing). The SmartCenter server using this license can only manage the internal enforcement module. If you have other enforcement modules that need to be managed, you cannot use this type of licensing. Different levels of licensing are available, based on the number of IP addresses that the FireWall-1 enforcement module will protect. Check Point currently offers 25, 50, 100, and 250 IP address licenses. It is important to understand that these IP addresses include every single device that is protected by the firewall; it does not just refer to devices that use the Internet. This includes servers, PCs, printers, IP phones, PDAs—anything with an IP address that is behind the firewall. If you have a private WAN connected to the LAN network that the internal interface of the firewall connects to, the IP addresses of all devices in the WAN are also counted as being protected. The Internet Gateway enforces licensing by listening to all IP transmissions on all interfaces except the defined external interface, and counting the number of different source IP addresses on internal networks (even if they are not connecting through the enforcement module). This means that it is important that you define the external interface correctly, which is achieved by placing the operating system device name of the external interface in a file called $FWDIR/conf/external.if. The enforcement module will continue to forward traffic if the maximum number of IP addresses specified by the license is exceeded, however the enforcement module will continuously generate log messages and email messages to the system administrator about the license being exceeded. This may slow down the enforcement module, so the license count issue should be addressed immediately.

If you have interface(s) that connect to a DMZ or an extranet partner, the IP addresses attached to these interfaces are still counted.

If you have more than 250 IP devices in your network, multiple enforcement modules, or you wish to separate the SmartCenter server and enforcement module components, you must purchase separate enterprise licenses for your SmartCenter server and enforcement module(s). An enterprise license allows for an unlimited number of protected IP devices, and permits a distributed topology with a SmartCenter server managing multiple enforcement modules.

Once you have purchased your Check Point product with the appropriate licensing, you will be provided with a *certificate key*, which is used to verify that you are entitled to a license. The certificate key is a 12-character alphanumeric string, and can only be used once to obtain a license. If you do not possess a certificate key, you cannot obtain a license for your software, so be sure that you receive a certificate key when purchasing VPN-1/ FireWall-1 NG.

If you purchase a Check Point evaluation media kit, a certificate key will be provided on the media kit, which can be used to obtain a 30-day evaluation license.

Once you have your certificate key, you can obtain a license from Check Point via www.checkpoint.com/usercenter. You must create a login and profile for your organization before registering your product, which enables you to keep track of any future license additions or modifications for your organization.

License Types

It is important to understand how Check Point licensing works. Historically licensing has been a facet of the Check Point product that has confused many people. VPN-1/FireWall-1 NG has two types of licenses available. The original type of licensing has been maintained for backward compatibility, and is referred to as a *local license*. The new license type is called a *central license* and is designed to make licensing much simpler to manage.

Central Licenses

Check Point introduced central licenses in VPN-1/FireWall-1 NG. The IP address associated with a license is now linked to the IP address of the Smart-Center server, rather than with each enforcement module, which is a major difference in licensing methods compared with previous versions. Each VPN-1/FireWall-1 host requires a central license. However, each license is linked to the IP address of the SmartCenter server, even if it is for an enforcement module. In a distributed environment where a separate SmartCenter server runs internally on the network with multiple enforcement modules running at Internet, extranet, or remote access entry points into your network, you no longer have to manage the multiple IP addresses of licenses associated with each of the multiple enforcement modules. Instead you only have to manage a single IP address of the SmartCenter server, and it is much less likely that this IP address will change in comparison to enforcement modules (if you change ISPs for example, you normally have to change the IP addressing on your enforcement modules). Using a central license provides the following benefits:

- Only a single IP address is needed for all licenses.
- You can modify the IP addressing of your enforcement modules without having to get a new license.
- Licenses can be removed from an enforcement module and moved to another enforcement module without requiring a new license.

The only scenario for a central license where you would need to reissue a license would be if you changed the IP address of your SmartCenter server.

Local Licenses

Local licenses are essentially the legacy method of licensing, where the IP address associated with a license is linked to the IP address of each host (whether it be an enforcement module or a SmartCenter server). Each VPN-1/FireWall-1 host (enforcement module and SmartCenter server) requires a local license that is linked to the IP address of each host. There are two types of local licenses:

NG Local The NG local license only applies to NG versions and can be imported into the license repository. NG local licenses can be installed and deleted via SmartUpdate.

4.1 Local A 4.1 local license only applies to 4.1 versions and can be imported into the license repository. 4.1 Local licenses can be installed via SmartUpdate, but cannot be deleted.

The license repository is located on the SmartCenter server and stores all licenses for the SmartCenter server and enforcement modules in your network. This enables centralized management of licenses. SmartUpdate is a product that includes a License Manager, which allows administrators access to the license repository.

Obtaining Licenses

You must obtain licenses via the Check Point User Center, which is a public website that handles all license requests and ongoing license management. Before obtaining a license, you must ensure that you have a valid certificate key for your product. If you do not have this information, contact your Check Point reseller.

With the previous methods of licensing, it was common for the Check Point reseller to obtain licenses on behalf of the organization installing Check Point. Access could be gained to licensing information simply by specifying the certificate key associated with the license. With the new method of licensing, all licenses are linked to a profile that is specific to the end user and requires a private user logon to gain access to licensing information. For this reason, it is recommended that the end user perform the process of obtaining licenses, instead of the reseller.

Once you have the certificate key for your Check Point product, contact the Check Point user center, which can be located via `http://www.checkpoint.com/usercenter`.

The Check Point User Center allows you to manage all Check Point licensing, software subscription agreements, and support agreements.

SmartUpdate

SmartUpdate is a part of the VPN-1/FireWall-1 SMART Clients and includes two components:

Installation Manager   Allows you to track the current versions of all Check Point and OPSEC products in your organization. You can also install or update Check Point and OPSEC products remotely from a central location.

License Manager   Provides access to the license repository and allows you to centrally manage licenses.

To use the Installation Manager, you must purchase a SmartUpdate license. You can purchase a license to manage a single Check Point host or an unlimited number of hosts. You do not need to purchase a SmartUpdate license to use the License Manager component.

SmartUpdate is managed via the SmartUpdate Check Point SMART client application, which you can install during SMART client installation. The SmartUpdate component on the SmartCenter server communicates with remote Check Point and OPSEC products by using the Check Point SVN Foundation (CPShared) component. Thus the CPShared component must be installed on all hosts that are managed via SmartUpdate. Check Point NG automatically installs the CPShared component—Check Point 2000 (4.1) Service Pack 2 and higher also supports the installation of the CPUtil component, which is the SVN foundation for Check Point 4.1. All communications between SmartUpdate and each managed host is via *secure internal communications (SIC)*. SIC must be initialized on the SmartCenter server and on each managed host before SmartUpdate can manage the host.

To enable SmartUpdate to communicate with Check Point 2000 (4.1) SP2 and higher hosts, you must use the older fw putkey method to enable management via SmartUpdate.

Figure 4.14 shows the SmartUpdate architecture.

FIGURE 4.14 Check Point SmartUpdate architecture

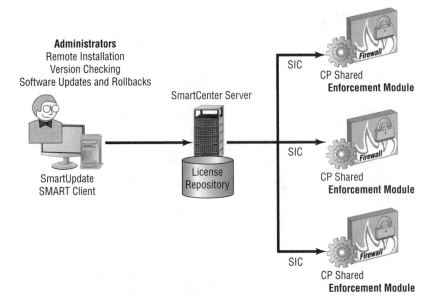

To use the Check Point SmartUpdate SMART client, you must have at least read-only permissions to the SmartUpdate permission level (configured via the Administrators tab of the cpconfig utility). The same authentication mechanism that is used for all other SMART clients (such as SmartDashboard) is applied for the SmartUpdate SMART client.

Installation Manager

The *Installation Manager* provides tracking of Check Point product versions installed throughout the enterprise, as well as enabling the installation and updating of Check Point and OPSEC products. The SmartUpdate SMART client provides access to the Installation Manager and enables administrators to perform all of the actions described above. Figure 4.15 shows the SmartUpdate SMART client with the Products tab selected, which provides access to the Installation Manager.

In Figure 4.15, a top-level object exists (labeled 172.20.1.1), which represents the SmartCenter server to which you are attached. Underneath this object are all the enforcement modules (and other SVN components) managed by the top-level SmartCenter server. Figure 4.15 shows a single enforcement module—nyfw01. You can see the various components that comprise the module and information about each component. For example, you can see that nyfw01 is installed with Windows .NET server (yes, Check Point VPN-1/FireWall-1 NG seems to work on Windows .NET server, but don't attempt to run this in a production environment!!) as the operating system (as indicated by the Windows 5.2 in the OS column) and is running Check Point VPN-1/FireWall-1 NG Feature Pack 3.

FIGURE 4.15   Products tab in Check Point SmartUpdate

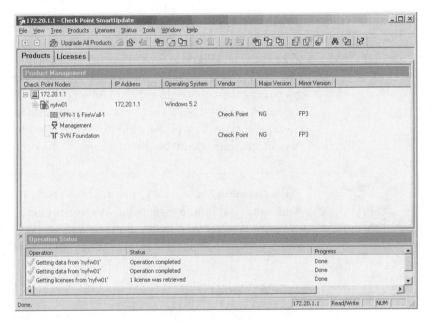

 When you first open SmartUpdate, detailed information is not displayed for each component. To get information about a component, you must explicitly do so by right-clicking the object and selecting Get Check Point Node Data. To get this information, you must make a read-write connection to the Smart-Center server security policy database, which means that you cannot have an administrator connected via SmartDashboard with read-write access at the same time as you attempt to get node data.

You can concurrently apply updates to multiple SVN components and track the status of each, with the ability to cancel an installation in progress or uninstall an update as required. The SmartUpdate Installation Manager obtains operating system and product information from each host to ensure only compatible updates are applied.

The SmartUpdate Installation Manager can also remotely apply Nokia IPSO operating system updates to Nokia firewall appliances.

Each update is applied via a SmartUpdate package, which is a compressed archive file that contains all the files necessary to install the update. Packages are available from the Check Point website, however you must have a registered software subscription contract to obtain access to the packages. Each package is digitally signed, ensuring an update is genuine and authentic. All packages are stored in a special folder called SUROOT in the root drive on the SmartCenter server, with the SmartUpdate SMART client automatically checking for any new packages in this folder. You merely need to copy new packages to the folder to be able to access and distribute them via SmartUpdate.

The Installation Manager also provides the ability to remotely install Check Point products. Before installation of a Check Point product, the CPShared component (SVN foundation) must be installed on the remote operating system, which enables communications with SmartUpdate.

License Manager

The *License Manager* allows you to manage licenses for your entire Check Point deployment. License Manager allows you to manage the license repository, which resides on the SmartCenter server and contains all the licenses for your Check Point products. You can manage both central and local licenses, as described above. License Manager allows you to perform the following functions:

- Add or remove licenses to the license repository.

- Attach or detach licenses to a remote enforcement module.

- View all licenses and their associated properties.

- Check for expired licenses.

Administrators can access License Manager by selecting the Licenses tab within the SmartUpdate SMART client. Figure 4.16 shows the SmartUpdate client with the Licenses tab selected.

FIGURE 4.16 License tab in Check Point SmartUpdate

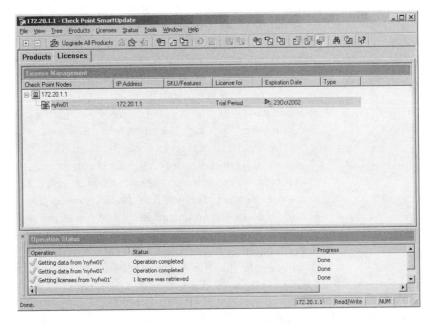

In Figure 4.16, you can see a license that is attached to nyfw01. Notice that this license is the 15-day trial license that comes with Check Point VPN-1/FireWall-1 NG Feature Pack 3. If a real license is installed, you will see IP address, features, expiration date, and other information for the license.

Prior to NG Feature Pack 3, you had to obtain an evaluation certificate key and register an evaluation license on the Check Point web site. In FP3, a 15-day evaluation license is included, making the whole process of evaluating Check Point VPN-1/FireWall-1 NG (or writing books about it!) much easier.

Before you can use the License Manager, you must license your Smart-Center server. This is normally performed during the SmartCenter server installation. However SmartCenter server licensing can be performed after installation using one of the following mechanisms:

- Using the cpconfig utility (the Check Point Configuration Tool on Windows)

- Using the `cplic put` command-line utility
- Using the `cprlic` remote command-line utility

When installing a new Check Point deployment, always install and license the SmartCenter server before any other components.

Once you have successfully licensed the SmartCenter server, you can next begin to install licenses for your Check Point enforcement modules and other products. How you install licenses for these products depends on the license type you have obtained. If you have obtained a central license for your enforcement module, you must add the license to the license repository on the SmartCenter server using the SmartUpdate License Manager. Next, you need to initialize secure internal communications (SIC) between the enforcement module and the SmartCenter server. To do this, you must create a security object (of type Check Point Gateway) for the enforcement module, and click the Communication button under the Secure Internal Communications section in the General Properties configuration screen of the Check Point gateway object (see Chapter 3). A dialog box titled Communication will next be displayed, which allows you to configure a one time activation key. Figure 4.17 shows the Communication dialog box.

FIGURE 4.17 The Communication dialog box

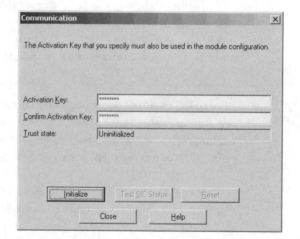

The one time activation key is a shared key configured on both the Smart-Center server and the enforcement module. On the enforcement module, during installation, you are asked to configure a one-time activation key for secure internal communications. This activation key must match the activation key configured for the enforcement module object on the Smart-Center server. The one-time activation keys essentially establish initial authentication that enables the SmartCenter server to issue a certificate to the enforcement module to protect subsequent communications.

You can reconfigure the one-time activation key on an enforcement module by running the cpconfig utility.

Once you have configured the activation key, click the Initialize button. This will instruct the SmartCenter server to attempt to establish communications with the enforcement module. The SmartCenter server and enforcement module will authenticate each other by using the one-time password (on the SmartCenter server) and the one-time password (on the enforcement module). The SmartCenter server will then issue a certificate to the enforcement module, which enables SIC. At this stage, the Trust State text box in Figure 4.17 should change to Trust Established, indicating SIC has been successfully established.

Once SIC has been established, you can attach the license added to the repository to the enforcement module using License Manager. During the attachment of the license, SIC is used to authenticate and protect the communications taking place. Once you have licensed your enforcement module, you can install a security policy on the module.

Using the CLI to Manage Security Policy

Check Point VPN-1/FireWall-1 originates from a Unix-based platform, and thus includes many command-line interface (CLI) utilities that can be used to manage security policy and enforcement. All of the CLI utilities available are stored either in the bin subdirectory of the directory in which VPN-1/FireWall-1 is installed, or in the bin subdirectory of the directory in which the SVN Foundation is installed.

On Windows-based systems, the default VPN-1/FireWall-1 NG installation path is C:\WINNT\FW1\NG (for the enforcement module and SmartCenter server) and C:\Program Files\CheckPoint\CPShared\NG (for the SVN Foundation). On Unix-based systems, the default VPN-1/FireWall-1 installation path is /opt/CPfw1-50 (for the enforcement module and SmartCenter server) and /opt/CPShared (for the SVN foundation). The VPN-1/FireWall-1 NG installation path is also described by the environment variable $FWDIR.

The common CLI utilities that you will use include cpstart, cpstop, fwstart, fwstop, cplic print, fwm load, fwm unload, fw fetch, fwm gen, fwc, fw ctl, and fw lichosts.

From VPN-1/FireWall-1 NG Feature Pack 2, the fwm command replaces the fw command for all commands that relate to the SmartCenter server component. The fw command is now used for all commands that relate to the enforcement module component. For the exam, be aware that you can still use fw commands for actions that relate to the SmartCenter server component.

cpstart

The cpstart CLI utility starts all the Check Point applications installed on a machine, excluding the cprid daemon, which is started separately during machine boot up. In a VPN-1/FireWall-1 installation, this starts the VPN-1/FireWall-1 components, as well as the SVN foundation.

cpstop

This utility is the opposite of the cpstart utility, in that it stops all the Check Point applications installed on a machine, excluding the cprid daemon, which is managed separately. In a VPN-1/FireWall-1 installation, this stops the VPN-1/FireWall-1 components, as well as the SVN foundation. Figure 4.18 demonstrates using the cpstop and cpstart utilities to restart all Check Point components on a host.

FIGURE 4.18   Using the cpstop and cpstart CLI utilities

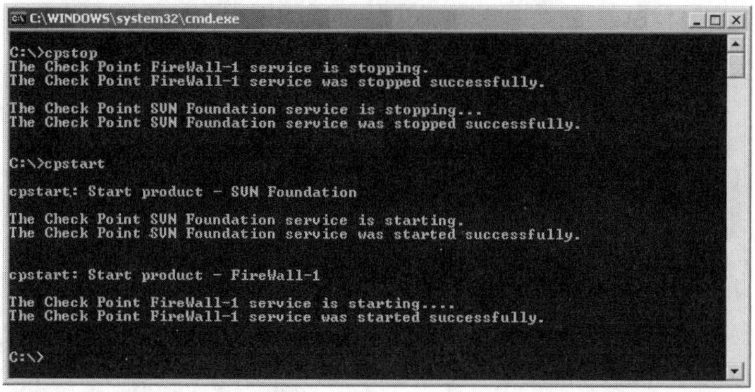

![Command prompt window showing cpstop and cpstart commands being run]

```
C:\WINDOWS\system32\cmd.exe

C:\>cpstop
The Check Point FireWall-1 service is stopping.
The Check Point FireWall-1 service was stopped successfully.

The Check Point SVN Foundation service is stopping...
The Check Point SVN Foundation service was stopped successfully.

C:\>cpstart

cpstart: Start product - SVN Foundation

The Check Point SVN Foundation service is starting.
The Check Point SVN Foundation service was started successfully.

cpstart: Start product - FireWall-1

The Check Point FireWall-1 service is starting....
The Check Point FireWall-1 service was started successfully.

C:\>
```

fwstart

The `fwstart` CLI utility starts all VPN-1/FireWall-1 components installed on a machine. VPN-1/FireWall-1 components including the enforcement module (`fwd`), the SmartCenter server (`fwm`), the VPN-1/FireWall-1 NG SNMP daemon (`snmpd`), and authentication daemons (such as `in.httpd`, which is used to provide an HTTP application-layer gateway daemon for authenticating HTTP access).

fwstop

This utility is the opposite of the `fwstart` utility, in that it stops all VPN-1/FireWall-1 components installed on a machine. This does not stop the SVN foundation, unlike `cpstop`. Figure 4.19 demonstrates using the `fwstop` and `fwstart` utilities to restart all VPN-1/FireWall-1 components on a host.

FIGURE 4.19   Using the `fwstop` and `fwstart` CLI utilities

Notice that the `fwstart` and `fwstop` only start/stop the FireWall-1 service, unlike `cpstart` and `cpstop`, which start/stop all Check Point components.

cplic print

The `cplic print` CLI utility prints information about Check Point product licenses. Figure 4.20 demonstrates the output of this utility on a SmartCenter server.

FIGURE 4.20 Using the cplic print CLI utility

In Figure 4.20, you can see that the SmartCenter server license is licensed to the IP address 172.20.1.1 and expired on the June 20, 2002. The features of the license indicate this license is an evaluation license.

fwm load

The fwm load CLI utility instructs a SmartCenter server to install the current security policy to one or more enforcement modules. This command has the following syntax:

```
fwm load [filter-file | rule-base] targets
```

The *rule-base* parameter specifies a security rule base file (identified by a .W extension), which is simply a text file that describes all of the security and address translation rules, as well as the security policy properties. The *filter-file* parameter specifies an *inspection script* (identified by a .pf extension), which is another text file that combines all of the security rules and policy with the required information about each object in the rules (obtained from the objects database). The inspection script essentially is a single file that contains all of the necessary information for the security policy and object information to be installed to an enforcement module, while a security rule base file only represents the security policy in the SmartCenter server (the objects database is separate). Both files are written in the C programming language, which is a high-level language used to write programs. The *targets* parameter defines the enforcement modules to which the policy should be installed. Before the policy is installed, the inspection file is compiled into an *inspection code* file, which is based on a low-level assembly language that contains the processor subroutines required on the enforcement module for policy enforcement.

Figure 4.21 demonstrates the use of the fwm load command on a Smart-Center server.

FIGURE 4.21 Using the fwm load CLI utility

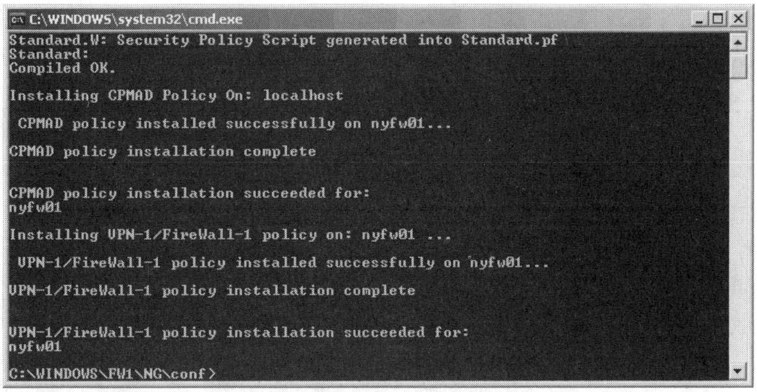

Notice that you must ensure that the fwm load utility can read the $FWDIR/conf directory for the rule base or filter file specified. In Figure 4.21, a rule base file is loaded (as indicated by the .W extension), which is compiled and then installed to the enforcement module specified (nyfw01).

> **NOTE** If SIC is not configured correctly between the SmartCenter server and enforcement module, you will receive an error "Authentication for command load failed." To resolve this issue, ensure SIC is configured correctly and re-initialize SIC communications if necessary. If communicating with enforcement modules prior to NG, this error means fw putkey needs to be run to ensure the correct secret keys are configured.

fwm unload

The fwm unload CLI utility instructs a SmartCenter server to uninstall the current security policy from one or more enforcement modules. This command has the following syntax:

    fwm unload *targets*

The *targets* parameter specifies the enforcement modules at which the policy should be uninstalled. When a policy is uninstalled, an enforcement module does not apply any security filtering, so it is recommended you only use this command for emergencies. Figure 4.22 demonstrates the use of the fwm unload command on a SmartCenter server to uninstall the security policy on an enforcement module called nyfw01.

fwm unload is especially useful for when an incorrect policy is installed that disrupts communications between enforcement and management modules. The command can be issued to unload the incorrect policy, after which the corrected version can be installed.

FIGURE 4.22 Using the fwm unload CLI utility

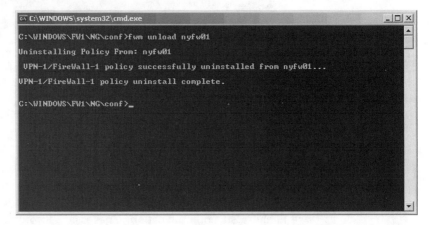

```
C:\WINDOWS\system32\cmd.exe                                    _ □ X
C:\WINDOWS\FW1\NG\conf>fwm unload nyfw01
Uninstalling Policy From: nyfw01
 VPN-1/FireWall-1 policy successfully uninstalled from nyfw01...
VPN-1/FireWall-1 policy uninstall complete.

C:\WINDOWS\FW1\NG\conf>_
```

fw fetch

The fw fetch CLI utility instructs an enforcement module to download and install the current security policy from the SmartCenter server. There is no fwm fetch command equivalent. The fw fetch command has the following syntax:

fw fetch *management-server*

The *management-server* parameter specifies the SmartCenter server from which the policy should be downloaded and installed. This command is an alternative to the fwm load command, where instead of the Smart-Center server pushing the policy, the enforcement module instead pulls the policy. Figure 4.23 demonstrates the use of the `fw fetch` command on an enforcement module to download the current security policy from a local SmartCenter server.

FIGURE 4.23   Using the fw fetch CLI utility

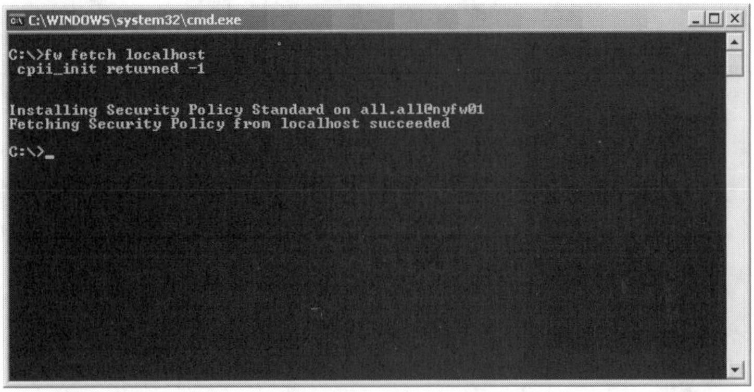

C:\WINDOWS\system32\cmd.exe

```
C:\>fw fetch localhost
 cpii_init returned -1

Installing Security Policy Standard on all.all@nyfw01
Fetching Security Policy from localhost succeeded

C:\>_
```

If you issue the fw fetch command and communications with the SmartCenter server fail, the enforcement module will simply use the last (current) security policy installed from the SmartCenter server. This ensures the current security policy is maintained until the SmartCenter server communications can be restored.

fwm gen

The `fwm gen` CLI utility instructs a SmartCenter server to generate an inspection script from a security rule base file. This command is useful for verifying that your security rules are valid. The command has the following syntax:

`fwm gen rule-base`

The *rule-base* parameter specifies the security rule base file (`*.W`) that should be generated into an inspection script. If you specify the command as above, the inspection script is output to the screen, so it is recommended you redirect the output to a file. Figure 4.24 demonstrates the use of the `fwm gen` command on a SmartCenter server, which generates an inspection script called `INSPECT.PF` in the `C:\Temp` directory from the `Standard.W` security rule base.

FIGURE 4.24 Using the fwm gen CLI utility

 The fwm gen command is the mechanism used when you verify your security policy from SmartDashboard by selecting Policy ➢ Verify.

fwc

The fwc CLI utility instructs a SmartCenter server to verify an inspection script by compiling it into inspection code. If the inspection script is valid, the compilation should take place without any error. The command has the following syntax:

    fwc filter-file

Notice that you must specify an inspection script (as indicated by the filter-file parameter), instead of a security rule base file. If you only have a rule base file, you must use the fwm gen command to generate the inspection script.

fw ctl

The fw ctl CLI utility sends or returns control information from the VPN-1/ FireWall-1 kernel module (INSPECT module). There is no fwm ctl command equivalent. This command has the following syntax:

    fw ctl [install | uninstall | pstat | arp | iflist]

The following describes each of the fw ctl options:

- fw ctl install—instructs the INSPECT module to intercept packets.

- fw ctl uninstall—instructs the INSPECT module to not intercept packets (effectively disabling the enforcement module).

- fw ctl pstat—displays internal statistics.

- fw ctl arp—displays any ARP entries in the local.arp file, which is used for network address translation on Windows-based VPN-1/FireWall-1 implementations.

- fw ctl iflist—shows the current interfaces that are known to the INSPECT module.

Figure 4.25 demonstrates the use of the fw ctl iflist command on an enforcement module, which lists all of the interfaces known to the enforcement module.

FIGURE 4.25 Using the fwm clt iflist CLI utility

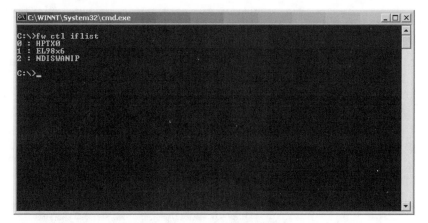

You can see in Figure 4.25 that three interfaces have been detected by the enforcement module. The NDISWANIP interface is associated with dial-up networking and is only present if you have some form of modem (analog, ADSL, or ISDN) attached to your computer.

fw lichosts

The fw lichosts CLI utility lists the hosts protected by VPN-1/FireWall-1. This is only relevant for VPN-1/FireWall-1 products that are licensed to protect a specific number of IP addresses. If you exceed the number of IP addresses that your VPN-1/FireWall-1 is licensed to protect, the enforcement module will stop permitting connections. You can purchase VPN-1/FireWall-1 to protect 25, 50, 100, or 250 IP addresses. For installations larger than this, you must purchase an Enterprise license (unlimited IP addresses), for which the fw lichosts command is not relevant.

On VPN-1/FireWall-1 enforcement modules that have a limit on the number of protected IP addresses, you must ensure that your external interface (i.e., the interface connected to the Internet) is configured correctly. This is because VPN-1/FireWall-1 counts the number of IP addresses associated with packets that are heard on all interfaces except the external interface, and checks that your license is not exceeded by the number of IP addresses counted (the enforcement module shouldn't count external IP addresses, as these are not protected devices within your organization). The $FWDIR/conf/external.if file defines the external interface name, which must be the operating system device name (case-sensitive) of the interface connected to the Internet.

The most common utilities you will use are fwstart and fwstop. Using these utilities represents the correct way in which to stop or start VPN-1/FireWall-1 NG. For some configuration changes, you may need to restart the VPN-1/FireWall-1 NG modules. Using fwstop followed by fwstart allows you to restart VPN-1/FireWall-1. Figure 4.26 shows an example of using the fwstop and fwstart utilities to restart VPN-1/FireWall-1 system.

FIGURE 4.26 Restarting a VPN-1/FireWall-1 system

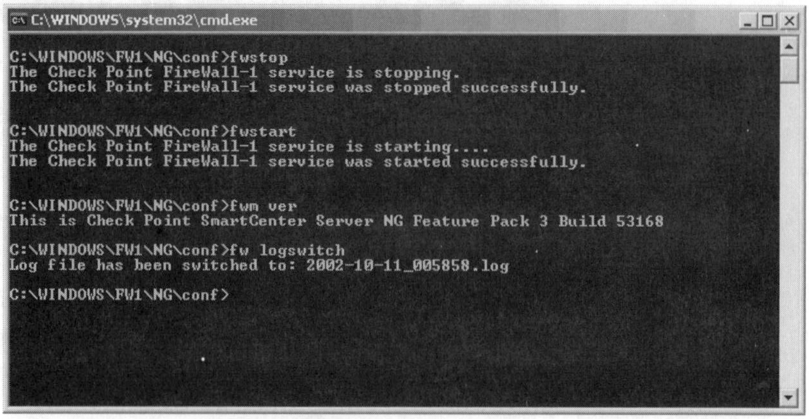

```
C:\WINDOWS\system32\cmd.exe                                          _ □ X

C:\WINDOWS\FW1\NG\conf>fwstop
The Check Point FireWall-1 service is stopping.
The Check Point FireWall-1 service was stopped successfully.

C:\WINDOWS\FW1\NG\conf>fwstart
The Check Point FireWall-1 service is starting....
The Check Point FireWall-1 service was started successfully.

C:\WINDOWS\FW1\NG\conf>fwm ver
This is Check Point SmartCenter Server NG Feature Pack 3 Build 53168

C:\WINDOWS\FW1\NG\conf>fw logswitch
Log file has been switched to: 2002-10-11_005858.log

C:\WINDOWS\FW1\NG\conf>
```

When you stop a VPN-1/FireWall-1 enforcement module, the internal network is still protected as IP routing (for example from the Internet interface to the internal interface) is disabled, while VPN-1/FireWall-1 is not running. The enforcement module itself is vulnerable to attack, however, as it has no security policy loaded to protect itself.

Figure 4.26 shows the `fwm ver` and `fwm logswitch` commands, which are explained in Table 4.1. As you can see, the `fwm` utility has a number of command-line switches that can be used to manage the Check Point security policy. Table 4.1 describes some other usages of the `fw` and `fwm` utilities.

TABLE 4.1 The *fw* and *fwm* Utility Command-Line Options

Command	Description
fw ver	Displays the VPN-1/FireWall-1 build version of an enforcement module.
fwm ver	Displays the VPN-1/FireWall-1 build version of a SmartCenter server.
fw putkey	Allows you to define shared secret keys that enable authentication between VPN-1/FireWall-1 systems. This method of authentication is not used by default in VPN-1/FireWall-1 NG. SIC is used instead.
fw log	Displays the security log files.
fwm logswitch	Allows you to rotate security log files. Using this option terminates the current log file and creates a new log file.
fwm logexport	Allows you to export security log files into an ASCII format for viewing by an external application or for export into a database.
fwm dbload	Downloads the user database to an enforcement module.

TABLE 4.1 The *fw* and *fwm* Utility Command-Line Options *(continued)*

Command	Description
fw lichosts	Lists the hosts protected by VPN-1/FireWall-1. This is only relevant for VPN-1/FireWall-1 products that are licensed to protect a specific number of IP addresses. If you exceed the number of IP addresses that your VPN-1/FireWall-1 is licensed to protect, your enforcement modules will still operate, however, you are in breach of your license.

EXERCISE 4.3

Using VPN-1/FireWall-1 Command Line Utilities

In this exercise you will learn how you can use command line utilities on nyfw01 to perform various system management tasks.

1. On nyfw01, start a command prompt by selecting Start ➢ Run and typing in **cmd**. Click OK, to invoke a command prompt.

2. Restart all Check Point applications (including the SVN foundation) by issuing the **cpstart** and **cpstop** commands.

3. Check the current version of VPN-1/FireWall-1 NG by issuing the **fwm ver -k** command.

4. Check the licenses installed on nyfw01 by issuing the **cplic print** command.

5. Unload the current security policy by using the **fwm unload nyfw01** command.

6. Change the command prompt path to the Check Point configuration directory ($FWDIR/conf) directory by typing in **cd \winnt\fw1\ng\conf** and then pressing Enter. This directory contains both rule base files (*.W files) as well as inspection script files (*.pf files). A rule base file is used to save security rules on the SmartCenter server that are viewed from SmartDashboard. An inspection script is generated from a rule base file and is downloaded to enforcement modules during Policy installation. By default, a single rule base called Standard.W and inspection script called Standard.pf

are used to house the security policy and inspection script. The security policy that you have configured so far in this book is stored in Standard.W and the Standard.pf file contains the inspection script that is used to enforcement security rules on the enforcement module. Install the Standard.W file to the enforcement module on nyfw01 by typing in **fwm load Standard.W nyfw01** command.

```
C:\WINDOWS\system32\cmd.exe                                    _|□|X|
C:\WINDOWS\FW1\NG\conf>fwm load Standard.W nyfw01
Standard.W: Security Policy Script generated into Standard.pf
Standard:
Compiled OK.

Installing CPMAD Policy On: localhost

 CPMAD policy installed successfully on nyfw01...

CPMAD policy installation complete


CPMAD policy installation succeeded for:
nyfw01

Installing VPN-1/FireWall-1 policy on: nyfw01 ...

 VPN-1/FireWall-1 policy installed successfully on nyfw01...

VPN-1/FireWall-1 policy installation complete


VPN-1/FireWall-1 policy installation succeeded for:
nyfw01
```

Notice in the graphic above that the Standard.W file is compiled into a Standard.pf file, which is then installed to nyfw01. You could specify a command of **fwm load Standard.pf nyfw01**, which would bypass the compilation of the Standard.W file; however any new changes to the Standard.W file would not be implemented.

7. Unload the current security policy again by using the **fwm unload nyfw01** command. Next, issue the **fw fetch nyfw01** command, which instructs the enforcement module component to fetch the current security policy from the SmartCenter server component. This is different to the fwm load command, which instead instructs the SmartCenter server to install a specific policy to an enforcement module.

8. You will now see how you can use the command-line to generate an inspection script, verify the script and then install the script, all in separate steps (unlike the fwm load command which performs all of these actions in a single step). Verify that the Standard.W file is valid by using the **fwm gen Standard.W > temp.pf** command, which will attempt to generate an inspection script.

EXERCISE 4.3 *(continued)*

The > character directs the output of the fwm gen command to the file temp.pf.

9. Verify that you can compile the temp.pf inspection script by using the **fwc temp.pf** command. This will compile the inspection script into inspect code (a very low-level assembly language that defines the CPU subroutines used on the enforcement module), which is stored in the $FWDIR/tmp directory. The inspect code is the actual code that is run by the VPN-1/FireWall-1 enforcement module.

10. Install the security policy in the temp.pf file to the enforcement module, by using the **fwm load temp.pf nyfw01** command.

11. Determine the current interfaces known to the VPN-1/FireWall-1 kernel by issuing the **fw ctl iflist** command.

Summary

When dealing with large and complex VPN-1/FireWall-1 security rule base, you need advanced rule management features to ensure you can customize your view of the security policy, as well as troubleshoot your security rule base when it is not working as expected. You can use features such as rule hiding and rule disabling in SmartDashboard to aid in rule management and troubleshooting. With the widespread availability of high-speed Internet access, VPN-1/FireWall-1 enforcement modules must be able to process large amounts of traffic quickly and efficiently. Because security rules are processed one by one from top to bottom, you should try and minimize the number of rules in the rule base, and move common rules to the top of the rule base so that they are matched faster. Also, avoid the excessive usage of the accounting tracking option, and only use complex services where they are required, to reduce the amount of traffic that must be inspected at the application layer.

From both an initial installation basis and on an ongoing basis, some system management tasks require attention. Each Check Point product must be licensed before it will operate. Check Point NG introduced a central license repository stored on the SmartCenter server that can be accessed via the License Manager in the SmartUpdate SMART client. From this repository licenses can be added or removed, and then attached or detached to remote

Check Point products. This simplifies and reduces the administrative overhead of maintaining licenses, especially in a complex Check Point topology. Licenses also are now bound to the SmartCenter server IP address, rather than the enforcement module IP address, which means you can change you IP addressing on enforcement modules without invalidating the VPN-1/FireWall-1 license. SmartUpdate also features the Installation Manager that allows you to manage Check Point product software upgrades and remote installations from a central point.

Finally, it is important to understand the common command-line utilities that can be used to configure and monitor both the VPN-1/FireWall-1 Smart-Center server and enforcement module. The `cpstart`, `cpstop`, `fwstart`, and `fwstop` utilities all can be used to stop and start VPN-1/FireWall-1 components. The `cplic` utility allows you to work with SmartCenter server licenses. The `fwm gen`, `fwc`, `fwm load`, `fwm unload`, and `fw fetch` utilities all deal with the verification, compilation, installation, or uninstallation of security policy, while the `fw ctl` command allows you to send or receive information from the INSPECT module kernel.

Exam Essentials

Understand how to manage rules.   Use the Rules menu to add, delete, disable, and hide rules. You can also right-click in the number column and manage rules from here. Hiding rules removes them from the SmartDashboard display, but the hidden rules are still enforced. Disabling rules does not hide them from the SmartDashboard display, but does prevent the rule from being enforced on enforcement modules.

Know how to optimize rule management.   You should always create a HOSTS file that specifies the IP address to hostname mappings for the security objects in your organization. This allows for easier management of IP addressing and reduces errors.

Know how to optimize rule processing on gateways.   Always try to keep the rule base as simple as possible and minimize the amount of rules. Place the most commonly used rules near the top of the rule base, and avoid heavy usage of the account tracking option. Only specify complex protocols where they are required.

Know the two types of NG Licenses.   NG introduced the central license, which is bound to SmartCenter server rather than enforcement module.

All central licenses are stored in a license repository located on the SmartCenter server. A local license is also available to maintain backward compatibility—the local license is bound to the enforcement module.

Know how to obtain a license. To obtain a license you must first purchase Check Point product. You will be provided with a certificate key, which you must specify on the Check Point User Center website when creating a new license.

Understand SmartUpdate. SmartUpdate is a Check Point SMART client that consists of two components. Installation Manager allows you to perform remote installations, software upgrades and rollbacks, and to check current software and OS versions. License Manager allows you to manage central licenses stored in the license repository. SmartUpdate communicates using SIC or `fwm putkey` (4.1 SP2 and higher). SmartUpdate requires the SVN foundation (`cpshared`) to be installed on all managed systems.

Understand common CLI utilities. `cpstart` and `cpstop` start and stop all Check Point products. `fwstart` and `fwstop` start and stop VPN-1/FireWall-1. The `fw` and `fwm` command has many options that get information about the VPN-1/FireWall-1 system. Make sure you understand exactly what each CLI utility can and cannot do.

Key Terms

Before you take the exam, be certain you are familiar with the following terms:

central licenses	Installation Manager
certificate key	Internet Gateway
database revision control	License Manager
Disable Rule	local licenses
fw	policy package
fwm	section title
hide a rule	secure internal communications (SIC)
inspection code	SecureUpdate
inspection script	SmartUpdate

Review Questions

1. Which of the following is recommended to reduce the administrative overheads of managing a complex rule base? (Choose all that apply.)

   A. Avoid the use of the accounting option.

   B. Use rule disabling.

   C. Maintain a HOSTS file.

   D. Place more frequently used rules near the top of the rule base.

   E. Use rule hiding.

   F. Use only complex protocols where required.

   G. Use DNS

   H. Use Section Titles

2. Which of the following is recommended to increase the *performance* of an enforcement module enforcing a complex rule base? (Choose all that apply.)

   A. Avoid the use of the accounting option.

   B. Use rule disabling.

   C. Maintain a HOSTS file.

   D. Place more frequently used rules near the top of the rule base.

   E. Use rule hiding.

   F. Use only complex protocols where required.

3. Which of the following is recommended to troubleshoot traffic that is being denied by an enforcement module incorrectly? (Choose all that apply.)

   A. Avoid the use of the accounting option.

   B. Use rule disabling.

   C. Maintain a HOSTS file.

   D. Place more frequently used rules near the top of the rule base.

   E. Use rule hiding.

   F. Use only complex protocols where required.

4. Which type of license would you use for a VPN-1/FireWall-1 4.1 enforcement module?

   A. Central

   B. Local

   C. Remote

   D. Distributed

5. You need to provide software build information to Check Point technical support. Which command should you use?

   A. fwm printlic

   B. fwm putlic

   C. fwm ver

   D. fwm version

6. You need to add a license for a Check Point NG enforcement module to a SmartCenter server. Using the *recommended* licensing scheme, which of the following represents the license type and the communications used to license the enforcement module? (Choose all that apply.)

   A. Central License

   B. Local License

   C. fwm putkey

   D. SIC

7. Which of the following can be used to license a SmartCenter server? (Choose all that apply.)

   A. cpconfig

   B. fwm putkey

   C. cprlic

   D. cplic put

8. You are constantly hiding the same rules to improve the readability of the rule base. This involves hiding about 20 or so rules and consumes a lot of time. Which of the following menu items could be used to save you time?

A. Rules ➤ Hide

B. Rules ➤ Unhide

C. Rules ➤ View Hidden

D. Rules ➤ Manage Hidden

9. You use the command `cp fetch` on an enforcement module. Which of the following happens?

A. SmartCenter server uploads security policy to the enforcement module.

B. Enforcement module downloads security policy from the Smart-Center server.

C. Enforcement module obtains the status of the SmartCenter server.

D. SmartCenter server obtains the status of the enforcement module.

E. Nothing

10. Which command should you use to install a policy on an enforcement module, if you are connected to the enforcement module?

A. `fwc`

B. `fw fetch`

C. `fwm gen`

D. `fwm load`

11. You wish to verify a security rule base using the CLI. How would you do this?

A. Attach to the SmartCenter server and run the `fwc` command.

B. Attach to the enforcement module and run the `fwc` command.

C. Attach to the SmartCenter server and run the `fwm gen` command.

D. Attach to the enforcement module and run the `fwm gen` command.

12. Which of the following extensions defines a security rule base file?

A. .c

B. .pc

C. .pl

D. .W

13. You have configured VPN-1/FireWall-1 for the first time. What is the default name of the inspection script?

A. Default.pf

B. Default.W

C. Standard.pf

D. Standard.W

14. You have installed an enterprise version of VPN-1/FireWall-1. Where is the external.if file located?

A. $FWDIR/bin

B. $FWDIR/conf

C. $FWDIR/database

D. None of the above

15. You save your current rule base as a separate rule base with a name of Backup and move the file to a folder called C:\Backup directory on your SmartCenter server. In the future, you attempt to load the Backup security rule base, but cannot see it as a valid option when selecting File ➢ Open from SmartDashboard. What should you do?

A. In the Open Policy dialog box, browse to the C:\Backup folder and choose the Backup.W file.

B. Move or copy the Backup.W file to the $FWDIR/bin directory.

C. Move or copy the Backup.W file to the $FWDIR/conf directory.

D. Nothing, the Backup.W file has obviously been deleted.

16. Which of the following commands would you use on a SmartCenter server to uninstall the security policy on an enforcement module?

    A. `fw ctl uninstall`

    B. `fwm uninstall`

    C. `fw ctl unload`

    D. `fwm unload`

17. An enforcement module loses communications with the SmartCenter server. What happens in terms of the security policy enforced after a reboot of the enforcement module, and communications are still down?

    A. The enforcement module shuts down.

    B. The enforcement module loads the last installed policy received from the SmartCenter server.

    C. The enforcement module does not forward traffic until it can communicate with the SmartCenter server.

    D. The enforcement module forwards all traffic.

18. You use the `fwm load` command to install a security policy to a VPN-1/ FireWall-1 NG enforcement module for the first time. However, you receive an error "command load failed." What would be the most likely cause?

    A. The enforcement module is down.

    B. The enforcement module has not run the `fwm putkey` command.

    C. The enforcement module object does not have a certificate.

    D. The enforcement module `fwd` daemon has crashed.

19. An enforcement module is running very slow and you have identified that a lot of traffic is hitting a single rule that is placed directly below the stealth rule. The rule specifies a destination element of Any, and in log viewer you can see that each connection is utilizing approximately 10MB of bandwidth. What should you do to improve performance?

    A. Move the rule to the top of the rule base.

    B. Move the rule to the bottom of the rule base.

    C. Turn off accounting for the rule.

    D. Disable the rule.

20. Which of the following licenses does not require an `external.if` file?

    A. 25 IP addresses

    B. 100 IP addresses

    C. 250 IP addresses

    D. Enterprise

Answers to Review Questions

1. **C, E, G, H.** To increase the manageability of a complex rule base, you should maintain some form of name resolution (e.g., HOSTS file or DNS), which allows you to quickly resolve the IP addresses associated with objects. You can also hide rules to increase readability. DNS is the preferred method, especially for larger, complex environments, as you can define all hostname to IP address mappings at a central DNS database, instead of having to manually configure HOSTS file on each device. Section Titles can also be used to group similar rules together, allowing for the security rule base to be collapsed as required to ensure easy management.

2. **A, D, F.** To increase the performance of enforcement modules, ensure that the most commonly matched rules at near the top of the rule base. Also avoid the excessive use of the accounting option, and only use complex protocols (such as H.323) where required.

3. **B.** If you are having problems with traffic being dropped incorrectly, you can disable rules temporarily, so that the disabled rules are not processed by enforcement modules, but are still present in the rule base to be enabled once the problem has been identified.

4. **B.** VPN-1/FireWall-1 NG supports central licenses and local licenses. Local licenses are used for backward compatibility with previous versions, and are bound to each specific enforcement module, rather than to a SmartCenter server.

5. **C.** The `fwm ver` command displays version information about VPN-1/FireWall-1.

6. **A, D.** The recommended licensing for NG components is to use *central* licensing, where licenses are managed centrally via the Smart-Center server. The SmartCenter server distributes central licenses to enforcement modules using SIC (secure internal communications).

7. **A, C, D.** The `fwm putkey` command is used to establish secure communications with older VPN-1/FireWall-1 components. All other utilities listed can be used to license a SmartCenter server.

8. **D.** The Rules ➢ Manage Hidden option allows you to save masks, which represent the collection of hidden rules currently applied to the rule base.

9. E. The `cp fetch` command does not exist. The `fw fetch` command would perform the action specified by B.

10. B. The `fw fetch` command is used on an enforcement module to "fetch" a policy from the SmartCenter server.

11. C. The SmartCenter server stores all security policy files, with the enforcement module only containing the inspection code file. The `fwm gen` command allows a SmartCenter server to generate the inspection script file from a rule base file, which will succeed if the rule base file is configured correctly, thus verifying the security rule base.

12. D. A security rule base file is saved as a `.W` file.

13. C. By default, the VPN-1/FireWall-1 security policy is called `Standard`, with the inspection script file therefore being called `Standard.pf`.

14. D. The `external.if` file is only used for VPN-1/FireWall-1 installations that use a license that limits the number of IP addresses that can be protected by the firewall (for these installations, the `external.if` file is stored in the `$FWDIR/conf` directory). The enterprise license has no restrictions, and thus does not require the `external.if` file.

15. C. When opening a security rule base, the available rule bases are determined by reading the `$FWDIR\conf` directory on the SmartCenter server for all files with a `.W` extension.

16. D. The `fwm unload` command is used on a SmartCenter server to uninstall an enforcement module security policy. The `fw ctl uninstall` command can be used on an enforcement module to configure the VPN-1/FireWall-1 INSPECT module to not intercept packets.

17. B. To ensure the last known good security policy is enforced in the event of a communications failure with the SmartCenter server, the enforcement module loads the last security policy received from the SmartCenter server.

18. C. There are two possibilities for this, `fwm putkey` has not been used to generate a secret keys for communications, or SIC has not been established. Because the enforcement module is version NG, it is most likely this is because SIC has not been established. SIC requires each communicating party to have a certificate.

19. C.   Because the rule is directly below the stealth rule, you can't optimize the rule further by placing it at the top of the rule base, because then you would be permitting access to your enforcement module. Because you can see the amount of bandwidth used by each connection, this means that accounting is enabled, which can be detrimental performance.

20. D.   An Enterprise license permits an unlimited number of protected hosts, which means the enforcement module does not have to monitor the number of source IP addresses making connections out of the external interface (defined in the `external.if` file).

Chapter

5

SmartView Tracker

THE CCSA EXAM OBJECTIVES COVERED IN THIS CHAPTER INCLUDE:

- ✓ Define the main SmartView Tracker components and icons.
- ✓ Explain the basic administrative operation of the SmartView Tracker.
- ✓ Explain blocking an intruder from accessing the network.

An important component of any network security system is the ongoing management of the security system. It is unfortunate that many organizations today purchase an expensive security system, configure it to enforce the security policy of the organization, and then lock it up in a server room, not touching it for months or years. This is a dangerous practice—the organization believes that its information systems are secure due to the network security system put in place. This might be a valid assumption for perhaps a month or two after the security system is installed; however, as time goes by and new vulnerabilities are discovered daily that provide new mechanisms for attackers to get into the network, the effectiveness of the security system becomes less and less sure. The threat of new vulnerabilities can be reasonably countered by the regular updates to the security system; however, just using this mechanism (and no other) as the only ongoing maintenance of your security systems is still lacking.

To truly ensure the security of your network, you must manage your security system on at least a weekly basis, if not a daily basis. The regular maintenance required consists of analyzing security logs, which contain a history of access permitted and rejected through the enforcement modules of your organization. A good security system should include a security logging subsystem that is accurate and easy to manage. By analyzing your logs for rejected and denied connections, you can detect direct attacks as well as reconnaissance scans. Reconnaissance scans are often a forewarning of a direct attack against your network—an attacker scanning your network looking for vulnerabilities to exploit. If you know what is going on in terms of your network security on a regular basis, you can easily identify whether or not your security policy needs to be modified to remove any possible vulnerabilities. You also will have a much better idea of who is responsible for an attack, which may aid law enforcement agencies in tracking down the culprits.

In this chapter, you will learn about *SmartView Tracker* (also known as the *Check Point Log Manager* and previously known as *Log Viewer* in prior versions), which is the Check Point management (SMART) client used to manage security logs. You will first learn about the Check Point logging architecture and how the SmartCenter Server and enforcement modules interact to ensure security logs are centrally maintained. Next, you will learn how to start SmartView Tracker and work with the Check Point security logs. You will learn how you can view the different security log databases and how to manipulate information within each database. Finally, you will learn how to temporarily block the systems associated with a connection that you suspect is malicious, without having to configure a new security rule.

Logging Architecture

Before working with SmartView Tracker, it is important to understand the logging architecture of Check Point VPN-1/FireWall-1 NG. Logging is much improved over previous versions of VPN-1/FireWall-1. A major issue with Check Point VPN-1/FireWall-1 4.1 and previous versions was the long response times experienced during Log Viewer updates. The screen update response times in NG are much faster, allowing for log viewing to be a much more user-friendly experience. VPN-1/FireWall-1 NG also includes mechanisms that allow third-party tools to work with log files, providing functions such as consolidated reporting and intrusion detection.

What Is Logging?

To begin the discussion of logging architecture, we must first define what logging actually is. Logging can be described as the process of writing *log records* to a log database in response to packets received or some Check Point security event. Log records are then consolidated into log events, with each event being displayed as a *log entry* in the SmartView Tracker.

Check Point security events that generate log entries include events such as rule matching, security policy configuration, and policy installation. Logging is invoked under the following circumstances:

- A new connection is matched against a rule that has a Track option specified (such as log, account, or alert).

- Another security event occurs, which is considered important enough that an alert notification or log entry is generated. Sample events include logging of implied rules, anti-spoofing detection on an enforcement module interface, or user authentication successes or failures.

- Administrative operations performed on the Check Point security policy database or security objects database—for example, the process of creating a security object or deleting a security rule.

The main source of log entries are rule-matching events. Every rule that has a tracking option configured will generate a log entry for each connection that matches the rule. Not all traffic that passes through VPN-1/FireWall-1 needs to be logged. An extremely useful feature of VPN-1/FireWall-1 NG is that all traffic the firewall processes does not have to be logged. Rules that do not specify a Track element option do not generate log events. This allows you to fine-tune the content of your log files, making them easier to analyze and manage.

If a rule is matched that specifies traffic should be logged, it is important to note that the log entries displayed in SmartView Tracker are based on each connection rather than each packet associated with a connection. For example, you might log HTTP connections through your firewall. When a connection is setup, an entry appears in the SmartView Tracker, indicating the various attributes associated with the connection and whether it was accepted, rejected, or denied. The subsequent packets sent during the life of the connection are not logged—this ensures that your log files do not become filled with useless information. Only packets that are part of a new connection generate a new log entry, as these represent a new connection entry in the stateful inspection engine of the enforcement module.

Now that you understand what logging is and when logging is invoked, it is important to understand where logging information is actually stored. The SmartCenter Server maintains all VPN-1/FireWall-1 NG security logging. The log file used in Check Point VPN-1/FireWall-1 NG is no longer a text-based flat file. It is now a true database complete with indexing features that allow information to be queried in the database at much faster speeds. There are actually three logging databases present on a VPN-1/FireWall-1 Smart-Center Server. SmartView Tracker refers to each of these databases as *log modes*. Each of the log modes are described below, with reference to the actual database filename provided (all the files reside in the $FWDIR\log directory):

Log (**fw.log**) The fw.log file represents the main security log database. All connections that match rules that specify a tracking option are logged as a log event in this database. Other security events such as user authentication and policy install on an enforcement module are also logged to this database.

In previous versions of VPN-1/FireWall-1, a separate accounting log file was used to store all events related to connections that matched a rule with a tracking option set to Account. In VPN-1/FireWall-1 NG, accounting records are integrated into the main security log database, and the accounting log file no longer exists. An Account Management predefined log query, which displays only accounting records can be applied to the fw.log database as required.

Active (fw.vlog)   The fw.vlog file holds a table of current connections active through the firewall. As new connections are established, the active log database updates to include log events related to the connection. Similarly, as a connection is torn down, the active log database updates the system to remove the log event related to the connection. This log mode allows you to block active connections that you suspect are malicious.

Audit (fw.adtlog)   The fw.adtlog file represents the audit log database. This database is new to VPN-1/FireWall-1 NG and provides auditing of administrator operations, such as security object configuration, rule base configuration, and policy installation and uninstallation. This feature is useful if you wish to track changes or need to rollback or identify unauthorized changes.

Other supporting files for each log database are also present in the $FWDIR\log folder, which provide indexing and transactional abilities, allowing incomplete transactions (for example, a log entry is half-written and a power outage shuts down the SmartCenter Server) to be rolled back.

Understanding the Logging Architecture

Now that you understand the basic concepts of logging, you can analyze the logging architecture that enables enforcement modules to generate log events and pass them to the SmartCenter Server for writing to the log database. Figure 5.1 shows the logging architecture on both an enforcement module and SmartCenter Server.

FIGURE 5.1 Logging architecture

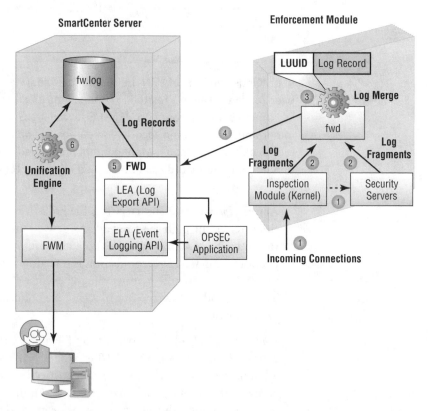

SmartView Tracker SMART Client

In Figure 5.1, the following events occur:

1. Incoming traffic associated with new or existing connections is received by the inspection module, which is part of the operating system kernel of the enforcement module. Incoming connections may also pass through other Check Point components, such as a security server (HTTP, FTP, or SMTP) or a FloodGate-1 module.

2. If the traffic matches a rule that specifies a tracking option, information about the traffic is passed to the fwd daemon, which runs in the *user mode* space of the operating system. Each *kernel mode* component (such as the inspection module) generates *log fragments*, which are pieces of information related to the traffic received.

3. The fwd daemon receives log fragments and merges information from the fragments into a log record. The log record is then stamped with a

Log Unique Unification ID (LUUID), which is a unique identifier that associates the log record with a particular connection. If a log record is generated for an existing connection, the same LUUID used for previous log records related to the connection are used for the new log record.

The VPN-1/FireWall-1 enforcement module components run in either kernel mode or user mode. Components such as the inspection module run in kernel mode, which gives the inspection module direct access to network traffic (before it reaches the operating system TCP/IP stack) and allows for higher performance. Kernel mode components cannot perform some tasks such as access files or initiate packets, so these tasks must be offloaded to a user mode component. The user mode component (e.g., fwd) is able to generate log messages that can be sent to the SmartCenter Server.

4. Each generated log record stamped with the LUUID by fwd is sent to the fwd daemon running on the SmartCenter Server.

5. The fwd daemon receives each log record and writes it to the security log database (fw.log). The fwd daemon also provides the *Log Export API (LEA)*, which allows log events to be exported to OPSEC applications, and the *Event Logging API (ELA)*, which allows OPSEC applications to write logging events to the security log database.

6. The unification engine links log records to a log entry by referencing the LUUID. The unification engine is responsible for updating the log entries shown in the SmartView Tracker application in real time (this is done via the fwm daemon, which is responsible for communicating with Check Point SMART clients). For example, when a log record representing a new connection is written to the fw.log database, the unification engine immediately displays a new log entry in SmartView Tracker via the fwm daemon. If the connection matched a rule that had a tracking option of Account, when the connection is terminated, the log entry for the connection is updated with the number of bytes associated with the connection.

In terms of logging architecture, there are two components in Figure 5.1 that you will commonly encounter:

Kernel Side *Kernel side* refers to the activities that take place on the enforcement module. Log fragments are generated by kernel components (such as the inspection module), which are then merged into log records with a LUUID by the fwd daemon.

Server Side *Server side* refers to the activities that take place on the SmartCenter Server. Log records either generate a new log entry (for new connections) or update an existing log entry (for existing connections). Any changes in the log database are updated in real time on the Smart-View Tracker SMART client.

Example of Logging Architecture

To understand how logging works, let's walk through a real life example. Let's say that a rule is defined in the security rule base that uses a URI (uniform resource indicator) resource object to log the URL's associated with HTTP connections. Using Figure 5.1 as a visual guide, the following lists what happens as traffic passes through the enforcement module:

1. The inspection module (kernel component) immediately sends a log fragment to fwd indicating HTTP traffic has been received.

2. HTTP traffic is passed to the HTTP security server for URL inspection. The security server sends log fragments to fwd as each URL is read.

3. fwd takes all fragments associated with the connection and combines them into a single log record that is stamped with a LUUID.

4. The record is passed to the fwd daemon on the management server.

5. The fwd daemon on the management server writes the log record to the fw.log database. The log record is matched against an existing HTTP log entry by virtue of the same LUUID. The unification engine monitors the log file for new records—as each new URL is processed, the unification engine adds the new URL information to the existing HTTP connection log entry, and updates the SmartView Tracker display.

6. In SmartView Tracker, as each URL using the same HTTP connection is accessed through the enforcement module, the log entry representing the connection is updated. The Info. field (you will learn about these fields later) is appended with each URL.

Working with SmartView Tracker

SmartView Tracker is installed by default during the Check Point SMART client installation and is considered an integral part of the SMART client suite.

Just as for all other SMART clients, to connect to a SmartCenter Server using SmartView Tracker, your system must be configured as a GUI client using the cpconfig utility.

In this section you'll learn how to start SmartView Tracker and will then be introduced to the basic components of SmartView Tracker.

Starting SmartView Tracker

To use SmartView Tracker, you must install the SmartView Tracker SMART client on a host whose IP address is an authorized GUI client. To start the SmartView Tracker application, select Start ➢ Programs ➢ Check Point SMART Clients ➢ SmartView Tracker. An authentication dialog box, similar to the dialog box presented when using SmartDashboard is presented, as shown in Figure 5.2. To establish a connection, enter in the appropriate credentials and IP address and click OK.

FIGURE 5.2   SmartView Tracker authentication dialog box

At this point the SmartView Tracker application establishes a connection to the SmartCenter Server, and receives a fingerprint to authenticate the Smart-Center Server. If this is the first time you have used any Check Point SMART client on the client system, you will be asked whether you want to accept the fingerprint. Assuming the SmartView Tracker application accepts the finger-print, encryption keys are negotiated and the credentials specified in Figure 5.2 are sent encrypted to the SmartCenter Server. The SmartCenter Server verifies the credentials against the user database, ensuring the username and password are both correct, and that you have the appropriate permissions to access SmartView Tracker.

To run SmartView Tracker and access security logs, an administrator account must possess at least read-only permissions for the Monitoring component. If read-only permissions are assigned, the administrator can view the log database, but cannot block connections or manage log files.

Assuming the credentials are okay and the administrator has the appropriate permissions to access the log database, the SmartView Tracker window appears, showing the fw.log database entries. Figure 5.3 shows SmartView Tracker after successful authentication.

FIGURE 5.3 The SmartView Tracker application

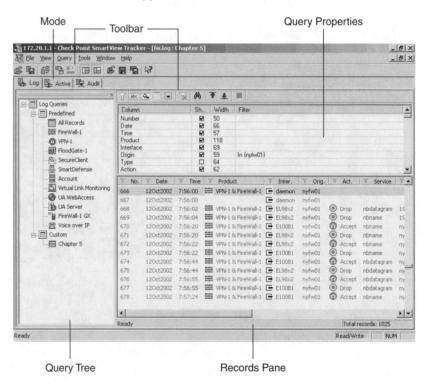

You can access SmartView Tracker from other SMART clients such as Smart-Dashboard by choosing Window ➢ SmartView Tracker. When you do this, the credentials you used to log in to the first SMART client are passed to Smart-View Tracker, meaning you don't have to re-authenticate and SmartView Tracker starts immediately.

Introduction to the SmartView Tracker Application

Figure 5.3 shows several important areas of the SmartView Tracker window. The following describes each component of the SmartView Tracker application:

Records Pane   The main component of the SmartView Tracker window is the *records pane*, which shows each log entry present in the log database file, based upon the current queries applied to the log database. Each log entry corresponds to a security event that has taken place, such as a connection being permitted or denied through an enforcement module, or the installation of a security policy on an enforcement module. The Smart-View Tracker records pane will often contain hundreds or thousands of log entries, and you can use the arrow keys as well as the PgUp or PgDn keys to navigate the log file as required.

Along the top of the log entry display is a list of column headers, each of which define specific fields that exist within each log entry. For example, the Date column is used to display the Date field contained within each log entry, which identifies the date on which the security event that generated the subsequent log event occurred. Often, a log entry field may reference objects contained within the security object database. For example, the Origin (Orig. in Figure 5.3) column indicates the enforcement module (Check Point gateway object) that a log entry was generated from. Sometimes, the SmartView Tracker display won't be able to show all columns within the same Window—you can use the scroll bars at the bottom and the side of the Records pane to view extra columns.

Check Point NG Feature Pack 3 introduces the capability to right-click on any rule-matching log entry (i.e., a log entry generated by a connection that matches a security rule) and choose an option called View Rule in SmartDash-board, which opens SmartDashboard and highlights the rule in the security rule base. For this feature to work, you must have enabled Database Revision Control feature in SmartDashboard global properties.

Mode   The Mode tabs are used to select the current security log database file that is being accessed. Three tabs are available—Log (`fw.log`—the main security log), Active (`fw.vlog`—the active connection log), and Audit (`fw.adtlog`—the audit log).

Query Tree   The query tree lists all *predefined queries* and *custom queries*. A *query* is describes a set of parameters that defines how records are displayed in the Records pane. These parameters are configured using the Query Properties pane.

Query Properties   This pane describes the parameters that define a query that has been opened from the Query Tree pane. A query describes each column or field that exists in log entries and describes the following parameters for each:

Show   Indicates whether or not a column is displayed in the Records Pane. For example in Figure 5.3, you can see that the Type column has been configured to not be displayed in the Records Pane, as the Show check box has been unchecked. You can also right-click on a column in the Records pane and select Hide from the menu that appears to remove the column from the display.

Width   Indicates the width of a column in pixels. You can specify a width in the Query Properties pane, or drag the bounds of a column in the Records pane to adjust width.

Filter   Describes criteria that can be used to filter the records displayed in the Records pane to only include records that match the criteria configured for the column. For example in Figure 5.3, you can see that the Origin column, which defines enforcement module that a log entry originated from, has a filter applied, with the criteria configured as `In {nyfw01}`. This filter means that only records that include an origin field of `nyfw01` (i.e., only log entries that have been generated by `nyfw01`) should be displayed. If you configure filters for multiple columns, all filters are combined using a logical AND operation, meaning the log records displayed meet all of the criteria for all filters. You can also modify the filter applied for a column by right-clicking on the column in the Records pane and selecting Edit Filter from the menu that appears.

Toolbar   The toolbar includes buttons that enable you to quickly perform actions within SmartView Tracker. In Figure 5.3, you can see that the toolbar is actually split into two sections. Figure 5.4 shows some of the important buttons located on the toolbar.

FIGURE 5.4   The SmartView Tracker toolbar

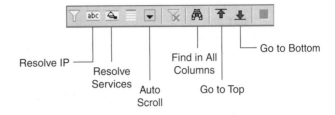

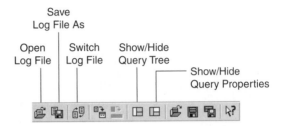

 You can show or hide the toolbar, Query Tree pane, and Query Properties pane by using the View menu in SmartView Tracker. This menu allows you to enable or disable visibility of each of these components. The visibility of the Records pane can never be disabled.

Table 5.1 describes each of the buttons indicated in Figure 5.4.

TABLE 5.1   SmartView Tracker Toolbar Buttons

Button	Description
Open Log File	Opens a historical log file that has been previously saved. When you open an historical log file, any new log events will not be displayed.
Save Log File As	Saves a copy of the current log file to a different log file, yet retains the current log file as the file that all current log entries are written to.
Switch Log File	Saves the current log file to a new file with timestamp and then creates a new log file that subsequent log entries are written to.

TABLE 5.1 SmartView Tracker Toolbar Buttons *(continued)*

Button	Description
Show/Hide Query Tree	Shows or hides the Query Tree pane.
Show/Hide Query Properties	Shows or hides the Query Properties pane.
Apply Filter	Applies all of the filters specified for a query to log entries in the Records pane. You can toggle this button on to selectively apply or remove filters.
Clear All Filters	Clear all of the filters specified for a query to log entries in the Records pane. After clicking this button, you cannot recover any filters that were previously configured.
Resolve IP	Resolves any log entry fields that contain IP addresses to either security objects in the VPN-1/FireWall-1 security policy or to host names using DNS or a HOSTS file.
Resolve Services	Resolves any log entry fields that contain service information, such as a TCP or UDP port, to a service object in the VPN-1/FireWall-1 security policy.
Show Null Matches	Enabling this option displays log entries that do not include a value in a column that is being filtered.
AutoScroll	Automatically scrolls the Records pane to ensure the latest log entries are displayed as they are generated.
Find in all Columns	Allows you to search for information in all columns displayed in the Records pane.
Go to Top	Takes you to the first entry (top) in the log file displayed in the Records pane.
Go to Bottom	Takes you to the most recent or last entry (bottom) in the log file displayed in the Records pane.

Displaying the Full Contents of a Field

SmartView Tracker shows log entries with many fields, all of which are displayed. As a result, you will often be unable to view all of the information contained within specific fields. SmartView Tracker provides a very quick mechanism to work around this problem, allowing administrators to quickly read detailed information about specific fields. You can view the entire contents of a single log entry by simply double-clicking the field, which displays the Records Details dialog box that includes all of the log entry information. Figure 5.5 shows an example of viewing the details of a single record.

FIGURE 5.5   Viewing the Details of a Single Record

In Figure 5.5, you can see all of the fields for a single log entry, which makes it very easy to extract information for a specific log entry. Only the columns that are currently displayed in the Records pane are listed as fields in the Record Details dialog box.

You can right-click any entry in the Records pane and select either Copy Cell or Copy Line from the menu that appears. The Copy Cell option copies the contents of the field that you right-clicked to the clipboard, while the Copy Line option copies the contents of the entire log entry to the clipboard in the following format:

Number:	8
Date:	12Oct2002
Time:	22:55:22
Product:	VPN-1 & FireWall-1

SmartView Tracker Modes

As described earlier in the Logging Architecture section, the log database actually consists of three separate log database files. The *SmartView Tracker mode* defines which of these three log database files you are currently viewing. You can select the appropriate mode by simply clicking on either the Log, Audit, or Active tabs located directly below the top toolbar in SmartView Tracker (see Figure 5.3). We will now discuss each of the SmartView Tracker modes in detail.

Log Mode

Log mode displays information contained within the `fw.log` file. This mode shows all security-related events that occur, such as rule matching, anti-spoofing, and VPN connection establishment. This mode is the default SmartView Tracker mode displayed when you first start SmartView Tracker. Referring back to Figure 5.3, you can see that the Log tab is currently selected, which indicates that the current display is Log mode. Each row displayed in the Records pane of Figure 5.3 represents a log entry, which in turn represents a single security event, such as the acceptance or denial of a connection that matches a specific rule, or the successful installation of a security policy on an enforcement module. Notice that within the Records pane, a number of columns exist, which define the fields contained within each log entry in the `fw.log` database. Each log entry contains information about a number of different parameters. For example, if a log entry represents a connection that has been processed by an enforcement module, parameters such as the source IP address, destination IP address, and whether the connection was accepted or denied are important. Each of the fields in a log entry include this type of information and more, ensuring you can effectively monitor the ongoing state of security.

Always remember that log entries that match a security rule always are generated on a per-connection basis, not on a per-packet basis.

By default, when you open SmartView Tracker, the Log mode view displayed includes a default selection of columns (fields) for each log entry. This selection is formally known as a *log query*, and the default log query is referred to as the *All Records log query*. This default log query is designed to include a suitable amount of information for each log entry to provide a general overview of the current security state of the various Check Point SVN components that are generating log events. Table 5.2 lists and describes each of the columns that are displayed in the All Records log query, which, by default, is displayed when you first open SmartView Tracker.

TABLE 5.2 All Records Log Query Columns

Column (Field)	Description
Number	Indicates the relative position of the log entry in the log file. For example, the first log entry has a number of 1, which increments for subsequent log entries as they are generated.
Date	Indicates the date the log entry was generated.
Time	Indicates the time the log entry was generated.
Product	Indicates the Check Point or OPSEC product that generated the log entry.
Interface	For rule-matching events, this field indicates the interface on which the connection request was received (i.e., the client side interface of the connection). You may also see a value of "daemon" for this field, which is used to indicate a control event, such as policy installation.
Origin	Indicates the Check Point or OPSEC host that generated the log entry.
Type	Indicates the type of security event the log entry represents. For rule-matching events, this column indicates the Track element specified for the rule (e.g., Log, Account, or Alert). The other value for this field that you may see is Control, which indicates a system control event, such as policy installation.

TABLE 5.2 All Records Log Query Columns *(continued)*

Column (Field)	Description
Action	Indicates the action that occurred with respect to the security event represented by the log entry. For rule-matching events, this column indicates the Action element specified for the rule (e.g., Accept, Drop, or Reject) place. Other security events may generate different actions. For example, VPN connections will generate Key Install, Encrypt, and Decrypt actions, while user authentication events will generate Authorize and Deauthorize actions.
Service	Used for rule-matching events and indicates the service (destination port) associated with the connection. This will normally specify a service object, if the Resolve Services button on the SmartView Tracker toolbar is selected.
Source	Used for rule-matching events and indicates the source IP address associated with the connection. This will normally specify a security object, such as a host node object, or a hostname, if the Resolve IP button on the SmartView Tracker toolbar is selected.
Destination	Used for rule-matching events and indicates the destination IP address associated with the connection. This will normally specify a security object, such as a host node object, or a hostname, if the Resolve IP button on the SmartView Tracker toolbar is selected.
Protocol	Used for rule-matching events and indicates the transport-layer protocol (e.g., TCP or UDP) associated with the connection.
Rule	Used for rule-matching events and indicates the rule number in the security rule base that the connection was matched against.
Source Port	Used for rule-matching events and indicates the source UDP or TCP port associated with the connection.

TABLE 5.2 All Records Log Query Columns *(continued)*

Column (Field)	Description
User	Used for authentication events and indicates the name of the user that attempted to authenticate.
Information	Provides further information about the log entry.

Predefined Log Queries

It is important to understand that the default view that SmartView Tracker displays does not include all columns (fields) available. SmartView Tracker provides many columns that you may find useful that are not included in the default Log mode view, to ensure the display is not too crammed and hard to read. SmartView Tracker allows you to define custom views that are based on the visibility of each column, the width of each column, and whether a filter (selection) is applied to each column. The set of columns that are displayed, the width of each column and the filters applied to each column is collectively known as a *log query*.

By default, the Log mode view displays what is known as the All Records predefined log query. This log query is designed to display an adequate amount of information for most products that generate log entries. If you are using SmartView Tracker to view log entries that are specific to a particular Check Point product, such as FireWall-1 or VPN-1, you will most likely want to view in-depth information for each log entry that is specific to the particular Check Point product. To accommodate this, SmartView Tracker includes several predefined log queries, which can display information in the Log mode view that is specific to a particular Check Point product or feature. In Figure 5.3, you can see each of these predefined log queries. Table 5.3 describes some of the important and common predefined log queries.

TABLE 5.3 SmartView Tracker Predefined Log Queries

Predefined Log Query	Description
All Records	The default log query that includes a selection of fields that are suitable for displaying an appropriate amount of information for log events generated by common Check Point products and features.

TABLE 5.3 SmartView Tracker Predefined Log Queries *(continued)*

Predefined Log Query	Description
FireWall-1	Displays information specific to the log entries generated by FireWall-1. This log query includes all of the columns displayed by the All Records log query, but applies a filter to the Product column so that only log entries generated by the VPN-1 & FireWall-1 product are displayed. Additional columns specific to FireWall-1, such as NAT rule number, XlateSrc, and XlateDst (all related to network address translation, which is discussed in Chapters 8 and 9) are also displayed
VPN-1	Displays information specific to the log entries generated by VPN-1. This log query includes the Product column with a filter applied that only includes log entries generated by VPN-1/FireWall-1.
SecureClient	Displays log entries generated by Check Point SecureClient PCs (remote access VPN users).
SmartDefense	Displays log entries generated by the new SmartDefense component of VPN-1/FireWall-1. SmartDefense is a new feature in VPN-1/FireWall-1 NG Feature Pack 3, and provides integrated intrusion detection for a number of reconnaissance, DoS, and unauthorized access attacks.
Account	Displays all rule-matching log entries that specify a Tracking element of Account. Accounting is used to record the number of bytes associated with each connection, allowing organizations to meter bandwidth usage on a per-system, per-application, and per-user basis.
Voice over IP	Displays log entries relating to Voice over IP calls made using the H.323 and Session Initiation Protocol (SIP) call control protocols. This view is very useful, as it includes information such as source IP phone and destination IP phone, allowing an organization to track Voice Over IP calls.

To apply a predefined selection log query, ensure that the Query Tree pane (see Figure 5.3) is displayed, either by selecting the Show/Hide Query Tree button on the toolbar (see Figure 5.4) or by selecting View ≻ Query Tree from the SmartView Tracker menu. In the Query Tree pane, right-click the log query that you wish to apply and select Open from the menu that appears. This will apply the log query to the current log file loaded in the Records pane. Figure 5.6 shows SmartView Tracker with the Account predefined log query applied. The SmartView Tracker display only shows the Records pane, so that you can see more columns in the Records pane.

FIGURE 5.6 The Account predefined log query

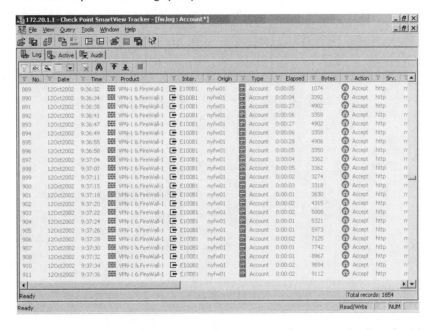

After applying the log query, the appropriate columns are displayed with filters applied where appropriate. For example in Figure 5.6, notice that the filter icon next to the Type label in the Type column has been filled with color (the color is green, but you can't see that because the figure is in black and white). This means that a filter has been applied to the column. For the Account predefined log query, the Type filter is filtered to only include log entries that specify a Type field of Account, for obvious reasons. Notice also that columns called Elapsed and Bytes have also been added to the Records pane, which provide information about the length of time a connection was established (the Elapsed column) and the number of bytes transferred by the connection (the Bytes column).

Logging HTTP Content

Because VPN-1/FireWall-1 possesses an HTTP security server, you can use this security server to inspect the content being requested in HTTP connections. This information can then be passed to the fwd daemon for logging purposes, which allows SmartView Tracker to display the URL requested in HTTP log entries. This feature demonstrates how VPN-1/FireWall-1 can be used to inspect and record application-layer information. To enable the logging of HTTP URLs, you must complete the following steps:

Create a Resource Object   Before you can log URLs, you must create a security rule that includes a resource object, which represents a service that is inspected at the application layer by the VPN-1/FireWall-1 security servers. Resource objects can be used not only for URL logging, but also for content filtering and anti-virus inspection by external OPSEC applications. To create a new resource object, select Manage ➢ Resources from the SmartDashboard menu, which will display the Resources dialog box. Click the New button and select URI from the menu that appears. This will display the URI Resource Properties dialog box as shown in Figure 5.7.

FIGURE 5.7   The URI Resource Properties dialog box

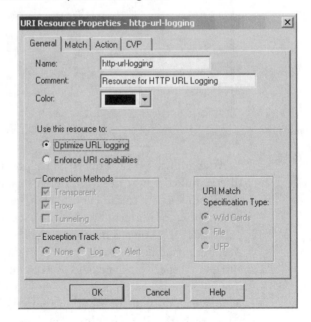

To create a resource object that is used for URL logging, you must select the Optimize URL logging option, as shown in Figure 5.7. This effectively disables all other options for the resource object, except for the describing fields such as name and comment. Once you have completed your configuration, click OK. Figure 5.8 shows the Resources dialog box with the resource object created in Figure 5.7 displayed.

FIGURE 5.8   The Resources dialog box

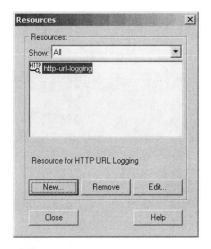

Create a Security Rule that Includes the Resource Object   Once you have created a resource object that is optimized for URL logging, you need to create or modify a security rule that includes the new resource object in the Service element of the rule. To add a resource object to the Service element of a security rule, right-click within the Service element for the rule, and select the Add With Resource option from the menu that appears. This will display the Service with Resource dialog box, which lists all services that support resource objects and allows you to choose a resource object. For HTTP URL logging, you must select the `http` service object, and then select a resource object that has been optimized for URL logging. Figure 5.9 shows the Service with Resource dialog box, with the `http` service object and the `http-url-logging` resource object created in Figure 5.8 selected.

Once you have added a service with resource to the Service element for a rule, you must also ensure that the Track element has an action of either

Log or Account configured. Figure 5.10 shows a completed security rule that will accept HTTP connections and log the URLs associated with each connection. Notice that the Service element indicates the `http` service object with an arrow pointing to the `http-url-logging` resource object, which indicates all packets matching the rule will be passed to the HTTP security server.

FIGURE 5.9 The Service with Resource dialog box

FIGURE 5.10 Example of a security rule that logs HTTP URLs

After you have configured your rule, ensure that you install your policy to each enforcement module.

View HTTP URL Information in SmartView Tracker Now that you have configured the appropriate resource object and security rule to implement HTTP URL logging, you can now use SmartView Tracker to view HTTP URLs. Entries that contain URL logging appear in Log mode, with URL information being displayed in the Info. field of each log entry. Figure 5.11 shows a log entry that contains URL information.

FIGURE 5.11   Viewing log entries with HTTP URLs in SmartView Tracker

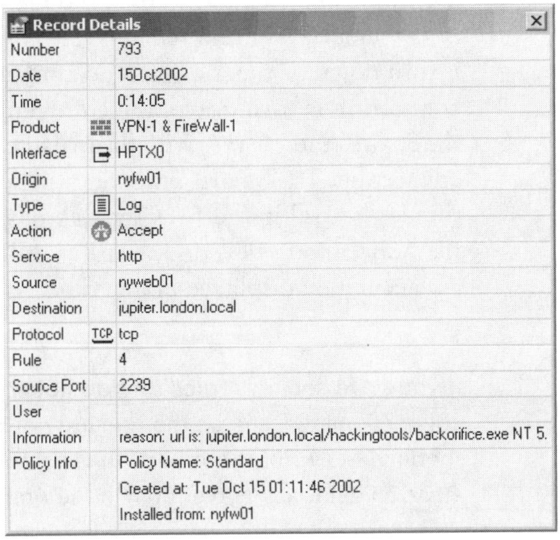

Record Details		✕
Number	793	
Date	15Oct2002	
Time	0:14:05	
Product	VPN-1 & FireWall-1	
Interface	HPTX0	
Origin	nyfw01	
Type	Log	
Action	Accept	
Service	http	
Source	nyweb01	
Destination	jupiter.london.local	
Protocol	tcp	
Rule	4	
Source Port	2239	
User		
Information	reason: url is: jupiter.london.local/hackingtools/backorifice.exe NT 5.	
Policy Info	Policy Name: Standard	
	Created at: Tue Oct 15 01:11:46 2002	
	Installed from: nyfw01	

In Figure 5.11 you see that an HTTP connection was established from nyweb01 to jupiter.london.local, and that the URL accessed (indicated by the Information field) was http://jupiter.london.local/hackingtools/backorifice.exe. The NT 5 portion at the end of the URL indicates that the client accessing the URL was a Windows 2000 client.

Detecting Anti-spoofing

Anti-spoofing tracking can be enabled on a per-interface basis within the topology screen of the enforcement module. The default setting is to generate log events, however a tracking option of none or alert is configurable. If anti-spoofing events are detected and anti-spoofing tracking is enabled, you should see the appropriate log or alert entry in the event viewer. If you inspect the Info. field of these entries, you should see a value of "message_info address spoofing;"

Active Mode

The *Active mode* view (also referred to as the *Active Connections Log*) displays information contained within the fw.vlog file. This mode shows all current connections that are being permitted through the enforcement modules managed by the SmartCenter Server. When a new connection is established through an enforcement module, log records are sent to the

SmartCenter Server with information about the new connection, and a new log entry is written to the `fw.vlog` file. This connection is displayed in the Active mode view, and remains until the connection between two devices is torn down or times out after a configurable period of inactivity. Once a connection is torn down, the enforcement module sends a log record to the SmartCenter Server with the LUUID of the original log record sent for the connection. The SmartCenter Server uses the LUUID to identify the connection log record in the `fw.vlog` database and removes it. The log entry in the Active mode view disappears as well, ensuring only current connections are accurately displayed at any time.

If you have security rules that do not specify a Track action, even though connections that match the rule are not logged in the `fw.log` database (Log mode view) while a connection is established, it will be registered in the `fw.vlog` database and shown in the Active mode view.

To access Active mode, click on the Active tab just underneath the top toolbar in SmartView Tracker (see Figure 5.3). Figure 5.12 shows an example of the Active mode view.

FIGURE 5.12 Active mode view

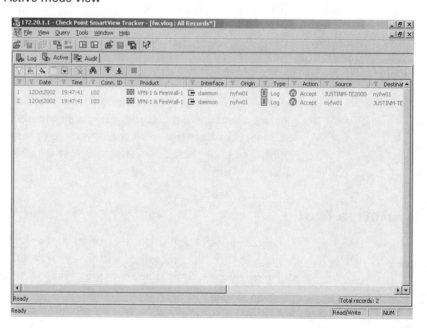

In Figure 5.12, notice that a new field called Conn. ID is specific to the Active mode view. You can't see all fields due to the size limitations of the Smart-View Tracker windows—the fields not shown in Figure 5.12 are the Service, Source Port, Elapsed, Bytes and Information field. Every connection displayed has a unique connection ID, even if the SmartCenter Server and enforcement modules have been rebooted. As new connections are displayed and as closed connections disappear, the log entry representing a current connection may change the No. field, depending on where the log entry is displayed in the log file. The connection ID ensures you can keep track of a particular connection while the SmartView Tracker Active mode display dynamically changes.

Because the Active mode view only shows connections, the fields shown are based on connection-based parameters. For example, the Interface field indicates the direction and interface through which a connection is based, while the Service and S_Port fields indicate the destination (server-side) and source (client-side) ports respectively. In Figure 5.12, notice that the value of all log entries for the Inter. field is daemon. This value is used when a connection originates from or terminates on an enforcement module (i.e., the enforcement module is the source or destination of a connection). In Figure 5.12, all connections specify either a Source or Destination of nyfw01, which is an enforcement module.

Audit Mode

Audit mode view (also referred to as the *Administrative Log*) displays information contained within the `fw.adtlog` file. This mode shows all administrative events related to configuring and managing the Check Point SmartCenter Server. Examples of these events include when an administrator logs in to (successfully or not) or logs out of the SmartCenter Server and any security policy changes (such as a security object modification or adding a security rule). To access the Audit mode view, click on the Audit tab located just below the top toolbar in SmartView Tracker. Figure 5.13 shows an example of Audit mode displayed in SmartView Tracker.

In Figure 5.13, you can see that in the title bar the actual database file you are viewing is listed—`fw.adtlog`. You can also see all the different fields in Figure 5.13 that make up Audit log events. Notice that some of these fields are also present in the Log mode view (compare with Figure 5.3), while other fields are new, specific to the Audit mode view. Table 5.4 describes the columns that are specific to Audit mode view.

FIGURE 5.13 Audit mode view

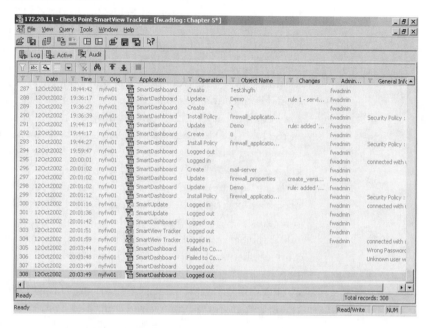

TABLE 5.4 Audit Mode Columns

Column	Description
Application	Describes the Check Point SMART client from which the audit event was generated. For example, in Figure 5.13, you can see events that have been generated by Smart-Dashboard, SmartUpdate, and SmartView Tracker
Operation	Describes the administrative operation that was performed. For example, in Figure 5.13, you can see that the operation associated with entry #290 is "Install Policy," which means that policy was installed to an enforcement module.
Object Name	Describes the object on which the administrative operation described by the Operation column is performed. For example, in Figure 5.13, you can see that for entry #296, the operation is Create and the object name is mail-server, which means a security object called mail-server was created.

TABLE 5.4 Audit Mode Columns *(continued)*

Column	Description
Changes	Describes any changes (if applicable) made to the object described by the Object Name column. For example in Figure 5.13, the Changes column of entry #291 indicates a rule was added to a security policy called Demo (as indicated by the Object Name column).
Administrator	Describes the VPN-1/FireWall-1 administrator that performed the operation. In Figure 5.13, this column is shown as "Admin…" and you can see that the administrator "fwadmin" has been responsible for most of the audit events
General Information	Lists any additional information associated with the event. For example in Figure 5.13, entry #305 shows a failed login attempt to SmartDashboard, with the General Information field indicating a wrong password was presented for an administrator.

If you wish to view all of the information for a specific entry, simply double-click the entry to open the Record Details dialog box. Figure 5.14 shows the Record Details dialog box that is displayed after double-clicking entry #298 in Figure 5.13.

FIGURE 5.14 The Record Details dialog box for an Audit Event

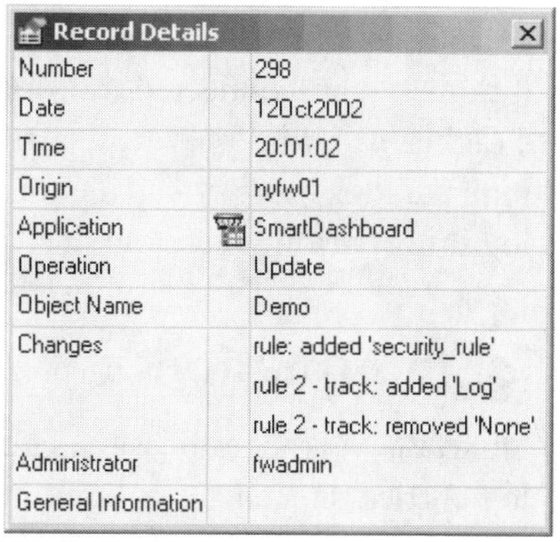

You can see in Figure 5.14 all of the information for entry #298. This entry describes an update to a security rule base called Demo from Smart-Dashboard. Notice in the Changes field that three changes are indicated. The first change ("rule: added 'security_rule'") indicates that a security rule has been added. The second change ("rule 2 – track: added 'Log'") indicates that an action of Log was added to the Track element of rule #2 and the final change ("rule 2 – track: removed 'None'") indicates that that the action of None was removed from the Track element of Rule 2.

Audit log entries are not generated until you save your changes. For example, if you delete a security rule, the log entry is not generated until the security rule base is saved or installed (which implicitly saves the rule base).

Manipulating Information Using SmartView Tracker

The default SmartView Tracker display may contain a lot of useless information, which can distract from security events that are important. This is certainly an issue if you are responsible for the daily analysis of log data-bases for unusual or suspect events. You might also wish to use SmartView Tracker to find security events related to a specific event that occurred over an approximate time frame, related to specific source, destination, and/or service parameters of a connection. For example, your organization's web server may have been breached during a certain time frame—you want to establish who connected the web server during the time frame. SmartView Tracker provides powerful search and filtering tools that enable you to manage logs more effectively on a day-to-day basis, as well as find specific log information when you need it.

Searching for Information

SmartView Tracker possesses a search utility that allows you to search for log entries on a single-column or all-column basis. For example, you might want to search for a log entry that includes a particular source object—you can search the Source column for the object. You might also want to find any object in the entire log database that starts with a particular pattern of characters. You can search all columns and specify a string pattern to search for.

Searching for Log Entries by Column

To search for log entries based on information contained within a single column, right-click in the column that you wish to search and select Find from the menu that is displayed. The Find by *<column>* dialog box will be displayed, with *<column>* replaced by name of the column that you are searching. For example, if you are searching within the Destination column, the Find by Destination dialog box is displayed. Assuming you are searching within the Destination column, Figure 5.15 shows the Find by Destination dialog box.

FIGURE 5.15 The Find by Destination dialog box

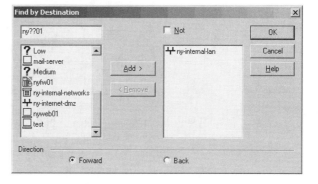

In Figure 5.15, notice that you can search for security objects, as well as specify a search string for wildcard searches. In Figure 5.15, the object ny-internal-lan will be searched for, and a pattern of ny??01 is being configured, with the ? wildcard character specified to match any single character. If you search for more than one object or search string, a match is found if any one of the search criteria is matched.

You can also use the * wildcard character, which matches any combination of one or more characters. For example, the regular expression *abc would match a value of aabc, ababc, or ab1abc, while the expression ?abc would match aabc but not ababc or ab1abc.

The Direction options allow you to select the direction in which you should search from. The Forward option specifies a search forward from the currently selected log entry in SmartView Tracker, while the Back option specifies a search backward from the currently selected log entry. The Not option negates all of the search criteria configured. For example, if Not is checked in Figure 5.15, all objects except for `ny-internal-lan` would be searched for. Once you have specified the appropriate search criteria and direction, click OK to begin searching the log database. If a successful match is found, the entry is selected and displayed in SmartView Tracker.

Depending on the column that you are searching within, the Find by *<column>* dialog box contents may change. Figure 5.16 shows the Find by Time dialog box, which is displayed when searching within the Time column.

FIGURE 5.16 The Find by Time dialog box

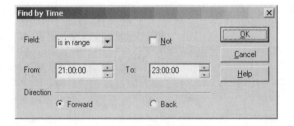

If you compare Figures 5.15 and 5.16, you can see that the search criteria options provided are customized to be relevant to the column that is being searched. In Figure 5.16, any log entry that has occurred within the time frame between 21:00 and 23:00 is being searched for.

If you wish to repeat a search using the same search criteria previously specified, you can press the F3 key, which searches for the next occurrence that matches the search criteria (i.e., Find Next).

Searching for Log Entries in All Columns

To search for log entries based on information contained within all columns, click the Find in All Columns button from the toolbar above the Records pane (see Figure 5.4). The Find in all columns dialog box is displayed, as shown in Figure 5.17.

FIGURE 5.17   The Find in all columns dialog box

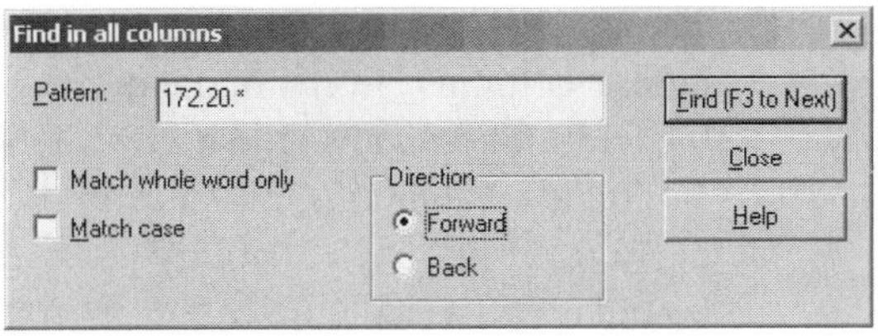

In Figure 5.17, IP addresses that belong to the 172.20.x.x networks (as indicated by the 172.20.* wildcard) are being searched for in all columns in the log file. Notice that for text-based searches, you can specify to match a whole word only or to match the case of the search string specified.

Filtering Information

You will often need to filter information to a specific subset to make analysis of log files easier. SmartView Tracker allows you to define *filters* for each column, which allow you to create a filter that shows only log entries that contain specific values in the field that the column represents. For example, you might want to only view log entries that relate to HTTP traffic—in this scenario you would define a filter on the Service column, which specifies only to include log entries whose Service field value is the HTTP service object. A filter is actually a parameter that belongs to a log query, which includes settings that define how information is displayed in the Records pane of SmartView Tracker. A log query includes information about the column order, visibility, width, and filters applied to each column in the Records pane. To understand the difference between a filter and a log query, consider the following example. A filter could be used to display all connections that relate to HTTP traffic, or could be used to display all connections that relate to HTTP traffic generated by a single source (this can be implemented by applying multiple filters to the appropriate columns). A log query can provide information based on both of filters listed above, but can also specify the width of columns and determine whether or not a column is displayed.

To define log queries, you can use one of following four methods:

- Create a log query using Columns.

- Create a log query using the Query Properties pane.

- Use Predefined log queries.

- Modify log query options.

Creating a Log Query Using Columns

The quickest way to generate your own custom view of log entries is to modify columns directly in the Records pane. You can hide columns, modify the width of columns, and apply filters to columns.

To hide a column, right-click in the column and select Hide from the menu that appears. To modify the width of a column, drag the left or right boundary of the column to the appropriate position. To filter information contained within a column, right-click on the column and select the Edit Filter option from the menu that appears. Depending on the column that you filter, a *<column>* Filter dialog box will appear that allows you to filter objects and information specific to the type of information presented in the column. For example, if you choose to filter information contained within the Source column, the Source Filter dialog box will be displayed, which will allow you to filter based on objects in the VPN-1/FireWall-1 security objects database, as these objects are always used in the Source element of rules. Figure 5.18 shows the Source Filter dialog box for the Source column.

FIGURE 5.18 The Source Filter dialog box

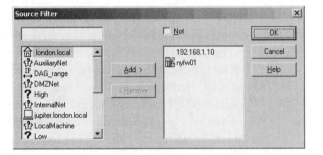

In Figure 5.18, notice that on the left side shows a list of all objects currently present in the security objects database of the SmartCenter Server. In Figure 5.18, the administrator is searching for all entries that specify a source of 192.168.1.10, which is an IP address not associated with any network object and therefore must be manually specified, or a source of the nyfw01 object. To add objects or values to the selection criteria, click the Add button, which then places them in the right side of the dialog box, which is a list of the criteria on which the filter will be based. You can add multiple objects or values as required.

Once you have specified the objects and values that you wish to use for selection criteria, you must choose whether you wish to view only the selection criteria, or if you wish to view everything but the selection criteria. This choice is determined by the Not checkbox, which is located in the top-center of the dialog box in Figure 5.18. The default setting for this is unchecked, which means that only log entries that include the objects or values specified in the selection criteria box (the right list) will displayed after the selection is defined. If you wish to view log entries that do not include the objects or values specified in the selection criteria box, you must check the Not check box. Once you have completed configuration of your selection, click Apply. Figure 5.19 shows the SmartView Tracker output after the selection defined in Figure 5.18 has been applied to the Source column.

FIGURE 5.19   SmartView Tracker after a selection has been applied

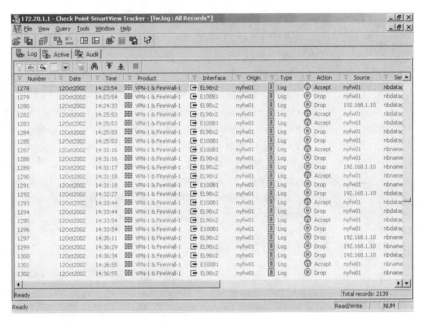

Take a close look at the Source field in Figure 5.19. Notice that all log entries include a source field value of 192.168.1.10 or nyfw01, reflecting the selection configured in Figure 5.18. The filter icon next to Source field header is now colored green (you won't be able to see this on the book page, only onscreen)—green means that a filter is currently applied to the column.

You can define multiple filters as required to each column, with each filter in place decreasing the number of log entries in SmartView Tracker to only include entries that match the criteria for all filters configured.

To remove a filter from a column, right-click in the column and select Clear Filter from the menu that appears. To remove all filters applied, click the Clear All Filters button from the toolbar above the Records pane (see Figure 5.4). This will permanently remove all filters applied, and if you wish to re-apply the filter you must re-create each of your filters.

If you wish to temporarily remove all filters applied to columns, click the Apply Filters button from the toolbar above the Records pane, which will toggle this button to an off state and temporarily remove the filters. To re-apply the filters, simple click the Apply Filters button again, which will toggle the button on an on state and re-apply the filters.

Saving Log Queries

A log query represents the collective visibility, width, and filter parameters applied to each column in the current SmartView tracker mode. When you modify the position of a column, remove a column from the Record pane, resize a column, or apply a filter to a column, all of these settings can be saved as a custom log query, which can be opened at a later date to quickly view a subset of information relevant to your environment. Custom log queries that have been saved are managed via the Query Tree pane. To save your current view settings to a custom log query, select Query ➢ Save As from the SmartView Tracker menu, which displays the Save Query As dialog box as shown in Figure 5.20.

FIGURE 5.20 Saving a log query

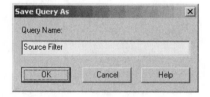

In Figure 5.20, the current settings are being saved as a log query called Source Filter. Once you have saved your log query, it is added to the Custom folder within the Query Tree pane. Figure 5.21 shows the Query Tree pane after the log query in Figure 5.20 has been saved.

FIGURE 5.21   Query Tree pane and custom log queries

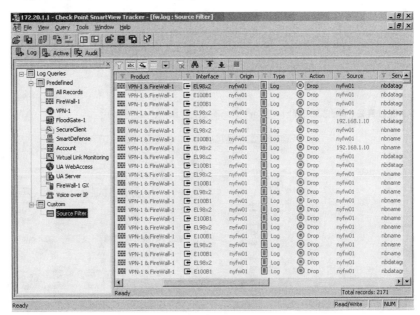

In Figure 5.21, notice that under the Custom folder in the Query Tree pane on the left, a log query called Source Filter is listed. To apply a custom log query to the Records pane, simply right-click on the appropriate log query in the Query Tree pane, and select Open from the menu that appears. You can also copy, rename, and delete log queries from this menu.

Because each mode in SmartView Tracker (i.e., Log mode, Active mode, and Audit mode) contains columns specific to each mode, custom log queries are only useable for the mode from which they were created.

Creating a Selection Using the Query Properties Pane

If you are creating views for SmartView Tracker that are complex and involve adjusting the visibility, width, order, and filters applied to multiple columns, a useful tool you can use is the Query Properties pane. The Query Properties pane lists each column, whether or not the column is visible, the width of the column, and any filters applied to the column. Because all of the settings that are applied to each column are available in a single view, this makes customization of complex views much easier. To display the Query Properties pane, select View ➤ Query Properties from the SmartView Tracker menu, or click the Show/Hide Query Properties button from the toolbar (see Figure 5.4). Figure 5.22 shows the Query Properties pane in the top right-hand corner, which allows you to define the visibility, width, and selection for each column.

FIGURE 5.22 The Query Properties Pane

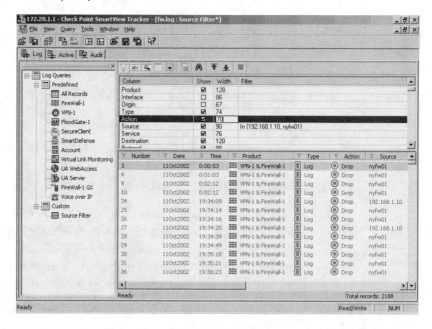

In Figure 5.22, notice that each column is listed, with the visibility settings (under the Show column), width settings, and filter settings for each column displayed. To specify that a column should be visible or hidden, simply check or uncheck the appropriate check box in the Show column of Figure 5.22. To modify the width of the column when it is displayed in SmartView Tracker, click in the Width column for the appropriate SmartView Tracker column and type in the desired width. Notice in Figure 5.22 that the Action column width is being modified to 70. To add a filter to a column, right-click on the appropriate column in the Query Properties pane (for example, the Source column) and select Edit Filter from the menu that appears. This will display the appropriate *<column>* Filter dialog box (see Figure 5.18), which allows you to define filter criteria for the column. Notice in Figure 5.22, selection criteria for the Source column has been defined to only include log entries that specify a source of 192.168.1.10 or nyfw01.

It is important to note that when you modify the Records pane display using the Query Properties pane (or by modifying columns directly as discussed in the previous section), you are modifying the current log query that is loaded. If you have started SmartView Tracker with the default log query (the All Records predefined log query), then you are modifying this log query. If you wish to save the modified log query, select Query ➢ Save or Query ➢ Save As from the SmartViewer menu. Remember that you cannot modify any predefined log queries, you must save a modified predefined log query to a new custom log query.

Using Predefined Log Queries

A predefined log query is a set of queries predefined by Check Point that display common views that you may use in SmartView Tracker. Refer to Table 5.3 for a description of predefined log queries included with SmartView Tracker. Predefined log queries ship with SmartView Tracker and cannot be modified, renamed, or deleted. You can modify or copy a predefined log query and then save it as a new log query. It is important to note that pre-defined log queries are only available for the Log mode view—no other log views (Audit and Active) have any predefined log queries available (in reality, they have a single predefined log query called All Records, but they have no other predefined log queries available). Predefined log queries can be loaded using Query Tree pane, by right-clicking on the appropriate predefined log query and selecting Open from the menu that appears. You can also use this menu to copy a predefined log query to a new custom query, which will inherit all of the predefined log query settings.

Modifying Other Log Query Options

There are some other log query options that affect how information is displayed in the Records pane, with these options also being saved within each log query that you define. Each of these options is configured using the toolbar that is above the Records pane (see Figure 5.4). The following lists each of the options that affect how information is displayed within the Records pane:

Apply Filter   Clicking this button toggles whether the filters configured for each column are applied. If you click the Apply Filter to remove all filters that are applied, you do not lose the configuration of those filters, meaning you can re-apply the filters by simply clicking the button once again.

Resolve IP Clicking this button toggles whether IP addresses in the Source and Destination columns should be resolved to security object names or host names (using DNS or a HOSTS file). Turning off the Resolve IP option can speed up the responsiveness SmartView Tracker, as name resolution does not need to take place.

Resolve Services Clicking this button toggles whether services in the Service and Source Port columns should be resolved to service object names.

Show Null Matches Clicking this button specifies whether log entries that do not have a value for a column that has a filter applied should be displayed. For example, control events (such as policy installation) have log entries that do not include an Action field. If you create a filter that only displays entries that have an Action field of accept, because the control events do not include an Action field, these events will be defined as null matches.

AutoScroll Clicking this button indicates that the Records pane display should be updated to display new log entries as they are generated. When this option is enabled, SmartView Tracker checks for new log entries every 5 seconds, and if it finds new log entries, automatically scrolls the Records pane to the bottom of the log file, ensuring the new log entries are displayed.

It is important to understand that each of the above options are configurable on a per-log query basis, meaning you can have one log query that resolves IP addresses and auto scrolls, and another log query that shows null matches and does not auto scroll.

EXERCISE 5.1

Using SmartView Tracker to View Security Events

The exercises in this chapter assume that you are working with the security topology that you have configured in Chapters 3 and 4. In this exercise, you will connect to the nyfw01 SmartCenter Server using SmartView Tracker and then you will generate security events and view the associated log entries in SmartView Tracker.

1. Start SmartView Tracker by selecting Start ➢ Programs ➢ Check Point SMART Clients ➢ SmartView Tracker NG. An authentication dialog box should appear. Enter the appropriate username and password, and specify a SmartCenter (management) server of **nyfw01**.

2. The SmartView Tracker application will now be started, with the Log mode view displayed. Security log entries should be displayed starting from the beginning of the log file. To view the most recent log entries, click on the Go To Bottom button on the toolbar above the Records pane.

3. Ensure that the Query Tree pane is displayed and change the current log query from the All Records predefined query to the FireWall-1 predefined query, by right-clicking the FireWall-1 predefined query from the Query Tree pane and selecting Open from the menu that appears. This will alter the current view, displaying log entries specific to FireWall-1 security events, with additional information displayed for each log entry.

4. From the jupiter.london.local host, establish an HTTP connection to nyweb01 (192.168.10.2). In SmartView Tracker, you should see a new log entry representing the new connection.

5. Select Window ➢ SmartDashboard from the SmartView Tracker menu, which will start SmartDashboard. For Rule 4 (permits ny-internal-lan to use web-services to any destination), remove the work-hours object from the Time element, and then install the new updated policy to nyfw01. This is to ensure that you aren't restricted to testing Rule 4 just inside working hours.

6. You will now establish a connection that matches Rule 4, but will include a tracking action of Account. Before you do this, open the Account predefined query from the Query Tree pane.

7. Ensure the Query Properties pane is open by selecting View ➢ Query Properties from the main menu. Using the Query Properties pane, hide the Date, Product, Interface, Origin, Protocol. Source Port, User, XlateSrc, XlateDst, XlateSPort, XlateDPort, and Information columns. Reduce the sizes of each column so that you can fit all the

remaining columns in the SmartView Tracker window. Once complete, choose Query ➢ Save As from the SmartView Tracker menu and save the custom log query as **Custom Accounting**. Doing this will allow you to load the current view in the future, without having to re-hide and readjust each column.

8. From the nyweb01 host, establish an HTTP connection to jupiter.london.local (172.20.1.2). If you can, download a large file. After download is complete, you should see a new log entry representing the new connection.

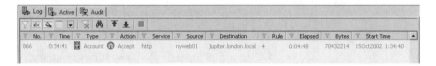

Notice that you can see that connection was established at 1:34:20 on the 15th October 2002 (as indicated by the Start Time column) and lasted for 4 minutes and 48 seconds (as indicated by the Elapsed column). You can also see that 70,432,214 bytes were exchanged during the connection (as indicated by the Bytes column).

9. Switch to Audit mode view by clicking the Audit tab located below the top toolbar in SmartView Tracker. Audit log entries should be displayed starting from the beginning of the log file. To view the most recent log entries, click on the Go To Bottom button in the toolbar above the Records pane. The three most recent entries should be related to the tasks you completed in Step 5, where you modified security Rule 4 (entry #83) and then installed the policy (entry #85—the intermediate entry #84 represents the creation of version 4 of the policy using the database revision control feature).

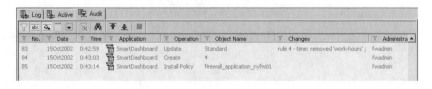

Log File Management

Log files can grow at an extremely rapid rate, particularly during busy periods or when your network is subject to attack. As a log file grows in size, the time it takes to both read and write from the log file increases. Over time, if you don't do something about the size of your log files, you will find that SmartView Tracker response will slow down, and the efficiency of your management tasks will be reduced.

You can reduce the size of log files by implementing "noisy" security rules that drop and do not produce log entries for traffic that is frequently transmitted on the network, but is of no use to capture in the log files. Examples of this traffic include DHCP traffic (generated when workstations connect to the network) and NetBIOS broadcast traffic (sent periodically by Microsoft Windows machines).

SmartView Tracker allows you to manage log files, with the ability to switch the current log file and create a new log file, as well as the ability to save the current log entries in a separate file and export the current log entries to an ASCII format.

The following log file management features are now examined:

- Enforcement module logging
- Log file location
- Log switching
- Saving log files
- Exporting log files
- Purging log files

Enforcement Module Logging

VPN-1/FireWall-1 NG has many enhancements over previous versions related to the way in which enforcement modules log security events. The Check Point objects representing both SmartCenter Servers and enforcement module now include a new screen called Logs and Masters, which allows you to control local logging, log file maintenance, and schedule the transfer of log files to the SmartCenter Server. Figure 5.23 demonstrates the Logs and Masters screen for a Check Point gateway object that represents an enforcement module.

FIGURE 5.23 The Logs and Masters screen for a Check Point Gateway object

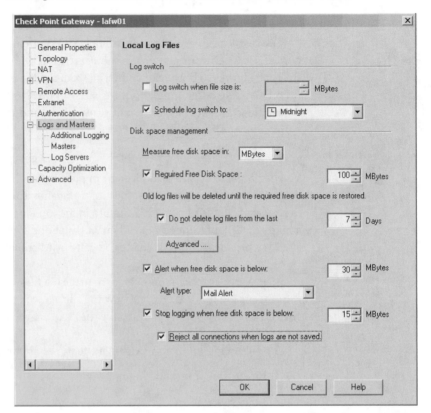

In Figure 5.23, notice that you can configure many useful log file management features. The log file is configured to be switched every night at midnight. To attempt to manage free disk space, the enforcement module is configured to attempt to free up disk space if free disk space falls below 100MB, by deleting old entries from the log file. To ensure recent entries are not deleted by this mechanism, only entries that are older than 7 days can be deleted. Notice that if free disk space falls below 30MB, a mail alert is configured, which would typically notify an administrator via SMTP mail. Logging will stop if free disk space falls below 15 MB, and the enforcement module is configured to reject all connections if logs are not saved (due to lack of disk space).

By default, none of the options shown in Figure 5.23 are applied to an enforcement module.

Notice in Figure 5.23 that under the Logs and Masters screen in the left window, the Additional Logging, Masters, and Log Servers screens also exist. The Masters and Log Servers screens are only available for enforcement module objects (a SmartCenter Server object only has the main Logs and Masters screen as well as the Additional Logging screen) and allows you to configure how an enforcement module is managed in a distributed environment, where the SmartCenter Server is separated from one or more enforcement modules. Figure 5.24 shows the Additional Logging screen:

FIGURE 5.24   The Additional Logging screen

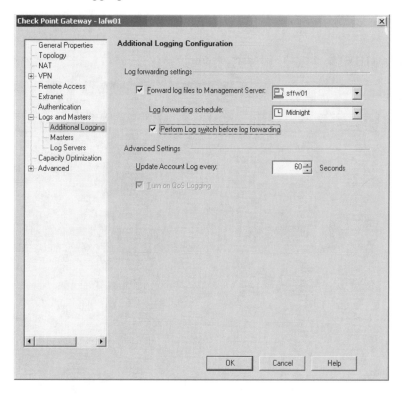

In Figure 5.24, the Forward log files to Management Server setting is only used when the enforcement module uses a local log file. This happens if the enforcement module is configured to log locally in the Log Servers screen (see Figure 5.26) or if the enforcement module cannot contact the log servers configured on the Log Servers screen. If local logging is enabled, the enforcement module will log to a local file, and will then forward this local file to the

SmartCenter Server specified in Figure 5.24 (`sffw01`), using the schedule defined under the Log forwarding schedule.

VPN-1/FireWall-1 NG includes a feature that enables SmartCenter Servers to collect Syslog messages from other devices. This enables the collection of security logging information from not just Check Point hosts, but also from other devices in the network that support Syslog, such as Unix hosts, routers, switches, and other network devices. You must enable this feature in the Additional Logging screen of your SmartCenter Server(s).

Figure 5.25 shows the Masters screen:

FIGURE 5.25   The Masters screen

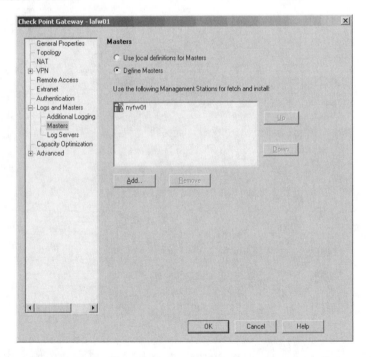

In Figure 5.25, you can configure how the enforcement module determines which SmartCenter Server should install and fetch security policy to and from the enforcement module. The SmartCenter Server that manages an enforcement module is also known as a *master*. The default and recommended selection is to choose the Define Masters option, which allows you to control who the masters are for the enforcement module from your security policy

database. In previous versions of VPN-1/FireWall-1, a local file called
`$FWDIR/conf/masters` was required on each enforcement module, which
simply contained a list of the SmartCenter Servers considered masters. By
choosing the Use local definitions for Masters option, you must create a
`masters` file on the enforcement module.

If it appears that all of your remote enforcement modules are not logging
to your SmartCenter Server, it is possible that a `masters` file containing the
SmartCenter Servers own IP address has been created on the SmartCenter
Server, which causes logging to fail. To fix this problem, remove the `masters`
file (located in `$FWDIR/conf`) from the SmartCenter Server.

Figure 5.26 shows the Log Servers screen, which allows you to configure
to whom the enforcement module should send logs.

FIGURE 5.26   The Log Servers screen for an enforcement module workstation object

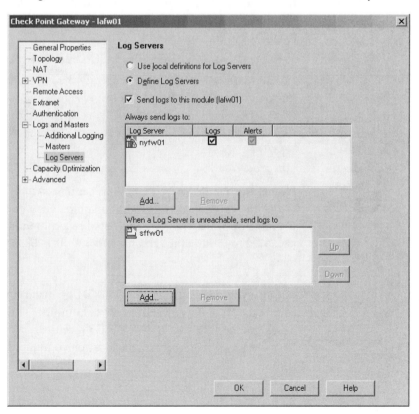

In Figure 5.26, the default and recommended selection is to choose the Define Log Servers option, which allows you to control the log servers for the enforcement module within the security policy database. Notice that you can configure the enforcement module to store log files locally (this option is not enabled by default). Also notice that sffw01 is configured as the destination to send logs if nyfw01 is unreachable. This parameter is similar to that configured on the Additional Logging screen, except that logging will be in real time (not scheduled, as you can define in the Additional Logging screen).

Log File Location

It is important that you understand where log files are stored by default and how you can modify this location. You have already learned that by default, all log files are stored in the $FWDIR\log directory on the SmartCenter Server. You may wish to modify this location, for example, storing log files on a separate partition or hard disk that has more disk space. On a Windows-based SmartCenter Server, you must create a string value called FWLOGDIR in the following Registry key:

HKEY_LOCAL_MACHINE\SOFTWARE\CheckPoint\FW1\5.0\

The value of FWLOGDIR must specify the full path that you wish to place the log files and must be a local drive. Figure 5.27 shows a newly created FWLOGDIR string value in REGEDT32 (a utility used to configure the Windows registry), which points the log files to the C:\Temp folder.

WARNING

Modify the Windows Registry with caution. Accidental misconfiguration or deletion of registry information could cause your system to become unstable or unusable. Microsoft also recommends that you only use REGEDT32 to modify the registry and not the REGEDIT tool that is commonly used.

Once you have created the FWLOGDIR entry in the registry, you must restart the VPN-1/FireWall-1 services running on the SmartCenter Server, using fwstop followed by fwstart. Once the SmartCenter Server services have been restarted, the new file location configured will be used for log file storage.

FIGURE 5.27   Changing the log file location on Windows

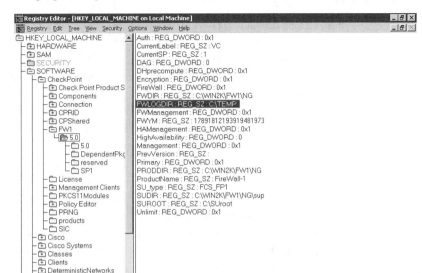

On a Unix-based SmartCenter Server, which has no concept of a registry, you can symbolically link the $FWDIR/log directory to another location. This means that $FWDIR/log still exists as a valid directory in the file system, but physically resides on a separate file system, with a symbolic link pointing to this location. The following shows the commands required on a Unix-based SmartCenter Server to change the log file location:

```
fwstop
mv $FWDIR/log $FWDIR/log.backup
ln -s /tmp/newlog/ $FWDIR/log
fwstart
```

In the example shown, you must first stop the VPN-1/FireWall-1 services. You then back up the current log file directory and then create a symbolic link using the ln command. In the example, the log files are physically stored in the /tmp/newlog location.

On both Windows and Unix SmartCenter Servers, once you have changed the log file location and specified a new one, the existing log files are closed and a new set of log files created in the new location.

Log Switching

Check Point VPN-1/FireWall-1 allows you to rotate your log files (known as log switching), meaning that you can close an existing, large log file and replace it with a new, empty log file. This process does not affect the ongoing operation of your SmartCenter Server or enforcement modules, ensuring log records are not lost during the log switch. To perform a log switch, select the File ➢ Switch Active File item from the SmartView Tracker menu, or click the Switch Log File button in the top toolbar (see Figure 5.4). When you perform a log switch, the current log file (e.g., fw.log) is closed and saved as a new file, with a filename that you can manually configure or a filename that is automatically generated and includes the current date and timestamp to ensure you know when the log file was switched. An example of a log file that has been log switched is 2002-10-11_005858_1.log. This filename indicates that the log switch was performed on October 11, 2002, at 00:58:53. A new log file is then created (e.g., fw.log), and fwd on the SmartCenter Server writes new log entries to this file. It is recommended that you configure automatic log switching, using the Logs and Masters screen (see Figure 5.24) on the Check Point Gateway objects representing your enforcement modules.

You can open previous log files that have been switched by selecting File ➢ Open or File ➢ Open in New Window from the SmartView Tracker menu.

The log file that you switch depends on the mode you are currently using in SmartView Tracker. For example, if you are in Log mode, you will switch the fw.log file. If you are in audit mode, you will switch the fw.adtlog file. You cannot log switch, save, or export the Active mode log file (fw.vlog).

You can use the fw logswitch CLI utility to perform log switching. This utility is used when you configure automatic log file switching on the Logs and Masters screen of a SmartCenter Server or enforcement module object.

Saving Log Entries

SmartView Tracker also allows you to save the current set of entries displayed in SmartView Tracker to a separate file. This is useful if you apply a selection to SmartView Tracker and wish to save the filtered log entries to a separate file, without affecting the current log files used for storing new log entries. To save the current set of log entries, select File ➢ Save As. You will be prompted for a location and filename where you wish to save the log file. You can also open any saved or rotated log file (any file that has a valid Check Point log database format) in SmartView Tracker, meaning that you are actually looking at historical data rather than real-time data. To open a log file, select File ➢ Open from the SmartView Tracker menu—you will be presented with a dialog box that asks to choose the log file to open, and also allows you to indicate whether all log entries or a specific range of log entries should be displayed. You can only have one log file per log mode open in SmartView Tracker at a time, unless you select File ➢ Open in New Window, which opens the log file in a new SmartView Tracker window. If you open an historical log file and wish to return to the current log file, select File ➢ Open and choose the `fw.log` file.

Exporting Log Entries

The Check Point log database files are saved in a format that cannot be easily understood by generic ASCII-based applications such as a text editor. You may wish to convert Check Point log files to a format that is suitable for export into a third-party database, to enable you to manage log files via the database system your company uses. You can export the current log entries displayed in SmartView Tracker (whether they are part of a current log file or an historical log file) by using the File ➢ Export menu item. You will be prompted to specify a path and filename for the exported text file. Once you have specified the path, the export process takes place. Any log entries that are not displayed due to selections in place are not exported.

WARNING

Avoid exporting large log files, as this places additional load on the SmartCenter Server and can take a long time.

Once complete, the exported text file will contain each log entry in a space-delimited file, with quotations wrapping each log field. Figure 5.28 shows an example of an exported log file.

FIGURE 5.28 Exported log file

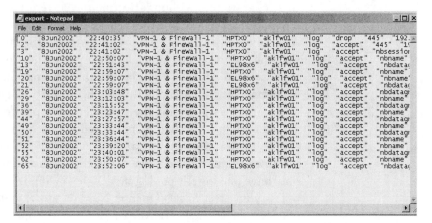

You can use the fw logexport CLI utility to export log files. This utility is much more flexible than using the log export functions provided by SmartView Tracker. For example you can specify your own choice of delimiter when using fw logexport, whilst using SmartView Tracker only exports to a space-delimited format.

Purging Log Entries

You can purge or delete all log entries from a log file. You can only use this feature to purge the current log file (e.g., fw.log)—you cannot purge historical log files. If you wish to purge historical log files, you must manually delete them via the file system interface of the SmartCenter Server.

To purge the current log file, select File ≻ Purge from the SmartView Tracker menu. If the current log file is not open, this option will be grayed out.

Purging log entries is generally not recommended, as it erases all record of security events that have occurred recently. You never know when you might need your security logs to track down unauthorized users who have gained access to your information systems.

Blocking Connections

Any effective security system must have the ability to block unauthorized access. You have learned to define security rules that enforce an organization's security policy, ensuring only authorized access is provided to the organization's information systems. Sometimes, unauthorized access can be masked as authorized access, fooling the security system. Machines are not perfect—they are only as good as the humans who create and configure them. Any good security policy document should define an intrusion response strategy, which is invoked in the event unauthorized access is gained to some or all of the information systems of the organization. A common intrusion response mechanism is to apply temporary blocking, where you temporarily block access from systems that you suspect are malicious in nature and have compromised your network. This section discusses how you can use the blocking feature of VPN-1/FireWall-1 NG.

Blocking Architecture

You normally implement blocking when you suspect that the integrity of the network has been breached by some unauthorized party. From a firewall security perspective, unauthorized access normally refers to an unauthorized connection that has (or is) established from a party outside the firewall to a party inside the firewall. You may have dedicated intrusion detection systems in place that detect intrusive activity and alert you to its presence. For example, let's say a hacker establishes an HTTP connection to a public web server that resides on a DMZ. The firewall permits the HTTP connection as this is the protocol used to communicate with the web server. The hacker is using a new vulnerability that has just been discovered with the web server operating system, which allows the hacker to gain system-level access by sending a particular sequence of traffic that causes a buffer overflow on the web server. An intrusion detection system monitoring network traffic on the DMZ segment is aware of the vulnerability, and detects the attack, alerting security administrators of the attack. At this point, you know of the attack and can respond according to the intrusion response procedures applicable for the situation. One way of thwarting the attack could be to unplug the web server from the network—effective but would also disrupt access to legitimate users. Another response might be to block access from the hacker system—if this response is used, you must have a suitable access control device that enforces the block. The obvious choice for blocking access from the hacker system is on the firewall through which the connection passes. Check Point VPN-1/FireWall-1 SmartView Tracker provides a powerful *blocking* feature that can be used to block access from attacking systems (or even block access to the target system).

It is important to note that you can only block access based on connections that are currently active. If you need to block access based on past connections, you must define security rules in the security policy that implement the required blocking. The blocking feature is only intended as a temporary measure until more permanent measures (such as creating a security rule) can be put in place.

Figure 5.29 shows an example of how you can use the blocking feature of VPN-1/FireWall-1.

In Figure 5.29 the following events occur:

1. An attacker (192.168.1.1) attempts to establish a connection to an internal web server. The firewall permits the connection as public access is permitted to the web server.

2. The attacker sends traffic that exploits a new vulnerability on the web server. The attacker gains system-level access to the web server.

3. An IDS application running locally on the web server detects the attack and issues an alert via some mechanism (such as e-mail or pager) to one or more security administrators.

4. A security administrator responds to the attack by establishing a SmartView Tracker connection to the SmartCenter Server. The administrator examines the active mode view and finds the connection that the attacker is currently using. The administrator blocks the source of the attack (192.168.1.1) indefinitely or for a configurable amount of time.

5. The SmartCenter Server instructs the enforcement module to block the attacker (192.168.1.1) for the amount of time specified by the administrator.

FIGURE 5.29 Blocking feature flowchart

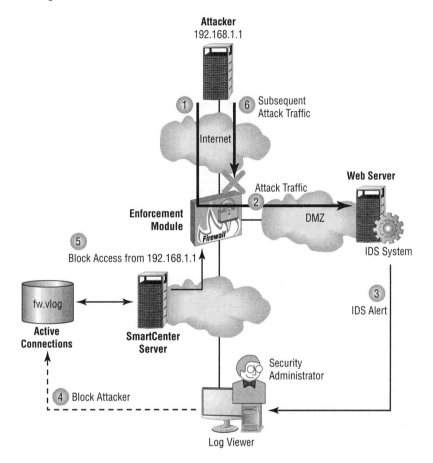

6. The attacker can no longer communicate with the web server—the attacker attempts to establish a new connection but fails, because all access from the 192.168.1.1 IP address has been blocked. The attacker is also blocked from gaining access to any other system while the block is in place.

The mechanism used by the SmartCenter Server to instruct the enforcement module to block the attacking system in Step 5 of Figure 5.29 is known as *suspicious activity monitoring (SAM)*. You use the `fw sam` command on an enforcement module to implement temporary blocking without modifying the security rule base, which is exactly how the SmartCenter Server instructs an enforcement module to implement blocking.

Real World Scenario

The *fw sam* Utility

You can use the fw sam utility in a script that is defined as the UserDefined tracking option in the security policy database. For example, you might specify the UserDefined tracking option for your stealth rule, which invokes a custom script that blocks access (using the fw sam command) for some configurable amount of time (e.g., 30 minutes) from any systems that try to establish a connection directly to an enforcement module. Use the power of the fw sam utility with caution—a wily hacker can spoof the IP address of attack attempts with the IP address of legitimate systems, tricking your enforcement module into blocking connections from these legitimate systems.

Using SmartView Tracker to Block an Intruder

The Check Point SmartView Tracker SMART client allows you to block current connections that are listed in the Active mode view (fw.vlog database).

You can only block connections if you are logged on as an account that has read-write access to the Monitoring component of the Check Point security policy. If you only possess read-only access to the monitoring component, you can view log files but you cannot manage them or block intruders.

If you identify a current connection that you believe is suspect and you wish to apply blocking, there are several parameters you must decide on before implementing blocking:

- Blocking scope
- Blocking timeout
- Where to apply blocking

First of all, you must determine what level of blocking you wish to apply, based on the systems associated with the connection. The level of blocking that you implement is referred to as the *blocking scope*. Check Point VPN-1/FireWall-1 allows you to block using one of the following three blocking scope options:

- Block only the connection (default)
- Block all access from the source of the connection
- Block all access to the destination of the connection

Most commonly you will block all access from the source of a connection, as this ensures that the rest of your network is protected from an attacking system. You might block all access to the destination of a connection if that connection has been established in an unauthorized fashion due to the prior compromise of a system—in this case the destination might be a system that the attacker owns or has access to. If you block only the connection, all subsequent traffic of the connection will be blocked, as well as any new connection attempts from the same source IP address to same destination IP address and port of the connection.

Once you have determined what you want to block (blocking scope), you must next decide for how long you wish the block to remain in force. The time during which a block is applied is known as the *blocking timeout*. You can set the blocking timeout to be indefinite, which means the block remains in place until the block is manually removed by a security administrator. Alternatively, you can apply a block for a configurable number of minutes—once the configured blocking timeout expires, the block is removed.

Finally, you must decide where you want to apply the block—you can either apply the block on the enforcement module through which the connection is currently active, or you can apply the block on all enforcement modules controlled by the SmartCenter Server. The latter is useful if you have multiple enforcement modules that secure multiple Internet access points—by applying the block at each enforcement module, the attacker cannot use another Internet connection to gain access to the target system.

Applying a Block

To use the blocking feature, you must use SmartView Tracker in Active mode view. To display Active mode view, select the Active tab located underneath the top toolbar in SmartView Tracker. Active mode will display all connections currently active through each enforcement module managed by the SmartCenter Server. You must determine which connection you wish to block. Once you have determined the connection you wish to block, select the connection in the Records pane and then select Tools ➢ Block Intruder from the SmartView Tracker menu. This will display the Block Intruder dialog box, as shown in Figure 5.30.

FIGURE 5.30 The Block Intruder dialog box

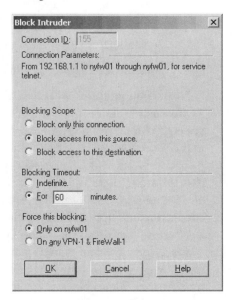

Notice in Figure 5.30 that the connection parameters are read to determine the source (192.168.1.1), destination (nyfw01), the enforcement module through which the connection is established (nyfw01), and service (telnet) associated with the connection. These parameters are used to determine what systems and services should be blocked. The *Blocking Scope* section allows you to choose whether you wish to only block the connection (and any subsequent connections from the source IP address to the destination IP address and service port), block all access from the source IP address, or block all access to the destination IP address. In Figure 5.30, all access from the source of the connection is to be blocked.

The default blocking scope is to block only the connection.

The *Blocking Timeout* section allows you to either apply the block indefinitely (the default) or for a configurable number of minutes. In Figure 5.30, the blocking timeout is configured as 60 minutes. Finally, the *Force this blocking* section allows you to configure which enforcement modules the blocking is applied to—in Figure 5.30 the non-default setting of On any VPN-1 & FireWall-1 enforcement module is selected. Once you have configured the parameters that you wish to apply for blocking, click OK to apply the block. If the block request was successful, a prompt will be displayed that confirms the request was successful.

Once the block is in place, all access defined by the blocking scope (see Figure 5.30) is blocked until the blocking timeout expires. In Figure 5.30, all access was blocked from the source (192.168.1.1) of the connection used for blocking. If any subsequent connection attempts are received from this system, the connection attempt will be blocked and a log entry will be generated in the main security log database (fw.log). Figure 5.31 shows the Log mode view of SmartView Tracker (which accesses the fw.log database) and the log entries generated by subsequent connection requests from the blocked system.

FIGURE 5.31 Log entries for connection requests from a blocked system

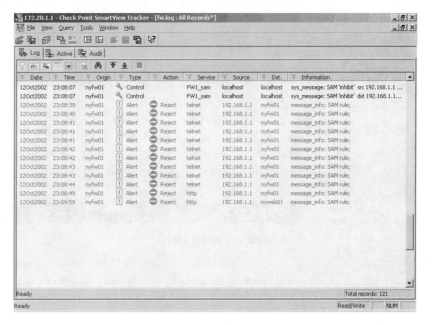

In Figure 5.31, notice that the first two entries are control entries (as specified in the Type field), with the Information field indicating that a SAM 'inhibit' (block) has been applied for the host 192.168.1.1 (both as a source and/or destination host) for 3600 seconds (60 minutes). After these entries, notice numerous log entries that specify an Action of reject and a source of 192.168.1.1 (the blocked system), in line with the block that has been applied. In the Information field for each of these reject log entries, a reason for the rejected connection is indicated by the text "message_info: SAM rule". This means that the connection was rejected due to a SAM rule in place—SAM rules are used to temporarily block access without manipulating the security rule base.

Removing a Block

As discussed in the previous section, you can apply a block indefinitely or for a configurable amount of time. If you wish to remove or clear a block (you must do so for indefinite blocks and you might wish to remove a timed block prematurely), you can do so from SmartView Tracker. Just as for when you apply a block, you must be in Active mode view to clear a block. Once you are in Active mode, select Tools ➤ Clear Blocking from the Smart-View Tracker menu. A warning will be displayed next, which informs you that all blocks that are currently applied will be removed. Click Yes to continue or No to cancel.

You cannot clear specific blocks and leave other blocks in place—if you wish to clear a specific block, you must remove all blocks.

Once you have cleared all blocks, a confirmation will be displayed indicated that all blocks were successfully cleared. Click OK to acknowledge the message. At this point, no blocks are in place and only your security rule base determines access through enforcement modules.

EXERCISE 5.2

Blocking Intruders

In this exercise, you will use SmartView Tracker to identify a connection that is currently active and you believe is unauthorized. You will block the source of the connection to protect your network and will verify that further connection attempts from the intruder are rejected.

1. Ensure that SmartView Tracker is started. To block an intruder, you must do so from an active connection. Switch to Active mode view by selecting the Active tab. Reduce the clutter of the view by hiding the Product, Interface, and Source Port columns and ensuring only the Records pane is displayed.

2. From the jupiter.london.local host, establish an HTTP connection to nyweb01 (192.168.10.2). In SmartView Tracker, you should see a new connection entry representing the new connection.

EXERCISE 5.2 *(continued)*

3. In the example, notice that the connection is represented as entry #4 can connection ID #15. To block the intruder system associated with the connection, select the connection and then select Tools ➢ Block Intruder from the SmartView Tracker menu. This will display the Block Intruder screen. In the Blocking Scope section, select the Block access from this source option, configure a blocking timeout period of 30 minutes and ensure the block is enforced on any VPN-1/FireWall-1 module. Click OK to apply the block.

4. Switch to Log mode view in SmartView Tracker by selecting the Log tab. Ensure that you are viewing the most recent log entries by clicking the Go To Bottom button on the toolbar above the Records pane.

5. From the jupiter.london.local host, attempt to establish another HTTP connection to nyweb01 (192.168.10.2). The connection should not succeed, as blocking has been applied. In SmartView Tracker, you should see a new log entry that indicates the connection attempt was rejected, with the Information field indicating this was because of a temporary SAM (blocking) rule.

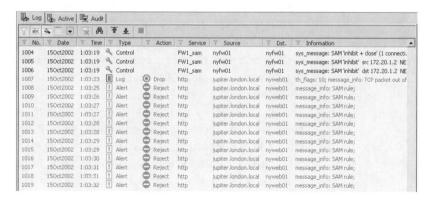

6. You will now remove the block applied in Step 3. Switch back to Active mode view and choose Tools ➢ Clear Blocking from the SmartView Tracker menu. You will be prompted to confirm that you wish to clear all blocks that are currently applied. Click Yes to clear all blocking.

7. From the jupiter.london.local host, attempt to establish another HTTP connection to nyweb01 (192.168.10.2). Because the block has been removed, you should be able to connect once again.

Summary

For a network security system to be effective, you must manage the security system on an ongoing basis. Good security is not just buying an expensive security product such as a firewall, configuring it, locking it in a cupboard, and then forgetting about it. Good security is a mix of using best-of-breed products and technologies, configuring those products and technologies using security best practices that meet your security requirements, and then monitoring the activity that is both permitted and denied through the security system. You can hardly justify the effectiveness of your security system without some ongoing proof provided by security and audit logs. One of the key strengths of the Check Point product is its integrated security logging and auditing feature. Just as the Check Point security policy is configured and stored centrally, and then distributed to multiple enforcement points, so to is the security and auditing log database. Check Point VPN-1/FireWall-1 also allows you to view all connections currently active through each enforcement module managed by a SmartCenter Server. This allows you to have a central view of the current state of the organization's network security, regardless of how distributed or complex the environment.

All log databases are stored on the SmartCenter Server, with each enforcement module generating and sending log records to the SmartCenter Server. Each enforcement module (kernel-side) attaches a Log Unique Unification ID (LUUID) to each log record that is generated by traffic. As new log records are received by the SmartCenter Server (server-side), the LUUID is used to ensure the log record can be associated with previous log records related to the connection that the traffic is part of. There are actually three log databases stored as separate files on the SmartCenter Server—fw.log (security logs), fw.adtlog (audit logs), and fw.vlog (active connection logs).

SmartView Tracker is the Check Point SMART client that is used to access the Check Point log databases on the SmartCenter Server. You must have at least read-only access to the monitoring component of Check Point. SmartView Tracker provides three modes, each of which displays log entries contained within each log database file. Log entries are generated in response to security events. A security event includes connections matching a security rule that has a tracking option, as well as control events such as policy installation. The Log mode (default) provides access to the security log database (fw.log). The Audit mode provides access to the audit log database (fw.adtlog), which is a new log database that is used to track administrative operations performed on Check Point products. The Active mode provides access to the active log database, which contains information about all of the active connections currently established through enforcement modules.

Each log entry contains fields, which provide information about the security event a log entry represents. Each field is represented by columns in SmartView Tracker—each mode in SmartView Tracker has different columns, some of which are unique to the nature of security events contained in the appropriate log database. SmartView Tracker allows you to customize each of these columns, including extra columns, hiding redundant columns, as well as modifying the width of columns. You can also apply a filter to a column, which enables you to filter log entries based on specific criteria related to the objects or values contained with a field. All of the various settings that control how information is displayed in SmartView Tracker are stored in log queries. SmartView Tracker includes predefined log queries, which are a preconfigured set of the above attributes designed to provide a function-specific or product-specific view of the security log database.

Another useful feature of SmartView Tracker is the ability to block active connections that you suspect are malicious in nature. Blocking uses the suspicious activity monitoring (SAM) feature of VPN-1/FireWall-1 to apply a temporary block without modifying the security rule base. You can block only a connection (and any subsequent connection requests that have identical parameters), block all access from the source of a connection, as well as block all access to the destination of a connection. To apply blocking, you must have read-write access to the monitoring component of VPN-1/FireWall-1. Blocking can only be applied to current connections that are displayed in the Active mode of SmartView Tracker. You can apply a block for a configurable number of minutes, or you can apply a block indefinitely, which remains in force until you explicitly remove the block. If you need to remove a block, you must remove all blocks—you cannot remove a specific block.

Exam Essentials

Understand the logging architecture of VPN-1/FireWall-1 NG. Only connections that match rules with a tracking option generate logs. As traffic is processed, kernel-side components such as the inspection module generate log fragments that are passed to the fwd daemon. The fwd daemon merges the fragments into a log record, attaches a LUUID, and forwards the log records to the fwd daemon running on the SmartCenter Server. The fwd daemon writes the records to the appropriate log database, with the unification engine updating SmartView Tracker, ensuring log entries associated with existing connections are updated rather than creating new log entries.

Know each of the log databases. The security log database (fw.log) contains security events such as rule matching events and control events. The audit log database (fw.adtlog) contains administrative events that track administrative operations performed on the security policy. The active log database (fw.vlog) contains a list of current connections active through each enforcement module managed by the SmartCenter Server.

Understand the permissions required for using SmartView Tracker. First of all, you must use SmartView Tracker from a system that has an IP address that is registered as a permitted GUI client via cpconfig. The account you use to connect must possess at least read-only access to the Monitoring component of VPN-1/FireWall-1. If you wish to possess the ability to block intruders, you must possess read-write access.

Understand how you can access each security log database. SmartView Tracker provides three modes that each provide access to a specific log database. The modes are Log (`fw.log`), Audit (`fw.adtlog`), and Active (`fw.vlog`).

Be able to work with SmartView Tracker to customize the information displayed. You can use predefined log queries (only in Log mode) to access common subsets of information such as FireWall-1 specific information or accounting information. You can use Query Properties pane to customize your view based on column visibility, width and selection criteria. You can also adjust the display of any column by right-clicking the column and choosing the appropriate configuration option.

Understand the fields contained within the various types of log entries. Make sure you have a good understanding of each of the fields unique to each log database. Also ensure you have a good understanding of common fields.

Understand how you can manage log files. Log switching provides the ability to seamlessly create a new log file and save the current log file to an historical file that is date and time stamped. This occurs without operation to the ongoing logging process. You can also save the currently displayed log entries to a log file for future analysis, as well as export the entries to an ASCII-based format for analysis using third-party tools. If you wish remove all entries from the current log file, you can use the purge feature.

Be able to block intruders. You can only block intruders from active mode—you must select a specific connection to block. To invoke blocking, use Tools ≻ Block Intruder.

Understand Blocking Scope and Blocking Timeout. Blocking Scope allows you to block the connection, all access from the source of a connection or all access to the destination of a connection. You can apply a block on only the enforcement module that the connection is active through, or on all enforcement modules. You can apply a block indefinitely or for a configurable amount of time.

Be able to remove a block. To remove a block, select Tools ≻ Clear Blocking in Active mode.

Key Terms

Before you take the exam, be certain you are familiar with the following terms:

Active Connections Log	Log Export API (LEA)
Active mode	log fragments
Administrative Log	Log mode
All Records log query	log modes
Audit mode	log query
blocking	log records
Blocking Scope	Log Unique Unification ID (LUUID)
blocking timeout	master
Check Point Log Manager	predefined log queries
custom queries	records pane
Event Logging API (ELA)	Server side
filters	SmartView Tracker
Force this blocking	suspicious activity monitoring (SAM)
kernel mode	Syslog
Kernel side	user mode
log entry	

Review Questions

1. Which of the following Check Point SMART clients is used to view security log information?

   A. SmartView Tracker

   B. SmartDashboard

   C. SecureUpdate

   D. SmartView Status

2. A log record can consist of multiple _____?

   A. Log entries

   B. Log events

   C. Log fragments

   D. LUUIDs

3. Where is the security log database located?

   A. Enforcement module

   B. Inspection module

   C. SMART client

   D. SmartCenter Server

4. Which of the following events could produce a log entry? (Choose all that apply.)

   A. Anti-spoofing violation with the tracking option set to None.

   B. Traffic matching an implied rule (assume the default implied rule configuration).

   C. Traffic matching an explicit rule that specifies a Track action of SnmpTrap.

   D. A policy being installed on an enforcement module.

5. You configure your security policy to log implied rules. What rule number is used in log entries for implied rules?

   A. 0

   B. 1

   C. 100

   D. 9999

6. Which of the following predefined selections can you apply to the Audit mode view? (Choose all that apply.)

   A. Account

   B. FireWall-1

   C. General

   D. VPN-1

7. Which of the following SmartView Tracker modes would you use to determine when a security object was created by an administrator?

   A. Account

   B. Active

   C. Audit

   D. Log

8. You are using SmartView Tracker and the title bar indicates that the current view is of the `fw.vlog` file. Which SmartView Tracker mode is currently displayed?

   A. Account

   B. Active

   C. Audit

   D. Log

9. The Proto. field represents which of the following?

   A. Application-layer protocol

   B. Data link layer protocol

   C. Session-layer protocol

   D. Transport-layer protocol

10. A firewall administrator creates a security rule. You are looking in the audit log database for the log event associated with the operation. Which of the following represents the correct value for the Operation field of the log entry?

   A. Create

   B. Delete

   C. Modify

   D. Update

11. An unauthorized administrative operation has been made on the security policy. Which of the following fields would be used to identify the system from which the operation was performed?

   A. Administrator

   B. Client

   C. Destination

   D. Source

12. Which of the following is used to uniquely identify log entries in active mode?

   A. Conn. ID

   B. No.

   C. Rule Number

   D. Origin

13. You wish to search for a log entry that includes a workstation named LEXICON or LEXICAN in either the Source or Destination fields. Which of the following searches should you use?

   A. Choose Edit ➤ Find and select both the source and destination fields to search in. Search for the pattern LEXIC*N.

   B. Choose Edit ➤ Find and select both the source and destination fields to search in. Search for the pattern LEXIC?N.

   C. Choose Edit ➤ Find and select the All Columns option. Search for the pattern LEXIC*N.

   D. Choose Edit ➤ Find and select the All Columns option. Search for the pattern LEXIC?N.

14. A selection in SmartView Tracker determines which of the following? (Choose all that apply.)

   A. Column height

   B. Column selection criterion

   C. Column visibility

   D. Column width

15. You wish to view all connections that were rejected during the lunch hour of the previous day. Which of the following columns must you apply a selection to? (Choose all that apply.)

   A. Action

   B. Date

   C. Time

   D. Type

16. You wish to quickly find out the column visibility, width, and selection settings for a predefined selection you have open in SmartView Tracker. How should you do this?

   A. Choose Selection ➤ Predefined Selection.

   B. Choose Selection ➤ Customize.

   C. Choose Edit ➤ Show Details.

   D. Choose Edit ➤ Show Selection.

17. Which SmartView Tracker mode must you use to block intruders?

    A. Account

    B. Active

    C. Audit

    D. Log

18. Which of the following lists valid blocking scope options? (Choose all that apply.)

    A. Block only a connection and subsequent connection requests using the same connection parameters.

    B. Block the destination of a connection.

    C. Block the source of a connection.

    D. Block the source network of a connection.

19. What Check Point feature is used to implement blocking?

    A. Implied Rules

    B. Explicit Rules

    C. Malicious Activity Detection (MAD)

    D. Suspicious Activity Monitoring (SAM)

20. You apply several blocks indefinitely and wish to remove the block from one connection only. What should you do?

    A. Select the connection and choose Tools ➤ Clear Blocking.

    B. Select the connection and choose Tools ➤ Block Intruder.

    C. Choose Tools ➤ Block Intruder.

    D. You must clear all blocks—you cannot clear only a single block.

Answers to Review Questions

1. A. SmartView Tracker is used for all security log management.

2. C. A log entry is generated by fwd from multiple log fragments generated by various components of the enforcement module.

3. D. The security log database is centrally held on the SmartCenter Server.

4. C, D. Option A will not generate a log entry because the tracking option is set to none. By default, implied rules are not logged, so Option B is incorrect. Any rule that specifies a Track action generates a log entry, and control events such as policy installation also generate log entries.

5. A. If logging of implied rules is enabled, a rule number of 0 is always used in the Rule field.

6. C. Both Audit mode and Active mode only have a single predefined selection called the General predefined selection.

7. C. Audit mode provides log entries that track administrative operations such as security policy and object configuration.

8. B. The Active mode view shows entries contained within the fw.vlog file.

9. D. The Proto. field indicates the transport-layer protocol (e.g. TCP, UDP, or ICMP). The Services field indicates the application-layer protocol.

10. D. Although the operation is to create a rule, this is described in the Audit log as an update of the security rule base.

11. B. The Client field lists the IP address or hostname of the system from which an administrator logs on to Check Point SMART clients.

12. A. Because the active log is dynamic, the Conn. ID field is used to assign a unique identifier for every connection (log entry) displayed in Active mode.

13. D. You can only search for information in a single column or all columns, hence you must search in all columns. The correct search pattern is LEXIC?N, as the ? character matches any single character, while * matches any one or multiple characters.

14. B, C, D. A selection describes the width, visibility, and selection criteria for each column.

15. A, B, C. The Action field determines whether a connection is accepted, dropped, or rejected. You filter entries during the lunch hour using a selection on the Time field, and to ensure only entries are shown from the previous day, you must use a selection on the Date field.

16. B. The Selection ➤ Customize menu item in SmartView Tracker opens a dialog box that allows you to view and customize the column visibility, width and selection settings for each column.

17. B. Only the systems associated with current connections can be blocked. All current connections are listed in active mode.

18. A, B, C. You cannot choose to block the network associated with the source of a connection.

19. D. The fw sam feature (SAM = suspicious activity monitoring) is used to implement blocking on enforcement modules without modifying the security rule base.

20. D. You cannot clear selective blocks—you must clear all blocks by using Tools ➤ Clear Blocking.

Chapter

6

User Authentication

THE CCSA EXAM OBJECTIVES COVERED IN THIS CHAPTER INCLUDE:

- ✓ Explain implementation for authentication.
- ✓ Describe creating users and user groups.
- ✓ Describe configuration for authentication parameters.

Authentication is a fundamental concept of security. The ability to identify a remote party is integral to the concepts of establishing identity and permitting access to information resources based on that identity. So far, you have seen how VPN-1/FireWall-1 identifies a remote party, based on the IP address of that party. Each object you have seen so far in the source and destination elements of VPN-1/FireWall-1 security rules has an IP address or represents a group of IP addresses. Although easy to implement and simple to understand, identifying a remote party based on IP address can be a flawed model, as an unauthorized party can easily masquerade as one of those IP addresses, and you have no control over who actually uses the device whose IP address you trust.

In this chapter, you will learn about the concepts of user-based authentication and how you can configure VPN-1/FireWall-1 with the necessary information to allow security policy to be configured not only on IP addresses (networks and hosts), but also on users. Authentication is also important for SecuRemote and SecureClient remote access VPNs, where VPN-1/FireWall-1 needs to be able to accurately identify remote users. You will also learn how you can create administrator objects within the VPN-1/FireWall-1 policy and control the level of access administrators have to VPN-1/FireWall-1 components. This chapter will focus on implementing authentication schemes, which define how a user is authenticated, and on configuring the VPN-1/FireWall-1 users database, which is a database that contains various user-related objects that are required for configuring authentication-based security rules, authenticating remote access VPN connections, and for enabling administrative access to VPN-1/FireWall-1 components.

The following topics will be presented in this chapter

- Authentication overview

- Authentication on VPN-1/FireWall-1 NG

- Enabling authentication on VPN-1/FireWall-1 NG

Authentication Overview

*A*uthentication is an integral concept that applies to all facets of security, not just computer and network security. For example, consider when you go to the bank to withdraw cash. When being served by the bank teller, you must present some form of identification that verifies you are the person that owns the account. This normally consists of your providing a signature, along with a legal document, such as a driver's license that also contains your signature and photo. The bank teller then compares the signature on the withdrawal slip with the signature you scrawled on the driver's license, as well as comparing you with your photo as an additional security measure. If the signatures are reasonably identical, the bank teller accepts that you are who you say you are and permits your request to withdraw money. In this scenario, you have essentially been authenticated, by virtue of the fact that your signature matches the signature of a legal document.

If you compare this to the authentication used for computer and network security, similarities can be drawn. For example, when you log on to a computer workstation, you must supply a username and password to gain access to both the workstation and other devices that are connected via the network. The username and password you supply are your *credentials*—equivalent to your bank account number, picture, and the signature that you sign in front of the teller in the bank example. After submitting your credentials, the computer (or another computer on the network) authenticates your credentials by comparing them with the credentials stored in an authentication database. It is important to note that in both examples, the authentication database must be trusted. If the authenticating party (i.e., the bank teller or the computer system to which you are logging on) trusts the authentication database, it therefore will trust any credentials provided by the authentication database. With the example of the driver's license, the bank knows that in order to obtain the driver's license with your photo and signature, you would have been subjected to rigorous identity checks to confirm that you are who you claim to be. If the credentials you supply match the credentials provided by the authentication database, you must be who you claim to be, because the authentication database is trusted.

If the authentication database is compromised, the whole concept of trusted authentication is broken. For example, if the driver's license is a very good fake, the fact that the bank teller trusts the driver's license can be exploited.

Other key security concepts related to authentication are *authorization* and *accounting*. Once a party has been successfully identified via authentication, it is important to next define exactly what that party can do. Authorization defines exactly what the permitted actions of an authenticated party are. For example, in the example of the bank, you might be only permitted to withdraw up to $5,000 in any single day. In the world of computer security, after logging into a computer system, you might be allowed to open applications such as Word or Excel, while being restricted from performing administrative functions such as creating new users or modifying passwords of existing users. In relation to network security and firewalls, authorization defines the networks, systems, and applications you are permitted to access after authentication.

Stepping back to the bank—so far you've established your identity and you have been advised you can only withdraw up to $5,000. Let's assume that you withdraw $5,000 and leave the bank. Next month, when you receive your bank statement, you will expect to see the withdrawal of $5,000. By providing you with a periodic record of account activity, the bank provides you with the necessary information to ensure that nobody else is accessing your account without your knowledge. This concept is known as accounting, and is important in computer and network security, as it provides a log of the actions an authenticated user performs. In relation to network security and firewalls, accounting allows you to track the networks, systems, and applications that are accessed by authenticated users.

It is important to understand that authorization and accounting are useless without first establishing identity via authentication. Authentication is a required component that must be completed before implementing authorization or accounting.

Authentication on VPN-1/FireWall-1 NG

Generally when you think about authentication, you think about users or groups. Users and groups are key entities in an organization—comprising the people that make up an organization and actually operate the systems. External users and groups also may play a part in an organization, as they may represent external customers, contractors, partners, or vendors. Many security policies are based on the functional groups within an organization (and the functional groups outside an organization—for example, marketing groups, sales groups, and engineering groups, which each represent individuals that play a different role within the same organization. Based on these security policies, the security devices in the network that enforce security must be able to identify not just networks, hosts, and services, but also users and groups.

So far in this book, you have examined how you can implement network security policy using security rules that define connections permitted for specific services between source and destination hosts/networks only, with no reference to users. If you actually think about it, security rules that specify hosts provide a form of authentication, albeit a less than obvious one. For example, let's assume a security policy exists that specifies a user called Alice, who works on a computer with an IP address of 192.168.1.1, is permitted to access a web server (10.1.1.1), but only for the purposes of browsing web pages. From the content you have learned so far in this book, there is only one way you can implement this policy on VPN-1/FireWall-1—create a rule that permits Alice's PC (source IP address of 192.168.1.1) to access only the web services (service of HTTP) running on the web server (destination IP address of 10.1.1.1). In this rule, authentication is performed based on the source IP address of the host. The firewall will only permit traffic matching this rule with a source IP address of 192.168.1.1, which essentially restricts access to Alice, as long as nobody else uses her machine. Authorization is also performed, as the authenticated host (192.168.1.1) is only permitted to access web services running on 10.1.1.1. If the rule specifies a tracking action such as log, accounting is also performed, as each connection made from the authenticated host to the authorized host and service will be logged in the security log.

If you are thinking that this is a particularly weak form of authentication, you are absolutely correct! One issue with the rule is that the parameter on which you are basing authentication (the source IP address of packets) can easily be faked or spoofed, which will trick the firewall into thinking spoofed packets are part of valid traffic being sent to the destination host. Another issue is that someone besides Alice might use Alice's PC, which will enable that user to gain unauthorized access to the web server, as the firewall has no way of identifying the user, only Alice's PC. By using security rules that specify hosts (IP addresses) as the source of each rule, you implement host-based authentication, whereas the security policy requires some form of user-based authentication. Consider what happens if Alice wants access from another machine—the IP address of the other machine must be added to the rule, introducing administrative overhead and increasing the chances of unauthorized access.

Clearly, when security policy is required that specifies permitted network services for users or groups, rather than the hosts that each user works on, it is desirable to be able to base your security rules on users and groups instead of hosts or networks. VPN-1/FireWall-1 NG allows for the creation of users and groups, which can be placed in the source element of rules, requiring enforcement modules to authenticate access to the objects in the destination and services element of the rule. It is important to understand that implementing user-based authentication for network access is much harder than just implementing rules that specify permitted source IP addresses. This is because IP (and transport protocols such as TCP and UDP) does not possess any user-based authentication features; hence, user-based authentication relies on either the authentication used in application-layer protocols, or by establishing some out-of-band authentication connection that can authenticate users and then enable access based on the Layer 3 (and in some cases Layer 4) parameters of IP traffic that emanates from the user. If you implement network access based on IP addressing, it is much easier to implement, as all IP traffic must have source and destination IP addressing. VPN-1/FireWall-1 implements user-based authentication in rules by supporting the authentication mechanisms used in common application-layer protocols (such as HTTP or TELNET) as well as supported out-of-band authentication connections, which can be applied for any type of network service. You will learn about how authentication works in rules in Chapter 7. In this chapter, the focus is on the process of actually performing authentication, whether it is performed in-band or via an out-of-band connection.

To successfully identify a remote party, you have seen that an authentication database is required. Many standards and protocols are available that provide authentication databases, and VPN-1/FireWall-1 supports many of them, as well as its own authentication database. In VPN-1/FireWall-1, an *authentication scheme* refers to the authentication database that is used and how VPN-1/FireWall-1 components communicate with authentication databases. VPN-1/FireWall-1 supports the use of different authentication schemes for different users, which makes it easy to support environments that have traditionally relied on many different authentication systems for different types of applications. When configuring authentication on VPN-1/FireWall-1, the first thing you must do is establish which authentication schemes you need to support and then configure support for them as required.

Once you have configured support for authentication schemes, you then need to define the actual users and groups that you expect to authenticate with VPN-1/FireWall-1. Just as VPN-1/FireWall-1 represents networks, systems, and services as objects, it also represents users and groups as objects. This allows user and group objects to be placed into security rules, just like a network or service object. Each user object you create represents a user, and you can configure which authentication scheme the user should use, as well as other parameters, such as the time of day the user can connect. After you configure user objects, you place them into group objects, which are a collection of user objects that share a common responsibility, or require similar levels of access. Group objects can then be placed in security rules, allowing for access to be granted based on users. You will now learn about authentication schemes and user objects, so that you possess a good understanding of these concepts before configuring VPN-1/FireWall-1 to support authentication. The following topics will be discussed:

- Understanding authentication schemes.
- Understanding user and group objects.

Understanding Authentication Schemes

Before discussing authentication schemes, it is important to understand that VPN-1/Firewall-1 stores all user-related objects it refers to in a *users database*, which is a database stored on the management server, managed via the Policy Editor management client, and distributed by the management server to each enforcement module. No matter how a user is authenticated, an object always exists in the users database, which defines how the user is to be authenticated and the specific VPN-1/FireWall-1 parameters that apply to the user. Authentication schemes relate to the specific issue of exactly how a user is to be authenticated. When you authenticate users, you must have a secure authentication database that you can use to ensure that the credentials presented by users are correct. The authentication database contains each trusted set of credentials—the credentials a user presents must match those stored in the authentication database. If the credentials presented by a user do not match those stored in the authentication database, the credentials are rejected and access is denied. VPN-1/FireWall-1 supports the concept of storing password information within the users database (effectively making the users database an authentication database), as well as the concept of supporting external authentication databases (at the same time if required). An authentication scheme essentially defines a particular type of authentication database, and also defines the protocols and communications that are required to interact with it. The following lists the authentication schemes supported by VPN-1/FireWall-1.

- VPN-1 & FireWall-1 Password
- OS Password
- RADIUS
- TACACS
- S/Key
- SecurID
- AXENT Pathways Defender

Out of the authentication schemes listed above, only the VPN-1 & FireWall-1 Password and S/Key authentication schemes store password information in the VPN-1/FireWall-1 users database. All of the other schemes store password information in an external authentication database, meaning the user objects are only used to define VPN-1/FireWall-1 parameters.

In addition to the schemes listed above, VPN-1/FireWall-1 also supports LDAP authentication, which is not considered an authentication scheme, but is considered an integral part of the users database if LDAP support is enabled. In this section, you will learn about each of the authentication schemes listed above, as well as LDAP authentication, and will also learn about hybrid mode authentication, which is important for authenticating remote access VPN connections.

VPN-1 & FireWall-1 Password

The simplest authentication scheme provided on VPN-1/FireWall-1 is the *VPN-1 & FireWall-1 Password* scheme. This scheme relies on a unique username and password to authenticate users, which are stored in the users database in a user object that represents each user. The users database is stored on the management server and is installed to each enforcement module by the management server. A username can be up to 100 characters in length and can use any alphanumeric character. The password must be between four to eight characters. Figure 6.1 shows how the VPN-1 & FireWall-1 Password scheme works.

FIGURE 6.1 VPN-1 & FireWall-1 Password authentication scheme

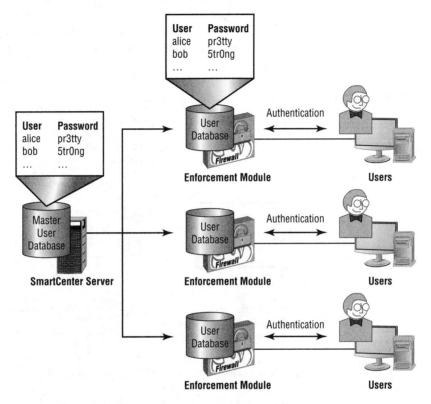

In Figure 6.1, the master VPN-1/FireWall-1 users database resides on the management server. Each enforcement module also maintains a local copy of the users database, which is installed from the management server master database. The user authentication database allows each enforcement module to authenticate users locally, without having to pass the authentication request back to the master users database on the management server. This increases the performance and responsiveness of the enforcement module when authenticating.

OS Password

The *OS Password* authentication scheme stands for operating system password, which as you might guess allows VPN-1/FireWall-1 enforcement modules to use the local operating system users database for authentication. This scheme relies on a unique username and password to authenticate users, which are stored in the operating system users database on each enforcement module. For example, on Windows NT-based VPN-1/FireWall-1 enforcement modules, the Security Account Management (SAM) database represents the operating system users database. Figure 6.2 shows how the OS Password scheme works.

FIGURE 6.2 OS Password authentication scheme

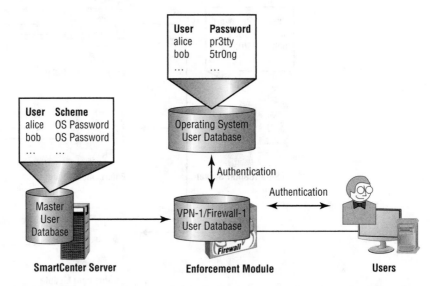

In Figure 6.2, notice that user objects still exist in the VPN-1/FireWall-1 master users database on the management server, which is downloaded to the enforcement module to allow local authentication. User objects are not configured with a password—instead the authentication scheme is configured as OS Password. When a user connects and specifies a username that matches a user object configured with OS Password, the enforcement module passes the username and password to the local operating system for authentication against the operating system authentication database. The passwords for each user must be configured at the operating system level, as all passwords reside in the operating system authentication database.

It is highly recommended you not use the OS Password authentication scheme for two reasons. The first and most important reason is that you are providing users with the local account information of enforcement modules. If a username and password is intercepted, it could give the eavesdropper account credentials to gain access to the enforcement module operating system. Clearly this is a major security risk for your enforcement modules. The second reason is that in an environment with multiple enforcement modules, if you want a user to authenticate against each enforcement module with the same username and password, you must ensure the OS password for the user is the same on each enforcement module. This is another security risk and introduces administrative overheads, as you must explicitly synchronize each enforcement module every time a password change occurs.

RADIUS

RADIUS stands for Remote Access Dial-in User Service and defines a protocol that enables authentication to be handled by a remote authentication database. The main benefit of RADIUS is that it centralizes authentication when you have many enforcement modules, by allowing you to configure each enforcement module to authenticate using a central RADIUS server. Figure 6.3 shows how RADIUS works.

RADIUS's Other Uses

RADIUS is common in ISP environments, where it is commonly used to authenticate point-to-point protocol (PPP) connections for dial-up and broadband users. In addition to providing an efficient authentication mechanism that enables RADIUS servers to scale for large environments, RADIUS also provides authorization features, which define what a customer can do once connected, as well as accounting features, which allow ISPs to measure the length of time connected and the amount of bytes transferred over customer connections. This accounting information is very important for billing purposes. VPN-1/FireWall-1 only supports RADIUS authentication and does not support RADIUS authorization or accounting.

In Figure 6.3, notice that user objects still exist in the VPN-1/FireWall-1 master users database on the management server, which is downloaded to the enforcement module to allow local authentication. User objects are not configured with a password—instead the authentication scheme is configured as RADIUS. When a user connects and specifies a username that matches a user object configured with RADIUS, the enforcement module passes the username and password to a RADIUS server, which authenticates the credentials and either accepts or rejects the authentication. The enforcement module and RADIUS server communicate using UDP, and each use a shared secret (that must match on both devices) to encrypt any passwords that are transmitted across the network.

FIGURE 6.3 RADIUS authentication scheme

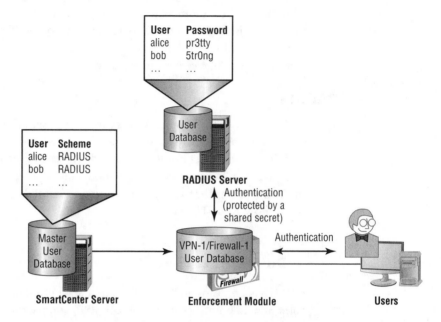

Although you don't have to manage the passwords for users authenticated via RADIUS, you still have to create objects for each user, as indicated in Figure 6.3. This step is required so that you can identify which group a user belongs to, ensuring the user is matched to the appropriate security rule (security rules only allow you to specify group objects rather than individual user objects).

 Real World Scenario

The *generic** Object

You can create a user object called generic*, which is used to match any usernames that are not represented in the VPN-1/FireWall-1 users database. You can configure the generic* object to use an authentication scheme such as RADIUS, which means users can be authenticated against an external database, without requiring explicit configuration of an object for each user. It is important to understand that any users authenticated by this feature inherit the VPN-1/FireWall-1 parameters configured for the generic* object; thus, authenticating users via this mechanism is less flexible as a single set of parameters (such as group membership or permitted logon times) will apply.

In NG Feature Pack 3, the `generic*` method of matching unknown users is replaced by a new type of user object called an external user profile, which can either match all unknown users (equivalent to `generic*`) or can match users belonging to a particular domain. For example, if a user authenticates using a user name of bob@ny.com, an external user profile can be created that recognizes the user belongs to the ny.com domain, strip the @ny.com from the username, and then forward the authentication data to authentication databases that belong to the ny.com organization.

The key advantage of using RADIUS is that it provides scalability in an environment where you must manage many enforcement modules (and other devices that required authentication). A single RADIUS server provides a central authentication database for hundreds of enforcement modules and other devices. If an organization has implemented a RADIUS infrastructure to provide authentication services for other devices, such as network access servers (that provide access for remote dial-in users), VPN-1/FireWall-1 can be configured to utilize the existing RADIUS infrastructure, eliminating the administrative overhead of managing a separate authentication database.

RADIUS also provides a simple means of communicating with internal authentication databases. For example, an organization using Windows NT may require internal users to authenticate with VPN-1/FireWall-1 for some services, but wants to ensure that the internal users use their internal domain credentials for authentication, to save them having to remember a new set of credentials. Instead of implementing the native internal authentication protocol (such as Windows NT authentication, which has security vulnerabilities and would require enforcement module membership to the internal domain), using RADIUS provides a very simple, standards-based front-end for authenticating users in the internal authentication database.

Internet Authentication Service (IAS)

Windows 2000 Server ships with a free RADIUS server, known as the Internet Authentication Service (IAS). If an organization has an internal Windows NT or Windows 2000 domain infrastructure, you can use the IAS to provide an interface for VPN-1/FireWall-1 to the internal domain authentication database, providing a single set of credentials for users, whether they are logging on to the domain or authenticating for access through the firewall. This saves users from having to remember multiple sets of credentials, and also saves the administrative overhead of having to maintain multiple sets of credentials for each user.

TACACS

TACACS stands for Terminal Access Controller Access Control System and defines a protocol that is commonly used to provide authentication, authorization, and accounting for terminal-based applications, such as TELNET. A terminal-based application session essentially consists of ASCII commands being issued by a client, with the server returning the appropriate information or feedback in response to each command. For example, if you telnet to a Unix host, you first authenticate, and then issue commands that enable you to perform tasks on the Unix hosts. The Unix host provides feedback or returns information based on the commands entered by the remote client. TACACS is designed to not only offer authentication of terminal-based sessions, but also to offer authorization and accounting for these sessions. The power of TACACS lies in its ability to restrict the commands or the level of access a user has when logging on. For example, you might configure a user profile on a TACACS server to only permit access to a specific set of commands, to ensure the user cannot perform tasks that are outside the users role. The accounting features allow you to keep track of what commands a user issues, so that you can trace any unauthorized actions performed on a host to a user.

VPN-1/FireWall-1 only supports TACACS authentication, where enforcement modules pass credentials from remote users to a remote TACACS server for authentication, much like how RADIUS works. The TACACS server compares the presented credentials with the credentials stored in the TACACS users database, and either accepts or rejects the authentication. Figure 6.4 shows how TACACS works with VPN-1/FireWall-1.

TACACS authentication is very similar to RADIUS authentication (see Figure 6.3 and Figure 6.4). User objects are defined in the VPN-1/FireWall-1 master users database on the management server, which is downloaded to the enforcement module to allow local authentication. User objects are not configured with a password. Instead, the authentication scheme is configured as TACACS. When a user connects and specifies a username that matches a user object configured with an authentication mechanism of TACACS, the enforcement module passes the username and password to a TACACS server, which authenticates the credentials and either accepts or rejects the authentication.

FIGURE 6.4   TACACS authentication scheme

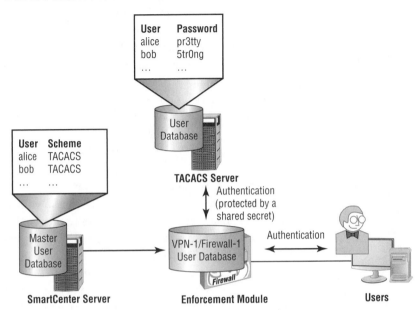

There are two versions of TACACS—TACACS and TACACS+. TACACS+ was invented by Cisco Systems and extended TACACS to provide many extra features. TACACS and TACACS+ are incompatible. When you define a TACACS security server object on VPN-1/FireWall-1, you must correctly specify the server as either a TACACS or TACACS+ server.

The enforcement module and TACACS server communicate using UDP (for TACACS) or TCP (for TACACS+), and each use a shared secret (that must match on both devices) to encrypt all TACACS communications. This is different from RADIUS, which uses UDP and only encrypts password information. Just like RADIUS, TACACS provides a centralized authentication database that can be used by multiple enforcement modules for authentication.

S/Key

S/Key is a *one-time password (OTP)* authentication scheme, which enables users to authenticate using a different password each time. One-time passwords ensure the security of credentials, especially in environments where credentials are sent in cleartext, making them vulnerable to sniffing. If you have a fixed password (i.e., your password is the same forever or for a relatively long period of time) and if you transmit this password across a network in cleartext, your password can easily be discovered by simply eavesdropping on the network. With one-time password schemes, each time you authenticate, the password you use is only valid once, meaning that an eavesdropper cannot reuse your password to falsely authenticate using your credentials (i.e., any intercepted passwords are useless).

S/Key works with each user initially selecting a secret key, which should only be known to each user and the S/Key server. The S/Key server is essentially the authenticating host—with VPN-1/FireWall-1 this is the enforcement module. On an S/Key client (the device requesting access to the S/Key server), the secret key is passed through a one-way hashing algorithm for a number of iterations, which generates a hash value that is unique to the secret key. The hash values generated for a secret key will never be the same as the values generated for a different secret key, so the hash value is unique to the secret key and thus identifies the secret key (and the user who is the only person that knows the secret key). Hashing algorithms are designed to be irreversible, meaning that it is virtually impossible to derive the original value (the secret key) from the output hash value. The hash value calculated is used as the one-time password, which is sent to the S/Key server. The S/Key server, which knows the secret key of the S/Key client, also performs the same hashing algorithm to generate a one-time password. If the one-time passwords generated by the S/Key client and S/Key server match, the user is authenticated.

S/Key on VPN-1/FireWall-1 supports the message digest 4 and 5 (MD4 and MD5) hashing algorithms. MD4 is known to be a weak hashing algorithm, so you should use MD5 where possible.

To ensure that a new one-time password value is generated each time a user connects, every time a user attempts to connect, the number or iterations of the hashing algorithm performed is decremented by one, meaning that a totally different hash output will be generated. As long as the S/Key server and S/Key client know how many iterations to perform, they will generate the same one-time password if the S/Key client has the correct secret key. In order to increase the security of the hashing algorithms, a *seed* value is also used in the hashing algorithm, which means that the hash output is generated from a combination of the secret key and the seed value, making it harder to determine the secret key by reversing the hashing algorithms.

When a user attempts to connect to a device that requires S/Key authentication, the S/Key server sends back a number and a seed value, which must be input to the S/Key client software running on the host the user is connecting from. The number defines the number of iterations that should be performed, and is always one less that the number used for the previous authentication. The seed is fed into the hashing algorithm along with the secret key, which also must be input by the user when authenticating. Figure 6.5 demonstrates how S/Key authentication works.

FIGURE 6.5 S/Key authentication scheme

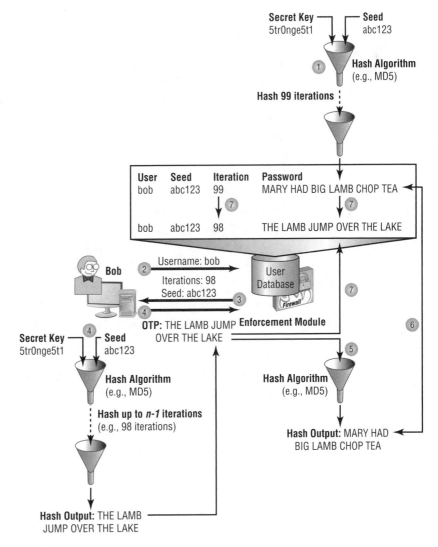

In Figure 6.5, the following events occur:

1. When the user object called bob is created in the VPN-1/FireWall-1 users database, the secret key for the user (5tr0nge5t1) is combined with the seed value abc123 (this seed value is configured per user and can be any value you choose) and passed through a hashing algorithm 99 times (this value is configurable). A hash output of MARY HAD BIG LAMB CHOP TEA is generated, and is stored in the users database along with the number of iterations (99) and the seed value. At this point the secret key is no longer needed, and is discarded, increasing the security of the secret key.

On VPN-1/FireWall-1, the secret key must be at least ten characters in length.

2. A user called bob attempts to access a service running on a host protected by the enforcement module. The enforcement module prompts for a username, and a username of bob is sent from the client host.

3. The enforcement module matches the username to an object that requires S/Key authentication. The enforcement module reads the seed value and the current iteration value (n). The seed value and the iteration value minus 1 ($n - 1$) is sent back to client. In Figure 6.5, you can see in the users database that the seed value is abc123 and that the iteration value is 99. This means an iteration value of 98 is sent back to the user, along with the seed value of abc123.

4. Bob runs an S/Key client application, which requires the user's secret key, the seed value returned in Step 2 and the iteration value returned in Step 2. Bob inputs the secret key (only known to Bob) of 5tr0nge5t1, the seed value of abc123, and an iteration value of 98. The S/Key application applies the hashing algorithm 98 times, generating a hash output of THE LAMB JUMP OVER THE LAKE. This hash output is sent to the enforcement module.

5. If the secret key entered by Bob in Step 4 is the same as the secret key used in Step 1 (and the seed value is also the same), the hash output received at the enforcement module represents the output that is generated before the last iteration (i.e., the 99th iteration) of the hashing performed in Step 1. This means that if the enforcement module

hashes the received hash output from Bob (THE LAMB JUMP OVER THE LAKE) one more time, an output of MARY HAD BIG LAMB CHOP TEA should be generated.

6. The enforcement module compares the current one-time password stored in the users database (i.e., the OTP generated from 99 iterations) with the OTP generated by hashing the received OTP from the client (which has been hashed 98 times) once. If these OTP values match, then the enforcement module knows that the secret key used on the client to generate the OTP is the same as that used on the enforcement module, effectively authenticating the user.

7. To ensure the next time the client authenticates a different OTP is required, the enforcement module writes the OTP value sent by the client (THE LAMB JUMP OVER THE LAKE) as the new OTP value in the users database, and also decrements the number of iterations by one (from 99 to 98).

The next time the user authenticates, the same steps occur as listed above. The user will be sent an iteration number of 97 (98 − 1), with the client generating an OTP based on 97 iterations and then sending it to the S/Key server. When the S/Key server receives the OTP generated by 97 iterations, by applying one more iteration, the OTP should then match the 98th iteration value stored in the users database. This process of decrementing the iteration number continues every time the user authenticates, until eventually the iteration value reaches 0. At this time, a new OTP must be initialized on the S/Key server by entering a new combination of seed and secret key, as described in Step 1 above.

The obvious advantage of S/Key authentication over other schemes such as RADIUS and OS Password is that the password used to authenticate changes each time, preventing an unauthorized user from attempting to use an eavesdropped password. Another advantage is that the secret key is not stored in the VPN-1/FireWall-1 users database, it is merely used to generate an initial OTP value as described in Step 1 of Figure 6.5. This means that if the users database is compromised for some reason, secret keys are not compromised because they are not stored in the database. The disadvantages of S/Key authentication are that an S/Key client application must be installed on each device a user wishes to authenticate from, and if the secret key is compromised, an unauthorized user can simply use the S/Key client application to generate the correct OTP values for authentication.

SecurID

SecurID is another one-time password authentication scheme; however, it differs in implementation from S/Key. SecurID works on the principle that a user must possess a hardware device or *token* to authenticate. For example, the SecurID tokens (also known as a FOB) are small electronic devices that look like a pager, which require a PIN (personal identification number) to activate and then generate an OTP that can be used for authentication. A SecurID server (known as an ACE/Server) is used to authenticate the OTP. The mechanism used to generate OTP values on both the SecurID client and ACE/Server is quite different from S/Key. When a SecurID token is initialized, a seed value (random value) is generated, which is input to the token, as well as the ACE/Server database. To ensure that each OTP generated for authentication is different, a value is used that is in common on both the ACE/Server and client but is different each time the user authenticates. The value used that varies is actually time—both the token and ACE/Server are time synchronized. A PIN is also generated, which is known only to the user and the ACE/Server. When a user wishes to authenticate, he or she enters the PIN into the SecurID token, which then performs a hash of the PIN, the seed value, and also the current time stamp. An OTP value is computed, which is then transmitted to the ACE/Server, which uses the PIN value and seed value stored in its local users database, as well as the current time to generate an OTP value. If both OTP values match, the user is authenticated.

VPN-1/FireWall-1 supports SecurID by acting as an ACE client, which in the SecurID architecture is similar to how VPN-1/FireWall-1 works for RADIUS and TACACS. If a user is defined as using SecurID authentication, VPN-1/FireWall-1 prompts the user for SecurID authentication, at which point the user sends the OTP generated by entering a PIN into the token. VPN-1/FireWall-1 then passes the OTP to the ACE/Server, which is defined as an object in the VPN-1/FireWall-1 security object database. The ACE/Server then either accepts or rejects the authentication.

SecurID is considered a very secure authentication mechanism, as you require a special hardware device to authenticate. This means that a hacker requires access to a valid users token, and must also know the PIN used to generate the correct OTP values. This is analogous to requiring a swipe card and a PIN to access a building. If you just required a PIN code to access a building, anybody who knows your PIN code can access the building. However if you also require a swipe card (i.e., a separate physical device) and a PIN code to access the building, an intruder must also gain access to your swipe card, making it much harder to break into the building.

Using this form of authentication is commonly referred to as 'Two Factor' or 'Strong' authentication, as it relies on more than one method of verifying a user's identity. A user must possess a token just to enable the capability to authenticate (something the user has) and must also know a PIN to unlock the token (something the user knows).

AXENT Pathways Defender

AXENT Pathways Defender is another token-based authentication scheme, similar to SecurID. AXENT was acquired by Symantec in 2000, and is now known as Symantec Defender.

The AXENT Pathways Defender authentication scheme is no longer supported from NG Feature Pack 3 onwards.

LDAP Authentication

LDAP stands for *Lightweight Directory Access Protocol*, and defines a standards-based architecture for implementing a global user directory. Both Novell NDS and Microsoft Windows 2000 Active Directory databases are LDAP-compliant, which means you can use VPN-1/FireWall-1 to authenticate these users via LDAP. LDAP uses a hierarchical tree structure to define users, which is designed in a fashion similar to DNS. LDAP databases consist of container objects and leaf objects—a container is an object that contains child objects (i.e. objects that belong to the container), while a leaf object is an object that actually represents a user. Each object can be identified by a distinguished name (DN), which essentially maps the object location in the LDAP database. The various subhierarchies in an LDAP database are called *organizational units* or OUs, which are essentially container objects for user objects or other OUs. In VPN-1/FireWall-1, you can define an LDAP server and a specific OU that you wish to read or manage. You can read the OU for user objects that can be used for authentication, and you can also manage user objects within the OU. Figure 6.6 demonstrates how LDAP is supported on VPN-1/FireWall-1.

In Figure 6.6, you can see an LDAP database for ABC Corp., with VPN-1/FireWall-1 configured to manage the Head Office Users organizational unit. On VPN-1/FireWall-1, when a user authenticates, the enforcement module first checks if any user objects exist in the VPN-1/FireWall-1 users database for the username. If not, VPN-1/FireWall-1 then queries the LDAP server, looking for a match on the username within the configured organization unit. Authentication occurs via LDAP, and the user is either accepted or rejected.

FIGURE 6.6 LDAP authentication

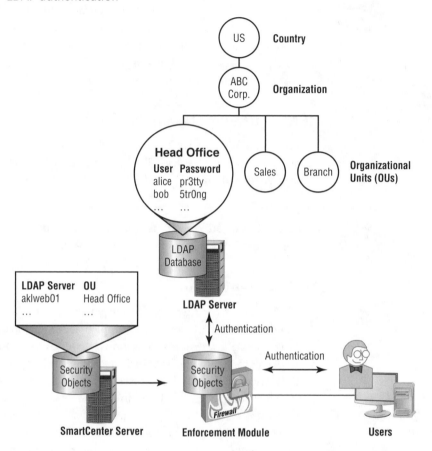

Check Point offers an add-on to VPN-1/FireWall-1 NG called the Account Management Module, which is an optional component that you can purchase. The Account Management Module is required if you wish to manage LDAP databases. If you are managing LDAP users, you can do so using the Users tab in the Object tree of SmartDashboard after defining the organization unit you are managing. You can still authenticate against an LDAP database (but manage it externally) without purchasing the Account Management Module.

Hybrid Mode Authentication

VPN-1/FireWall-1 supports user-based authentication for both security rules and for remote access (SecuRemote or SecureClient) VPN connectivity. Remote access VPNs allow users to establish a secure and encrypted connection across the Internet to a VPN-1/FireWall-1 enforcement module, and then tunnel native traffic to the internal network through this tunnel. VPN-1/FireWall-1 supports two VPN protocols that can be used for remote access VPNs:

FWZ Encryption   Check Point's original proprietary encryption protocol. Normally, FWZ only supports payload encryption, which means the payload of each IP packet is encrypted. This causes problems for VPNs, which require native IP packets to be tunneled to the internal network and which may use private IP addressing. To enable FWZ to be used for remote access VPNs, FWZ encrypted packets can be tunneled over Check Points proprietary FW1 encapsulation protocol, which has an IP protocol number of 94. This tunneling is disabled by default and must be enabled on each VPN-1/FireWall-1 enforcement module. FWZ remote access VPN connections can utilize any VPN-1/FireWall-1 authentication scheme to authenticate access.

FWZ Encryption is no longer supported from NG Feature Pack 2 onwards.

IPSec   IPSec is a standards-based encryption and VPN protocol for IP traffic, defined by the IETF (Internet Engineering Task Force). For all VPN connections, the IPSec standard only supports the use of pre-shared keys or certificates for authentication. This means that standards-based IPSec VPNs are not compatible with VPN-1/FireWall-1 authentication schemes, such as RADIUS or TACACS.

Hybrid mode authentication enables VPN-1/FireWall-1 to use any authentication scheme for VPN-1/FireWall-1 remote access VPN connections. Hybrid mode extends the IPSec standard by implementing proprietary exchanges in the IKE (Internet Key Exchange) negotiations, which enable users to pass their username and password to the VPN-1/FireWall-1 enforcement module securely. These credentials can then be authenticated via any scheme, such as RADIUS or SecurID. It is important to understand that hybrid mode authentication is not an authentication scheme, it is merely an extension to the negotiation of IPSec-based remote access VPN connections that enables any scheme to be used for authenticating the connection.

IKE is a protocol designed to authenticate and negotiate IPSec security associations, which are a unidirectional VPN flow. Check Point has proposed the hybrid mode extensions as a standard to the IETF.

Understanding User Objects

Now that you understand authentication schemes, which define how a user is authenticated, it is important to understand the objects that comprise the VPN-1/FireWall-1 users database. Just as you must define security objects before you can create VPN-1/FireWall-1 NG rules that represent systems and networks, you must also define user objects before you can create security rules that include users or groups. VPN-1/FireWall-1 NG provides a users database, which is configured on the management server but installed to the management server and each enforcement module, enabling authentication to be performed on an enforcement module. The users database includes the following types of objects:

Users A *user object* represents a single user, and is used for the purposes of verifying authentication-based security rules and remote access VPN connections. Each user object is configured with a specific authentication scheme, which determines how the user should be authenticated.

Groups A *group object* represents a collection of user objects that each share some common privilege. All security rules that specify an authentication action are configured with a source element that specifies a group object. You cannot configure security rules with user objects—you must use group objects. A group object only has one parameter—the user objects that belong to it. All other parameters (such as authentication scheme) must be configured separately on each user object in the group.

User templates A *user template object* allows you to define common configuration parameters from which you can base new user objects on. When you create a new user object, you can choose the template on which you wish common parameters to be inherited from. For example, you could use a user template to define group membership for user objects, or you could configure a specific authentication scheme that would be inherited by user objects created from the templates. Using templates saves time when having to create many users who share common attributes.

Administrators An *administrator object* is new to VPN-1/FireWall-1 NG and allows you to create administrative accounts that are permitted access to the VPN-1/FireWall-1 management clients. In versions prior to NG, you could only configure administrators via the `cpconfig` utility. Administrator objects cannot be used in authentication rules in the security rule base.

Before we proceed to the next section of the chapter, where you will learn how to configure authentication schemes and the users database, it is important that you have a clear understanding of what has been discussed so far in the chapter. You should now be familiar with the following concepts:

- Authentication schemes define how a user is authenticated.

- The users database is separate from an authentication database, except for the case of the VPN-1 & FireWall-1 Password authentication scheme, where the users database also acts as an authentication database for users configured with this scheme.

- Every user is represented by a user object in the users database.

- Every user object is configured with a single authentication scheme.

- Different authentication schemes can be configured for different users, allowing multiple authentication schemes to be supported at the same time.

Configuring Authentication

To configure authentication on VPN-1/FireWall-1 NG, you must follow a series of configuration steps in the correct order. The following identifies each of the steps:

1. Configure authentication schemes.

2. Configure the users database.

3. Install the users database.

4. Configure authentication-based security rules.

In this section you will learn how to perform the first three configuration tasks. In Chapter 7, you will learn how to configure the various authentication-based security rules.

Configuring Authentication Schemes

To configure support for a particular authentication scheme, you must ensure that your enforcement module supports the authentication scheme, and that the enforcement module can communicate with any remote servers that might be associated with the authentication scheme. The following describes the tasks that you must perform to enable an enforcement module to support an authentication scheme:

- Configure support for the authentication schemes you wish to use on each enforcement module.

- Configure server objects for any authentication schemes that require authentication from an external server.

- Configure any external servers that are used for authentication.

- Install the security policy.

Enabling Support for the Authentication Scheme

VPN-1/FireWall-1 allows you to selectively enable or disable support for each authentication scheme on each enforcement module. The enforcement module object in the objects database on the management server includes a screen called Authentication, which enables you to enable or disable support for each authentication scheme. To configure an enforcement module object, select Manage ➤ Network Objects from the SmartDashboard main menu, then select the appropriate enforcement module object from the Network Objects list, and then click the Edit button to display the properties for the object. Enforcement module objects include an Authentication screen, which enables you to configure the authentication schemes supported on the enforcement module. Figure 6.7 shows the Authentication screen on a workstation object that represents a VPN-1/FireWall-1 enforcement module.

In Figure 6.7, the default settings of the Authentication screen are shown. You can see a section called Enabled Authentication Schemes, which allows you to selectively enable or disable the authentication schemes that the enforcement module supports. By default, the Secure ID, RADIUS, and TACACS authentication are enabled. To enable or disable a scheme, simply check or uncheck the appropriate schemes and click OK.

Notice that LDAP is not considered an authentication scheme. You must enable LDAP authentication globally, by configuring the LDAP Account Management screen in the Policy ➤ Global Properties dialog box within SmartDashboard. In this screen is a setting called Use LDAP account management, which by default is disabled and must be enabled to support LDAP authentication.

FIGURE 6.7   The Authentication screen

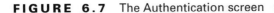

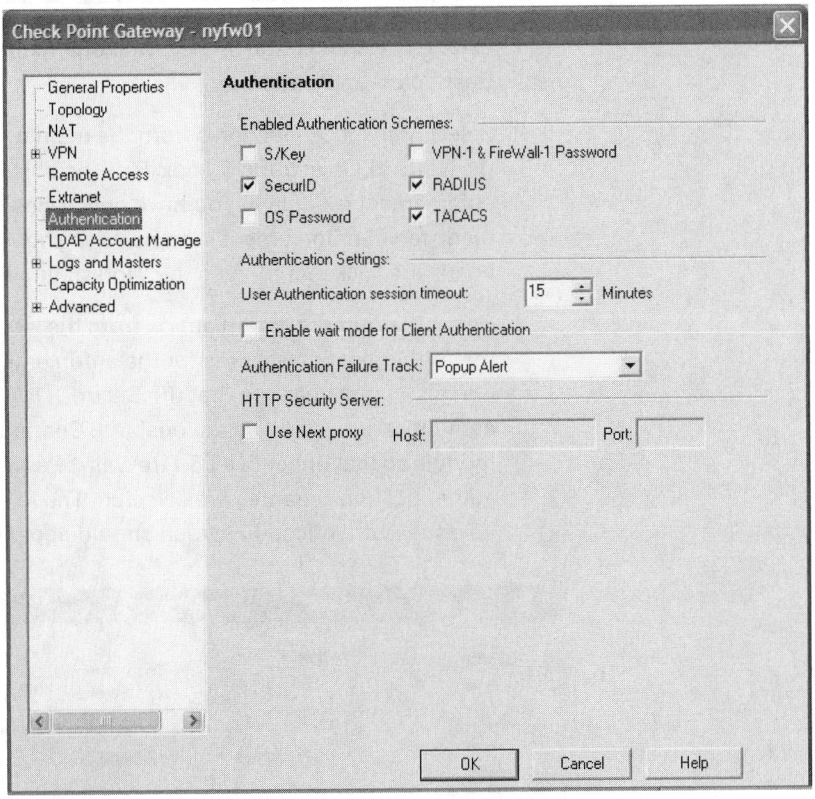

EXERCISE 6.1

Configuring Authentication Scheme Support on an Enforcement Module

The exercises listed in this chapter continue the exercises configured in previous chapters and therefore assume you are familiar with the topology used in previous exercises. Specific assumptions and new topology changes for the exercises in this chapter include the following:

- An object called nyweb01 exists in the objects database.

- Assume that nyweb01 includes RADIUS server software, which will allow RADIUS authentication to be configured.

1. Establish a connection to your management server via the Smart-Dashboard application.

2. Select Manage ➢ Networks from the main menu, which will open the Network Objects dialog box. Find the object that represents your enforcement module (if you have only a single combined management server/enforcement module, then choose the object for this host), and click Edit to open the Workstation Properties dialog box.

3. Select the Authentication option from the left pane, which displays the Authentication scheme for the enforcement module object. By default, you should see that the SecurID, RADIUS, and TACACS authentication schemes are enabled. Configure the enforcement module so that only VPN-1 & FireWall-1 Password and the RADIUS authentication schemes are selected. The following demonstrates how the Authentication screen should appear:

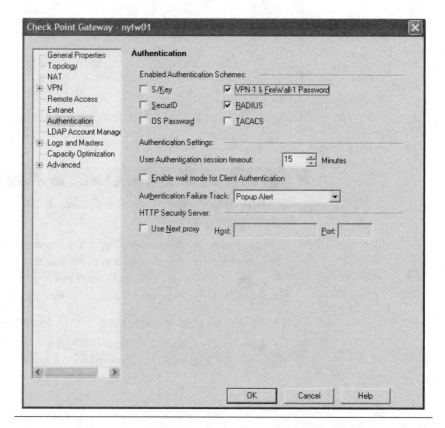

Configuring Server Objects

Some authentication schemes require the use of an external server that hosts an authentication database. To support these authentication schemes, you must define *server objects* that represent the external server. The RADIUS and TACACS authentication schemes all require at least one server object to be defined before they can be used to successfully authenticate users. To create a server object, you must first ensure that you create a simple workstation object for the server, which only requires the IP address of the server to be configured. Then you create the server object, defining parameters required to ensure communications between the enforcement module and the server, and selecting the appropriate workstation object that represents the IP address of the server. For example, you might have a RADIUS server called NYAUTH. You would first create a workstation object called NYAUTH, with an IP address of the server configured in this object. Next, you would create a server object (with a different name, such as NYAUTH-RADIUS), define the various RADIUS parameters (such as shared secret), and bind the server object to the correct workstation object.

To create a server object, select Manage ➢ Servers from the SmartDashboard main menu, which opens the Servers dialog box. Click the New button, and select the appropriate server type from the dropdown list that appears. Figure 6.8 shows the process of selecting the appropriate server type.

FIGURE 6.8 Creating a server object

You can see the various types of server objects that you can create in the dropdown list displayed by clicking the New button. Figure 6.8 shows that a RADIUS server is about to be created. Figure 6.9 shows the RADIUS Server Properties dialog box, which is displayed if the New ➢ RADIUS option is selected in Figure 6.8.

FIGURE 6.9 The RADIUS Server Properties dialog box

In Figure 6.9, you can see that a RADIUS server object called nyweb01-radius. You see that the Host dropdown box is used to select the appropriate workstation object that is bound to the server object. The Shared Secret text box allows you to configure the shared secret that will be used to encrypt passwords transmitted across the network to the RADIUS server. Once you have completed your configuration, click OK.

EXERCISE 6.2

Configuring a RADIUS Server Object

1. Establish a connection to your management server via the Policy Editor application.

2. Select Manage ➢ Servers from the main menu, which will open the Servers dialog box. By default, you should only see an object called internal_ca, which represents the internal certificate authority on the management server. Click New, and select RADIUS from the dropdown menu.

EXERCISE 6.2 *(continued)*

3. The RADIUS Server Properties dialog box will be displayed, which allows you to define a RADIUS server. Configure the object with the following parameters:

   - Name: nyweb01-radius
   - Comment: RADIUS Service on NYWEB01
   - Host: aklweb01
   - Shared Secret: firewall

4. Click OK to complete your configuration of the object, and then click Close.

Configuring the External Authentication Server

If you are configuring support for an authentication scheme that uses an external server, after you have created the appropriate server object on VPN-1/ FireWall-1, you may need to configure the external server as well. For example, if you are enabling support for an external RADIUS server, you must configure each enforcement module as a RADIUS client on the RADIUS server and ensure that the shared secret configured in Figure 6.9 is configured for the RADIUS client.

Once you have enabled the appropriate authentication schemes on an enforcement module, any users that are configured to use a supported authentication scheme can be authenticated by the enforcement module. If a user is configured with an authentication scheme that is not enabled on the enforcement module, user authentication will always fail (even if the credentials are valid) until the authentication scheme is enabled.

Installing the Security Policy

Once you have configured or created any objects in the security objects database, or modified any policy properties, you must install the security policy to each enforcement module to ensure the modifications to the security policy are applied to each enforcement module.

Now that authentication schemes and necessary server objects are configured, you must install your security policy to apply the new configuration to the enforcement module. Select Policy ➢ Install from the main menu in SmartDashboard, and install your security policy to the enforcement module that you just configured. This ensures that the enforcement module will only support the VPN-1 & FireWall-1 Password and RADIUS authentication schemes and is configured with a RADIUS server object.

Configuring the Users Database

You can create and configure the various objects in the users database via the SmartDashboard management client, by selecting Manage ➢ Users and Administrators from the main menu, which displays the Users dialog box. Figure 6.10 shows the Users dialog box.

FIGURE 6.10 The Users dialog box

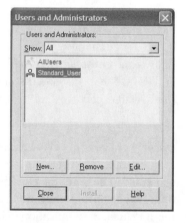

In Figure 6.10, you can see a user template object called Default, which is the only object present in the users database after a new VPN-1/FireWall-1 NG installation. This template allows you to create users with default parameters. From the Users dialog box shown in Figure 6.10, you can create the following objects:

- User
- User template

- Administrator

- Group

- External group

- External user profiles (not covered in this book, see the real-world scenario for more details)

The configuration of each of the above objects (excluding external user profiles) is now discussed in detail.

Configuring Users

To create a user, you simply click the New button in the Users dialog box (see Figure 6.10), choose the User by Template option, and then select the appropriate template on which you wish to create the new user. Figure 6.11 demonstrates selecting the appropriate options to create a new user object.

FIGURE 6.11 Creating a user object

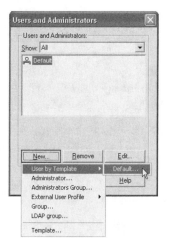

In Figure 6.11, you can see that only one template is available for selection (Default). If you create custom user templates, they will appear in the list alongside the Default template. Once you select the appropriate template, the User Properties dialog box is displayed, which allows you to configure all the parameters associated with the user. You can also display the User Properties dialog box for an existing user object by selecting the user object and clicking the Edit button. Figure 6.12 shows the User Properties dialog box.

FIGURE 6.12 The User Properties dialog box

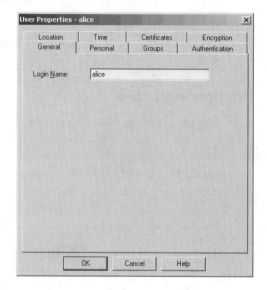

In Figure 6.12, you can see that the User Properties dialog box has eight different tabs, each of which allows you to configure various parameters for the user.

General Allows you to configure the name of the user object. In Figure 6.12, you can see that a user object called `alice` is being created.

 Both usernames and passwords are case-sensitive in VPN-1/FireWall-1.

Personal Allows you to configure the following parameters for the user.

Expiration Date The date on which the user account will expire and is no longer considered valid. This date must be specified in dd-mmm-yyyy format.

The default expiry date for the Default template is the 31st of December in the year in which the VPN-1/FireWall-1 management server is installed.

Comment   Describes the user object. This is normally the full name of the user.

Color   Can be used to differentiate the role of the user. For example, you might configure accounting user objects with one color, and VPN user objects with another color.

Figure 6.13 shows the Personal tab within the User Properties dialog box.

FIGURE 6.13   The Personal tab in the User Properties dialog box

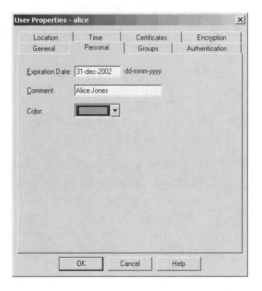

Groups   Allows you to configure the groups to which the user belongs. Groups are used in security rules, which means you can control the access privileges of a user object by placing it in the appropriate groups. Figure 6.14 demonstrates the Groups tab.

In Figure 6.14 you can see that the user object currently belongs to no groups, and a group called accounting is present in the users database.

FIGURE 6.14 The Groups tab in the User Properties dialog box

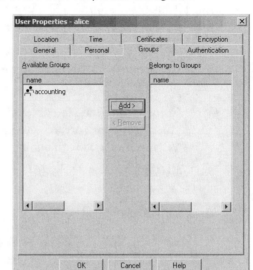

 VPN-1/FireWall-1 places all users into a hidden group called All Users, which cannot be modified or deleted.

Authentication Allows you to configure the authentication schemes that are valid for the users. Available schemes include SecurID, VPN-1/ FireWall-1 Password, OS Password, RADIUS, S/Key, and TACACS. Figure 6.15 shows the Authentication tab, with the option of VPN-1 & FireWall-1 Password chosen.

 You can define any authentication scheme that you like for a user; however, be aware that the appropriate authentication scheme must also be enabled on the enforcement module to which the user will connect and authenticate.

Notice in Figure 6.15 that you can configure the password for the user object when the VPN-1 & FireWall-1 authentication scheme is selected. To configure a password, click the Change Password button, which

displays the Enter Password dialog box. From this screen you can specify
a password for the user that will be stored locally in the VPN-1/FireWall-1
users database.

FIGURE 6.15 The Authentication tab in the User Properties dialog box

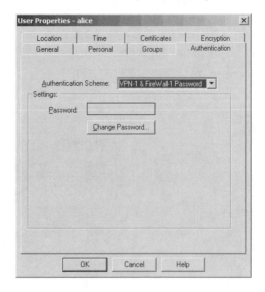

 VPN-1/FireWall-1 passwords must be between four and eight characters in
length.

It is important that you understand that you must configure an authentication scheme for a user object, so that users can be authenticated
appropriately.

 Creating a user object for a remote access VPN user who wishes to use
the pre-shared method of authentication for IPSec is the only exception
to configuring an authentication scheme for a user object.

Location Allows you to configure the source objects (IP addresses) from
which the user can authenticate, as well as the destination objects (IP
addresses) the user can access once authenticated. By default, the user can

authenticate from any IP address and can also access any destination IP address. Figure 6.16 shows the Location tab.

> **NOTE**   Security rules that use authentication in the rule base must be explicitly con-figured to permit access to the allowed locations specified for a user object. This means that although a user object defined in the user database might be permitted access to any location, if there are no rules in the rule base that permit the user access to the location, the user cannot gain access.

FIGURE 6.16   The Location tab in the User Properties dialog box

Time   Allows you to configure the days of the week and the time of the day during which the user is permitted access. By default, a user can connect at any time on any day of the week.

Certificates   Allows you to generate certificates for the user object that are signed by the internal CA, which means that the certificate will be trusted as a means of identifying the user on any enforcement module managed by the local management server. Figure 6.17 shows the Certificates tab in the User Properties dialog box.

FIGURE 6.17 The Certificates tab in the User Properties dialog box

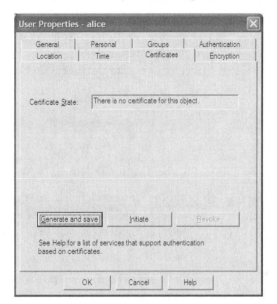

To generate a certificate for a user, click the Generate and Save button. At this point you will be prompted for a password, which is a one-time password that is used to lock the certificate until it reaches the user. Once the certificate is received, the same one-time password configured during certificate creation must be specified by the user receiving the certificate to unlock the certificate. This process ensures the security of the certificate.

Once a user or administrator object has a certificate, you cannot rename the object unless you revoke the certificate.

Encryption   The final tab allows you to configure the valid encryption schemes that the user is permitted to use. This tab is solely for the configuration of remote access VPN users.

Once you have completed configuring a user object, you must install the users database on the management server and enforcement modules. This installation is separate from the security policy installation, and can be performed without reinstallation of the normal security policy.

Minimum Requirements

When you need to create user objects, you might be wondering what the required configuration parameters are to create a user object correctly. When configuring a user object, you must configure the following minimum parameters to ensure the user is configured correctly:

- Login name (via General tab)

- Expiration date (via Personal tab)

- Group membership (via Groups tab)

- Authentication scheme (via Authentication tab)

It is important to understand that all of the above parameters, except for Login name, can be defined in a user template object, which is used to create user objects that have common configuration parameters.

Configuring group membership is not a requirement; however, if you do not configure this, the user will be placed into the All Users group only, or into any groups defined by the template object if a custom template object is used to create the user object.

Configuring User Templates

When you need to configure many users, you should first create user templates that contain common settings that will be applied to all users. For example, you might be creating users that each belong to three different groups. By creating a user template object that is configured to belong to each group, user objects can be created based on the template and will inherit the group membership settings.

If you create user objects based on a user template object, and then modify the user template object, changes made to the template are not propagated to existing user objects that were created from the template. The exception to this is if you are using LDAP account management, where you create special templates to create LDAP users, with any changes to the template being propagated to user objects created from the template.

To create a user template, simply click the New button in the Users dialog box (see Figure 6.10), and select the Template option. The User Template Properties dialog box is now displayed, which looks very similar to the User Properties dialog box shown in Figure 6.12. You can also display the User Template Properties dialog box for an existing user template object by selecting the user template object and clicking the Edit button. Figure 6.18 shows the User Template Properties dialog box.

FIGURE 6.18 The User Template Properties dialog box

In Figure 6.18, notice that all tabs for a user object are present for a user template object, with the exception of a certificates tab (a certificate is something that is generated uniquely for each user, and therefore cannot be configured in a template). The General tab is selected, and a login name of `marketing user` has been configured, which means that the template will have a name of `marketing user`. The following describes each of the configuration tabs that are present for a user template object:

General, Personal, Groups, Location, Time, Encryption   Each of these tabs contains the same configuration parameters that are present on the corresponding tabs of the User Properties dialog box (see Figure 6.12). See the previous section for descriptions of each of the parameters on these tabs. When you configure any of these parameters, any user objects that are created based on the template object inherit the parameters configured. For example, Figure 6.19 shows the Groups tab of the user template object being created in Figure 6.18. Because the template object is configured to belong to the `marketing` group, any user object that is created based on the `marketing user` template object will belong to the `marketing` group.

FIGURE 6.19 The Group tab in the User Template Properties dialog box

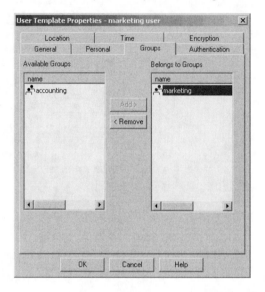

Authentication The authentication tab on a user template object is slightly different from the authentication tab on a user object when an authentication scheme of VPN-1 & FireWall-1 Password is chosen. In Figure 6.15, you saw the authentication tab for a user object with an authentication scheme of VPN-1 & FireWall-1 Password chosen. On the user object, you also had to configure a password, which should only be known to the user and the administrator configuring the password. For a user template object, because the object applies common settings to multiple users, you cannot configure the password on the authentication tab of the user template object, as each password must be individually configured for each user. Figure 6.20 shows the Authentication tab with the VPN-1 & FireWall-1 Password scheme chosen.

FIGURE 6.20 The Authentication tab

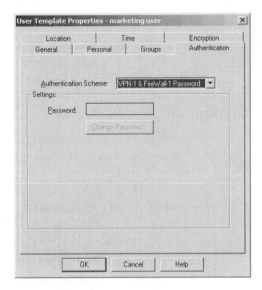

Notice in Figure 6.20 that the Change Password button is grayed out, preventing you from configuring a password for the template object. When you create a user object based on this user template, you must configure the password for each individual user object.

If you are using any other authentication scheme than VPN-1 & FireWall-1 Password (i.e., a remote authentication database), you do not need to configure the password for any users created from the template object, as these passwords are stored on the remote authentication databases, not locally on VPN-1/FireWall-1.

Minimum Requirements

When configuring a user template object, you must configure the same minimum parameters to ensure user objects created from the template object are created correctly:

- Login name (via General tab)
- Expiration date (via Personal tab)

- Group membership (via Groups tab)

- Authentication scheme (via Authentication tab)

The login name parameter merely gives the template object a unique name that you can identify it by—it does not affect the login name parameter of user objects created from the template.

Configuring Administrators

Administrators are a new type of object available from VPN-1/FireWall-1 NG Feature Pack 1. An administrator object represents a user that has some level of administrative rights to configure and manage VPN-1/FireWall-1 components. In previous versions of VPN-1/FireWall-1, administrators were only configured from the cpconfig utility. By using the users database to store administrative accounts, you can configure new administrators without physical access to the management server (as is required when using cpconfig). Administrator objects support some useful features of user objects, such as restricting the hours and days that an administrator can log on. A very important feature of administrator objects is that they provide the ability to use certificates for authentication, rather than just a username, which increases the security of permitting remote administrative connections to the security policy. You cannot configure certificates for an administrator if they are created using the cpconfig utility. Another very important feature of using administrator objects is that you can now use RADIUS as an external authentication database to authenticate administrative access to VPN-1/FireWall-1 security policy. This is useful for environments that already have RADIUS servers that provide centralized authentication, authorization, and accounting, and wish to control and monitor the management of administrative access to VPN-1/FireWall-1 via the existing RADIUS infrastructure.

To create an administrator, you simply click the New button in the Users dialog box (see Figure 6.10), choose the Administrator by Template option and then choose the appropriate user template object that you wish to create the administrator object from. User template objects can be used to create both user objects and administrator objects. The Administrator Properties dialog box will be displayed, which is shown in Figure 6.21. You can also display the Administrator Properties dialog box for an existing administrator object by selecting the object and clicking the Edit button.

FIGURE 6.21 The Administrator Properties dialog box

In Figure 6.21, notice the reduced number of tabs available for an administrator object (compare with Figure 6.18). The Admin Auth tab is equivalent to the Authentication tab for a user object, and the Admin Certificates is equivalent to the Certificates tab for a user object.

The Location tab does not apply for administrator objects, as the location from which an administrator can configure the VPN-1/FireWall-1 management server is still controlled by the GUI Clients tab in the cpconfig utility.

An administrator called bob is being created. Notice the Permissions Profile dropdown box, which you must configure before configuring any other parameters. A permissions profile is a collection of permissions that apply to the various VPN-1/FireWall-1 components and other Check Point product components. By default, no permissions profiles are configured, so if you are creating your first administrator object, you must create a permissions profile by clicking the New button. This will display the Permissions Profile Properties dialog box, which allows you a new permission profile object. Figure 6.22 shows the Permissions Profile Properties dialog box that is displayed after you click the New button in Figure 6.21.

You can also create and manage permissions profiles by selecting Manage ➤ Permissions Profiles from the main menu in Policy Editor.

FIGURE 6.22 The Permissions Profile Properties dialog box

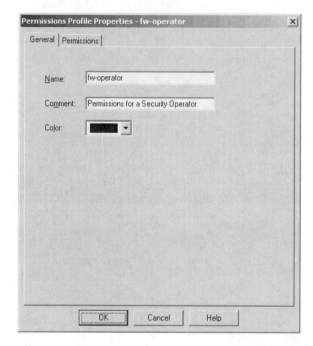

In Figure 6.22, you can see that two tabs are present, which are described below.

General Allows you to configure a name, comment, and color for the permissions profile. You must configure a name that is unique in the context of any security object. For example, if you have a workstation object called `fw-operator`, you cannot name the permissions profile `fw-operator`.

Permissions Allows you to configure permissions for access to each of the various VPN-1/FireWall-1 components and other Check Point product components. Figure 6.23 shows the Permissions tab.

FIGURE 6.23 The Permissions tab

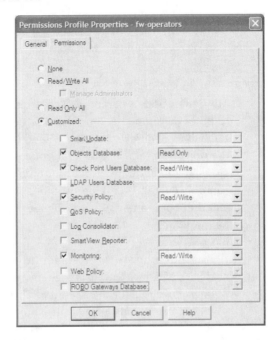

In Figure 6.23 you can see four sets of permissions that you can configure for a permissions profile object:

None Grants no permissions for accessing any component. Any administrator object with a permissions profile that has None configured cannot access any Check Point component. This is useful for temporarily disabling an administrator account.

Read/Write All Grants full access to all Check Point components. This is the Check Point equivalent of a superuser or root account.

Read Only All Grants Read Only access to all Check Point components. Administrator objects with these permissions can view Check Point component configuration and monitor components, but can not make any configuration changes.

Customized Allows you to configure custom permissions for each Check Point component. You can assign None, Read Only, and Read/Write permissions, which have the same meaning as the definitions above, except that they only apply for a single component. In Figure 6.23, the permissions profile object is granted Read Only access to the objects database (contains security objects such as workstation, network, and service objects), Read/Write access to the Check Point users database (the subject of this chapter), Read Only access to the security policy (security rules and policy properties), and Read Only access to monitoring components (Log Viewer and System Status).

The SecureUpdate component controls the permissions that can be assigned to other components. If no permissions or Read Only permissions are applied to SecureUpdate, only Read Only permissions can be applied to the objects database, however you can customize all of the other permissions. If you configure Read/Write permissions for SecureUpdate, you can only customize the permissions for the monitoring component, with all other components being granted Read/Write permissions that cannot be modified.

It is important to understand the components that affect access to the VPN-1/FireWall-1 management clients. For an administrator to log on to Policy Editor, the Security Policy component must have at least Read Only permissions applied. It is important that you enable at least Read Only access to the security policy, if you have assigned rights to either the objects database or Check Point users database. These databases are configured via Policy Editor and if no permissions are granted for the security policy component, the administrator will not be able to log on to Policy Editor at all, effectively blocking access to the databases. The monitoring component affects access to the Log Viewer and System Status applications. Read/Write access to the monitoring component allows an administrator to block connections (and remove blocks) from Log Viewer.

Once you have completed configuration of the new permissions profile object, you will be returned to the Administrator Properties dialog box. Figure 6.24 shows the Administrator Properties screen after a permissions profile object has been created (and applied).

As you can see, the `fw-operator` permissions profile shown in Figure 6.22 and Figure 6.23 is now applied to the administrator object. You can click the View Permissions Profile button to view the permissions that are applied.

Looking at the other tabs in Figure 6.24, all of these tabs except the Authentication tab are identical to the tabs present for a User Object. (Refer to the Configuring Users section for more information on these tabs.) Figure 6.25 shows the Authentication tab.

FIGURE 6.24 The Administrator Properties dialog box

FIGURE 6.25 The Authentication tab

In Figure 6.25, the Authentication Scheme dropdown list is shown, and you can see that SecurID, VPN-1 & FireWall-1 Password, OS Password, and RADIUS are the only available schemes for configuration. In comparison, a user object has the S/Key and TACACS schemes available as well. These schemes are not supported for administrator object authentication, and therefore are not present in the Authentication Schemes dropdown list on the Authentication tab of an administrator object.

As previously mentioned, VPN-1/FireWall-1 NG Feature Pack 1 introduces the ability for VPN-1/FireWall-1 administrators to use a certificate rather than a username for authentication. The Certificates tab (which is identical to the Certificate tab for a user object and is shown in Figure 6.17) allows you to create a certificate for an administrator.

An administrator object uses certificates for management client authentication purposes, while a user object uses certificates for remote access VPN authentication purposes.

When a certificate has not been created for a user or administrator, the Certificate State field indicates this by the text "There is no certificate for this object." If you click the Generate button on the Certificates tab, the internal certificate authority (CA) that resides on the management server will create a certificate for the administrator object that can be used for identification purposes when using Check Point management clients. After clicking the Generate button, you will be advised that the generation of a certificate for the administrator object cannot be undone, unless you revoke the certificate. Once you acknowledge this message, you will be presented with the Enter Password dialog box, which is shown in Figure 6.26.

FIGURE 6.26 The Enter Password dialog box

The password configured in Figure 6.26 is used to protect the private keys associated with the certificate. You should ensure that the password is known only to the user who the certificate is assigned to. After you have configured the private key password, the certificate will be generated by the internal CA, and you will next be prompted to save the certificate as a file. Figure 6.27 shows the process of saving the certificate to disk.

The certificate will be saved to disk on the Policy Editor host from which the configuration is being performed.

FIGURE 6.27 Saving a certificate to disk

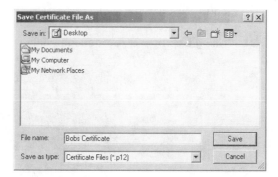

Once the certificate has been saved, you are returned to the Certificate tab on the Administrator Properties screen. The Certificate State field should now indicate the object has a certificate as shown in Figure 6.28. You can use the Revoke button to revoke the certificate at any time.

FIGURE 6.28 Administrator object with a certificate

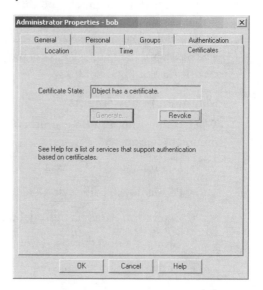

Once you have a certificate for identification purposes, you can use the certificate instead of a username for authentication. To use a certificate for identification, you must have file system access to the certificate file generated in Figure 6.27 from the management client host. The path to the certificate must be specified at the management client authentication dialog box, and certificates must be specified as the method of identity. Figure 6.29 demonstrates using certificates for identification for management client authentication.

FIGURE 6.29 Using a certificate for management client authentication

It is important to understand that the password required in Figure 6.29 is the password for the authentication scheme configured under the Authentication tab of the administrator object for the administrator (see Figure 6.25). The password in Figure 6.29 is *not* the password you configure to unlock the certificate (see Figure 6.26).

Minimum Requirements

When configuring an administrator object, you must configure the following minimum parameters:

- Login name (via General tab)
- Permissions Profile (via General tab)
- Expiration date (via Personal tab)
- Group membership (via Groups tab)
- Authentication scheme (via Admin Auth tab)

It is important to understand that just as for user objects, all of the above parameters, except for Login name and Permissions Profile, can be defined in a user template object, which can be used to administer objects that have common configuration parameters.

Configuring Groups

Groups are important in VPN-1/FireWall-1, as they constitute the only objects in the users database that can actually be configured in security rules. A group object is simply an object that consists of multiple user or group objects. Instead of allowing you to configure specific user objects in security rules, VPN-1/FireWall-1 only allows you to configure group objects in security rules. This is because security policies rarely apply to a specific user—instead they apply to a specific role or function within the organization that may be the responsibility of more than one user. Taking this approach also ensures that new users can easily be configured for access by adding the users to a group object configured for the appropriate rule, without having to modify the rule base, only the users database. To create a group, you simply click the New button in the Users dialog box (see Figure 6.10) and then choose the Group option, which will display the Group Properties dialog box. You can also display the Group Properties dialog box for an existing group object by selecting the group object and clicking the Edit button. The Group Properties dialog box is shown in Figure 6.30.

FIGURE 6.30   The Group Properties dialog box

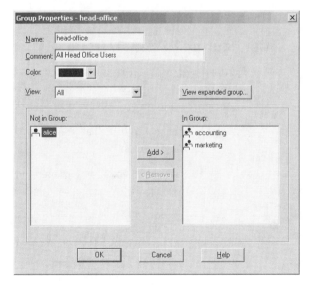

In Figure 6.30, a group called `head-office` is being created, which represents all head office users. The In Group box lists the objects that are a member of the group, while the Not in Group box lists the objects that are not currently part of the group, but are available to be added to the group. Notice that you can nest groups (configure a group to belong to another group) as well as provide a container for user objects. For example, in Figure 6.30 the `accounting` and `marketing` groups (you can tell these are group objects as indicated by two people being pictured in the group object icon) belong to the `head-office` group. You can add or remove group members by selecting the appropriate object and clicking the Add or Remove buttons. Notice that the user object called Alice (you can tell this is a user object because only a single person is depicted for the user object icon) is not part of the group. Once you have completed your configuration, click OK. After you have added a user object to a group object, any security rules that include the group object the user object is a member of will automatically apply to the user.

The View dropdown box allows you to show only objects of a particular type in the Not in Group and In Group boxes. For example, you can alter the view to only display user objects, meaning that all other objects, such as other group objects are not displayed. The View expanded group button allows you to view the parent groups that the current group may belong to.

Configuring External Groups

External groups allow you to represent LDAP organization units as VPN-1/FireWall-1 groups, which you can then configure in security rules. To configure external groups, you must first complete the following tasks:

1. Purchase and install an Account Management Module license on your management server.

2. Enable LDAP account management via the Policy ➢ Global Properties ➢ LDAP Account Management screen in SmartDashboard.

3. Create an LDAP server object(s) in the security object database.

Once you have completed the above tasks, you are ready to authenticate using an LDAP database. You can create external groups by selecting the New ➢ External Group option from the Users dialog box (see Figure 6.10), which displays the External User Group (LDAP) Properties dialog box. From this screen you can choose to include all users within the base organizational unit configured for an LDAP server, or you can filter to only authenticate against specific groups within an organizational unit. Figure 6.31 demonstrates the External User Group (LDAP) Properties dialog box.

FIGURE 6.31 The External Group Properties (LDAP) dialog box

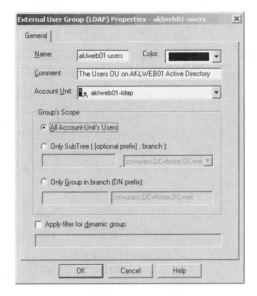

EXERCISE 6.3

Creating Objects in the Users Database

In this exercise you will learn how to create each type of object. We'll assume that two groups of users exist, marketing and sales. All marketing users are to be authenticated via VPN-1 & FireWall-1 Password and only permitted access during working hours (Monday–Friday, 8 A.M.–6 P.M.). All sales users are to be authentication via RADIUS and have no restrictions applied for access.

1. Establish a connection to your management server via the Policy Editor application.

2. Select Manage ➢ Users and Administrators from the main menu, which will open the Users dialog box. If this is a new VPN-1/ FireWall-1 installation, you should only see a single object called Default. Click New and select the Group option from the dropdown list, which will display the Group Properties dialog box for a new group object. Configure a group name of **marketing**, a comment of Marketing Users, and a color of dark blue.

3. Create another group called **sales**, with a comment of Sales Users, and a color of red. After creating this group, you should be able to see the marketing and sales groups in the Users dialog box.

4. Click New and select the Template option from the dropdown list, which will display the User Template Properties dialog box for a new user template object. Click on the General tab, and configure a login name of **Marketing User**.

5. Select the Personal tab, configure an expiration date of December 31, 2010; configure a comment of Marketing User; and change the color to dark blue.

6. Click on the Groups tab and add the marketing group to the Belongs to Groups column.

7. Click on the Authentication tab, and configure an authentication scheme of VPN-1 & FireWall-1 Password.

8. Select the Time tab, and configure permitted access times to only be during the week between 8 A.M. and 6 P.M.

9. Click OK to complete your configuration. Repeat Steps 4 to 7 to create another user template object called Sales User with the following parameters.

   - Login Name: Sales User
   - Expiration Date: April 30, 2005
   - Comment: Sales User
   - Color: Red
   - Belongs to Group: Sales
   - Authentication Scheme: RADIUS (using AKLWEB01-RADIUS)

Apart from the authentication scheme, the entire configuration required for the above parameters is straight forward. The graphic below demonstrates the configuration required to configure RADIUS as the authentication scheme for the template, using the aklweb01-radius server object created in Exercise 6.2.

10. Once you have completed your configuration of both user template objects, the Users dialog box should now display the group objects and user template objects for sales and marketing.

You are now ready to create user objects for specific users. You will create a user called **alice** that belongs to the marketing group and a user called **bob** that belongs to the sales group.

11. Click New and select the User by Template ➤ Marketing User option from the dropdown list. This will display the User Template Properties dialog box for a new user object that is based on the Marketing User template object. Click on the General tab, and configure a login name of **alice**.

12. If you click on the Groups tab, you should see that the user object is a member of the marketing group, because the object has inherited this setting from the Marketing User template object.

13. Because the Marketing User template defines VPN-1 & FireWall-1 Password as the authentication scheme, you must configure a password for the user object. Select the Authentication tab, click the Change Password button, and configure a password of **alice123**.

14. Click OK to complete your configuration. Create another user object by clicking New and selecting the User by Template ➤ Sales User option from the dropdown list. Configure the user object with a login name of **bob**. Because the object is based on the Sales User template, you don't need to configure authentication as the authentication scheme is RADIUS, which means the password is managed externally on the RADIUS server.

15. Create an administrator object by selecting New ➤ Administrator by Template ➤ Default. This will display the Administrator Properties dialog box. Click on the General tab, configure a login name of **administrator**, and then click on New to create a new permissions profile object.

> **EXERCISE 6.3** *(continued)*
>
> 16. Configure the permissions profile object with a name of `full-access`, and then click on the Permissions tab. Select the Read/ Write All permission and then click OK to return to the Administrator Properties dialog box.
>
> 17. The administrator object should now have a permissions profile of `full-access` assigned. Click on the Authentication tab, configure an authentication scheme of VPN-1 & FireWall-1 Password, and configure a password of **admin123**. Once complete, click OK to create the administrator object. At this stage, the Users dialog box should contain all objects created in this exercise. Click Close to close the Users dialog box and return to the main view in Policy Editor.

Installing the Users Database

Once you have completed configuration of the users database, you must install it to the applicable enforcement modules to ensure that each has the most up-to-date users database available. The users database in VPN-1/ FireWall-1 is installed separately from the security rule base. This means that if you install a policy to an enforcement module, the current users database is not installed to the enforcement module as well. If you refer back to the Users dialog box shown in Figure 6.10, you can see an Install button. You must install the users database separately by clicking on the Install button in Figure 6.10. Figure 6.32 shows the Install Users Database dialog box, which is displayed after you click the Install button.

You can also install the users database by selecting Policy ➢ Install Users Database from the main menu in SmartDashboard.

Notice that the dialog box in Figure 6.32 is very similar to the dialog box displayed when you choose the enforcement modules on which a security policy is installed. Once you have selected the appropriate enforcement modules, click OK to begin the process of installing the users database to each enforcement module. Figure 6.33 shows the Install Users Database dialog box after installation of the users database has been successfully completed on an enforcement module.

FIGURE 6.32 The Install Users Database dialog box

FIGURE 6.33 The Install Users Database dialog box

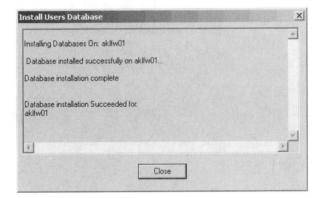

 You do not need to install the users database to enforcement modules when you only create or modify administrator objects, as these objects are only used by the management server. If you do not install the users database, you must however ensure you save the current policy in SmartDashboard by selecting File ➤ Save from the main menu. When you install the users database, it is automatically saved on the management server.

EXERCISE 6.4

Installing the Users Database and Testing Authentication

In the previous exercises you have configured the appropriate authentication schemes, server objects, and user database to support authentication. You must now install the users database to your enforcement module to complete the configuration required to enable authentication. You will test administrative access to VPN-1/FireWall-1 using the administrator object you created in Exercise 6.4.

1. Select Policy ➤ Install Users Database from the main menu, which will open the Install Users Database dialog box that should include your enforcement module. Ensure the ak1fw01 enforcement module is checked and then click OK.

2. At this point, installation of the database to the enforcement module will proceed. The Install Users Database dialog box will show the status of this. Click Close once installation has succeeded.

3. Exit and restart SmartDashboard. When prompted for authentication, specify a username of **administrator** and password of **admin123** (i.e., the administrator object credentials you created in Exercise 6.3), and then click OK to authenticate. You should authenticate successfully and be able to connect with full access rights.

Summary

Authentication provides you with powerful control over who can access your network on a per-user basis rather than just a per-host or per-device basis. On VPN-1/FireWall-1 NG, user-based authentication can be used for authenticating access to networks and services via security rules, as well as authenticating SecuRemote and SecureClient remote access VPN connections.

To enable user-based authentication, several prerequisites must be met. First, you must have an authentication database, which is a trusted store of user credentials, typically containing a username and password for each user. The type of authentication database used and the manner in which VPN-1/FireWall-1 interacts with an authentication database defines an authentication scheme. VPN-1/FireWall-1 supports its own internal authentication scheme (VPN-1 & FireWall-1 Password) as well as many other authentication schemes, such as OS Password, RADIUS, TACACS, S/Key, and SecurID. By purchasing the optional Account Management Module, the VPN-1/FireWall-1 can integrate with LDAP-compliant databases, allowing VPN-1/FireWall-1 to both manage LDAP databases and authenticate using LDAP. By default, VPN-1/FireWall-1 enforcement modules support RADIUS, TACACS, S/Key, SecurID, and AXENT Pathways Defender authentication schemes. If you wish to use another authentication scheme, or if you wish to disable an unused authentication scheme, you must configure the workstation object representing each enforcement module. Some authentication schemes use an external authentication database, such as RADIUS and TACACS, so to enable support for these schemes you must also configure objects that represent the servers that provide the interface to the external authentication database. In VPN-1/FireWall-1 NG, these objects are referred to as server objects.

Once you have enabled the appropriate authentication scheme(s), you must configure the users database, which is an internal VPN-1/FireWall-1 database maintained and managed by the management server. The users database includes user, user template, administrator, and group objects. User objects represent users that will authenticate at enforcement modules, while user template objects define common settings that you can apply to new users created from a template object. Each user object has an authentication scheme configured, which determines how the user will be authenticated. Depending on the authentication scheme, user passwords may be stored in the users database, or may be stored in an external authentication database. Administrator objects represent VPN-1/FireWall-1 administrators that will authenticate at the management server, for the purposes of using management clients such as SmartDashboard and Log Viewer. Group objects allow you to place user objects (and other group objects) that share a common set of privileges together. All authentication-based security rules on VPN-1/FireWall-1 require the use of group objects as opposed to user objects, so these objects are very important. The users database is managed centrally at the management server, but a copy is distributed to each enforcement module, which allows every enforcement module to authenticate users. When you make any changes to the users database on the management server, you must install the users database to each enforcement module to ensure the most up-to-date configuration is used.

Once you have enabled the authentication schemes that your VPN-1/FireWall-1 topology will use, and configured the appropriate objects in the VPN-1/FireWall-1 users database to represent the users and groups relevant to your network, you have the necessary base configuration to implement user-based authentication security rules. In the next chapter, you will learn how to implement these rules.

Exam Essentials

Understand authentication. Authentication is the process of accurately verifying that a remote party or user is who they claim to be. Authentication establishes the trusted identity of a remote party or user.

Know the authentication schemes supported by VPN-1/FireWall-1. VPN-1/FireWall-1 supports the VPN-1 & FireWall-1 Password, OS Password, RADIUS, TACACS, S/Key, and SecurID authentication schemes. VPN-1/FireWall-1 also supports authentication via LDAP if the account management module is installed.

Understand the VPN-1/FireWall-1 users database. The users database is configured and stored on the management server. The management server users database is the master copy of the users database, and a copy of the users database is installed to each enforcement module, ensuring that authentication can be performed locally by each enforcement module.

Know the authentication schemes supported for remote access (SecuRemote or SecureClient) VPN connections. If using FWZ, any authentication scheme is supported. If using IPSec, nonstandard authentication schemes are not supported (only pre-shared keys and certificates are supported), unless you enable hybrid mode authentication, which permits any authentication scheme to be used with IPSec VPNs.

Understand the different types of objects in the users database. The users database includes user objects, administrator objects, user template objects, group objects, and external group objects. User objects are used to represent users that wish to access systems and services protected by an authentication-based security rule, or for users that wish to connect via a remote access VPN connection. Administrator objects are used to define users that can administer VPN-1/FireWall-1 components. User template objects are used to define a set of common parameters that can be applied to any user or administrator objects that are created based on the template. Group objects are used to represent a collection of user, administrator, and other group objects, and are important as they are used for security rules that require authentication. External group objects are used for LDAP authentication.

Know the default objects present in the users database. By default, the users database includes a user template object called Default, and a group object called All Users.

Understand the various configuration parameters for each object in the users database. User objects include General, Groups, Location, Time, Encryption, Authentication, and Certificates configuration parameters. Administrator objects include all of the parameters for user objects, except for Encryption parameters. User template objects allow you to define any setting that can be commonly applied to multiple user and/or administrator objects.

Understand the order in which you must configure authentication. You should configure support for authentication as follows: First, enable support for the desired authentication schemes. Next, configure the users database and install the users database. Finally, configure authentication-based security rules.

Know how to enable support for authentication schemes. To enable support for authentication schemes, you must do so via the Authentication screen of the workstation object properties for each enforcement module.

Key Terms

Before you take the exam, be certain you are familiar with the following terms:

Account Management Module	organizational units
accounting	OS Password
administrator object	RADIUS
authentication	seed
authentication scheme	server objects
authorization	TACACS
credentials	token
group object	user template object
hybrid mode authentication	user object
Lightweight Directory Access Protocol	users database
one-time password (OTP)	VPN-1 & FireWall-1 Password

Review Questions

1. Which of the following authentication schemes is enabled by default? (Choose all that apply.)

   A. RADIUS

   B. TACACS

   C. OS Password

   D. LDAP

   E. VPN-1 & FireWall-1 Password

2. Which of the following mechanisms uses one-time passwords? (Choose all that apply.)

   A. RADIUS

   B. Certificates

   C. S/Key

   D. SecurID

   E. LDAP

   F. VPN-1 & FireWall-1 Password

3. VPN-1/FireWall-1 supports which of the following features of RADIUS and TACACS? (Choose all that apply.)

   A. Authentication

   B. Authorization

   C. Accounting

   D. Revocation

4. What is the maximum length of a VPN-1 & FireWall-1 Password?

   A. 7

   B. 8

   C. 12

   D. 14

5. Which of the following correctly defines case-sensitivity in VPN-1/FireWall-1?

   A. Both username and password are not case-sensitive.

   B. Username is not case-sensitive; password is case-sensitive.

   C. Username is case-sensitive; password is not case-sensitive.

   D. Both username and password are case-sensitive.

6. Which of the following authentication schemes uses passwords configured locally on each enforcement module?

   A. RADIUS

   B. OS Password

   C. TACACS

   D. VPN-1 & FireWall-1 Password

7. Which of the following authentication schemes uses an external authentication database?

   A. VPN-1 & FireWall-1 Password

   B. S/Key

   C. SecurID

   D. OS Password

8. You wish to authenticate network access to a sales database. Which of the following objects must you create? (Choose all that apply.)

   A. User objects to represent each sales user.

   B. An administrator object to represent the sales team leader.

   C. A user template object to ease the creation of sales users.

   D. A group object to represent the sales users.

9. Which of the following must be configured when creating a user object? (Choose all that apply.)

   A. Permitted login times

   B. Login name

   C. Authentication scheme

   D. VPN-1 & FireWall-1 Password

10. You wish to restrict the login times of a VPN-1/FireWall-1 administrator. Which method would you use to create the account for the administrator?

    A. cpconfig

    B. fwconfig

    C. Users database

    D. Security objects database

11. You wish to restrict the locations from which a VPN-1/FireWall-1 administrator can administer the management server. Which method would you use to create the account for the administrator?

    A. cpconfig

    B. fwconfig

    C. Users database

    D. Security objects database

12. You create a administrator object called carmen, configure an authentication scheme of VPN-1 & FireWall-1 Password, and configure a password of carmen123. The user specifies the correct username and password when authenticating; however, authentication fails. Access works from the same machine using another account. What could be the possible causes? (Choose all that apply.)

    A. Expiration date is in the past.

    B. User object is disabled.

    C. Users database has not been installed to the enforcement module.

    D. Security policy has not been installed to the enforcement module.

    E. System from which Carmen is connected is not an authorized GUI client.

13. An organization has five hundred users, which will use five different security rules. Each security rule will permit access for one hundred of the users, and each user will only be permitted for a single security rule. Which of the following objects should you create to enable access, and allow you to create the objects in the shortest amount of time? (Choose all that apply.)

   A. 500 administrator objects

   B. 5 user objects

   C. 500 user objects

   D. 5 group objects

   E. 500 group objects

   F. 1 user template object

   G. 5 user template objects

14. Which of the following is unique to an administrator object?

   A. Certificate

   B. Login name

   C. Permissions profile

   D. Permitted access times

15. True or False. A group object can be a member of another group object.

   A. True

   B. False

16. Which of the following must you create to represent a RADIUS server? (Choose all that apply.)

   A. Group object

   B. OPSec applications object

   C. Server object

   D. Workstation object

17. True or False. RADIUS protects password information transmitted between a RADIUS client and a RADIUS server by encrypting all communications with a shared secret.

    A. True

    B. False

18. Which of the following objects would you create to represent LDAP users?

    A. Administrator

    B. External group

    C. Group

    D. User

19. Which of the following authentication schemes would require a user to possess an external device separate from the computer that they are using to connect?

    A. RADIUS

    B. S/Key

    C. SecurID

    D. TACACS

20. VPN-1/FireWall-1 uses the users database for which of the following? (Choose all that apply.)

    A. Establishing a remote access VPN connection.

    B. Authenticating access to a particular service running on an internal system.

    C. Adding licenses to the management server.

    D. Adding new user objects to the users database.

Answers to Review Questions

1. A, B. By default, SecurID, RADIUS, and TACACS are enabled.

2. C, D. S/Key and SecurID use one-time passwords.

3. A. RADIUS and TACACS authentication is only supported. VPN-1/FireWall-1 performs its own authorization and accounting.

4. B. A VPN-1 & FireWall-1 Password must be between four and eight characters in length.

5. D. Both the username and password are case-sensitive on VPN-1/FireWall-1.

6. B. Be careful with this question. Notice that the question uses the word *configured*, which means that password configuration is performed locally on the enforcement module. This is not the case with RADIUS or TACACS, and with VPN-1 & FireWall-1 Password, password configuration is performed at the management server and then copied out to each enforcement module.

7. B, D. Both VPN-1 & FireWall-1 Password and S/Key store all credential information, including passwords (or last OTP for S/Key) in the users database. The other schemes all use an external authentication database.

8. A, D. Remember, all security rules that use authentication must use group objects, so you must create a group object. A group object that contains no members is useless, so you must also create user objects to represent each sales user. Although a user template object is not required to create user objects, they are recommended to ease the administrative overheads of creating users.

9. B, C. By default, a user object is permitted access at any time, so A is ruled out. You must configure a unique login name, as this identifies each user and you must also configure an authentication scheme for the user object, so that the enforcement module knows how to authenticate the user. You only need to configure VPN-1 & FireWall-1 Password if this authentication scheme is configured for the user object.

10. C.   Only administrator objects in the users database give you the capability to restrict the times during which a VPN-1/FireWall-1 administrator may log in.

11. A.   The GUI Clients tab in the `cpconfig` utility restricts which hosts (IP addresses) can configure and manage the management server. The location parameters for administrator objects (in the users database) are ignored by VPN-1/FireWall-1.

12. A.   You must ensure that the expiration date of any user object is in the future, otherwise the user object is considered invalid. A user object cannot be disabled, you must either remove it or alter the expiration date. Because this is an administrator object, you don't actually need to install the users database to enforcement modules (you only need to save the policy in Policy Editor, which automatically saves any changes to the users database on the management server). Because administrative access works from the same machine using a different username, options D and E cannot be correct.

13. C, D, G.   You must create an object for each user (i.e., 500 user objects), to allow VPN-1/FireWall-1 to authenticate each user. Security rules only use group objects, so you must create at least five group objects, one for each rule. To enable you to create all of these objects as quickly as possible, you must also create five user template objects, with each template object defining membership to a unique group object.

14. C.   The permissions profile parameter is unique to administrator objects, as it defines the privileges an administrator has to various VPN-1/FireWall-1 components.

15. A.   VPN-1/FireWall-1 NG permits the nesting of groups within each other.

16. C, D.   A server object represents the RADIUS service running on a host. In a server object, the host on which the RADIUS service is running must be represented by a workstation object.

17. B.   RADIUS only encrypts password information, but does not encrypt any other information, unlike TACACS which encrypts all information.

18. B.   External group objects represent users within an LDAP organizational unit.

19. C.   SecurID is a token-based authentication scheme that uses external devices to generate one-time passwords.

20. A, B, D.   User and group objects allow VPN-1/FireWall-1 to authenticate SecuRemote and SecureClient remote access VPN connections, as well as authenticate access to services and systems via security rules. Administrator objects allow for administrators to configure and manage the management server, including the users database. To add licenses, you must run the `cpconfig` utility, with access to this utility being controlled by administrative access to the operating system of the management server or enforcement module.

User, Client, and Session Authentication

THE CCSA EXAM OBJECTIVES COVERED IN THIS CHAPTER INCLUDE:

- ✓ Describe configuration for authentication parameters.
- ✓ List types of services supported by VPN-1/FireWall-1 NG requiring username and password.
- ✓ Describe implementation for client authentication.
- ✓ Describe implementation for session authentication.

Security policies are predominantly defined in terms of users and groups within the organization and outside the organization, and the systems and services that each can access. In the firewall world, many administrators are used to working with security rules based on source IP addresses rather than users, and consequently rules are defined that map the concept of a user to an IP address. This mapping works fine if a single user always uses the same IP address, but becomes inaccurate as soon as a user moves to a different IP address (common in DHCP environments) or if multiple users use the same machine. VPN-1/FireWall-1 provides authentication rules that allow you to define security policy based on users and groups, rather than source IP address, which ensures your security rules are tightly integrated with the security requirements of an organization.

Before you can authenticate users, you must prepare your VPN-1/FireWall-1 systems for authentication. In the previous chapter, you were introduced to the concept of authentication and you learned how to implement the necessary authentication schemes, as well as the user and group objects required for your organization. With this underlying configuration in place, you can implement authentication rules in your security policy. In this chapter, you will learn how you can implement security rules that control access based on users and groups, rather than just on IP addresses.

VPN-1/FireWall-1 supports a number of different *authentication types*, which determine how authentication is performed, the bounds of authentication, and the services supported by authentication. This chapter will examine user, client and session authentication, which comprise the authentication types supported on VPN-1/FireWall-1.

Concepts of Authentication Rules

To understand authentication-based security rules, it is important to review the basic security model used by VPN-1/FireWall-1. Figure 7.1 shows a network topology, where access is required to be controlled by a VPN-1/FireWall-1 enforcement module. A user called Alice is a web operator that needs to administer websites running on Server-A using HTTP.

FIGURE 7.1 Network topology

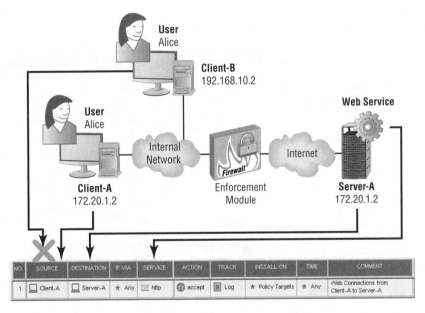

NO.	SOURCE	DESTINATION	IF VIA	SERVICE	ACTION	TRACK	INSTALL ON	TIME	COMMENT
1	Client-A	Server-A	✱ Any	TCP http	accept	Log	✱ Policy Targets	✱ Any	Web Connections from Client-A to Server-A

In Figure 7.1, a user called Alice on the inside of the enforcement module wishes to connect to a specific service (HTTP) on Server-A, which is connected externally to the enforcement module. The rule below the figure shows how you would permit this connection, based on the content covered so far in this book. Because Alice is using a computer called Client-A, which has an IP address of 192.168.10.2, the source element of the security rule specifies an object called Client-A (configured with an IP address of 192.168.10.2) as the permitted source. Alice wishes to establish a connection with Server-A, which has an IP address of 172.20.1.2; therefore, the destination element specifies an object called Server-A (configured with an IP address of 172.20.1.2). Because Alice only needs to access web services running on Server-A, the service element of the rule specifies that only the

HTTP service is permitted. The rule shown in Figure 7.1 grants Alice access to the web server running on Server-A, but this access is only granted access by virtue of the fact that she is located on Client-A. If Alice moves to Client-B, she will not be able to connect, as Client-B has not been configured as a permitted source. The problem with the rule is that it is based on the connecting host (IP address) rather than the connecting user—the enforcement module has no concept of Alice. So far in this book, you have learned how to approach the security policy requirement for Figure 7.1 in the manner described above. Figure 7.2 shows how you can use security rules to identify users, rather than the hosts that users are located on.

FIGURE 7.2 A user-based security rule

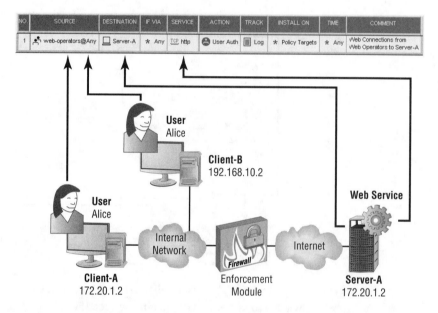

In Figure 7.2, you can see that the entity web-operators@any is defined in the Source element of the rule. Notice also that the Action element specifies an action of User Auth, rather than Accept. The web-operators@any expression means that the user group web-operators (as defined by the web-operators portion of the expression) is permitted from any IP address (as defined by the any portion of the expression). This means that the Source element of the rule has been extended to identify not only permitted source IP addresses, but also a permitted group of users. The destination and service elements are the same as the rule in Figure 7.1, which means the only thing that has changed is that VPN-1/FireWall-1 identifies who is making HTTP connections to Server-A based on users and the IP address of the hosts from which each is connecting from, rather than just IP address. VPN-1/FireWall-1 defines user access in security rules by using groups rather than individual users, as security policy should always be defined in terms of a functional group, instead in terms of an individual user. For example, there may be another web operator called Bob, who also needs to administer websites on Server-A. If you created a rule that only specified the user object representing Alice, Bob would not be able to administer Server-A without a new rule being added. By creating a group that defines the role or purpose of users that require access and then granting the group the appropriate access via security rules, you can then simply add users to the group as required, and each user will inherit the security access configured in security rules that include the group.

User-Based Authentication

You might ask why you would provide user-based authentication at a firewall, instead of the destination systems that a user is attempting to access. The answer is scalability and ease of management. If an organization has a single web server that requires authentication, it is easy to implement authentication on that server and maintain it on a regular basis. If an organization has a thousand web servers however, implementing authentication on each web server becomes difficult to manage. By implementing authentication on the security gateway of the network (i.e., a VPN-1/FireWall-1 enforcement module), you introduce a single point of authentication, which makes management easy and also integrates the access policies for your web servers into your network security policy.

You might be wondering now how VPN-1/FireWall-1 matches new connections to an authentication-based rule and then identifies users to verify they are authorized for the rule. With traditional security rules, VPN-1/FireWall-1 matches connections to security rules by comparing the following parameters:

- Source IP address of received packet with Source element

- Destination IP address of received packet with Destination element

- IP protocol and source/destination TCP/UDP ports of received packet with Service element

Of course, once a connection has been matched to a security rule and permitted, the connection parameters above are written to the connection table on the INSPECT module, which ensures return traffic for the connection can be permitted. This operation works for all types of traffic, as all IP traffic has at least a source IP address, destination IP address, and an IP protocol number (if the IP protocol number indicates TCP or UDP, source/destination TCP/UDP ports are also always present).

When you throw in authentication to this model, it starts to become a bit more difficult. Most Layer 3/4 protocols, including the most common protocols (IP, TCP, and UDP) do not include any authentication mechanism that can identify the user that has actually caused a packet to be generated. Because of the inability of IP, TCP, and UDP to identify users, if a network application wishes to identify users and grant access based on a connecting user (rather than just an IP address), application-layer protocols must include their own mechanisms. For example, HTTP includes a mechanism for authenticating users. If you go to a website and are prompted for a username and password, you are being identified from a user perspective rather than an IP address perspective. Unfortunately not all application-layer protocols include a mechanism to authenticate users, which means if you wish to enforce a security policy that requires you to control access based on users and groups, rather than IP address, you have a problem.

To support common protocols that include their own authentication mechanisms, as well as protocols that do not, VPN-1/FireWall-1 provides two generic methods of authentication: in-band and out-of-band.

In-band authentication   *In-band authentication* means that authentication is provided within the application-layer protocol that a user is attempting to use. Many application-layer protocols define methods by which users can be authenticated, because the inventors of these protocols have recognized the need to establish identity. For a firewall to implement in-band authentication, it must have an understanding of the application-layer protocol it is required to authenticate access for. Consider the case of HTTP. If an HTTP client attempts to access an HTTP server through a firewall, and the firewall is configured to authenticate the connection, the firewall must emulate the HTTP server the client is accessing, as the HTTP server would normally challenge the client for authentication if authentication was enabled on the HTTP server. For each application-layer protocol that a firewall needs to authenticate, the firewall must run a server-side implementation of the protocol, to ensure it can authenticate an incoming connection on behalf of a protected system. VPN-1/FireWall-1 provides *security servers*, which are application-layer services or daemons that can provide authentication services for common protocols, by intercepting the initial connection requests, authenticating the requests, and then allowing the connection to proceed.

Out-of-band authentication   *Out-of-band authentication* means that authentication is provided externally from the application-layer protocol that a user is attempting to use. Some protocols do not specify mechanisms for authentication, which means it is impossible to implement in-band authentication. It is also very difficult for a firewall to understand the many application-layer protocols in use today and how to authenticate each of these, according to the authentication mechanisms provided within the protocol. To implement the code necessary for a firewall to support authentication for the various protocols would take a very large effort, with the complexity reducing the stability and performance of the firewall. For these reasons, VPN-1/FireWall-1 only supports in-band authentication for a few very common application-layer protocols, and supports out-of-band authentication for all other protocols. This means that for a user who needs out-of-band authentication, the user must first establish a connection to the VPN-1/FireWall-1 enforcement module. Once authentication is successful, the user is authorized to make connections to the destination systems and services specified in the authentication rule on the enforcement module.

In both of the authentication methods listed above, it is important to understand that authentication is performed only when a connection is initiated. Once authentication is successful, the connection is allowed to be established and the Layer 3/4 parameters associated with the connection are written to the connection table. Subsequent packets exchanged during the life of the connection are identified based on parameters such as source/ destination IP address and source/destination TCP/UDP port and matched to an existing connection in the connection table, and there is no concept at this stage of users or authentication.

If a new connection is initiated from the host that the user is located on, depending on the type of authentication implemented, the new connection may or may not require authentication once again. This is discussed later in the chapter.

VPN-1/FireWall-1 supports several types of authentication, which can be categorized as either an in-band authentication or out-of-band authentication.

If you refer back to Figure 7.2, you will notice that the Action element of the security rule specifies an action of User Auth. This refers to user authentication, which is one of the types of authentication supported by VPN-1/FireWall-1. In total, there are three types of authentication that exist on VPN-1/FireWall-1 NG:

- User authentication
- Client authentication
- Session authentication

The Action element in a security rule defines which of the above types of authentication is implemented. Each of these authentication types will be discussed in detail in this chapter.

Transparent and Non-Transparent Authentication

Each authentication type supported on VPN-1/FireWall-1 can be classified as *transparent* or *non-transparent*. These terms refer to how authentication is actually implemented and how intrusive the authentication process is to the user. Let's start by first examining transparent authentication.

Transparent authentication occurs when a user attempts to establish a connection to the desired system and service the user wishes to connect to, after which the user is then challenged for authentication. The user thinks that the destination system is prompting the user for authentication, when really an enforcement module in the middle of the connection is prompting the user for authentication. The user has no concept that the enforcement module exists; hence, it is transparent to the user. Figure 7.3 demonstrates transparent authentication.

FIGURE 7.3 Transparent authentication

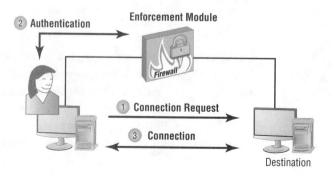

Destination

In Figure 7.3, the following events occur:

1. The user attempts to establish a connection with the desired destination system.

2. The enforcement module matches the connection to a rule that requires authentication. The enforcement module challenges the user for authentication, holding the connection request until authentication has been completed. The user sends his or her credentials to the enforcement module, which authenticates them and ensures the user is permitted access to the destination.

3. Assuming authentication is successful, the original connection request sent in Step 1 is passed to the destination system, and a connection can now be established.

Non-transparent authentication occurs when a user first establishes a connection with an enforcement module, authenticates, and then attempts to connect to the desired destination. With non-transparent authentication, once the user has authenticated, the user is then authorized to establish connections to the desired destination. Because the user must explicitly connect to the enforcement module, the enforcement module is non-transparent to the user, hence the name. Figure 7.4 demonstrates non-transparent authentication.

FIGURE 7.4   Non-transparent authentication

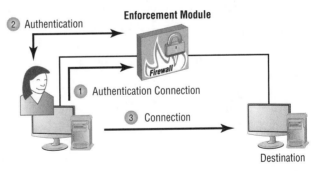

In Figure 7.4, the following events occur:

1. The user establishes a connection to the enforcement module for the purposes of authentication.

2. Authentication information is passed from the user to the enforcement module. The enforcement module authenticates the user and then looks up any rules that the user is permitted to access. Because the user has authenticated successfully, these rules are now authorized for the user.

3. The user attempts to connect to the desired destination. Because authentication was successful in Step 2, the enforcement module permits the connection.

Each authentication type on VPN-1/FireWall-1 can be defined as transparent or non-transparent. It is important to understand the concepts of transparency and non-transparency, as it has a direct impact on how intrusive and complex it is for users to authenticate.

Understanding Rule Processing Order with Authentication Rules

It is very important that you understand how authentication rules are processed in relation to normal security rules. Regardless of the type of authentication being configured for a security rule, all authentication rules are processed by an enforcement module *after* security rules, which means that even if an authentication rule is configured above a security rule in the security rule base, a connection matching both rules will be matched against the security rule first. For example, if an incoming connection can be matched to both an authentication rule and a security rule, the connection is always matched against the security rule first, regardless of whether or not the authentication rule is higher in the rule base. If the security rule specifies an action of Accept, the connection will be permitted and authentication will not take place. If the security rule specifies an action of Reject or Drop, the connection will only then be matched against the authentication rule if the authentication rule is higher in the rule base than the rejecting or dropping security rule.

When configuring authentication rules, you must be very careful that connections you wish to authenticate do not match other normal security rules, as the connections may be permitted without authentication. Remember that this can happen, even if the security rule is below the authentication rule.

User Authentication

*U*ser authentication provides native, in-band authentication of HTTP, FTP, TELNET, and RLOGIN connections. The VPN-1/FireWall-1 enforcement module provides security servers for each of these protocols, which are application-layer daemons that can both emulate server-side connections from a client (for the purposes of challenging the client for authentication information) and spawn client-side connections to a server, on behalf of other clients (after successful authentication). When user authentication is configured for a rule, connection requests that match the rule are intercepted and forwarded to the appropriate security server. For example, when an HTTP request is sent from a client to a destination web server, the enforcement module intercepts the request and passes it to the HTTP security server, which establishes an HTTP connection with the client (the client thinks that it has established a connection with the destination web server). The HTTP security server then challenges the client for authentication details. The client returns authentication information, which is authenticated by the authentication scheme defined for the user object that matches the username supplied by the client. Once authentication is successful, the security server establishes a new connection to the destination web server, and passes back to the source any HTTP traffic from the destination. All subsequent traffic is passed over two connections—one from the web client to the security server and the second from the security server to the web server. Figure 7.5 demonstrates user authentication over an HTTP connection.

FIGURE 7.5 User authentication

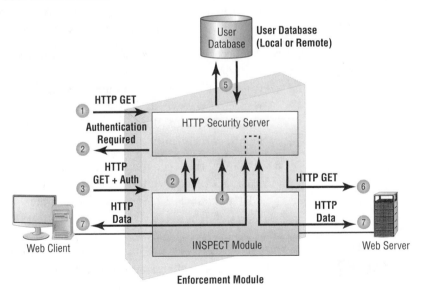

In Figure 7.5 the following events occur:

1. The web client initiates a TCP connection to port 80 (i.e. an HTTP connection) on the web server. This connection setup is received by the enforcement module, which matches the traffic to a rule that specifies user authentication should take place. The connection setup request is passed to the security server and the connection is actually established to the security server (which essentially pretends to be the web server)— the key point is that the web client thinks it has formed a basic HTTP connection with the web server. The web client sends an HTTP GET request, which requests the content of a URL on the web server.

2. The HTTP GET request is received by the enforcement module and matched to a connection in the connection table pending authentication. The GET request is passed to the security server, which sends back a response to the web client that advises the web client authentication is required.

3. The web client prompts the user for a username and password. The user specifies his or her credentials and a new HTTP GET request is sent, this time including authentication data.

4. The HTTP GET request is received by the enforcement module and matched to a connection in the connection table pending authentication. The GET request is passed to the security server.

5. The security server extracts the authentication data and passes it to a local or remote (e.g., RADIUS) authentication database for authentication. This database contains a list of valid usernames and their respective passwords. The credentials supplied by the web client will either be rejected (this is then indicated to the web client, who can try and re-authenticate) or will be accepted.

6. Assuming the credentials are correct, the security server now establishes a TCP connection to the web server and forwards the HTTP GET request sent in Step 4 with the authentication data stripped out.

A TCP connection is not established from the security server to the destination specified in a user authentication rule until after the source has authenticated successfully with the security server.

7. The web client and web server can now communicate. It is important to understand that all traffic from the web client is passed to the

security server, which then forwards this traffic to the web server, and vice versa. This is because the web client sends authentication data in every HTTP packet, which must be stripped by the security server before forwarding to the web server (as the web server is not expecting authentication from the client).

Although the security server is involved in every HTTP transaction exchanged between the web client and web server, the web client (and web server) have no idea that the security server exists. As described in Figure 7.5, the client has a connection with the security server, and the security server has another connection to the server. The same process described for HTTP in Figure 7.5 applies to the other services supported by user authentication. This means that user authentication is considered transparent.

At this point, it is important to introduce the concept of *authorization scope*. When any type of authentication is performed in VPN-1/FireWall-1, authorization takes place after successful authentication. It is very important that you understand exactly what is authorized after authentication for each of the authentication types. The authorization scope defines exactly what is authorized after authentication and for how long. For user authentication, only the connection that is authenticated is authorized. This means that any new connections require another authentication. This also means that user authentication is very secure, but is intrusive, as the user must authenticate every new connection. Although this may not be a problem for protocols that operate over a single connection, it is a problem for protocols that use multiple connections. The major example of this is HTTP—when a user opens a web page, many HTTP connections may be opened to other web servers, as some content on the web page may not reside on the web server hosting the page. This means that the web browser client must open new HTTP connections to other web servers, which means the user must re-authenticate for each new connection. This will become very intrusive and irritating for the user.

Most web browsers will cache authentication information for a particular web server they are communicating with. This means your web browser can open multiple connections to the *same* web server without requiring re-authentication, as the browser will attach cached authentication information in the HTTP packets sent over the new connections. Your web browser will not cache authentication data for other web servers that you connect to; hence, you need to authenticate at least once per web server that is connected to. If you shut down your browser and restart it, you will lose the cached authentication information.

Configuring User Authentication

Before you configure user authentication rules, you must ensure that you have configured the following prerequisites, which you should recall from the discussion in Chapter 6:

- Configured the appropriate authentication schemes.

- Created user objects for users that you wish to identify.

- Created group objects that represent the functional groups (collection of users) that share a common privilege level.

- Installed the users database to your enforcements modules.

Once you have configured the above prerequisites, you have the necessary supporting configuration to implement user authentication. To configure user authentication rules, you should perform the following actions:

- Configure global user authentication parameters.

- Create a user authentication rule.

- Customize user authentication rule parameters.

Each of these tasks is now discussed in detail.

Configuring Global User Authentication Parameters

For user authentication, there are several parameters that can be either configured globally for all user authentication rules installed on a single VPN-1/FireWall-1 enforcement module, or configured globally for *all* enforcement modules. These parameters include the following:

- Security server welcome messages

- Failed authentication attempts

- User authentication session timeout

Security Server Welcome Messages

You can modify the banners used by the TELNET, FTP, and RLOGIN security servers displayed during authentication, which allows you to display custom text that may be relevant to your organization. To modify the welcome messages displayed, choose Policy ➤ Global Properties from the SmartDashboard menu, and then select the FireWall-1 ➤ Security Server screen. Within this screen, you should see fields that allow you to specify a welcome message

file for the TELNET, FTP, and RLOGIN security servers. Figure 7.6 shows
the Security Server screen.

FIGURE 7.6   The Security Server screen

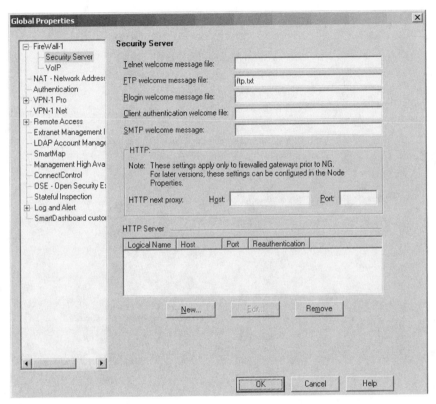

In Figure 7.6, notice that the filename ftp.txt is specified as the welcome
message file for the FTP security server. When configuring message files,
ensure that you place the file in the $FWDIR/conf directory of your manage-
ment server, and then specify only the filename in the appropriate welcome
message file field in Figure 7.6. The welcome message file is simply a text
file that includes the custom banner that you wish to be displayed. The
welcome message file text will be appended to the normal welcome messages
displayed by the security server; it will not replace the normal welcome
messages. The welcome messages are also configured globally for all security
servers running on all enforcement modules.

Having a banner that warns off unauthorized access is important in some jurisdictions for prosecuting parties that have illegally gained access to your systems.

Failed Authentication Attempts

For all authentication types (user, client, and session authentication), you can globally configure the maximum number of *failed authentication attempts* before a connection is torn down. These settings are configured from the Authentication screen within the Global Properties dialog box, which is opened by selecting Policy ➢ Global Properties from the SmartDashboard menu. Figure 7.7 shows this screen.

FIGURE 7.7 The Authentication screen

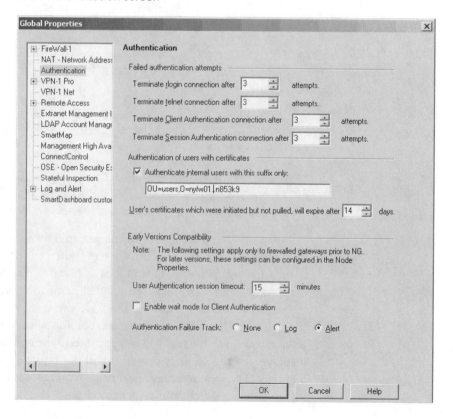

In Figure 7.7, the Failed authentication attempts section allows you to define the number of failed authentication attempts permissible for RLOGIN and TELNET connections. The default setting for each of these is three attempts. If a user fails authentication for three attempts, the connection is torn down, and the user must establish a new TELNET or RLOGIN connection.

User Authentication Session Timeout

The *User Authentication session timeout* parameter has a different meaning depending on the protocol the timeout is applied to. For FTP, TELNET, and RLOGIN connections, the User Authentication session timeout parameter represents the amount of time a single connection is idle (no activity is detected) before the connection is torn down. If an idle connection is torn down, the user must reestablish the connection and re-authenticate. For HTTP connections, the User Authentication session timeout parameter is used to extend the validity of a one-time password (OTP) for the time period configured. For example, if user authentication is invoked for an HTTP connection, and the user authenticates using an OTP scheme such as SecurID, the user is authorized for the user authentication session timeout period for subsequent connections, meaning the user does not need to re-authenticate new connections during this time period.

The User Authentication session timeout parameter is defined on a per-gateway (enforcement module) basis on VPN-1/FireWall-1 NG; however, for all versions prior to NG, this parameter is defined globally (see Figure 7.7). To configure the User Authentication session timeout parameter for a VPN-1/FireWall-1 NG enforcement module, first select Manage ➢ Network Objects from the SmartDashboard menu to open the Network Objects dialog box. From here, select the appropriate Check Point object representing the enforcement module that you wish to configure, and then click the Edit button. This will display the Check Point Gateway dialog box for the enforcement module object. The User Authentication session timeout parameter is present on the Authentication screen, as shown in Figure 7.8.

In Figure 7.8, you can see that the user authentication session timeout is set to 15 minutes (the default). This means that if a user leaves a user-authenticated FTP, TELNET, or RLOGIN connection idle for 15 minutes, the connection will be torn down.

FIGURE 7.8 Configuring user authentication session timeout

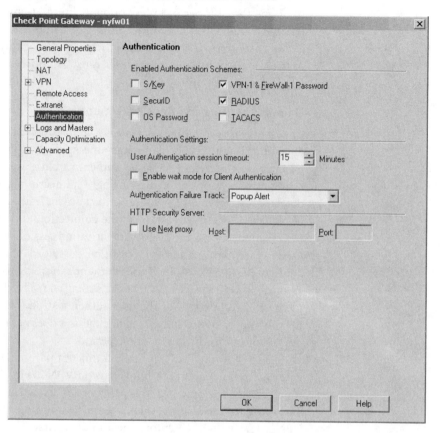

To configure the User Authentication session timeout parameter for enforcement modules prior to NG, open the Global Properties dialog box by selecting Policy ➢ Global Properties from the SmartDashboard menu, and then display the Authentication screen. On this screen you can configure the User Authentication session timeout parameter, which will apply to all enforcement modules prior to NG.

Creating a User Authentication Rule

Once you have defined the appropriate global user authentication parameters, you can begin to create your user authentication rules. All authentication-based rules only support the use of the Source element of a rule for defining the permitted groups of users for the rules. You cannot define users as the Destination element of a rule, as there is no way for VPN-1/FireWall-1 to authenticate the destination of a connection. To create a user authentication rule, first of all create a new security rule, by selecting the appropriate option (Bottom, Top, Below, or Above) from the Rules ➢ Add Rule submenu within SmartDashboard. This will create a default rule that drops all traffic. The following describes how you should configure each of the elements in the rule to implement user authentication:

Source Element   To add user access to the Source element of the rule, right-click within the Source element and select the Add Users Access from the menu that appears. This will display the User Access dialog box, which allows you to select the user group object that you wish to specify in the rule. Figure 7.9 shows the User Access dialog box.

FIGURE 7.9   The User Access dialog box

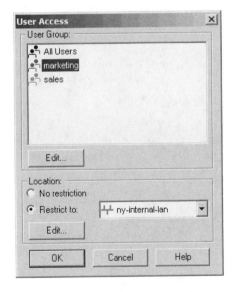

In Figure 7.9, all of the User Group objects in the user database are displayed, with the `marketing` group is selected. The Location parameters allow you to restrict the permitted IP addresses that the user can authenticate from, which provides the additional security of limiting access based on both source IP address and user authentication. By default, the Location is set to No restriction, which means a user can authenticate from any IP address. Notice in Figure 7.9 that the Location has been restricted to the `ny-internal-lan` network object, meaning users can only authenticate from hosts on that network. Once you have completed your configuration, click OK to add the access specified to the Source element of the rule you have just created.

You can add multiple user group objects to the Source element of a rule.

Destination Element   The next element of the rule you will configure is the Destination element, which is configured in the same manner as a normal security rule. For example, you might specify a network object in the Destination element, which represents the destination network the users specified in the Source element are trying to access.

Service Element   For the Service element, you must ensure that the services you configure only include one or more of the services that are supported by user authentication (`http`, `ftp`, `telnet`, and `rlogin` service objects).

VPN-1/FireWall-1 includes a predefined service group object called `Authenticated`, which includes each of the services supported by user authentication.

Action Element   Next you will configure the Action element, which is where you specify that the rule is an authentication-based rule, rather than a normal security rule. To specify that user authentication is to be invoked, right-click in the Action element and select the User Auth option.

Track, Install On, Time, and Comment Elements   The remaining security rule elements (Track, Install On, Time, and Comment) are configured identically to the manner in which you configure normal security rules.

Figure 7.10 demonstrates a user authentication security rule, which includes user access configured in the Source element and an Action element of User Auth.

FIGURE 7.10   A user authentication security rule

NO.	SOURCE	DESTINATION	IF VIA	SERVICE	ACTION	TRACK	INSTALL ON	TIME	COMMENT
1	marketing@ny-internal-lan	✱ Any	✱ Any	Authenticated	User Auth	Log	✱ Policy Targets	✱ Any	User Authentication Rule

In Figure 7.10, notice that the Source element specifies a permitted group of `marketing@ny-internal-lan`. This group represents users that belong to the `marketing` group that are authenticating from a host within the `ny-internal-lan` network. Users in the group that authenticate from a host outside the `ny-internal-lan` network are not permitted access. Notice that the Service element specifies the `Authenticated` service group, which is a group object including the HTTP, FTP, TELNET, and RLOGIN services. The Action element of User Auth tells the enforcement module that any new connections matching this rule should be passed to the user authentication security servers for authentication.

After completing the configuration of a user authentication security rule, you must install the policy to your enforcement modules for the rule to take effect.

Customizing User Authentication Rule Parameters

In Figure 7.10, you saw how to create a simple user authentication rule. When you create a user authentication rule, you can customize a number of parameters for the specific rule. To customize a user authentication rule, right-click on the User Auth action in the Action element of the rule, and select the Edit properties option to display the User Authentication Action Properties dialog box. This dialog box allows you to customize how user authentication is implemented for the rule. Figure 7.11 shows the User Authentication Action Properties dialog box.

FIGURE 7.11 The User Authentication Action Properties dialog box

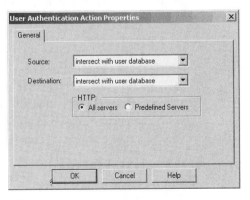

You can see in Figure 7.11 that there are three parameters you can define (Source, Destination, and HTTP), which are now discussed in detail.

Source and Destination

The source parameter in Figure 7.11 allows you to configure how access should be determined if the Location specified in the Source element of the rule (see Figure 7.9) is not part of the permitted source locations configured for the user object that represents the user that is authenticating on the rule. If you refer back to Chapter 6, remember that you can restrict the source location that a user is permitted access from. If the location permitted in the Source element of the rule is not a permitted location in the user object, the Source parameter in Figure 7.11 determines how this "conflict" is handled. The Source dropdown box allows you to choose two options:

Intersect with user database   The default setting, which defines that the locations restricted for the user object should be enforced. This means that if the source IP address of the host from which the user is authenticating is not included within the sources defined on the Locations tab for the user object, access will be denied, even if the source IP address of the host is permitted in the locations parameter of the Source element for the security rule.

Ignore user database   Choosing this option means that the Locations tab on the user object is ignored, meaning the source IP address of the host from which the user is authenticating must only be within the locations defined in the Source element of the security rule.

The Destination parameter in Figure 7.11 has the same definition and configuration options as the Source parameter, except this applies to the Destination element of the user authentication rule and the Destinations parameter in the Location tab of the user object.

HTTP

The HTTP parameter defines how HTTP connections should be handled by the HTTP security server after user authentication is successful. This setting only affects HTTP connections, and does not affect FTP, TELNET, or RLOGIN connection. As you can see in Figure 7.11, there are two configurable options, Predefined Servers and All servers

PREDEFINED SERVERS

The default setting is the Predefined Servers option, which defines that all incoming HTTP connections are handled according to the configuration of the HTTP Server section under the FireWall-1 ➢ Security Server screen in the global properties of the security policy. To access this screen, select Policy ➢ Global Properties from the SmartDashboard menu, which displays the Global Properties dialog box. You can then navigate to the FireWall-1 ➢ Security Server screen, which includes the HTTP Server section as shown in Figure 7.12.

FIGURE 7.12   The Security Servers screen

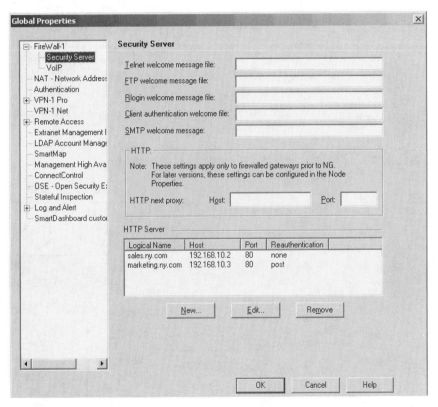

In Figure 7.12, you can see in the HTTP Server table that two *logical servers* are configured—sales.ny.com and marketing.ny.com. You can think of a logical server as a virtual web server or a website—a feature of many web servers is that they can host many websites while operating on a single IP address. For example, a web server might host a website called abc.com as well as a website called xyz.com, which are totally separate and unrelated. To allow a web server to determine which website connecting clients wish to see, a client specifies the logical server name (e.g., abc.com) in the HTTP

GET request sent. The web server will then serve the appropriate website content to the client.

The Host field is the field in the HTTP GET request that specifies the logical server a web client wishes to connect to.

When the Predefined Servers feature is configured for a user authentication rule, HTTP connections are only permitted to the logical servers listed. In addition to this restriction, all incoming HTTP connections must be directed to the external IP address on the VPN-1/FireWall-1 enforcement module. Each incoming HTTP connection will be examined by the security server, which will determine the website (logical server) that the connecting client wishes to connect to, and will then establish a connection on behalf of the client to the appropriate host specified in Figure 7.12. For example, consider Figure 7.13.

FIGURE 7.13 Using the Predefined Servers feature

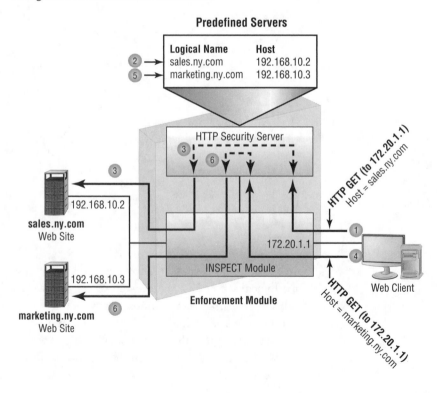

The following describes the events that occur in Figure 7.13.

1. In order for the Predefined Servers feature to work, the web client must resolve both the sales.ny.com and marketing.ny.com hostnames to 172.20.1.1, which is the external IP address of the enforcement module. Let's assume that the web client first wants to access the sales.ny.com website. The web client establishes an HTTP connection with the external IP address of the enforcement module, which is passed to the HTTP security server. The web client sends an HTTP GET request that includes a host field configured with the name of the website (logical server) the web client wishes to access (i.e., sales.ny.com).

2. At this point, authentication will occur. Assuming user authentication is successful, the enforcement module reads the host field in the HTTP GET request, and determines that the web client wishes to access the sales.ny.com website. The security server reads the Predefined Servers table (as defined in the HTTP Server section of Figure 7.12) and determines that the internal web server hosting this website is 192.168.10.2.

3. The HTTP security server establishes a connection to the web server at 192.168.10.2 and relays the HTTP GET request originally sent from the web client. The website content is returned to the security server, which then relays this content back to the web client. All subsequent HTTP traffic for the connection is always processed by the HTTP security server and relayed to the web client or web server.

4. Now the web client wants to access the marketing.ny.com website. The web client establishes an HTTP connection with the external IP address of the enforcement module, which is passed to the HTTP security server. The web client sends an HTTP GET request that includes a host field configured with the name of the website (logical server) the web client wishes to access (i.e., marketing.ny.com).

5. At this point, authentication will occur. Assuming user authentication is successful, the enforcement module reads the host field in the HTTP GET request, and determines that the web client wishes to access the marketing.ny.com website. The security server reads the Predefined Servers table (as defined in the HTTP Server section of Figure 7.12) and determines that the internal web server hosting this website is 192.168.10.3.

6. The HTTP security server establishes a connection to the web server at 192.168.10.3 and relays the HTTP GET request originally sent from the web client. The website content is returned to the security server, which then relays this content back to the web client. All subsequent HTTP traffic for the connection is always processed by the HTTP security server and relayed to the web client or web server.

The Predefined Servers feature means that your firewall can front-end all of your web servers and route all incoming web requests to the appropriate web server based on the website being accessed. Notice in Figure 7.12 that you can also specify the port to connect to on the internal web server hosting the web site content. You can also specify re-authentication options, which allow you to define how connections to the website are re-authenticated. In Figure 7.12, connections to `sales.ny.com` are not re-authenticated after initial user authentication (as indicated by the "none" setting), whereas connections to `marketing.ny.com` require re-authentication by the enforcement module if a POST request is sent from the web client to the web server (i.e., the client tries to write data to the server).

Use the Predefined Servers feature for user authentication rules that permit external users accessing internal web servers.

ALL SERVERS

The All servers setting in Figure 7.11 permits access to any web server after user authentication. When using this option, web clients do not connect to the IP address of the enforcement module, instead they connect to the desired destination web server. The enforcement module will intercept these connections and pass them to the HTTP security server for authentication. Assuming authentication is successful, the HTTP security server will then establish a connection to the original destination web server on behalf of the client, and then relay all content between the web client and web server. All Servers is useful when you are permitting access to unknown or a large number of web servers; however, it does not allow for re-authentication features. Figure 7.14 demonstrates how HTTP user authentication works when the All servers option is configured for a user authentication rule.

FIGURE 7.14   Using the All servers feature

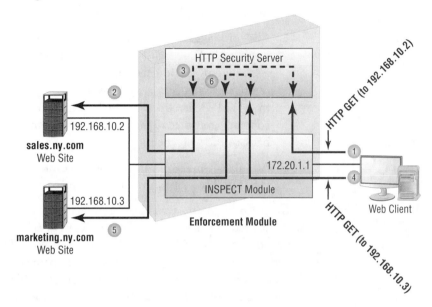

The following describes the events that occur in Figure 7.14.

1. Let's assume that the web client wants to access the sales.ny.com web site. Because the All servers feature is configured, the web client must establish an HTTP connection with the IP address of the actual web server hosting the website. The web client sends an HTTP GET request to the 192.168.10.2 address.

2. The enforcement module intercepts the HTTP GET request and passes it to the HTTP security server. At this point, authentication will occur. Assuming user authentication is successful, the security server will establish a connection to the web server at 192.168.10.2 and relay the HTTP GET request originally sent from the web client. The website content is returned to the security server, which then relays this content back to the web client.

3. All subsequent HTTP traffic for the connection is always processed by the HTTP security server and relayed to the web client or web server.

4. Now the web client wants to access the marketing.ny.com website. Because the All servers feature is configured, the web client must establish an HTTP connection with the IP address of the actual web

server hosting the website. The web client sends an HTTP GET request to 192.168.10.3.

5. The enforcement module intercepts the HTTP GET request and passes it to the HTTP security server. At this point, authentication will occur. Assuming user authentication is successful, the security server will establish a connection to the web server at 192.168.10.3 and relay the HTTP GET request originally sent from the web client. The website content is returned to the security server, which then relays this content back to the web client.

6. All subsequent HTTP traffic for the connection is always processed by the HTTP security server and relayed to the web client or web server.

If you compare the events of Figure 7.14 with Figure 7.13, notice that with the Predefined Servers feature, the HTTP security server takes the additional step of reading the host field in the HTTP GET request, to determine which logical server the web client wishes to connect to. This requires every logical server to be defined in the HTTP Server table in the Security Server screen of the Global Properties dialog box. If you are implementing user authentication for web clients that are connecting to any number of web servers on the Internet, clearly it would be impossible to configure all of these in the HTTP Server section. For this reason, you should configure the All servers feature when you are implementing user authentication for web clients that are accessing a large number of web servers. Referring back to Figure 7.11, the HTTP parameter is configured as All servers, as the Destination element in Figure 7.10 is configured as Any, indicating the user authentication rule applies to a large number of destination web servers.

Use the All servers feature for user authentication rules that permit internal users accessing Internet web servers.

The User Authentication Process

Now that you have learned how to configure user authentication, it is important that you understand the process that a user must participate in when user authentication is required. The protocols supported by user authentication all support their own authentication mechanisms, which may be configured at the destination systems configured in a user authentication rule. Having a security server provide authentication in the middle of a connection can cause some issues, especially if authentication is required at the destination (server), as well as by the security server on the enforcement module. For example, if you establish a TELNET connection to a host, you normally are authenticated by that host before being granted access. If you are using user authentication for the TELNET connection, both the VPN-1/ FireWall-1 TELNET security server and the destination TELNET server require authentication. How does a user authenticate against both the security server and destination server? The following sections describe how authentication at the destination is handled for each protocol when user authentication is implemented.

HTTP

When a web client establishes an HTTP connection to a web server, and the security rule matching the traffic specifies that user authentication is required, the HTTP connection from the client is passed to the HTTP security server, which challenges the web client for authentication information. Normally, the web client simply enters the username and password of a user object configured on the enforcement module. Figure 7.15 shows the authentication prompt displayed when a web client attempts to access a web server and user authentication is configured.

FIGURE 7.15 User Authentication prompt for HTTP

In Figure 7.15, the web client is attempting to connect to the website `www.checkpoint.com`. This connection has matched a user authentication rule on an enforcement module in between the client and destination web server, which passes the connection to the HTTP security server. The web client is then challenged for authentication information as shown in Figure 7.15. The user has specified a username of `alice` and the appropriate password. Assuming the credentials are correct, the HTTP security server will accept the connection and then establish a connection to `www.checkpoint.com` on behalf of the web client. The method described in Figure 7.15 works for destination web servers that do not require authentication. If a destination web server does require its own authentication, then the web client must authenticate in a different manner.

When a web client connects to a destination web server that requires authentication, you might expect the user to be prompted for authentication again after successfully authenticating via user authentication. This in fact will happen if you attempt to authenticate as demonstrated in Figure 7.15 on the enforcement module. After successful authentication, the destination web server will prompt for authentication, which will be relayed to the web client. Even if the client enters valid authentication information, the connection will not work, due to the way HTTP authentication works. When HTTP authentication is used by a web client, the client attaches HTTP authentication information to every packet that is sent from the client. This is quite unlike other protocols, such as TELNET or FTP, where authentication information is only sent initially to establish a connection. In the scenario described above, when the web client specifies authentication data for the destination web server, the authentication data sent in each packet to the HTTP security server is overwritten. The HTTP security server can no longer validate that the HTTP packets sent are authenticated, as they now include credentials for a different system (the destination server), and the packets are rejected.

For situations where authentication is required at both the HTTP security server and the destination web server, you must specify both usernames and both passwords when authenticating with the HTTP security server. You might be wondering exactly how the web client supplies two sets of credentials rather than one. This is achieved by separating each set of credentials with the @ symbol, for both the username and password. The following describes the syntax required for the username and password parameters when you establish an HTTP connection that requires user authentication with a both an HTTP security server and destination web server:

Username   Specify ***\<destination-user>*@*\<fw1-user>*** as the username.

Password   Specify a password of ***\<destination-password>* @*\<fw1-password>***.

For example, let's assume that you are a web client attempting to connect to a destination web server called `sales.ny.com`. You require a username and password of `administrator` and a password of `admin` to access the web server. An enforcement module protects the HTTP server and has a rule that requires user authentication for HTTP access to the server. You are provided with a username of `alice` and a password of `alice123` to authenticate with the HTTP security server on the enforcement module. Figure 7.16 demonstrates how you authenticate with the HTTP security server when prompted for authentication in your web browser.

FIGURE 7.16   User Authentication prompt for HTTP

In Figure 7.16, the username is specified as `administrator@alice`, which indicates that `administrator` is the username on the destination web server and `alice` is the username on the enforcement module. You can't see what is input for the password in Figure 7.16—this should be in the format of `<destination-password>@<fw1-password>`, which is `admin@alice123`. Once you click OK, the combined credentials are sent to the HTTP security server, which separates the two sets of credentials. The HTTP security server authenticates the credentials for the username `alice`, and then connects to the destination web server, sending the `administrator` credentials specified in Figure 7.16.

FTP

When an FTP client establishes an FTP connection to an FTP server, and the security rule matching the traffic specifies that user authentication is required, the FTP connection from the client is passed to the FTP security server, which then presents its own username and password prompt back to the FTP client. Because the destination FTP server will also require authentication, the FTP client user must specify a valid username and password for user authentication (i.e., a valid account that can be authenticated by the security server) as well as a valid username and password for authentication by the destination FTP server (this username and password is normally unrelated to the username and password required for user authentication on the security server). To prevent FTP clients from having to authenticate in two separate steps, when the clients authenticate at the FTP security server, you supply both sets of credentials to the FTP security server. The FTP security server takes one set of credentials and authenticates them. Assuming the credentials are valid, the FTP security server establishes a connection to the destination FTP server and passes the second set of credentials supplied by the FTP client for authentication. Assuming the second set of credentials are valid, the FTP connection is established and the FTP client does not need to authenticate for a second time on the destination FTP server. All connection traffic is passed from the FTP client to the FTP security server, from the FTP security server to the FTP server, and vice versa.

To specify two sets of credentials, a similar method to that used for HTTP authentication is implemented. Each set of credentials is separated with the @ symbol, for both the username and password. An important addition is that the destination FTP server (name or IP address) must be included in the username sent to the FTP security server. The following describes the syntax required for the username and password parameters when you establish an FTP connection that requires user authentication with a VPN-1/FireWall-1 FTP security server:

Username Specify *<destination-user>@<fw-user>@<destination>* as the username.

Password Specify a password of *<destination-password>@ <fw1-password>*.

For example, let's assume that you are an FTP client attempting to connect to a destination FTP server with an IP address of 192.168.10.2. You require a username and password of administrator and a password of admin to access the FTP server. An enforcement module protects the FTP server and has a rule that requires user authentication for FTP access to the server. You are provided with a username of alice and a password of firewall to authenticate with the FTP security server on the enforcement module. Figure 7.17 demonstrates how you would connect to the FTP server and supply the correct credentials.

FIGURE 7.17 User authentication for FTP connections

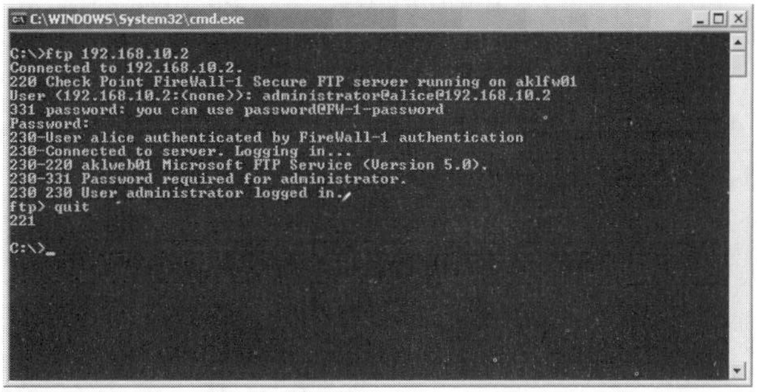

In Figure 7.17, you first attempt to establish an FTP connection to 192.168.10.2. You can see that this connection is intercepted by the FTP security server, as indicated by the banner that is presented (220 Check Point FireWall-1 Secure FTP server running on aklfw01). You then specify a user-name in the format of *<destination-user>*@*<fw-user>*@*<destination>*, which is administrator@alice@192.168.10.2—notice that you must specify the destination host to which you are connecting, even though you initially attempted to connect to that host. The FTP security server then prompts you to specify the passwords for both the destination FTP server and the firewall user. You can't see what is input for the password in Figure 7.17—this should be in the format of *<destination-password>*@ *<fw1-password>*, which is admin@alice123. At this point, the firewall credentials (username = alice, password = alice123) are authenticated. If these credentials are correct, the FTP security server then establishes a con-nection to the destination FTP server and passes the FTP server credentials (username = administrator, password = admin). You can see that on the destination FTP server, a username of administrator has been used as indicated in the welcome banner presented after successful authentication.

TELNET

If a TELNET client attempts to establish a TELNET connection to a TELNET server through a VPN-1/FireWall-1 enforcement module that requires user authentication, the TELNET connection is passed to the TELNET secu-rity server, which immediately prompts the TELNET client for username and password. The username and password that the client specifies must be that of a valid account that the security server can authenticate. Once this authentication is successful, the TELNET security server then establishes a connection to the destination TELNET server. Depending on the TELNET server, authentication may or may not be required. For example, Cisco routers by default only require a password for TELNET servers, and can be configured so that no password is required. Because of these possibilities, the TELNET security server does not pass any authentication information to the destination TELNET server, and instead just forwards whatever authentication prompts are required back to the TELNET client. This means that when a TELNET client connects to a TELNET server through an enforcement module that requires user authentication, the TELNET client must authenticate twice—once with the TELNET security server and then again with the destination TELNET server. This is different from FTP connections, where you only specify authentication information once (although you are actually specifying two sets of credentials). Figure 7.18 demonstrates how a TELNET client connects to a TELNET server through a VPN-1/FireWall-1 enforcement module that requires user authentication for the connection.

FIGURE 7.18   User authentication for TELNET connections

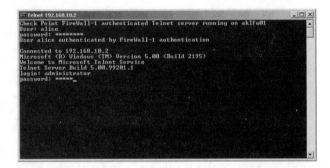

In Figure 7.18, you can clearly see that authentication with the TELNET security server on the VPN-1/FireWall-1 enforcement module is performed. After successful authentication, the TELNET security server establishes a connection with the destination TELNET server and passes back the authentication prompt back to the TELNET client, which then enters the credentials required to access the destination TELNET server.

RLOGIN

RLOGIN is considered a legacy protocol similar to TELNET, in that it provides a remote shell (or console session) running on a remote host. RLOGIN is only used for accessing Unix hosts, and due to many security flaws with the RLOGIN protocol, is seldom used today, with TELNET or Secure Shell (SSH is essentially encrypted TELNET) being favored for gaining remote shell access to a Unix system. When RLOGIN is used in conjunction with user authentication on VPN-1/FireWall-1 NG, the authentication process works in an identical manner to how TELNET works with user authentication.

Configuring User Authentication

For all exercises in this chapter, it is assumed that you have completed the exercises for Chapter 6, in which you created the appropriate user objects and enabled the appropriate authentication schemes.

1. Delete any security rules that are currently in the rule base.

2. Create a new security rule that invokes user authentication for HTTP connections established from marketing users located on nyweb01. The rule should be configured as follows:

   - Source = marketing@nyweb01

   - Destination = Any

   - Service = http

   - Action = User Auth (Ensure that the HTTP section of the user authentication action properties is configured as All servers)

3. The following shows the rule that you should have created:

4. Install the security policy and then attempt to establish an HTTP connection from nyweb01 to jupiter.london.local. You should be prompted for authentication in your browser—if you specify a marketing users credentials (e.g., alice with a password of alice123), you should be authenticated successfully and connect to jupiter .london.local (in Chapter 6, remember that you restricted access for marketing to between 8 A.M. and 6 P.M., Monday–Friday, so bear this in mind).

5. Attempt to establish another HTTP connection, but this time use the credentials of a sales user (e.g., bob with a password of bob123). Because the rule only permits marketing users, authentication should fail.

Client Authentication

You have learned that user authentication only works for HTTP, FTP, TELNET, and RLOGIN services. But what happens when you want to authenticate access to another service? User authentication is not compatible with any other services, because security servers do not exist for any other services.

SMTP is the exception to this. SMTP as it used today on the Internet does not use any authentication, and the SMTP security server is used for securely providing a mail exchanger on the Internet for internal domain e-mail, instead of being used for authentication purposes.

Check Point VPN-1/FireWall-1 provides two other authentication methods, which provide authentication for any service. The first of these is *client authentication*, which provides authentication for any service by using out-of-band authentication, rather than in-band authentication (which is used for user authentication). With user authentication, all authentication is performed within the HTTP, FTP, TELNET, or RLOGIN connection on the client host—this means that authentication is performed in-band, as part of the application-layer protocol. With client authentication, a user on a client host must first of all establish a separate connection to the enforcement module and authenticate, after which the client can then establish a connection using the permitted services in the client authentication rule on the enforcement module. The authentication is totally separate from the actual application-layer protocols that the user is accessing, hence the term out-of-band. The out-of-band connections to the enforcement module can be established using either of the following mechanisms:

HTTP   You can point your web browser to Port 900 on the enforcement module, which provides a connection to the HTTP security server for client authentication purposes. A special web page is presented, which allows you to specify your username and password, after which you can choose to gain access to all services permitted in the client authentication rule, or specific hosts and services on each.

TELNET   You can establish a TELNET connection to Port 259 on the enforcement module, which provides a connection to the TELNET security server for client authentication purposes. You specify your username and password, after which you can choose to gain access to all services permitted in the client authentication rule, or specific hosts and services on each.

Once a user has successfully authenticated, access to the hosts and services specified by the client authentication rule (or access to the hosts and services specified by the user during the authentication process) is provided. It is important to note that the IP address of the host is permitted, meaning that one or more users on the host can establish as many connections to permitted hosts and services as they like. For example, if a user called alice on a PC with an IP address of 192.168.1.10 performs client authentication successfully, another user could use Alice's PC and be permitted access through the enforcement module, even though the access is intended for alice. This is less secure than user authentication, where access is granted on a per-connection basis. With client authentication, although authentication is performed on a user basis, access is actually granted on a per–IP address basis. Figure 7.19 demonstrates how client authentication works.

FIGURE 7.19   Client authentication

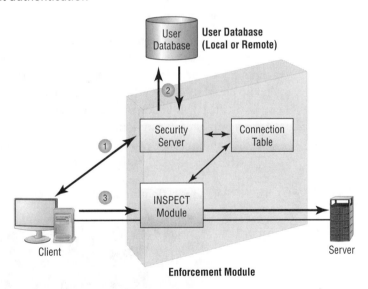

In Figure 7.19 the following events occur:

1. A user on the client host establishes an out-of-band connection to either the HTTP or TELNET security server on the enforcement module. The security server prompts the user for credentials and the user supplies these details to the security server.

2. The security server authenticates the credentials supplied, using either a local or remote authentication database. If the user is successfully authenticated, the user is notified, and the user can now select whether to gain access to all hosts and services permitted by client authentication rules for the user, or to gain access to specific hosts and services within the permitted hosts and services. Once the user selects the level of access required, the security server authorizes this access, which enables new connections from the user to be permitted without required re-authentication.

3. The client host now initiates the desired connections to the hosts and services protected by the enforcement module. The enforcement module permits the traffic, because the appropriate rules have been authorized by the security server in Step 2. It is important to understand that *any* user or application on the client host (authorized IP address) can gain access to the hosts and services permitted by client authentication rules for the user that authenticated in Step 1. In other words, the authorization scope of client authentication is per IP address, rather than per connection (as is the case for user authentication).

Client authentication is considered a non-transparent form of authentication, as the user must explicitly establish a connection to the enforcement module for the sole purposes of authentication. After authentication is complete, the user can then connect to the desired destination.

Now that you understand how client authentication works, let's view a few examples of it in action. First, let's have a look at how a user establishes out-of-band authentication. Figure 7.20 demonstrates how a user uses TELNET out-of-band authentication.

FIGURE 7.20 TELNET authentication for client authentication

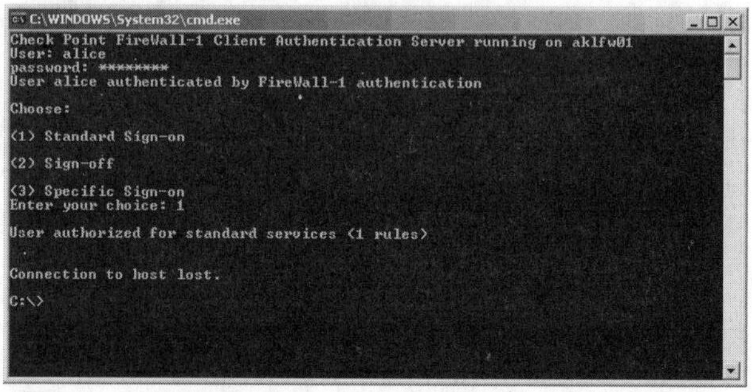

TELNET client utilities use port 23 by default for TELNET connections. On most TELNET client utilities, you can specify a custom port by including it as a parameter after specifying the name or IP address of the TELNET server. For example, the command `telnet x.x.x.x 259` (where `x.x.x.x` is the IP address of the enforcement module) attempts to establish a TELNET connection to port 259 on the enforcement module.

In Figure 7.20, a TELNET connection has been established to port 259 on the enforcement module (you can't see the `telnet` command issued, as the Windows telnet utility clears the screen immediately after a connection is established). You can see that the connection is passed to the TELNET security server as indicated by the banner presented to the user. A username and password are specified, which authenticate successfully. The user is then presented with three options:

Standard Sign-on   Indicates to the security server that all access permitted in each client authentication rule that relates to the user should be granted.

Sign-off   Indicates to the security server that all access permitted from a previous authentication by the user should be removed.

Specific Sign-on   Indicates to the security server that the user wishes to specify the hosts and services that he or she wishes to gain access to. The hosts and services specified must fall within the hosts and services of a client authentication rule that is permitted for the user.

In Figure 7.20, an option of 1 is selected (Standard Sign-on), after which the connection is closed. At this point, the client host can access any hosts and services permitted by client authentication rules for the user. By default, permitted access via client authentication is limited to 30 minutes, after which the user must authenticate again via the out-of-band TELNET or HTTP method. This time limit is known as *authorization timeout* and is configurable per client authentication rule.

Now let's take a look at how a user uses the HTTP out-of-band authentication mechanism. Figures 7.21a through d demonstrate the HTTP authentication process.

In Figure 7.21a, you can see that an HTTP connection has been made to port 900 on the enforcement module. The syntax in most web browsers for establishing an HTTP connection to a custom port on an HTTP server is `http://<server>:xxx`, where *xxx* is the custom port number. For example, in Figure 7.21a, the URL specified is **http://172.20.1.1:900**, which indicates to the browser to establish an HTTP connection to port 900 on 172.20.1.1 (the enforcement module).

FIGURE 7.21 HTTP authentication for client authentication

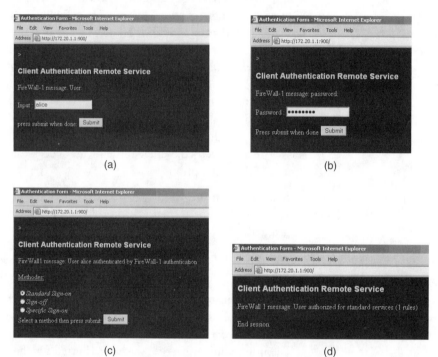

(a)

(b)

(c)

(d)

If you compare Figures 7.21 a through d with Figure 7.20, you can see that the authentication process for HTTP is identical to the process used for TELNET authentication. Once client authentication is completed, the client (IP address of the host the user has authenticated from) is authorized for any rules that are configured for the user (assuming the user signs in using the standard sign-on method as shown in Figures 7.20 and 7.21c).

Configuring Client Authentication

Before you configure client authentication rules, you must ensure that you have configured the user database with the appropriate user and group objects, so that you can populate client authentication rules with the correct objects, and enabled the appropriate authentication schemes on your enforcement modules.

Once you have configured these prerequisites, you have the necessary supporting configuration to implement client authentication. To configure client authentication rules, you should perform the following actions:

- Configure global client authentication parameters.

- Create a client authentication rule.

- Customize client authentication rule parameters.

Each of these tasks is now discussed in detail.

Configuring Global Client Authentication Parameters

For client authentication, a couple parameters can be configured globally for all client authentication rules for all enforcement modules. These parameters include the following:

- Failed authentication attempts

- Wait mode

Failed Authentication Attempts

As discussed in the user authentication section, you can globally configure the maximum number of failed authentication attempts for all types of authentication (including client authentication) before a connection is torn down. These settings are configured from the Authentication screen within the Global Properties dialog box, which is opened by selecting Policy ➤ Global Properties from the SmartDashboard menu. If you refer back to Figure 7.7, you can see the Terminate Client Authentication connection after x attempts setting, which has a default setting of three attempts. If a user fails client authentication for three attempts, the connection is torn down, and the user must establish a new TELNET or HTTP client authentication connection.

Wait Mode

If you refer back to Figure 7.7 and Figure 7.8, notice a setting called Enable wait mode for Client Authentication. By default, this setting is disabled and is configured via individual enforcement module objects in VPN-1/FireWall-1 NG (see Figure 7.8) or via the Global Properties ➤ Authentication screen for prior versions to VPN-1/FireWall-1 NG (see Figure 7.7). Wait mode is a feature that can only be used when a client authenticates using the TELNET client authentication mode. When enabled, once a user has authenticated via TELNET, the TELNET client authentication session is maintained, and must be left open for the duration that the client authentication rules specified. If the TELNET client authentication session is closed, the authorization for the client is immediately removed. During the authorization period, the VPN-1/ FireWall-1 enforcement module pings the client regularly to ensure the client is still up. If the client is not up for some reason (i.e., the client host has crashed), the TELNET client authentication session is closed and the authorization for the rule is removed. This ensures authorized rules do not remain open in the event that the authorized client loses connectivity and cannot sign off (when a client signs off, all authorizations for the client are removed).

Creating a Client Authentication Rule

To create a client authentication rule, you configure the rule in the same fashion as a user authentication rule except that you must specify an action of Client Auth in the Action field and you can specify any service in the Service element. You also do not need to configure user access in the source element of the rule, although this is recommended. An important caveat of client authentication is that you ensure that client authentication rules are placed *above* any rules that deny access to enforcement modules (such as the stealth rule). This ensures that connections to the TELNET and HTTP client authentication servers are permitted, as any rule with an action of Client Auth implicitly permits access to these authentication servers.

If you restrict the location that users can authenticate from in the client authentication rule, the TELNET and HTTP security servers will only accept authentication connections from the permitted locations. All other authentication connection requests from other IP addresses not within the permitted location are dropped.

If you do not wish to place your client authentication rules above your stealth rule, you can create an explicit rule that permits access to the client authentication services, placing this above your stealth rule, which then allows you to place client authentication rules below the stealth rule.

You can place user and session authentication rules below your stealth rule and they will still work. Only client authentication rules must be placed above your stealth rule.

Figure 7.22 demonstrates a client authentication rule.

FIGURE 7.22   A client authentication rule

Notice that the service element specifies any service, unlike user authentication rules, which are limited to only HTTP, FTP, TELNET, and RLOGIN services.

Customizing Client Authentication Rule Parameters

Once you configure an action of Client Auth, you can modify the way in which client authentication is implemented for the rule by right-clicking on the Client Auth action and selecting Edit properties from the menu that appears. This will display the Client Authentication Action Properties dialog box, which is shown in Figure 7.23.

FIGURE 7.23   The Client Authentication Action Properties dialog box

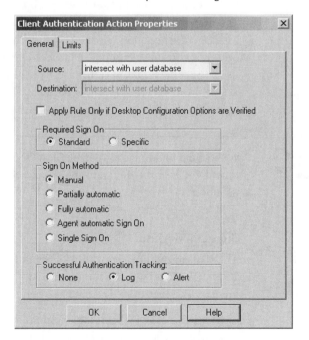

You can see in Figure 7.23 that there are several parameters that you can define on the General tab including Source, Destination; Required Sign On; Sign On Method, and Successful Authentication Tracking.

We'll now discuss these parameters, as well as the parameters presented on the Limits tab in Figure 7.23.

Source, Destination

Source, Destination allows you to configure how access should be determined if the Location specified in the Source element of the rule (see Figure 7.9) is not part of the permitted source locations configured for the user object that represents the user who is authenticating on the rule. These parameters work in an identical fashion to how they work for user authentication rules.

The Destination parameter is only configurable if the Specific Sign On option is configured.

Required Sign On

The Required Sign On option determines whether a user can be authorized for all destinations and services specified by the rule (the Standard option), or whether a user must specify the destinations and services he or she wishes to access during client authentication (the Specific option). If the Standard option is chosen in Figure 7.23, the user can choose either the Standard Sign On or Specific Sign On options during authentication (see Figures 7.13 and 7.14). If the Specific option is chosen, the user cannot choose the Standard Sign On option during authentication.

When a user chooses a Specific Sign On, the list of destinations and services must be within the destinations and services configured in the client authentication rule.

Sign On Method

The sign on method determines how a user actually authenticates with the VPN-1/FireWall-1 enforcement module for client authentication. The following describes each option:

Manual   This is the default setting, and means that a client must initiate a client authentication session with the enforcement module using either TELNET to port 259 or HTTP to port 900, before the user can access the destinations and services specified in the rule. So far in this section on client authentication, the manual sign on method has been described.

Partially Automatic   This option, also known as *implicit client authentication*, allows users to use user authentication using HTTP, FTP, TELNET, or RLOGIN in place of the manual client authentication process described above. If a connection matches the client authentication rule that is HTTP, FTP, TELNET, or RLOGIN based (i.e., a user authentication service), authentication is performed in-band using user authentication via the security servers on the enforcement module. If user authentication is successful, the client is then authorized for the client authentication rule (including services outside of the user authentication services). If users wish to establish a connection permitted by a client authentication rule that specifies a partially automatic sign on method, and the connection is not a user authentication service (i.e., HTTP, FTP, TELNET, or RLOGIN), you must use the manual client authentication sign on method before attempting the connection. Choosing this option enables you to perform client authentication using a user authentication mechanism rather than manual client authentication. For example, a user may need to access a TELNET server behind a gateway, and also access an SQL server. If you want to authenticate this access, you can't use user authentication, as the SQL access cannot be authenticated using this method. If you created a partially automatic client authentication rule, which permitted TELNET access to the TELNET server and SQL access to the SQL server, the user could first authenticate with the enforcement module using TELNET-based user authentication. This would not only grant the client access to the TELNET server, but would also authorize the client for access to the SQL server. See "Providing Transparent HTTPS Authentication" Real World sidebar for another example of where you might configure this option.

A partially automatic client authentication rule is also commonly referred to as implicit client authentication, as the client authentication rule is implicitly authorized after user authentication.

Fully Automatic   This method uses the session authentication agent to provide authentication for the client authentication rule. If a new connection matches a client authentication rule that is currently not authenticated for the requesting client, the enforcement module will invoke session authentication back to the requesting client. Once the user successfully authenticates via session authentication, all destinations and services permitted in the client authentication rule are authorized for the client IP address. Note that the client must have the session authentication agent installed.

If you specify a fully automatic sign on method and the first connection that matches a client authentication is a user authentication service (HTTP, FTP, TELNET, or RLOGIN), user authentication is invoked (in the same manner as partially automatic authentication), instead of session authentication. For all other services, session authentication is invoked.

Agent Automatic Sign On This is similar to the fully automatic sign on method, except all services are authenticated by the session authentication agent, including HTTP, FTP, TELNET, and RLOGIN. The client must have the session authentication agent installed.

Single Sign On Systems This method is used in connection with Check Point's optional address management product, which maps users to IP addresses on the network. If a connection request matches a client authentication rule with this sign on method, the address management database is referenced to determine the user associated with the IP address. If the user currently associated with the IP address is a member of any of the permitted user groups in the Source element of the rule, the client IP address is authorized for the rule. This method involves no authentication at all from a client perspective, as authentication has previously occurred that has mapped the user to an IP address in the address management database.

 Real World Scenario

Providing Transparent HTTPS Authentication

A common request from users of VPN-1/FireWall-1 is the ability to authenticate HTTPS (SSL) connections at the VPN-1/FireWall-1 enforcement module, without requiring users to manually authenticate using client authentication or the session authentication agent. Instead users authenticate using a method similar to HTTP authentication, which is native to all modern web browsers.

VPN-1/FireWall-1 provides transparent HTTP authentication natively using user authentication; however, this cannot be extended to HTTPS as all information in an HTTPS connection is encrypted end-to-end between the web client and the web server. You can configure a client authentication rule with a partially automatic sign on method to provide authentication of HTTPS connections without requiring web clients to authenticate to the enforcement module using the manual client authentication sign on methods. The following illustration shows a rule that provides this.

NO.	SOURCE	DESTINATION	IF VIA	SERVICE	ACTION	TRACK	INSTALL ON	TIME	COMMENT
1	marketing@Any	nyweb01	✶ Any	TCP http / TCP https	Client Auth	Log	✶ Policy Targets	✶ Any	Partially Automatic Client Authentication Rule

The Client Auth action is configured with a partially automatic sign on, which means a user authentication service (such as HTTP in the above picture) can be used to provide client authentication, rather than manual client authentication. The following illustration demonstrates how a user would connect to an HTTPS server using the rule in the previous illustration.

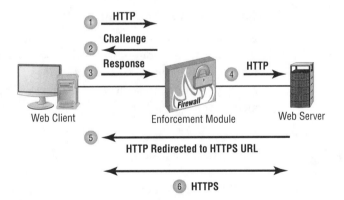

1. The web client initiates an HTTP connection to the destination web server. Because the rule shown in the graphic specifies HTTP as a service, the connection is matched against the rule on the enforcement module. The connection is passed to the HTTP security server for authentication, as the sign on method for the rule is configured as partially automatic.

2. The HTTP security server challenges the web client for authentication information.

3. The web client authenticates using HTTP to the enforcement module.

4. If authentication is successful, the client authentication rule is now authorized for the IP address of the web client, which means the web client can now establish an HTTPS connection to the web server. The HTTP connection request sent in Step 1 is forwarded to the web server.

5. The web server is configured to redirect the HTTP connection permitted in Step 4 to a new HTTPS-based URL on the web server.

6. The web client attempts to connect to the web server via HTTPS. Because the client authentication rule was authorized in Step 4, the HTTPS connection is permitted to the web server.

Notice that the web client does not need to manually authenticate with the enforcement module over HTTP port 900 or TELNET port 259. The authentication is provided via HTTP, which is useful as all modern web browsers support HTTP authentication. It is important to note that the authentication information passed to the enforcement module during Step 2 is not encrypted, as the authentication is performed using HTTP.

Successful Authentication Tracking

Referring back to Figure 7.23, notice the Successful Authentication Tracking section at the bottom of the dialog box. This allows you to configure whether or not successful authentications are tracked via logging in the security log file (Log mode view in SmartView Tracker) or via alerting (pop-up alert in SmartView Status).

Any unsuccessful authentication tracks are always logged.

Figure 7.24 demonstrates log entries in SmartView Tracker that show a successful and unsuccessful authentication attempt.

In Figure 7.24, the first entry indicates successful authentication by the user alice. Notice the action is authorize, which means that a client authentication rule has been successfully authorized. The next log entry demonstrates a connection being permitted due to the authorization. The next four entries indicate failed authentication attempts, with the final entry showing a deauthorize action, where the user has signed off via the TELNET or HTTP security servers.

Limits

The Client Authentication Action Properties dialog box includes a Limits tab, which is shown in Figure 7.25. This tab defines the authorization parameters in terms of how long the client authentication rule is authorized and the number of authorized sessions permitted before client authentication must take place again.

FIGURE 7.24   Authentication entries in SmartView Tracker

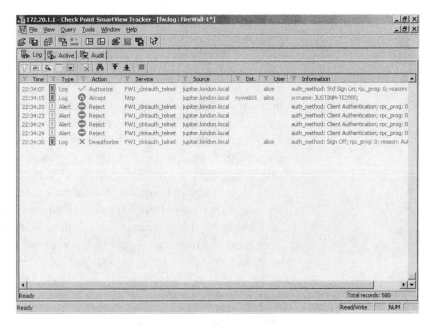

FIGURE 7.25   Client authentication limits

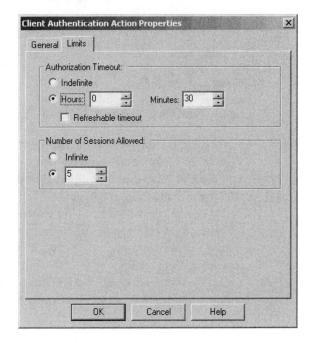

The following describes the configuration parameters shown in Figure 7.25:

Authorization Timeout   Determines how long the client authentication rule is authorized for after successful client authentication. The default setting is 30 minutes, which means that an authorized client can establish new connections for up to 30 minutes, after which time connections will be rejected unless the rule is re-authenticated. Notice that you can configure an option of Indefinite, which means that once a client has authenticated, the rule is authorized indefinitely. Choosing this option is not recommended, as a client only ever needs to authenticate once to be authorized, and you are relying on the client to sign off to remove the authorization. If the client does not sign off, the client could reconnect in days or weeks without requiring authentication again (you would need to stop and start your enforcement module to remove the authorization). The Refreshable timeout parameter (disabled by default) resets the authorization timeout timer every time a new authorized connection is established that matches the client authentication rule. Note that this does not mean that the authorization timeout timer is reset every time an existing connection exchanges traffic—only when a new authorized connection is established.

Number of Sessions Allowed   Defines how many sessions are authorized after successful client authentication. The default setting is five sessions, which means that up to five sessions (that fall within the elements of the client authentication rule) will be permitted by the enforcement. If this limit is reached, the client must re-authenticate the client authentication rule.

Real World Scenario

Implementing Authentication for HTTP Connections

If you wish to implement authentication for HTTP connections to external web servers from internal web clients, it is recommended that you configure a partially automatic client authentication rule, which specifies a refreshable authorization timeout and an infinite number (or very large number) of allowed sessions. If you implement user authentication for the HTTP connections, every new HTTP connection must be re-authenticated, disrupting the user. By using a partially automatic rule, users can be authorized for web access to any server after the first HTTP connection is authenticated via user authentication with the HTTP security server. By configuring a refreshable authorization timeout, users only need to re-authenticate if they are idle (not making any new HTTP connections) for the authorization timeout period configured. Because HTTP makes many connections over the course of a user browsing the web, you must set the number of allowed sessions very high to avoid frequent re-authentication.

EXERCISE 7.2

Configuring Client Authentication

1. Reconfigure the security rule created in Exercise 7.1 to use client authentication for HTTP and Terminal Server (ms-rdp) connections from marketing users located on nyweb01 to any destination. The rule should be configured as follows:

   - Source = `marketing@nyweb01`
   - Destination = Any
   - Service = `http, ms-rdp`
   - Action = Client Auth (leave Client Auth properties as default)

2. The following shows the rule that you created:

3. Install the security policy and attempt to establish an HTTP connection from nyweb01 to `jupiter.london.local`. This should fail as you have not authenticated (notice that you are not prompted for authentication in your browser as you were in Exercise 7.1).

4. Establish an HTTP connection to port 900 via the browser on nyweb01. Authenticate with the appropriate marketing credentials (e.g., **alice** with a password of **alice123**) and ensure that you select the standard sign-on method.

5. Attempt to establish an HTTP connection to `jupiter.london.local`. This time the connection should succeed.

6. Establish another HTTP connection to port 900 via the browser on nyweb01. Authenticate with the appropriate marketing credentials (e.g., **alice** with a password of **alice123**) and then log off the user.

7. Configure the client authentication rule to use implicit client authentication. You can do this by right-clicking the Client Auth action element and selecting Edit Properties. In the dialog box that appears, change the Sign On Method to Partially automatic and then click OK.

8. Reinstall the security policy and again attempt to establish an HTTP connection from nyweb01 to jupiter.london.local. Instead of the connection failing as it did in Step 3, you should now be presented with an authentication prompt in the browser. This is because implicit client authentication allows user authentication to be used to authorize client authentication rules. Enter the appropriate marketing credentials, after which you should successfully connect to jupiter.london.local.

9. Attempt to establish a Terminal Server connection to jupiter.london.local. The connection should succeed, because the user authentication in Step 8 has authorized the client authentication rule.

Session Authentication

*S*ession *authentication* represents the third and final option for providing user-based authentication to determine access through a VPN-1/FireWall-1 enforcement module. Session authentication is an out-of-band authentication mechanism (the other out-of-band mechanism is client authentication) that is designed to address the flexibility issues of user authentication and the security issues of client authentication. With user authentication, you learned that this mechanism only applies for HTTP, FTP, TELNET, and RLOGIN services, which rules it out as an authentication mechanism for other services. Client authentication provides flexibility by providing authentication for any service, but has issues with security as access is provided on a per-host (per-IP address) basis, allowing any number of connections from an authenticated host, regardless of the user on the host.

NOTE   User authentication does not have the security issues of client authentication, as HTTP, FTP, TELNET, and RLOGIN access is only provided on a per-connection basis, meaning another user cannot obtain unauthorized access by establishing a new connection from the host on which the previous user authenticated.

Session authentication provides the security of per-connection authentication for any service, making it appear as the most obvious choice for authenticating access to services outside of HTTP, FTP, TELNET, and RLOGIN. The only downside to session authentication is that it requires a custom application to be installed on each client host using session authentication. This application, which is written by Check Point, is called the *session authentication agent*, and provides out-of-band authentication for each connection (or session) that requires authentication on an enforcement module. When the session authentication agent is installed and running, it listens on TCP port 261, which allows enforcement modules that need to authenticate a user for session authentication to contact the agent for authentication information. Figure 7.26 demonstrates how session authentication works.

FIGURE 7.26   Session authentication

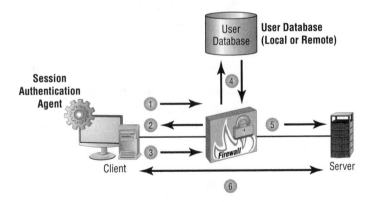

The following describes the events that occur in Figure 7.26:

1. A user on the client attempts to make a connection through the enforcement module to the server. The enforcement module matches the traffic to a rule that specifies session authentication.

2. The enforcement module establishes a session authentication connection back to the client host (the enforcement module knows the IP address of the host, as this is indicated in the source IP address of the original packet seen by the enforcement module). Because the session authentication agent is running and listening on TCP port 261, the connection from the enforcement module is successful.

If the client running the session authentication agent is behind a network address translation (NAT) device that is performing NAT for the client before traffic reaches the enforcement module, you must ensure that the NAT being performed is static NAT (one-to-one), so that the enforcement module initiates and establishes a session authentication connection back to the client. If hide NAT (or PAT) is being performed, the enforcement module will not be able to connect to the client. NAT is discussed in Chapter 8.

3. The enforcement module challenges the session authentication agent for authentication. The agent pops up a dialog box to the user, requiring a username and password to authenticate access for the connection. The user enters the appropriate username and password, which are collected by the session authentication agent and then passed back to the enforcement module over the session authentication connection established in Step 2.

4. The enforcement module receives the authentication information and authenticates it against a local or remote authentication database.

5. Assuming authentication is successful, the connection is added to the connection table, and the original packet sent by the client in Step 1 is forwarded on to the destination server.

6. Subsequent traffic generated between the client and server for the connection initiated in Step 1 is permitted by the enforcement module. It is important to note that the client must separately authenticate any new connections through the enforcement module to the same destination server or other destinations, which is unlike client authentication, where the client could establish any number of new connections after authentication.

Although session authentication includes an out-of-band authentication mechanism, it is considered transparent, as the user does not need to establish the out-of-band authentication mechanism (the enforcement module does this). The user merely needs to attempt to connect to the desired destination, and session authentication will be invoked (much like user authentication, except with user authentication, the authentication is provided in-band).

Configuring Session Authentication

Before you configure session authentication rules, you must ensure that you have configured the user database with the appropriate user and group objects, so that you can populate session authentication rules with the correct objects, and enabled the appropriate authentication schemes on your enforcement modules. Once you have configured these prerequisites, you have the necessary supporting configuration to implement session authentication. To configure session authentication, you should perform the following actions.

- Configure global session authentication parameters.
- Create a session authentication rule.
- Customize session authentication rule parameters.
- Install and configure the session authentication agent.

Each of these tasks is now discussed in detail.

Configuring Global Session Authentication Parameters

For session authentication, there is only a single parameter that can be configured globally for all session authentication rules on all enforcement modules. This is the Failed authentication attempts for Session Authentication parameter that is configured from the Authentication screen within the Global Properties dialog box, which is opened by selecting Policy ➤ Global Properties from the SmartDashboard menu. If you refer back to Figure 7.7, you can see the Terminate Session Authentication connection after *x* attempts setting, which has a default setting of three attempts. If a user fails session authentication for three attempts, the connection attempt that invoked session authentication on the client is torn down, and the user must establish a new connection that invokes session authentication.

Creating a Session Authentication Rule

To configure a session authentication rule, you configure the rule in the same fashion as a user or client authentication rule, except that you must specify an action of Session Auth in the Action field. Just as you can with client authentication, you can specify any service in the Service element of the rule. Unlike the client authentication rule, a session authentication rule can be placed below the stealth rule, as it is the enforcement module that actually makes authentication connections back to the session authentication agent. Figure 7.27 demonstrates a rule configured for session authentication.

FIGURE 7.27 A session authentication rule

NO	SOURCE	DESTINATION	IF VIA	SERVICE	ACTION	TRACK	INSTALL ON	TIME	COMMENT
1	marketing@Any	nyweb01	✱ Any	✱ Any	Session Auth	Log	✱ Policy Targets	✱ Any	Session Authentication Rule

Notice that just like client authentication, the service element can specify any service, unlike user authentication rules, which are limited to only HTTP, FTP, TELNET, and RLOGIN services.

Customizing Session Authentication Parameters

Once you configure an action of Session Auth, you can modify the way in which session authentication is implemented for the rule by right-clicking on the Session Auth action and selecting Edit properties from the menu that appears. This will display the Session Authentication Action Properties dialog box, which is shown in Figure 7.28.

FIGURE 7.28 The Session Authentication Action Properties dialog box

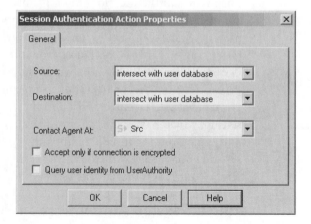

You can see in Figure 7.28 that there are several parameters that you can define:

Source, Destination   Allows you to configure how access should be determined if the Location specified in the Source element of the rule (see Figure 7.9) is not part of the permitted source locations configured for the user object that represents the user that is authenticating on the rule. These parameters work in an identical fashion to how they work for user authentication and client authentication rules.

Contact Agent At   This option allows you to specify the session authentication agent that should be contacted for authentication information by the enforcement module. The default setting is to contact the source of the connection (as specified by the Src object in Figure 7.28), which means that the client initiating the connection must authenticate (as is the case with user and client authentication). You can configure the enforcement module to contact an agent running on a different host, such as the destination system of the connection, or any other workstation object defined in VPN-1/FireWall-1. If you choose to configure the agent that is contacted to not be the Src object, you must ensure that a user is present on the machine that hosts the agent that is contacted, so that authentication can take place when the connection request is attempted.

Installing and Configuring the Session Authentication Agent

The session authentication agent is the software that must run on each client that authenticates using session authentication. The agent is very simple, and when loaded runs in the background until a user must supply authentication information. The session authentication agent installation software for Windows is available on the VPN-1/FireWall-1 CD, under the windows\CpSessionAgt-50 directory. Setup is performed in a few simple steps and once installed, the session agent is configured to automatically start whenever the computer starts. When the agent is running, you will see an icon within the system tray. Figure 7.29 shows the session authentication agent icon in the system tray (on the right).

FIGURE 7.29   Session authentication agent system tray icon

If the session authentication agent is not started, you can start it by selecting Start ➤ Programs ➤ FireWall-1 ➤ Session Authentication Agent NG. By default, the session authentication agent is configured to start automatically when a user logs on.

To work with the agent, simply right-click the icon in the system tray. This will present you with a Configuration option, which allows you to configure the agent, as well as an Exit option, which allows you to close the agent. Figure 7.30 shows the Configuration dialog box, which is displayed if you right-click the system tray icon and select the Configuration option.

FIGURE 7.30 Session authentication agent Configuration dialog box

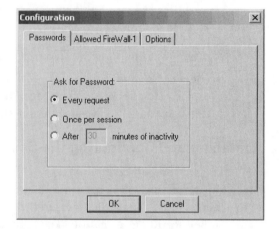

Notice in Figure 7.30 that the Passwords tab is displayed by default, which allows you to configure how the agent performs session authentication. The agent can be configured in different modes, which in essence controls how the agent caches user credentials. You can configure the agent so that connections requiring session authentication can be automatically authenticated without requiring user intervention. Although transparent to the user, in the background every new connection is being authenticated by the enforcement module, regardless of the configuration of the session authentication agent. The session authentication agent either supplies the enforcement module with cached credentials, or prompts the user for new credentials, depending on the configuration. The following lists the different authentication modes displayed in Figure 7.30:

Every request   This option is the default setting and means that each new connection established from the client to hosts and services permitted in the session authentication rule on the enforcement module will require re-authentication by the user. This option is identical to how user authentication works in terms of requiring separate authentication for each new connection, and is the most secure, but most intrusive method of session authentication.

Once per session   Enabling this option is similar to client authentication, in that any new connections are authenticated automatically by the session authentication agent using the credentials supplied when a connection was initiated for the first time. This option is less secure, but is less intrusive to the user, as a user only has to authenticate once and can establish multiple connections afterwards. Each new connection established by the user requires session authentication from the firewall; however, the agent simply passes cached credentials, keeping the process hidden from the user. Using this option is still more secure than client authentication, as authentication is only provided while the session authentication agent is running. For example, if an authenticated user logged off, and another user immediately accessed the machine, the session authentication agent would be restarted and would require authentication credentials from the new user. This is unlike client authentication, where the new user could gain authenticated access without being authenticated, as client authentication works on a per–IP address basis.

After *x* minutes of inactivity   Enabling this option is similar to the once per session option; however, it allows you to configure an inactivity timer, which protects against an unauthorized user using an authenticated session of a user who has left their PC unattended with the session authentication agent still running. Re-authentication is required for any new connections established after the inactivity timer expires.

Figure 7.31 shows the Allowed FireWall-1 tab within the Configuration dialog box.

FIGURE 7.31 The Allowed FireWall-1 Tab in the Session authentication agent Configuration dialog box

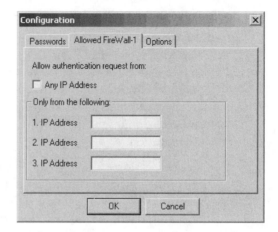

In Figure 7.31, you can configure the permitted enforcement modules from which the session authentication agent will accept authentication requests. By default, no options are configured, which means that any authentication requests will be rejected. The Any IP Address option permits authentication requests from any IP address, which makes life easier in terms of configuration, but is not recommended in terms of security best practices. Because session authentication involves the enforcement module to establish a connection back to the session authentication agent for authentication purposes, an attacker could send a fake authentication request to the agent, which would either prompt the user for authentication details or send back cached authentication details, depending on the configuration of the agent (see Figure 7.30). This could be used by the attacker to gain unauthorized access to user credentials. By manually configuring the IP addresses of known, trusted enforcement modules, you prevent this form of attack from occurring.

EXERCISE 7.3

Installing the Session Authentication Agent

For this exercise you will need access to the Check Point VPN-1/ FireWall-1 NG CD-ROM.

EXERCISE 7.3 *(continued)*

1. On nyweb01, insert the Check Point VPN-1/FireWall-1 NG CD-ROM, browse to the windows\CpSessionAgt-50 folder, and run the setup.exe program. Follow the setup program to install the session authentication agent.

2. Once setup is complete, the session authentication agent icon should appear in the system tray. Right-click the icon and select Configuration from the menu that appears. On the Allowed FireWall-1 configuration tab, configure the agent to accept authentication requests from the internal IP address of nyfw01 (192.168.10.1).

Session Authentication Process

Once you have finished installing and configured session authentication on both the enforcement module and the session authentication agent client, you should test session authentication to ensure it is working as expected. Testing is simple—all you need to do is ensure the session authentication agent is running on the client and then attempt to establish a connection to a destination system and service configured in a session authentication rule. At this point, assuming the enforcement module matches the connection against a session authentication rule, the enforcement module will establish a session authentication connection to the agent, requesting authentication data. The agent will then display a prompt to the user, who must specify a valid username and password. Figure 7.32 demonstrates the session authentication agent prompt.

FIGURE 7.32   Session authentication agent prompt

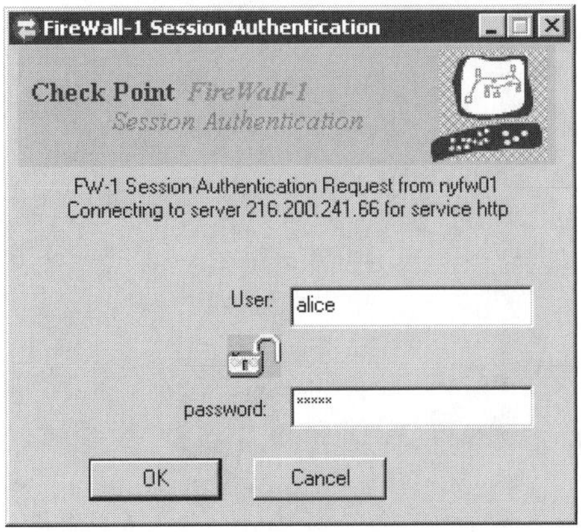

In Figure 7.32, a username of `alice` is being specified along with password information for the user. This information is then passed back to the enforcement module, where it is authenticated. Assuming the client is authenticated, the connection the client made is permitted. Any new connections have the same process applied to them (i.e., re-authentication must take place), except the information provided for the user.

EXERCISE 7.4

Configuring Session Authentication

1. Reconfigure the security rule created in Exercise 7.2 to use session authentication. The rule should be configured as follows:

   - Source = `marketing@nyweb01`
   - Destination = Any
   - Service = `http, ms-rdp`
   - Action = Session Auth (leave Session Auth properties as default)

2. The following shows the rule that you created:

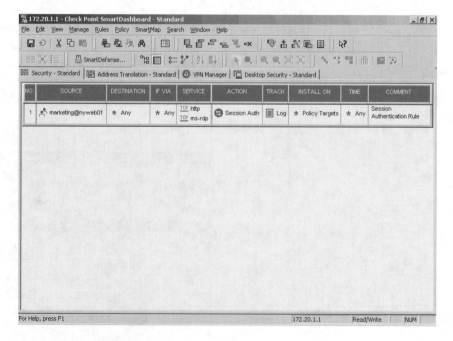

3. Install the security policy and attempt to establish an HTTP connection from nyweb01 to jupiter.london.local. The session authentication agent should prompt you for authentication. Enter the appropriate marketing credentials (e.g., alice with a password of alice123). Once you have authenticated, the HTTP connection should be established.

4. Attempt to establish a Terminal Server connection to jupiter .london.local. Again, you should be prompted for authentication by the session agent, as session authentication applies per connection, unlike client authentication.

Selecting the Appropriate Authentication Type

For the CCSA exam, it is important to understand which authentication type you should use, given a set of security requirements. This section explains the key differences between each authentication type, the advantages and disadvantages of each, and describes the situations when you should use each.

There are several considerations that help define whether or not a particular authentication type is appropriate:

- Supported services

- Authorization scope

- Transparency

- Performance

- Compatibility

Table 7.1 describes each of these key considerations and how each authentication type meets (or does not meet) them.

TABLE 7.1 Authentication Type Comparison

	User Auth	Client Auth	Session Auth
Supported Services	HTTP, FTP, TELNET, RLOGIN	All	All
Authorization Scope	Connection	IP Address	Connection
Transparency	Transparent	Non-transparent	Transparent
Performance	Worst	Best	Medium
Specific Requirements	None	None	Session Authentication Agent Required

Each of these considerations is now discussed in depth for each authentication type.

The CCSA exam tests heavily on selecting the appropriate type of authentication for a given situation or requirement. Make sure you are very clear as to the features and limitations of each authentication type.

When to Use User Authentication

User authentication is recommended when you only need to support HTTP, FTP, TELNET, and RLOGIN services, as authentication is secure (authentication is required per connection) and transparent (users don't need to know of the enforcement modules existence). In terms of performance, user authentication is not as scalable as other authentication types, because the enforcement module security servers proxy connections between the source and destination of each connection. The following section describes the considerations of Table 7.1 and how they affect whether user authentication is appropriate for a given situation.

Supported Services for User Authentication

Because user authentication is limited to only HTTP, FTP, TELNET, and RLOGIN services, if you have a service outside of these that you wish to authenticate, you have ruled out user authentication. If you need to support services other than those supported by user authentication, you must use either client or session authentication.

Security for User Authentication

User authentication is considered secure, because authorization only applies to a single connection. If an attacker somehow gains access to the host system, the attacker cannot establish a new connection masquerading as the authenticated user, because each new connection must be authenticated. Although this is good from the point of view of security, user authentication is the most intrusive, because each new connection must be authenticated. User authentication is not recommended for HTTP access, as each HTTP connection must be authenticated. Because many web pages have content that is obtained from multiple web servers, if user authentication is configured, the user must authenticate each new connection to each web server. This is very obtrusive for users, as they may need to authenticate 10 or 20 times just to display a single web page.

Transparency for User Authentication

User authentication is transparent, which means that a user only needs to connect to the desired destination system, without first establishing a separate connection to the enforcement module for the purposes of authenticating.

Performance for User Authentication

The enforcement module intercepts any connections that require user authentication, passing them to the appropriate security servers, which authenticate the connection and then proxy the connection transparently. Because the security servers are proxying each connection, performance and scalability becomes an issue for larger deployments, as the security servers must maintain an application-layer connection to both the source and destination of the connection.

When to Use Client Authentication

Client authentication is best suited for users that require access to many systems and services behind an enforcement module and do not want to have to authenticate each new connection. It is also suited to applications and services that may run a script that authenticates the host, allowing the application or service to then connect to a remote service running on a destination system. Be aware that client authentication is the least secure of all authentication types, as an IP address is authorized, rather than a connection. This means that another user on the client machine could exploit the authorized status of an IP address, gaining unauthorized access. Because of this, client authentication is recommended for single-user machines only (as opposed to multiuser machines). In terms of performance, client authentication is the most scalable of all authentication types, as authentication only occurs once per client authentication session, with all other connections that are part of the authorized session being processed in the same manner as normal security rules.

You must consider four very important requirements when selecting the type of authentication that should be implemented, and how client authentication meets or does not meet these requirements: supported services, security, transparency, and performance.

Supported Services for Client Authentication

Client authentication supports all services, so along with session authentication represents the only choices for authentication if you need to authenticate services outside of HTTP, FTP, TELNET, and RLOGIN.

Security for Client Authentication

Client authentication is considered the least secure of all authentication types. By default, if a client authenticates successfully, the IP address of the client is authorized to make connections to any destination system and service specified in the client authentication rule. Client authentication has limits, which define how long a client authentication rule is authorized for and the maximum number of authorized connections that can be made. By default, a rule remains authorized for 30 minutes, meaning that the authenticated client IP address is permitted to make connections to the destination systems and services specified in the rule during for 30 minutes, without requiring new authentication. The maximum number of authorized connections made during this time frame is configured as five by default. Once this limit has been reached, the client must re-authenticate to authorize any new connections. By ensuring your limits match your security requirements with small amounts of tolerance, you can normally circumvent these risks. For example, if a client needed to authorize a single connection (and did not need to make any further connections), you should configure the authorization timeout period for the rule to be very low (e.g., five minutes) and the number of connections permitted to be very low as well (e.g., one or two). This ensures that the requirements of the legitimate clients are met, and reduces the amount of time the authorization is open to exploitation.

You can also reduce the vulnerability of client authentication by training your users to sign off immediately after they have established their required connections. Users can sign off by connecting to the client authentication daemons and selecting the sign-off option (see Figures 7.20 and 7.21c). Once a user signs off, the authorized client IP is de-authorized, meaning that any further connections from the client are rejected unless a new client authentication sequence occurs. The connection established during the time that the client was authorized is maintained, even after the user logs off.

If you have a requirement to implement client authentication rules that support a large number of destination systems and services (e.g., you need to specify any service in the Service element, and an entire network or group of networks in the Destination element), it is recommended that you configure the client authentication rule to require Specific Sign-On as the Required Sign-On parameter in the Client Authentication Action Properties dialog box for the rule (see Figure 7.23). If you permit standard sign-on in this scenario, once a client has been authorized, that IP address will be permitted to make connections to all of the destination systems and services specified in the client authentication rule, which increases the vulnerability of your networks. When you configure a client authentication rule to require a specific sign-on, during the client authentication process, the client must choose the specific sign-on option and then specify the required destination systems and services that the client must be authorized for. If you refer back to Figures 7.20 and 7.21c, you can see that a specific sign-on option exists. Figure 7.33 shows process of choosing the Specific Sign-on option using TELNET client authentication.

FIGURE 7.33 Specific Sign-on for TELNET client authentication

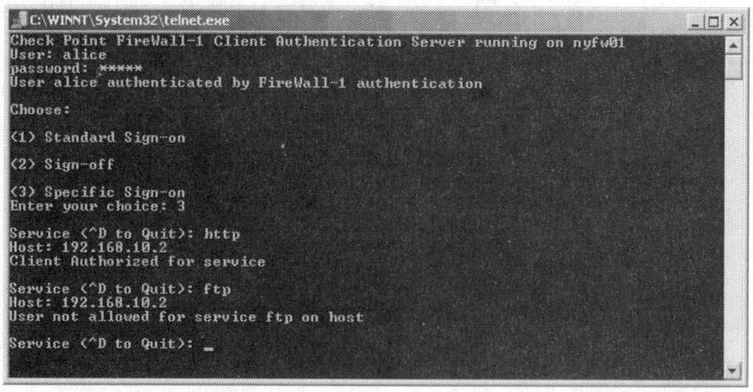

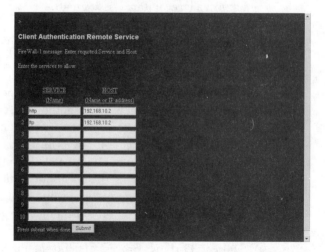

In Figure 7.33, Option 3 is selected, which means Specific Sign-on is invoked. The client is then prompted to specify the service and the host on which the specified service should be authorized. In Figure 7.33, the client is authorized to access the HTTP service running on 192.168.10.2 if the client specifies a destination host and service that is not configured in the client authentication rule, the authorization is rejected, as shown in Figure 7.33 for FTP running on 192.168.10.2. Figure 7.34 shows the Specific Sign-on screen for HTTP client authentication, which is invoked if the Specific Sign-on option is selected in Figure 7.23.

FIGURE 7.34 Specific sign-on for HTTP client authentication

In Figure 7.34, the same services and hosts configured for authorization in Figure 7.33 are specified. Once you have configured the list of authorized services and hosts, click the Submit button. Figure 7.35 shows the page that is displayed after clicking the Submit button.

FIGURE 7.35   Specific sign-on results for HTTP client authentication

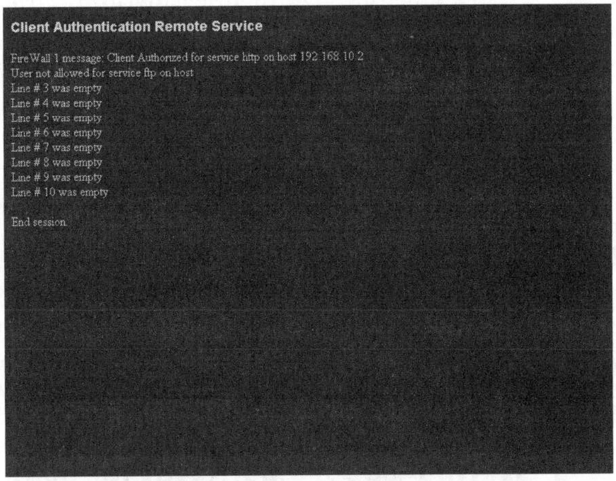

You can see that the client has been authorized for the HTTP service running on 192.168.10.2; however, the authorization for the FTP service running on 192.168.10.2 has been rejected, because this service is not specified in the client authentication rule.

Transparency for Client Authentication

In its default state (manual client authentication), client authentication is non-transparent, which means that a user must connect to an enforcement module for the purposes of authentication, before attempting to connect to the desired destination system and service. You can change the sign-on method for client authentication to partially automatic or fully automatic (see Figure 7.23), which enables client authentication to become transparent, yet still retain the other features of client authentication.

When you enable partially automatic client authentication, you can use HTTP, FTP, TELNET, or RLOGIN connections to transparently authenticate via user authentication, which then authorizes the remaining destination systems and services in the client authentication. If users wish to initially connect using a service that is not supported by user authentication, then manual client authentication must be performed first to authorize the client authentication rule.

If you enable fully automatic client authentication, users can establish a connection of any service to transparently authenticate via session authentication, which then authorizes the access to the other destination systems and services in the client authentication rule. Fully automatic client authentication obviously requires a session authentication agent to be installed on the machine of the authenticating user, although an agent is not required if HTTP, FTP, TELNET, or RLOGIN connections are used for authentication, as these are authenticated using user authentication rather than session authentication.

With regards to fully automatic client authentication, you might be wondering why you would use this over session authentication. The main reason is if you wish for your users to only authenticate transparently once with the session authentication agent, after which the client machine the user is working from is permitted to make other connections without authentication.

Performance for Client Authentication

With manual client authentication, only a single connection to an enforcement module security server is required, after which all authorized connections are not processed by any security servers, and are instead processed in the same way as connections matching normal security rules. With partially automatic and fully automatic client authentication, the authenticating connection may be performed in-band (for HTTP, FTP, TELNET, and RLOGIN) or may be performed via session authentication. This means that client authentication does not suffer the performance hit of user authentication, as only a single connection is needed per client to authorize the client, after which all connections are processed by the INSPECT module (running in kernel mode), instead of by security servers (running in user mode). This allows client authentication to support many more authorized connections than user authentication.

When to Use Session Authentication

Session authentication is best suited to authenticating users for access to services not supported by user authentication, and when you only want authentication to be applied per connection, rather than per IP address. You can also use session authentication to provide authentication from a different location, other than the source of the connection. For user and client authentication, all authentication must be performed by the source of the connection—with session authentication, authentication is performed by the source of the connection by default, but can be configured to be performed at the destination or any other workstation object known to VPN-1/FireWall-1. An organization must again consider supported services, security, transparency, and performance when selecting the type of authentication that should be implemented, and how session authentication meets or does not meet these requirements.

Supported Services for Session Authentication

Session authentication supports all services, so along with client authentication represents the only choices for authentication if you need to authenticate services outside of HTTP, FTP, TELNET, and RLOGIN.

Security for Session Authentication

Session authentication is considered as secure as user authentication, because each connection must be separately authenticated. For each new session authentication connection, the enforcement module will contact the session authentication agent. The session authentication agent also controls the level of security, as it can be configured to prompt for each new connection (default), to only prompt once per session (the duration the agent is running), or to prompt after a configurable period of inactivity. For HTTP traffic, the default setting (prompt on each new connection) is unsuitable, as the user will suffer the same obtrusiveness that user authentication introduces with HTTP. The recommended setting that ensures the best security and is least obtrusive is to configure re-authentication only after an idle period of time. It is important to understand that the session authentication agent is only loaded when a user logs on and is closed when a user logs off. This ensures that another user cannot log in to a machine after a user has logged off and gain unauthorized access, because the session authentication agent closes down when the original user logs off.

Transparency for Session Authentication

Session authentication is transparent, as users do not need to establish a separate authentication connection prior to the connection that they wish to establish. Instead, this is handled after user attempts to connect to the desired destination system and service, with the enforcement module making a connection back to the session authentication agent. At this point, the agent will prompt the user for authentication, which is entered and returned to the enforcement module. If authentication is successful, the original connection made from the user is permitted.

Performance for Session Authentication

Session authentication requires an enforcement module to make a connection to a session authentication agent every time a new connection is made that matches a session authentication rule. This means that the performance penalty of session authentication is higher than client authentication (with client authentication, only a single authentication connection is made, after which subsequent connections are passed through the INSPECT module), but is not as high as user authentication, because an authentication connection is only required at the establishment of each connection, after which all traffic passed through the enforcement module is handled in the same manner as normal traffic matching a normal security rule connection. With user authentication, *all* connection traffic is passed through security servers, which increases the performance penalty associated with user authentication.

Summary

There are three different types of authentication: user, client, and session authentication. User authentication provides authentication for HTTP, FTP, TELNET, and RLOGIN connections only, with authentication being provided transparently by the appropriate security servers on enforcement modules. Each connection requires authentication, which makes user authentication secure as new connections from the same IP address require new authentication.

Client authentication provides authentication for all services, but its default form (known as manual client authentication) requires users to explicitly establish a connection to the TELNET or HTTP security server for authentication. Once authentication is complete, the IP address of the machine the user authenticates from is authorized for the client authentication rule, which means the user can establish new connections to other systems and services defined in the rule without requiring re-authentication. Although this is more flexible, it is less secure than authenticating per connection, as another user may gain access to the authorized machine and be able to gain unauthorized access to machines behind the enforcement module. Client authentication can be configured to be partially automatic or fully automatic, which enables authentication to be performed in a transparent fashion, meaning the user does not need to first establish a connection for authentication purposes, instead attempting to connect directly to the desired destination and then being prompted for authentication, either via a user authentication mechanism (partially automatic) or via session authentication (fully automatic).

Session authentication provides the best of both user authentication and client authentication. User authentication is secure, because it only authenticates per connection, but is restrictive because it only supports HTTP, FTP, TELNET, and RLOGIN. Client authentication is flexible, because it supports all services, but authenticates an entire host (IP address), which makes it easy for other unauthorized users to exploit. Session authentication provides authentication on a per-connection basis (like user authentication) and also supports all services (like client authentication). A session authentication agent is required on the user machine, which listens for authentication connections from enforcement modules. When a user attempts a new connection that matches a session authentication rule, the enforcement module challenges the session authentication agent for authentication, which is provided by the user and then returned back to the enforcement module. If authentication is successful, the connection is permitted. If a new connection is matched against a session authentication rule, the same process happens again.

Exam Essentials

Understand the types of authentication.   The authentication types include user, client, and session authentication.

Know how to configure an authentication rule.   Authentication rules require user groups to be defined as the permitted source objects. You can add user access to the Source element of a rule by adding user group objects, and further restrict the hosts (IP addresses) a user can authenticate from. The Action element of an authentication rule specifies the appropriate type of authentication. Remember that you must ensure a normal security rule is not present that matches the connections you wish to authenticate, as the connections will be matched to this rule, even if they are below the authentication rules.

Know how to customize an authentication rule.   Each authentication type allows you to configure both global parameters and parameters that apply only for a specific rule. You can customize the authentication parameters for a rule by right-clicking the authentication type configured in the Action element (e.g., User Auth) and selecting the Properties option.

Understand where to place your authentication rules.   You must place client authentication rules above your stealth rule or any rule that blocks access to your enforcement modules. This restriction does not apply for user authentication and session authentication rules.

Understand user authentication.   User authentication is transparent (users connect directly to the desired destination to invoke authentication) and is performed by security servers on the enforcement module. It only supports HTTP, FTP, TELNET, and RLOGIN, and authentication is required per connection, which makes it secure. All connections authenticated via user authentication actually consist of two connections per connection—one from the client to the security server and the other from the security server to the destination server.

Understand client authentication.   Client authentication in its default form (manual client authentication) is non-transparent, in that users must first establish a connection to the enforcement module to authenticate, using either the TELNET security server listening on port 259 or the HTTP security server listening on port 900. It supports all services, and authentication is required on a per–IP address basis, which means once a user has authenticated, the IP address of the host is authorized to make new connections to other destination systems and services specified in the client authentication rule. This makes client authentication the least secure method of authentication. All authorized connections permitted by client authentication are permitted directly through the enforcement module (in the same fashion as normal security rules permit connections), making client authentication more scalable than user authentication.

Understand the different types of client authentication.   There are three main types of client authentication. Manual (the default) requires users to authenticate in a non-transparent fashion (to either the HTTP or TELNET security server). Partially automatic allows users to establish an HTTP, FTP, TELNET, or RLOGIN connection and authenticate transparently using user authentication, which then authorizes the client authentication rule. Fully automatic allows users to establish a connection with using any service, with the enforcement module authenticating the user via session authentication. Once authenticated, the client authentication rule is authorized. Both partially automatic and fully automatic client authentication are methods of making client authentication transparent.

Understand session authentication. Session authentication is designed to combine the best features of both user and client authentication. Just like client authentication, session authentication supports all services; however, authentication is performed per connection (just like user authentication), which is more secure than client authentication. The only downside to session authentication is that it requires a session authentication agent on the source machines. When a new connection matches a session authentication rule, the enforcement module connects to the session authentication agent on the source machine, and the agent then challenges the user for authentication. This means that the enforcement module establishes an out-of-band authentication connection to the agent for each connection.

Know which type of authentication to choose given a set of requirements. The exam focuses heavily on selecting the correct authentication type. Key factors that determine the selection of authentication type include the services by the authentication type, the authorization scope (per connection or per IP address), security (determined by the authorization scope), transparency, and performance.

Key Terms

Before you take the exam, be certain you are familiar with the following terms:

authentication types	logical servers
authorization scope	non-transparent authentication
authorization timeout	out-of-band authentication
failed authentication attempts	session authentication client
host	transparent authentication
implicit client authentication	user authentication
in-band authentication	User Authentication Session Timeout

Review Questions

1. You wish to authenticate connections on an enforcement module to an FTP server behind the enforcement module. Client PCs may host multiple users. Which authentication type should you implement?

   A. User authentication

   B. Client authentication

   C. Implicit client authentication

   D. Session authentication

2. You need to authenticate web access to the Internet from web clients behind an enforcement module. Users should only have to authenticate once, and should only re-authenticate if they leave their machines for a certain amount of time. Which authentication type should you configure? (Select the best option.)

   A. User authentication

   B. Client authentication

   C. Implicit client authentication

   D. Session authentication

3. You have concerns about the security of client authentication as you do not wish to authorize access on a per–IP address basis. You need to provide authentication for SMTP connections. Which authentication type should you configure?

   A. User authentication

   B. Client authentication

   C. Implicit client authentication

   D. Session authentication

4. What is the maximum number of connections that can be authorized by user authentication?

    A. 1

    B. 2

    C. 10

    D. Unlimited

5. Client authentication in its default state is considered which of the following? (Choose all that apply.)

    A. Automatic

    B. Manual

    C. Non-transparent

    D. Transparent

6. You configure an authentication rule at the top of your rule base, but HTTP connections that should be authenticated are being permitted through the enforcement module without authentication. Which of the following is the most likely cause?

    A. Implied rules are permitting the connections.

    B. A normal security rule is configured below the authentication rule that is matching the connections.

    C. A normal security rule is configured above the authentication rule that is matching the connections.

    D. Your enforcement module is not licensed for authentication.

7. You create a client authentication rule, but users cannot connect to the TELNET or HTTP security servers. How should you resolve this?

    A. Create a rule that permits TCP connections to ports 259 and 900 on the enforcement module. Place the rule directly above the client authentication rule.

    B. Configure user authentication—client authentication doesn't work with HTTP or TELNET.

    C. Ensure the enforcement module is licensed for authentication.

    D. Place the client authentication above the stealth rule.

8. You need to implement transparent authentication that authorizes per IP address for any service. Which authentication type should you implement?

   A. Client authentication

   B. Implicit client authentication

   C. Fully automatic client authentication

   D. Session authentication

9. Which of the following describes the user authentication session timeout? (Choose all that apply.)

   A. Determines the amount of idle time between connections being established before authorization is removed.

   B. Determines the amount of idle time within a connection before authorization is removed.

   C. Is configurable on a per-enforcement module basis.

   D. Is configurable on a global basis only.

10. Which of the following are features of client authentication? (Choose all that apply.)

   A. Authorization scope is per IP address

   B. Suitable for authorizing multi-user client machines

   C. Transparent

   D. Requires agent on client machines

11. You configure a user authentication rule for a user that needs to make 20 TELNET connections to various TELNET servers. How many connections will exist in total, in terms of the client machine and enforcement module?

   A. 1

   B. 20

   C. 21

   D. 40

12. By default, how many connections are authorized by successful client authentication?

    A. 1

    B. 5

    C. 10

    D. Unlimited

13. You implement manual client authentication using the TELNET security server, but have had heard of attacks where an attacker crashes an authenticated client machine and then exploits the authorized status of the client IP address. How can you alleviate this, ensuring you support any service and no agent software is required?

    A. Configure user authentication.

    B. Configure session authentication.

    C. Enable wait mode.

    D. Configure a low authorization timeout.

14. For session authentication rules to work, where should you place the rules?

    A. Above the stealth rule

    B. Below the stealth rule

    C. Above any security rules that explicitly deny the connections

    D. Anywhere in the rule base

15. Where can session authentication be performed? (Choose all that apply.)

    A. At the source of the connection

    B. At the destination of the connection

    C. At any workstation object defined in VPN-1/FireWall-1

    D. At the enforcement module

16. Which of the following describes how session authentication connections are formed by default?

    A. Authentication connection is formed from source host to enforcement module.

    B. Authentication connection is formed from enforcement module to source host.

    C. Authentication connection is formed from destination host to enforcement module.

    D. Authentication connection is formed from enforcement module to destination host.

17. You configure the source of a user authentication rule to grant access to the group a user belongs to from a location that the user connects from. The user is presenting the correct credentials, but is being rejected. Further examination reveals that the user object representing the user is not permitted network access from the location configured in the rule. How should you rectify the situation, without modifying the user object at all?

    A. In the user authentication properties of the rule, configure the Source parameter to intersect with the user database.

    B. In the user authentication properties of the rule, configure the Destination parameter to intersect with the user database.

    C. In the user authentication properties of the rule, configure the Source parameter to ignore the user database.

    D. In the user authentication properties of the rule, configure the Destination parameter to ignore the user database.

18. Which Global Properties screen allows you to configure custom banners for user authentication?

    A. Authentication

    B. FireWall-1

    C. Security Servers

    D. VPN

19. You configure user authentication for FTP connections to a remote FTP server with an IP address of 172.16.1.1. The FTP server requires its own authentication as well. A user has an account called `alice` on the enforcement module, an account called `ftp-user` on the FTP server. What should be specified at the username prompt when the user authenticates with the FTP security server?

   A. `alice@ftp-user`

   B. `alice@ftp-user@172.16.1.1`

   C. `ftp-user@alice`

   D. `ftp-user@alice@172.16.1.1`

20. You create a user authentication rule for HTTP access from internal clients to web servers on the Internet. You have not customized the rule in any way, and users are complaining that authentication fails, even though users are adamant they are passing the correct credentials. What is the cause of the problem?

   A. Users are specifying invalid credentials.

   B. HTTP is not supported by user authentication.

   C. The user authentication rule is configured to only permit HTTP connections to predefined servers.

   D. The rule is below the stealth rule.

Answers to Review Questions

1. **A.** FTP is a supported service for user authentication, so you should use this type, as authentication is performed on a per-connection basis, which is important given that multiple users may reside on client machines.

2. **C.** Although user authentication supports HTTP, it required authentication per connection, which means users will be constantly authenticated when accessing web pages, due to the nature of HTTP. You could use client authentication; however, implicit client authentication is better, as users can be authenticated transparently via HTTP user authentication once, which then authorizes further HTTP connections from the client IP address. Session authentication is not ideal, as it requires installation of an agent and requires authentication per connection.

3. **D.** The question has effectively ruled out client authentication, so you need to choose between user authentication and session authentication. SMTP is not supported by user authentication so you must use session authentication.

4. **A.** User authentication authorizes a single connection.

5. **B, C.** By default, client authentication is manual, which means users must connect to the enforcement module directly to authenticate (thus authentication is non-transparent), prior to connecting to desired systems and services behind the enforcement module.

6. **B.** The default implied rules do not permit HTTP connections. The question says that the authentication rule is at the top of the rule base, so C cannot be the answer. Authentication does not require licensing. Security rules are processed before authentication rules, even if the authentication rules are above the security rules.

7. **D.** Always remember that client authentication rules should be placed above the stealth rule, as they implicitly permit authentication connections to the enforcement module. Although A could rectify the situation, it will not, because the rule is placed directly above the client authentication rule, which means it will still be below the stealth rule.

8. C. Because authorization is required per IP address, you must implement some form of client authentication. To make client authentication transparent, you can implement implicit client authentication (works only for HTTP, FTP, TELNET, and RLOGIN) or fully automatic client authentication (works for all services, requires session authentication agent). Because the question specifies all services, you must use fully automatic client authentication.

9. B, C. User authentication session timeout defines the amount of time a connection can be idle (no traffic is exchanged) before the connection will be torn down. It is configurable on a per-enforcement module basis for NG enforcement modules.

10. A. Client authentication authorizes rules on a per–IP address basis. It is not suitable for multiuser machines, as authorization is per IP address, which could allow an unauthenticated user on a machine to gain unauthorized access while another authenticated user is on the machine. Client authentication is non-transparent by default and does not require any agents on client machines.

11. D. Because user authentication is implemented, for each TELNET connection that is made, the client has a connection to the TELNET security server on the enforcement module, and the TELNET security server has another connection to the destination TELNET server. This means there are actually two connections in place per TELNET session.

12. B. By default, client authentication authorizes five connections.

13. C. By enabling wait mode, the enforcement module maintains the TELNET client authentication session with an authorized host. If that session goes down, any authorized client authentication rules are immediately de-authorized. The enforcement module also pings the client machine, and if there are no replies, the TELNET session is torn down. If the client is down due to a DoS attack, it will not reply to the pings from the enforcement module, which means the enforcement module will tear down the TELNET client authentication session and de-authorize any rules associated with the client machine.

14. C. User and session authentication rules can be placed below the stealth rule but must be placed above any rules that explicitly deny connections that match the authentication rules.

15. A, B, C. Session authentication allows you to authenticate connections not only at the source of the connection (default), but also at the destination or at any workstation object known to VPN-1/FireWall-1.

16. B. By default, session authentication occurs at the source of the connection. The enforcement module detects a connection that requires session authentication and establishes a connection to the session authentication agent on the host for authentication purposes.

17. C. The issue here is with the source of the rule. By default, VPN-1/ FireWall-1 checks both the location specified in the source of the object and the locations permitted for the user object. If the IP address the user is connecting from is not permitted in either of these, the connection is not permitted. By configuring the rule to ignore the user database, the locations permitted for the user object are ignored, with the locations configured for the user authentication rule only being honored.

18. C. The Security Servers screen allows you to configure welcome banners for the various security servers.

19. D. When you need to pass authentication information to both the enforcement module FTP security server and destination system FTP server, you must specify username credentials as *<destination-account>@<fw1-account>@<FTP server IP address>*.

20. C. By default, a user authentication rule only permits HTTP connections to predefined servers. Because the access in this question is from the internal network to the Internet, the rule must be configured to permit HTTP connections to all servers.

Chapter

8

Network Address Translation

THE CCSA EXAM OBJECTIVES COVERED IN THIS CHAPTER INCLUDE:

✓ List the reasons and methods for NAT.

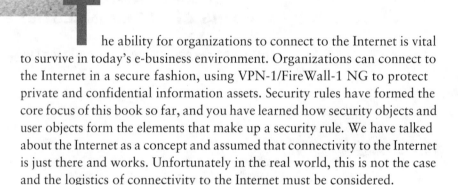

he ability for organizations to connect to the Internet is vital to survive in today's e-business environment. Organizations can connect to the Internet in a secure fashion, using VPN-1/FireWall-1 NG to protect private and confidential information assets. Security rules have formed the core focus of this book so far, and you have learned how security objects and user objects form the elements that make up a security rule. We have talked about the Internet as a concept and assumed that connectivity to the Internet is just there and works. Unfortunately in the real world, this is not the case and the logistics of connectivity to the Internet must be considered.

The subject of this chapter is *network address translation* or *NAT*, which is a technique used by devices that form the gateway between the Internet and the private IP network of an organization (such as a VPN-1/FireWall-1 enforcement module) to ensure internal devices can communicate with the Internet. Many organizations use private IP addresses, which are a range of IP addresses open for use by anybody but considered invalid on the Internet to avoid IP addressing conflicts caused by the unregulated use of private IP addresses. The reuse of private IP addresses by the multitude of organizations throughout the world ensures valid IP addresses are conserved, which must be globally unique on the Internet. NAT enables private IP addresses to be translated to valid IP addresses, which allows external devices on the Internet to think they are communicating with a device that has a valid IP address, instead of a private IP address. VPN-1/FireWall-1 provides the ability to implement NAT, which provides a solution that enables connectivity to and from the Internet (using NAT) and also restricts the connectivity provided to specific networks, hosts, applications, and users. In this chapter, you will learn about the various types of NAT available on VPN-1/FireWall-1 and how they work. Once you have a firm grasp of how NAT works, you will be ready to move on to Chapter 9, "Manual and Automatic NAT," where you will configure NAT on VPN-1/FireWall-1.

Understanding Network Address Translation

Before you learn about how NAT works, you must understand why you would implement NAT. You should also know a bit of the background as to how NAT has become an important requirement in today's networks. Network address translation is used for the following reasons in networks today:

- Allows devices with private IP addresses to connect to the Internet.

- Provides security for the devices on the internal network.

Each of the above reasons will now be discussed in detail.

Private IP Addressing

With the explosive growth of the Internet, many organizations today implement their networks based on IP. IP has it roots in the Internet—it was developed to enable the global network that the Internet has become. An important component of IP is addressing—as with any form of communications protocol, whether it be computer-related or something like the postal system, addressing provides the ability to uniquely identify each party that is connected to or part of the communications network. On the Internet, this means organizations need to ensure that the IP addresses they configure are unique, so that they can communicate with any other device on the Internet. As with any global communications network, such as the traditional telephony network or the global postal system, addressing is controlled in a hierarchical fashion, to ensure that addresses are allocated efficiently and uniquely. IP is currently deployed based on IP version 4, or *IPv4*, which has been in place since the early days of the Internet. IPv4 uses a 32-bit address space, which can support a maximum of approximately 4 billion or so devices. With the explosive Internet growth in the early 1990s, the globally unique address space would have been exhausted within years without some mitigation. Many organizations were looking to deploy IP throughout their networks to thousands of devices, yet not all of these devices required connectivity to the Internet. Allocating globally unique addresses to each of these devices wasted address space on those devices that only needed IP connectivity within the organization. There needed to be some mechanism that allowed specific IP addresses to be reused by organizations (i.e., more than one organization could use the IP addresses), yet still enable connectivity to the Internet.

To facilitate this mechanism, the Internet Engineering Task Force (IETF) created RFC1918, which defines a private IP addressing scheme that can be used by any organization wishing to set up a private network based on IP, without requiring the allocation of globally unique address space. RFC1918 defines three ranges of addressing, designed to suit the IP addressing requirements of any sized organization:

- 10.x.x.x

- 172.16.x.x–172.31.x.x

- 192.168.x.x

RFC1918 specifies that these IP addresses are illegal on the Internet and should only be used for organizations that wish to implement a private IP network. The whole purpose of RFC1918 is to define IP addresses that can be used by any organization wishing to use IP on their private network, without the organization's having to worry about obtaining public address space that does not conflict with other public address space. In other words, Organization X can use IP addressing of 10.x.x.x (e.g., have a host with an IP address of 10.1.1.1) and Organization Y can use the same IP address of 10.x.x.x (and also have a host with an IP address of 10.1.1.1). Because both networks are private, in theory they have no concept that the other exists; hence, it does not matter if either use the same IP addressing that would normally cause conflicts on the public Internet.

Private IP addressing works fine if the private network is isolated from other public networks such as Internet; however, most organizations want to connect their private networks to the Internet. Because RFC1918 states that private IP addressing is illegal on the Internet, this causes a problem for an organization that has implemented private IP addressing and also wants to connect to the Internet. This is where NAT comes into the picture. NAT allows an organization to implement a device that connects to both the private network and the Internet. This NAT device is normally implemented on the firewall that protects the organization from the Internet (e.g., VPN-1/FireWall-1). The NAT device can be viewed as a gateway between the public address space implemented on the Internet, and the private address space implemented for the internal network of the organization. At this point, although it has already been mentioned, it is important to formally define that a private address space and public address space exists. IP addresses within these address spaces can be defined as follows:

- Private IP addresses—part of the private address space defined by an organization.

- Valid IP addresses—part of the globally unique address space that forms the Internet.

Figure 8.1 demonstrates the concept of private IP addresses and valid IP addresses:

FIGURE 8.1 NAT boundaries

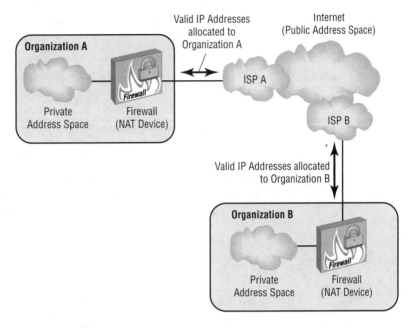

In Figure 8.1, you can see that each organization maintains its own private IP addressing on the internal network protected by the firewall, while the firewall provides a connection to the public address space of the Internet. The organization's ISP allocates a pool of valid IP addresses, which are used to represent devices to the Internet.

NAT works by modifying the IP addresses of packets sent from private IP addresses to valid IP addresses, to ensure that all IP addresses include valid IP addressing on the Internet. NAT essentially provides a valid identity on the Internet for a private device, with the NAT device rewriting IP address fields to masquerade as the private device. For example, if a private device with an IP address of 10.1.1.1 needs to connect to a device on the Internet with a valid IP address of 199.1.1.1, the NAT device must translate the source IP address of the packets from 10.1.1.1 to some valid IP address that is allocated to the organization. For packets that need to be sent from the Internet to private devices, NAT allows you to use a valid IP address that represents a private device, so that any packets sent to that valid destination IP address are translated back to the private device.

Providing Security for Internal Devices

Although NAT is primarily designed for connecting devices with private IP addresses to the Internet, NAT also provides a basic level of security from external devices on the Internet, by concealing the internal addressing of the network from the Internet. If you do not conceal the internal addressing of your networks, attackers can determine your inner network topology and generate attacks, masquerading as an internal device. NAT provides security in the event that your internal network is suddenly exposed to the Internet. Because internal devices connecting to the Internet through a NAT device have private IP addresses, if the NAT device fails for some reason, connectivity between internal devices and the Internet is severed, as packets will be sent out to the Internet with a private IP address. Although this might sound bad, because connectivity has been broken, it can also be considered good from a security point of view. Figure 8.2 demonstrates two different ways that an organization could implement a DMZ network that provides access to some public servers (e.g., web servers) for an organization from the Internet.

FIGURE 8.2 NAT security

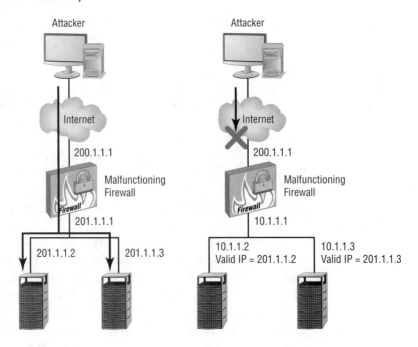

In Figure 8.2, the network on the left has configured valid IP addressing on the DMZ, which means no NAT is required for the web servers to communicate with the Internet. If the firewall for some reason malfunctions and permits any access to the protected DMZ (i.e., acts like a router), any device on the Internet now has full network access to the servers because the DMZ servers have valid IP addressing, making them extremely vulnerable to attack. The network on the right has configured private IP addressing on the DMZ, which means that the firewall provides NAT to enable the web servers to communicate with the Internet. If the firewall malfunctions, which stops any access control or NAT from being applied, although the firewall is open, external devices can't communicate with the web servers because they have private IP addressing, which is illegal on the Internet. If an external device attempts to connect to one of these private IP addresses, the next-hop router in the Internet will most likely drop the packet, because it will have no concept of the private IP addressing configured for the organization's DMZ network.

NAT also provides security via a special type of NAT called hide NAT. Hide NAT allows multiple private IP addresses to be "hidden" behind a single valid IP address—hence the term hide NAT. Hide NAT enables internal devices to make connections out to the Internet, but does not enable external devices to connect to internal devices whatsoever. In other words, hide NAT only works in one direction—from the internal network to the Internet. This ensures that external devices cannot initiate connections to internal devices—they can only accept connections from them.

NAT in VPN-1/FireWall-1

VPN-1/FireWall-1 supports network address translation, enabling devices with private IP addresses that are protected by VPN-1/FireWall-1 enforcement modules to be represented with a valid IP address on the Internet. Two types of NAT are supported on VPN-1/FireWall-1:

- Static NAT
- Hide NAT

Static NAT

Static NAT is the easiest method of NAT to understand, as it translates IP addresses in a one-to-one fashion. This means that a single private IP address is translated to a single valid IP address. Figure 8.3 demonstrates a network topology and how static NAT maps private IP addresses to valid IP addresses in a one-to-one fashion.

FIGURE 8.3 Static NAT

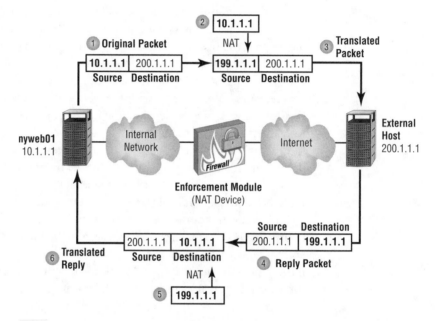

In Figure 8.3 the following events occur:

1. A host called nyweb01 on the internal network sends an IP packet to an external device on the Internet. The source IP address of the packet is 10.1.1.1 and the destination IP address of the packet is 200.1.1.1.

2. The IP packet is received at the VPN-1/FireWall-1 enforcement module. An address translation rule is configured that translates the source IP address of any packet with a source IP address of 10.1.1.1 to 199.1.1.1. The enforcement module rewrites the source IP address of the packet generated in Step 1, replacing 10.1.1.1 with 199.1.1.1. The 199.1.1.1 IP address is a valid address on the Internet, and is allocated to the VPN-1/FireWall-1 enforcement module by the organization's ISP.

3. The translated packet is sent to the Internet and eventually arrives at the external device. The external device believes it has received a packet from 199.1.1.1 rather than 10.1.1.1.

4. The external device sends a reply packet back towards nyweb01, with a source IP address of the external device (200.1.1.1), which identifies that the packet was generated by the external device. Because the source IP address of the packet received by the external device in Step 3 was 199.1.1.1, the reply packet has a destination IP address of 199.1.1.1.

5. Because the destination IP address of the reply packet is a valid address (199.1.1.1), the reply packet is eventually routed through the Internet back to the VPN-1/FireWall-1 enforcement module. To ensure the reply packet is forwarded on to the internal device, the destination IP address of 199.1.1.1 must be translated to 10.1.1.1. This ensures that the return traffic for traffic generated by nyweb01 has the correct IP addressing when it arrives back at nyweb01.

6. The translated reply packet is forwarded by the enforcement module towards nyweb01. Because the destination IP address is now 10.1.1.1, nyweb01 will receive the packet, and know that it is a reply packet from the external device, as the source IP address of the received packet is 200.1.1.1.

In Figure 8.3, an IP address of 199.1.1.1 has essentially been allocated to nyweb01, which enables nyweb01 to communicate on the Internet using an identity of 199.1.1.1, instead of the its real private identity (10.1.1.1). This valid IP address can also be used by external devices wishing to connect to nyweb01—an external device simply has to send a connection request to the valid IP address representing nyweb01, and the enforcement module will translate the destination IP address from the valid IP address to the actual internal IP address configured on nyweb01.

It is important to note that Figure 8.3 demonstrates a connection between nyweb01 and an external device that consists of bidirectional communications. Therefore NAT must be able to handle not only packets that are sent from nyweb01 to the external device, but also the return packets of the connection. In other words, NAT needs to be connection-aware rather than just packet-aware.

In Figure 8.3, you saw how NAT can enable an internal device with a private IP address to establish connections with external devices on the Internet. In VPN-1/FireWall-1, two forms of NAT relate to the direction in which a connection is established:

Source NAT   *Source NAT* represents address translation rules for connections established from devices with private IP address to devices with valid IP addresses. Source NAT is named so because the packets that are sent from the source of the connection to the destination of the connection require the source IP address to be translated.

Destination NAT *Destination NAT* represents address translation rules for connections established from devices with valid IP addresses to devices with private IP addresses. Destination NAT is named so because the packets that are sent from the source of the connection to the destination of the connection require the destination IP address to be translated.

Figure 8.3 demonstrated source NAT, because the connection was established from a device with private IP addressing to a device with valid IP addressing. Even though in Step 5 of Figure 8.3 the destination IP address of the reply packets were translated, the processes of Step 5 are not referred to as destination NAT, as the reply packets are part of a source NAT connection. If, however, the external device in Figure 8.3 needs to establish a connection to nyweb01, destination NAT is required, as the connection is being established from a device with a valid IP address to a device with a private IP address. The required translations for this connection would be the same as for Figure 8.3, except the packet flow would start from the external device, rather than nyweb01.

It is very important that you think of NAT in terms of connections rather than packets on VPN-1/FireWall-1. These concepts are identical to the concepts that apply for security rules. You have learned that security rules are configured based on connections, rather than packets, with the return packets of a connection not requiring a security rule that matches the Layer 3/4 parameters of the packets. In an identical fashion, address translation rules are configured based on connections, with the direction of the connection used to define terms such as source NAT and destination NAT.

Now that you understand how static NAT works for a single internal device, what happens when you want multiple internal devices with private IP addresses to communicate on the Internet? Let's assume in Figure 8.3 that another host called nymail101 has an IP address of 10.1.1.2 and wants to connect to the Internet. You can't use the 199.1.1.1 valid IP address, because this is already allocated to nyweb01. To provide nymail101 with a public identity, you need to allocate another valid IP address. Assuming 199.1.1.2 is not in use, you can allocate this valid IP address to nymail101, which means that nymail101 will appear to have an IP address of 199.1.1.2 to any external device. If you extend this concept of a one-to-one mapping, you will find that if you wish to use static NAT to connect to the Internet, you need one IP address per internal device. For example, if you had an internal subnet with an address of 10.1.1.x/24, if you wanted each device (254 in total, 10.1.1.1–10.1.1.254) on this subnet to communicate on the Internet using static NAT, you would need 254 valid IP addresses. In Figure 8.3, you might allocate the 199.1.1.x address range to the 10.1.1.x internal subnet. This would mean that valid IP addresses would be allocated to each internal device as follows:

- 10.1.1.1 ➤ 199.1.1.1

- 10.1.1.2 ➤ 199.1.1.2

- 10.1.1.3 ➤ 199.1.1.3

- ...

- 10.1.1.254 ➤ 199.1.1.254

Many organizations do not have large amounts of public address space allocated, so static NAT should only be reserved for those hosts that need it. Static NAT is normally only used for hosts that require the ability for external devices to connect to them. Examples of such devices include mail servers, web servers, and DNS servers. Because static NAT provides a one-to-one mapping, if an enforcement module receives a connection request addressed to a certain valid IP address, the enforcement module can map that valid IP address back to an internal device, translate the destination IP address, and forward the packet on to the correct internal device (i.e., static destination NAT). In Figure 8.3, any connection request addressed to 199.1.1.1 is mapped to nyweb01, allowing external devices to connect to nyweb01.

Issues with Static NAT

Some restrictions apply to static NAT, and it is important that you are aware of these before you implement static NAT. The following lists common issues with static NAT:

- Incompatible application-layer protocol support

- Lack of valid address space

Application-Layer Protocol Support for NAT

Some application-layer protocols are incompatible with NAT, as they either transmit IP address information within the application data stream or use

IP addresses for some function of the protocol. Figure 8.4 demonstrates how an application-layer protocol that transmits IP addressing information within the application data stream can be "broken" by NAT.

FIGURE 8.4 Application-layer protocol NAT issues

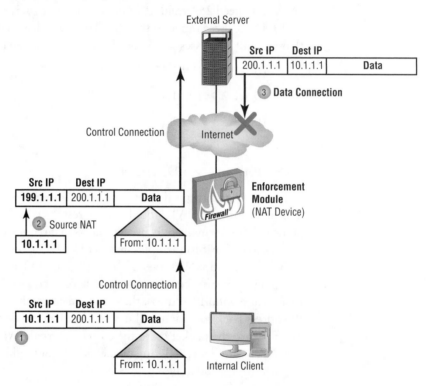

In Figure 8.4 the following events occur:

1. An internal client with a private IP address of 10.1.1.1 makes a control connection to an external server. A separate control connection is used in some protocols to pass control information (e.g., commands). The packet has a source IP address of 10.1.1.1 and a destination IP address of 200.1.1.1. Let's assume that the client wishes to receive data from the server, and the protocol requires a separate data connection to be established. To enable the separate data connection, the client includes its IP address (10.1.1.1) in the application data stream.

2. The packet arrives at the enforcement module, which performs static NAT based on the security policy configuration. The source IP address

of the packet is rewritten to the valid IP address 199.1.1.1. Because the enforcement module only normally works with Layer 3/4 information, it has no idea that the private IP address of the client is also included in the application data stream, and this is not translated.

3. The external server receives the packet and processes the application-layer data. Rather than using the source IP address of the packet received (i.e., 199.1.1.1, the valid IP address of the client) to determine where the data connection should be established to, the server uses the private IP address (10.1.1.1) within the application data stream. The server therefore sends a connection setup request to a destination IP address 10.1.1.1, which fails because this is an illegal address on the Internet. The next-hop router that receives this packet from the server has no idea where 10.1.1.1, and will normally drop the packet.

To ensure the application-layer protocol in Figure 8.4 works correctly, the enforcement module needs to not only translate the source IP address of packets being sent from the client, but also translate the private IP address included as part of the application data stream. Unlike IP addresses, which are always in the same position within a packet, the position of a private IP address within the application data stream can vary, depending on the application-layer protocol. This means that for each application-layer protocol that requires NAT within the application data stream, specific code must be written that tells the enforcement module where to look within a packet and under which circumstances a rewrite should occur within the application data stream. An example of a protocol that VPN-1/FireWall-1 NG supports that sends IP addressing information within the application-layer data stream is NetBIOS over TCP/IP (NetBT).

Limited Address Space

Static NAT provides one-to-one mappings, which means that for each device that requires a valid IP address, the valid IP address that is assigned to that device cannot be used by another device. This means that if you configure static NAT and you want some internal devices with private IP addresses to communicate with external devices on the Internet, you require one valid IP address per private IP address. If you have a limited number of valid IP addresses available to you, this causes a problem if you have more internal devices that require Internet connectivity than valid IP addresses. You could, of course, obtain more valid IP addresses, but this will cost you more money. You could also implement hide NAT (discussed in the next section), which allows multiple internal devices to use a single valid IP address; however, hide NAT is only supported for connections initiated from internal devices to external devices on the Internet and not for the reverse.

If you have more internal devices that must be available to receive connections from the Internet than valid IP addresses, you can configure a static NAT translation to apply only to a specific service, rather than an entire IP address. For example, let's assume an organization has a single valid IP address of 199.1.1.1 available, but has a separate web server, mail server, and FTP server located internally, which all require connectivity from the Internet. VPN-1/FireWall-1 NG could be configured to translate any incoming HTTP connections addressed to 199.1.1.1 to the web server, any incoming SMTP connections addressed to 199.1.1.1 to the mail server, and any incoming FTP connections address to 199.1.1.1 to the FTP server.

Hide NAT

Static NAT is easy to understand, because a one-to-one relationship exists between an internal IP address and a valid IP address. Unfortunately, public address space is limited, and many organizations do not have enough public address space to configure static NAT for each internal device that needs to connect to the Internet. For example, if an organization has 10,000 internal devices to connect to the Internet, if static NAT is configured, 10,000 public addresses are required for static NAT to work. Clearly this is not feasible due to the limited availability and cost of public address space, so another solution is required. That solution is called *hide NAT*, which is also commonly referred to as *dynamic NAT*. Hide NAT provides *many-to-one* mapping, which means that multiple private IP addresses can be represented by a single valid IP address.

For example, if you had a single valid IP address of 199.1.1.1 allocated to your organization, and had ten internal devices with private IP addresses of 10.1.1.1–10.1.1.10 to connect to the Internet, by using hide NAT, all of these hosts can connect to the Internet using the single valid IP address of 199.1.1.1. You might be wondering exactly how this is possible—the answer is that hide NAT doesn't just translate IP addresses, it also translates Layer 4 ports—specifically, TCP and UDP ports or ICMP identifiers.

ICMP includes an Identifier field, which is used to differentiate between different ICMP sessions on the same host.

When NAT translates both Layer 3 (e.g., IP addresses) and Layer 4 (e.g., TCP ports) information, it is commonly referred to as *port address translation* or

PAT. Figure 8.5 demonstrates a network topology and how hide NAT (or PAT) maps many private IP addresses to a single valid IP address (many-to-one).

FIGURE 8.5 Hide NAT

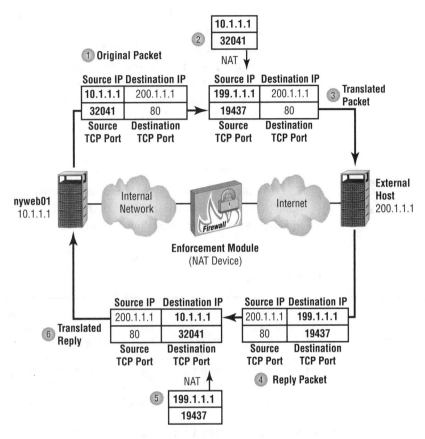

In Figure 8.5 the following events occur:

1. A host called nyweb01 on the internal network needs to connect to an external web server. The host generates a TCP connection request packet. This packet has a source IP address of 10.1.1.1 and a destination IP address of 200.1.1.1 (the external web server). The host generates a random TCP port number locally that will be used for the connection, and places this port number (32041) in the source TCP port field of the packet. The destination TCP port of the packet is the well-known port 80, which represents the HTTP service running on the external web server.

2. The IP packet is received at the VPN-1/FireWall-1 enforcement module. An address translation rule is configured that translates a pool of private IP addresses (including 10.1.1.1) to the valid IP address of 199.1.1.1. The source IP address of the packet is therefore rewritten to 199.1.1.1. The source TCP port is also rewritten to a value that is not in use by any other translations currently active on the enforcement module. In Figure 8.5, the source TCP port of the original packet is altered from 32041 to 19437. A NAT table is present on the enforcement module, which holds all current translations that are in use for other connections. Table 8.1 is a sample table and shows the entry that is written for the translated packet received from nyweb01.

 The NAT table shown in Table 8.1 is for demonstration purposes only and reflects the functional composition of the NAT table. The true composition of the NAT table in VPN-1/FireWall-1 differs from this.

TABLE 8.1 NAT Table

ConnID	Src IP	Src Port	Dest IP	Dest Port	Xlate Src IP	Xlate Src Port	Xlate Dest IP	Xlate Dest Port
1	10.1.1.3	3492	200.1.1.1	80	199.1.1.1	32041	–	–
	200.1.1.1	80	199.1.1.1	32041	–	–	10.1.1.3	3492
2	**10.1.1.1**	**32041**	**200.1.1.1**	**80**	**199.1.1.1**	**19437**	–	–
	200.1.1.1	**80**	**199.1.1.1**	**19437**	–	–	**10.1.1.1**	**32041**
...	...							
	...							

In Table 8.1, notice that a couple of entries represent each connection from an internal device to an external device. The Conn ID field identifies a connection, the Src IP, Src Port, Dest IP, and Dest Port columns represent the fields in the original packet, and the Xlate Src IP, Xlate Src Port, Xlate Dest IP, and Xlate Dest Port columns represent the values used in the address translation process. There is a connection for another internal device (Connection 1), and the first entry for this connection indicates the source IP address of the host (10.1.1.3) is translated to the Xlate Src IP value (valid IP address) of 199.1.1.1. The second entry for Connection 1 ensures that return packets for the connection are translated appropriately so that the packets arrive at the correct internal device. The connection highlighted in bold represents the new connection information that is written to the table in Step 2. Notice that the first connection in the table has a translated source port value of 32041, which is the same as the original source port used in the IP packet sent by nyweb01 in Step 1. To ensure that the translated source port for the IP packet sent by nyweb01 is unique, the original source port is translated from 32041 to a unique Xlate Src Port value (19437). If the enforcement module did not translate the source port, two connections would have same Xlate Src Port value, and the enforcement module will not be able to differentiate between return packets of either connection.

The process of populating the NAT table with connections is dynamic; hence, hide NAT is often referred to as dynamic NAT. With static NAT, permanent translation entries are present in the NAT table.

3. The translated packet is sent to the Internet and eventually arrives at the external web server. The external web server believes it has received a packet from 199.1.1.1 rather than 10.1.1.1 (nyweb01). The external web server also believes that nyweb01 is using a TCP port of 19437 for the connection, and hence will reply using this value.

4. The external web server sends a reply packet back towards nyweb01, with a source IP address of itself (200.1.1.1) and a source TCP port of 80, which identifies that the external web server from the HTTP service generated the packet. Because the source IP address of the packet received by the external device in Step 3 was 199.1.1.1 and the source TCP port was 19437, the reply packet has a destination IP address of 199.1.1.1 and a destination TCP port of 19437.

5. Because the destination IP address of the reply packet is a valid address (199.1.1.1), the reply packet is eventually routed through the Internet

back to the VPN-1/FireWall-1 enforcement module. The source and destination IP addresses and TCP port information is read and matched to a connection in the dynamic NAT table (see Table 8.1). Because the source IP address is 200.1.1.1, source TCP port is 80, destination IP address is 199.1.1.1, and the destination TCP port is 19437, the enforcement module identifies the packet as a return packet of the second connection listed in Table 8.1. The enforcement module translates the destination IP address to 10.1.1.1 and the destination TCP port to 32041, per the information contained in the dynamic NAT table. This ensures that the return traffic for the connection initiated by nyweb01 has the correct IP addressing when it arrives back at nyweb01.

6. The translated reply packet is forwarded by the enforcement module towards nyweb01. Because the destination IP address is now 10.1.1.1 and the destination TCP port is now 32041, nyweb01 will receive the packet and know that the packet is related to the connection initiated in Step 1, based on the source and destination IP addresses and TCP port information.

In Figure 8.5, an IP address of 199.1.1.1 has essentially been allocated to multiple internal devices, which enables these devices to communicate on the Internet using an identity of 199.1.1.1. The enforcement module is able to differentiate between each connection for return traffic address to 199.1.1.1 by ensuring that the source TCP or UDP port of each connection is unique. The dynamic NAT table maintains the IP address and port mappings for each connection, allowing the enforcement module to make the correct translations for return traffic. Notice that connection entries are generated as new connections are made from internal devices to external devices. This ensures that any return traffic for the connections can be matched to the correct connection and the appropriate translations made.

Port numbers are dynamically assigned from two pools of numbers: 600–1023 and 10,000–60,000. If the original source port of a connection is less than 1024, the translated port is chosen from the first range (600–1023). If the original source port is greater than 1024, the translated port is chosen from the second range (10,000–60,000). Based on these pools, the theoretical maximum number of connections supported by a single valid IP address used for hide NAT is 50,425.

Figure 8.5 demonstrated what happens for outbound connections, from the internal network to external devices, but what happens for connections from external devices that need to communicate with internal devices? The answer is that they won't work—hide NAT cannot be used to enable communications for connections initiated from an external device (valid IP address) to an internal device. Let's assume in Figure 8.5 that the external web server is trying to connect to the web server running on nyweb01, and sends a connection request packet to 199.1.1.1. The destination IP address of the packet will be 199.1.1.1 and the destination port will be 80 (HTTP). When the packet arrives at the enforcement module, the enforcement module will not be able to match the connection to any current connections in the dynamic NAT table, because this is the first packet in a new connection. This means that the enforcement module does not know what to do with the packet—it has no way in determining which private IP address the destination IP address of the packet to be translated to, because there is no matching connection in the dynamic NAT table.

Because hide NAT can only be used for connections from private devices to public devices, it only supports source NAT and does not support destination NAT.

To allow connections from external devices to internal devices with private IP addressing, static NAT must be used. With static NAT, the translation mappings are static (not dynamic); hence, the incoming connection request can be translated based on the static NAT information that is always in the NAT table. For example, if static NAT is configured in Figure 8.5, Table 8.2 shows the translations that are always present in the NAT table.

TABLE 8.2 Static NAT Entries in the NAT Table

Src IP	Src Port	Dest IP	Dest Port	Xlate Src IP	Xlate Src Port	XLate Dest IP	Xlate Dest Port
10.1.1.1	–	–	–	199.1.1.1	–	–	–
–	–	199.1.1.1	–	–	–	10.1.1.1	–

In Table 8.2, if a connection is initiated from an external device, the enforcement module knows how to translate the connection, as the required address translation is already in the NAT table, and each valid IP address maps back to a single private IP address. Notice, however, that only the device with an IP address of 10.1.1.1 can make outgoing connections using 199.1.1.1 as a valid IP address. This demonstrates that although static NAT enables connections to be made from valid IP addresses to private IP addresses, it only provides a one-to-one mapping.

Remember that hide NAT can only be used for outbound connections from internal private IP addresses to external devices on the Internet. If you need to enable inbound connections from a valid IP address to an internal device with a private IP address, you must use static NAT.

Issues with Hide NAT

There are some restrictions to using hide NAT, and it is important that you are aware of these before you implement hide NAT. The following lists common issues with hide NAT:

- NAT table expiration
- Limited support for protocols other than TCP, UDP, and ICMP
- No support for connections that are established from external devices
- Complex protocols
- No support for protocols using fixed source ports

NAT Table Expiration

Because hide NAT provides many-to-one translations, it is conceivable that a single IP address could be supporting thousands of connections at a time. You saw in Table 8.1 how each connection is included in the NAT table. In other words, the NAT table holds a translation per connection, rather than per IP address. The NAT table on VPN-1/FireWall-1 by default has a limit of 25,000 connections that it can support. This limit can be extended to 50,000. Because the NAT table is a finite resource, VPN-1/FireWall-1 NG includes an expiration timer for each connection, which ensures entries for invalid connections to not consume space in the NAT table. If a connection is idle for long enough to expire, the entry in the NAT table is removed. By default, the NAT expiration timer for TCP connections is 3600 seconds and the NAT expiration timer for UDP connections is 330 seconds.

In Chapter 4 you learned that the connection table implements session timeout timers, which define how long a connection (any connection, whether it is subject to NAT or not) must remain idle until it is no longer considered valid. By default, the TCP session timeout is 3600 seconds and the UDP session timeout is 40 seconds. It is important that you understand that both of these timers are separate to NAT expiration timers and that you must ensure the NAT expiration timers are never lower than the session timeouts. If the NAT expiration timers are lower than the session timeouts, it is possible that the NAT entry for a connection can expire, yet the connection is still valid in the security connection table. This would mean that packets of the connection would be permitted by the enforcement module, but address translation would not occur, breaking the connection. The `fwx_tcp_expiration` and `fwx_udp_expiration` kernel variables control the NAT expiration timers that apply for all connections in the NAT table. You can modify these on Unix-based machines using the CLI; however, you cannot modify these variables on Windows-based enforcement modules. To ensure NAT expiration timers are never lower than session timeout timers, it is recommended that you modify TCP session timeout and UDP session timeout values instead of NAT expiration timers, which can be controlled from SmartDashboard on a global or per-service basis.

Limited Support for Protocols Other than TCP, UDP, and ICMP

Hide NAT works for TCP, UDP, and ICMP traffic, as these transport layer protocols include port numbers (TCP and UDP) or identifiers (ICMP) that can be translated by the enforcement module to uniquely identify connections associated with the same public source IP address. Other transport layer protocols, such as those used by IPSec, do not include port numbers and therefore have limited compatibility with hide NAT. For all transport layer protocols other than TCP, UDP, and ICMP, VPN-1/FireWall-1 only supports a single connection per unique combination of translated public source IP address, destination IP address, and IP protocol number (transport protocol). For example, encapsulating security payload (ESP) is a transport protocol used by IPSec that has an IP protocol number of 50. If an internal device with a private IP address attempts to connect to an external VPN server and hide NAT is applied, the connection will work, as the valid IP address, destination IP address, and IP protocol number can be mapped back to the internal device. However, if another device attempts to connect to the same VPN server, it will not be able to (the other device can connect to a different external VPN server that is currently not specified in another hide NAT connection).

Real World Scenario

Hide NAT and Virtual Private Networks

A common issue experienced in the real world is the incompatibility of hide NAT with IPSec traffic, which is used for VPNs. IPSec traffic uses transport layer protocols called authentication header (AH) and encapsulating security payload (ESP). These protocols do not support the concept of ports, meaning they are incompatible with hide NAT (although VPN-1/FireWall-1 has limited support for these protocols with hide NAT, many other vendors do not support hide NAT with these protocols at all). With the increasing availability of broadband Internet connections, many SOHO users how have NAT devices providing Internet access for multiple internal devices. By default, these NAT devices are normally only configured for hide NAT (PAT). If an employee of an organization is trying to gain access to the corporate network from home via a remote access VPN, a VPN connection cannot be established because of the incompatibility of hide NAT with IPSec protocols. One solution is to configure static NAT for the internal device from which the user is connecting; however, this normally restricts Internet access to a single device, as many home Internet connections are only permitted a single IP address (and hence single static NAT one-to-one mapping). The other solution is to encapsulate IPSec traffic in TCP or UDP, which ensures the traffic is compatible with hide NAT. The corporate VPN gateway must understand the TCP or UDP encapsulation, so that it can strip it off and then decrypt the native IPSec traffic. VPN-1/FireWall-1 supports UDP encapsulation of IPSec traffic, which ensures remote access VPN compatibility with hide NAT. This solution adds extra overhead to the VPN connection, but ensures that multiple devices can still be supported behind the NAT device.

No Support for External Connections

As already described, hide NAT is only supported for connections that are initiated from devices with private IP addresses to devices with valid IP addresses. It cannot be implemented for connections initiated from devices with valid IP addresses to devices with private IP addresses. To support these connections, you must implement static NAT.

Complex Protocols

You saw previously in Figure 8.4 that static NAT can cause issues for complex protocols that transmit IP addressing information within the application data stream. This is a generic problem that applies to both static NAT and hide NAT. Hide NAT also has problems with complex protocols that establish *back connections* from the server (i.e., the device on the Internet) to client (i.e., the internal device). Hide NAT can only be used for connections that are initiated from devices with private IP addressing to devices with valid IP addressing. If an external device attempts to connect to the valid IP address that is used for hide NAT, the enforcement module has no way of telling which internal device the connection is intended for because this valid IP address is used for many internal devices. Figure 8.6 shows what happens in Figure 8.4 with hide NAT, even with application-layer NAT support enabled on the enforcement module.

FIGURE 8.6   Complex protocol issues with hide NAT

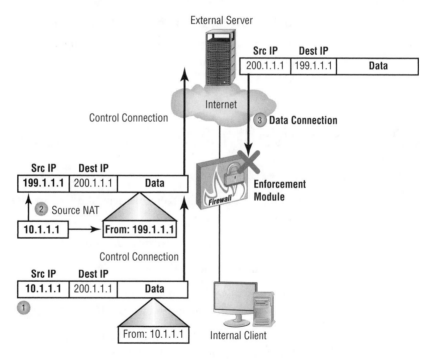

In Figure 8.6, notice that in Step 2, the enforcement module rewrites both the source IP address and the private IP address contained within the packet. Because of this, the server attempts to establish a data connection back to 199.1.1.1, instead of the private IP address of the client. When this packet arrives at the enforcement module, the enforcement module does not know what to do with the packet, as 199.1.1.1 is used for hide NAT, and the new connection request will not be in the NAT table. If static NAT was configured, the 199.1.1.1 address would map back to the internal client, and the enforcement module would translate the destination IP address from 199.1.1.1 to 10.1.1.1 and forward the packet on. Because hide NAT is configured, the enforcement module drops the connection request, and the protocol is broken.

For complex protocols to work with hide NAT, the enforcement module must understand the mechanics of the protocol and whether any back connections may occur. If the enforcement module understands this information, when a connection is added to the NAT table for a complex protocol, the enforcement module can also add in the appropriate translation entry for return connections, which enables the enforcement module to associate back connections with the appropriate internal device. Common complex protocols supported for hide NAT by VPN-1/FireWall-1 include FTP, H.323, and SIP (SIP is supported in NG Feature Pack 2 onwards).

No Support for Protocols that Use Fixed Source Port Numbers

Hide NAT cannot work with protocols that work with fixed source port numbers, as the client source port of a connection is always translated with hide NAT.

VPN-1/FireWall-1 NG NAT Enhancements

VPN-1/FireWall-1 NG has significantly improved support for NAT, making it much easier to implement and less prone to error. Enhancements include the following:

- The ability to perform address translation at the ingress interface
- The removal of the requirement to configure ARP

Historically with previous versions of VPN-1/FireWall-1, you have had to configure the following to ensure NAT works correctly:

- Destination NAT required configuration of the operating system route table
- All forms of NAT normally required ARP configuration

Enhancements to Destination NAT

In versions prior to VPN-1/FireWall-1 NG, for destination NAT to work, the operating system of the enforcement module has to have a static route configured, which allows the operating system to route the external valid IP address representing an internal device to the correct interface associated with the path to the internal device. Figure 8.7 demonstrates the reasoning behind this.

FIGURE 8.7 Destination NAT prior to NG

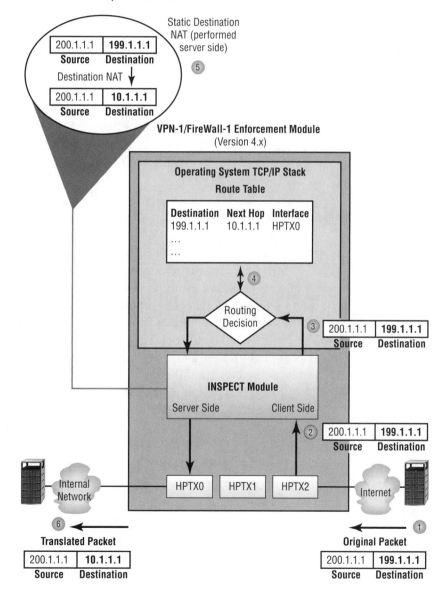

In Figure 8.7 a packet is being sent from an external device (200.1.1.1) to the valid IP address (199.1.1.1) representing an internal device (10.1.1.1). The following events take place:

1. The external device generates an IP packet with a source IP address of 200.1.1.1 (itself) and a destination IP address of 199.1.1.1 (the valid IP address for the internal device).

2. The packet is received on the external interface of the enforcement module (HPTX2) and is passed to the VPN-1/FireWall-1 INSPECT module for inspection.

3. The INSPECT module checks the IP packet against the connection table (to determine whether the packet is part of an existing connection), followed by the security rule base (if the packet represents a new connection). Assuming the packet represents a new connection, the packet is matched against a security rule that permits the connection, and the packet is forwarded to the operating system TCP/IP stack for routing.

4. The operating system TCP/IP stack now routes the packet. Routing is based on destination IP address—at this time, the destination IP address of the packet is still 199.1.1.1. If the destination IP address is part of the external segment from which the packet arrives, the operating system will attempt to route the packet back out the ingress interface. For example, in Figure 8.7, if the external interface of the enforcement module is configured with an IP address of 199.1.1.100 and a subnet mask of 255.255.255.0, with the default routing table generated by the operating system, the IP address of 199.1.1.1 will be considered attached to the external interface, and the packet will be routed back out the external interface. Therefore, a *host route* must exist that associates the destination IP address of 199.1.1.1 with the correct egress interface (a host route is simply a route that refers to an individual host rather than a network). In Figure 8.4, the route for 199.1.1.1 points to the internal device 10.1.1.1, which ensures the correct egress interface (HPTX0) is selected for routing.

5. The packet is routed towards the egress interface and is passed to the INSPECT module once again. At this point, network address translation occurs. Based on a static destination NAT rule configured on the enforcement module, the destination IP address of the packet is rewritten from 199.1.1.1 to 10.1.1.1, ensuring the packet will reach the internal device.

6. The packet is forwarded out the egress interface towards the internal device. The packet now contains a destination IP address of the private IP address of the internal device (10.1.1.1), ensuring the packet reaches the internal device.

In Figure 8.7, notice that address translation is performed within the INSPECT module at the egress interface, *after* the routing decision made by the operating system, meaning the operating system has to have a host route configured for the valid IP address that represents the internal device. This requirement means incurs extra administrative overhead on VPN-1/FireWall-1 enforcement modules prior to NG, and is also prone to misconfiguration errors. Notice in Figure 8.7 the terms *client side* and *server side*. These terms describe the point at which the INSPECT module receives a packet. The client side refers to when the INSPECT module receives a packet immediately after it has been first received on the ingress interface—the term client side is used because the packet is received from the interface facing the source of the packet (i.e., the client). The server side refers to when the INSPECT module receives a packet that has been routed by the operating system to the appropriate egress interface—the term server side is used because the packet is about to be sent out the interface facing the destination of the packet (i.e., the server).

In previous versions of VPN-1/FireWall-1, destination NAT is referred to as server-side destination NAT, because destination NAT is performed on the server side. In VPN-1/FireWall-1 NG, you now have the option of performing destination NAT within the INSPECT module at the ingress interface (i.e., at the client side), which means that the operating system now routes based on the private IP address of internal devices, as opposed to the valid IP address. Figure 8.8 demonstrates this.

In Figure 8.8, the destination NAT is performed at the ingress interface (step 2), before the packet is passed to the TCP/IP stack for routing. This means that the operating system receives a packet with a destination IP address of an internal device (step 3), as opposed to the valid IP address, and therefore only requires a route to the internal device. You would normally expect all internal routes to be already configured on your enforcement modules, as the enforcement module needs to know where to route packets for internal devices. The requirement to configure a host route for each valid IP address (as shown in Figure 8.7) is counterintuitive, and often is overlooked when configuring address translation. The ability of VPN-1/FireWall-1 NG to perform destination NAT at the ingress interface before the packet is routed means that you don't need to update the operating system route table each time you configure NAT. In VPN-1/FireWall-1 NG, this feature is referred to as client-side destination NAT, because destination NAT occurs at the client side.

FIGURE 8.8 Destination NAT in VPN-1/FireWall-1 NG

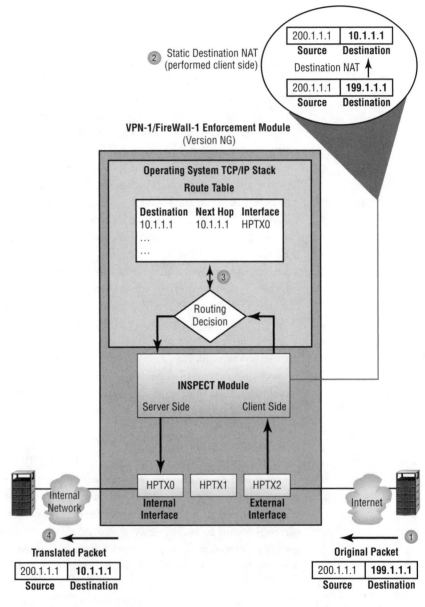

If you are wondering what happens in the case of source NAT (translation of the source IP address of packets), address translation occurs after the packet has been routed by the operating system and passed to the INSPECT module before being forwarded out the egress interface (i.e., server side). This happens in both VPN-1/FireWall-1 NG and previous versions and this behavior cannot be modified. Performing source NAT on the server side does not cause the same problems as those experienced for destination NAT, because routing is only performed based on the destination IP address rather than source IP address.

Enhancements to ARP Support

Address resolution protocol (ARP) is a fundamental component of IP communications between systems on Ethernet networks, which is often overlooked as it is very much behind the scenes and normally just works. ARP is used for a single purpose—to associate the IP address of a system with the *MAC address* of the network card that connects the system to the Ethernet network. Ethernet communications do not use IP addresses, instead using the MAC address. Therefore, if two hosts on an Ethernet segment need to communicate using IP, they must somehow determine each other's MAC address. ARP is the protocol that they use.

With most VPN-1/FireWall-1 installations, all interfaces on the enforcement module will be Ethernet interfaces, meaning that ARP is always in use. When you configure NAT, you must consider some issues with ARP. Figure 8.9 demonstrates how NAT affects ARP.

FIGURE 8.9 NAT and ARP

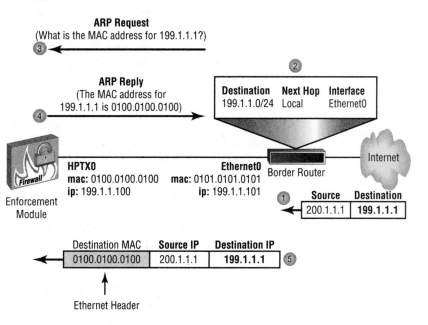

In Figure 8.9, an external device with an IP address of 200.1.1.1 is sending an IP packet to the valid IP address 199.1.1.1, which represents an internal device behind the enforcement module that has a private IP address. The following events occur:

1. A packet is sent from an external device (200.1.1.1) to 199.1.1.1. The IP address 199.1.1.1 is part of the valid address space allocated to the organization. The packet arrives at the border router that belongs to the organization, which connects the organization to the Internet. An Ethernet segment joins the border router to the external interface of the organization's enforcement module. An IP subnet of 199.1.1.0 with a network mask of 255.255.255.0 (199.1.1.0/24) is configured on the segment. The external interface of the firewall is configured with an IP address of 199.1.1.100 and the ISP router is configured with an IP address of 199.1.1.101. The IP addressing on this segment represents the valid address space allocated to the organization (199.1.1.1–199.1.1.254).

2. The packet received is routed by the border router. The border router consults its local routing table, and determines that the destination IP address of the packet (199.1.1.1) is attached locally via the Ethernet0 interface. This is because the segment between the border router and the enforcement module is configured with an IP subnet of 199.1.1.0/24, and 199.1.1.1 falls within this subnet. Even though the real device that is represented by the 199.1.1.1 IP address is actually not attached to the segment (it is behind the firewall), the router believes that the device is locally connected, according to the rules of IP.

3. Because 199.1.1.1 is locally connected, the border router determines that it must forward the packet directly to the host with an IP address of 199.1.1.1. To do so, the border router must forward the IP packet in an Ethernet frame, containing the appropriate destination MAC address for the host with the IP address of 199.1.1.1. The border router checks a local ARP cache, which contains a cache of IP address to MAC address mappings that have recently been used. Assuming this is the first packet delivered to 199.1.1.1 (therefore the ARP cache is empty), the border router generates an *ARP request*, which is broadcast to all devices attached to the segment. This ARP request basically asks for the MAC address of the host that has an IP address of 199.1.1.1.

4. In a normal Ethernet network, a host with an IP address of 199.1.1.1 would actually be connected to the segment and would reply to the border router, indicating its MAC address. However in Figure 8.9,

this is not the case, because the 199.1.1.1 IP address is actually a virtual IP address representing a host that is elsewhere in the network. For the IP packet to be delivered to the internal device represented by the 199.1.1.1 IP address, the enforcement module must receive the packet, so that it can perform the appropriate address translation and forward the packet on to the internal device. For this reason, the enforcement module sends an *ARP reply* to the border router, indicating that the MAC address of its external interface (0100.0100.0100) represents the host with the 199.1.1.1 IP address.

5. The border router receives the ARP reply and now has the necessary information to forward the IP packet to what it believes is the final destination of the packet. An Ethernet frame is generated, which includes a destination MAC address of 0100.0100.0100 and the IP packet. This frame is forwarded onto the Ethernet segment and is accepted by the external interface of the enforcement module, as it is addressed to the MAC address of the external interface. At this point the packet is subject to inspection and address translation by the enforcement module, and is eventually forwarded onto the appropriate internal device.

The crucial point in Figure 8.9 is that the enforcement module must answer ARP requests for any valid IP addresses that have been configured for NAT, even though the actual IP address of the external interface of the enforcement module is different. By responding with the MAC address of the external interface, the border router will then forward IP packets destined for the valid IP addresses to the enforcement module, ensuring the packets can be subject to the appropriate address translation and forwarded to the correct internal device.

In Figure 8.9, you could also configure host routes on the border router that explicitly route any traffic destined for the 199.1.1.1 IP address to the enforcement module. You could also configure permanent ARP entries in the ARP cache of the border router, mapping the MAC address of the external interface of the enforcement module to 199.1.1.1 IP address. Using either of these methods has the disadvantage of requiring you to configure and maintain two separate devices (the enforcement module and the border router) when you configure NAT.

The process of sending an ARP request on behalf of another device is referred to as *proxy ARP*. In versions prior to VPN-1/FireWall-1 NG, you had to manually configure the operating system of the enforcement to proxy ARP for valid IP addresses that required address translation. On Unix-based systems, this required the configuration of manual ARP entries in the local ARP cache, and on Windows-based systems, this required the configuration of a file called $FWDIR\state\local.arp. The following demonstrates a local.arp file:

```
199.1.1.1    01-00-01-00-01-00
199.1.1.2    01-00-01-00-01-00
199.1.1.3    01-00-01-00-01-00
199.1.1.99   01-00-01-00-01-00
```

Each entry indicates the IP address that the enforcement module should proxy ARP for (i.e., respond to ARP requests), with the corresponding MAC address indicating the MAC address that should be returned in the ARP reply. This MAC address must be the MAC address of the interface on the enforcement module that should receive packets addressed to the valid IP address. In the example shown above, the enforcement module will proxy ARP for the IP addresses 199.1.1.1, 199.1.1.2, 199.1.1.3, and 199.1.1.99. In each case, the enforcement module will specify a MAC address of 0100.0100.0100 in the ARP reply generated.

In VPN-1/FireWall-1 NG, the requirement for a local.arp file (Windows) or manual ARP entries (Unix) has been removed. VPN-1/FireWall-1 NG now supports a feature called *automatic ARP*, which allows VPN-1/FireWall-1 to automatically take care of the proxy ARP configuration for you when you configure NAT. This means that you do not have to manually configure the proxy ARP feature as in previous versions, reducing the administrative overhead and possibility of misconfiguring NAT on VPN-1/FireWall-1 NG.

Automatic ARP is only supported for automatic NAT rules in VPN-1/FireWall-1 NG. Any manual NAT rules require the configuration of a local.arp file on Windows, or the appropriate manual ARP entries on Unix.

Summary

Network address translation enables organizations that use private IP addressing to connect to the Internet. Many organizations use private IP addressing, as the valid IP address space is in short supply, and is normally only allocated in small amounts to each organization. NAT also provides security from the Internet, by hiding the internal IP addressing of an organization.

There are two basic types of NAT—static NAT and hide NAT. Static NAT provides one-to-one mapping between a private IP address and valid

IP address, and can be used for both connections from a private IP address to a valid IP address and also for connections in the reverse direction. Hide NAT provides many-to-one mapping between multiple private IP addresses and a valid IP address, and can only be used for connections established from a private IP address to a valid IP address (and not for the reverse). Hide NAT uses port address translation (PAT), which allows a single valid IP address to represents multiple private devices by translating not only source IP addressing, but also source TCP/UDP port numbers.

The directions in which NAT connections are made differentiate source NAT and destination NAT. Source NAT describes NAT that is applied to connections established from a private IP address to a valid IP address. For these connections, packets sent from the private IP address must have a valid identity on the Internet to communicate with the intended destination. This means that the source IP address of packets must be translated, hence the name source NAT. Destination NAT describes NAT that is applied to connections that are established from a valid IP address to a private IP address. For these connections, packets sent from the valid IP address must be addressed to a valid IP address that represents the private IP address. This means that the destination IP address of packets must be translated.

When you implement NAT, you must be aware of that some protocols are not compatible with NAT, or require extra intelligence on the NAT device to ensure correct protocol operation. Such protocols include those that transmit IP addressing information within the application data stream, as well as protocols that establish multiple connections (e.g., a control connection and data connection) between communicating parties.

Exam Essentials

Understand why NAT is required. NAT is primarily required to connect devices with private IP addresses to the Internet. NAT also provides security by hiding an organization's internal IP addressing from the Internet.

Understand the difference between private and valid IP addresses. Private IP addresses are defined in RFC1918 and include 10.x.x.x, 172.16.x.x–172.31.x.x, and 192.168.x.x. These IP addresses are intended for private use only and are illegal on the Internet. Organizations can implement private IP addresses freely. Valid IP addresses form the address space present on the Internet, and include most IP addresses outside of the RFC1918 address space. Valid IP addresses are allocated to ISPs that in turn allocate a portion of this address space to their customers.

Valid IP addressing requires that every device on the Internet have a unique IP address, to ensure devices can be uniquely identified by their IP addresses.

Understand the two basic types of NAT. Static NAT provides a one-to-one mapping, from a single private IP address to a single valid IP address. Static NAT can be used to allow devices with private IP address to connect to devices with valid IP addresses and can also enable devices with valid IP addresses to connect to devices with private IP addresses. Hide NAT provides many-to-one mapping, which means multiple private IP addresses can be represented by a single valid IP address. NAT devices that implement hide NAT manage this by using port address translation (PAT), where the source TCP or UDP port of a connection is also translated to allow the device to uniquely identify each private IP address associated with a valid connection. Hide NAT can only be used to enable devices with private IP addresses to connect to devices with valid IP addresses, and not vice versa (unlike static NAT).

Understand source NAT. Source NAT refers to when packets sent in the direction of a connection (i.e., from source to destination) require the source IP address to be translated, which means source NAT is used for connections originating from devices with private IP addresses to devices with valid IP addresses. Source NAT also covers the required translations for return packets associated with the connection. Both static NAT and hide NAT support source NAT.

Understand destination NAT Destination NAT refers to when packets sent in the direction of a connection (i.e., from source to destination) require the destination IP address to be translated, which means destination NAT is used for connections originating from devices with valid IP addresses to devices with private IP addresses that are represented by a valid IP address. Destination NAT also covers the required translations for return packets associated with the connection. Only static NAT supports destination NAT.

Understand the issues associated with NAT. Both static NAT and hide NAT break application-layer protocols that send IP addressing information in the application data stream, unless of course the NAT device understands these protocols and can make the appropriate translations within the application data stream. Hide NAT can also break complex protocols that require back connections or return connections to be established to a private device.

Understand NAT expiration timers.   VPN-1/FireWall-1 implements NAT expiration timers for hidden UDP and TCP connections (connections that require hide NAT), which are separate from the session timeout values configured for the connections. You should always ensure your NAT expiration timers are always equal or longer than the matching protocol session timeout parameter.

Understand client side and server side.   Client side refers to the interface on an enforcement module that faces the source or client of a connection. Server side refers to the interface on an enforcement module that faces the destination or server of a connection. VPN-1/FireWall-1 processes packets both client side and server side, and NAT can occur at either of these points.

Understand enhancements to NAT in VPN-1/FireWall-1 NG.   VPN-1/FireWall-1 NG includes the ability to perform destination NAT on the client side, which means the operating system of the enforcement module does not need host routes for each valid IP address that point to the next-hop internally that is closest to the private IP address represented by the valid IP address. Automatic ARP is also supported, which removes the requirement to configure ARP support manually (via `local.arp` or proxy ARP).

Key Terms

Before you take the exam, be certain you are familiar with the following terms:

address resolution protocol (ARP)	IPv4
ARP reply	MAC address
ARP request	many-to-one
automatic ARP	network address translation (NAT)
back connections	port address translation (PAT)
client side	proxy ARP
destination NAT	server side
dynamic NAT	source NAT
hide NAT	static NAT
host route	

Review Questions

1. Which of the following describes how NAT provides security for networks? (Choose all that apply.)

   A. Provides access control.

   B. Can hide network topology behind a single valid IP address.

   C. If NAT stops working, prevents devices from connecting directly to internal network.

   D. Enables private networks to connect to the Internet.

2. Which of the following is a private IP address? (Choose all that apply.)

   A. 1.1.1.1

   B. 10.1.1.1

   C. 100.1.1.1

   D. 192.1.1.1

   E. 192.168.1.1

3. Which of the following defines private IP addresses?

   A. RFC1066

   B. RFC1918

   C. RFC1999

   D. RFC2182

4. A device on the Internet with an IP address of 200.1.1.1 connects to an IP address of 199.1.1.1, which represents an organization's mail server that has a configured IP address of 10.1.1.1. Which of the following statements describe which IP addresses are private and valid with respect to the mail server?

   A. 10.1.1.1 is the private IP address; 200.1.1.1 is the valid IP address.

   B. 10.1.1.1 is the valid IP address; 199.1.1.1 is the private IP address.

   C. 10.1.1.1 is the valid IP address; 200.1.1.1 is the private IP address.

   D. 10.1.1.1 is the private IP address; 199.1.1.1 is the valid IP address.

5. Which of the following are modified for static source NAT? (Choose all that apply.)

A. Source IP address of original packets

B. Destination IP address of reply packets

C. Source port of original packets

D. Destination port of reply packets

6. You configure hide NAT for an internal web server. Which of the following statements are true? (Choose all that apply.)

A. The server can make outgoing connections to the web.

B. External devices can make connections to the web server.

C. The server cannot make outgoing connections that required fixed TCP or UDP source ports.

D. The server can run any application that transmits IP address information within the application data stream.

7. A connection is established from an internal device with a private IP address to an external device on the Internet. What form of NAT is required to support this?

A. Automatic NAT

B. Destination NAT

C. Manual NAT

D. Source NAT

8. On VPN-1/FireWall-1, how are address translation rules are applied?

A. Per connection

B. Per frame

C. Per fragment

D. Per packet

9. You need to support 70,000 NAT connections from the internal network to the Internet at the same time. External devices do not need to establish connections to internal devices. Which of the following lists the minimum requirements? (Choose all that apply.)

   A. Two valid IP addresses

   B. Two enforcement modules

   C. Two SmartCenter Servers

   D. Two ISPs

10. What is ARP used for?

    A. Resolve a given MAC address to an IP address.

    B. Resolve a given IP address to a MAC address.

    C. Resolve a given hostname to an IP address.

    D. Resolve a given IP address to a hostname.

11. Which of the following does NAT provide? (Choose all that apply.)

    A. Access Control.

    B. Access to the Internet for devices with private IP addresses.

    C. Prevents devices on the Internet from connecting to internal devices.

    D. Conserves public address space.

12. An organization uses internal IP addressing of 172.168.10.x. Which form of NAT is required for this organization to connect to the Internet?

    A. Static NAT

    B. Hide NAT

    C. Automatic NAT

    D. Manual NAT

    E. None of the above

13. Which of the following describes hide NAT? (Choose all that apply.)

    A. One-to-one

    B. Many-to-one

    C. Static

    D. Dynamic

    E. Enables private devices to access public devices

    F. Enables public devices to access private devices

14. Which of the following describes static NAT? (Choose all that apply.)

    A. One-to-one

    B. Many-to-one

    C. Fixed entries in NAT table

    D. Dynamic entries in NAT table

    E. Enables private devices to access public devices

    F. Enables public devices to access private devices

15. Which of the following configuration requirements does VPN-1/ FireWall-1 NG remove for destination NAT? (Choose all that apply.)

    A. Configuring an IP address on the enforcement module

    B. Configuring a `local.arp` file on the enforcement module

    C. Configuring routes for internal networks on the enforcement module

    D. Configuring host routes for valid IP addresses on the enforcement module

16. Which of the following kernel variables would you use to extend the NAT expiration timer for hidden TCP connections?

    A. `fwd_tcp_expiration`

    B. `fwx_tcp_expiration`

    C. `nat_tcp_expiration`

    D. `fwnat_tcp_expiration`

17. What is the default NAT expiration for dynamic UDP connections?

    A. 30 seconds

    B. 40 seconds

    C. 330 seconds

    D. 3600 seconds

18. Users are making connections to the Internet and complaining that when they leave their PCs for half an hour or so, their connections don't work any more and they have to reconnect. You check the TCP connection timeout setting, and this is set to 3600 seconds. What is the most likely cause of the problem?

    A. The users are using hide NAT.

    B. The users should have a continuous PING running to the destination to ensure the connection stays up.

    C. The rule for hide NAT is only configured for certain periods of the day. Users are staying connected outside of these times.

    D. The NAT expiration timer for hidden TCP connections is too low.

19. A connection is made from an internal device and hide NAT is applied to the connection. The connection has a source port of 3678 and a destination port of 80. Which of the following describes the port translations that occur for packets sent from the internal device to the external device? (Choose all that apply.)

    A. The source port of the connection is translated to a number in the range of 10,000–60,000.

    B. The source port of the connection is translated to a number greater than 1024.

    C. The destination port of the connection is translated to a number between 600 and 1023.

    D. The destination port of the connection is translated to a number between 0 and 599.

20. A friend has heard that VPN-1/FireWall-1 NG doesn't need separate ARP configuration and route configuration on the enforcement module operating system. Which of the following types of NAT does this apply to? (Choose all that apply.)

A. Automatic hide NAT

B. Automatic static NAT

C. Manual hide NAT

D. Manual static NAT

Answers to Review Questions

1. B, C. NAT provides security by allowing devices to use private IP addresses, yet still connect to the Internet. If the NAT stops working, because your internal network uses private IP addresses, external devices will not be able to communicate with your network. You can use hide NAT to enable outgoing connections to the Internet to appear as if they are all coming from a single host. This only works for outgoing connections not incoming connections, which ensures internal devices can connect to the Internet without exposing these devices by enabling connectivity in the reverse direction.

2. B, E. The private IP address range includes 10.x.x.x, 172.16.x.x–172.31.x.x, and 192.168.x.x.

3. B. RFC 1918 defines private IP addresses.

4. D. The mail server is configured with an IP address of 10.1.1.1, which is a private IP address. Because 199.1.1.1 represents the mail server on the Internet, this is considered its valid IP address.

5. A, B. Static NAT is one-to-one mapping, meaning only IP addresses are translated. Source NAT means that the source IP address of the original packet of a connection will be translated, and return packets for the connection will have the destination IP address translated back to the original source IP address.

6. A, C. Hide NAT only permits outbound connections (from private network to public network) and because it provides many-to-one translation, must also modify TCP/UDP source port numbers. This causes problems with applications that required fixed TCP or UDP port numbers. Any form of NAT causes problems for protocols that transmit IP addressing information within the application data stream.

7. D. Source NAT is required for this connection, as the source IP address of the connection is private and requires translation to a valid IP address.

8. A. NAT rules on VPN-1/FireWall-1 are applied on a per-connection basis, which means a single NAT rule can accommodate both the forward and return packets associated with a connection.

9. A, B.   For this scenario, hide NAT can be used, which saves valid IP address usage. VPN-1/FireWall-1 only supports 50,000 hide NAT connections in the NAT table, so you must implement two enforcement modules, which also means you must have at least two valid IP addresses available for hide NAT use.

10. B.   ARP is used to determine the MAC address associated with an IP address.

11. B, D.   Security rules provide access control, and private IP addresses (not NAT) prevent devices from connecting to internal devices. NAT permits devices with private IP addresses to connect to the Internet and conserves public address space (e.g., hide NAT).

12. E.   172.168.10.x (don't get confused with the 192.168.x.x private addressing) is valid IP addressing, meaning NAT is not required for this organization to connect to the Internet.

13. B, D, E.   Hide NAT provides many-to-one address translation, and is dynamic, because the NAT table (part of the connection table) that holds all current translations, is built dynamically as connections are subjected to hide NAT. Hide NAT only enables private devices access to the Internet; it cannot enable public devices to be able to access private devices.

14. A, C, E, F.   Static NAT provides one-to-one address translation and uses fixed entries in the NAT table that map a private IP address to a valid IP address, and vice versa. Hide NAT enables private devices access to the Internet, as well as enable public devices access to private devices.

15. B, D.   In VPN-1/FireWall-1 NG, destination NAT is performed client side, which means that the enforcement module operating system does not need host routes configured for each valid IP address used with destination NAT. Automatic ARP is also supported, removing the need to configure proxy ARP on the operating system (e.g., configuring a `local.arp` file).

16. B.   The `fwx_tcp_expiration` and `fwx_udp_expiration` kernel variables control the NAT expiration timers for hidden (dynamic or hide NAT) TCP and UDP connections.

17. C.   The default NAT expiration timeout for UDP connections is 330 seconds and for TCP connections is 3600 seconds. Don't get confused with the UDP connection timeout for the connections permitted by the security rule base, which by default is 40 seconds (the TCP connection timeout is 3600 seconds, the same as the NAT expiration timeout).

18. D.   The most likely cause is that the NAT expiration timer for hidden TCP connections is too low (e.g., 30 minutes), which means that although the connection is still a valid connection in the connection table, the NAT translations expire too early. You should always ensure that the NAT expiration timers are equal or higher for connections that have hide NAT applied.

19. A.   With hide NAT, only the source port of packets sent from the client (private device) to the server (public device) of a connection is translated. The destination port is not translated, as this indicates the service that the client wishes to connect to on the server. If the original source port is greater than 1024, the port is translated to a value in the range of 10,000–60,000.

20. A, B.   The new automatic ARP and client-side destination NAT features are only available with automatic NAT (both hide NAT and static NAT are supported).

Chapter

9

Configuring Network Address Translation

THE CCSA EXAM OBJECTIVES COVERED IN THIS CHAPTER INCLUDE:

- ✓ Describe setup for static NAT.
- ✓ Describe setup for hide NAT.
- ✓ Describe basic network configuration using NAT.

In the previous chapter you were introduced to the concepts of network address translation (NAT) and how NAT provides the ability for organizations with private IP networks to connect to the Internet. For VPN-1/FireWall-1 NG enforcement modules that provide connectivity to the Internet, you will almost always need to configure and manage NAT to ensure connectivity. Many organizations today implement private IP addressing internally, so NAT is mandatory if an organization wants to connect to the Internet. In this chapter, you will learn about the options available to VPN-1/FireWall-1 administrators for implementing NAT, which option you should use based on your requirements, and how to configure NAT.

The Address Translation Rule Base

Now that you have been introduced to NAT and understand how it works, it's time to learn how to configure NAT on VPN-1/FireWall-1. The heart of the NAT configuration on VPN-1/FireWall-1 is the *address translation rule base*, which is made up of *address translation rules*. Address translation rules are very similar to security rules, except they define how packets should be network address translated, rather than which packets should be permitted access (as is the case with security rules). The address translation rule base is configured via SmartDashboard, and is represented as a separate rule base. Figure 9.1 shows the address translation rule base within SmartDashboard.

The address translation rule base is accessed via the Address Translation tab at the top of the rule bases, as shown in Figure 9.1. In Figure 9.1, a single address translation rule is configured. You can see the various fields and elements that make up each rule. Notice that some elements (such as Original Packet) possess subelements. Table 9.1 describes each of the elements and subelements that comprise an address translation rule.

FIGURE 9.1 The address translation rule base

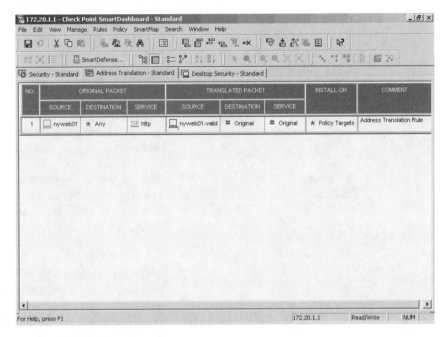

TABLE 9.1 Address Translation Rule Elements

Element	Subelement	Description
No.	–	Indicates the number of the rule in the address translation rule base. Address translation rules are processed in order from the lowest number to the highest number.
Original Packet	–	Specifies the Layer 3/4 parameters of packets that are classified by the address translation rule. The original packet always defines a packet that has been received by an enforcement module.

TABLE 9.1 Address Translation Rule Elements *(continued)*

Element	Subelement	Description
	Source	Defines the source IP address required to match a rule for packets that are being inspected against the address translation rule base.
	Destination	Defines the destination IP address required to match a rule for packets that are being inspected against the address translation rule base.
	Service	Defines the service required to match a rule for packets that are being inspected against the address translation rule base.
Translated Packet	–	Defines how an original packet is translated. The translated packet always defines the packet that is forwarded on by an enforcement module.
	Source	Specifies the new source IP address that the original packet source IP address should be translated to. This subelement also defines whether to apply static NAT (as indicated by the subscript *S* in Figure 9.1), or whether to apply hide NAT (this would be indicated by the subscript *H*).
	Destination	Specifies the new destination IP address that the original packet destination IP address should be translated to. Only static NAT can be applied for destination NAT.
	Service	Specifies the new service that the original packet service should be translated to.
Install On	–	Indicates the enforcement module(s) that the address translation rule should be installed on.
Comment	–	User comment that describes the address translation rule

In Figure 9.1, if you examine the Original Packet element, it indicates that any packets received by the enforcement module that have a source IP address of nyweb01, a destination IP address of any IP address and a destination TCP port of 80 (as defined by the service object http) will be matched against the rule. The Translated Packet element defines the translations that will take place on the original packet before it is forwarded towards its destination. In Figure 9.1, the source IP address of the original packets will be translated to the IP address defined for the nyweb01-valid object, and you can see that static NAT will occur (a one-to-one mapping), as indicated by the subscript *S*. The destination IP address and TCP ports will not modified, as indicated by the = Original (i.e. equals Original) values. Figure 9.2 demonstrates the address translation that occurs for the rule shown in Figure 9.1, assuming nyweb01 is configured with an IP address of 192.168.10.2 and nyweb01-valid is configured with an IP address of 172.20.1.102.

FIGURE 9.2   Address translation for rule in Figure 9.1

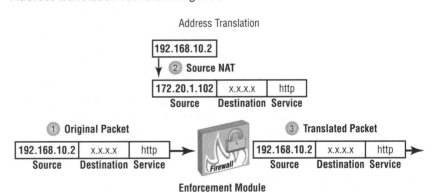

In Figure 9.2 the following events occur:

1. An HTTP Packet is sent from nyweb01 towards the enforcement module. For the packet to be matched against the original packet parameters of the address translation rule in Figure 9.2, the source IP address of the packet must be 192.168.10.2 and the service of the packet must be HTTP. The destination IP address can be anything.

2. The enforcement module receives the packet and compares the packet against the address translation rule base. The packet is matched to

the original packet parameters of the address translation rule in Figure 9.2 and is thus translated according to the translated packet parameters of the rule. This means that the source IP address of the packet is translated to the IP address of the `nyweb01-valid` object (172.20.1.102).

3. The translated packet is forwarded towards its destination.

Notice that the original packet is the packet sent toward the enforcement module (or received by the enforcement module) and the translated packet is the packet sent from the enforcement module. The original packet represents a packet that an enforcement module has been received and is about to be inspected. The translated packet represents a packet that has been inspected by the enforcement module, has had the appropriate address translations take place, and is about to be forwarded from the enforcement module toward the packet destination.

It is very important that you understand that address translation rules are only applied against the first packet in a new connection. Once the packet is permitted, an entry representing the new connection is written to the connection table. Subsequent packets of the connection are matched to the entry in the connection table and permitted by virtue of the fact that they are part of an established, permitted connection, and hence are not processed against the security rule base. The connection entry contains all the necessary NAT information required to ensure packets for both directions of the connection are translated correctly.

Automatic NAT

Now that you have an understanding of how address translation is implemented on VPN-1/FireWall-1, you can examine how to configure address translation rules. VPN-1/FireWall-1 NG supports two methods for configuring NAT:

- Automatic NAT

- Manual NAT

Automatic NAT represents the simplest and recommended method of implementing NAT on VPN-1/FireWall-1 for most situations. When you configure automatic NAT, you don't actually configure address translation rules—they are automatically configured for you by VPN-1/FireWall-1. So how does VPN-1/FireWall-1 know what address translation rules should be applied? The answer is that when you configure automatic NAT, you do so via security objects.

You are already familiar with security objects and the significant role they play in VPN-1/FireWall-1. Security objects represent the networks, systems, users, and applications that are relevant to the security policy requirements of your organization. Each security object possesses various configuration properties, which define the characteristics of the object. For example, a host node object contains an IP address property, which defines the IP address of the host represented by the host node object. Similarly, a network object contains both an IP address and network mask property, which together define the network address of the subnet represented by the network object. If you have previously configured security objects, in the properties dialog box for some objects, you may have noticed the presence of a configuration tab or configuration screen called NAT. The NAT configuration tab is present for some security objects, and allows you to configure automatic NAT for these objects. The following lists the types of security objects that can be configured for automatic NAT:

- Check Point objects
- Node objects
- Network objects
- Address range objects

In addition to configuring security objects, you can also configure some global properties that apply for automatic NAT operation on all VPN-1/FireWall-1 enforcement modules. Before you configure any of the above objects for automatic NAT, it is important that you understand some of the global NAT properties that apply to automatic NAT and how you can modify them.

For each of the various types of objects that can be configured for NAT, a scenario will be first introduced, which explains an example network topology and how you can implement NAT by configuring automatic NAT for the appropriate security object. After you have learned how to configure automatic NAT for each type of object, you will then learn how to configure the appropriate security rules to permit connections that are subject to automatic NAT.

Configuring Global NAT Properties

VPN-1/FireWall-1 NG defines several parameters related to automatic NAT that apply globally across all enforcement modules. These parameters are configurable within SmartDashboard, and are accessed by selecting Policy ➢ Global Properties and then selecting the Network Address Translation screen within the Global Properties dialog box (see Figure 9.3).

FIGURE 9.3 The Network Address Translation screen

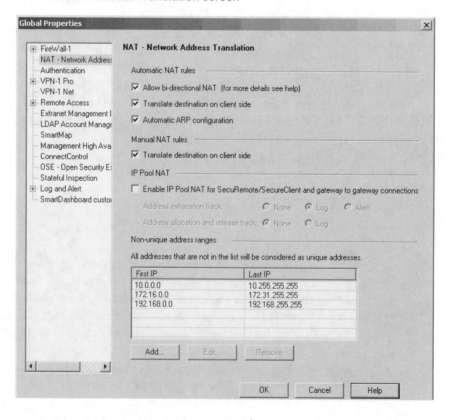

In Figure 9.3, notice that there are several sections within the Network Address Translation screen. This section discusses the Automatic NAT rules and IP Pool NAT sections.

Configuring Global Automatic NAT Rules Properties

The Automatic NAT rules section defines global parameters for any NAT rules that are generated by configuring automatic NAT (discussed in the next section). The following describes each parameter within the Automatic NAT rules section shown in Figure 9.3:

Allow bi-directional NAT   This parameter applies when an enforcement module receives a connection that has both a source IP address and destination IP address with matching objects that each has automatic NAT configured. In other words, this parameter applies to any packets that require both source NAT and destination NAT applied to the source and destination IP addresses of the connection respectively. When this parameter is enabled (the default setting), both the source NAT and destination NAT will take place. If Automatic rules intersection is disabled, then only one of the address translations will take place (the first automatic NAT rule that the connection matches).

Translate destination on client side   This parameter is enabled by default and specifies that for any automatic NAT rules, destination NAT (i.e., translation of the destination IP address of a packet) takes place on the client side, as opposed to the server side. When destination NAT is performed on the client side, address translation is performed by the INSPECT module immediately after the packet has been received by the enforcement module. This means that destination NAT takes place before the packet is passed to the TCP/IP stack for routing, which means you don't need to configure routes for valid IP address on the enforcement module operating system. Note that this setting only applies for automatic NAT rules and only applies to destination NAT. All source NAT occurs on the server side (i.e., after a packet has been routed by the operating system). For further clarification as to how destination NAT works on the client side, refer back to Chapter 8.

Automatic ARP configuration   This parameter enables the VPN-1/FireWall-1 enforcement module to automatically implement the appropriate proxy ARP configuration required for packets addressed to valid IP addresses that require NAT to be delivered to the enforcement module from upstream routers that receive the packets. This means that you don't have to configure the operating system separately by adding manual ARP entries (Unix) or configuring a `local.arp` file (Windows), which was required in previous versions of VPN-1/FireWall-1. The reasoning behind the need for proxy ARP was discussed earlier (see Chapter 8). The Automatic ARP configuration parameter is enabled by default and only applies to automatic NAT rules.

Automatic ARP is not supported on Linux-based and Nokia enforcement modules.

You normally should leave the Automatic NAT rules parameters enabled, as they make life easier for you as the VPN-1/FireWall-1 administrator, and there are no good reasons why you should ever need to disable them. If for some reason you do need to disable the Perform destination translation on the client side parameter, you will need to configure routes in the operating system route table of all enforcement modules that ensure packets addressed to valid IP addresses are routed to the correct egress interface. If you need to disable the Automatic ARP configuration setting (this is required for manual NAT, which is discussed later), you will need to manually configure the operating system of each enforcement module to support the proxy ARP mechanisms required (e.g., configure a `local.arp` file on Windows) to ensure packets addressed to a valid IP address are sent to the enforcement module.

It is important that you understand that the Automatic NAT rules parameters (obviously) only apply to automatic NAT rules. Because of the benefits of these parameters, it is recommended that you configure automatic NAT rules instead of manual NAT rules where possible. Also be aware that when you upgrade from version 4.1, the "Translate destination on client side" parameter is not enabled by default.

Configuring Global IP Pool NAT Properties

The IP Pool NAT section in Figure 9.3 applies to VPN-1 SecuRemote/SecureClient connections. By default, the Enable IP Pool NAT for SecuRemote/SecureClient and VPN connections parameter is disabled. If you enable this parameter, you enable VPN-1/FireWall-1 enforcement modules to NAT decrypted traffic received from SecuRemote/SecureClient VPN clients. Figure 9.4 demonstrates this feature.

FIGURE 9.4   IP Pool NAT for SecuRemote/SecureClient VPN connections

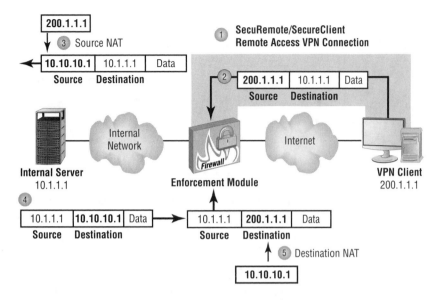

In Figure 9.4, a SecuRemote VPN client is connected to the VPN-1/
FireWall-1 enforcement, enabling a remote employee to securely access the
internal network. The enforcement module is configured to perform IP Pool
NAT for SecurRemote/SecureClient VPN connections. The following events
take place in Figure 9.4:

1. A remote employee establishes a remote access VPN connection to the
    corporate VPN-1/FireWall-1 enforcement module. This VPN connec-
    tion encrypts and encapsulates private communications between the
    VPN client and the internal network.

2. The VPN client sends a packet to an internal server with an IP address
    of 10.1.1.1. Because the VPN client has connected to the Internet and
    obtained an IP address of 200.1.1.1, the source IP address of the packet
    is 200.1.1.1. This packet is encrypted, encapsulated, and forwarded
    over the VPN connection to the enforcement module.

3. The enforcement module decrypts the packet received from the VPN
    client and removes any encapsulation, which should produce the original
    IP packet generated by the VPN client in Step 2. Because IP Pool NAT
    is configured on the enforcement module, the VPN client source IP
    address is mapped to an address from a pool of IP addresses assigned
    to the enforcement module. For example, let's assume the pool of

addresses is 10.10.10.1–10.10.10.100. The enforcement module maps the first available address from the pool (assuming all addresses are free, this will be 10.10.10.1) to the VPN client source IP address. The enforcement module then performs source NAT on the packet received from the VPN client, translating the source IP address from 200.1.1.1 to the address chosen from the pool (10.10.10.1). The packet is then forwarded to the internal server.

4. The internal server receives the packet, and believes it is communicating with 10.10.10.1. The internal server replies to the packet and addresses the reply to 10.10.10.1. This packet is forwarded toward the enforcement module.

5. The enforcement module receives the packet from the internal server and performs destination NAT on the packet to ensure the VPN client understands the packet. The destination IP address of the packet is translated from 10.10.10.1 to 200.1.1.1, and the packet is then forwarded over the VPN connection back to the VPN client.

IP Pool NAT enables SecuRemote/SecureClient VPN clients to appear as part of the internal network. This is particularly useful if you wish to identify VPN clients internally on your network. Without IP Pool NAT, the source IP address of packets sent by SecuRemote/SecureClient VPN clients is the same as the actual IP address of the VPN client interface connected to the Internet. Because the VPN client may be connecting from anywhere in the world, you typically have no control over the IP addresses allocated to VPN clients, so if you wish to identify VPN clients with IP Pool NAT, it is almost impossible.

You can log address exhaustion events (when a pool of IP addresses is exhausted) and address allocation and release events by configuring the IP Pool NAT track section on the NAT screen.

Configuring the IP Pool NAT parameter shown in Figure 9.3 merely enables the ability to use the feature on VPN-1/FireWall-1 enforcement modules managed by the SmartCenter server. To actually enable IP Pool NAT on an enforcement module, you must also perform the following tasks:

Configure an address range object An address range object represents a range of IP addresses, and can be created by selecting Manage ➢ Network Objects from the SmartDashboard menu. An address range object represents all IP addresses between a configured lower bound and upper bound.

This address range object is used to defined the pool of IP addresses used for the IP Pool NAT feature. For example, Figure 9.5 shows an address range object called `pool-nat` that represents the IP addresses between 192.168.1.1 and 192.168.1.100, inclusive.

FIGURE 9.5   An address range object

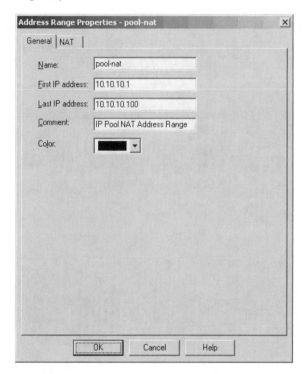

Enable IP Pool NAT on the appropriate enforcement module   The final step is to configure IP Pool NAT on the enforcement module. This is performed via the NAT screen within the host node object representing the enforcement module. Once you have globally enabled support for IP Pool NAT by checking the Enable IP Pool NAT for SecuRemote/Secure-Client and VPN connections parameter on the NAT screen, an IP Pools section appears. From there you can enable IP Pool NAT, and select the appropriate address range object for performing pool NAT on SecuRemote/SecureClient VPN connections. Figure 9.6 shows the NAT screen for an enforcement module called `nyfw01`, with IP Pool NAT having been enabled and the `pool-nat` address range object created in Figure 9.5 configured as the range to allocate IP addresses from.

You must ensure that your internal routers have the appropriate routes installed to route the IP addresses used for pool NAT back to the appropriate enforcement modules. IP Addresses used for pool NAT also are not supported by Automatic ARP, so you may need to implement proxy ARP on enforcement modules, or add static ARP entries/host routes on routers.

FIGURE 9.6 Configuring IP Pool NAT on an enforcement module

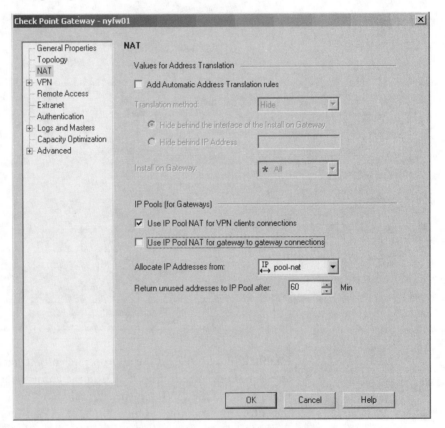

Configuring Automatic NAT for Check Point and Node Objects

As discusses previously, you can configure automatic NAT for Check Point, node, network, and address range objects. If you need to configure automatic NAT for a specific device, you must ensure a host node object exists that represents the device, so that you can implement the appropriate automatic NAT configuration for the device.

The automatic NAT configuration for all types of Check Point and Node objects follows the same concepts as the host node object configuration demonstrated in this section.

Figure 9.7 demonstrates a network topology where an internal device nyweb01 needs to initiate HTTP connections to devices on the Internet, and also requires external devices on the Internet to be able to establish HTTP connections to nyweb01.

FIGURE 9.7   Sample NAT topology for host node objects

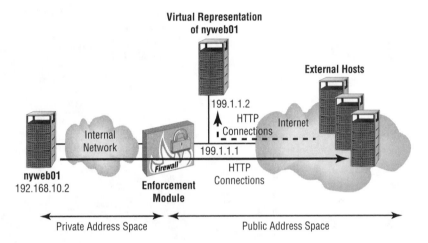

In Figure 9.7, the enforcement module provides the boundary between the private address space of the organization and the public address space of the Internet. In order for nyweb01 to communicate with devices on the Internet, it must possess a valid IP address on the Internet. To meet this requirement, automatic NAT must be configured so that nyweb01 is assigned a valid IP address of 199.1.1.2. This means that external devices will think that nyweb01 has an IP address of 199.1.1.2, instead of the internal private IP address of 192.168.10.2. Because external devices must be able to establish connections to nyweb01, a static one-to-one mapping is required between the internal private IP address and the external valid IP address of nyweb01. This means that static NAT must be configured for nyweb01.

To configure automatic NAT for a host node object, select Manage ➢ Network Objects from the SmartDashboard, which opens the Network Objects dialog box. From here, select the host node object that you wish to configure and click the Edit button, which will open the Host Node Properties dialog box for the object. The NAT screen within the Host Node Properties dialog box allows you to configure automatic NAT for the host node object. Figure 9.8 shows the NAT screen on the Host Node Properties dialog box for nyweb01.

FIGURE 9.8   The NAT screen on the Host Node Properties dialog box

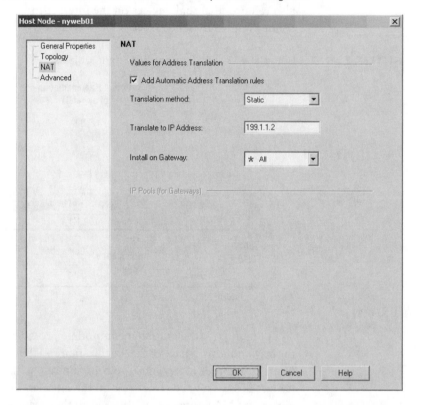

In Figure 9.8 within the NAT screen, notice the Values for Address Translation section, which enables you to configure automatic NAT. To enable automatic NAT, you must check the Add Automatic Address Translation rules option. Once you enable this option, you can configure the other parameters within the Values for Address Translation section. The following describes each of these parameters:

Translation method   The translation method defines if the automatic NAT configuration for the object specifies Static NAT (one-to-one mapping and the default setting) or Hide NAT (many-to-one mapping). Because external devices must be able to connect to nyweb01 in Figure 9.8, the translation method for nyweb01 must be configured as Static.

The hide translation method is more commonly used for network objects, as hide NAT is a many-to-one translation. You can also configure a host node object for hide NAT, which means that the workstation can establish outgoing connections to the Internet, but external devices on the Internet cannot establish connections to the configure network valid address.

Translate to IP Address   Defines the valid IP address that is assigned to the object. For packets received that have a source IP address for private IP address of the object (i.e., packets sent from the object), the source IP address is translated to the configured network valid address. For packets received by the enforcement module that are addressed to the network valid address (e.g., packets sent from the external devices to the valid IP address of nyweb01), the destination IP address of the packets is translated from the network valid address to the private IP address of the object. In Figure 9.8, the translated IP address is configured as 199.1.1.2, which means that any packets sent by nyweb01 will have the source IP address translated to 199.1.1.2, and any packets that are sent to 199.1.1.2 will be translated to the internal address of nyweb01 (192.168.10.2). When you configure a translation method of static NAT, the translated IP address configured should not be used as the translated IP address for any other objects. This is because static NAT is a one-to-one mapping.

If you configure the hide translation method, the Translate to IP Address field changes to a Hide behind IP address field, with a Hide behind the interface of the Install on Gateway field above it (this will be discussed later in this Chapter). With hide NAT, you can use the same hiding IP address for multiple objects because hide HAT is a many-to-one mapping.

Install on Gateway   Refers to the enforcement modules that the automatic NAT rules generated by the configuration should be installed on. In Figure 9.8, the automatic NAT rules generated by the configuration will be applied to all enforcement modules managed by the SmartCenter server currently being configured.

Once you click OK on the NAT screen in the Host Node Properties dialog box, the appropriate address translation rules will be generated automatically by VPN-1/FireWall-1 in the address translation rule base. If you select the address translation tab in SmartDashboard, you should see the address translation rules that have been automatically generated. Figure 9.9 shows the address translation rule base after the configuration described in Figure 9.8 is applied (assuming no other NAT rules exist).

FIGURE 9.9 The address translation rule base for a host node object

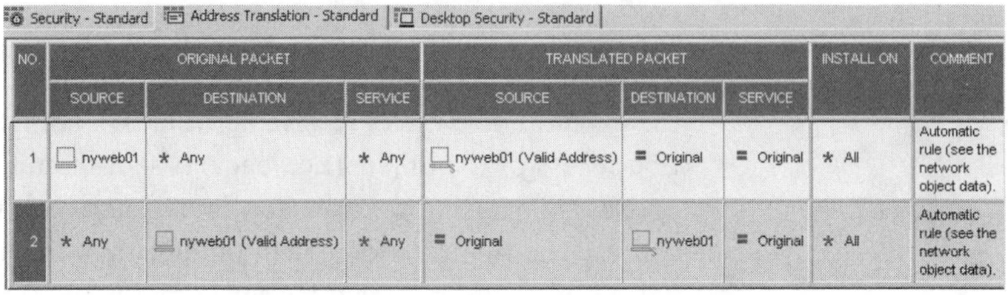

NO.	ORIGINAL PACKET			TRANSLATED PACKET			INSTALL ON	COMMENT
	SOURCE	DESTINATION	SERVICE	SOURCE	DESTINATION	SERVICE		
1	nyweb01	✱ Any	✱ Any	nyweb01 (Valid Address)	= Original	= Original	✱ All	Automatic rule (see the network object data).
2	✱ Any	nyweb01 (Valid Address)	✱ Any	= Original	nyweb01	= Original	✱ All	Automatic rule (see the network object data).

The rules shown in Figure 9.9 are automatically generated based on the configuration of Figure 9.8. You can't modify automatic NAT rules—to modify them you must modify the NAT configuration for the object the rules apply to. Notice that the Comment field for each rule indicates the rules are automatic and should be configured via the security object. The first rule specifies the appropriate translation for connections that are initiated from nyweb01 to the Internet. Notice that the translated packet source is listed as nyweb01 (Valid Address), which refers to the network valid address configured on the NAT screen of the host node object (199.1.1.2—see Figure 9.8). Also notice that the translated packet source object has a subscript S, which indicates the translation is a static NAT. All address translation rules are based on connections, which means that the first rule also takes care of return packets associated with the connection.

The second rule specifies the appropriate translation for connections that are initiated from external devices to the valid IP address of nyweb01. This rule ensures that external devices can initiate connections to nyweb01. Notice that the original packet destination is listed as nyweb01 (Valid Address) and the translated packet destination is listed as nyweb01$_S$. This means that any packets addressed to the valid address configured for nyweb01 (199.1.1.2) are translated to the internal address of nyweb01 (192.168.10.2). The subscript S indicates that the translation is a static NAT. Any return packets of these connections are automatically taken care of by the second rule.

Based on the rules generated in Figure 9.9, you can see that for automatic static NAT, both a source NAT rule (source IP address is translated) and a destination NAT rule (destination IP address is translated) are created.

After you have configured automatic NAT for any type of object, for the automatic NAT rules generated to take effect, you must install the security policy to your enforcement modules.

Configuring Automatic NAT for Network Objects

Often you will need to enable NAT for all devices within a subnet or network, rather than just a single device. VPN-1/FireWall-1 allows you to configure automatic NAT for network objects so that any device within the network is enabled for NAT. Figure 9.10 demonstrates a network topology where internal devices on the internal network need to initiate connections to devices on the Internet. There is no requirement for external devices to be able to connect to the internal devices.

FIGURE 9.10   Sample NAT topology for network objects

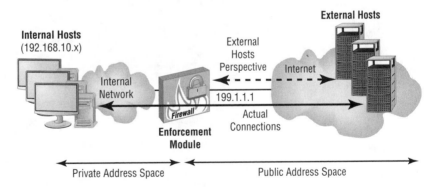

In Figure 9.10, devices on the internal network only need to establish connections to external devices on the Internet and no connections need to be established from the Internet to the internal devices. Because of this, hide NAT can (and should) be implemented, as it only permits outbound connections to be made and only requires a single valid IP address for multiple internal devices. By only permitting outbound connections, hide NAT prevents external devices from being able to connect to your internal devices. If you configure static NAT for each internal device, a security rule misconfiguration could leave your internal devices vulnerable to external devices. Therefore for network objects (see Figure 9.10), hide NAT is to be configured, with the external IP address of the enforcement module (199.1.1.1) to be used as the valid IP address.

Let's assume that a network object called `ny-internal-lan` exists, which represents the 192.168.10.x subnet. To configure automatic NAT for a network object, select Manage ➢ Network Objects from the SmartDashboard, which opens the Network Objects dialog box. From here, select the network object that you wish to configure and click the Edit button, which will open the Network Properties dialog box for the network object. Across the top of the dialog box, you should see a tab called NAT—click this tab to display it, which allows you to configure automatic NAT for the network object. Figure 9.11 shows the NAT tab on the Network Properties dialog box for `ny-internal-lan`.

FIGURE 9.11 The NAT tab for a network object

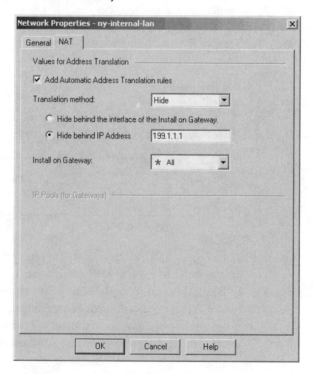

If you compare the NAT tab for a host node object (Figure 9.8) with that for a network object (Figure 9.11), you will notice that the configurable parameters are very similar. Notice in Figure 9.8 that the translation method is selected as Hide (which means hide NAT is configured), and that by choosing this translation method, the next parameter has changed. Instead of a network valid address parameter being present, as was the case for host node objects (Figure 9.8), you can see that this has been replaced by two new parameters:

Hide behind the interface of the Install on Gateway   Choosing this interface means that the valid IP address will be determined by the IP address of the server side interface of the enforcement module that each connection passes through. For example, in Figure 9.10, connections pass from the internal network to the external network, with the external interface on the enforcement module being the server side interface for this connection. If this option was configured, the hiding IP address of these connections will therefore be 199.1.1.1. This option is explained in more depth later in this chapter.

Hide behind IP Address   A fixed IP address that the object being configured will be hidden behind. Depending on the translation method you choose, the text describing the valid IP address changes as demonstrated in Figures 9.8 and 9.11. In Figure 9.11, the hiding IP address is 199.1.1.1, which means that for any outgoing packets received by the enforcement module that have a source IP address that falls within the range of the network object (192.168.10.x), the source IP address of the packet will be translated to 199.1.1.1, and port address translation will also take place.

Prior to NG Feature Pack 2, the Hide behind the interface of the Install on Gateway option did not exist, with only an option called Hiding IP Address (equivalent to the Hide behind IP Address option) provided. To provide the functionality of the Hide behind the interface of the Install on Gateway option for all versions prior to NG Feature Pack 2, specify a Hiding IP Address of 0.0.0.0

Once you click OK on the NAT tab, the appropriate address translation rules will be generated automatically by VPN-1/FireWall-1 in the address translation rule base. If you select the Address Translation tab in

SmartDashboard, you should see the address translation rules that have been automatically generated. Figure 9.12 shows the address translation rule base after the configuration in Figure 9.11 is applied.

FIGURE 9.12 The address translation rule base for a network object

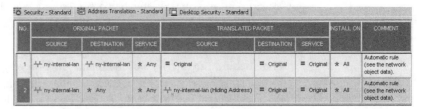

If you have multiple objects configured for automatic NAT, the automatic NAT rules are ordered by host node object, address range object, and then network object. Within objects of the same type, alphabetical order is used to order rules.

In Figure 9.12, notice that two address translation rules are automatically generated. Let's skip the first rule for now and move on to the second rule. Notice that the translated packet source indicates a value of ny-internal-lan (Hiding Address), which refers to the Hiding IP Address parameter configured in Figure 9.11 (199.1.1.1). This means that for packets sent from the 192.168.10.x network (ny-internal-lan) to any destination and service, the source IP address of these packets will be translated to 199.1.1.1. The subscript *H* in the translated packet source indicates that the translation performed will be hide NAT, meaning the source TCP/UDP ports of the packet will also be translated.

Now let's look back at the first rule. This rule looks a little strange, as it specifies that packets with a source IP address of 192.168.10.x (ny-internal-lan) and a destination IP address of 192.168.10.x should not be translated. This rule is always generated for network objects, whether static NAT or hide NAT is configured for the object, and is always placed above the actual address translation rules. Having this rule ensures that any internal communications between devices that both belong to the network object are not translated. Figure 9.13 demonstrates a situation when this rule is useful.

FIGURE 9.13 Situation where NAT should not occur

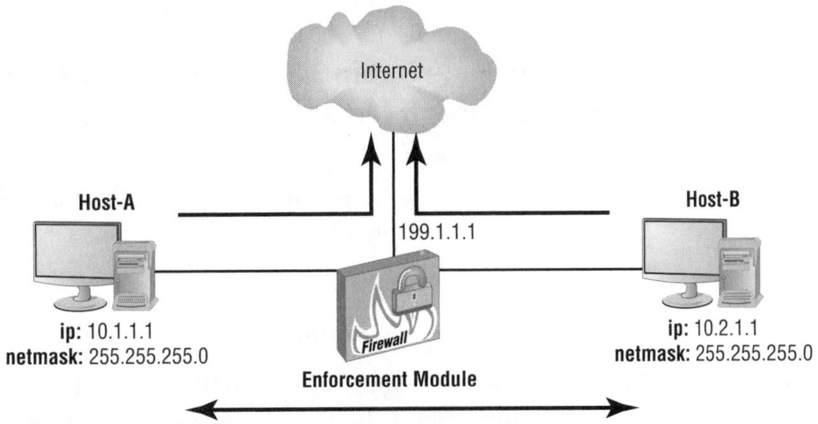

In Figure 9.13, both Host-A and Host-B wish to connect to the Internet. To accommodate this, automatic hide NAT is configured for a network object that includes all 10.x.x.x addresses. When Host-A or Host-B needs to connect to the Internet, the hide NAT rule takes place and the source IP address of each host is hidden behind the 199.1.1.1 address. Now consider what happens when Host-A and Host-B need to communicate with each other. When Host-A and Host-B communicate with each other, packets are sent through the enforcement module, even though both hosts are internal devices. Without the first rule shown in Figure 9.12, packets sent from Host-A to Host-B would by matched against the hide NAT rule, meaning the source IP address of the packets would be translated to 199.1.1.1. If anti-spoofing is configured, this will cause a violation when return packets are received back on the interface facing Host-B, as 199.1.1.1 represents the IP addressing of another interface. Even if anti-spoofing is disabled (this is not recommended), translating internal traffic is not recommended, because, for starters, it doesn't provide any benefit and, NAT normally is incompatible with these protocols because many internal communications use protocols that are more complex than those typically used on the Internet. The first rule in Figure 9.12 ensures that internal communications between Host-A and Host-B are not address translated, which removes any potential issues with anti-spoofing and protocol incompatibility with NAT.

The rules that are automatically generated in Figure 9.12 indicate that for automatic hide NAT, only a source NAT rule is generated (not a destination NAT rule), as indicated by the second rule in Figure 9.12. This is inline with the concept that hide NAT cannot support connections initiated from devices with valid IP addresses to internal devices.

Using the Hide behind the interface of the Install on Gateway Option (0.0.0.0) for Hide NAT

When you configure automatic hide NAT for a security object, you have several choices for configuring the hiding IP address field on the NAT tab for the object (see Figure 9.11). If you configure a specific hiding IP address:

- Hide behind IP Address
- Hide behind the interface of the Install On Gateway

If you choose the Hide behind IP Address option, you must specify a valid IP address. This valid IP address can be any of the following IP addresses:

- External IP address of the firewall
- Any valid IP address owned by the organization

If the Hide behind IP Address option is selected, the most common option used is to hide behind the external IP address of the firewall (see Figure 9.11). You can also use any valid IP address owned by the organization to hide behind, as long as that address is routable to the organization's enforcement module.

Note that you can also specify to choose the option to Hide behind the interface of the Install on Gateway, which means that private IP addresses will be hidden behind the IP address of the server-side interface of each connection on the enforcement module. Figure 9.14 demonstrates this.

In Figure 9.14, assume that the network object for ny-internal-lan has been configured with a hide NAT option of Hide behind the interface of the Install on Gateway Option in Figure 9.11. If any device on ny-internal-lan makes a connection to the Internet (i.e., Connection A), for that connection, the internal interface is considered the client-side interface for the connection and the external interface is considered the server-side interface for the connection (because the external interface faces the server side of the connection). This means that any connections made to the Internet, such as Connection A, will be hidden behind the valid IP address of the external interface (199.1.1.1). If any device in ny-internal-lan makes a connection to the External Partner network (i.e., Connection B), this time the DMZ interface is considered the server-side interface for the connection, and the valid IP address used will be 198.1.1.1 instead.

FIGURE 9.14   Using the Hide behind the interface of the Install on Gateway Option

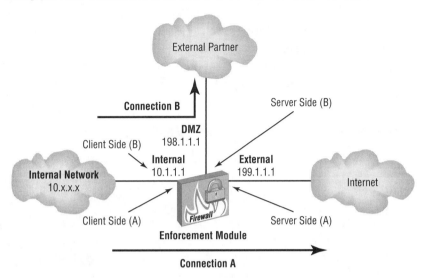

By configuring the Hide behind the interface of the Install on Gateway, the actual hiding IP address used for each connection is dynamically generated, depending on the interface that faces the destination of the connection. This provides the following advantages:

- If you change the IP addressing of any interface on the enforcement module, you don't need to update any objects that use this option, as new connections will automatically use the new IP addressing.

- If you have a complex environment where connections may be made from an internal object on different interfaces on the enforcement module, using this option to generate the hiding IP address ensures the correct hiding IP address is used relative to the destination for each individual connection (as demonstrated in Figure 9.13 for connections to the Internet as opposed to connections to the external partner network).

Configuring Automatic NAT for Address Range Objects

The final security object that can be configured for automatic NAT is the address range object. The address range object is similar to a network object, except it represents a *contiguous* range of IP addresses that is not limited to the subnet boundaries a network object is limited to. For example, an address range object can represent the IP addresses of 10.1.1.3–10.1.1.9, or the IP addresses of 1.1.1.1–99.9.9.9. Figure 9.15 demonstrates a network topology for address range objects, which is similar to the sample NAT topology for network objects in Figure 9.10, where internal devices on the internal network need to initiate connections to devices on the Internet. Unlike for the network objects, however, external devices need to be able to connect to the internal devices represented by address range objects.

FIGURE 9.15 Sample NAT topology for address range objects

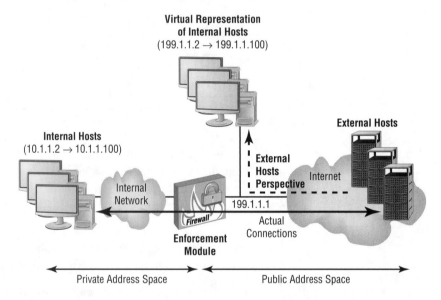

In Figure 9.15, the internal devices 10.1.1.2–10.1.1.100 on the internal network need to be able to establish connections to external devices on the Internet. External devices also need to be able to establish connections to each of these hosts, meaning that static NAT is required (a one-to-one mapping is required for each internal device). You could create 99 host node objects and configure a unique valid IP address for each object; however, this would be very time consuming and prone to error. Address range objects allow you to configure a contiguous range of addresses and then configure automatic NAT for the address range. A contiguous range of addresses means a continuous range of addresses. For example, the range 10.1.1.2, 10.1.1.3, 10.1.1.4, and 10.1.1.5 is contiguous, while the range 10.1.1.2, 10.1.1.4 and 10.1.1.6 is not contiguous, because the range of addresses is not continuous.

In Figure 9.15, the range 10.1.1.2–10.1.1.100 is a contiguous range, so you can create an address range object to represent these hosts. To configure automatic NAT for an address range object, select the address range object from within the Network Objects dialog box and click the Edit button, which will open the Address Range Properties dialog box for the address range object. Across the top of the dialog box, you should see a tab called NAT—click this tab to display the NAT configuration tab, which allows you to configure automatic NAT for the address range object. Figure 9.16 shows the NAT tab on the Address Range Properties dialog box for an address range object called ny-internal-range, which represents the address range of 10.1.1.2–10.1.1.100.

FIGURE 9.16   The NAT tab for an address range object

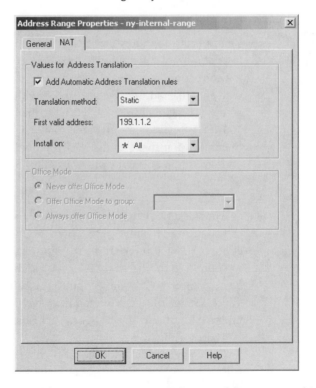

When you configure automatic NAT for an address range object, and specify a translation method of Static, a parameter called the First valid address must be configured, which defines the start of the valid address range that will be mapped to the internal address range specified by the address range object. Once you configure a first valid address, one-to-one mappings are automatically generated for each internal IP address within the address range. For example, notice in Figure 9.16 that First valid address is configured as 199.1.1.2, which means that one-to-one static NAT mappings are automatically generated as follows:

- 10.1.1.2–199.1.1.2
- 10.1.1.3–199.1.1.3
- 10.1.1.4–199.1.1.4
- …and so on, until…
- 10.1.1.100–199.1.1.100

You can also configure static NAT for a network object, which means that the host portion of the private IP address will map directly to the host portion of the corresponding valid IP address. For example, if you have a network object with private IP addressing of 10.1.1.0 (with subnet mask of 255.255.255.0), and a network valid address of 199.1.1.0, the IP address 10.1.1.1 is translated to 199.1.1.1, 10.1.1.2 is translated to 199.1.1.2, and so on. Using this method of configuring many static NAT translations is not as flexible as using an address range object, as the translation can only be applied to the bounds of a subnet.

The static NAT mappings generated above ensure that each internal device can connect to devices on the Internet, and also ensures external devices can connect to each internal device. For example, if an external device needs to connect to the internal device with an IP address of 10.1.1.61, the external device can do so by connecting to the valid IP address 199.1.1.1. In short, address range objects save you from having to configure automatic NAT for multiple host node objects, when each host node object is part of a contiguous IP address range.

Once you click OK on the NAT tab, the appropriate address translation rules will be generated automatically by VPN-1/FireWall-1 in the address translation rule base. If you select the address translation tab in Smart-Dashboard, you should see the address translation rules that have been automatically generated. Figure 9.17 shows the address translation rule base after the configuration in Figure 9.16 is applied.

FIGURE 9.17 The address translation rule base for address range objects

Security - Standard | Address Translation - Standard | Desktop Security - Standard

NO.	ORIGINAL PACKET			TRANSLATED PACKET			INSTALL ON	COMMENT
	SOURCE	DESTINATION	SERVICE	SOURCE	DESTINATION	SERVICE		
1	ny-internal-range	ny-internal-range	* Any	= Original	= Original	= Original	* All	Automatic rule (see the network object data).
2	ny-internal-range	* Any	* Any	ny-internal-range	= Original	= Original	* All	Automatic rule (see the network object data).
3	* Any	ny-internal-range	* Any	= Original	ny-internal-range	= Original	* All	Automatic rule (see the network object data).

In Figure 9.17, notice that a first rule similar to the first rule created in Figure 9.12 is automatically created. Again, this first rule ensures that any communications within the address range are not translated.

TIP

Whenever you configure automatic NAT for network objects or address range objects, a rule is automatically generated that prevents internal communications between hosts within the network or address range object from being address translated.

The second and third rules define the necessary address translation rules for static NAT. Notice that the static NAT rule is identical in concept to the static NAT rule that was automatically configured for the host node object in Figure 9.9 for host node objects, except that the rules in Figure 9.17 specify an address range object instead of a host node object. The first rule defines source NAT for connections initiated by internal devices, and the second rule defines destination NAT for connections initiated from external devices to internal devices.

Understanding VPN-1/FireWall-1 Packet Flow with Automatic NAT

It is important to understand how packets flow through the enforcement module when automatic NAT is configured. By understanding the packet flow, you will know how to configure security rules that work your automatic NAT configuration and understand how automatic NAT removes some of the manual configuration previously associated with NAT in prior versions of VPN-1/FireWall-1 NG.

Automatic Static NAT Packet Flow

With automatic NAT, NAT can be applied for the source IP address (source NAT) or for the destination IP address (destination NAT). Figure 9.18 shows the packet flow through an enforcement module when automatic NAT is configured and source NAT takes place.

FIGURE 9.18 Automatic static source NAT

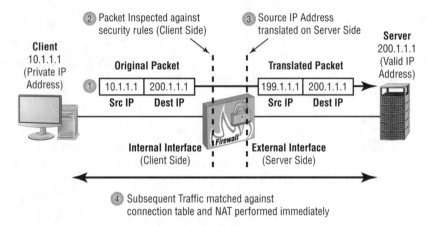

In Figure 9.18, the following events take place:

1. A client with a private IP address initiates a connection to an external server. A packet is sent that includes the private IP address of the client as the source IP address.

2. The packet is received by the internal interface of the enforcement module and passed to the INSPECT module. This is the client side of the connection, as the interface faces the client. The packet represents a new connection, so the packet is processed against the security rule base. This means that a security rule must be configured that permits the original packet sent in Step 1. An anti-spoofing check also takes place, which verifies the source IP address is valid for the interface. Assuming the original packet matches a permitted security rule and passes the anti-spoofing check, a new connection is entered into the connection table and the packet is passed to the operating system for routing.

3. The operating system routes the packet based upon the destination IP address of the packet, with the packet being routed to the egress interface. The INSPECT module receives the packet from the operating system on the egress interface (server side). Because an entry was added to the connection table in Step 2, the packet is matched to this connection and implicitly permitted. Since automatic source NAT occurs server-side, the source IP address of the packet is translated to a valid IP address. The connection table is also updated with NAT information and the translated packet is forwarded to the destination.

4. All subsequent packets associated with the connection are permitted and translated appropriately as soon as the enforcement module receives the packets, because the connection table has the appropriate address translation information present for the connection. For example, return packets require the destination IP address to be translated to the private IP address of the client. This occurs when the packet is received on the external interface (server side), as the packet is immediately matched to a connection in the connection table at this point.

Figure 9.19 shows the packet flow through an enforcement module when automatic NAT is configured and destination NAT takes place.

FIGURE 9.19   Automatic static destination NAT

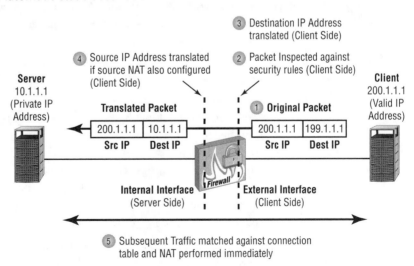

In Figure 9.19, the following events take place:

1. An external client with a valid IP address initiates a connection to an internal server. A packet is sent that includes the valid IP address of the internal server as the destination IP address.

2. The packet is received by the external interface of the enforcement module and passed to the INSPECT module. This is the client side of the connection, as the interface faces the client. The packet represents a new connection, so the packet is processed against the security rule base. This means that a security rule must be configured that permits the original packet sent in Step 1. Assuming the original packet matches a permitted security rule, a new connection is entered into the connection table. An anti-spoofing check also takes place, which verifies the source IP address is valid for the interface.

3. Because automatic destination NAT takes place on the client side by default, the destination IP address is translated to the private IP address of the internal server, before the packet is passed to the operating system for routing. The connection table is also updated with NAT information, and the translated packet is forwarded to the operating system for routing.

NOTE

If you disable client-side destination NAT, you must configure a host route in the operating system for the valid IP address associated with each private IP address.

4. The operating system routes the packet based on the private IP address of the internal server and routes the packet to the correct egress interface (server side). Once again the INSPECT module receives the packet and because an entry was added to the connection table in Step 2, the packet is matched to this connection and implicitly permitted. If source NAT is configured for the object represented by the source IP address, the source IP address of the original packet will also be translated and the connection table updated appropriately, and the translated packet is forwarded to the destination.

5. All subsequent packets associated with the connection are permitted and translated appropriately as soon as the enforcement module receives the packets, because the connection table has the appropriate address translation information present for the connection. For example, return

packets require the source IP address to be translated to the valid IP address of the client. This occurs when the packet is received on the internal interface (server side), as the packet is immediately matched to a connection in the connection table at this point.

In versions prior to VPN-1/FireWall-1 NG, an anti-spoofing check of the destination IP address of outgoing packets also takes place *before* destination NAT (remember destination NAT occurs server side prior to NG). Because the anti-spoofing check is applied before the destination IP address is translated, the valid IP address must be included in the list of valid IP addresses for the outgoing interface. For example in Figure 9.19, you would normally expect the list of valid IP addresses for the internal interface to be 10.x.x.x. In any version prior to VPN-1/FireWall-1 NG, you also have to ensure the list of valid IP addresses includes the IP address 199.1.1.1 as this the IP address present in the packet when the anti-spoofing check of the outgoing packet takes place.

Notice in Figures 9.18 and 9.19 that the client side and server side changes, depending on where the connection is being initiated. The client side always faces where the connection is initiated from (i.e., the client) and the server side always faces where the connection is being initiated to (i.e., the server).

Automatic Hide NAT Packet Flow

Automatic hide NAT only supports source NAT, where the private IP address of an internal device is translated to a valid IP address. This source NAT is always performed on the server side and is identical to the packet flow shown in Figure 9.18.

Configuring Security Rules for Automatic NAT

Because security rule processing always takes place first at the client-side interface, you must configure your security rules based upon the original packet received. With automatic NAT, it is important to understand that when you configure automatic NAT for an object, the object now possesses another IP address that the security rule base can also match. For example, assume that you configure a host node object with an IP address of 10.1.1.1 and do not configure automatic NAT for the object. You create a security rule that specifies the host node object as the destination. This means that only packets with a destination IP address of 10.1.1.1 will match the host node object specified in the rule. Now assume that you configure for automatic static NAT for the object and configure a valid IP address of 199.1.1.1. Now, any packets with a destination IP address of 10.1.1.1 or 199.1.1.1 will match the host node object specified in the rule.

Because security rules can reference all of the IP addresses configured for a security object (both the private IP address and the valid IP address), your security rules only need to reference a single security object, regardless of whether you are permitting access based upon the private IP address or valid IP address of the object.

Referring back to the topology shown for host node objects in Figure 9.7, after automatic NAT has been configured for the host node object nyweb01, the appropriate security rules need to be configured. HTTP connections are to be permitted from nyweb01 to external devices on the Internet, and HTTP connections are also to be permitted from external devices to nyweb01.

Consider the rule required to permit HTTP access from nyweb01 to the Internet. Remember – always configure security rules based upon the original packet received by the enforcement module. In Figure 9.7, this will represent packets with a source IP address of nyweb01, a destination IP address of any and a service of HTTP. Figure 9.20 demonstrates the appropriate rule for permitting HTTP access from nyweb01 to the Internet:

FIGURE 9.20 Security rule required for automatic static source NAT

Notice that the rule in Figure 9.20 corresponds to the original packets that are sent by nyweb01.

Now consider the rule required to permit HTTP access from external devices to nyweb01. Again – always configure security rules based upon the original packet received by the enforcement module. In Figure 9.7, this will represent packets with any source IP address, a destination IP address of 199.1.1.2 and a service of HTTP. Because the nyweb01 object has been configured for automatic static NAT, it has two IP addresses that identify the object:

- 192.168.10.2 – the private IP address of nyweb01, configured on the General screen of the host node properties

- 199.1.1.2 – the valid IP address of nyweb01, configured on the NAT screen of the host node properties

Because the nyweb01 object contains the IP address 199.1.1.2, it can be used for the rule to permit access from the Internet to the valid IP address of nyweb01. Figure 9.21 demonstrates the appropriate rule (Rule 2) for permitting HTTP access from external devices to nyweb01.

FIGURE 9.21 Security rule required for automatic static destination NAT

The rule in Figure 9.21 is quite counterintuitive, as it implies that the rule accepts packets sent to the private IP address of nyweb01. However, because a valid IP address has been configured within the object for automatic NAT, this valid IP address will also be matched by the rule.

The second rule permits HTTP access to both the valid IP address *and* private IP address of nyweb01. This is undesirable, as only access to the valid IP address is required. To circumvent this potential security hole, you can create a new host node object that has a general IP address configured as the valid IP address of nyweb01 (e.g. nyweb01-valid, IP address = 199.1.1.2). Performing these actions however starts to break the "automatic" concept associated with automatic NAT.

EXERCISE 9.1

Configuring Automatic NAT

In this exercise you will configure automatic NAT so that any device on the ny-internal-lan network can access http services on the Internet, using the external IP address of the enforcement module. You will also ensure that nyweb01 can be accessed from the Internet via the 172.20.1.10 address. Once you have configured automatic NAT, you will configure the appropriate security rules to permit connections that are configured for NAT.

1. Delete all security rules that you have configured for previous exercises.

EXERCISE 9.1 *(continued)*

2. Select Policy ➢ Global Properties and open the Network Address Translation screen from within the Global Properties dialog box. Ensure that the Automatic ARP configuration and Perform destination translation on the client side settings are enabled. Click OK.

3. Configure automatic hide NAT for the ny-internal-lan network by selecting Manage ➢ Network Objects, opening the ny-internal-lan network, and selecting the NAT configuration tab. Enable automatic NAT by checking the Add Automatic Address Translation rules option, ensuring the translation method is set to Hide and that the Hide behind the interface of the Install on Gateway option is selected (i.e., the IP address of the server-side interface for a connection). Click OK once complete.

4. Open the nyweb01 object and select the NAT screen from the workstation properties dialog box. Enable automatic NAT by checking the Add Automatic Address Translation rules option, ensuring the translation method is set to Static and that the network valid address is set to 172.20.1.10. Click OK.

5. Verify the appropriate automatic NAT rules have been added by viewing the address translation rule base.

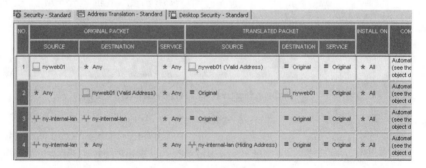

6. Now you must create the appropriate security rules. To enable outgoing HTTP access for internal devices, create a new rule with the following parameters:

  - Source = **ny-internal-lan**
  - Destination = **Any**
  - Service = **http**
  - Action = **accept**

7. To enable incoming HTTP access to nyweb01, create a new rule with the following parameters:

   - Source = **Any**
   - Destination = **nyweb01**
   - Service = **http**
   - Action = **accept**

8. Your configuration is nearly complete. Verify that your rules are correct and the install the policy. After policy installation, verify that jupiter.london.local can establish an HTTP connection to nyweb01 using its valid IP address of 172.20.1.10 (this verifies the second NAT and second security rule). Use the FireWall-1 predefined log query within SmartView Tracker to ensure that HTTP connections established from nyweb01 to jupiter.london.local have the appropriate source NAT (192.168.10.2–172.20.1.10) applied (this verifies the first NAT and first security rule).

NO.	SOURCE	DESTINATION	SERVICE	ACTION	TRACK	INSTALL ON	TIME	COMMENT
1	ny-internal-lan	✴ Any	TCP http	🌐 accept	▤ Log	✴ Policy Targets	✴ Any	Permit HTTP connections from internal LAN to Internet
2	✴ Any	nyweb01	TCP http	🌐 accept	▤ Log	✴ Policy Targets	✴ Any	Permit HTTP connections from Internet to nyweb01

Manual NAT

You have seen how you can configure automatic NAT rules, by simply modifying security objects that support automatic NAT. Automatic NAT is intuitive, as you have a single security object that can be configured with both an internal identity (i.e., a private IP address or network address) as well as an external identity (i.e., a valid IP address). Once you have configured the valid IP addresses for a security object, NAT rules are automatically created, and for network objects and address range objects, an automatic NAT rule is even added to prevent address translation of communications between devices within the object. Configuring automatic NAT enables client-side destination NAT, so you don't have to configure routes for each valid IP address on your enforcement modules. Automatic NAT also eliminates the need to manually configure proxy ARP on your enforcement module, with VPN-1/FireWall-1 NG handling this for you automatically.

After reading the above paragraph you are probably thinking automatic NAT is great—and it is. You are probably also thinking why you would ever think of configuring NAT in any other way, given all of the benefits listed above. Unfortunately, there is one drawback to automatic NAT—you can't modify the NAT rules that are automatically generated by automatic NAT. Although automatic NAT rules may meet your requirements most of the time, sometimes you will need the ability to customize NAT rules for specific requirements. When this need arises, you must configure manual NAT, which allows you to define your own address translation rules. For example, you may wish to translate incoming connections to a valid IP address to an internal device, but only if the incoming connections are SMTP connections. You can only do this by specifying the smtp service in the appropriate address translation rules in the address translation rule base—this is not possible using automatic NAT (all automatic NAT rules specify a service of Any).

Configuring manual NAT involves quite a number of tasks. It is more complex than automatic NAT, because many of the tasks required to implement NAT in general that are handled automatically by VPN-1/ FireWall-1 for automatic NAT must be manually configured for manual NAT. The following lists each of the tasks you must perform to configure manual NAT:

- Configure the enforcement module operating system to support manual NAT.

- Configure VPN-1/FireWall-1 NG to support manual NAT.

- Create security objects that represent the valid IP addresses of internal objects.

- Create the required manual NAT rules in the address translation rule base.

- Configure the appropriate security rules.

Before you perform any of these tasks, you should have a good idea as to the address translations that you wish to perform, as you will need to know valid IP addresses and internal IP addresses when you configure the operating system of the enforcement module. Figure 9.22 shows a network topology that will be used to demonstrate the configuration of manual NAT in this section.

FIGURE 9.22   Sample network topology for manual NAT

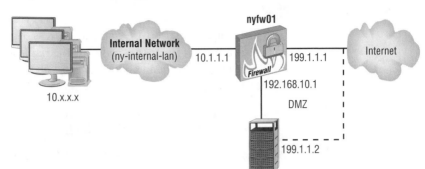

In Figure 9.22, the administrator of nyfw01 wishes to enable static NAT for the web server nyweb01, which is located in the DMZ network. The private IP address of nyweb01 is 192.168.10.2, and nyweb01 should appear as if it is connected to the Internet with the valid IP address of 199.1.1.2 (the dotted line connecting nyweb01 to the Internet in Figure 9.22 does not represent a physical interface and is only intended for illustration purposes). The administrator only wishes to enable static NAT for web services, to ensure that external devices on the Internet cannot gain access to nyweb01 if security rules are misconfigured. User PCs on the internal network (represented by the ny-internal-lan object) also need to connect to the Internet for web browsing , but do not require the ability for external devices to establish connections. The administrator wishes to restrict address translation for outgoing user connections to only web-related services (e.g., domain-udp, http, https, and ftp), and all connections must be translated to the external IP address of the enforcement module (199.1.1.1). To meet the security requirements of the administrator of the topology in Figure 9.22, you cannot simply use automatic NAT, as you will not be able to restrict the services permitted for the automatic NAT rules generated. For this reason, you must configure manual NAT to ensure the security requirements can be met.

Configuring the Enforcement Module Operating System to Support Manual NAT

When you configure manual NAT, there is some configuration of the enforcement module operating system required. As you learned in Chapter 8, in previous versions of VPN-1/FireWall-1, the following operating system configuration is required:

- Host routes that route the valid IP address of an internal device to the private IP address of the device or the next-hop router that leads to the device. This is required for any valid IP addresses used in destination NAT rules.

- Proxy ARP configuration to ensure that the enforcement module will answer ARP requests for the valid IP address of an internal device

Automatic NAT in VPN-1/FireWall-1 NG removes the requirement to configure each of the above, with client-side destination NAT translating the valid destination IP address of packets to an appropriate private destination IP address *before* the packet is passed to the operating system for routing, meaning the operating system only needs to know how to route to the private IP address of the packet, as opposed to the valid IP address. Automatic ARP is also provided in VPN-1/FireWall-1 NG, which automatically configures the operating system to answer ARP requests for valid IP addresses that are not physically configured on the enforcement module.

In VPN-1/FireWall-1 NG Feature Pack 1 and Feature Pack 2, if you configure manual NAT, as opposed to automatic NAT, you must manually configure hosts routes for the valid IP addresses of devices and also configure proxy ARP manually. Host routes are required because in these versions, manual destination NAT is only configured server-side, just like previous versions of VPN-1/FireWall-1 NG. Proxy ARP configuration also must be configured manually.

In VPN-1/FireWall-1 NG Feature Pack 3, client-side destination NAT is now supported for manual NAT as well as automatic NAT, removing the requirement to configure host routes for the valid IP addresses of internal devices. You can enable/disable client-side destination NAT for manual NAT using the NAT screen within the Global Properties dialog box of SmartDashboard (see Figure 9.3). This setting is enabled by default. With manual NAT in Feature Pack 3, you must still manually configure proxy ARP, as automatic ARP is still only a feature supported by automatic NAT.

Referring back to Figure 9.22, notice that there are two valid IP addresses that will be used for address translation:

- 199.1.1.1 (for internal PCs)

- 199.1.1.2 (for nyweb01)

Because 199.1.1.1 is the external IP address of the enforcement module, you do not need to configure proxy ARP for this IP address. If an external device (e.g., a border router) sends an ARP request to 199.1.1.1, the enforcement module will answer the ARP request, as 199.1.1.1 is the real IP address of the external interface. You also don't need to configure a host route for the 199.1.1.1 address, as you will only be configuring hide NAT for this address, meaning return packets that require destination NAT will be translated on the client side, as the return packets will be matched on the client side to a connection in the connection table. For the 199.1.1.2 external IP address, you need to configure proxy ARP to ensure the enforcement module answers ARP requests for the 199.1.1.2 IP address. You will also need to configure a host route for the address on the enforcement module operating system, but only if client-side destination NAT for manual NAT is disabled, to ensure packets are routed to the correct egress interface.

Configuring Host Routes

Because you may not always work with NG Feature Pack 3 installations, it is important you understand how to configure host routes, which are required to enable manual destination NAT for all versions prior to NG Feature Pack 3. Remember that if you are using NG Feature Pack 3 or higher, and client-side destination NAT for manual NAT is enabled (the default), then you do not need to configure host routes as per this section, and only need to configure proxy ARP.

To configure a host route, you must perform the appropriate operating system commands for adding routes. On both Windows and Unix, you use the *route add <valid IP> <Next Hop>* command to configure host routes. The following shows how you would configure a host route on a Windows-based enforcement module for the valid IP address of nyweb01:

```
route add -p 199.1.1.2 192.168.10.2
```

The –p option specifies that the route should be permanently added to the route table (i.e., the route will be present even after the enforcement module is rebooted). The first IP address represents the destination IP address of the packet being routed (in this case, the valid IP address 199.1.1.1) and the second IP address represents the next-hop device. This means that the route specifies for any packets with a destination IP address of 199.1.1.1 to route those packets to 192.168.10.2 (the private IP address of nyweb01). This ensures that the packet will be routed out the DMZ interface towards nyweb01, at which point it will be intercepted by the enforcement module and the appropriate address destination NAT (199.1.1.1 to 192.168.10.2) will take place. After you have configured the host route, you can use the `route print` command to display the operating system routing table verify your configuration.

The following demonstrates how you would configure a host route on a Unix-based enforcement module:

```
route add 199.1.1.1 192.168.10.2 1
```

The last parameter (1) specifies the hop count (number of routing hops required to reach the destination IP address). Notice that the -p option is not supported on Unix systems, which means that you must configure any custom `route add` commands in the appropriate startup scripts on your Unix enforcement module.

Configuring Proxy ARP

To configure proxy ARP on Windows-based systems, you must create a file called `local.arp` that contains each valid IP address that you are translating on the enforcement module and the MAC address of the external interface of the enforcement module. To determine the MAC address of the external interface, use the `ipconfig /all` command, as shown below:

```
C:\> ipconfig /all
Windows 2000 IP Configuration

        Host Name . . . . . . . . . . . . : nyfw01
        Primary Dns Suffix . . . . . . . :
        Node Type . . . . . . . . . . . . : Hybrid
        IP Routing Enabled. . . . . . . . : No
        WINS Proxy Enabled. . . . . . . . : No


Ethernet adapter External:

        Connection-specific DNS Suffix . :
        Description . . . . . . . . . . . : HP Ethernet 10/100
        Physical Address. . . . . . . . . : 00-10-A4-E0-1E-D3
        Dhcp Enabled. . . . . . . . . . . : No
        Autoconfiguration Enabled . . . . : No
        IP Address. . . . . . . . . . . . : 199.1.1.1
        Subnet Mask . . . . . . . . . . . : 255.255.255.0
        Default Gateway . . . . . . . . . : 199.1.1.2
```

In the example above, the Physical Address field displays the MAC address (00-10-A4-E0-1E-D3) for the external interface. Once you know the appropriate MAC address, you can then create the local.arp file, which must be placed in the $FWDIR\conf directory on the enforcement module.

If you are creating a local.arp file, make sure you are aware that for VPN-1/ FireWall-1 NG you must place the file in the $FWDIR\conf directory, as opposed to the $FWDIR\state directory for previous versions.

This file contains entries that map a valid IP address to the MAC address of the external interface. Each entry has the syntax <valid IP address> <MAC address>. The following demonstrates configuring the local.arp file on a Windows-based enforcement module for the valid IP address 199.1.1.2.

```
199.1.1.2     00-10-A4-E0-1E-D3
```

Notice that you must configure the MAC address exactly as it is displayed in the ipconfig /all command output. Once you have saved the local.arp file, you must stop and start the FireWall-1 service (using fwstop and fwstart).

To configure proxy ARP on a Unix-based system, you use the arp Unix command. The syntax of this command is *arp -s <valid IP> <external MAC> pub*. The -s parameter specifies that the mapping configured should be added to the operating system ARP cache. The pub parameter specifies that the enforcement module should proxy ARP (answer ARP requests) for the valid IP address specified. To determine the MAC address of the external interface, use the ifconfig command, which is demonstrated on a Red Hat Linux system below:

```
# ifconfig eth0
eth0   Link encap:Ethernet HWaddr 00:01:02:3C:88:7A
       inet addr:199.1.1.1 Bcast:199.1.1.255 Mask:255.255.255.0
       UP BROADCAST RUNNING MULTICAST MTU:1500 Metric:1
       RX packets:1872435 errors:0 dropped:0 overruns:0
       TX packets:1029384 errors:0 dropped:0 overruns:0
```

In the example above, the ifconfig command is used to display information about the external interface called eth0. The first line of the output includes the HWaddr field, which indicates the MAC address of the external interface is 00:01:02:3C:88:7A. Once you know the MAC address of the external interface, you can configure the appropriate proxy ARP entries.

The following demonstrates the appropriate proxy ARP entry for the valid IP address 199.1.1.2 on a Red Hat Linux enforcement module:

```
# arp -s 199.1.1.2 00:01:02:3C:88:7A pub
```

 To ensure the proxy ARP entries required for manual NAT on a Unix system are present in the ARP cache after an enforcement module has been rebooted, you must configure the required arp commands in the appropriate startup scripts.

Configuring VPN-1/FireWall-1 NG to Support Manual NAT

On Windows-based systems, if you wish to use a local.arp file for manual NAT, you must disable the automatic ARP feature that is enabled by default. To disable automatic ARP, select Policy ≻ Global Properties, which will display the Global Properties dialog box. Select the Network Address Translation screen and then uncheck the Automatic ARP configuration parameter (see Figure 9.7). Bear in mind that this will disable automatic ARP globally for all enforcement modules, so you will need to implement the appropriate proxy ARP configuration (e.g., local.arp on Windows) on all enforcement modules for valid IP addresses, regardless of whether automatic or manual NAT is being used.

Creating the Appropriate Security Objects for Manual NAT

When you configure a manual NAT rule, you must be able to specify the both the IP address of the original packet and the valid IP address that you wish to translate the original packet to (i.e., the private IP address and valid IP address of each device that address translation is to be configured for). With automatic NAT, you specify both the private IP address and valid IP address within the same security object. When you configure manual NAT, you must create separate objects to represent the private IP address and valid IP address respectively.

Referring back to Figure 9.22, let's assume that the objects nyweb01 and ny-internal-lan, which include the private IP addresses of the devices represented by each object, have already been created. This means that the nyweb01 host node object is configured with an IP address of 192.168.10.2, and the ny-internal-lan network object is configured with an IP address of 10.0.0.0 and subnet mask of 255.0.0.0 (i.e., 10.x.x.x). Now consider the valid IP addresses required for each of these objects. The valid IP address that represents nyweb01 is to be 199.1.1.2—therefore a host node object must be created that represents this IP address. When you create a security object that represents the valid IP address of another security object, you generally use the same name for the object, and add an appropriate prefix or suffix to indicate the new object represents the valid IP address of the other security object. For example, for the topology of Figure 9.22, you could create a host node object called nyweb01-valid, which is used to represent the valid IP address (199.1.1.2) of nyweb01. Figure 9.23 shows the Host Node Properties dialog box for a host node object created to represent the valid IP address of nyweb01.

FIGURE 9.23   The host node object representing the valid IP address of another host node object

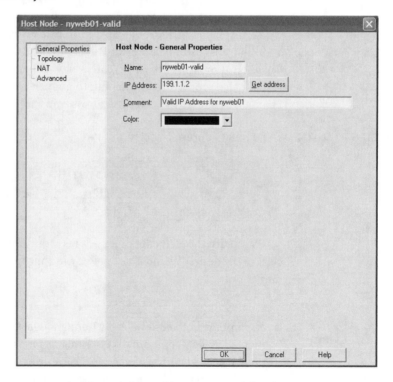

Now consider the valid IP address required for the ny-internal-lan object. The administrator for the network in Figure 9.22 requires that devices on the internal network should be translated to the external IP address of the nyfw01 enforcement module (199.1.1.1). An object must

already exist for nyfw01 (because it is an enforcement module), which will be configured with the external IP address of nyfw01. Therefore you do not need to create a new object that represents the valid IP address to be used for address translating connections from devices on the internal network (ny-internal-lan).

Configuring Manual NAT Rules

Once you have configured the enforcement module operating system to support manual NAT and you have the appropriate security objects in place that represent both the private IP address and valid IP address of devices in the network, you can proceed to configure manual NAT rules in the address translation rule base.

Working with address translation rules is very similar to working with security rules in the security rule base. To work with address translation rules, ensure that the Address Translation tab in SmartDashboard is selected, which displays the address translation rule base. To configure your first address translation rule, select Rules ➢ Add Rule ➢ Top from the Smart-Dashboard menu. This will create a new rule at the top of the rule base, which will be configured by default to not perform address translation at all. Figure 9.24 shows the default address translation rule that is created.

FIGURE 9.24 The default address translation rule

NO.	ORIGINAL PACKET			TRANSLATED PACKET			INSTALL ON	COMMENT
	SOURCE	DESTINATION	SERVICE	SOURCE	DESTINATION	SERVICE		
1	✱ Any	✱ Any	✱ Any	≡ Original	≡ Original	≡ Original	✱ Policy Targets	

To modify the elements of an address translation rule, you simply right-click in the desired element and select the appropriate option from the menu that appears.

WARNING

If you combine both automatic NAT and manual NAT rules, be aware that configuring an object for automatic NAT means the automatically generated NAT rules are placed at the top of the rule base above manual NAT rules. You cannot move existing manual rules to the top of the rule base above automatic rules. If you wish for manual NAT rules to be higher than automatic NAT rules, you must first configure automatic NAT and then create manual rules, using Rules ➢ Add Rule ➢ Top to create manual NAT rules above automatic NAT rules.

Configuring a Manual Static NAT Rule

Now let's configure the necessary rules for the address translation requirements of nyweb01 in Figure 9.22. First of all we'll examine the requirements for the nyweb01 web server, which requires static NAT. The administrator would like external devices to be able to access HTTP services running on nyweb01 and to enhance the security of the network; address translation should only be performed for HTTP connections. In VPN-1/FireWall-1 NG, just like security rules, address translation rules work on a per-connection basis, which means that you don't need to configure rules for the return traffic of a connection. This means that you only configure address translation rules with regards to the packets received when the connection is initiated from the source of the connection (the client) to the destination of the connection (the server). Once a connection has been translated and installed into the INSPECT module connections table, and return packets for the connection are translated appropriately to ensure packets arrive back at the source of the connection.

For the requirements of nyweb01 in Figure 9.22, you only need to create an address translation for connections from external devices on the Internet to the HTTP service running on nyweb01. If you think about what the original packet will look like for this traffic before address translation takes place, the source address could be anything (the connection is being established from undefined external devices on the Internet), the destination address will be the valid IP address of nyweb01 (199.1.1.2), and the service will be HTTP. Now if you think about what the translated packet should look like after it leaves the enforcement module and is sent towards nyweb01, the source address should not be modified (these addresses are valid in the original packet), the destination address should be translated to the private IP address of nyweb01 (192.168.10.2), and the service should not be modified. Table 9.2 lists the original packet parameters and the address translations that are required before the translated packet is forwarded on towards nyweb01.

TABLE 9.2   Address Translation Requirements for nyweb01

Original Packet			Translated Packet		
Source	Destination	Service	Source	Destination	Service
Any	199.1.1.2	HTTP	Any	192.168.10.2	HTTP

Let's walk through the configuration required to create a rule that performs the necessary address translation for the entry indicated in Table 9.2. Assume that you have already added a default rule (see Figure 9.24) and that you will be configuring this rule.

1. To create the rule for the entry in Table 9.2, the Original Packet ➢ Source element does not need to be modified, as this by default is configured as Any. To add the IP address 199.1.1.2 (represented by the object nyweb01-valid) to the Original Packet ➢ Destination element, you need to right-click within the element and click Add from the menu that appears, which will display the Add Object dialog box as shown in Figure 9.25. Once you have selected the appropriate object (in Figure 9.25 this is nyweb01-valid) click OK.

FIGURE 9.25 The Add Object dialog box

2. Next you need to configure the Original Packet ➢ Service element, adding the http service. To add a service object, simply right-click within the Original Packet ➢ Service element and select Add from the menu that appears. Again the Add Object dialog box will appear, however this time you can only select from service objects. For this example you need to select the http object and then click OK to add the HTTP service to the rule.

3. In Step 1 and 2 you have seen how to configure the parameters for the original packet, which is the packet that is received by the enforcement module before address translation. Now you need to configure the

translated packet parameters, which define how the original packet should be address translated. Because the entry in Table 9.2 refers to packets sent to the valid IP address, you only need to configure destination NAT, which means that the Translated Packet ≻ Source element should not be modified (i.e. = `Original`), which means no address translation takes place on the source IP address of the original packet. To configure translation on the destination IP address of the original packet, you need to add the appropriate object to the Translated Packet ≻ Destination element. After you right-click in this element, you need to choose the Add (Static) option from the menu that appears. This means that you are adding a static NAT rule (remember static NAT is the only option available for destination NAT). Again the Add Object dialog box is displayed. For this example, you need to select the `nyweb01` object from the list and click OK, which ensures the destination IP address of the original packet (199.1.1.2) is translated to the private IP address of `nyweb01` (192.168.10.2).

4. Because you only need to translate the destination IP address of the original packet, you should leave the Translated Packet ≻ Service element to = `Original`, to ensure the service indicated by the packets remains as HTTP.

Figure 9.26 shows the correct rule for enabling address translation for connections to `nyweb01`.

FIGURE 9.26   Address translation rule for incoming connections to nyweb01

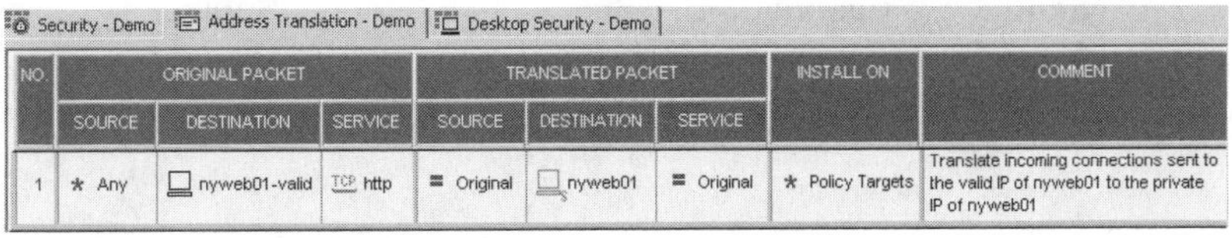

Notice that in the Translated Packet ≻ Destination element, a subscript S is displayed, which means that the rule specifies static NAT (a one-to-one mapping).

Configuring a Manual Hide NAT Rule

The second requirement for the topology of Figure 9.22 is to enable internal PCs to connect to the Internet using common web-based services. There is no requirement for enabling connectivity from external devices to the internal PCs, so static NAT is not necessary. Because the administrator wants all connections from internal devices to the Internet to appear as if they are coming from the external IP address of nyweb01 (i.e., many-to-one), hide NAT must be configured.

Because address translation rules are connection-based, you only need to define a single address translation rule, which will cater to return packets of translated connections as well. For the requirements of internal devices in Figure 9.22, you only need to create an address translation for connections from internal devices to external devices using common web services. If you think about what the original packet will look like for this traffic before address translation takes place, the source address could be the private IP address of any internal device (i.e., 10.x.x.x), the destination address should be anything (internal devices must be able to connect to any device on the Internet), and the services should be domain-udp, http, https, and ftp. Now if you think about what translated packets should look like after they leave the enforcement module and are sent to the Internet, the source address should be the external IP address of the enforcement module (to ensure external devices can reply to the packets), the destination address should not be modified, and the services should not be modified. Table 9.3 lists the original packet parameters and the address translations that are required before the translated packet is forwarded on from internal devices to the Internet.

TABLE 9.3 Address Translation Requirements for ny-internal-lan

Original Packet			Translated Packet		
Source	Destination	Service	Source	Destination	Service
10.x.x.x	Any	domain-udp http https ftp	199.1.1.1	Any	domain-udp http https ftp

Let's walk through the configuration required to create a rule that performs the necessary address translation for the entry indicated in Table 9.3.

1. To create a new rule you can right-click in the No. element of an existing rule (e.g., Rule 1 created in Figure 9.26) and select the Add Rule below or Add Rule above option from the menu that appears. This will create a new address translation rule below or above the existing rule you right-clicked within.

2. In Table 9.3, the source IP address of the original packets that the rule applies to should be 10.x.x.x (represented by the `ny-internal-lan` object). To configure this, you need to right-click in the Original Packet ➢ Source element and select the Add option. This will display the Add Object dialog box, from which you can choose the `ny-internal-lan` object.

3. The next parameter that requires configuration is the Original Packet ➢ Service element. Notice in Table 9.3 that multiple services need to be configured. Unlike security rules, address translation rules do not allow you to add multiple objects to any element, which means that you must create group objects if you wish to represent multiple objects within a rule element. Let's assume that a group object called `web-services` has been created, which includes the `domain-udp`, `http`, `https`, and `ftp` service objects. To add this group object to the element you need to right-click within the Original Packet ➢ Source element, select Add from the menu that appears, and choose the `web-services` object.

4. Now you need to configure the translated packet elements. Referring back to Table 9.3, the only parameter that requires translation is the source IP address, which should be translated to 199.1.1.1 (represented by the `nyfw01` object) using hide NAT (many-to-one). To configure this translation, you need to right-click in the Translated Packet ➢ Source element, which displays a menu. This menu will include an Add (Static) and an Add (Hide) option, because you can configure either static NAT or hide NAT for source NAT. For this example, you need to select the Add (Hide) option, and then choose the `nyfw01` object from the Add Object dialog box.

Figure 9.27 shows the correct rule for enabling address translation for connections from internal devices to the Internet for the topology of Figure 9.22.

FIGURE 9.27 Address translation rule for outgoing connections from `ny-internal-lan`

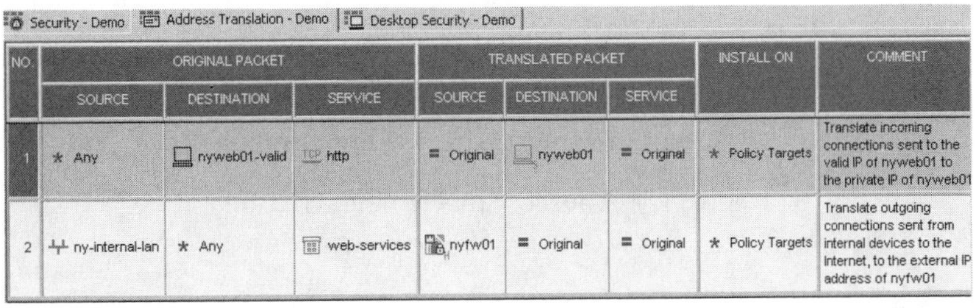
Security - Demo | Address Translation - Demo | Desktop Security - Demo

NO.	ORIGINAL PACKET			TRANSLATED PACKET			INSTALL ON	COMMENT
	SOURCE	DESTINATION	SERVICE	SOURCE	DESTINATION	SERVICE		
1	* Any	nyweb01-valid	http	= Original	nyweb01	= Original	* Policy Targets	Translate incoming connections sent to the valid IP of nyweb01 to the private IP of nyweb01
2	ny-internal-lan	* Any	web-services	nyfw01	= Original	= Original	* Policy Targets	Translate outgoing connections sent from internal devices to the Internet, to the external IP address of nyfw01

Notice that in the Translated Packet ➤ Source element, a subscript *H* is displayed, which means that the rule specifies hide NAT (a many-to-one mapping).

Configuring the Appropriate Security Rules

Before address translation rules will work, you must configure the appropriate security rules. You have already seen how packets are handled by the enforcement module when automatic NAT is configured, and you have learned that you should always configure security rules for automatic NAT based upon the original packet received. We'll now discuss how the packet flow through an enforcement module with manual NAT configured, so that you understand exactly when address translation occurs while a packet is being processed by an enforcement module.

Manual NAT Packet Flow

With manual NAT, static and hide NAT can be applied for the source IP address (source NAT) or static NAT can be applied for the destination IP address (destination NAT). Prior to NG Feature Pack 3, manual static destination NAT takes place on the server side. In NG Feature Pack 3, manual static destination NAT now takes place on the client side by default, which is identical to how automatic static destination NAT works (see Figure 9.19). For manual static and hide source NAT, NAT always occurs on the server side, which is also identical to how the equivalent types of NAT occur with automatic NAT. Configuring Security Rules for Manual NAT.

Because security rule processing always takes place first at the client-side interface, you must configure your security rules based upon the original packet received. With manual NAT, all IP addresses referenced are only the primary IP addresses of the objects (configured on the General screen). This means that for manual destination NAT, you must create separate objects that represent internal devices and their respective valid IP addresses.

If you consider the NAT rule specified in Table 9.3 and configured in Figure 9.27, based upon the fact that you always configure security rules based upon the original packet received, you must configure a security rule that includes the following elements:

- Source = ny-internal-lan

- Destination = Any

- Service = web-services

Notice that each of these security rule elements is identical to the Original Packet elements for the address translation rule in Figure 9.27.

You don't necessarily have to identically match each element of the security rule identically to the address translation rule. You must only ensure that the elements configured in the security rule are a subset of the elements configured in the address translation rule, which will then ensure all connections matched against the security rule are translated appropriately.

If you consider the NAT rule for the rule specified in Table 9.2 and configured in Figure 9.26, based upon the fact that you always configure security rules based upon the original packet received, you must configure a security rule that includes the following elements:

- Source = Any

- Destination = nyweb01-valid

- Service = http

Again, notice that each of these security rule elements is identical to the Original Packet elements for the address translation rule configured in Figure 9.26. Figure 9.28 shows the required security rules to permit access for the connections that are also configured for both address translation rules in Figure 9.27.

FIGURE 9.28   Security rules to enable access for connections that require NAT

Notice in Figure 9.28 that for each of the security rules, the source, destination, and service elements are identical to the Original Packet source, destination, and service elements for the corresponding address translation rule in Figure 9.27.

Configuring Manual NAT

In this exercise you will configure manual NAT for the same rules that you configured in Exercise 9.1.

1. Remove the automatic NAT configuration you configured for each object in Exercise 8.1 by unchecking the Add Automatic Address Translation rules option on the NAT tab for each object (ny-internal-lan and nyweb01).

2. Determine the MAC address of your external interface by using the ipconfig /all command.

3. Create a local.arp file in the $FWDIR/conf directory and configure an entry that maps the valid IP address of 172.20.1.10 (represents nyweb01) to the MAC address of the enforcement module external interface (obtained in Step 2). You must ensure you specify the correct format (see earlier in this chapter) for the file. Once complete, stop and start the firewall.

4. Add a host route that routes the valid IP address of nyweb01 (172.20.1.10) to the private (real) IP address of nyweb01 (192.168.10.2). The command you need to enter is **route add 172.20.1.10 192.168.10.2**.

5. Ensure that the enforcement module will use the local.arp file. You will need to disable automatic ARP via the NAT screen in the Global Properties dialog box, which can be opened by selecting Policy ➤ Global Properties from the SmartDashboard menu.

6. Create a new host node object called nyweb01-valid with an IP address of 172.20.1.10.

7. Create an address translation rule that enables devices within ny-internal-lan to establish HTTP connections to the Internet, using hide NAT. The address translation rule needs to be configured as follows:

   - Original Packet Source = **ny-internal-lan**
   - Original Packet Service = **http**
   - Translated Packet Source = **nyfw01** (using hide NAT)

8. Create another address translation rule that enables external devices to establish HTTP connections to the valid IP address of nyweb01. The address translation rule needs to be configured as follows:

   - Original Packet Destination = **nyweb01-valid**
   - Original Packet Service = **http**
   - Translated Packet Destination = **nyweb01** (using static NAT)

The following shows the address translation rule base after creating the two address translation rules.

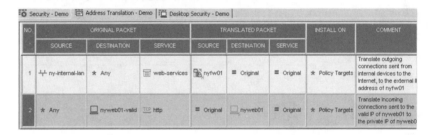

9. Now you need to ensure the current security rules are configured correctly for the manual NAT rules. The first rule you created in Exercise 9.1 for enabling HTTP connectivity from ny-internal-lan will still work, as source NAT is applied in the same manner for both automatic NAT and manual NAT. The second rule, however, will not work, as manual destination NAT works differently than automatic destination NAT. With manual destination NAT, the NAT rule is applied after packets are inspected against the security rule base, meaning the security rule must be configured for packets sent to the valid IP address of nyweb01, as opposed to the private IP address of nyweb01. Ensure the second security rule is configured as follows:

   - Source = **Any**
   - Destination = **nyweb01-valid**
   - Service = **http**
   - Action = **accept**

EXERCISE 9.2 *(continued)*

The following shows the security translation rule base after modifying the second security rule:

10. Install the security policy and verify that `jupiter.london.local` can still establish HTTP connections to the valid IP address of nyweb01. Use FireWall-1 predefined selection within SmartView Tracker to ensure that HTTP connections established from nyweb01 to `jupiter.london.local` have the appropriate source NAT (192.168.10.2 to 172.20.1.1) applied.

Verifying NAT

After you have configured your address translation rules (whether they be automatic or manual NAT rules), you must install the security policy (which includes security rules and address translation rules) to your enforcement modules. Once the new policy has been installed, you can verify that the appropriate address translations are taking place by using SmartView Tracker. Within SmartView Tracker, the FireWall-1 predefined log query in the Log mode view includes several columns that are relevant to address translation. To load the FireWall-1 predefined log query, ensure the Query Tree pane is displayed and right-click on Log Queries ➢ Predefined ➢ FireWall-1 and select Open from the menu that appears. The following describes columns within this selection that are relevant to address translation:

Source Represents the source IP address of the original packet of a connection.

Destination Represents the destination IP address of the original packet of a connection, before translation.

Source Port Represents the source TCP/UDP port of the original packet of a connection, before translation.

Service   Represents the destination TCP/UDP port of the original packet of a connection, before translation.

NAT rule number   Represents the rule number of the NAT rule that a connection matches. This field is new to NG Feature Pack 3.

NAT additional rule number   Represents the rule number of a second NAT rule that a connection matches. For example, NAT rules may be defined that translate both the source and destination IP address of the packet. This field is new to NG Feature Pack 3.

XlateSrc   Represents the translated source IP address of a packet after it has been translated.

XlateDst   Represents the translated destination IP address of a packet after translation.

XlateSPort   Represents the translated source TCP/UDP port of a packet after translation.

XlateDPort   Represents the translated destination TCP/UDP port of a packet after translation.

Based upon the configuration implemented in Figures 9.26–9.28, Figure 9.29 demonstrates the record details for a log entry in SmartView Tracker for a connection established from the Internet (jupiter.london.local) to the ny-internal-lan network (nyweb01).

FIGURE 9.29   Verifying NAT in SmartView Tracker

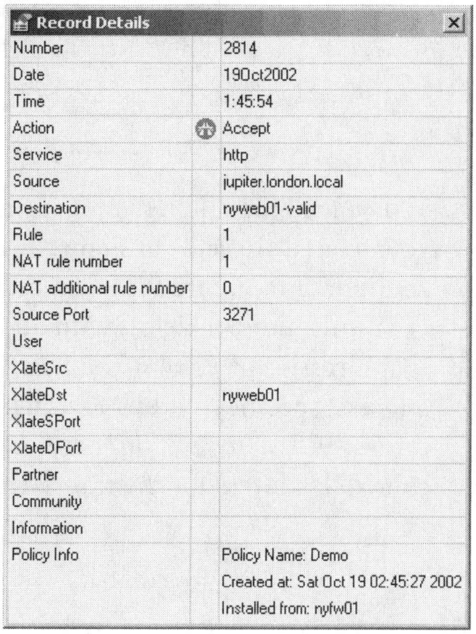

Record Details		
Number	2814	
Date	19Oct2002	
Time	1:45:54	
Action	Accept	
Service	http	
Source	jupiter.london.local	
Destination	nyweb01-valid	
Rule	1	
NAT rule number	1	
NAT additional rule number	0	
Source Port	3271	
User		
XlateSrc		
XlateDst	nyweb01	
XlateSPort		
XlateDPort		
Partner		
Community		
Information		
Policy Info	Policy Name: Demo	
	Created at: Sat Oct 19 02:45:27 2002	
	Installed from: nyfw01	

In Figure 9.29, the log entry (#2814) represents a connection that matches the rule you created in Figure 9.26. The address translation rule that you configured was a static destination NAT rule—notice that the Destination field (the original destination IP address) specifies nyweb01-valid and the XlateDst field indicates the destination IP address was translated to nyweb01. Also notice that NAT rule number 1 was matched.

Figure 9.30 demonstrates the record details for a log entry in SmartView Tracker for a connection established from the ny-internal-lan network (nyweb01) to the Internet (jupiter.london.local).

FIGURE 9.30 Verifying NAT in SmartView Tracker

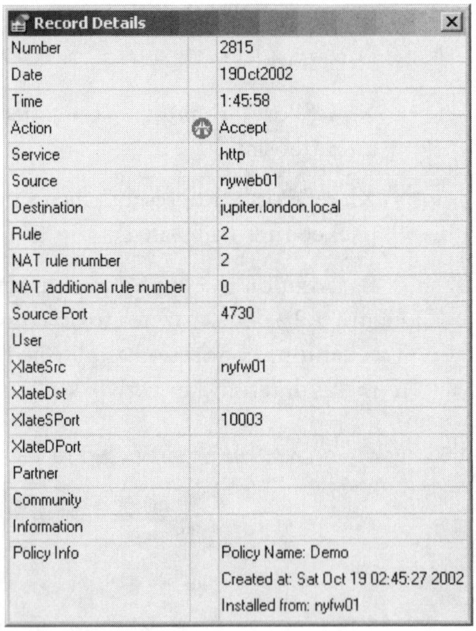

Record Details		✕
Number	2815	
Date	19Oct2002	
Time	1:45:58	
Action	🌐 Accept	
Service	http	
Source	nyweb01	
Destination	jupiter.london.local	
Rule	2	
NAT rule number	2	
NAT additional rule number	0	
Source Port	4730	
User		
XlateSrc	nyfw01	
XlateDst		
XlateSPort	10003	
XlateDPort		
Partner		
Community		
Information		
Policy Info	Policy Name: Demo	
	Created at: Sat Oct 19 02:45:27 2002	
	Installed from: nyfw01	

The log entry (#2815) represents a connection for that matches the rule you created (Rule 2) in Figure 9.27. The address translation rule that you configured in Figure 9.27 is a hide NAT rule (rule #2 as indicated in the NAT rule number field), with address translation configured on the source IP address. Notice that the Source field (the original packet source IP address) specifies nyweb01, which is a device with an IP address that belongs to the ny-internal-lan network. The XlateSrc field indicates that the source IP address for the translated packet is translated to nyfw01. Because the address translation rule configured in Figure 9.27 is a hide NAT rule, port address translation also takes place on the source port, to allow a many-to-one mapping. Notice that the Source Port field for log entry indicates that the source (TCP) port for the original packet is 4730 and that the XlateSPort field indicates that the source TCP port is translated to 10003. With the static NAT log entry in Figure 9.30, no ports were translated, as static NAT operates on a one-to-one mapping and only requires translation of IP addresses.

The XlateSPort field should only ever have a value present if hide NAT has occurred.

Summary

VPN-1/FireWall-1 NG provides two methods for implementing NAT, which can be used to implement NAT simply and quickly, or can be used to implement NAT in a manner that is fine-tuned and customized to your organization's security requirements. Automatic NAT provides a very simple mechanism by which you can configure security objects for NAT, with VPN-1/FireWall-1 generating automatic NAT rules for each configured object. This allows you to configure security objects with both a private IP address and a valid IP address, meaning only one security object is required to represent two different IP addresses. Automatic NAT provides other useful features in VPN-1/FireWall-1 NG, such as the ability to perform client-side destination NAT, which eliminates the need to configure operating system host routes for each valid IP address, and the ability to automatically generate ARP replies to any ARP requests for a valid IP address, instead of manually configuring the enforcement module operating system to do it. For all its benefits, automatic NAT has some downsides, the major downside being the inability to directly edit automatic NAT rules so that they can be fine-tuned to match an organization's requirements.

When automatic NAT doesn't meet the needs of an organization, you can use manual NAT, which as the name suggests, allows you to have full control over NAT rules by enabling you to manually create each rule. By implementing manual NAT, you can restrict NAT rules to only apply for connections that match specific Layer 3/4 parameters. When you implement manual NAT, you must configure the appropriate supporting mechanisms for NAT, which are handled automatically in automatic NAT. This includes configuring host routes for each valid IP address (in FP3 you no longer need to do this) and the appropriate operating system configuration of proxy ARP. Once you have configured either automatic NAT or manual NAT, you need to ensure that the appropriate security rules are in place to permit the connections defined by NAT. Always configure security rules based upon the original packet received by an enforcement module.

Exam Essentials

Understand how NAT is implemented on VPN-1/FireWall-1 NG. VPN-1/FireWall-1 uses a separate address translation rule base to implement NAT. This rule base consists of address translation rules that each define how one or more of the source, destination and service elements of the original packets of a connection should be translated. Address translation rules can be added automatically by VPN-1/FireWall-1 (automatic NAT) or manually by administrators (manual NAT).

Know that NAT rules are connection-based. Remember that NAT rules are connection-based, rather than packet-based, meaning a single NAT rule matches the bidirectional packet flow of a connection and handles NAT for both packets sent from the source of a connection to the destination, as well as the return packets of the connection.

Understand automatic NAT. Automatic NAT allows VPN-1/FireWall-1 to automatically configure the appropriate NAT rules for you, based on the NAT configuration you specify for a security object. Host node objects, network objects, and address range objects all support automatic NAT. You cannot modify automatic NAT rules—all automatic NAT configuration is controlled via objects. Automatic NAT supports both static NAT and hide NAT.

Understand how automatic NAT performs destination NAT. In VPN-1/FireWall-1 NG, automatic destination NAT is applied client side by default, as opposed to server side in previous versions. This means that the operating system of enforcement modules does not need host routes configured for each valid IP address that is used for destination NAT.

Know how to configure automatic NAT. Global automatic NAT properties are configured via the Network Address Translation screen in the Global Properties dialog box (accessed via Policy ≻ Global Properties in SmartDashboard). From here you can control automatic rules intersection, whether or not to perform client side destination NAT, and whether or not to enable automatic ARP. To configure automatic NAT for a particular device, network, or set of devices, you configure the NAT tab on the appropriate workstation, network, or address range object.

Understand how to configure security rules to support automatic NAT rules. Always configure security rules based upon the original packet received of a connection. Objects configured for automatic NAT have both private and valid IP addresses that can both be matched by security rules, meaning you can use a single object for rules that need to match the valid IP address of the object.

Understand the Hide behind the interface of the Install on Gateway automatic hide NAT option. When you configure automatic NAT for an object and configure hide NAT to use the Hide behind the interface of the Install on Gateway option, VPN-1/FireWall-1 dynamically hides the private IP addresses of the object behind the IP address of the server side interface of the enforcement module for each connection that matches the automatic NAT rule for the object. This ensures that IP address changes on the enforcement module do not required reconfiguration of NAT (prior to Feature Pack 2 this feature was configured by configuring 0.0.0.0 as the hiding IP address).

Understand manual NAT. Manual NAT requires you to create your own NAT rules. You must also configure the enforcement module operating system to support manual NAT, enable proxy ARP, and ensure the appropriate host routes exist for the destination valid IP addresses associated any manual destination NAT rules (in Feature Pack 3, you can enable client-side destination NAT, which eliminates the host route requirement). Although manual NAT requires more work, it does permit customization of NAT rules. For example, you can limit the services to which a manual NAT rule applies, whereas an automatic NAT rule applies for all services.

Understand how to configure the appropriate security rules for manual NAT. Security rules must be configured based on the original packet that is received by the enforcement module.

Understand the limitations of using manual NAT and automatic NAT together. To implement manual NAT, you must use the `local.arp` file on Windows-based enforcement modules, which requires automatic ARP to be disabled. At present, this is a global setting, so it applies to all enforcement modules, even if they are not Windows-based. Also beware that automatic NAT rules are always placed above manual NAT rules, so if you want manual NAT rules to be placed above automatic NAT rules, configure automatic NAT rules first, and then create manual NAT rules at the top of the rule base.

Understand how to verify NAT. The FireWall-1 predefined selection for Log mode view in SmartView Tracker contains fields that indicate how packets are translated if NAT is implemented for a particular connection. These fields include NAT rule number, XlateSrc, XlateDst, XlateSPort, and XlateDPort.

Key Terms

Before you take the exam, be certain you are familiar with the following terms:

address translation rule base   contiguous

address translation rules

Review Questions

1. An NG Feature Pack 1 enforcement module has an external IP address of 199.1.1.1, with a subnet mask of 255.255.255.0. Which of the following can you configure as the hiding IP address for a network object if you wish to permit devices within the network to establish connections to the Internet? (Choose all that apply.)

   A. 0.0.0.0

   B. 199.1.1.1

   C. 199.1.1.255

   D. 255.255.255.255

2. To which of the following types of objects can you apply NAT? (Choose all that apply.)

   A. Host Node

   B. Domain

   C. Address range

   D. Network

   E. Server

3. You wish to enable external devices to connect to internal devices, which are configured with IP addresses between 10.1.1.10 and 10.1.1.50. You have a pool of valid IP addresses with 199.1.1.13 to 199.1.1.100 currently not allocated. Which is the quickest method of configuring NAT?

   A. Configure an address range object and configure the starting IP address as 199.1.1.13.

   B. Configure a network object and configure the finishing IP address as 199.1.1.53.

   C. Create a host node object for each device, and allocate a unique valid IP address to each.

   D. Create a host node object for each device, and configure it to use a free IP address from an address range object representing the pool of valid IP addresses.

4. You configure automatic NAT for an object and leave the default global NAT parameters in place on your new VPN-1/FireWall-1 NG installation. Where is destination NAT performed for the object?

   A. Client side

   B. Server side

   C. TCP/IP stack

   D. None of the above

5. Which of the following statements are correct with respect to address translation rules? (Choose all that apply.)

   A. You can place a network object in the original packet source element.

   B. You can specify multiple service objects in the original packet service element.

   C. You can choose which enforcement modules a rule should be installed on.

   D. You can restrict the time during which address translation rules are valid.

6. A customer is using a Linux-based enforcement module and phones you advising automatic ARP is not working, even though it is enabled. What is the cause of the problem?

   A. Manual NAT rules exist.

   B. You must configure static ARP entries on your border routers.

   C. You must configure a `local.arp` file.

   D. Automatic ARP is not supported on Linux.

7. You configure automatic NAT for an object. Which of the following do you also need to do to ensure connections work for the object? (Choose all that apply.)

   A. Configure a `local.arp` file.

   B. Configure host routes on the enforcement module operating system for the valid IP address.

   C. Configure security rules that permit the connections required for the object.

   D. Install the security policy.

8. You wish to configure automatic NAT for an object. Which of the following should you configure?

   A. An address translation rule

   B. A security rule

   C. The IP address property for the object

   D. The NAT configuration page for the object

9. You configure manual NAT rules and notice that ARP requests are not being answered by the enforcement module. You have created the correct `local.arp` file, stopped and started the firewall, and installed the policy. What is the most likely cause of the problem?

   A. A host route is not configured on the enforcement module.

   B. The Automatic ARP property is enabled on the Global Properties ➢ NAT screen.

   C. A security rule is configured that is blocking ARP.

   D. There is no security rule that permits the connections configured for NAT.

10. Which of the following is true about automatic NAT rules? (Choose all that apply.)

   A. They are hidden.

   B. They are automatically created for objects that have NAT configured.

   C. Automatic rules can be modified by administrators.

   D. Destination NAT is performed client side by default.

11. When would you configure IP Pool NAT?

   A. To enable hide NAT

   B. To enable NAT for an address range object

   C. To enable SecuRemote clients to appear as if they are using an internal IP address

   D. To enable static NAT

12. You need to ensure the internal devices represented by a network object can make connections to the Internet, and also need to ensure that devices on the Internet can make connections to a single device located within the network object. How should you configure automatic NAT to support these requirements? (Choose all that apply.)

   A. Configure automatic static NAT for the network object.

   B. Configure automatic hide NAT for the network object.

   C. Create a host node object for the device and configure static NAT for the object.

   D. Create a host node object for the device and configure hide NAT for the object.

13. An address range object is defined with a first IP address of 172.16.1.1 and a last IP address of 172.16.1.50. On the NAT tab for the object, the hiding IP address is configured as 200.1.1.1. What is the valid IP address for the internal device with a private IP address of 172.16.1.10?

   A. 200.1.1.1

   B. 200.1.1.10

   C. 200.1.1.11

   D. 200.1.1.50

14. You create a manual static destination NAT rule that uses a valid IP address of 200.1.1.1 to represent a private IP address of 10.1.1.1. The IP address of the enforcement module is 200.1.1.254 externally and 10.1.1.254 internally. What should the destination IP address of the security rule configured to enable the NAT rule be configured as?

   A. 10.1.1.1

   B. 10.1.1.254

   C. 200.1.1.1

   D. 200.1.1.254

15. An internal device with a private IP address of 10.1.1.1 makes a connection to an external device with an IP address of 200.1.1.1. Automatic static NAT is configured for the object, with a valid IP address of 199.1.1.1 configured. Which of the following identifies the correct packet rewrite?

   A. Source IP address of 10.1.1.1 translated to 200.1.1.1

   B. Destination IP address of 200.1.1.1 translated to 199.1.1.1

   C. Source IP address of 10.1.1.1 translated to 199.1.1.1

   D. Destination IP address of 200.1.1.1 translated to 10.1.1.1

16. The following indicates some of the different types of address translation rules.

    1. Automatic hide NAT rules

    2. Automatic static NAT rules

    3. Manual hide NAT rules

    4. Manual static NAT rules

Which of the following represents the order that each are placed in the rule base if you configure all manual NAT rules first, with manual hide NAT rules initially configured above manual static NAT rules?

    A. 1, 2, 3, 4

    B. 3, 4, 1, 2

    C. 2, 1, 3, 4

    D. 2, 4, 1, 3

17. You configure automatic static NAT for an address range object. How many automatic NAT rules are created?

    A. One

    B. Two

    C. Three

    D. Four

18. A Windows-based enforcement module has manual NAT rules configured and the `$FWDIR` folder is regularly backed up. The enforcement module fails, and a new enforcement module is built. The `$FWDIR` folder is then restored, and connectivity works, except for connections that match any manual destination NAT rules. What could be the cause of the problem?

    A. The `local.arp` file needs to be re-created.

    B. Proxy ARP entries need to be configured on the operating system.

    C. The `local.def` file needs to be re-created.

    D. Host routes need to be configured on the enforcement module.

19. You create an automatic hide NAT rule for a host node object called nyweb01 that has an IP address of 10.1.1.1, and configure a hiding IP address of 200.1.1.1. The destination IP address of a web server is 201.1.1.1. In SmartView Tracker, you verify that you can see connections to the web server are being accepted. What is the value of the XlateDst field for each connection in SmartView Tracker?

A. 10.1.1.1

B. 200.1.1.1

C. 201.1.1.1

D. None of the above

20. A friend has heard that VPN-1/FireWall-1 NG doesn't need separate ARP configuration and route configuration on the enforcement module operating system. To which of the following types of NAT does this apply? (Choose all that apply.)

A. Automatic hide NAT

B. Automatic static NAT

C. Manual hide NAT

D. Manual static NAT

Answers to Review Questions

1. **A, B.** You can configure 0.0.0.0 as the hiding IP address, which represents the external interface of the enforcement module. You could, of course, also configure the actual IP address of the enforcement module (199.1.1.1).

2. **A, C, D.** NAT is supported for Check Point, node, network, and address range objects.

3. **A.** The quickest way is to create an address range object that includes the IP addresses 10.1.1.10 to 10.1.1.50 and configure a starting IP address of 199.1.1.13.

4. **A.** Automatic destination NAT is applied client side by default (for new installations only, for upgraded installations this setting is disabled by default).

5. **A, C.** NAT rules support the use of check point, host node, network, address range, and group objects in the source/destination elements. You can only specify a single object in any element, which means if you want to support multiple service objects, you must specify a single group object that includes each service. You can specify which enforcement modules a rule should be installed on, but you cannot restrict the time during which the rule is valid.

6. **D.** Automatic ARP is not supported for VPN-1/FireWall-1 NG enforcement modules running on Linux.

7. **C, D.** Automatic NAT removes the need to configure proxy ARP and routes on the enforcement module operating system. You still need to ensure the appropriate security rules are in place and that the security policy is installed after the automatic NAT and security rule configuration. You also must ensure your enforcement module operating system will work with automatic NAT (Linux and Nokia IPS do not support automatic NAT).

8. **D.** To configure automatic NAT, you configure the NAT configuration page or screen for supported objects. NAT rules are then automatically created.

9. B.   The problem here is with ARP, which means packets aren't even being delivered to the enforcement module for inspection. This rules out A (routing occurs after inspection), C, and D. When you configure manual ARP, you must disable the automatic ARP feature.

10. B, D.   Automatic NAT rules are shown in the address translation rule base, but cannot be modified directly. The rules are created automatically when NAT is configured for an object. Destination NAT is performed client side (before OS routing) in NG by default.

11. C.   IP Pool NAT translates the source IP address of native packets decrypted by a VPN-1/FireWall-1 enforcement module sent by SecuRemote/SecureClient VPN clients. A pool of IP addresses is defined using an address range object, and each client is assigned a unique IP address from this pool.

12. B, C.   Devices within the network only need to make outgoing connections to the Internet, so you should configure hide NAT for the network object, to save valid IP address usage. To enable external devices to connect to the internal device, you must create a host node object for the specific device and configure static NAT, as this supports destination NAT. Automatic static NAT rules are always placed above automatic hide NAT rules, so connections to and from the device will be correctly matched to the static NAT rules first.

13. A.   Careful here—the question states the hiding IP address is configured, which means that hide NAT (many-to-one) is configured. This means that all private IP addresses in the range will be translated to a single IP address (the hiding IP address). If static NAT was configured (one-to-one) and the first valid address was configured as 200.1.1.1, then the correct answer would be 200.1.1.10.

14. C.   Always configure security rules based upon the original packet received.

15. C.   Because the connection is initiated by the internal device, the source IP address of the connection is 10.1.1.1 and the destination address is 200.1.1.1. To ensure the external device can reply back to the internal device, the source address must be translated to the valid address— that is, 10.1.1.1 to 199.1.1.1.

16. C. Automatic NAT rules are always placed above existing manual NAT rules, with automatic static NAT rules being placed above automatic hide NAT rules. Manual NAT rules are not reordered at all by VPN-1/FireWall-1; hence, the manual hide NAT rules remain above the manual static NAT rules.

17. C. Separate NAT rules are implemented to enable static source NAT and static destination NAT. Another rule is placed above the static NAT rules that specifies not to translate packets sent between devices that both reside within the address range object.

18. D. The question clearly states that only the $FWDIR directory is being backed up. This directory contains the local.arp file (local.def does not exist). Windows-based enforcement modules also do not support proxy ARP configuration. Host routes are required for manual destination NAT rules, but are stored within the operating system, separate from the $FWDIR directory.

19. D. Because hide NAT does not support destination NAT, you will never see connections in Log Viewer that have an IP address in the XlateDst field.

20. A, B. The new automatic ARP and client-side destination NAT features are only available with automatic NAT (both hide NAT and static NAT are supported).

Chapter

10

VPN-1/FireWall-1 System Management

THE CCSA EXAM OBJECTIVES COVERED IN THIS CHAPTER INCLUDE:

✓ Explain the files and procedures necessary for backing up critical VPN-1/FireWall-1 NG information.

✓ Describe the procedure for uninstalling VPN-1/FireWall-1 NG.

✓ Explain monitoring the security policy with the SmartView Status view.

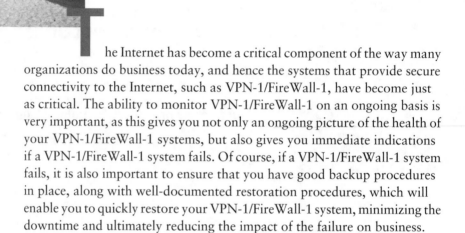

he Internet has become a critical component of the way many organizations do business today, and hence the systems that provide secure connectivity to the Internet, such as VPN-1/FireWall-1, have become just as critical. The ability to monitor VPN-1/FireWall-1 on an ongoing basis is very important, as this gives you not only an ongoing picture of the health of your VPN-1/FireWall-1 systems, but also gives you immediate indications if a VPN-1/FireWall-1 system fails. Of course, if a VPN-1/FireWall-1 system fails, it is also important to ensure that you have good backup procedures in place, along with well-documented restoration procedures, which will enable you to quickly restore your VPN-1/FireWall-1 system, minimizing the downtime and ultimately reducing the impact of the failure on business.

In this chapter, you will learn how to back up VPN-1/FireWall-1, so that you can restore VPN-1/FireWall-1 SmartCenter servers and enforcement modules if a failure or corruption occurs. It cannot be stated enough how very important it is that you back up VPN-1/FireWall-1 on a regular basis (daily is recommended)—as a VPN-1/FireWall-1 administrator you want to be able to restore a VPN-1/FireWall-1 installation quickly and accurately, ensuring the most recent or a very recent configuration is restored. An important skill associated with the backup and restoration of VPN-1/FireWall-1 is the ability to uninstall VPN-1/FireWall-1. You will also learn how to uninstall VPN-1/FireWall-1 in this chapter, which is useful if you need to restore a working VPN-1/FireWall-1 configuration on a system that has a corrupted VPN-1/FireWall-1 installation.

In the final part of this chapter, you will learn about SmartView Status, which is a Check Point SMART client that provides real-time monitoring and alerting information for VPN-1/FireWall-1 systems. SmartView Status gives you a complete, yet concise, picture of the current status of all VPN-1/FireWall-1 systems, allowing you to identify any immediate or imminent problems.

Backing Up VPN-1/FireWall-1

As with any critical system in an organization's network, performing regular backups of VPN-1/FireWall-1 is important to ensure that if your SmartCenter server or enforcement modules fail, you can restore your current security policy quickly, minimizing the downtime and its associated impact on the business. As a CCSA, you need to understand how to back up (and restore) critical files for the following VPN-1/FireWall-1 NG components:

- SmartCenter servers
- Enforcement modules

Apart from performing backups on a regular basis, before upgrading or installing a new service pack on VPN-1/FireWall-1, you should always ensure you take a complete backup of the VPN-1/FireWall-1 SmartCenter server and enforcement module configuration, so that you can rollback your installation quickly if problems occur.

Before examining the backup and restoration procedures for VPN-1/FireWall-1 NG SmartCenter servers and enforcement modules, it is important to understand the `$FWDIR` environment variable that is used in this chapter to refer to the location where VPN-1/FireWall-1 is installed. The following lists the full file system path to `$FWDIR`, if VPN-1/FireWall-1 has been installed in the default location:

Windows-based Systems   `$FWDIR` represents the `<systemroot>]fw1\ng` directory. On a default Windows NT/2000 installation, `<systemroot>` is `c:\winnt`, which means that on most default VPN-1/FireWall-1 NG installations, `$FWDIR` will refer to `c:\winnt\fw1\ng`.

Unix-based Systems   On Solaris, `$FWDIR` represents the `/opt/CPfw1-50` directory for VPN-1/FireWall-1 NG installations. You can also access this directory via `/etc/fw`, which is a symbolic link to the actual VPN-1/FireWall-1 installation directory (`/opt/CPfw1-50`).

Backing Up the SmartCenter Server

The SmartCenter server is a key component of VPN-1/FireWall-1 NG, as it houses the global security policy configured for an organization and also centrally stores security log events from enforcement modules distributed throughout the network.

To ensure the appropriate backup of the security policy database, you must at a minimum back up the $FWDIR/conf directory. This directory contains the following files that define security policy configuration:

objects.C   Defines the object database, which includes all security objects, such as network objects and service objects that are required for enforcement module operation, and is derived from the objects_5_0.C file.

objects_5_0.C   Defines the master object database as used by the management server, which includes all security objects. This file is used to derive the objects.C file for enforcement module operations.

*.W   All files that have a .W extension represent a particular security and address translation rule base. VPN-1/FireWall-1 NG supports multiple security/address translation rule bases.

rulebases.fws   Consolidates the various security rule bases into a single file.

fwauth.NDB*   These files define the user object database.

fwmusers   Lists all administrators that have been defined using the cpconfig utility and the permissions assigned to each.

gui-clients   Lists all GUI clients that are authorized to manage the SmartCenter server using a VPN-1/FireWall-1 SMART client. This list is configured using the cpconfig utility.

Another important directory on the SmartCenter server is the $FWDIR/lib directory, which contains the various libraries used to define the security logic of VPN-1/FireWall-1. Sometimes you may need to modify the files in this directory, so if you do this, you must back up these files as well.

When installing a new service pack or upgrading, VPN-1/FireWall-1 NG will overwrite files in the $FWDIR/lib directory. If you have modified any of these files, you will need to make the modifications once again in the new library files.

You should always back up your VPN-1/FireWall-1 NG licenses, as these are required for VPN-1/FireWall-1 NG to work. A good mechanism to ensure you will always have your licensing information backed up is to ensure that all licenses your organization owns are kept up to date in the Check Point User Center. The User Center is an online license repository that allows you to manage your licenses (e.g., request license details, move an IP address, or request an upgraded license) and can be accessed via http://www.checkpoint.com/usercenter.

Restoring a SmartCenter Server

The impact of the failure of the SmartCenter server varies, depending on whether your organization implements a SmartCenter server that is integrated with an enforcement module, or if your SmartCenter server is completely separated from your enforcement modules. If your SmartCenter server is completely separated from your enforcement modules, a SmartCenter server failure will normally have no visible impact on the network from a user perspective. Each enforcement module will continue to provide external connectivity, enforce the current security policy, and will cache security log events locally until the SmartCenter server can be restored.

If, however, your SmartCenter server is integrated with an enforcement module, the SmartCenter server failure will affect any connections between networks and the SmartCenter server/enforcement module. In this scenario, you will obviously be under more pressure to restore the SmartCenter server, to ensure the enforcement module component of the system can start functioning again.

When you need to restore a SmartCenter server, you need to perform the following steps:

1. If you need to restore the SmartCenter server operating system, ensure the IP address is configured the same as the previous system and that the name of the server is identical to the previous system. It is a good idea to restore the operating system to its previous version and service pack level, and apply any other custom configuration parameters to the operating system that were previously applied (e.g., security hardening).

2. Install VPN-1/FireWall-1 with the same options as the original installation.

3. During installation, enter the appropriate license for the SmartCenter server.

4. If you are using central licenses, after installation is complete, add all licenses for enforcement modules into the license repository via SecureUpdate.

5. Install the appropriate VPN-1/FireWall-1 service packs to ensure the new installation is at the same service pack level as the prior system.

6. Stop VPN-1/FireWall-1.

7. Restore the backed up files.

8. Start VPN-1/FireWall-1.

9. Install the security policy to enforcement modules.

If your SmartCenter server also includes an enforcement module, consider the implications and requirements for restoring enforcement modules.

Backing Up the Enforcement Module

If you are working with a VPN-1/FireWall-1 installation that includes the SmartCenter server and enforcement module components on the same server, you do not need to separately back up the enforcement module, as backing up the SmartCenter server also backs up the appropriate enforcement module information. There are, however, some considerations you must understand for all enforcement modules, whether dedicated or integrated with the Smart-Center server. On all enforcement modules, you need to back up the following operating system information:

Operating system route table Required if manual NAT rules are configured, although it is good practice to back up even if manual NAT is not implemented. On Windows-based machines, use the `route print` command to print the current route table and save the output to a file so that you can add the appropriate routes after restoration. On Unix-based machines, locate the appropriate startup script file that builds the routing table and back up this file.

Persistent Routes (routes that are installed even after bootup) on Windows-based machines are stored in the Windows registry, under the `HKLM\System\CurrentControlSet\Services\Tcpip\Parameters\PersistentRoutes` key.

Proxy ARP configuration Only required on Unix-based machines if manual NAT rules are configured (on Windows-based machines, the `$FWDIR/conf/local.arp` file controls ARP for manual NAT rules, so if you back up the `$FWDIR/conf` directory, you also back up the `local.arp` file). Locate the appropriate startup script file that configures the proxy ARP entries and back up this file.

If your enforcement module is separate from your SmartCenter server, then to back up VPN-1/FireWall-1 on an enforcement module, you should back up, at a minimum, the `$FWDIR/conf` directory. Although much of the security configuration is stored on the SmartCenter server, this directory includes important information such as the enforcement module certificates (used for Secure Internal Communications).

Restoring an Enforcement Module

The failure of an enforcement module generally has a much bigger visible impact on the organization than if a SmartCenter server fails, as the enforcement module is actually required for Internet connectivity or connectivity between networks attached to the enforcement module (this statement assumes your enforcement modules are separate from your SmartCenter server). To ensure the fastest restoration time, consider using appliance-based enforcement modules, such as the Nokia platform or the Check Point SecurePlatform, which can normally restore the enforcement module within 30 minutes or less.

Check Point SecurePlatform is a bootable CD-ROM that includes a security-hardened version of Red Hat Linux and Check Point VPN-1/FireWall-1 NG software. At the time of writing, this product is free (except for the cost of the media) and provides a great appliance-type option for organizations that wish to deploy VPN-1/FireWall-1 on an Intel-based server. Installation takes 10 minutes or so.

If you don't use appliance-based enforcement modules, consider scripting your enforcement module operating system installation to minimize the time required for operating system installation and configuration.

Only enterprise licensed (unlimited IP addresses) VPN-1/FireWall-1 installations support the separation of the SmartCenter server and enforcement module. If your organization possesses an enterprise license, you should take advantage of this capability and separate your SmartCenter server from your enforcement modules. This ensures that if your policy database becomes corrupted, or your SmartCenter server fails, your enforcement modules (and the network connectivity enabled by them) can still operate, and also ensures faster restoration times for your enforcement modules. It also increases the security of your SmartCenter server, as it can be placed in a secure area inside your network, instead of being exposed to the Internet if it is co-installed with an enforcement module.

When you need to restore an enforcement module that is separate from your SmartCenter server, you need to perform the following steps:

1. If you need to restore the enforcement module operating system, ensure all IP addressing is configured the same as the previous system and that the name of the enforcement module is identical to the previous system.

2. Restore the appropriate operating system routes and proxy ARP configuration as required.

3. Install VPN-1/FireWall-1 with the same options as the original installation.

4. Install the appropriate service packs to ensure the new installation is at the same service pack level as the prior system.

5. Stop VPN-1/FireWall-1.

6. Restore the backed up files.

7. Start VPN-1/FireWall-1.

8. Fetch the security policy from the SmartCenter server.

If your SmartCenter server and enforcement module are integrated, you need to ensure that any restoration tasks required for the SmartCenter server are also implemented.

EXERCISE 10.1

Backing Up VPN-1/FireWall-1 NG

In this exercise, you will back up the required files on nyweb01 to ensure you can restore nyweb01 in the event of a failure.

1. On nyweb01, stop VPN-1/FireWall-1 totally by issuing the `cpstop` command.

2. Copy the `$FWDIR/conf` directory to an alternate location, and then restart VPN-1/FireWall-1 by issuing the `cpstart` command.

3. Open Policy Manager and connect to the SmartCenter server. Take a quick note of the current security rule base and then make a modification to the rule base, such as deleting several rules. Ensure that you install the new policy.

EXERCISE 10.1 *(continued)*

Let's assume that the modifications made in Step 3 have caused problems for some users, and you wish to restore the previous security policy from the backup made in Step 2.

4. Stop VPN-1/FireWall-1 again by issuing the `cpstop` command.

5. Replace the current `$FWDIR/conf` directory (which includes the modified rule base) with the `conf` directory that was backed up in Step 2.

6. Restart VPN-1/FireWall-1 by issuing the `cpstart` command. Open Policy Manager and connect to the SmartCenter server—the security rule base should be configured as it was previously before you made the modifications in Step 3. This confirms that the security policy has been restored from a backup.

Uninstalling VPN-1/FireWall-1

Sometimes you may need to uninstall VPN-1/FireWall-1. A common scenario where you might need to do this is if your VPN-1/FireWall-1 installation becomes corrupted, and you wish to reinstall VPN-1/FireWall-1 and restore a previous configuration from backup. When uninstalling VPN-1/FireWall-1, always uninstall components in the reverse order from which you installed them. For example, when you install a VPN-1/FireWall-1 SmartCenter server and/or enforcement module, the following components are installed in the listed order:

1. SVN Foundation (CPShared)

2. VPN-1/FireWall-1 NG components (e.g., SmartCenter server, enforcement module)

3. Backward Compatibility (if selected during installation)

4. SMART clients (if selected during installation)

Backward Compatibility is a component that can only be installed on Smart-Center servers. It allows a SmartCenter server to manage previous versions of VPN-1/FireWall-1 enforcement modules.

To uninstall VPN-1/FireWall-1, you therefore uninstall each of the components listed above in reverse order:

1. SMART clients (if installed)

2. Backward Compatibility (if selected during installation)

3. VPN-1/FireWall-1 NG components (e.g., SmartCenter server, enforcement module)

4. SVN Foundation (CPShared)

Uninstalling VPN-1/FireWall-1 on Windows

Uninstalling VPN-1/FireWall-1 on Windows is very straightforward, using the same mechanism that is used for uninstalling any Windows program. To uninstall VPN-1/FireWall-1, select Start ➢ Control Panel ➢ Add/Remove Programs, which will activate the Add/Remove Programs applet. Figure 10.1 shows the Add/Remove Programs applet window.

In the applet window, you should see the various VPN-1/FireWall-1 components that are installed. For example, in Figure 10.1, you can see separate SMART client, SVN Foundation, and VPN-1/FireWall-1 components. To remove a VPN-1/FireWall-1 component, select the desired component (remember the order in which you must uninstall VPN-1/FireWall-1) and then click the Change/Remove button. In Figure 10.1, you can see that the Check Point SMART clients NG Feature Pack 3 component has been selected—to uninstall this component, simply click the Change/Remove button. After uninstall is complete, restart the system to ensure all components are removed correctly.

If you upgraded from a previous version of VPN-1/FireWall-1 when you installed VPN-1/FireWall-1 NG, if you uninstall VPN-1/FireWall-1 NG, the previous version will be restored.

FIGURE 10.1   The Add/Remove Programs applet window

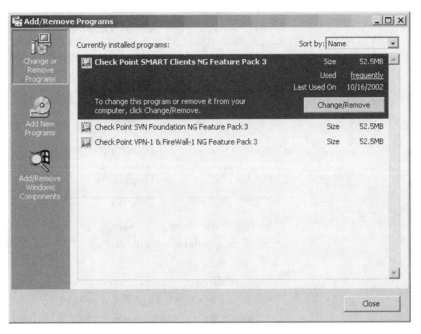

Uninstalling VPN-1/FireWall-1 on Unix

The procedure for uninstalling VPN-1/FireWall-1 on Unix-based platforms varies depending on the flavor of Unix installed.

On Solaris systems, you use the `pkgrm` (package remove) command, specifying the appropriate VPN-1/FireWall-1 package name as a parameter within the command. Table 10.1 lists the Solaris package names VPN-1/FireWall-1 components commonly installed on a SmartCenter server or enforcement module.

TABLE 10.1   Solaris Packages for VPN-1/FireWall-1 Components

Solaris Package	VPN-1/FireWall-1 Component
CPshrd-50	SVN Foundation
CPfw1-50	VPN/FireWall-1 NG

TABLE 10.1 Solaris Packages for VPN-1/FireWall-1 Components *(continued)*

Solaris Package	VPN-1/FireWall-1 Component
CPfwbc-41	VPN-1/FireWall-1 4.1 Backward Compatibility
CPclnt-50	SMART clients
CPtdps-50	Policy Server
CPrt-50	Reporting Module
CPfg1-50	FloodGate-1

The following shows an example of removing a VPN-1/FireWall-1 component from a Solaris system. Note that package names are case-sensitive on Solaris.

```
# pkgrm CPfw1-50
The following package is currently installed:
   CPfw1-50    Check Point VPN-1 & FireWall-1 Next Generation
               Feature Pack 3

Do you want to remove this package? y

Removal of <CPfw1-50> was successful.
```

After uninstall is complete, restart the system to ensure all components are removed correctly.

On Linux systems, you use the rpm -e command, specifying the appropriate VPN-1/FireWall-1 package name as a parameter within the command. Table 10.2 lists the Linux package names VPN-1/FireWall-1 components commonly installed on a SmartCenter server or enforcement module.

TABLE 10.2 Linux Packages for VPN-1/FireWall-1 Components

Linux Package	VPN-1/FireWall-1 Component
CPshared-50	SVN Foundation
CPFireWall1-50	VPN/FireWall-1 NG

TABLE 10.2 Linux Packages for VPN-1/FireWall-1 Components *(continued)*

Linux Package	VPN-1/FireWall-1 Component
FireWall-1_BC_4.1	VPN-1/FireWall-1 4.1 Backward Compatibility
CPPolicySrv-50	Policy Server
CPFloodGate1-50	FloodGate-1

The Check Point SMART clients and Reporting Module are not supported on Linux.

The following shows an example of removing a VPN-1/FireWall-1 component from a Linux system. Note that package names are case-sensitive on Linux.

```
# rpm -e CPFireWall1-50
```

After uninstall is complete, restart the system to ensure all components are removed correctly.

If you upgraded from a previous version of VPN-1/FireWall-1 when you installed VPN-1/FireWall-1 NG on a Solaris or Linux system, if you uninstall VPN-1/FireWall-1 NG, the previous version will be restored.

SmartView Status

The need to monitor the operational status of your enforcement modules is paramount in determining the availability of both internal and external access to and from your information systems that is regulated by enforcement modules. VPN-1/FireWall-1 NG offers the *SmartView Status* SMART client, which allows you to monitor the status of a VPN-1/FireWall-1 enforcement module, as well as check the status of the underlying operating system for the enforcement module. Just like each of the other SMART clients you have learned about so far (SmartDashboard and SmartView Tracker), the SmartView Status SMART client establishes a connection with the SmartCenter server. The SmartCenter server then provides status information back to the SmartView Status SMART client for each enforcement module it manages. In this section, you will learn how you can use SmartView Status to monitor Check Point hosts on an ongoing basis, as well as learn how you can manage alerts generated by security events.

Using SmartView Status

To use SmartView Status, you must install the SmartView Status SMART client on a host whose IP address is an authorized GUI client. To start the SmartView Status application, select Start ➢ Programs ➢ Check Point SMART clients ➢ SmartView Status. An authentication dialog box, similar to the dialog box presented when using SmartDashboard or SmartView Tracker is presented, as shown in Figure 10.2. To establish a connection, enter in the appropriate credentials and IP address and click the OK button.

 To use SmartView Status, an administrator account must possess at least read-only permissions for the monitoring privilege of VPN-1/FireWall-1.

FIGURE 10.2 SmartView Status authentication dialog box

Assuming the credentials are okay and the administrator has the appropriate permissions to use SmartView Status, the SmartView Status window appears, as shown in Figure 10.3.

 You can access SmartView Status from other SMART clients such as SmartDashboard by choosing the Window ➢ SmartView Status menu item. When you do this, the credentials you used to login to the first SMART client are passed to SmartView Tracker, meaning you don't have to re-authenticate and SmartView Tracker starts immediately.

FIGURE 10.3 The SmartView Status application

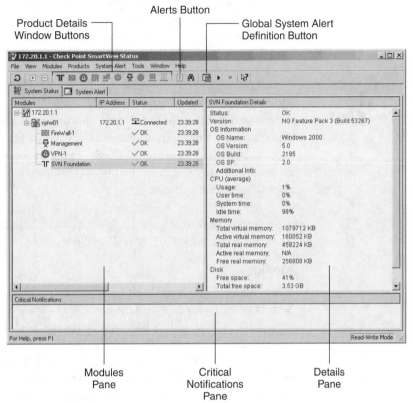

The SmartView Status application presents information using different panes or windows, which are just a particular method of displaying status information. The following lists each of the panes/windows available in SmartView Status:

- Modules pane

- Details pane

- Product Details window

- Critical Notifications pane

Modules Pane

In Figure 10.3, the pane on the left side is called the *Modules pane*, which provides a hierarchical listing of the top-level SmartCenter server (which SmartView Status is connected to) for all Check Point hosts (referred to as *workstations*) and the installed Check Point products (referred to as *modules*). SmartView Status supports many Check Point products, including FireWall-1 enforcement modules, VPN-1 gateways, SmartCenter servers, FloodGate-1 gateways, and Policy Servers (used for SecureClient policy). You can also monitor OPSEC applications using SmartView Status.

The SVN Foundation installed on all Check Point hosts is used to provide SmartView Status with the current status and information related to the Check Point products installed on each host. If you need to monitor OPSEC applications using SmartView Status, the SVN Foundation must also be installed on the OPSEC host to allow the host to communicate status and information back to SmartView Status.

Referring back to Figure 10.3, notice that there are four columns in the Modules pane, which are now described.

Modules

Hierarchically lists the Check Point workstation objects managed by the SmartCenter server to which the SmartView Status client is connected. Each Check Point host will include one or more Check Point components, or modules, which can be viewed in the Modules column by expanding a host. In Figure 10.3, you can see a top-level object labeled 172.20.1.1, which represents the SmartCenter server that the SmartView Status client is connected to. Underneath this object is a single workstation object called nyfw01, which represents a Check Point host. The nyfw01 object is expanded, which reveals the major Check Point components (modules) installed on the host. You can see that nyfw01 is a combined SmartCenter server and enforcement module, because it has the FireWall-1 (and VPN-1) modules listed, as well as the Management module.

IP Address

Indicates the IP address of each Check Point host object and is not applicable for the modules installed on each host. In Figure 10.3, you can see that the nyfw01 host has an IP address of 172.20.1.1. Notice that no modules have an IP address value.

Status

Indicates the current status of the host or module. There are various states that exist for the Status column, which all depend on whether or not you are looking at a host (workstation object) itself (e.g., nyfw01) or a particular module installed on a workstation object (e.g., VPN-1). An icon and a type represent each status. Table 10.3 lists the possible states indicated in the Status column for each workstation object.

TABLE 10.3 SmartView Status Module View States for Workstation Objects

Icon	Status Type	Description
⧗	Waiting	This status is shown when SmartView Status starts and is attempting to determine the state of a module. This status will show for no more than 30 seconds during SmartView Status startup.
	Connected	The SmartCenter server can communicate with the workstation object.
	Disconnected	The SmartCenter server cannot communicate with the workstation object.
	Untrusted	Indicates that SIC has failed. The machine is reachable but is not managed by the current SmartCenter server that is monitoring the workstation object.

The states displayed in Table 10.3 only apply for workstation objects. In Figure 10.3, the nyfw01 object is considered a workstation object, and you can see that the current status of the object is Connected. Table 10.4 lists the possible states indicated in the Status column for each module object.

TABLE 10.4 SmartView Status Module View States for Module Objects

Icon	Status Type	Description
✓	OK	The module is installed on the machine and is responding to status requests from the SmartCenter server.
✓	Attention	The module is installed on the machine and is responding to status requests from the SmartCenter server; however, there is some minor problem on the module.

TABLE 10.4 SmartView Status Module View States for Module Objects *(continued)*

Icon	Status Type	Description
⏳	Waiting	This status is shown when SmartView Status starts and is attempting to determine the state of a module. This status will show for no more than 30 seconds during SmartView Status startup.
?	Unknown	The module cannot be reached or there is no Check Point agent installed on the host.
⚐	Untrusted	The machine is reachable but is not managed by the current SmartCenter server that is monitoring the module object.
✗	No Response	Indicates that there are no Check Point modules installed on the machine or that the module is corrupted.
!	Problem	The module is installed on the machine and is responding to status requests from the SmartCenter server; however, there is some major problem on the module (e.g., policy is not installed on the FireWall-1 module).

The states displayed in Table 10.4 only apply for module objects. In Figure 10.3, the FireWall-1, Management, VPN-1, and SVN Foundation objects are all considered module objects, and you can see that the current status of each of these modules is OK. Figure 10.4 shows what happens if you uninstall the security policy from the enforcement module on nyfw01 and then stop the VPN-1 module.

You can use the vpn drv on and vpn drv off CLI utilities to load and unload the VPN-1 driver on an enforcement module.

Notice that the FireWall-1 module on nyfw01 has a status of No Policy, which indicates that no security policy is installed on the enforcement module. The icon for the status is an exclamation mark, which indicates a status type of Problem (see Table 10.4). Also notice that the VPN-1 module has a status of No Response, which indicates that the VPN-1 module is down or not responding to status requests from the SmartCenter server.

FIGURE 10.4 The Modules pane after uninstalling a policy

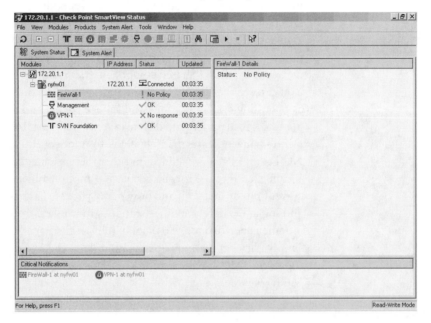

Updated

The Updated column indicates the last time that the information shown in SmartView Status viewer was updated. SmartView Status updates all information every 60 seconds; however, you can manually update specific workstations or modules by selecting the appropriate object and then clicking the Update Selected button in the toolbar (see Figure 10.3), or by right-clicking the appropriate object and selecting Update from the menu that appears. If you update a workstation object, all the module objects that belong to that workstation are automatically updated as well.

You cannot modify the update interval (60 seconds) for SmartView Status from within SmartView Status itself. If you need to update information outside of this interval, you must manually update a specific workstation or module by selecting the object and then pressing the Update Selected button (the left-most button on the toolbar). You can modify the update interval globally for all SmartView Status clients by using the Log and Alert screen in Global Properties dialog box within SmartDashboard.

Details Pane

Referring back to Figure 10.3, the pane on the right side is called the *Details pane*, and provides detailed information for the object that is currently selected in the Modules pane on the left side. Depending on the type of module selected, the Details pane will display different information. For example, in Figure 10.3, the SVN Foundation module object is selected, which displays information about the nyfw01 operating system. This information is communicated from the CPShared component that resides on every Check Point host. You can see that the SVN Foundation provides you with information such as operating system versions and service packs, and the current state of the host's CPU, memory, and disk resources. In Figure 10.3, the SVN Foundation Details pane indicates that nyfw01 is a Windows 2000 server with Check Point NG Feature Pack 3 installed and that there is currently 41% free disk.

The Details pane for the FireWall-1 module object provides details on the current policy installed and how many packets have been accepted, dropped, and logged. There are other statistics that relate to how the enforcement module is performing. To display the Details pane for a FireWall-1 module, simply click on the appropriate module in the Modules pane. Figure 10.5 shows the Details pane for the FireWall-1 module of the nyfw01 object in the Modules pane.

FIGURE 10.5 The Details pane for a FireWall-1 module

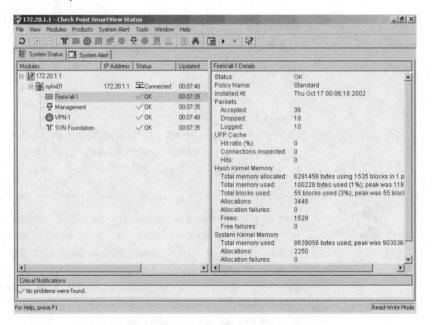

In Figure 10.5 you can see that the current policy installed is called "Standard" and that it was last installed on Thursday, October 17, 2002, at 00:06:18. You can also see that the enforcement module has accepted 36 packets, dropped 18 packets, and logged 10 connections.

For the Management module, the Details pane provides the status of the SmartCenter server and also indicates if any SMART clients are connected to the SmartCenter server. To display the Details pane for a FireWall-1 module, simply click on the appropriate module in the Modules pane. Figure 10.6 shows the Details pane for the Management module of nyfw01 object in the Modules pane.

FIGURE 10.6 The Details pane for a Management module

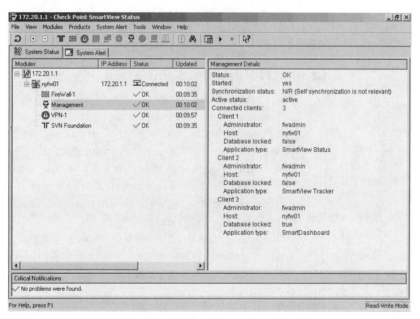

In Figure 10.6, you can see the current status of the SmartCenter server and that it is started. The Synchronization status field is only relevant if you are using the high availability feature, where a primary and secondary SmartCenter server must synchronize the security policy database. The Connected clients field indicates any SMART clients that are currently connected to the SmartCenter server. In Figure 10.6, currently three SMART clients are listed as being connected to the Management module. You can see that each of the connections is made from the local host (nyfw01) itself (as indicated by the Host entry for each connected client), the administrator connected for each connection is `fwadmin` (as indicated by the Administrator entry for each connected client), and that the connections include SmartView Status, SmartView Tracker, and SmartDashboard connections (as indicated by the Application type entry for each connected client). Notice that the third connection indicates that the Database locked parameter is true, which indicates that this client is currently connected with read/write access to the security policy database using SmartDashboard.

When an administrator connects to a SmartCenter server using Smart-Dashboard with read/write access (the default), the security database is locked, which prevents other administrators from connecting at the same time with read/write access (other administrators must connect with read-only access). This is to ensure that the security policy database does not become corrupted.

Critical Notifications Pane

The *Critical Notifications pane* is used to display any monitored workstations or modules that have currently have some problem or other critical status. Referring back to Figure 10.3, you can see the Critical Notifications pane at the bottom of SmartView Status. Notice in Figure 10.3 that the Critical Notifications pane indicates that there are currently no problems with any monitored workstations or modules, which is verified by the Modules pane, which indicates the `nyfw01` workstation is connected and all modules on `nyfw01` have a status of OK.

If you refer back to Figure 10.4, which demonstrates what happens when a security policy is uninstalled from a FireWall-1 enforcement module and VPN-1 is stopped, notice that the Critical Notifications pane shows two notifications:

- FireWall-1 at nyfw01

- VPN-1 at nyfw01

The "FireWall-1 at nyfw01" notification indicates that there is a problem with the FireWall-1 module on the `nyfw01` workstation object, while the "VPN-1 at nyfw01" notification indicates a problem with the VPN-1 module on `nyfw01`. If you double-click on a critical notification, the affected module that belongs to the indicated workstation object will be displayed in the Modules pane, which allows you to quickly navigate to the source of the notification, without having to search through the hierarchy of workstations and modules until you find the affected workstation and module.

Product Details Window

The *Product Details window* allows you to view logical groups of information related to the various Check Point products (or modules in SmartView Status terminology) supported by SmartView Status. The Modules pane provides you with a view based on the various Check Point hosts monitored by SmartView Status. The Product Details window instead allows you to view information about Check Point hosts based on a specific product, such as FireWall-1 or VPN-1. The Product Details windows are not shown by default in SmartView Status. To open the Product Details window for a particular product, you can use the Products menu or you can click the appropriate button in the Smart-View Status toolbar (see Figure 10.3). For example, to view the Product Details window for FireWall-1 modules, you can select Products ➤ FireWall-1 from the SmartView Status menu or you can click the FireWall-1 Details button on the SmartView Status toolbar (see Figure 10.3). Figure 10.7 shows the Product Details window for FireWall-1, which is titled FireWall-1 Details.

FIGURE 10.7   The FireWall-1 Details window

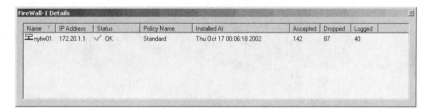

In Figure 10.7, each Check Point host monitored by SmartView Status that has a FireWall-1 module is displayed (you can only see a single host in Figure 10.7 as only a single host is being monitored). Each entry displays the most important information relevant to the product. For example, Figure 10.7 shows important information relevant to FireWall-1, because the Product Details window is being displayed for the FireWall-1 product. You can see that information such as the current status, current policy, and the number of packets accepted and dropped is shown, which gives a quick summary as to the current status of the FireWall-1 module. In Figure 10.7, notice that the Name column header has a small gray arrow in it, which is pointing downwards. This indicates that the information displayed in the FireWall-1 Details window is sorted in descending order by the Name column. You can sort in either ascending or descending order by simply clicking in the column header (e.g., the Name field) that is currently being sorted, which simply toggles the current sort order from ascending to descending or vice versa. You can also sort based on any column shown in the Product Details window. Simply click in the column header field for the appropriate column.

If you are tasked with managing many Check Point hosts, the Product Details window gives you a single view that enables you to quickly ascertain the current state of each host.

Other important Product Details windows include the SVN Foundation, VPN-1, and Management Details windows (each displayed by the appropriate product from the Products menu or by clicking the appropriate button in the toolbar). You can display multiple Product Details windows at once, which enables a management status to present information for different Check Point products at the same time. Figure 10.8 demonstrates displaying the SVN Foundation Details, VPN-1 Details, and Management Details windows at the same time.

FIGURE 10.8   Displaying multiple Product Details windows

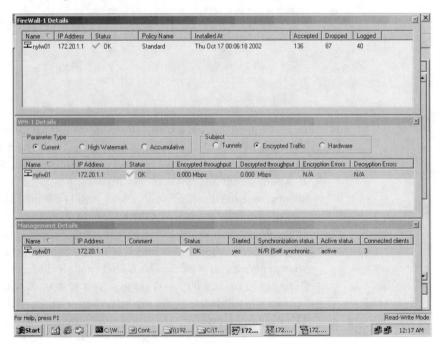

Managing Alerts Using SmartView Status

In previous chapters, you have learned that a security rule can define a tracking option of alert, and that other security events can also generate alerts. You can configure VPN-1/FireWall-1 to generate pop-up alerts in SmartView Status, which is very useful if you have firewall operators who use SmartView Status on an ongoing basis. For example, you could configure a specific security rule to generate an alert if the rule is matched, which could then be displayed in a pop-up window on a SmartView Status SMART client. Similarly, you might block an intruder using SmartView Tracker and then wish to be alerted to any future unauthorized access attempts while the block is imposed.

When a pop-up alert is generated in SmartView Status, the Alerts window is displayed (or popped up), which maintains a list of all alerts that have been generated since SmartView Status started. Figure 10.9 shows the Alerts window after an alert has been generated.

FIGURE 10.9   The Alerts window

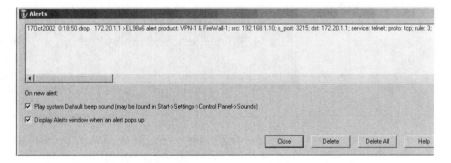

In Figure 10.9, you can see an alert that has been generated at 00:18:50. The alert includes information about what caused it. In Figure 10.9, the information contained within the alert indicates it was generated due to a security rule being matched. You can see that the connection was dropped (as indicated by the text "drop" after the timestamp), that the source of the connection was 192.168.1.10, and the destination of the connection was 172.20.1.1. Notice that you can configure SmartView Status to beep when an alert is generated (this is enabled by default), and you can also enable or disable the Alerts window from "popping" up when an alert is generated (this is also enabled by default). The Delete and Delete All buttons at the bottom of the Alerts window allow you to delete one or all alerts.

You can also view the Alerts window at any time by selecting Tools ➢ Alerts from the SmartView Status menu, or by clicking the Alerts button in the SmartView Status toolbar.

Generating Alerts in SmartView Status

VPN-1/FireWall-1 allows you to generate alerts in SmartView Status for the following security events:

Security Rules   If you wish to generate pop-up alerts in SmartView Status for connections that match specific security rules in the VPN-1/FireWall-1 security rule base, you simply need to configure the Track element of the appropriate rules with the Alert option. Any connections that match security rules with a Track element of Alert configured will generate a pop-up alert in SmartView Status. For example, Figure 10.10 shows a rule configured with the Track element configured with the Alert option.

FIGURE 10.10   A security rule with a Track element of Alert

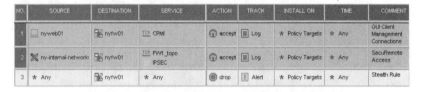

Anti-spoofing   There are other security events other than rule matching that you can define alerting for. For example, you can configure VPN-1/FireWall-1 to generate an alert if an anti-spoofing violation is detected, by configuring the Anti-spoofing section of the Topology tab in the Interface Properties dialog box. Figure 10.11 shows how you can configure an alert to be generated in SmartView Status if an anti-spoofing violation occurs.

In Figure 10.11, the Spoof Tracking parameter is configured as "Alert," which means an alert will be popped up in SmartView Status if an anti-spoofing violation occurs.

Other Security Events   There are many other security events that you can define alerting actions for. The alerting options configured for these events are configured by selecting Policy ➢ Global Properties from the SmartDashboard menu and then selecting the Log and Alert screen. Figure 10.12 shows this screen.

FIGURE 10.11 Configuring alerts for anti-spoofing violation

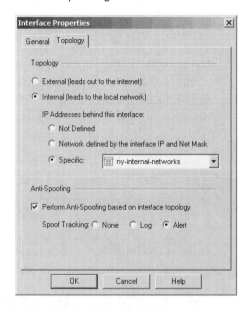

FIGURE 10.12 The Log and Alert screen

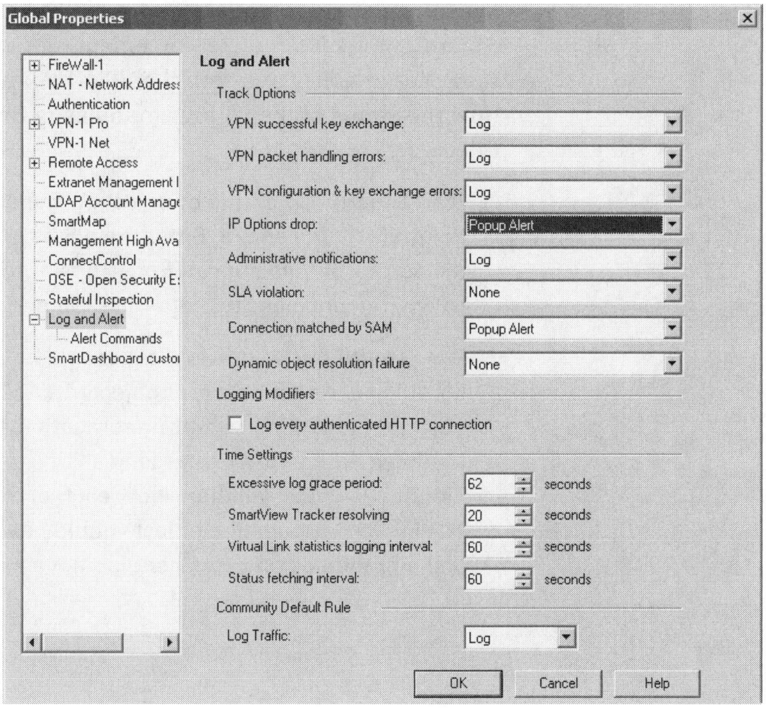

In Figure 10.12, the Track Options section defines various security events and the tracking options that are invoked for each event. If you wish to generate a pop-up alert in SmartView Status for any of these events, select the Popup Alert option from the dropdown box for the appropriate events. For example, in Figure 10.12, the IP Options drop and Connection matched by SAM events are configured to generate a pop-up alert in SmartView Status. Examples of other tracking options include Log (generate an entry in the security log), Mail Alert (generate an SMTP message), and User Defined Alert (generate a custom script or executable file).

A Connection matched by SAM event is matched for any intruders that attempt unauthorized access after a block has been applied for the intruder.

Notice in Figure 10.12 a section called Time Settings. Under this section, you can see a parameter called Status fetching interval, which defines how often the status information in SmartView Status is updated.

EXERCISE 10.2

Using SmartView Status to Monitor Check Point Hosts

In this exercise, you will use SmartView Status to monitor the nyfw01 SmartCenter server and enforcement module. You will uninstall the security policy and stop the VPN-1 component, and then see how the status of the various modules in SmartView Status are affected.

1. Start SmartView Status by selecting Start ➢ Programs ➢ Check Point SMART clients ➢ SmartView Status NG. An authentication dialog box should appear. Enter the appropriate username and password, and specify a SmartCenter server of nyfw01.

2. The SmartView Status application will now be started, with the Modules pane listing a root object of 172.20.1.1 with a single host object representing nyfw01 underneath the root object. Select Modules ➢ Expand All to expand all trees within the Modules pane hierarchy, which will then show each of the modules on nyfw01. The nyfw01 workstation object should have a status of connected, and all modules on nyfw01 should have a status of OK.

3. You will now uninstall the security policy on nyfw01 and see how SmartView Status reacts. Open a command prompt on nyfw01 and issue the fw unload nyfw01 command. This will uninstall the security policy on the FireWall-1 module of nyfw01.

4. The SmartView Status view may not update immediately, as it refreshes every 60 seconds. Force an update of the nyfw01 object by right-clicking the nyfw01 object and selecting Update from the menu that appears.

5. In the Modules pane, the FireWall-1 module of nyfw01 should now indicate a Problem status, with a description of No Policy. The Critical Notifications pane should also display a critical notification for the FireWall-1 module on nyfw01.

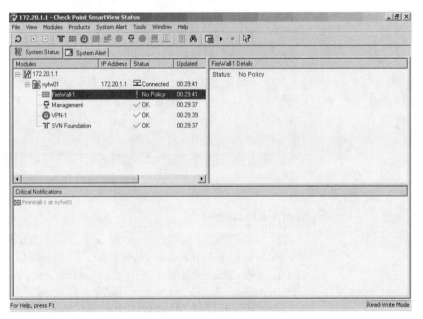

6. You will now stop the VPN-1 module nyfw01 to see how Smart-View Status reacts. Open a command prompt on nyfw01 and issue the vpn drv off command. This will stop the VPN-1 module on nyfw01.

EXERCISE 10.2 *(continued)*

7. Update the nyfw01 object. In the Modules pane, the VPN-1 module of nyfw01 should now indicate a No Response status. The Critical Notifications pane should now display a critical notification for the FireWall-1 module on nyfw01 and VPN-1 module on nyfw01.

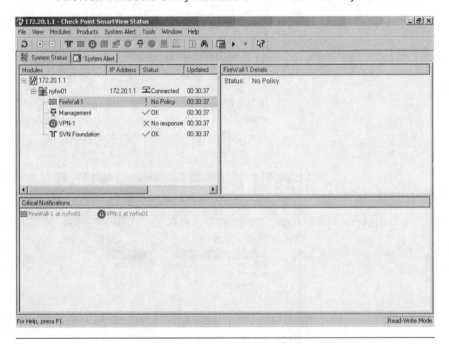

System Alerts

VPN-1/FireWall-1 NG Feature Pack 2 introduced a new feature to Smart-View Status, called *system alerts*. System alerts allow you to define custom alerts for system-related events that SmartView Status detects. Prior to NG Feature Pack 2, System Status could not actually define alerts for system events; it could only display alerts that were defined in the security policy using SmartDashboard.

The system alerts feature is based on the cpstat_monitor utility installed in the $FWDIR\bin directory.

System alert allows you to define alert parameters based on the following Check Point products:

- FireWall-1

- SmartCenter Server

- SVN Foundation

- FloodGate-1

Global System Alert Definitions

When you configure system alerts, you can configure both global system alert definitions (which apply to all Check Point hosts) as well as individual system alert definitions for specific hosts. To configure global system alert definitions, click on the Global System Alert button or select System Alert ≻ Global from the main menu. This will display the Global System Alert Definition dialog box, as shown in Figure 10.13.

FIGURE 10.13   The Global System Alert Definition dialog box

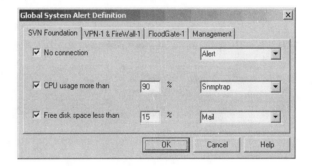

Notice in Figure 10.13 each of the tabs represent the various products you can monitor. The SVN Foundation tab is selected in Figure 10.13, and you can see that SmartView Status is configured to generate an alert (pop-up) if no connection can be made to the SVN Foundation. An SNMP trap is configured if CPU usage grows more than 90% and that an e-mail alert is generated if free disk space falls under 15%.

Figure 10.14 shows the VPN-1 & FireWall-1 tab of the dialog box shown in Figure 10.13.

In Figure 10.14, you can see various parameters that relate to VPN-1/ FireWall-1. If no policy is installed on an enforcement module, an alert of "User-defined 1" is defined, which is a configurable alerting action defined in the Global Properties of the VPN-1/FireWall-1 security policies.

FIGURE 10.14 The Global System Alert Definition dialog box

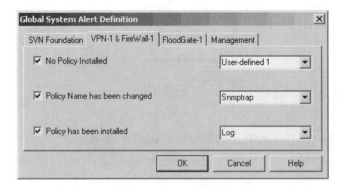

Host-Specific System Alert Definitions

SmartView Status enables you to override global system alert definitions and use custom alert configurations for each Check Point host configured. To configure customized alerts, click the System Alert tab underneath the toolbar, which opens the System Alert screen within SmartView Status. Figure 10.15 shows this page.

FIGURE 10.15 Host-specific System Alert window

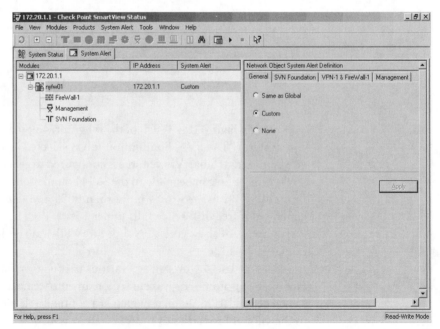

In Figure 10.15, notice that the nyfw01 Check Point host has been detected. The right pane allows you to define the system alert definition for each specific Check Point host, with the ability to define that all parameters should be updated based on the Global System Alert Definitions (by choosing the Same as Global option). If you select the Custom option in Figure 10.15, you are then able to modify each of the specific product tabs shown in Figure 10.15.

If all of the parameters on the SVN Foundation, VPN-1 & FireWall-1, and Management tabs are grayed out, ensure that the Same as Global option on the General tab is not enabled (this is the default).

Starting System Alert

The final step in enabling the system alert feature is to actually start it. By default, it is not running and must be explicitly started. To start system alert, select System Alert ≻ Start from the main menu.

Summary

Understanding how to back up and how to restore VPN-1/FireWall configuration is critical to ensure the ongoing availability and uptime of your VPN-1/FireWall-1 systems. VPN-1/FireWall-1 is simple to back up, with the $FWDIR/conf and $FWDIR/lib folders only requiring backup on a SmartCenter server. On an enforcement module, you only need to back up the $FWDIR/conf directory, although you also need to ensure you have backed up the operating system route table and any proxy ARP configuration. Although this information is enough to restore the specific VPN-1/ FireWall-1 configuration, you should also ensure information such as your VPN-1/FireWall-1 licenses and operating system configurations, versions, and service pack levels are well-documented. Knowing this information will ensure that you can restore an identical system to the previous system, without any new compatibility issues being introduced.

If a failure does occur and you need to restore a system from backup, as part of the restoration procedure, you may find that you need to uninstall VPN-1/ FireWall-1. This process is very simple for VPN-1/FireWall-1 NG—simply use the appropriate operating system method of removing VPN-1/FireWall-1 components, ensuring that you uninstall components in the reverse order that they were installed (e.g., always remove the SVN Foundation last, as this is always installed first).

SmartView Status is a Check Point SMART client that enables you to monitor in real-time the status and health of your VPN-1/FireWall-1 systems. Information such as operating system versions and load can be determined via the SVN Foundation component on a VPN-1/FireWall-1 installation, with other components providing information specific to that component. For example, you can see the number of packets dropped when looking at the statistics displayed for a FireWall-1 enforcement module. SmartView Status also provides real-time alerting information, with a pop-up alert mechanism that can be invoked every time a security event occurs (such as a security rule being matched or anti-spoofing detection) that has an alerting action defined.

Exam Essentials

Understand which files you must back up for VPN-1/FireWall-1 NG. On a SmartCenter server, you must back up the $FWDIR/conf directory and possibly the $FWDIR/lib directory if any library files have been modified. On an enforcement module, you must back up the $FWDIR/conf directory and should also ensure the operating system route table and any proxy ARP configuration is backed up.

Understand how to restore a backup of VPN-1/FireWall-1 configuration files. Restoration is straightforward—simply restore the host system to its previous state and then install VPN-1/FireWall-1 (if required). Once installed, stop VPN-1/FireWall-1 and replace the $FWDIR/conf (and possibly $FWDIR/lib) directory of the new installation with the backed up $FWDIR/conf directory.

Know how to uninstall VPN-1/FireWall-1. On Windows systems, uninstall is performed from the Add/Remove programs control panel applet. On Unix systems, uninstall is performed using the pkgrm utility (Solaris) or the rpm -e utility (Linux)

Understand how you can monitor Check Point hosts in real-time. The SmartView Status SMART client provides real-time monitoring and alerting for Check Point hosts and products.

Understand each of the views in SmartView Status. SmartView Status provides different views to represent information in different ways. The Modules pane provides a hierarchical tree that lists each Check Point host managed by the SmartCenter server and the associated Check Point products installed on each. The Details pane provides information about a particular host or product, and the Product Details window lists all hosts and a set of key statistics based on a specific product, such as FireWall-1, VPN-1, or SVN Foundation. The Critical Notifications pane indicates a critical status on a module for a particular host.

Understand each of the possible statuses for workstations and modules in SmartView Status. A workstation object can have a status of Waiting, Connected, Disconnected, and Untrusted. A module object can have a status of OK, OK/Problem, Waiting, No Response, Unknown, Untrusted, and Problem. Ensure that you understand what each of these means and when you might see each in SmartView Status.

Understand how alerts are generated in SmartView Status. SmartView Status provides pop-up alerts, which pop up in the Alerts window on the SmartView Status console. A security rule that specifies a Track element of Alert will generate a pop-up alert, and other security events such as anti-spoofing can be configured to generate a pop-up alert.

Key Terms

Before you take the exam, be certain you are familiar with the following terms:

Critical Notifications pane	Product Details window
Details pane	SmartView Status
modules	system alerts
Modules pane	workstations

Review Questions

1. You are using SmartView Status to monitor an enforcement module, and you notice a Problem status on the FireWall-1 module. What is the most likely cause of this?

   A. SIC has not been established with the enforcement module.

   B. The FireWall-1 services on the enforcement module have failed.

   C. No security policy is installed on the enforcement module.

   D. The network connection to the enforcement module has gone down.

2. Which of the following requires backup on an enforcement module? (Choose all that apply.)

   A. $FWDIR/bin

   B. $FWDIR/conf

   C. $FWDIR/lib

   D. $FWDIR/state

3. Which of the following commands is used to remove VPN-1/FireWall-1 on a Linux-based enforcement module?

   A. cpconfig

   B. pkgadd

   C. pkgrm

   D. rpm

4. You recently implemented a fix on VPN-1/FireWall-1 that involved modifying the base.def file. Last night you had to restore VPN-1/FireWall-1 from backup and notice that the fix has disappeared. What is the most likely cause?

   A. The $FWDIR/bin directory was not backed up.

   B. The $FWDIR/conf directory was not backed up.

   C. The $FWDIR/lib directory was not backed up.

   D. The $FWDIR/state directory was not backed up.

5. An organization has a distributed VPN-1/FireWall-1 installation and experiences a SmartCenter server failure. Which of the following is *not* true?

    A. Enforcement modules will continue to accept permitted connections.

    B. Enforcement modules will save logs locally until the SmartCenter server has been restored.

    C. Enforcement modules will continue to operate but will cease to accept any new connections.

    D. Enforcement modules will continue to apply NAT rules to traffic.

6. Which of the following files represents the users database?

    A. fwauth.NDB

    B. objects.c

    C. Standard.W

    D. users.c

7. You are about to install a new VPN-1/FireWall-1 service pack on your SmartCenter server. You perform a backup of all folders in the $FWDIR directory before the upgrade. Which of the following folders should you restore after the upgrade, assuming the upgrade is successful?

    A. $FWDIR/bin

    B. $FWDIR/database

    C. $FWDIR/conf

    D. $FWDIR/lib

8. Which of the following files represents a security policy rule base?

    A. fwauth.NDB

    B. objects.c

    C. Standard.W

    D. users.c

9. You need to back up an enforcement module and have backed up the
   $FWDIR/conf directory. What other information should you back up?
   (Choose all that apply.)

   A. $FWDIR/bin

   B. $FWDIR/lib

   C. Operating system route table

   D. Operating system proxy ARP configuration

10. Which of the following represents the directory where VPN-1/
    FireWall-1 is installed on a Windows-based platform, assuming default
    parameters?

    A. c:\fw1

    B. c:\fw1\ng

    C. c:\winnt\fw1

    D. c:\winnt\fw1\ng

11. When uninstalling VPN-1/FireWall-1 NG, which component should
    you remove last?

    A. SMART clients

    B. SVN Foundation

    C. VPN-1/FireWall-1

    D. FloodGate-1

12. Which of the following commands is used to remove VPN-1/FireWall-1
    on a Solaris-based enforcement module?

    A. cpconfig

    B. pkgadd

    C. pkgrm

    D. rpm

13. Which view in SmartView Status lists the VPN-1/FireWall-1 work-stations and modules managed by a SmartCenter server?

  A. Critical Notifications

  B. Details

  C. Product Details

  D. Modules

14. Which of the following components is required on OPSEC applications if you wish to monitor them using SmartView Status?

  A. SVN Foundation

  B. OPSEC Foundation

  C. VPN-1/FireWall-1 NG

  D. Log Export Agent

15. A workstation in the Modules pane of SmartView Status indicates a status of disconnected. What is the most likely cause of this?

  A. SIC has not been established with the enforcement module.

  B. The FireWall-1 services on the enforcement module have failed.

  C. No security policy is installed on the enforcement module.

  D. The network connection to the enforcement module has gone down.

16. Which of the following would you use to generate customized SNMP traps in response to specific system events on an enforcement module, such as low disk space? (Choose all that apply.)

  A. cpconfig

  B. cpstat_monitor

  C. SmartView Tracker

  D. SmartView Status

17. Which of the following SmartView Status views provides information about all hosts that have a common VPN-1/FireWall-1 product installed?

    A. Critical Notifications

    B. Details

    C. Product Details

    D. Modules

18. You want a pop-up alert to appear in SmartView Status every time a new connection is established from the Internet to an internal protected host. How do you achieve this in SmartDashboard?

    A. Configure the Log and Alert screen in the Global Properties dialog box.

    B. Configure alerting in the anti-spoofing tracking options of the enforcement modules external interface topology.

    C. Configure a security rule that includes a tracking option of User-Defined Alert.

    D. Configure a security rule that includes a tracking option of alert.

19. Executing which of the following commands would cause a status of Problem for a FireWall-1 module in SmartView Status?

    A. cpconfig

    B. cpstop

    C. fwstop

    D. fw unload

20. Which of the following panes/windows are alerts that are generated by connections matching security rules displayed in? (Choose all that apply.)

    A. Details pane

    B. Critical Notifications pane

    C. Alerts window

    D. Product Details window

Answers to Review Questions

1. C. The Problem status is indicated when the SmartCenter server can communicate with the enforcement module over trusted connections, but some problem exists. The most common example of the Problem status is when no security policy is installed on an enforcement module.

2. B. Only the `$FWDIR/conf` directory requires backup on an enforcement module.

3. D. On Linux, the `rpm -e` command is used to remove VPN-1/FireWall-1 components.

4. C. The `$FWDIR/lib` directory contains definition files (`.def` extension) that are normally not modified, but should be backed up if they do require modification.

5. C. When a remote SmartCenter server fails or cannot be contacted, enforcement modules continue to operate with no restrictions, using the most recent security policy that was installed. Any log entries generated are cached locally until the SmartCenter server is restored.

6. A. The `$FWDIR/conf/fwauth.NDB*` files represent the users database in VPN-1/FireWall-1 NG.

7. D. The `$FWDIR/lib` directory holds library files that sometimes may need to be modified. Installing a service pack overwrites these files, so to ensure any customized library files are maintained, you need to restore this directory.

8. C. Any file with a `.W` extension represents a security policy rule base.

9. C, D. Only SmartCenter servers require the `$FWDIR/lib` directory to be backed up. On an enforcement module you should back up the OS route table and proxy ARP configuration in addition to the `$FWDIR/conf` directory.

10. D. The `c:\winnt\fw1\ng` directory represents the default installation path for VPN-1/FireWall-1 NG on Windows.

11. B. The SVN Foundation should always be uninstalled last (and always installed first).

12. C. On Solaris, the `pkgrm` command is used to remove VPN-1/FireWall-1 components.

13. D. The Modules pane provides a hierarchical listing of all Check Point hosts (workstations) and installed components (modules) on each host.

14. A. The SVN Foundation is required on all Check Point and OPSEC-compliant systems that are to be monitored by SmartView Status.

15. D. The disconnected state refers to any scenario where the Smart-Center server cannot communicate with a Check Point host. Although you might also consider B as the answer, in the scenario described by B, the SVN Foundation may still be running, and the status of the workstation object would be connected, with the FireWall-1 module having a status of No Response.

16. B, D. The `cpstat_monitor` utility can be used to generate customized alerts based on system events. SmartView Status now also supports this functionality.

17. C. The Product Details window provides information about a specific VPN-1/FireWall-1 component or product, listing each host that has the component installed and providing product-specific information for each.

18. D. The tracking option of alert by default defines a pop-up alert in SmartView Status. Because the requirement is based on specific connections being passed through the enforcement module, you must define alerting based on a security rule.

19. D. If `cpstop` is executed, the workstation object will go into a state of Disconnected. If `fwstop` is executed, the status of the FireWall-1 module will go into a state of No Response. If the `fw unload` command is used to unload the current security policy, the status of the FireWall-1 module will change to Problem.

20. C. The Alerts window displays any security events generated that have an action of Alert defined.

Glossary

accept An action defined for security rules in VPN-1/FireWall-1. The accept action permits connections matching a security rule to be established. See also: *deny* and *reject*.

access rules See: *security rules*.

Account Management Module A VPN-1/ FireWall-1 component that enables Smart-Dashboard to manage LDAP directories. See also: *Lightweight Directory Access Protocol (LDAP)*.

accounting A method of security logging where each connection is logged along with the number of bytes transferred during the connection. Accounting can also be defined as the process of auditing the actions a user (e.g., an administrator) performs.

Active Connections Log (fw.vlog) Log file that contains all current connections active through VPN-1/FireWall-1 enforcement modules managed by a SmartCenter server. Compare with: *Administrative Log*.

Active mode A view in SmartView Tracker that displays the Active Connections Log file. See also: *Active Connections Log*.

actualize A process used in SmartMap to create network objects based on the implied network objects generated by an enforcement modules or external gateways topology configuration. See also: *implied network object*.

address range object A security object that can be used to represent any contiguous range of IP addresses, without having to conform to subnet boundaries. Address range objects are useful for quickly configuring a pool of valid IP addresses that maps to each private IP address in the address range object.

address resolution protocol (ARP) Integral component of IP communications where an IP device sends an ARP request, which asks for the Layer 2 (MAC) address associated with an IP device attached to the local network. When you configure NAT on VPN-1/FireWall-1, ARP must be considered to ensure that VPN-1/FireWall-1 answers ARP requests for valid IP addresses that require NAT.

address translation rule A set of conditions (elements) that classifies the original parameters of a connection that must be matched, and the NAT actions to perform on the packet. See also: *address translation rule base*.

address translation rule base Collection of address translation rules, that is applied in order from top to bottom. See also: *address translation rule*.

Administrative Log (fw.adtlog) Log file that contains auditing information that includes administrative actions performed by security administrators within the VPN-1/FireWall-1 security policy. See also: *Active Connections Log* and *Security Log*.

administrator object A type of object that exists in the users database that defines VPN-1/ FireWall-1 administrators. See also: *users database*.

Advanced Encryption Standard (AES) An encryption algorithm also known as Rjindael (named so after the inventor of the algorithm), which has been designated as the future standards-based encryption algorithm by the NSA, succeeding the well-known DES and Triple DES encryption algorithms. AES provides stronger encryption than triple DES (AES currently supports up to 256-bit key lengths, as opposed to 168-bit for triple DES) and is also less computationally intensive than triple DES, increasing the throughput capabilities of encryption devices. See also: *Data Encryption Standard (DES)*.

Alerts windows   A window in SmartView Status used to view pop-up alerts generated by security rules that specify a tracking option of alert, as well as other security events that are configured to generate pop-up alerts.

amplification attack   Common DoS attack that uses weaknesses in the IP protocol to amplify a stream of packets generated by an attacker hundreds or thousands of times, which has the effect of bringing down the target system.

anti-spoofing   A security feature on VPN-1/FireWall-1 that protects from attackers who generate IP packets with fake or spoofed source/destination IP addresses.

application-layer gateway   A generic type of firewall device that provides application-layer proxying of connections between a protected network and external networks. For example, if an internal device makes an application-layer connection to an external device, the connection is terminated by the application-layer gateway, which then establishes a separate application-layer connection to the external device, effectively making the connection of behalf of the internal device. See also: *packet filtering firewall* and *stateful inspection technology*.

ARP reply   An ARP message that is used to indicate to a requesting device the Layer 2 address of the IP device that was queried in the original ARP request message. See also: *ARP request* and *address resolution protocol*.

ARP request   An ARP message that is used to query all devices on a locally connected network for the Layer 2 address of an IP device. See also: *ARP reply* and *address resolution protocol*.

asymmetric encryption   Describes an encryption algorithm that uses one key for encryption and a different key for decryption. See also: *symmetric encryption*.

Audit mode   A view in SmartView Tracker that displays the administrative log file. See also: *Administrative Log*.

authentication   The process of establishing identity and verifying identity. Authentication is an integral component of any form of security.

authentication scheme   Defines the mechanism used by VPN-1/FireWall-1 to authenticate a user. Examples of authentication schemes include VPN-1/FireWall-1 authentication, operating system authentication, and RADIUS authentication. See also: *authentication*.

authentication types   VPN-1/FireWall-1 supports several types of authentication—user, client, and session authentication. See also: *user authentication*, *client authentication*, and *session authentication*.

authorization   Defines the systems and applications that a user can access once he or she has been authenticated. See also: *authentication*.

authorization scope   Used in conjunction with client authentication rules. Defines the services and destination systems within the client authentication rule that an authenticated user is authorized to use or access. See also: *client authentication*.

authorization timeout   Used in conjunction with client authentication rules. Defines how long an authenticated user can establish new connections to the authorized services and destination systems defined within the client authentication rule. See also: *client authentication*.

automatic ARP   Feature introduced for automatic NAT rules in VPN-1/FireWall-1 NG that eliminates the requirement to configure operating system ARP support.

automatic NAT   Feature provided by VPN-1/FireWall-1 that enables you to configure the valid IP address on the same object that represents the internal device, with VPN-1/FireWall-1 configuring the appropriate NAT rules for you automatically. Automatic NAT rules cannot be modified and apply for all services. Compare with: *manual NAT*.

Before Last   A location in the Check Point security rule base used to place implied security rules. Any implied security rules configured to be placed Before Last are placed before the last explicit security rule.

bidirectional   The communication flow of a connection between two devices. A bidirectional connection means that both devices can send information to each other (i.e., each device is both a sender and receiver). If a connection is *unidirectional*, only one device can send information to the other (i.e., one device is the sender and one device is the receiver). UDP and TCP connections are bidirectional connections.

binding order   The order in which network interfaces are bound to the TCP/IP protocol stack in Microsoft Windows systems.

blocking   The process of blocking connections from the source of an active connection in the Active Connections Log, which you suspect is an intruder attempting to gain access to your network. See also: *blocking scope*, *blocking timeout*, and *Force this blocking*.

blocking scope   Scope to which a block applies. The scope can be to a specific type of connection, from the source of a blocked connection, or to the destination of a blocked connection. See also: *blocking*.

blocking timeout   Length of time a block should be applied. This can be indefinite or a configurable amount of minutes. See also: *blocking*.

central licenses   The new and recommended type of licensing in VPN-1/FireWall-1 NG, where all licenses for all VPN-1/FireWall-1 components are centrally licensed to the SmartCenter server IP address. These licenses are only supported on VPN-1/FireWall-1 NG systems. Compare with: *local licenses*.

certificate   An electronic document that verifies the identity of a computer system, application, or user. Certificates are issued and signed by a certificate authority (CA) and work on the premise that if you trust the CA, you trust the entity presenting a signed certificate to you. See also: *certificate authority (CA)* and *public key infrastructure (PKI)*.

certificate authority (CA)   An integral component of a PKI that is responsible for maintaining and issuing certificates for computer systems and users. See also: *certificate* and *public key infrastructure (PKI)*.

certificate key   A numeric value that identifies a specific VPN-1/FireWall-1 license that has been sold to a customer. The certificate key is used to generate the license and is similar in concept to a serial number.

Check Point configuration tool   Configuration utility also known as cpconfig that is used to perform system-level configuration of VPN-1/FireWall-1, such as licenses, GUI clients, and administrators.

Check Point Log Manager   See: *SmartView Tracker*.

Check Point objects   Security objects used in SmartDashboard to represent Check Point systems. Common types of Check Point objects include Check Point gateways, which represent enforcement modules and Check Point hosts, which typically represent a SmartCenter server. See also: *enforcement module*, *gateway*, and *SmartCenter server*.

cleanup rule   A recommended security rule that is matched last in the security rule base and ensures any traffic not matched by rules in the security rule base is dropped and logged.

client authentication   A type of authentication on VPN-1/FireWall-1 that provides authentication for all services, but by default requires users to explicitly authenticate with either the HTTP or TELNET security server (i.e., client authentication is non-transparent). Once authenticated, a user is authorized for access to all services and destination systems specified in the rule, or a subset of these, depending on how the user signs in. Derivatives of client authentication exist that make client authentication transparent. Compare with: *user authentication* and *session authentication*.

client side   The point at which the INSPECT module examines a packet. Client-side inspection occurs immediately after a packet has first been received at the ingress interface. Compare with: *server side*.

connection persistence   Behavior of enforcement modules after a new policy is installed. If connections are currently active that are no longer permitted by a new policy, the connection persistence configuration determines if the existing connections are immediately dropped, or if the existing connections are permitted to continue until the connection is no longer required.

Content Vector Protocol (CVP)   A Check Point protocol that enables enforcement modules to forward HTTP, SMTP, and FTP content to external content security servers for anti-virus checking and content filtering.

control decisions   Used in the stateful inspection engine of VPN-1/FireWall-1 to determine how a packet should be handled. Examples of control decisions include accepting a packet and rejecting a packet. See also: *stateful inspection technology*.

CPShared   See: *SVN Foundation.*

credentials   Most commonly the unique combination of username and password that identifies a user to an authentication server and verifies that the user is who he or she claims to be. Credentials may also include other formats, such as a certificate.

Critical Notifications pane   A pane in Smart-View Status that displays any events that are considered critical. See also: *SmartView Status.*

Critical Notifications view   Provides critical notifications in a separate view, which are generated in response to status changes of workstations and or modules.

custom log query   A customized view in SmartView Tracker that displays fields and includes filters showing information specific to the needs of administrators. Custom queries are saved and can be applied at any time as required, providing a convenient mechanism to quickly filter information. See also: *filters*, *log query*, and *predefined log query.*

daemons   Server-side application-layer services that run on a system. In a client/server protocol, the service that provides the server-side functionality of the protocol can be referred to as a daemon. Application-layer gateways implement daemons for each application-layer protocol that they must proxy, which causes scalability and performance issues if many application-layer protocols must support. See also: *application-layer gateway.*

Data Encryption Standard (DES)   An encryption algorithm originally used by the U.S.

military but now commonly used throughout the world. The original DES algorithm uses 56-bit key strengths; however, 40-bit DES is widely deployed, which is due to previous export restrictions that were in place for encryption technologies outside the U.S. The 40-bit and 56-bit versions of DES are no longer suitable for data privacy functions, as DES crackers can now crack encrypted information within hours by brute force. Triple DES is a derivative of the DES algorithm, and essentially uses three 56-bit keys to pass data through the DES algorithm three times, providing an effective key strength of 168 bits. Although much more secure than DES, triple DES is computationally intensive and thus affects the maximum throughput of encryption devices. The Advanced Encryption Standard (AES) has been chosen as the successor to triple DES, which provides stronger keys (up to 256-bit currently) and is much less computationally intensive than triple DES. See also: *Advanced Encryption Standard (AES).*

data integrity   Feature provided by secure communications protocols, such as IPSec, which ensures that data sent from one device to another is not tampered with in transit, or another device does not impersonate the sending device by replaying packets sent. See also: *authentication, Encapsulating Security Payload,* and *IPSec.*

default rule   A hidden rule that is applied always at the end of the rule base. The default rule drops any traffic not matched by the security rule base, without logging the dropped traffic. It is recommended that you implement a cleanup rule just before the default rule, which ensures dropped traffic is also logged.

denial of service (DoS) An attack against an organization's information systems that is designed to disrupt and/or deny access to the services provided by those systems. DoS attacks have recently been popular in the press, with many successful DoS attacks affecting notable websites on the Internet.

deny An action defined for security rules in VPN-1/FireWall-1. Any connection requests that match a security rule that has an action of deny configured are dropped. See also: *accept* and *reject*.

destination NAT Refers to NAT that is required to translate the destination IP address for connections that are initiated to the valid IP address representing an internal device. Compare with: *source NAT*.

Details pane A pane in SmartView Status that displays specific details relating to a module on a specific workstation in the Modules pane. See also: *modules, Modules pane, SmartView Status*, and *workstations*.

Details view A view in SmartView Status that displays detailed information for the current workstation or module selected in the Modules view. See also: *Modules view*.

Diffie-Hellman A key generation algorithm that allows two parties to securely generate a shared session key that can be used for symmetric encryption, without having to exchange the shared session key across a network. This

algorithm is used in protocols such as IPSec. See also: *IPSec* and *symmetric encryption*.

Disable a Rule The process of disabling a rule in the security rule base, which means the rule will not be enforced by enforcement modules, but still exists in the security policy. Compare with: *Hide a Rule*.

distinguished name Defines the full path of an object identified by a certificate in an X.500 directory, using X.500 nomenclature. All certificates are issued to objects that exist within an X.500 directory. See also: *certificate, certificate authority (CA)*, and *public key infrastructure (PKI)*.

dynamic NAT See: *hide NAT*.

e-business Organizations and individuals conducting business electronically over the Internet.

eitherbound Packets being analyzed by a VPN-1/FireWall-1 enforcement module are inspected inbound (when the packet is received) and outbound (when the packet is sent) by the INSPECT module. Eitherbound is the default mode of inspection in VPN-1/FireWall-1 NG. See also: *INSPECT module, inbound*, and *outbound*.

Encapsulating Security Payload (ESP) An IP transport-layer protocol that forms part of the IP Security (IPSec) standard. ESP provides authentication, confidentiality, data integrity, and non-repudiation services for the encrypted payload of IPSec packets. See also: *authentication, data integrity*, and *IPSec*.

Enforcement Module   Component of VPN-1/FireWall-1 that normally forms a gateway between the internal networks of an organization and external networks such as the Internet. Enforces the security policy distributed by the SmartCenter Server component and also generates security log events and forwards these to the SmartCenter Server. See also: *SmartCenter Server*.

Event Logging API (ELA)   An API that third-party developers can use to enable OPSEC applications to generate security log events and store these in the VPN-1/FireWall-1 security logs. Compare with: *Log Export API*.

explicit rules   Any security rule that has been manually defined by a security administrator. Contrast with: *implied rules*.

external interface   The network interface on a firewall that connects to the Internet.

extranet virtual private network (VPN) A virtual private network that securely connects the internal networks of two separate organizations together, using a public network (such as the Internet). See also: *virtual private network*, *intranet VPN*, and *remote access VPN*.

failed authentication attempts   Used in conjunction with client authentication rules. Defines the number of consecutive failed authentication attempts that must occur before a client authentication connection to the VPN-1/FireWall-1 security servers is terminated. See also: *client authentication*.

filters   A filter forms part of a log query, and defines the information that should only be displayed within a specific column in the SmartView Tracker records pane. See also: *log query*, *Records pane*, and *SmartView Tracker*.

fingerprint   A field on a certificate that includes a hash of the contents of the certificate, which can be used to identify the system presenting the certificate. The fingerprint is used in VPN-1/FireWall-1 to allow SMART clients to ensure that the SmartCenter server they are connecting to is legitimate.

firewall   A generic device that provides a gateway between the internal networks of an organization and external networks, such as the Internet. A firewall implements access control for connections between connected networks, ensuring that only connections permitted by the security policy of the organization are permitted. See also: *application-layer gateway*, *packet filtering firewall*, and *stateful inspection technology*.

flows   A connection between two devices. Internet communications generally follow a client/server paradigm, where a client (also known as the source of the connection) establishes a connection to a server (also known as the destination of the connection) for the purposes of exchanging information. A flow implies direction and is defined as the direction from the client (source) to the server (destination); however, flows (connections) are bidirectional, with traffic flowing from the client to the server and return traffic flowing from the server to client.

Force this blocking   Defines where blocking should be applied. Choices include only on the enforcement module that hosts the blocked connection or on all enforcement modules. See also: *blocking*.

fragmentation The process by which IP packets are split into fragments, to ensure that the MTU of the Layer 2 media that the IP packet is being placed onto is not exceeded. Fragmentation is used in many DoS attacks and can be used to bypass a firewall's access control mechanism. See also: *maximum transmission unit (MTU)*.

fully automatic Used in conjunction with client authentication rules. Permits session authentication to authorize access to all other services and destinations described in the client authentication rule. This means that users don't have to manually connect to the security servers for client authentication, instead they use the session authentication agent installed locally. See also: *manual* and *partially automatic*.

gateway A computer system or network device that includes more than one network interface and, therefore, provides a gateway between two or more networks. Enforcement modules are commonly referred to as gateways. Compare with: *host*. See also: *Check Point objects* and *enforcement module*.

group object A type of object that exists in the users database that is used to group user objects and administrator objects. Group objects are the only objects in the users database that can be defined in security rules. See also: *users database*.

hash See: *message digest*.

Hide a Rule The process of hiding a rule in the security rule base, which makes the security rule base easier to read and manage, but still enforces the rule on enforcement modules. Compare with: *Disable a Rule*.

hide NAT A form of NAT that is used to hide the private IP addresses of many internal devices behind a single valid IP address (many-to-one). Hide NAT can only be used for source NAT (connections established from the private IP addresses to external valid IP addresses). Compare with: *static NAT*.

host A workstation, computer system, or machine that only has a single network interface connection. Compare with: *gateway*.

host route A route that specifies the next-hop IP address of a single host. Host routes are required for manual NAT rules on VPN-1/FireWall-1.

hybrid mode authentication Defines authentication where two different authentication mechanisms are combined. In VPN-1/FireWall-1 NG, hybrid mode authentication enables remote access VPN connections to be authenticated at both a machine level and at a user level by supporting any user-based authentication scheme, such as RADIUS.

implicit client authentication Used in conjunction with client authentication rules and describes partially automatic client authentication rules. See also: *partially automatic*.

implied network object A network object in SmartMap that is automatically generated via the topology configuration for an enforcement module or gateway. Implied network objects cannot be configured and must be actualized to enable configuration of these objects. See also: *actualize*.

implied rules (implicit rules)   Any security rule that has been automatically generated by VPN-1/FireWall-1 NG. Implied rules are configured via Policy ➤ Global Properties ➤ FireWall-1 in the SmartDashboard. Compare with: *explicit rules*.

in-band authentication   Authentication that occurs within an application-layer protocol. Protocols such as HTTP and TELNET support in-band authentication. VPN-1/FireWall-1 provides in-band authentication for HTTP, TELNET, FTP, and RLOGIN connections. Compare with: *out-of-band authentication*.

inbound   Defines the point at which packets being received by an enforcement module are being inspected by the INSPECT module. See also: *INSPECT module, eitherbound*, and *outbound*.

INSPECT   A high-level scripting language used by VPN-1/FireWall-1 that defines security rules and policy on an enforcement module. See also: *inspection script* and *INSPECT module*.

INSPECT module   The kernel-mode component of a VPN-1/FireWall-1 enforcement module that is responsible for intercepting packets received from or sent out a network interface and applying security inspection of those packets. See also: *INSPECT* and *inspection script*.

inspection code   The low-level machine language generated by from an inspection script, that contains the CPU commands used to implement security policy. See also: *INSPECT* and *inspection script*.

inspection script   A script written in INSPECT that defines the security policy enforced by the INSPECT module. See also: *INSPECT* and *INSPECT module*.

installation manager   A component of the SmartUpdate SMART client, which is used for managing VPN-1/FireWall-1 software installations, service pack upgrades, version upgrades, and rollbacks. See also: *SmartUpdate*.

internal certificate authority (ICA)   An internal certificate authority that ships with VPN-1/FireWall-1 NG, allowing VPN-1/FireWall-1 NG to issue certificates to SmartCenter servers and enforcement modules out of the box, without deploying a separate PKI. The ICA is only used for securing communications between Check Point products.

Internet Gateway   A VPN-1/FireWall-1 product that integrates the SmartCenter server and enforcement module onto a single platform and is licensed to protect up to 250 IP addresses. For installations that require protection for more than 250 IP addresses, or that need to separate the SmartCenter server and enforcement module, an Enterprise version of the product is required.

intranet VPN   A virtual private network that securely connects separate departments, business units, or geographical locations, using either a private or public network (such as a

Service Provider network). See also: *virtual private network*, *extranet VPN*, and *remote access VPN*.

IP Version 4 (IPv4)   The current implementation of IP used throughout the world. IPv4 defines a 32-bit address space, which has caused problems with limited address space being available for the continuously increasing number of organizations being connected to the Internet.

IPSec (Internet Protocol Security)   A set of transport-layer protocols that provide a framework for providing secure communications over an IP network. IPSec provides authentication, data confidentiality, data integrity, and non-repudiation features. See also: *authentication*, *data integrity*, and *Encapsulating Security Payload*.

Kernel mode   Indicates that a software application runs as part of the operating system kernel, which provides faster performance. The INSPECT module is a kernel mode component of an enforcement module. Compare with: *User mode*

kernel side   The log event generation process and describes the enforcement module components that generate log fragments.

License Manager   A component of the SmartUpdate SMART client, which is used for managing VPN-1/FireWall-1 central licenses. See also: *SmartUpdate*.

Lightweight Directory Access Protocol (LDAP)   A protocol used for accessing X.500 databases, which store information about the entities within an organization and also include the hierarchical structure of the organization. See also: *Account Management Module*.

local licenses   Represents the historical type of licensing used in versions of VPN-1/FireWall-1 prior to NG, where each VPN-1/FireWall-1 component is licensed locally to a local IP address. Compare with: *central licenses*.

local.arp   File used on Windows systems to provide proxy ARP functionality. This is required for installations that use manual NAT.

log entry   A representation of a security event in SmartView Tracker. See also: *log fragments*.

Log Export API   An API that third-party developers can use to enable OPSEC applications to capture security log events and perform analysis of those events. Compare with: *Event Logging API*.

log fragments   Logging information specific to a logging record that is generated by the various enforcement module components as a packet is passed through an enforcement module. Log fragments are consolidated into logging records, which ensure all logging information is associated with a connection. See also: *log entry*.

Log mode   A view in SmartView Tracker that displays the security log file. See also: *Security Log*.

log query   A set of attributes that defines a specific view in the SmartView Tracker Records pane. A log query defines any filters applied to columns, the visibility of columns, and the width of columns. See also: *filters, Records pane,* and *SmartView Tracker.*

log records A collection of log fragments that are generated as a packet passes through an enforcement module. Each log record is associated with a connection, and is passed to the SmartCenter server. Log records are then combined into the log entry that represents an existing connection, or a new log entry is generated if the log record describes a new connection. See also: *log fragments* and *log entry.*

Log Unique Unification Identifier (LUUID) An identification field that is attached to each log record to identify log records sent by an enforcement module to the SmartCenter server. See also: *log records.*

Log Viewer See: *SmartView Tracker.*

Logical Server Provides a virtual representation of an internal group or cluster of servers providing a common service (such as web servers). VPN-1/FireWall-1 includes licensed features that enable it to load balance and redirect connections to the Logical Server, ensuring a single server does not get overloaded while other servers remain idle.

MAC address The Layer 2 Ethernet address used for uniquely identifying a host on the Layer 2 network.

management clients See: *SMART clients.*

management server See: *SmartCenter server.*

manual Used in conjunction with client authentication rules. Requires users to authenticate with the HTTP or TELNET security server to authorize access to the services and destinations defined in the client authentication rule. See also: *partially automatic* and *fully automatic.*

manual NAT Implemented when administrators define their own NAT rules. Manual NAT rules enable you to fine-tune NAT rules, but require configuration of the operating system route table and proxy ARP configured, and the disabling of automatic ARP globally on the SmartCenter server. Compare with: *automatic NAT.*

many-to-one NAT as provided by hide NAT. Many refers to many private IP addresses and one refers to a single valid IP address. See also: *hide NAT.*

master In a distributed VPN-1/FireWall-1 installation, each enforcement module has the concept of a master, which defines the SmartCenter server that the enforcement module receives security policy from and also where the enforcement module sends log records to.

maximum transmission unit (MTU) The maximum size of frames that can be sent on a Layer 2 media, such as Ethernet or ATM. For example, Ethernet networks have an MTU of 1500 bytes, meaning up to 1500 bytes of data can be sent in a single Ethernet frame. If upper-layer protocols (such as IP) present packets that exceed the MTU, fragmentation can take place, which involves splitting the packet into fragments. See also: *fragmentation.*

message digest Also known as a hash, this is the output of a hashing algorithm. A hashing algorithm is a one-way algorithm that takes a variable-length message as input and produces a fixed-length output (message digest) that is unique to the original message, but cannot be used to derive the message (hence the term one-way). A message digest can be attached to a message to ensure that the original contents of the message are not altered in transit, providing assurances of the integrity of the data. See also: *data integrity*.

module   Used in SmartView Status to refer to a Check Point component installed on a workstation. See also: *SmartView Status*.

Modules   Represent specific Check Point products installed on Check Point systems being monitored by SmartView Status. See also: *Modules pane*, *SmartView Status*, and *workstations*.

Modules pane   A pane in SmartView Status that displays all workstations (Check Point systems) and modules (Check Point products) being monitored via SmartView Status. See also: *modules*, *SmartView Status*, and *workstations*.

Modules view   A hierarchical view in SmartView Status that displays each Check Point workstation managed by the Smart-Center server to which SmartView Status is connected and the module that resides on each workstation.

network address translation (NAT)   A technique used to translate the source/destination IP addresses of packets to ensure that private devices can communicate with devices on the Internet with a valid IP address.

network objects   Network objects have two contexts in the security objects database of VPN-1/FireWall-1. In the first context, they are used to generically describe security objects such as Check Point objects, node objects, address range objects, and domain objects. In the second context, they are used to describe networks or subnets, such as a 192.168.1.0/24 subnet.

Next Generation (NG)   The current version of VPN-1/FireWall-1.

node objects   Security objects used in Smart-Dashboard to represent non–Check Point systems. Two types of node objects exist—a gateway node object (includes more than one network interface) and a host node object (only has a single network interface). See also: *Check Point objects*, *host*, and *gateway*.

noisy rule   A recommended security rule that drops traffic that is frequent and normal in the network, without logging the drop events to avoid unnecessary clutter of the security log files. Examples of this include NetBIOS traffic and DHCP broadcast traffic.

non-repudiation   Removes the ability for a party to dispute that they were the originators of some data. For example, non-repudiation might be used by a bank, so that a customer could not deny that they had withdrawn some money when in fact they had. Non-repudiation is a feature provided by IPSec. See also: *IPSec*.

one-time password (OTP)   A strong authentication mechanism used by the S/KEY and SecurID authentication schemes that requires users to specify a different password each time they authenticate (i.e., a given password is only valid one-time for a single authentication). This ensures that attackers that sniff password information cannot use that password information to gain unauthorized access to systems protected by authentication. See also: *token*.

Open Platform for Security (OPSEC) A framework provided by Check Point that allows third-party developers to integrate their products with Check Point products, enhancing the functionality of both products. See www.opsec.com for more details.

Open Security Extension (OSE) A licensed VPN-1/FireWall-1 feature that enables a SmartCenter server to manage access control lists on third-party routers, such as Cisco routers.

organizational units Objects within an LDAP database that define the hierarchical structure of an organization. The account management module is used to manage specific organization units. See also: *Account Management Module* and *LDAP*.

OS Password A VPN-1/FireWall-1 authentication scheme that uses the enforcement module operating system authentication database to authenticate users. See also: *authentication scheme*.

outbound The point at which packets being sent out a network interface of an enforcement module are being inspected by the INSPECT module. See also: *INSPECT module*, *eitherbound*, and *inbound*.

out-of-band authentication Authentication that occurs outside of the application-layer protocol connection that a user wishes to establish. On VPN-1/FireWall-1, client authentication provides out-of-band authentication by requiring users to first establish connections to the HTTP or TELNET security servers, authenticate, and then authorize access to the services and destination systems listed in the client authentication rule. Compare with: *in-band authentication*.

Packet filtering firewall A generic type of firewall that inspects packets up to Layer 3/Layer 4 and then either permits or rejects the packet. Packet filtering firewalls represent the most basic form of firewalls and do not understand that connections are bidirectional flows, instead analyzing all traffic packet by packet, without any concept of a connection. See also: *application-layer gateway*, *firewall*, and *stateful inspection technology*.

partially automatic Used in conjunction with client authentication rules. Permits user authentication to be used for any HTTP, FTP, TELNET, or RLOGIN connections specified in the rule, which then automatically authorizes access to all other services and destinations described in the client authentication rule. This means that users don't have to manually connect to the security servers for client authentication. See also: *manual* and *fully automatic*.

permissions A set of rights defined for VPN-1/FireWall-1 administrators that describes the level of access each has to various VPN-1/FireWall-1 components. See also: *read-write* and *read-only*.

policy definition point   Where security policy rules are defined and configured. In VPN-1/FireWall-1 NG, both the SMART clients and SmartCenter server represent the policy definition point. See also: *policy distribution point* and *policy enforcement point*.

policy distribution point   Where security policy rules are converted into a format suitable for a policy enforcement point and then distributed out to each policy enforcement point. In VPN-1/FireWall-1 NG, the SmartCenter server represents the policy distribution point. See also: *policy distribution point* and *policy enforcement point*.

Policy Editor   See: *SmartDashboard*.

policy enforcement point   Where security policy rules are enforced at gateways between the internal networks of an organization and external, untrusted networks. In VPN-1/FireWall-1 NG, the enforcement module represents the policy enforcement point. See also: *policy distribution point* and *policy enforcement point*.

port address translation (PAT)   Used by hide NAT and translates both the source IP address and source TCP/UDP port of a connection, enabling the translated source TCP/UDP port to uniquely identify the private device internally. See also: *hide NAT*.

predefined log query   A predefined view in SmartView Tracker that displays fields and includes selections (filters) that show information specific to a VPN-1/FireWall-1 product or feature, such as FireWall-1 or accounting records.

Product Details view   A view in SmartView Status that allows you to view the various workstations that have a particular type of Check Point product installed (e.g., FireWall-1) and also view quick statistics specified to the product.

proxy ARP   Describes when a device responds to an ARP request on behalf of another system. Proxy ARP is required for NAT, to ensure that enforcement modules respond to ARP requests for the valid IP addresses configured for NAT. Proxy ARP is automatically implemented by automatic ARP, but requires operating system configuration for manual ARP. See also: *address resolution protocol*.

public key infrastructure (PKI)   An infrastructure that stores and provides X.509 certificates that authenticate the identity of computer systems and individuals. Certificates can be used for authentication, data confidentiality, data integrity, and non-repudiation features. See also: *certificate* and *certificate authority (CA)*.

public/private key pair   Used to provide the authentication, data confidentiality, data integrity, and non-repudiation services provided by certificates. Each system or user in a PKI possesses a public/private key pair, with the private key only known to each system/user, and the public key freely available to anybody (this is included the certificate issued to each system/user). Public/private keys provide the foundation of asymmetric encryption. See also: *certificate*, *public key infrastructure (PKI)*, and *asymmetric encryption*.

quality of service (QoS)   The level of service provided to an application by the network. QoS on the network can be defined in terms of bandwidth, packet loss, latency, and jitter. For example, an ERP application might have strict bandwidth requirements of 128Kbps per session, while a voice application has strict latency and jitter requirements. FloodGate-1 is a Check Point product that provides QoS to network applications.

RADIUS   The Remote Access Dial-in User Service protocol. Provides centralized authentication services for multiple enforcement modules to a RADIUS server that hosts a central authentication database. RADIUS is also useful for integrating VPN-1/FireWall-1 authentication into the internal authentication database systems for an organization (e.g., Active Directory). VPN-1/FireWall-1 supports RADIUS as an authentication scheme. Compare with: *TACACS*.

read-only   A permission defined for VPN-1/FireWall-1 administrators that allows a specific component (e.g. security object) or function of VPN-1/FireWall-1 to be viewed but not modified. See also: *permissions*.

read-write   A permission defined for VPN-1/FireWall-1 administrators that enables full access to a specific component or function of VPN-1/FireWall-1. See also: *permissions*.

Records pane   A pane in SmartView Tracker that displays security log entries. See also: *filters*, *log query*, and *SmartView Tracker*.

reject   An action defined for security rules in VPN-1/FireWall-1. Any connection requests that match a security rule that has an action of reject configured are dropped, with a notification being sent back to the requesting system. See also: *accept* and *deny*.

remote access VPN   A virtual private network that securely connects remote employees to the internal network of an organization, using the Internet as a transport medium. See also: *virtual private network*, *extranet VPN*, and *intranet VPN*.

resource object   A security object used in SmartDashboard to forward common application-layer protocol traffic to security servers for inspection. A resource object is always associated with a service object, and can be used to enforce application-layer security as well as URL logging. See also: *security servers* and *service objects*.

rule elements   These make up the various components or fields of a security rule. Each security rule has a source, destination, service, action, track, time, install on, and comment element. See also: *security rule*.

Secure Internal Communications (SIC)
The mechanism used to implement secure communications between Check Point components in VPN-1/FireWall-1 NG. Provides authentication, integrity and confidentiality services.

secure sockets layer (SSL)   Popular protocol used commonly for secure web transactions that is used by VPN-1/FireWall-1 to provide authentication, data integrity, and data confidentiality for Secure Internal Communications. See also: *Secure Internal Communications (SIC)*.

Secure Virtual Network (SVN)   The umbrella of Check Point products that combined together provide a true end-to-end security solution for any type of organization.

SecureUpdate See: *SmartUpdate*.

Security Log (`fw.log`) Log file that contains all security events that have occurred on VPN-1/FireWall-1 enforcement modules managed by a SmartCenter server. Compare with: *Active Connections Log* and *Administrative Log*.

security objects Networks, systems, applications, and users in the VPN-1/FireWall-1 security policy. The `objects.C` file stores all network, system, and application objects, while the `fwauth.NDB*` files store all user objects. See also: *network objects*, *service objects*, and *user objects*.

security policy Normally a document that defines the network security policies and procedures of an organization. Security policies can be very broad in scope, defining anything from physical access security to acceptable Internet usage policy for employees.

security rules A set of conditions (elements) that classifies specific types of connections and then defines the actions that an enforcement module should take for any matching connections. See also: *rule elements*.

security rule base A collection of security rules that makes up the complete list of security rules that are enforced by an enforcement module. See also: *security rules*.

security servers Application-layer daemons or services that reside on Check Point enforcement modules, providing application-layer security services for HTTP, FTP, SMTP, TELNET, and RLOGIN services.

seed A variable that is used to introduce randomness into the output generated by

combining the seed and the encryption key and passing them through an encryption algorithm.

selections A selection is similar to a filter, in that it defines a filter that should be used to display only specific information within a column in SmartView Tracker. A selection also defines column width and column visibility.

self-signed Refers to the certificate of the root CA of a PKI. The root CA is the trusted entity in a PKI that generates a certificate that identifies itself and then signs the certificate itself, hence the term self-signed. The internal CA of VPN-1/FireWall-1 generates a self-signed certificate to enable it to issue certificates to other VPN-1/FireWall-1 components. See also: *certificate*, *certificate authority*, *public key infrastructure*, and *internal certificate authority*.

server objects Security objects in VPN-1/FireWall-1 that are used to define backend services such as RADIUS authentication. Each server object requires a workstation object to be defined.

server side A point at which the INSPECT module examines a packet. Server-side inspection occurs after a packet has been received and routed by the operating system to the appropriate egress interface. Compare with: *client side*.

service objects Objects in VPN-1/FireWall-1 used to represent transport-layer and application-layer protocols. See also: *security objects*.

session authentication A type of authentication on VPN-1/FireWall-1 that enables per-connection authentication of any service, but requires a session authentication agent on the authenticating client. See also: *session authentication agent*.

session authentication agent   Check Point software that resides on a client workstation (authenticating device) and is required for session authentication. When session authentication occurs, the enforcement module establishes a connection to the session authentication agent automatically, requesting authentication information from the authentication device. See also: *session authentication*.

session state   Describes the state of a session or connection in a stateful inspection firewall. For example, a connection may be in a connecting state, indicating that the connection is in the process of being established. A connection might also be in an established state, indicating the connection has been established. Session state information also includes information about Layer 3 and Layer 4 parameters of a connection, such as source port, destination port, and TCP sequence number. See also: *stateful inspection technology*.

signature (digital signature)   A field within a certificate that contains a hash of the certificate contents that has been encrypted using the signing certificate authorities private key. This means that the encrypted hash can only be decrypted using the CA's public key. The contents of the certificate are then hashed, and the resulting hash output is compared with the decrypted hash (signature). If the two hashes do not match, the authenticating device knows that the certificate has either been tampered with or signed by an invalid certificate authority. The signature provides authentication and data

integrity services. See also: *certificate, certificate authority*, and *public/private key pair*.

SMART clients   Used to provide a GUI to the VPN-1/FireWall-1 security policy defined on a SmartCenter server (using SmartDashboard), as well as accessing security logs (using SmartView Tracker) and monitoring the status of VPN-1/FireWall-1 hosts and products (using SmartView Status). Previously known as management clients. See also: *SmartCenter server* and *enforcement module*.

SmartCenter server   Central component of VPN-1/FireWall-1 that stores the security policy database, distributes the appropriate security policy to each enforcement module, and stores security log events generated by enforcement modules. Security administrators use SMART clients to configure and manage the security policy defined at the SmartCenter server. Previously known as management server. See also: *SMART clients* and *enforcement module*.

SmartDashboard   A Check Point GUI SMART client that is used to configure security policy on a VPN-1/FireWall-1 SmartCenter server. Previously known as Policy Editor. See also: *SMART clients* and *SmartCenter server*.

SmartMap   A licensed graphical application that is part of SmartDashboard, which maps out the IP topology of the entire internetwork as configured in VPN-1/FireWall-1. This view provides a logical representation of the network and can be used to identify the flows between systems that are permitted or rejected by security rules.

SmartUpdate   Check Point SMART client that is used to manage licenses centrally and also Check Point product versions and upgrades. Previously known as SecureUpdate. See also: *SMART clients*.

SmartView Status A Check Point SMART client used to provide real-time monitoring and alerting of Check Point systems. Previously known as System Status. See also: *SMART clients*.

SmartView Tracker The Check Point SMART client used for managing and viewing the various Check Point security log files. Previously known as Log Viewer. See also: *SMART clients*.

SmartView Tracker Mode SmartView Tracker contains different modes, which define the security log file that is being viewed within SmartView Tracker. See also: *Active mode*, *Audit mode*, and *Log mode*.

source NAT NAT that is required to translate the source IP address for connections that are initiated from devices with private IP addresses. Compare with: *destination NAT*.

stateful inspection technology Describes the patented technology used in Check Point VPN-1/FireWall-1 firewalls. A stateful inspection firewall provides the intelligence of application-layer gateways, yet combines these features with the speed of packet filtering firewalls to provide a high performing, scalable, and intelligent firewall solution. Stateful inspection technology uses a connection table to store session state to all connections currently established through the firewall, ensuring return traffic for each connection is permitted and also ensuring complex protocols, such as H.323 can open dynamic connections securely. See also: *application-layer gateway*, *packet filtering firewall*, and *session state*.

static NAT A form of NAT that provides a single one-to-one mapping between a private IP address and external valid IP address. Static NAT does not conserve address space like the many-to-one hide NAT, but does enable connections to be established from external devices to internal devices represented by their corresponding valid IP address. Compare with: *hide NAT*.

stealth rule A recommended security rule that should be placed at the top of the security rule base. It protects enforcement modules from attack by explicitly denying any connections to the enforcement module.

subnet broadcast A broadcast that is sent to all hosts within an IP subnet. This is represented by the last IP address available with an IP subnet and is used in some DoS attacks. See also: *denial of service*.

Suspicious Activity Monitoring (SAM) A feature provided on enforcement modules that enables temporary security rules to be put in place, without modifying the normal security policy. This feature is used to implement blocking. See also: *blocking*.

SVN Foundation Common Check Point component shared across all Check Point NG products, which provides common functionality, Secure Internal Communications, and monitoring functions.

symmetric encryption An encryption algorithm that uses the same key for encryption and decryption. DES and AES are examples of symmetric encryption algorithms. See also: *asymmetric encryption.*

SYSLOG   A protocol commonly used by Unix-based systems that defines the format by which a system should generate system error and information messages and how those messages should be stored. Most systems that support SYSLOG send all SYSLOG messages to a central SYSLOG server, which consolidates system log events for the entire network. VPN-1/FireWall-1 NG supports the capability of accepting SYSLOG messages and storing them in the security log.

system alerts   Feature new to Check Point NG Feature Pack SmartView Status SMART Client, which allows customized alerts to be defined on specific system management events. See also: *SmartView Status.*

System Status   See: *SmartView Status.*

TACACS   The Terminal Access Controller Access Control System protocol. Similar to RADIUS in that it provides centralized authentication services for multiple enforcement modules to a TACACS server that hosts a central authentication database. TACACS traditionally is used to provide authentication, authorization, and accounting services for terminal-based access to hosts. VPN-1/FireWall-1 supports TACACS as an authentication scheme. Compare with: *RADIUS.*

token   A software or hardware device that is used to generate one-time passwords for users that require one-time passwords (OTP) for authentication. Products such as SecurID implement tokens for OTP authentication. See also: *one-time passwords.*

transitive   How implicit trust relationships are formed between entities. For example, if A trusts B and B trusts C, and if the trust is transitive, A also trusts C implicitly. Transitive trusts form an integral concept of a PKI. See also: *public key infrastructure.*

transparent authentication   Occurs when a user establishes a connection to the desired end-system, and is then prompted for authentication automatically. Compare with: *non-transparent authentication.*

non-transparent authentication   Occurs when a user must establish an out-of-band connection for the purposes of authenticating, prior to establishing a connection to the desired end-system. Compare with: *transparent authentication.*

user authentication   A type of authentication on VPN-1/FireWall-1 that provides transparent authentication for HTTP, TELNET, FTP, and RLOGIN connections. User authentication only applies on a per-connection basis. Security servers for each of these protocols exist on VPN-1/FireWall-1, and act similarly to transparent application-layer proxies, by transparently terminating each client connection on the appropriate security server and then establishing another connection to the destination on behalf of the client. Compare with: *client authentication* and *session authentication.*

user authentication session timeout   The amount of time an authenticated user authentication session can reaming idle before the connection is deemed invalid and torn down.

User mode   Indicates that a software application runs outside of the operating system kernel, providing slower performance but enabling interaction with other applications and the network. The fwd daemon and security servers on an enforcement module are User mode components of an enforcement module. Compare with: *Kernel mode*.

user object   A type of object that exists in the users database that is used to define a specific user. See also: *users database*.

user template object   A type of object that exists in the users database that is used to define a template that can be used to create user objects and administrator objects with common attributes. See also: *users database*.

users database   Stores all user, administrator, user template, and group objects for VPN-1/FireWall-1 in files called $FWDIR/conf/fwauth.NDB*.

virtual private network (VPN)   Describes the collective virtual network formed by connecting two or more private networks securely across a public network, such as the Internet. Although all private networks are connected to the public network, communications are only permitted between devices in each private network, forming a virtual private network. See also: *extranet VPN*, *intranet VPN*, and *remote access VPN*.

VPN-1 & FireWall-1 password   A VPN-1/FireWall-1 authentication scheme that uses passwords stored for user objects in the users database to authenticate users. See also: *authentication scheme*.

workstations   Used in SmartView Status to refer to a Check Point system. See also: *SmartView Status*.

Index

Note to the Reader: Throughout this index **boldfaced** page numbers indicate primary discussions of a topic. *Italicized* page numbers indicate illustrations.

D

V

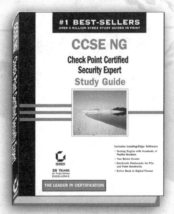

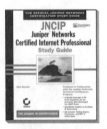

The Official
Juniper Networks™ Certification Study Guides
From Sybex

The Juniper Networks Technical Certification Program offers a four-tiered certification program that validates knowledge and skills related to Juniper Networks technologies:

- JNCIA (Juniper Networks Certified Internet Associate)
- JNCIS (Juniper Networks Certified Internet Specialist)
- JNCIP (Juniper Networks Certified Internet Professional)
- JNCIE (Juniper Networks Certified Internet Expert)

The JNCIA and JNCIS certifications require candidates to pass written exams, while the JNCIP and JNCIE certifications require candidates to pass one-day hands-on laboratory exams.

Key Selling Points

- **The Only OFFICIAL Juniper Networks Study Guides Are From Sybex**

  Written and reviewed by Juniper employees, the Juniper Networks Study Guides are the only official Study Guides for the Juniper Networks Technical Certification Program. Each book provides in-depth coverage of all exam objectives and detailed perspectives and insights into working with Juniper Networks technologies in the real world.

- **A Franchise on the Ground Floor**

  The combination of Juniper Networks and Sybex is an awesome partnership, bringing together a networking market leader and the most respected certification publisher.

- **Juniper Endorsed and Marketed**

  Juniper Networks will advertise, market, and publicize the Juniper Networks Study Guides to its 500 carrier and service provider customers in the USA and around the world, via its equipment sales force, web sites, customer programs, trade shows, public relations, customer service center, and training program.

TELL US WHAT YOU THINK!

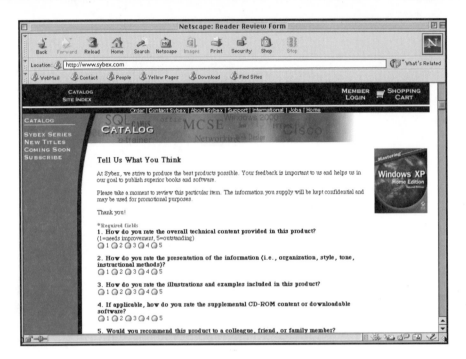

Your feedback is critical to our efforts to provide you with the best books and software on the market. Tell us what you think about the products you've purchased. It's simple:

1. Go to the Sybex website.
2. Find your book by typing the ISBN or title into the Search field.
3. Click on the book title when it appears.
4. Click **Submit a Review.**
5. Fill out the questionnaire and comments.
6. Click **Submit.**

With your feedback, we can continue to publish the highest quality computer books and software products that today's busy IT professionals deserve.

www.sybex.com

SYBEX Inc. • 1151 Marina Village Parkway, Alameda, CA 94501 • 510-523-8233